D0342700

THE CORRESPONDENCE OF

George, Prince of Wales 1770–1812

VOLUME IV 1799–1804

The Prince of Wales
by Vigée-Lebrun

THE CORRESPONDENCE OF

George, Prince of Wales 1770-1812

VOLUME IV 1799-1804

EDITED BY

A. Aspinall, C.V.O., M.A., D.Litt.

CASSELL · LONDON

UNIVERSITY OF VICTORIA
LIBRARY
Victoria, B. C.

CASSELL & COMPANY LTD
35 Red Lion Square · London WC1
and at Melbourne · Sydney · Toronto
Johannesburg · Cape Town · Auckland

© A. Aspinall 1967
First published 1967

Made and printed in Great Britain by
William Clowes and Sons, Limited
London and Beccles
F.167

Editor's Preface

I should like to express once more my gratitude to the owners of MSS. from which I have quoted either in the body of the work or in footnotes. Again it is my pleasant duty to express my thanks to Mr. R. Mackworth-Young, M.V.O., Her Majesty's Librarian, for the valuable assistance and advice which he has given me; to Miss Jane Langton, Registrar of the Archives, who has answered many queries most helpfully; to Mr. Oliver Millar, C.V.O., F.S.A., Deputy Surveyor of the Queen's Pictures, for advice about illustrations; and to the Rev. S. B.-R. Poole, who has been good enough to read the proofs of this volume and provide valuable material for footnotes.

In view of the increasing political importance of this correspondence, a select list of officeholders has been included and will form a feature of the remaining volumes. The dates given are approximate: there was often a considerable interval between the date of appointment and the date when the appointee actually took over from his predecessor or began to receive his salary.

In the case of some quotations from MSS. in the British Museum, folio numbers are not invariably given; even when they are, they may, in the case of recently acquired MSS., be provisional only.

Contents

Genealogical Tables

Illustrations

I   1799

Ever since the break-up of his marriage in April 1796 the Prince had
been seeking a reconciliation and reunion with Mrs. Fitzherbert, as the
only cure for his disordered, tortured mind, but she had considered his
marriage as placing an insuperable barrier between them. 'The link
once broken could never be re-joined,' she declared. Lady Jersey too had
passed out of his life. He was oppressed by a sense of loneliness which
became almost unendurable; there was no end, either, to the wickedness
of the Princess, his wife, and he was suffering from persecution mania
which, according to his own testimony, was driving him almost insane.
The report of Mrs. Fitzherbert's death at Bath in February 1799 made
him frantic, and the contradiction of the report still left him 'in a dreadful
state'. Full of remorse for his shabby treatment of her, full of promises
for the future (promises which, like most of those he ever made, were
kept only so long as it suited him) he wrote a hysterical letter to her on
11 June, imploring, demanding, that she should return to him, protesting
his utter devotion to her, threatening to kill himself unless she came
back, reminding her of her marriage vows (though he had broken his
own), and going so far as to threaten to reveal to the world his 'marriage'
with her, notwithstanding the severe penalties to which such a revelation
would expose her uncle and brother, the witnesses of the unlawful
ceremony. Time was to reveal, as usual, the worthlessness of his protestations.

Mrs. Fitzherbert, indeed, would have liked the truth about her marriage to be made known, but she could not have faced the ruinous
consequences both to the Prince and to her family. She temporized with

2

him, promised to reconsider the situation provided that he would do nothing rash in the meantime; and with this answer he had to be satisfied. Her own family, and even the Royal Family favoured a reconciliation; the Duke of Kent actively promoted it, and Princess Augusta told her brother how creditable it would be for both of them that *old friends sincerely and unalterably attached* should come together again.' The Queen too, who had never approved of her daughter-in-law, countenanced the idea. But Mrs. Fitzherbert's religious scruples remained to be overcome. The matter was referred to the Pope, who eventually pronounced her to be the Prince's canonical wife and said she was at liberty to rejoin him if he was sincerely penitent for his sins. Had the fact been revealed that she had appealed to Rome for guidance, Protestant feeling would have been inflamed, but the matter, like the marriage ceremony, was kept secret. Before the end of the year the reconciliation had taken place, and on 11 December the Prince sent her the copy of the Will which he had made in her favour nearly four years earlier. Amongst the presents she received from him was a gold bracelet, and inside the attached locket was a painting of his right eye, said to be by Cosway. On the bracelet were engraved the words, *rejoindre ou mourir.*

The Prince was luckier than he deserved to be. Prince Adolphus was less fortunate. He had fallen deeply in love with his cousin, Princess Frederica of Mecklenburg-Strelitz, who had been widowed at the age of eighteen, her husband, Prince Louis of Prussia, the brother of King Frederick William III, having died in December 1796. Prince Adolphus offered her his hand, and in January 1798 the offer was accepted. But when the Prince, indirectly through Dundas, asked his father's permission to marry, he was told that he must not even mention the matter again until peace was made. The Princess, however, was not prepared to remain a widow indefinitely, and she at once formed a connexion with one of her German friends, Prince Frederick of Solms-Braunfels, with the result that she became pregnant in the summer of 1798. A secret marriage was arranged, the ceremony taking place, apparently, on 7 January 1799,[1] and the child was born in March. Prince Adolphus was heart-broken, but with his usual generosity he soon forgave her. Though perfectly happy and contented in Hanover he was disappointed at not being allowed to accompany his brother Frederick on the expedition to the Helder.

In the spring of 1798 the King had ordered Prince Augustus to leave Naples, and at the end of May he had arrived at Vienna via Trieste, after a severe illness on the road. Then he was instructed to go to Berlin, where he arrived before the end of October. In the Prussian capital he was miserable and inconsolable because 'his heart's dearest delight' and her son were not allowed to join him; suffering severely, too, from

1. But on 10 December 1798, according to some authorities.

3

asthma which compelled him to sleep in an armchair for months together; mentally tortured because he felt that he was living in banishment and denied that parliamentary grant which would have made him financially independent of his father, and such as had been given to his brothers Edward and Ernest. Lady Hamilton was not renowned for her truthfulness, but she may well have been accurate in saying that Prince Augustus had left Naples owing her a good deal of money. 'Twelve years of my life I was . . . almost Queen of Naples.' When the Prince was there, 'I spent all my husband's and all my own money for seven years in treating and giving him respectability, *which sometimes he wanted. We never were repaid anything.*' The Prince disliked Livingston and Robert Arbuthnot, the two Gentlemen, not of his own choice, with whom he was compelled to live, and he was as yet unable to face the fact that he must give up Lady Augusta as his wife if he wished to return home and be again received by his offended family. Lady Augusta, risking the loss of her pension (which in any case was not being regularly paid) secretly joined him in Berlin on 10 August, travelling under the name of Mrs. Ford, and pretending, on arrival, that she had come to take a last farewell of her husband who, she alleged, had been reported to be dying. He then asked Lady Dunmore, her mother, then in London, to send over his son, who arrived in Berlin on 17 September, but, in accordance with the King's orders, the boy was taken back to England shortly afterwards by his mother. Prince Augustus threatened to publish 'for the amusement of the public' all the correspondence on the subject of his 'marriage' unless Lady Augusta's debts were paid and she was given an adequate income. The pension of £1,200 a year, dating from 27 July 1796 (she herself said it was one of £900, a calculation which perhaps allowed for more than the usual deductions), was obviously insufficient, even when regularly paid, to enable her to educate her son and to live like the Princess she chose to believe herself to be. The King ordered Lady Dunmore to hand over her grandson otherwise 'very unpleasant consequences' would follow. The Prince of Wales generously undertook to educate the boy at his own expense, but Prince Augustus declined the offer. In October he agreed that his brother, Lady Augusta and Lord Thurlow should be the joint guardians of his son. The Prince of Wales was now finding it expedient to establish more friendly relations with the King, with the result that Prince Augustus, to his astonishment and mortification, received no support from any member of his family in his efforts during the year to secure recognition of his marriage. The Prince of Wales told him bluntly that the King would never recognize it, that the law of the land would not be altered to suit his convenience, and that Lady Augusta's family too would feel the weight of the King's displeasure. 'Our lot by birth and station . . . makes us all amenable to it:' a sentiment which would have done the Prince more credit had it been

4

in his mind in 1785. Prince Augustus, he said, ought to be satisfied, like the Duke of Kent, with a mistress, in which case 'neither the King nor the world would ever have interfered or questioned' him. This, however, was not quite accurate, for the Duke of York, as Commander-in-Chief, warned his brother Edward (13 December 1799) that the world had talked a good deal 'of the public manner in which you went everywhere accompanied by Mme. de St. Laurent' when in England. 'This may be done abroad . . . it cannot be done at home.' The Duke of Kent was soon to make the unpleasant discovery that to live in this open manner with a lady not his wife was to disqualify himself from high military command at home.

The Duke of Kent, back in Nova Scotia on 6 September after a passage of forty-three days, found it a dreary place compared with the beauty and attractions of London. The climate did not suit him, and he suffered from rheumatism. He hoped within a year to be recalled and given employment at home—to be appointed Commander-in-Chief in Ireland if the projected Union was accomplished and the office of Lord Lieutenant abolished, as Pitt at one time contemplated, was his 'favourite wish'. Alternatively, he would have liked a similar command in Scotland or in one of the Military Districts in England, or else an appointment on the Staff, but his connexion with Mme. de St. Laurent proved to be an insuperable obstacle. Like all his brothers he was in low water financially. In March he inquired anxiously of Pitt whether he could be given, like his brother the Duke of Clarence, a free supply of candles, fuel and food whilst in residence at St. James's Palace, and he was told that for a whole year the cost to the Board of Green Cloth would be about £3,500 (it had been only about £2,000 in the case of the Duke of Clarence because he had spent a considerable part of the year in the country). He reminded Pitt that his brother Prince Ernest, ever since his return to England, had occupied his (Prince Edward's) apartments in St. James's Palace, and had enjoyed every allowance to the same extent as the Duke of Clarence, his dinner alone excepted. 'I, on the other hand,' declared the Duke of Kent, 'have had nothing allowed me but house here alone, having been obliged both at the house which his Majesty took for me in St. James's Street and since, at my apartments at Kensington Palace, to provide my fuel, candles and every other article for the expenditure of my house without receiving anything in compensation, and when I have wished to have a friend to dine with me I have been under the necessity of sending for my dinner to a tavern.' He had to give Thomas Coutts £2,000 every quarter for the liquidation of his debts, and told him, 'It certainly will be a severe sacrifice to give up again three of the best years of my life to pass them in that dreary quarter of the globe, but I think it a point of honour to clear off my incumbrance.' And he was making financial provision for Mme. de St. Laurent in the form of superannuation benefit. He had already bought £6,000 of Government Stock for her, which, with compound interest, would eventually produce an income of £300 a year.[1]

In the summer the Duke of York was put in charge of the expedition to the Helder.[2] Various circumstances combined to ensure its failure after the initial success of the capture of the Dutch fleet in the Texel. Delays in the arrival of the Russian contingent enabled the French and the Dutch republicans to organize their defence, and the expected aid from the Dutch royalists failed to materialize. The attack on Bergen was repulsed, and on 18 October the Duke felt obliged to make the Convention of Alkmaar, by the terms of which he evacuated Holland and surrendered his prisoners but retained the Dutch fleet. The expedition, though strategically sound, was badly planned and executed, but Ministers did not blame the Duke, Lord Grenville, for example, saying that he 'had no other fault . . . than that of following, perhaps too implicitly, the advice of those whose advice he was desired to follow. In many things he has certainly done extremely well.'

In the Prince's own letters there are few references to the progress of the war. He may well have been more concerned about his own troubles and frustrations, and especially his indebtedness. He did, however, occasionally review his Regiment, but he would not have been allowed to accompany it to Holland had it been sent there. He loyally defended his brother's reputation after the failure of the expedition.

In Wurtemberg his sister's situation was becoming increasingly uncomfortable as French 'monsters' invaded her husband's territory. Her letters were necessarily guarded in tone except on the rare occasions when she found a safe means of conveyance. From Princess Amelia the Prince heard of 'dear Royal's' enormous size, which almost disabled her from walking up or down stairs. 'This is out of compliment, I suppose, to *her Duke*.'

By this time the Duke of Clarence had completely changed his views, and now thought the war to be no longer one of choice but of necessity. His confidence in the ultimate outcome was as optimistic as Pitt's had been years earlier. He was sure that the Archduke Charles and Suvoroff would quickly liberate Italy, very hopeful that the Helder expedition would result in the expulsion of the French from Holland and the Netherlands. 'Bonaparte and his army are no more.' France was

1. His appeal to Pitt was obviously unsuccessful, for he wrote in a similar strain to Addington on 28 February 1802, making the additional point that he had suffered repeated losses at sea by shipwreck and enemy action whilst employed abroad.

2. It was believed, said Lord Bathurst, that only a loan of £50,000 from the Government, to be repaid by quarterly instalments of £1,000 starting in 1805, enabled him to leave the country. Some people, added Bathurst, 'go the length of doubting whether the advantage was worth so much money.'

incapable of withstanding the Allies and peace must soon be restored to Europe. Like Pitt he had still much to learn.

1417 THE PRINCE OF WALES TO MRS. NUGENT

Tuesday night, 1 Jan. 1799

Your kind note reached me just as I was in the middle of my dinner and hurrying to the Play, and I am only this instant returned home, or I should have answered it sooner. I am afraid it will be impossible for me to be in town till Tuesday at soonest, but should I come on Sunday I hope I need not say how truly happy I shall be to dine with you not only on that day, but whenever you are so good as to wish *it*. You had best not think of me though on Sunday at any rate, and as soon as I return I will make a point of calling upon you and arranging a day for *a quiet party* with you. My best compliments to the Admiral.[1] Ever dear Mrs. Nugent's very sincere friend[2] (Kingston Hall MSS.).

1418 THE PRINCE OF WALES TO THE DUKE OF YORK

4 Jan. 1799

I empower you to receive from Hugh Watts, Esqr. such sums of money as may fall due to me, as shares of the loan in which I bear a share. (43926)

1419 THOMAS TYRWHITT TO THE PRINCE OF WALES

Carlton House, 4 Jan. 1799

A rumour prevailed this morning that there had been an oversight in the Income Bill respecting the usual clause of exempting the Royal Family from the operations of it.[3] I immediately came home & read through the

1. Admiral Nugent. See No. 1403.

2. The Prince wrote to Lady Elgin on the 1st: 'I shall be most happy to see you & the dear child in town by twelve tomorrow, when I will settle everything touching her removal to London. A happy new year to you. I am just arriv'd from Windsor'. (49231)

3. On 5 December 1798 the Government had brought in a Bill to repeal the assessed taxes of the previous year and to substitute a graduated income tax at a maximum rate of two shillings in the pound, producing, it was estimated, about £10,000,000. The tax was to be levied on incomes exceeding £60 a year at a rate of five-sixths of one per cent on incomes between £60 and less than £65, and ten per cent on incomes of £200 and upwards.

Bill, & to my extreme surprize I find no such exemption. I mentioned it to several persons in the House, & it seems as if it was the intention of Ministers that they should pay. With great submission, however, to their better judgment, I think this is taking the Royal Family by surprize, & debarring them of that credit with the public which doubtless they would have gained by a spontaneous proposal, should Ministers have thought such a step necessary.

I cannot imagine for a moment that his Majesty is aware the public will know his actual revenue from the Funds, & your Royal Highness I know will excuse me from observing that I think the tax will fall far too heavy on the younger branches of the Royal Family, whose incomes, without the diminution of a tenth, are too disproportionate. If Lord Thurlow had attended, I should have requested him to have asked the simple question, 'Had his Majesty been consulted upon the point?' Should this be the case, & it is understood by their Majesties, your Royal Highness will I trust pardon my zeal in that which I felt a call of duty to state.

The only Lord in opposition in the House is Lord Holland,[1] & there are not twelve of their Lordships alltogether.

I must apologise to your Royal Highness for the haste with which this is written as I wish to save the post.

I enclose a note from Gascoigne.[2] I hope to see your Royal Highness return on Tuesday as well as when I took leave of you. (39550-1)

1420   THE QUEEN TO THE PRINCE OF WALES, AND A REPLY

Queen's Lodge, Windsor, 7 Jan. 1799

I must follow the dictates of my heart, my dearest son, by congratulating you upon the return of this day. I have not the talent of a Sévigné [3] else I would make a sonnet for the 7th, but what I wont in elegance I hope to make up in attachment & truth, & wish most sincerely that little Charlotte may become besides outward elegance & beauty, both good &

1. Henry Richard Fox, 3rd Lord Holland (1773–1840), Charles James Fox's nephew. Succeeded his father, 1774. Lord Privy Seal, October 1806–March 1807; Chancellor of the Duchy of Lancaster in the Reform Ministry, 1830–4, and 1835–40. In July 1797 he married Elizabeth (1775–1845), daughter of Richard Vassall, of Jamaica, and the divorced wife of Sir Godfrey Webster, who obtained £6,000 damages in an action of *crim. con.* against Lord Holland.

2. Possibly Isaac Gascoyne, M.P.; but, more likely, J. Gaskoin, Clerk of the Prince's Stables.

3. The Queen thought that Mme. de Sévigné's manner of relating trifling circumstances made her *Letters* interesting and pleasing to the reader (*R. F. Greville's Diaries*, p. 52, ed. by F. M. Bladon).

8

virtuous, by which she must become a comfort to you, a blessing to those around her, & an ornament to her sex, & lastly may she prove to you as affectionate as you are to me which is the earnest wish of [etc.].

I give a Ball to the servants in honor of the day.[1] (36502)

1. The Prince evidently thought it unnecessary to be at home for his daughter's birthday. He was paying a visit to his friend the Duchess of Rutland at Belvoir, having left London on 2 January. He wrote to his friend Arthur Paget from Belvoir on the 7th: 'Though I wrote you, my dearest Arthur, a letter of sixteen or eighteen pages about six weeks ago, & though I have received no answer to it as yet, still I cannot help writing a few lines to you from this place, amidst all its bustle & confusion. The Lady of the Mansion on the Birthday was dressed more superbly, look'd more nobly, *dans le grand genre*, as it should be, & more beautifully than I have seen her for months & indeed almost I may say years, & she did the honours of that immense fête in a manner that no one but herself knows how to do. I really figured to myself what with the ancient appearance of the Castle, the prodigious concourse of the natives without, & the numbers of the bettermost sort within doors, together with the illuminations, the music, the noise & the bustle, that I was transported in a dream to some of those scenes which we have read the description of having existed in the days of chivalry. But to return to the Lady of the House, though she exerted herself to the utmost, still it was evident that there was a gloom that hung about her, which she could not conquer & which deadened every pleasing event that took place, & which she would have supremely enjoyed under other circumstances. I am almost the only person, she tells me, that she can venture to talk to. Of course I need not add, my dear friend, that we have had much, much conversation. On my soul I think I never did see any creature in all my life so perfectly attached as she is; indeed, my dear Arthur, you never will be able to shake it off. I almost, from the manner in which she talks of you, the animation, the passion with which she dwells upon your name, & upon every circumstance that regards you, should think you to blame were you to attempt ever to break through it, as I am confident it would cost her her life, & I am persuaded you never could nor would forgive yourself. She is beginning to get one of her nasty coughs again; pray write & preach up Sir Walter [Farquhar] and everything that is proper, but I am afraid there is but one remedy that could be of any essential avail and that would be yourself. Why that should not be the case, my beloved Arthur, I cannot really see; why bury yourself alive, so loved, esteemed, & liked as you are by all that know you? Why not entirely decline the line you are in, & by adhering to the parliamentary cause, look, through the interest of your friends, besides your own abilities, forwards to an honourable situation at one of the Boards, which perhaps though not quite equal in point of emolument to what you may in a year or two meet with as a Foreign Minister, still you will enjoy your friends, they will enjoy you, which must be quite out of the question as long as you are to be one of the *sanctioned spies & hidden lamps of Lord Grenville*.

Weigh this well over, & let me know your sentiments. The less you hesitate now, I am confident, the better it will be for you, & the appointment of Mr. Grenville to Berlin I should hope might furnish you with a sufficient excuse. Indeed, indeed, dear Arthur, you know not also how I miss you each hour of the four & twenty, & all that your friends can say that inspires them with any pleasing feelings in their convivial moments, is either, don't you remember dear Arthur's saying so, or doing so, or how he would like to be with us, or what would Arthur say or think, or how would he act upon such & such a circumstance? I expect there is no explaining or telling you how we all feel about you. Therefore you ought a little to weigh, at the same time that you consider for yourself, what so deeply interests & concerns the happiness of your friends. After this long prosing sermon which I hope you will forgive me for, my dear Arthur, though you may rate it a bore, I must write you in order to extort a smile before I conclude some little account of *Chig* [Mr. Chester]. He arrived on the Saturday in the

9

Carlton House, 6 o'clock [? *c. 3 Feb. 1799*]

Accept, my dearest mother, my best thanks for your kind & considerate letter which I have just received. I am certainly much better, & so much so that I trust, with the assistance of a bandage, to be able to be out tomorrow. Keate, who has just left me, finds not the smallest symptom of anything that resembles gout, but pronounces it positively nothing but the old strain, & perhaps from having walked much of late & remained with wet boots on, some degree of rheumatism, if I have any in my habit, may have paid me a trifling visit in that part which is certainly the weakest owing to repeated accidents. I trust I shall be well enough to present myself at Windsor on Monday, & may I entreat of you, my dearest Madam, to inform Eliza so, & to say I should most certainly have written had I not been afraid of detaining your servant too long. The joy I feel at the arrival of my beloved Emely, & at the good tidings I have of her is really quite inexpressible, & the instant I can waddle out, it will be to satisfy myself with a peep at her. Ernest, who is in the room, my dearest madam, whilst I am writing, is extremely anxious that as I have not the good fortune of seeing you myself, that I should mention to you in writing what I am confident you will agree with me in, & that is, that in case certain subjects should be mention'd to you in which he is most personally interested *for your opinion*, & that a diminution of the appointments which have ever attended the Peerages of the Royal Family should appear to be in agitation, you would just hint that these are not moments to lower any of the branches of the Royal Family by putting them upon a footing inferior to what they had ever hitherto been, & to which their birth so justly gives them a right to look up to & expect. You cannot doubt from my general sentiments respecting the interests of my family, that I must have most deeply impressed upon my mind the impolicy, the indelicacy, & the impropriety of such a publick measure, should it be

last week, from Ireland; on Sunday he dined with me & a party to commemorate how happy we used to be with you last year, & hope to be for many many years to come; the party were viz., Bathurst, Brummell, Chig, & Bob Mongomery. After the first glass after dinner every round was a bumper to you in the very best Claret I had. Chig thought it too weak. Of course stronger, the old Queen's House Claret, was produced for him which he swore was the b-pup-pup-pup-pest Cha-a-a-teau Margeau he had ever ta-a-asted, & tumbled about ten o'clock smack on his face, and was obliged to be carried off between two servants. The rest were bad enough, God knows, except myself, though my every glass was a bumper to your health, I can safely swear I never flinched one, dear Arthur, & you well know I am not even upon indifferent occasions a *shirker*. Since that day, the old girl has never ceased being tipsy twice a day, first at dinner & on—but after supper—for she always makes a regular supper first—& a couple of bottles of iced Champagne, after a couple of quarts of small beer which she calls, you know a swig of beer, has completed about six in the morning the old gentlewoman since she has been with us here. Upon my word, I am quite ashamed of the length of this scrawl. I will therefore only say that there is no one existing, my dear Arthur, who loves you more truly or sincerely than your ever affectionate George' (*Paget Papers*, i,148–50).

intended to be brought forward, as big with every species of mischief to our family. (42278–9)

1421 THE DUKE OF BEDFORD TO THE PRINCE OF WALES

Woburn, 3 Feb. 1799

I have the honor to acknowledge the receipt of your Royal Highness's letter and am extremely concerned to learn that I have been deprived of the honor of receiving your Royal Highness by so unpleasant a circumstance, tho' I trust all danger is past.[1] I must entreat of your Royal [Highness] not to consider any engagement to me further than is consistent with your own perfect convenience and that your Royal Highness will believe that at all times I shall be most happy to receive you. The weather is so dreadfully bad and the roads in such a wretched state (added to the situation of Prince Ernest)[2] that I fear your Royal Highness could not leave London without its being attended with great inconvenience; if so I beg of your Royal Highness not to think of it but that you will have the goodness to fix any other time more suitable to you.[3] I shall with punctuallity deliver your Royal Highness's message. Chester is not here.

1. Probably a reference to the Prince's illness.

2. Prince Ernest had been indisposed, but he was well enough to dine with the Duke of Clarence on the 4th. The following letter from Prince Ernest to the Prince of Wales, dated merely, 'St. James, Sunday, 5 o'clock', may well have been written on Sunday, 4 February: 'I had just sent to Carlton House to enquire after you, not having heard anything I doubted your being gone to Wooburn. But judge of my astonishment at hearing this moment from McMahon of your being ill. My first intention was directly to have gone to you, but McMahon insisted on my not doing so, and assured me upon his honour there was *no* danger, otherwise no earthly power or self consideration should prevent my directly coming to attend you, not merely from gratitude for your very kind attention to me during my illness, but from *real* love, which will never cease for you as long as *I live*.

I return you many many thanks for the enclosed, I received yesterday evening a few lines in which a recapitulation of thanks, and the firmest gratitude to you for your goodness in writing [*sic*]. I also thank you for your goodness, Pemberton has assured me *today* the babies *sic*] is perfectly well.

When I once obtain my Dukedom I know that in spite of all endeavours I never should have got it but for your conversation with the Queen; that settled the whole business and *your* having settled Edward's folly will now arrange the whole. If you should be any ways worse pray send to me that I may directly come; never mind me, *je suis un pauvre Sire*, but recollect you are of the greatest consequence to us all.

I am *better* today though very weak. I was feverish last night & emetic till ¼ past 11 o'clock doubted your coming or else should certainly not have failed staying up; as it was I passed a bad night. God bless you, dearest brother; for Heaven's sake take care of yourself, do not think now of quitting your house till Nussy [see No. 1587] allows it, and let me know this evening how you are.' (42276–7)

3. The Prince of Wales was at Woburn from Sunday, 3 March to the 7th.

I cannot conclude, Sir, without assuring your Royal Highness that I shall ever retain a lively sense of the many kind expressions contained in your letter, in which sentiment I beg leave to subscribe myself [etc.]. (39552–3)

1422 THE PRINCE OF WALES TO THE DUCHESS OF RUTLAND

12 Feb. 1799

I cannot, my dear Duchess, sufficiently express my thanks to you for your kind letter which I received quite safely by the post yesterday. Indeed, indeed, my dear friend, I am most truly grateful to you in particular, as well as to *our other friend*, for the interest you are so good as to take in the most *essential* circumstance, really the *only one* that can *ever* give me *a taste again for life*, & if I do not express myself as strongly as I ought to you for all your kindness, beleive me, it is not from want of the just & due sense I entertain of it, but from being totally inadequate to the expressing myself as I could wish. Much & great I am aware will be the difficulties I shall have to rencounter [*sic*] in the accomplishment of *that object* that is *nearest & dearest* to my heart, but nevertheless it is a duty I owe myself to endeavour to *levy every obstacle however great* & to *convince* you as well as every relation and friend of *hers* of *my sincerity & attachment for her*, & that *at no period, however misrepresented*, there *never was an instant in which I did not feel for her*, as I am afraid she *never* felt for me.[1] Let me conjure of you to thank our friend in the warmest manner possible for the affectionate & kind part she takes respecting me, & assure her that if I do not write myself to thank her it is merely to comply with her own wishes on that head. She may most positively rely on my not only not mentioning her name, but not even hinting at the smallest communication ever having taken place between us on this or even on any other circumstance, further than merely alluding to the satisfaction I felt to the very bottom of my soul that by our fortunately having met at Belvoir, all passed misunderstandings had been committed to oblivion, & that we were once more upon *that footing* which it *ever shall be* one of the principal objects of my life *to preserve* as it is *one* of the *only ones* that does afford me any sort of comfort or consolation. I need not, I am sure, entreat of you, my dearest friend (if you will permit me to call you so) to continue, whenever you can get the smallest scrap of intelligence, to convey it to me, as everything, *you well know in our situation*, even the *merest trifle*, becomes of the *utmost*

1. For some time the Prince had been most anxious that Mrs. Fitzherbert should rejoin him, but as yet she had rejected his overtures. Her dangerous illness during this month brought him to a state bordering on desperation if not insanity.

consequence. Our friend I trust likewise will continue her good offices, & not cease either by word of mouth through you or by letter to afford me such intelligence as she may pick up, for it is of the utmost consequence to me to know everything in order not to get upon wrong grounds, not even for an instant. As to the hints respecting the *old lady* [1] I shall most carefully & distinctly guide my conduct by them; & indeed I think it will be of extreme consequence that as soon as *the other* has left B[ath] our friend should write to intimate to the old lady that when at Belvoir I had enquired after her, & spoken of her with so much affection that in case I should intimate a wish to call on her, which she did not doubt I should *wish* to do, it would be extremely unkind not to see me.

And now I must entreat forgiveness of you for having talked so much of myself, but I could not help it, *c'est plus fort que moi.* One word more & I will have done, & that is, that you may either read all this part of my letter to *our* friend if you choose to do so, as I have nothing concealed from either of you *now* upon this head; besides, there is another circumstance I have to mention to you & which you may likewise hint at, even assert if you please, that everything *is finally at an end* IN ANOTHER QUARTER,[2] so far so that I think there is but little probability of my even visiting there in a common way much more, & that a few weeks will even conclude that.

Now for other topics. I was in hopes to have given you by this time some account of a letter or letters which I might have received from Munich,[3]

1. Mrs. Fitzherbert's mother (Mrs. Smythe).

2. The reference is probably to Lady Jersey.

3. Probably from Arthur Paget, who had been sent to Munich in September 1798 on an Extraordinary Mission. The Duke of York wrote to him on 5 February 1799: 'I am very sorry to hear that you find Munich so dull. It must be very much altered indeed since I was there, which may be owing to the extreme age of the Elector, otherwise it certainly was, after Vienna, the pleasantest place I was in in Germany' (Add.MSS.48383). In May 1799 Paget withdrew from Munich to Ratisbon, in obedience to instructions. He was presented at Court on 31 May on his return home. He was M.P. for Anglesey, 1794–1807, *Chargé d'Affaires* at Berlin, 1794–5; Minister to Sicily, 1800–1; to Austria, 1801–6; Ambassador to Turkey (Special Mission), 1807. G.C.B.,1815.

There are some undated letters to Paget from the Prince of Wales in Add.MSS.48383:

(i) '5.30. I write from Albemarle Street. I do beg, entreat, & insist upon your calling here tonight after the Play. I never saw the Dss. look half so handsome in all my life, & if you saw with my eyes which I am convinced you must do, I *know what must be the* infallible consequence. God bless you.'

(ii) *Carlton House*, 7.30.

'I am but this instant return'd home & have found your kind note. By hunting you all day I have missed of you [*sic*]. However, I will return, though I acknowledge my imprudence is of the greatest, break up your family party, call therefore on me a little before ten here at *Carlton House*, & I will be at home purposely to see you. Adieu, ever dearest Arthur.'

(iii) '3.15. If the Peer should not dine, will you ask Shelley, & will you have Somerset or not? Shelley has been here but I did not ask him as I did not know what Lord Uxbridge would do.'

but not a mail is arrived, consequently I have heard not a syllable, excepting from *his brother*[1] who dined with me the other day, & from him I understood that *he* had written de la pluie et du beau temps about horses and common occurrences, but nothing particularly about himself; so much so that he was rather inquisitive of me whether *he* seem'd happy or pleas'd with his situation, saying that he was confident he would write & had written more openly & frankly to me about himself than he would to any of his own family. My answer was generally that he did not seem very comfortable as I fear'd *he* thought *his* being *there* was owing to some of his family not wishing him to be in England, & certainly not having acted by him as he had a right to expect & as he had deserved of them. This is all, my dear Duchess, that is in my power to tell you, as it *is all* that I know. However, you may depend the very first instant I hear anything I will that same moment communicate it to you.

And now I should think you must be tired of my horrid scrawl; however, before I conclude I cannot help offering you my sincerest congratulations on the Duke's intended marriage with Lady Elizabeth Howard,[2] & which I understand he announced yesterday publicly; not having seen him yet, I have written to him to express my best wishes, & you know me sufficiently to be well convinced how truly interested I ever must feel in the happiness & prosperity of everything that is related *to you*, & to which *you are attached, let the ties be what they may*. I have seen & examined the boxes myself; everything was properly & carefully deliver'd, so for Heaven's sake set your mind at rest on that head. I will not tresspass any further, therefore will only say God bless you, my dearest friend.

P.S. I go in two or three days at furthest[3] (Rutland MSS.).

1423   THE PRINCE OF WALES TO THE DUKE OF RUTLAND, AND THE REPLY

Carlton House, 12 Feb. 1799

I learnt late last night, my dear Duke, that you had publicly announced your marriage with Lady Elizabeth Howard. I therefore seize the earliest opportunity of expressing my sincere congratulations to you, &

1. Probably Lord Paget.

2. The Duke of Rutland married Lady Elizabeth Howard (1780–1825), daughter of the 5th Earl of Carlisle, on 22 April.

3. His journey to Bath was deferred in order that he might be present at the investiture of Lord Spencer as a Knight of the Garter on 1 March. So few Knights had been installed, it was said, that a Chapter of the Order could not be held without the Prince's presence (*The Times*, 22 February).

14

of assuring you that in every event of life no one has more your interest & happiness at heart, than [etc.] (Rutland MSS.).

THE DUKE'S REPLY
Albemarle Street, 12 Feb. 1799
Allow me to express in faint terms the sense which I entertain of the kindness with which your Royal Highness condescends to congratulate me upon the event which is likely to take place in a short time. Amongst the numerous instances of friendship with which your Royal Highness has ever honoured me, & which, with the truest gratitude and pride I acknowledge, none has so sensibly affected me as the present. Your Royal Highness will excuse the mean terms in which I endeavour to express my feelings; the only merit they can claim is that of being the heartfelt sentiments of one who begs permission to subscribe himself with humble sincerity [etc.]. (39554)

1424   W. PEARCE[1] TO [?]
Admiralty Office, 18 Feb. 1799
In the uncertainty that your stay at Bath would not have been lengthened beyond a week or ten days, I forbore troubling you with a letter expressing my sense of the very friendly conduct of Colonel McMahon. Upon his speaking to the Prince, his Royal Highness desired him to inform Miss Gainsborough,[2] which he did in a very handsome manner, that he should keep one of the pictures to shew his regard for the memory of honest Gainsborough, and that to serve her more essentially he would recommend the Duke of Bedford to purchase the other two.

This proceeding in his Royal Highness has fully justified the opinion you have ever zealously professed of his steady & generous attachments.

The point upon which I am induced again to resort to your interference is that the Duke's decision may be obtained. I do most solemnly assure you that the whole of those pictures would have been purchased long since (two for Mr. Beckford[3] & one by Mr. Farrington[4]) had not it been Miss Gainsborough's pride in accordance to her father's wishes that the

1. A clerk in the Admiralty Office.

2. Margaret Gainsborough, elder daughter of Thomas Gainsborough (1727–88), the painter.

3. William Beckford (1760–1844), of Fonthill fame. M.P. for Wells, 1784–90; for Hindon, 1790–4 and 1806–20.

4. Joseph Farington (1747–1821), the landscape painter and diarist.

15

Prince should have one of his best landscapes in his possession. Pray, dear Sir, do what you can on this subject.

I am sorry to say that poor Miss Wood died this morning. (39555–6)

1425 THE PRINCE OF WALES TO THE DUCHESS OF RUTLAND

Saturday night, 12 o'clock [? *23 Feb. 1799*]

I was too ill yesterday, my dearest Duchess, to be able to hold a pen, or I should have written to you. Your feeling heart I know will feel for my distress when you know that yesterday morning's newspapers contain'd an account that SHE *had died* at Bath the Wednesday evening preceeding.[1] To discribe my feelings, to talk even of the subject is totally impossible, for I could neither feel, think, speak; in short, there was almost an end to my existence. Indeed, it was a mercy of Providence that I was thus bereft of all sense, for had I not, I am convinc'd, frantic as I should have been, I should have put an end to my existence myself; my younger brother E[rnes]t happen'd to see the newspaper, &, reading the article, posted off to my house, hoping to have prevented my seeing the papers till he had been able to find out the truth respecting the article. However, in this shocking state he found me as the papers had been brought me before he arrived; he instantly sent up to the Paper Office to find by what authority or from whence this article had been introduced at such full length; three horrid letters were sent us, all from different people at Bath, mentioning the circumstance, & another from someone at Bath to my attorney who is hers likewise, a very long one upon law business, at the end of which these words were introduced quite at the bottom of the fourth side of paper ('Alas! poor Mrs. F—— is just gone'). Think only all this time of me. It then occurr'd to my brother to run up *to her cousin's* Mrs. Butler[2] in Portman Square, there he flew. She said her accounts were even on the Wednesday & of the most favourable kind from the old lady,[3] which letter he brought with him. To be sure, it was most satisfactory but still the anxiety whether this letter might not have been written an hour or two before those that had come to the Post Office & which also bore the date of Wednesday was quite insupportable, till in about two hours afterwards, this good natur'd lady sent me another

1. On Tuesday the 26th *The Times* stated that the report in some of the daily papers of Mrs. Fitzherbert's death was contradicted by accounts from Bath dated Friday the 22nd.

2. Little seems to be known about Mrs. Fitzherbert's cousin Elizabeth, daughter of the 5th Lord Langdale by his wife Constantia Smythe, sister of Walter Smythe (father of Mrs. Fitzherbert). She married Robert Butler of Ballyragget. The Prince first met Mrs. Fitzherbert at her house. She is mentioned once in Wilkins' *Mrs. Fitzherbert and George IV.*

3. Mrs. Fitzherbert's mother.

16

letter from the old lady & which the post had brought to her since my brother had been with her, & dated on the Thursday saying that she was quite out of danger & mending rapidly. Oh my God it was almost *too great happiness such* that to have her continue *quite well*, I do not know whether I would not sacrifice what I have most at heart in the world, the giving up all hope of ever passing another moment in the course of my life with her. And today, my dearest & most amiable friend, *I myself* have had a letter from *the old lady*, though rather short, still civil & kind, to assure me that her daughter, though she had been so very ill, still was not only now quite out of danger, but every hour visibly mending. I forgot to tell you that on Wednesday I was told she was very ill at Bath, which determin'd me to write to enquire after her, of the old lady, & which, though she did not answer by the return of post as I had entreated her to do, still she did yesterday & that was the letter I got this morning, whereas had she written, as I say, by the return of post, I should have received it yesterday & that of course would have put my mind at rest, as much as it could be after so terrible a shock, & which by her not doing left me under a certain degree of apprehension that there might be some grounds for the report, as she had not complied with the request contain'd in my letter. However, thank God that all is as it is, notwithstanding I acknowledge myself to be in a dreadful state still, & I can hardly write my two lines to her, to tell her that the paragraph in the newspapers was a fabrication without any sort of grounds. I am just still able, my dearest Duchess, to return you my most unfeigned thanks for your last kind letter as well as every other instance of your kindness to me, but I really am so fatigued with writing, not having eaten since the day before yesterday & only now rising out of my bed to send you this shocking scrawl, that I must conclude, & will therefore only add that though my heart is now almost fuller than ever, still there is a corner which will ever be solely devoted to the most affectionate attachment & love for you. Say everything I conjure you from me to dear, dear Fanny.[1]

No posts arriv'd as yet.

I will however in a few days write to you a letter all about yourself or what will appear I dare say better in your eyes, about *your other self*. God bless you (Rutland MSS.).

1. Mrs. Butler's cousin.

Saturday evening, 2 Mar. 1799

I wanted most exceedingly to see you yesterday and I waited at the Theatre for that purpose several hours, very much to the inconvenience of my own business which, of course, being of a public concern, I must and ought to attend to.

My business with you was merely an intermediate communication with H.R.H., whom I myself do not like to break in upon. I knew that a Message was to be brought down to Parliament for a provision to the two younger Royal brothers,[2] which is all very right and proper, but I think that no proper opportunity should be lost of representing to the country the real and true situation of H.R.H., which is simply and truly this; that during his minority the country benefitted nearly about £500,000 by H.R.H.'s revenue going into the Civil List, which would otherwise have gone so much more in arrear. Now, what have his Majesty's Ministers done? They have obliged H.R.H. under an Act of Parliament (little short of an Insolvent Bill) to pay his own debts out of his own income, leaving him without any provision whatever, that I know of, to provide for the Establishment of the Princess Royal [*sic*], his daughter, now presumptive heiress to the Crown of these Realms, an expence that must encrease as that Royal infant advances in years. I am perfectly aware that more proper persons than myself ought to have been employed in such a business, but why not attend to it, at least as far as my opinion & advice could aid the general cause?

I entreat you to mention these circumstances & ideas to H.R.H., and if agreeable to that Rl. personage, I should like, in matters of business, to have a more ready communication than at present exists between us, if H.R.H. is of opinion that my attachment may be useful & convenient to H.R.H.'s interests. (39557–8)

1. William Taylor (?1754–1825), 'Opera Taylor', described by Huskisson as 'little fat Taylor'. M.P. for Leominster, 1797–1802; for Barnstaple, 1806–12. Manager and principal proprietor of the Opera House. In 1796 he had hoped that Pitt would help him to obtain a seat, but he came in for Leominster on the interest of the Duke of Norfolk and on the Prince of Wales's recommendation. If Farington is to be believed, difficulty was experienced in finding two Members to present him to the Speaker, and the Duke soon regretted his choice. There was no consistency about his subsequent political affiliations. As a result of his connection with the Opera House, he became fraudulently bankrupt by 1819.

2. On 1 March the following Message was presented to the House by Pitt: 'His Majesty, being desirous of making competent provisions for the honourable support and maintenance of his dearly beloved sons, Prince Edward and Prince Ernest Augustus, which the monies applicable to the purposes of his Majesty's Civil Government would be insufficient to defray; and being also desirous of being enabled to extend to his beloved daughter, the Princess Amelia, the provision which he has been enabled to make out of the hereditary revenue for the other branches of his Royal Family, desires the assistance of Parliament...' (*House of Commons Journals*, liv, 255).

Woburn, 5 Feb. [*? Mar.*]¹ *1799*

Ten thousand thanks, my dear Duchess, for your kind letter, which I had no means of answering till today, & I am afraid that even now you will think I write too shortly [?] upon the many interesting topics that it contains, and though confin'd very much as to time I will endeavour, however, to make the most of it, & to prove to you that I do not feel or think less of my friends than I do of myself.

I will begin therefore by your concerns before I advert to my own. In primis, though there are accounts of Mr. Grenville's² safety, an officer in a small vessel having been sent over to Heligoland to enquire, & having there acquired the information to which I have already alluded of Grenville's being safely arrived at Copenhagen, though the vessel in which he sailed & thirteen of the crew had perished, still by a letter I have this instant received from London I am informed that no mails are as yet arrived; indeed, further than it being very *uncomfortable* I do not conceive you have *any*, or indeed *the smallest reason* to make yourself uneasy, my dearest Duchess, about our friend, as, though absent from us, still he is in an exceeding safe and retired spot, & far from the scene of warfare & confusion. You will, I am thoroughly convinced, receive one or two letters by each mail & whatever is contained in mine, you may depend upon my faithfully informing you of.

As to there being the smallest grounds to suppose that either I have or intend to resign my regiment to my brother or to anyone else, I do on my honour assure you I have never for a single instant had an idea of the sort, & there is no more truth in this report than there is at any part of it being order'd to Portugal,³ forty horses have been drafted out of the regiment as a part of a remount for the Twelfth L[igh]t D[ragoo]ns, and which have marched with a detachment of men under the command of little Charles Manners to Southampton, there to be deliver'd over to an officer of the Twelfth Regiment. As to myself, my dearest Duchess, I hardly as yet know ou j'[illegible]; however, as you may suppose, I am much easier from the accounts I have heard, or else I should not write

1. See note 2 for the date; also No. 1421, *n.* 3.

2. Thomas Grenville (1755–1846), Lord Grenville's elder brother. M.P. for Buckinghamshire, 1779–84 and 1813–18; for Aldeburgh, 1790–6; for Buckingham, 1796–1810. President of the Board of Control, July–September 1806; First Lord of the Admiralty, September 1806–March 1807. He and Fox had parted company in 1793 on the issue of the war. Extraordinary Mission to Vienna, 1794. In December 1798 he was sent on another Special Mission to Berlin in the hope of bringing Prussia into an anti-French coalition. After a series of mishaps, including shipwreck, he reached Berlin on 17 February 1799. The news of his safe arrival in Germany did not reach England until March.

3. The Spanish Government was believed to be contemplating an invasion of Britain's ally, Portugal, and during the year the British Government was planning the despatch of an expeditionary force for the protection of Lisbon. The attack, however, did not then materialize.

from hence; my mind wanted a little rest & change of scene, & I there fore I came [*sic*] here till Thursday.[1] Mrs. B[utler], the cousin of our friend Fanny, has been more humane, kind & attentive to me than I can possibly find words to express. On Saturday last she had the best possible accounts, & on Sunday morning I saw the servant of the person indisposed who [illegible (? came)] himself to acquaint me with the pleasant intelligence he had received by letters from Bath, & the post this morning brought me a letter from the same man with further good accounts from Bath as late as yesterday. This I will entreat of you to tell Fanny with many thanks for all her kindness, & if she will but write to her & tell her what she knows of what my sufferings have been, I think it will be *of immense consequence & do much good*, but if she could press her in consequence *to do or to say something to me* which would lead to putting things in a train, it would be delightful. Of this, though, she must judge for herself whether she can venture or not to go so far. Pray let me hear from you soon again as soon as you know anything either of what Fanny has written, or intends to write, or what she may have heard as to the effect that all this may have had on the other's mind. Forgive this horrid scrawl as I write in the utmost hurry, & beleive me ever, my dearest Dss [etc.] (Rutland MSS.).

1428   MAJOR-GENERAL WILLIAM GARDINER[2] TO THE PRINCE OF WALES

Norwich, 7 Mar. 1799

After an absence of fourteen years and some months I have at length the honor of addressing your Royal Highness once more from this country, and my satisfaction in regard to this article would be complete could I add to it the hope of shortly throwing myself at your Royal Highnesse's feet, and assuring you, Sir, in person of the unalterable continuance of my devoted attachment, but no person knows better than your Royal Highness the risk I should run by attempting such a measure, which could only produce immediate destruction to myself and give pain to those who are so good as still to take some interest in my situation. Perhaps I run nearly as great a hasard in going to Ireland, but I found something decisive was absolutely necessary to be done, as it had been frequently

1. See No. 1421, *n*. 3.

2. William Gardiner (1748–1806), brother of the 1st Viscount Mountjoy. Colonel, 1783; Major-General, April 1794; Lieutenant-General, June 1799. 'Gardiner is come over', wrote Cornwallis on the 20th. 'I mean to propose to recommend him ... for the Staff in this country, and to place him next in command to Lake in the Province of Munster (*Cornwallis Correspondence*, iii.77). Cornwallis had a high opinion of his military capacity, but thought he drank too much. At the time of his death he was Commander of the Forces in Nova Scotia and New Brunswick, and Governor of Kinsale.

signified to me, and even from high authority, that I could receive no advantage in the military line as long as I continued abroad, and I had a fatal proof of this in the last promotion of Lieutenant-Generals, which stopped almost at my name, though I had had the preceding rank the same year as many of those then appointed, and was a Field Officer before a number of the present Major-Generals were in the Army. All, then, that remains for me in the actual circumstances in which I find myself is to throw myself on your Royal Highnesse's protection, for though I have received many acts of marked kindness from the Duke of York and that I am persuaded both of his Royal Highnesse's justice and good offices, yet you, Sir, cannot fail to have great weight, and particularly since you have taken a military carreer, in which I am happy to hear from everybody (what I can most perfectly believe myself) that your Royal Highness is distinguished for attention, discipline, and knowledge of the profession beyond any officer in the service.

I took the respectful liberty of sending your Royal Highness by Colonel Anstruther,[1] who left Yarmouth yesterday morning for London, a real Damascus blade, taken by the Cosaks from a Turkish bastian at the Battle of Rimnicki,[2] gained the last war by the Marshal Suvarow;[3] the blade was sold in its simple state to a Polish nobleman, and probably had been very richly mounted, as is the custom with the Turks, but such as it is it was given to me by the then possessor as a mark of gratitude for some attention I was so fortunate as to have it in my power to shew him and his family during the Revolution, and if it proves acceptable to your Royal Highness I shall be doubly recompensed.

I am now on my way to Ireland and shall repair there with the utmost expedition; it is more than three months since I quitted Warsaw and was detained above two parts of that time at Hambourg and Cuxhaven, at the latter of which places I believe I should have died had it not been for the society of Colonel Anstruther, who was my companion in all my latest distresses.

Excuse, Sir, the liberty I have taken in writing you this long letter and be assured of the high respect and inviolable attachment with which [etc.]. (39559–60)

1. William Anstruther, Colonel since 1795.

2. On 22 September 1789 the Prince of Coburg, supported by Suvoroff, defeated the main Turkish army on the Rimnik. The Russo-Turkish war dragged on until the final peace treaty was signed at Jassy in January 1792.

3. Count Alexander Suvoroff (1729–1800), Russian Field-Marshal. In 1799 he was sent into Italy to help the Austrians against the French. He defeated Moreau on the Adda, Macdonald at the Trebbia, and Joubert at Novi, but lack of concerted action from the other Allied forces ensured the failure of his campaign to liberate Switzerland.

1429 THOMAS TYRWHITT TO THE PRINCE OF WALES

Boodles, 7 p.m., 8 Mar. 1799

The debate¹ is just over & the division upon the £12,000 pr. ann. was 83 for & 5 against (Mr. Tierney,² Sr. G. Schuckborough,³ Mr. Martin,⁴ Mr. Wilberforce Bird⁵ & Mr. Hobhouse⁶). Col. Lowther⁷ adverted to an expression of Mr. Tierney respecting the Princess Charlotte, & remarked 'That it would be highly satisfactory in any person in the situation about H.R.H. that could say H.R.H. had incurred no new difficulties'. Well aware that by my silence malevolence might have fancied a debt of £100,000, I got up & stated things as they are to the House. I am not vain enough to say I did it well, but thus much I can assure your R.H., that the House expressed uncommon satisfaction when I sat down, & I have since been told that it has pleased as much I was in hopes it would.⁸

I shall not fail to see your R.H. early in the morning & say how much I am your affec. servant. (39561)

1430 THE PRINCE OF WALES TO THE EARL OF MORNINGTON

Carlton House, 18 Mar. 1799

Having ordered Tyrwhitt to mention to you the names of three gentlemen for whom various friends of mine have requested me to interest

1. See No. 1426, and *Parliamentary Register*, liii.221–36. According to this source, and to *The Times*, the minority numbered four, but this cannot be checked from the *Journals*, the House being then in Committee of Supply. There is no report in the *Parliamentary History*.

2. George Tierney (1761–1830), whig M.P. for Colchester, 1789–90; for Southwark, 1796–1806; for Athlone, 1806–7; for Bandon, 1807–12; for Appleby, 1812–18; for Knaresborough, 1818–30. Treasurer of the Navy, 1803–4; President of the Board of Control, end September 1806–April 1807; Master of the Mint, 1827–8.

3. Sir George Augustus William Shuckburgh, afterwards (1793) Shuckburgh-Evelyn, 6th Baronet (1751?–1804). M.P. for Warwickshire, 1780–1804.

4. James Martin (1738–1810), M.P. for Tewkesbury, 1776–1807. Banker and country gentleman. His 'incorruptible integrity compensated for the mediocrity of his talents' (Wraxall, iv, 81).

5. William Wilberforce Bird (*c.* 1759–1836), M.P. for Coventry, 1796–1802.

6. Sir Benjamin Hobhouse (1757–1831), 1st Baronet. M.P. for Bletchingley, 1797–1802; for Grampound, 1802–6; for Hindon, 1806–18. Chairman of the Committee of Ways and Means, 1807. Created Baronet, 1812. He was the father of Byron's friend John Cam Hobhouse.

7. James Lowther (1753–1837), M.P. for Westmorland, 1775–1812; for Appleby, 1812–18. Colonel of the Westmorland Militia. He was a cousin of Lord Lonsdale, and Equerry to the Duke of Gloucester, 1782–90.

8. Tyrwhitt stated that the Prince, ever since the late settlement of his affairs, had strictly complied with the terms of that agreement; and that he maintained the young Princess without incurring one shilling of debt.

22

myself, and whom I am persuaded you will take under your protection, I cannot resist expressing my hearty satisfaction at hearing the climate of India has not proved unfavourable to your constitution, but that on the contrary you feel yourself better than when in this country.

European news you will, I am persuaded, have so much in detail from various quarters that I shall not detain you with any; assuring you therefore of my hearty wishes for your prosperity, I am [etc.].[1] (Add. MSS. 37414, f. 4)

1431 PRINCESS ELIZABETH TO THE PRINCE OF WALES

Windsor, 19 Mar. 1799

I have just received mama's commands to enclose you a letter she is very desirous you sd. receive. She orders me to tell you with her love that had she not been hurried to death it would have been much better wrote, but she knows yr. good nature & relies on you to forgive it; if you answer her, she begs you will enclose it to *me*. (Add. Georgian 11/80)

1432 THE QUEEN TO THE PRINCE OF WALES, AND THE REPLY

Windsor, 19 Mar. 1799

A circumstance happened on Sunday night in my room when we had a matter of eight ladies with us which I was very anxious to communicate to you as yesterday morning, but my time was so taken up from eight o'clock till past twelve which so fretted me that could I without making the world, who is ever ready to watch the Royal Family more watchful, gone to you or send a message I should have done it [*sic*], particularly as I expected Ernest, who had promised to come & would have made it so easy to have done, but he failed & I was obliged to leave London quite unhappy to myself.

The Kg. took notice of Ldy. Cholmondeley's children[2] at Church, admired them, & said in the evening how glad he was to see her so constantly at Chapel, & then asked if she had a particular place allowed

1. This letter was dictated to, and written by Tyrwhitt.

2. Lady Cholmondeley had three children: George Horatio, Viscount Malpas (1792–1870) who succeeded his father as 2nd Marquess on 10 April 1827; Charlotte Georgiana (?1795–1828) who, in 1818, married Lieutenant-Colonel Hugh Seymour, a cousin of the 3rd Marquess of Hertford and brother of Minny Seymour; and William Henry Hugh (1800–84), who married, 28 February 1825, his cousin, Charles Arbuthnot's daughter Marcia Emma Georgiana (1804–78), and who succeeded his brother as 3rd Marquess of Cholmondeley, 8 May 1870.

by Ldy. Mary Cook[1] in the Closet. Ldy. Bath said that she was only there during Lent, & when the Royal Family was absent she as well as many other of the Peers' Ladies sat in the Peers' seat below. The Kg. answered she must find that a much colder seat, upon which he was answered that Ldy. C., being very attentive to the young ladies which were with her, could not bring them upstairs, & therefore preferred staying with them below. He then inquired the names of those ladies & was told Miss Seymor & Miss Fellows. He then said, 'I know the last, but who is the first?,' & was answered, Lrd. C. natural daughter. He asked me if I knew that. I answered I understood she was a ward of his, & then several of the others said No, she was his daughter. This I thought was my duty to mention to you, but I was still more anxious to inform you of my having received a letter from Ldy. C. yesterday morning in which she renews her request about Miss McKenzie, & then returns me thanks for allowing Miss Seymour to be presented at Court, & inquires whether I continue of the same oppinion. Now, my dear, you must remember that I iṁediately said to you, why present her at all? upon which you answered me it will be just like Mademoiselle le Clair,[2] & I made the remark, God knows so many people come to Court that I do not think the Kg. would mind it much, particularly as he does not know her. But I do not remember that I ever said, *I gave leave that she should be presented, & you know that step I never should take without the Kg.'s leave at any time*, nor did I understand it in that light, else I should immediately have given for answer that I did not dare give leave without the Kg., & before you left me I again repeated, why present her at all? You will I hope be convinced that I can have no personal dislike to a young woman well brought up & unknown to me, but after what passed on Sunday I think it my particular duty to prevent Ldy. C.'s taking a step which might offend the Kg., & also to clear myself of the mistake of my having given leave for a presentation at Court without the Kg. being made acquainted with it.

I am so convinced of your judgement & regard to decency that you will approve of my intention to see Ldy. Cholmondeley on Thursday to explain myself upon the subject, as I must own that I never saw a more sensible & respectfull letter than hers is to me.

I hope you will enjoy this fine weather in the country & amuse yourself

1. Edward Coke, Viscount Coke (1719–53), only son of Thomas, Earl of Leicester (1697–1759), married, 1747, Mary (1727–1811), fifth daughter of the 2nd Duke of Argyll. She was supposed to be half crazy, but she had been badly treated by her husband: they were separated in 1750.

2. The 3rd Duke of Richmond (1735–1806), who was succeeded as 4th Duke by his nephew, had three daughters by his housekeeper. Of one of them, Miss Le Clerc, Farington said that 'she lives at the Duke's and the Duchess is very fond of her. She has been introduced at Court.'

well. The exercise I hope will cure all bilious disorders which will give great pleasure to [etc.]. (36503–4)

THE PRINCE OF WALES'S REPLY

Critchill, 21 Mar. 1799

Your kind letter reached me by the post this morning & I return home from hunting purposely to answer it, to keep you in as little suspense as possible. Your statement of *everything that passed between you & me respecting Miss Seymour is* PERFECTLY CORRECT, & I am not a little astonished that Lady Cholmondeley should have been imprudent enough, however well intention'd, to say one single word to you upon the subject, especially as I have not to the best of my recollection ever had one single word of conversation with her upon it. Cholmondeley I certainly had some conversation with, but merely general with respect to you, such as saying you were *very kind to me* when I spoke to you, & I advised him as I told you I should, not to ask any questions, but to bring her to Court when Mrs. Arbuthnot[1] was to be presented & to present her as *a ward of his*. This is *specifically* ALL that passed between us. However, I shall now write to him directly myself, but not shew your letter. There is one mode before I write to him which I think still it might be effected by, which is, Cholmondeley's saying what is *perfectly true*, that *she is no daughter of his*, but *his ward*, & contradict by that means what she has been by some people supposed to be. Pray send me a few lines in answer whether you think this might not be done by either a letter or message thro' one of your Ladies from Lady Cholmondeley, who may have been supposed to be acquainted with the general idea of the world, & fearing that you & the King might have heard it, & this to be done by way of explanation previous to the girl's presentation, fearing that you might both be prejudiced against her. Excuse this scrawl, as I write in the utmost haste, fearing I shall otherwise be too late for the post & consequently not get my letter to Cholmondeley. Do not be the least uneasy, I conjure you, my dearest mother, at the idea of my being displeased. I assure you I shall not whichever way the circumstance turns out. I certainly do wish the girl well, & it certainly will be the surest means, her being presented at Court, the getting her probably well settled hereafter, which is no inconsiderable reflection to me. However, I will not have *you* stand in the *smallest degree committed*. Pray let me hear from you as soon as you have had it in your power to turn the circum-

1. Charles Arbuthnot married, 23 February 1799, Marcia (1774–1806), daughter of William Clapcott-Lisle and of Hester, who was a granddaughter of the 3rd Earl of Cholmondeley. She was presented at Court on 3 April.

stance over in your mind as I have stated it to you. I write though to Cholmondeley immediately, merely to suspend Georgiana's presentation till he hears again from me. Adieu, my ever dearest mother, I say nothing either for or of myself, except, that I am what is no news to you, ever [etc.]. (42270–2)

1433 THE PRINCE OF WALES TO PRINCESS ELIZABETH, AND THE REPLY

Critchill, 21 Mar. 1799

I have sent a long scrawl to the dear Queen which I will beg of you to desire her to shew you, & as soon as you conveniently can, to get me an answer.

Edward came here yesterday evening & is gone this morning back to London.[1]

In the utmost haste I am [etc.]. (42273)

FROM PRINCESS ELIZABETH

Queen's House, Good Friday evening [? *22 Mar. 1799*]

I am commanded by mama, my dearest brother, to tell [you] that much as she has longed to see you she has never had a moment since she returned from Windsor which she could call her own. She grieves most exceedingly at your continuing to suffer so much & she flatters herself that you will *really* take *care* & follow Keate's orders most exactly. By her going to Kew tomorrow she will return so late that she again will be prevented from calling on you; therefore flatters herself that by giving yourself entirely up for these next ten days there may be a chance of seeing you at our return from Windsor. We all eat of the bunn you sent us through your dear little Charlotte who was quite delightfull. My sisters & mama join in love. (Add. Georgian 11/81)

1434 THE QUEEN TO THE PRINCE OF WALES

Queen's House, 23 Mar. 1799

Yr. answer arrived late last night to my great astonishment, as I really hardly could believe that my letter had reached you. I have had my

1. *The Times* reported on the 20th that his carriage had been attacked by highwaymen at Langley.

26

interview with Lady C. & fairly told her of the accidental conversation which happened in my room on Sunday night, as also a remark of the Kg.'s which I forgot to mention to you, how highly he approved of Ldy. Willoughby & her conduct in never having attempted to present Miss Bertie until she was married, & she agreed with me that after this it would be improper to think of presenting Miss Seimour. That is all that passed between her & me upon the subject, for as we understood one another perfectly well I thought it better to drop that subject. She talked with great delight of yr. goodness to herself & family, & expressed every possible attachment & affection for yr. person. As to the proposal you make about the manner in which the Kg. might be undeceived about the suspicion of M.S. being Lrd. C.'s daughter, I will fairly own, as you wish me to speak the truth, that you will act more kindly towards her by giving it up entirely, for you know how difficult it is to deceive the Kg., & should by any accident which cannot now be foreseen, (but yet may happen) the real truth ever come to light, I am convinced the dear Kg. never would forgive it. All this my own conscience bids me say, & by yr. letter I am justifyed not only in doing so, but I feel truely happy to have it in my power of preventing your taking any step which might with reason offend the Kg.

I am just come from Ldy. Elgin where we took leave of Chasse.[1] We are all sorry to part with her, I hope she will be happy. Ldy. Elgin keeps up her spirits wonderfully & when she begins to get low she goes to dear little Cha[2] to recover her spirits, in which she is quite right, for anything so good or so engaging I never saw before, & yesterday she was *unique*.

I must now quit you & prepare myself for leaving town tomorrow. I wish you a happy Easter & beg you to remember [etc.]. (36505)

1435   THE EARL OF CHOLMONDELEY TO THE PRINCE OF WALES

London, 23 Mar. 1799

Lady Cholmondeley had the honor of taking her children to the Queen's

1. Lady Elgin's daughter Charlotte (*d.* 1816). She was one of the Ladies of the Bedchamber to the elder Princesses. At noon on Saturday the 23rd the Queen and the Princesses paid a visit to Lady Elgin and Lady Charlotte Bruce at the Countess's house in Downing Street, where, said *The Times*, they partook of an elegant breakfast. On the 28th Lady Charlotte married Captain, afterwards Admiral Sir Philip Charles Durham, at her mother's house. Her wedding dress was a gift from the Queen. The bridesmaids were Lady Frances Bruce and Lady Charlotte Belasyse. 'Captain Durham', suggested *The Times*, 'a great admirer of *Anson's* Voyages, is now studying *Bruce's* Travels'.

She was now succeeded as a Lady of the Bedchamber to the elder Princesses by Lady Matilda Wynyard.

2. Princess Charlotte.

House on Friday last, when her Majesty was graciously pleased to enter on the subject of Miss Seymour's presentation at St. James. But as I understand it may be unpleasant to the King, I am sure your Royal Highness will approve of its being dropt for the present.

Your Royal Highness has been very good to us upon the occasion, and I am well aware of the great advantage that would result to Miss Seymour if she could have been presented without difficulty at St. James'.

People in general have been very kind to Lady Cholmondeley & indeed almost without exception Miss Seymour is constantly invited everywhere. I have every reason to hope that her beauty & accomplishments will procure her a good establishment such as she deserves, and I am sure your Royal Highness, with your usual goodness, will at all times honor her with your protection.

You will be sorry, Sir, to hear that a roguish Attorney is trying all in his power to deprive poor Mrs. Elliot of the small annuity settled upon her by Sir John Elliot[1] & I fear the long process of a Chancery suit will alone force him to pay her what is her due.

It seems certain that Mr. Grenville cannot succeed with the King of Prussia in persuading him to come forward, & without his assistance the Emperor is in a very disagreable situation.[2] The weakness of his Cabinet is realy unaccountable in not forseeing the villainous intentions of the French, and the certainty of their breaking every Treaty & every promise the moment they found it was to their advantage so to do.

I was in hopes to have had the honor of paying my duty to your Royal Highness at Bath where I go tomorrow for two or three days with Lady Cholmondeley to see her sister, but Mr. Churchill tells me he thinks your Royal Highness will not be there so soon, which I am very sorry to hear. (50832–3)

1436 THE PRINCE OF WALES TO THE DUCHESS OF RUTLAND

Critchill, 23 Mar. 1799

I have now time & opportunity to answer your last letter the receipt of which was one reason that I had not written to you as yet; however, I should have written to you before you wrote to me, immediately upon

1. Possibly Sir John Elliot (1736–86) who was knighted, 31 May 1776, who became Physician in Ordinary to the Prince of Wales, and was created a Baronet, 25 July 1778. On 19 October 1771 he married Grace, daughter of Hew Dalrymple, Attorney-General of Grenada. In 1774 she was divorced for *crim. con.* with Viscount Valentia, afterwards Earl of Mountnorris [I.]. She, who was known as 'Mrs. Elliot', subsequently intrigued with the Prince of Wales and many others; and died, 16 May 1823, near Sèvres.

2. See No. 1427*n*.

receiving a letter from Munich,[1] had it not contain'd *such matter* which I shall advert to presently, that I thought it *fairer & more honorable by you* to let the impression of what *he might have written* to you, have fair play with you before I wrote, in order not to put you under any difficulties with respect to me. Our friend in this instance has done, as I have in many instances before known him do, take up circumstances *too hastily* & without giving himself time to ponder upon them & rather foresees, from a lively imagination & apprehension, what he fears may happen, than attends to the case as it is. Now the truth of this *is*, my dear Duchess, perfectly well known to yourself. You were *my confidante, not an agent*, to whom I open'd my whole heart & soul, just *as he* might have been to me, or *as I have been to him*. As to his judgment of the result of the case in question respecting my happiness, I cannot admit him to be as good a judge as I myself am. No man can know the interior of my mind as I know it myself. Long experience must have taught me THAT which no rhetorick or persuasion, however great my affection may be or my opinion of the person who may attempt doing so, can make me see or feel in another point of view. He, I can easily perceive, was afraid that I wish'd to embroil *you*. Do me the justice to agree that it never was so. You have indeed been *my friend, my most confidential friend*, but that I have to no one (excepting only one who you know also) ever hinted that I had ever open'd my lips to you upon such a subject. I have likewise had the honor of being thought worthy by you of being the repositor of your feelings respecting him. Whatever I have heard from any quarter that I thought might be either important or interesting to you to know respecting him I have always consider'd it a *duty incumbent upon me from the friendship you was so good to express for me & the confidence you reposed in me, instantly to communicate to you.* And in this further respect I may have gone beyond what there was any occasion for you ever to have done by me, & that is that I have written to him touching yourself, but nevertheless I cannot consider myself *as an agent* employed by you, an agent *of what*? Is he not perfectly aware of your attachment to him, & are not you completely sensible of the perfect return of his affection?[2] I could not acquaint either of you of what you did not already know & feel, but I have talked of him to you de vive voix & to him of you by letter, & merely repeated things that I thought might be pleasing & interesting to both parties, but still I cannot consider myself as any agent of yours. In

1. From Arthur Paget.

2. For the Duchess's many admirers see No. 877n. Dr. John Ford, writing sometime in 1796 to William Roscoe the historian and M.P. for Liverpool, said that Chester was crowded with nearly a thousand soldiers from Ireland. The Duke of Rutland was their Colonel, and his beautiful Duchess caused a great sensation whenever she appeared. Duchesses, he added, were so seldom seen in Chester that he believed the inhabitants expected some superior kind of being (Roscoe MSS. No. 1558).

what does your situation therefore towards me, differ from mine towards you? In none that I see. You had the same confidence, the same friendship repos'd in you that was reposed in me; you only communicated what you heard that might be interesting & that too from *one channel only*, & that also *merely for a time that it would or could be necessary*; therefore I might insist upon it, as it appears to me, that there is nothing in our respective situations towards each other, circumstanced as we are, that we have both of us done, which, from the friendship we have mutually acknowledged & felt for each other, & the confidence we had placed in each *other, we were not entitled to expect from one another, at least from liberal minds, which I am confident both of ours are*. This I must beg of you to place in a proper point of view to him, that you was merely (to use the same word again by way of explanation that I have done in a former part of my letter) the *repositor* of the innermost *secrets, thoughts & feelings of my heart, my confidante*, ALL *in one word* MY FRIEND, *& no agent*. Recollect also, my dear Duchess, that when you ask'd me whether I had ever hinted anything upon the subject to him, I told you I had talk'd over all former circumstances with him, which at the same time you informed me he had never divulged to you. You may likewise recollect you ask'd me whether I had any objection to your touching upon it towards him. I told you you might mention the circumstance, indeed, as I should have done had he been present, for you well know that there is hardly anything I ever keep from him, but it would have been merely acquainting him with the circumstance itself & with my feelings, but not by way of consulting or asking an opinion about it at all; for what advice can ever be of any service if one feels oneself *really* attached? I do not consider our affection as being in our power; perhaps a passion form'd at first sight may be got the better of by advice, or by cool reasoning at the very first moment if your mind is capable of such reasoning & thought, but where an attachment has lasted for years, & though perhaps smother'd for a time bursts forth afresh, that alone affords sufficient proof that it is stronger in the heart & mind than anything that either advice or reasoning could bring against it. Allow me, dear Duchess, to think you will admit I am fair in my way of seeing & representing everything; were anyone to attempt to advise you *to think no more of Arthur*, in the first place I do not think you would consider them much longer as *your friend*. I think you would justly hold them in estimation *as a* fool, & as to theirs or any other advice, I think if I know you, it would *have as little effect upon you as upon anybody, or, as I cannot but say what our friend's opinion has at the present moment upon my feelings*, be just & fair to me & in your letter when you write to him tell him how good humor'dly at least & how justly I have argued with you, & at the same time not allowing myself to be in the least out of humor with him.

The agitation & hurry I have been in for the last ten days owing first to her being expected in town, & then afterwards her arrival in London [1] & a thousand circumstances which naturally attended that arrival, has been such that I never have had it in my power to write to you, which I now do, as soon as I have had a couple of days quiet in the country, & have been able to collect my thoughts & ideas a little & to quiet in some degree my nerves, which, as you may easily believe, have not been a little shatter'd from the continued state of irritation they have been in, & the severe trials I have had to go through for a considerable time past. As to the rest of his letter, he answers in no one point as to his returning home except that he shall treasure up & bear most carefully in his mind my advice. As to you, he talks of you with an affection & as I really think you deserve, as *the greatest angel that ever was*, & acknowledges that in many instances previous to the present moment his conduct to you had not been such as you merited, & as he wished it had been. In short, though his letter was so far communicative & friendly, still I think it savour'd too much of the ministerial tone of an old Foreign Minister, or Minister writing a lecture to a young Prince just entering life, & this I beg you will tell him, as I shall likewise, I assure you.

By this time I should think, my dear Duchess, you must be completely tired of seeing my handwriting; however, I cannot help, before I conclude, asking you one question, and that is, whether I am to understand by your letter that there is to be an end to that friendship & confidence which has so pleasingly to my feelings subsisted between us for so long a time, & that we are only to be upon that kindly [?] sort of footing so loosely defined by the word friendship but which more properly shd. be called acquaintance, as in that case, however severely I may feel such a circumstance, still I shall never attempt to intrude upon you either myself or my concerns in any shape; if you think this is Arthur's wish & your intention, & the construction you put upon what he has written, pray say so frankly, as tho' painful, still it will save both you & me much awkwardness & uncomfort [*sic*]. But to be quite sure, you had better before you exactly define what you intend, ask him fairly the question after telling him what I have said in this letter to you.

I really am quite ashamed of the immense length of this epistle, but when I profess it I am very sincere, in being in *friendship* & I trust in every transaction of life, it is therefore that I have ventured to trespass so long upon your patience to be the more explicit; for when I have placed my affection, friendship & confidence as I have in you, my dear Duchess, & not lightly too, I do not think it should be lightly overthrown, either for want of explanation or understanding between us. I ever shall remain, my dear Duchess's very sincere friend & humble servant.

1. Mrs. Fitzherbert arrived at Lord Wentworth's house in Seymour Street from Bath on Friday the 15th.

P.S. Pray let me hear from you from again [*sic*] & direct to me at my house in town at all times, for there all my letters come safe. I am quite ashamed upon looking back at the number of erasures & inaccuracies in this hasty scrawl, but I have not time to write it over again. Therefore you must have the goodness to forgive me (Rutland MSS.).

1437   PRINCE ADOLPHUS TO THE PRINCE OF WALES

Hannover, 27 Mar. 1799

Though it is a very long time since I have had the pleasure of writing to you, yet I trust you know me too well to think me capable of neglect or forgetfulness, and that you will attribute my silence to the true reason, the fear of troubling you. I have also of late not been in a great humor to write, having been very much out of spirits on account of a subject which you undoubtedly will have heard of, & which has hurt me so much that I have not touched it to anybody but to those who were informed of the whole affair from the beginning to whom I was obliged to write.[1] Ernest has received an account of the whole busyness, which I desired him to mention to you, it being too painful a task for me to give twice a detailed account of these particulars: and for this reason I hope, dear brother, you will excuse my not having written to you before on this subject. My first intention was to inform you of everything, but on my receiving an order not to mention the subject to anybody, I put off writing to you till I should have some hopes that the match could take place, when you undoubtedly should have been the first person to have been informed of it: but as the whole affair has been broke off, I own I was too much moved to write on the subject except to those who were already implicated in the affair. This is the real reason why you have not heard from me on this subject, and I hope, my dearest brother, that you are too

1. *The Times* had this paragraph on the 29th: 'A story is related in one of the morning papers of yesterday, and will probably be copied into other papers of this day, of Prince Adolphus having joined Mr. Grenville at Hanover by appointment, and accompanied him to Berlin, where it was intended he should have settled the preliminaries with the King of Prussia for the marriage of his Royal Highness with the widow of the late Prince Lewis; but that on arriving at Berlin, it was found she was married to the Prince de Salm. That Prince Adolphus may have been enamoured of the Princess above-mentioned, and that he formerly solicited the leave of his Royal father to marry her, is very possible, but that he lately went to Berlin with Mr. Grenville in order to negociate the completion of this business is wholly unfounded. The Prince de Salm has been married to the widow of Prince Lewis full three months, and it is reported from pretty good authority that though there were many reasons for wishing to bring this match to a conclusion, the whole circumstance was not very satisfactory to the King of Prussia. His Majesty, however, settled £6,000 a-year on the Princess de Salm, who has retired with her husband to a distance from the Capital, where they live quite secluded.'

much persuaded of my attachment for you to think that my silence could come from neglect. God knows I love you from the bottom of my heart and that there is nothing I would not do for to prove it you. Pray let me soon hear from you, and be assured that nothing can render happyer your [etc.].[1]

I hoped to have been able to give you some good news of the operations of the Austrian Army. The last account we received was that the two Armies were very near one another not far from Constance; and therefore it is highly [? probable] that an action will have taken place by this time. General Hotze who commands in Swisserland has been twice attacked in his position at Feldkirch, but he has defeated the ennemy, and according to the French reports they have lost very near 4000 men. The Archduke has sent great reinforcements to this General, the ennemy seeming determined to drive the Austrians out of Swisserland. Poor Royal is in a very disagreeable situation at this moment, the French having entered the Dutchy of Wertemberg: it seems though that for the present they do not intend to molest that country, and for this reason my sister has resolved to remain at Ludwigsburg, a Castle three leagues from Stuttgard, from whence she can get in a very few hours into the Prussian dominions. (48532-3)

1438   THE PRINCE OF WALES TO THE DOWAGER COUNTESS OF ELGIN
Bath, 1 Apr. 1799
Accept, my dear Countess, my very best congratulations & good wishes in the late event that has taken place in your family;[2] no one, you know, feels more for you at all times than I do, but particularly upon so trying an occasion as the late one.[3] At the same time that this must in some degree have been painful to you it was attended with something to

1. Mrs. Richard Trench, who met Prince Adolphus in Berlin in 1799, described him as 'extremely handsome, tall and finely formed; his complexion fair, yet manly; his features regular yet expressive. His manners bear that stamp of real goodness which no art can imitate, no other charm replace; and though he presents himself with suitable dignity, his address immediately inspires ease and confidence. His conversation is fluent, various and entertaining' (*Remains of Mrs. Trench*, ed. by Dean of Westminster, p. 37).

2. Her eldest surviving son, Thomas (1766-1841), who had succeeded his brother as 7th Earl of Elgin in July 1771, married Mary, daughter of William Hamilton Nisbet, of Dirleton and Belhaven, Haddingtonshire, on 11 March 1799. The marriage was dissolved in 1808, and she immediately married Robert Ferguson, of Raith (1768?-1840), M.P. for Fifeshire, 1806-7; for the Dysart Burghs, 1831-4, 1837-40, and for Haddingtonshire, 1835-7. She died 9 July 1855.

3. The reference may be to the shipwreck of the *Proserpine* frigate in January, which was carrying Lord Elgin's official recall from his Berlin Embassy, dated 25 January.

balance it a little, the pleasure you must have experienced at seeing Elgin again with his amiable wife. I trust they are both as well as you can wish them, & I beg you will mention me kindly to them both. As for poor dear Chassey I shall not say anything at all about her except that I hope most truly *she will be happy*, for if I was to hazard anything *in my own way*, you would just treat me as you did at the coach door, when you drove me away in the Park. I hope my dear little Charlotte continues quite well; pray give my most affectionate love & blessing to her. (49232)

1439   PRINCESS AMELIA TO THE PRINCE OF WALES
Queen's Lodge, 2 Apr. 1799
My dearest Prince of Wales or Eau de Miel:[1] knowing how ready you always are to do a good-natured action I take this opportunity of troubling you with a few lines to beg if you can procure two tickets for Mrs. Hope's Ball for Ly. Anne Wombwell & Sir George as they are just come to town & desirous to set out in the coach at once. I should likewise have asked for one for dear Charlotte Belly[2] but mama intends leaving me here tomorrow as they return on Friday & therefore Belly is so good as to stay with me. If you can get these tickets send them if you please at once to Ly. Anne, No. 13, Cavendish Square. We hear *you are the man* to apply to.

We are all very well & as to myself I am much the same. What horrid weather.

Ernest came last Monday & remained till Sunday when he went to Lord Abercorn's. I long to see you again, my dear perfect *Eau de Miel*. Lord Uxbridge has been here. All my sisters, particularly dear Miny, desire their kindest love & beleive me ever, dear Eau de Miel, your affte. friend.[3] (Add. Georgian 14/22)

1440   LETTERS FROM THE EARL OF CHOLMONDELEY TO THE PRINCE OF WALES
London, 2 Apr. 1799
I have much satisfaction in being able to inform your Royal Highness

1. He was given this affectionate nickname because he sent her gifts of honey-water.

2. Lady Charlotte Belasyse (1767–1825), one of the Ladies of the Bedchamber to the younger Princesses.

3. The Prince had gone to Bath from Critchell on Friday, 29 March, on a private visit (to take the waters). He complained of being far from well.

that Admiral Payne[1] is considerably better than I expected to find him. Sir Walter Farquhar[2] says considering the very severe shock he has received, he is much better than he himself expected, but to bring him round will be work of time & much attention.

I went this morning to Brompton & found the Admiral in bed. He seems still to think that his complaint is a dumb & unformed gout. He desired me in the strongest manner to assure your Royal Highness of his gratitude for your goodness to him; indeed, I am very sure it has had the best effect possible upon his mind.

The Hamburg mail is not yet arrived. The wind is so strong it is supposed it cannot come in. People are very anxious to hear the news confirmed. That events have happened advantageous to the Austrian arms cannot I think be doubted. If they amount to the general expectation it may give a fortunate turn to the late unforseen & unfortunate events. If the French are realy retreating in disorder their army will be annihilated as they must not expect mercy from the irritated inhabitants.

The taking of Corfu at this moment is a most lucky incident. The passage from that arsenal to Italy is so short that the Russians may easily send a sufficient force to oblige the French to abandon their new conquests in the Neapolitan dominions.

It is supposed the Russians were not in the late engagement with the Archduke, but that they are gone with Suvorow into Italy. (39562-3)

Piccadilly, 4 Apr. 1799
I am very sorry to inform your Royal Highness that by letters received from the Continent, & particularly one from Mr. Grenville dated Berlin 27th it appears that all the late accounts of advantages gained over the French armies are destitute of any foundation.

The last letter from Stutgard dated the 20th states that Genl. Vandamme,[3] who had his Headquarters at Ebingen, had changed them the preceding day to Heckengen. Gen. Jourdan was on the 18 at Phulendorff. After this movement of the French armies their advanced posts were immediately opposite to those of the Austrians & news may be expected in a few days of an action. Hitherto there has not been, nor could there

1. Payne, who had been restored to favour since 1794, was made a Rear-Admiral on 14 February 1799. Lord Minto wrote (24 January 1799): 'The Prince lately met Jack Payne for the first time since his disgrace, and spoke to him with great cordiality and affection' (*Life and Letters of Lord Minto*, iii.48).

2. Physician to the Prince of Wales, 1796; created Baronet, 1796. (1738-1819)

3. Dominique Joseph Vandamme (1770-1830) commanded a division under Soult at Austerlitz in 1805; was defeated and taken prisoner at Kulm in 1813. Exiled after the second restoration in 1815, he died at Cassel in July 1830.

have been any action from the armies having been so distant from each other on the 14 & 15, when it was reported Jourdan had received a check.

After the above account, it appears very singular that Jacobi should have sent the account from Radstadt to Berlin, that Mr. Grenville forwarded by express to London.

Lord Auckland told Lady Cholmondeley last night at the Duchess of Gordon's that he did not himself beleive that Massena had been worsted in the Grisons.

I am going to the Drawing Room, & if the other mail arrives in time for the post I will have the honor of making the news known to your Royal Highness.

I sent this morning to Admiral Payne, and I am happy to say he has sent a good account of himself. (39564–5)

1441 PRINCESS AMELIA TO THE PRINCE OF WALES

Queen's Lodge, 7 Apr. 1799

My dearest dear Eau de Miel: It is quite out of my power to express to you how obliged I feel myself for the very kind letter you wrote me. Sr. George[1] & Ly. Anne beg me to return you many thanks as well as Charlotte *Belly*. My perfect Miny begs a thousand loves as well as my other sisters.

I am glad the waters agree so well with you, my dear Eau de Miel, but am very sorry your *nasty* spasms still continue. No one will rejoice more than your own child (meaning myself) to hear you have lost them, for they are not at all *dunfuass*[2] companions.

Dear Louisa[3] was to come to town yesterday for a day or two. I think dear mama very well. Our last letters from dear Royal were dated the 12th of March & everything was quiet; she was still at Lewisburg. Don't tell, but I hear she is so prodigiously large, she can scarcely walk up or downstairs. This is out of compliment I suppose to *her Duke*:[4] very romantic, but if I was her I would not if I could help it shew my affection in this manner.

What a dear perfect creature you are, my dear *Eau de Miel*. I hear dear little Charlotte was vastly well on Thursday. Charlotte Belly begs many duties & thanks & beleive me [etc.]. (Add Georgian 14/23)

1. Wombwell.

2. An invented word.

3. The reference may be to Lady Louisa Paget. *See* No. 1187.

4. The Duke of Wurtemberg was himself amazingly round, and Napoleon is said to have remarked, rather unkindly, that he believed that God had created this Prince to demonstrate the utmost extent to which the human skin could be stretched without bursting.

1442 THE EARL OF CHOLMONDELEY TO THE PRINCE OF WALES

London, 8 Apr. 1799

As your Royal Highness must be very anxious to ascertain the truth of the many & contradictory reports that have been propogated relative to the events that have taken place between the Austrian & French armies, I take the liberty of informing your Royal Highness that there can no longer be a doubt that the Archduke had a considerable advantage over the centre of the French army on the 20th & 21st since which the latter have regained some advantage; the extent we are ignorant of.

The French had pushed forward with success a body of men into the Tyrol; they have been obliged to retire again into the Grisons with a considerable loss.

I am very happy to tell your Royal Highness that I yesterday saw a letter from Vienna, where they are not alarmed; on the contrary, the Archduke's army is both numerous & well disposed. Considerable corps of Russians are *certainly* on their march, and if the Archduke can only keep in check the French army, everything may be expected in Italy in the course of the campaign.

I shall be most truly happy to hear your Royal Highness receives every benefit from the Bath waters. (39566–7)

1443 LORD PAGET TO THE PRINCE OF WALES

Guildford, 10 Apr. 1799

I cannot sufficiently express my obligation for the very kind letter that I received this morning from your Royal Highness & which I have taken the liberty to send to Ld. Uxbridge that he may be equally sensible of your goodness to us. As however I was allowed to leave town on the day after I received a summons to attend the Second Reading of the Copper Bill, I imagine that such arrangements have taken place as may render the measure palatable to all parties and do away the necessity of giving any further trouble to our friends.[1]

Your Royal Highness mentions that the newspapers have revived the stale and uninteresting subject of Watson's court martial. I have only seen its publication announced and do not think that a man in his senses would under such circumstances have taken this step.

1. There were complaints in March that the price of copper had risen by 20 per cent during the previous six months, and by 40 per cent since 1797: a rise which added greatly to the cost of sheathing ships' bottoms. On 20 March the House decided that a Bill should be introduced to prohibit the exportation of copper and to permit its importation duty free, for his Majesty's service. The Bill was read a first time on 21 March but was abandoned for that session on 18 June.

The weather has been so bad that I have not yet been out with the 7th. I flatter myself that so many this summer have the advantage of acting in line with the 10th. I feel confident that we shall derive the greatest benefit from it and from being under your Royal Highness's command. (17905–6)

1444   THE PRINCE OF WALES TO THE QUEEN, AND A REPLY

Bath, 10 Apr. 1799

I cannot delay, my dearest mother, troubling you with a few lines in consequence of the very kind enquiries my brother Ernest inform'd me, on his arrival yesterday evening, you had been so good as to make after me, & of which I assure you I am most truly sensible. Would it were in my power to write anything that could either interest or amuse you from hence, but of all the dull séjours I ever experienc'd, this certainly at the present moment is the dullest. Perhaps my having been a good deal indispos'd since I have been here, & which always to a certain degree leaves a species of gloomy impression on the mind, makes me consider this place as stupider than it really is. However, I understand that in the opinions of most people it really *is* so, & perhaps the more so, from the comparative very gay & crowded winter which has fallen to the lot of this water-drinking place during the last three or four months, the like of which I am inform'd has never before been known. As to myself, not to tresspass too long upon you, I certainly am better & gradually getting better every day, my spasms, from the good effect of the waters, certainly decreasing much as to their violence as well as the frequency of the visits they have been so kind as to make me. The life I lead is the most regular possible, always in bed at half past eleven, up a little after seven, & I have stinted myself to only one pint of wine, pour tout pottage. I go as little out as I possibly can; to avoid singularity one must occasionally go to the Rooms, or, properly speaking, to the Balls, for half an hour, which is the utmost time I have staid, as there is hardly a creature I ever saw before in all my life that go there, & the two Balls that I have hitherto been at so crowded, so hot, & so stinking, that I was absolutely gasping for fresh air, & dying to get away from the moment I came into the Rooms.[1] I hope my dear little Charlotte is quite well & continues to be a *good girl*, I have much, my dear madam, to say to you respecting *her* when I again return to town, as well as upon *other topics* which I shall

1. The Prince of Wales and Prince Ernest on the 12th became members of that 'delightful institution', the Bath Harmonic Society. 'After supper, the President gave a bumper to each of the Royal brothers, with three times three, followed up with the songs and chorusses of *Rule Britannia* and *Britons strike Home*, which were sung with great spirit and *éclat*.'

not touch till we meet. Pray let me know if there is anything that either you or any of the dear girls would wish to have from this place; if there is, I hope it is not necessary for me to add that I trust you will allow me to be your comīssionaire. I am not very gay, therefore I will now conclude with signing myself [etc.]. (42274-5)

Queen's House, 10 [?12] Apr. 1799
I will not leave London without returning you thanks for yr. kind letter, & in particular for the good account you give me of yr. state of health. My fears about the Bath waters being taken improperly are so great that I sent for Turton & ordered him to write you good advice which I hope you have received by this time & need not add how much I wish you to follow his prescriptions.

Comparisons between the Metropolis & Bath would I suppose be lèse Majesté, but I may be allowed to say that what yr. present habitation is to[o] dull, London I fear is to[o] gay for the health & strength of many of the young ladies, for there are at least five or six more a comming so thick one after another for fear of the beaux going away, that those who go to all must have Herculean strength to bear up with the fatigue.

One good, however, has arisen from this gaiety which is the declared match of Lrd. Bagot & Amely [*sic*] Fitzroy, an event in which I am sure you will rejoice sincerely,[1] & it is thought that, provided it is well managed, that this may bring about a reconciliation between Ldy. Southampton & Mrs. Allen. The death of the Dowager Dutchess of Beaufort[2] brought about that between the Dutchess of Rutland & Ldy. Elyzabeth Norman[3] & I understand nothing can equal the joy of the daughter. I do not hear that Mr. Norman has as yet been admitted, but if he is prudent & silent upon the subject, perhaps sensible conduct may do much for him. The poor Duke of Dorset had a stroke of the palsy on Wednesday. He did walk about the room yesterday, but had not recovered the use of his hand or speech last night & is declared in great danger.[4]

Dear little Charlotte becomes more engaging every day & I think that of late the hesitation in her speech is much less, & by watching her much

1. William, 2nd Lord Bagot (1773-1856), who succeeded his father in 1798, married, 30 May 1799, Emily (1770-1800) fourth daughter of the 1st Lord Southampton. She died of consumption.

2. Charles, 4th Duke of Beaufort (1709-56), married, 1740, Elizabeth, sister of Norborne, Lord Botetourt, and daughter of John Symes Berkeley. She died on 8 April 1799, aged 80.

3. Lady Elizabeth Manners (1776-1853), the Duke of Rutland's sister, married Richard Norman in August 1798.

4. The Duke died on 19 July.

39

& strengthening her body she will I make no doubt get the better of it.

I hope when next you write to hear that you are quite well & that you drink even sparingly of water according to orders, which I must still recommend as the preservation of yr. health is uppermost in the thoughts of [etc.]. (36506–7)

1445 THE MARQUESS OF ABERCORN TO THE PRINCE OF WALES

11 Apr. 1799

The time is now come when I may, without even the appearance of any indelicacy, beg your Royal Highnesses acceptance of my most sincere & ardent thanks for those most gracious & flattering proofs of interest & kindness with which you have honoured me.

When I found two days ago that in consequence of Mr. Sutton's absence your Royal Highness had not the due notice you were pleased to command of the second reading of the Bill[1] which I have had the misfortune of being obliged to bring forward, I felt much hurt lest you should for a moment doubt my sense of the value of your Royal Highnesses countenance & friendship upon that as well as every occasion, but as everything passed as unanimously & respectfully as I could possibly have wished, I now cannot but rejoice that your Royal Highnesses goodness to me has not been the occasion of trouble, though it is indeed a pride to me to feel convinced that if it had you would not have grudged it.

All I could say in return would very imperfectly express what I feel, but I am sure your Royal Highness gives me credit for the impression which your uniform kindness must make upon my mind, & the gratification I must feel in being honoured with such constant marks of your friendship & esteem.

I trust your Royal Highness does justice to the disinterested & affectionate attachment as well as gratitude with which I subscribe myself [etc.]. (39568–9)

1446 LORD LOUGHBOROUGH (THE LORD CHANCELLOR) TO THE PRINCE OF WALES

24 Apr. 1799

Your Royal Highness was pleased in reference to a writing that had been

1. On 21 March he was given leave to introduce a Bill to dissolve his marriage. Captain Joseph Copley was the co-respondent. The Bill was read a second time on 10 April and received the royal assent on 10 May (*House of Lords Journals*, xlii.108, 200).

delivered by Mr. Bicknell to Mr. Cotes about the 14th of February 1796 & which when authenticated I understood was proposed to be presented by me to his Majesty as a Petition of Right, to direct at my humble request that your Attorney & Sollicitor General should communicate with me upon the opinion I entertained that it did not belong to the Office of Chancellor to receive & present a Petition of Right to his Majesty.

I stated that opinion to these learned gentlemen with the reasons on which it was founded, and the precedents which seemed to prove that the proceeding on a Petition of Right did not & could not without manifest error commence in the manner proposed; I added that if upon the result of my farther research into a proceeding which had been in disuse for almost two centurys they should discover any precedent that could justify my assuming a function which I took to be inconsistent with the duty assigned to me in the course of the suit, I should consider with the utmost attention the authority of any such precedent.

I have had no communication since with these gentlemen upon the subject till I had the honour of receiving your Royal Highness's letter of the 19th instant when I took the earliest opportunity of inquiring of them whe[the]r they had found any other precedent, which they said they had not, & of recalling to their recollection the result of the former interview three years ago which they very clearly understood.

The writing is still in Mr. Cotes's custody but it has always remained at Mr. Bicknell's disposal whenever he chose to take it away, returning the receipt which he required Mr. Cotes to give at the time he delivered it to him. (39570–1)

1447 THE PRINCE OF WALES TO THE DOWAGER COUNTESS OF ELGIN

Bath, 24 Apr. 1799

Many thanks for your kind letter of yesterday to which I only reply a few lines, my dear Countess, as the post is going out. You rejoice me quite with so good an account of the dear child, but I am dissatisfied with your account of yourself. Pray let me have a letter from you soon. As to myself, I have been between ourselves *very ill indeed*, & it is little known *how ill*, but I thank God I am able to go out again, though I continue *weak & low* from the extreme severe discipline I have been obliged to undergo. For God's sake do not alarm my mother, but I tell you the truth. How does the dear Queen do? Pray let me know. Let me beg of you to send the enclosed to my beloved Mary as soon as you get it. I wish her to get it as early as possible as it contains the best wishes of my heart but ill & faintly expressed on her birthday. Oh *what an angel she is*, my dear Lady, how gifted in body *& mind* by Providence, & what a *blessing* *she is to us all.* I say not this with a view of disparaging any of the rest of *my beloved sisters, as they are all equally dear to me,* but as her birthday is tomorrow & I have of course *been thinking much of her,* therefore she is more immediately under my *mind's eye,* & therefore I cannot help talking of her, as I think, know, & with conscious pride feel *as her brother* that she truly deserves.

P.S. My love to Chasse if she is with you. (49233)

1448   THE QUEEN TO THE PRINCE OF WALES, AND THE REPLY

Q[ueen's] H[ouse], 24 Apr. 1799

At my arrival in London on Munday I was told you was arrived the night before & that unexpectedly, which made me put off writing that day, & in the evening I was rejoiced to hear that Mr. Jerningham had given a very excellent account of yr. health to Lrd. Harcourt, which I trust will encourage you of going on with the waters in a temperate way as the best means of insuring success. You ask me about the report of the Duke of York's house being upon sale, & desire me for once not to be too prudent. What I know about it at present I was told by yr. brother Ernest, & that it was beleived by the world that the Kg. had granted him some ground in the Park for building; that the Duke, however, denied both the selling his house & the grant. Two years ago I remember hearing that a great builder was about York House, & instead of paying down the money, he was for the value to build a new house for the Duke near Whitehall. This was told me by the Kg. as a scheme of which he himself had no great opinion, & in a few weeks after that all idea of this was given up. Last year when we breakfasted at his Office he said that he was so well lodged at Whitehall that he had thoughts of putting up a bed there & make it his entire habitation, to which I answered, 'Why not!—for as you live at present a great house is useless, for as the Dutchess cannot be there yr. family is always divided.' This is all that passed between him, the Kg. & me, but I beleive nothing has passed this winter more particularly, only that variety of furniture has been transported from London to Oatlands, which probably has given rise to the report, at least for renewing it. The Dutchess has been so very ill that the Duke was sent for on Saturday last. She has kept her bed for four days & was not to attempt getting up till yesterday. I mean to send today to make inquiries after her. Yr. two brothers are to go to the Levée *pour les baise mains.*[1] Well, it has lasted long enough before it came so far.

1. On Wednesday the 24th Prince Edward and Prince Ernest kissed the King's hand at the Levée on being created Duke of Kent and Duke of Cumberland respectively. On 26 August

Old Mac is arrived safe & well, to live with her nephew. She talks of taking a better house, of subscribing to the Opera, & to see company every Saturday night, as it is but fair to be quiet one night in the week. Happy she who enjoys such spirits at 81.

The Duke of Rutland's wedding was very quiet at Lrd. Carlisle's house. They young couple [*sic*] are gone to Cheveley, & if I am well informed, are not to be presented untill the deep mourning is over,[1] which of course cannot be till after the Duke's return from Ireland.[2] Ldy. Elyzabeth & Mr. Norman are both with the Dowager Dutchess at Belvoir & very happy, c'est une bonne perspective pour Monsieur Forest. Ldy. Antrim[3] is to be married tomorrow. Oh! how I wish that Lrd. Marc Kerr was arrived to marry Ldy. Charlotte, her sister.[4] She is but in a bad state of health, & the incessant balls & hot rooms I fear will injure her much.

& now for poor Mrs. Barker, *indeed if I would I could not grant her request*. The applications are without exaggeration above 20, some of which of an old date, & others of such a nature as to require some delicacy in choosing without offending, & she is right in saying her age is against her.

I have seen little Charlotte. She was delightfull & declared she would not leave the house till she had seen us go to the Play. She grows very tall indeed.

& now I think it is time to release you, & I will finish by wishing you fine weather, which is very essential to make the waters beneficial, & to clear my head, which is very dull, but not so dull as not to feel the pleasure of subscribing myself [etc.]. (36508–9)

The Times declared that the Duke of York had disposed of his house in Piccadilly.

1. The reference must be to the death of the Duchess Dowager of Beaufort, in her 81st year on 8 April. She was the widow of the 4th Duke (1709–56), and the mother of Mary, Duchess of Rutland (1756–1831).

2. It was on 10 July that the Duke was presented to the King on his return from Ireland.

3. Anne Katharine, *suo jure* Countess of Antrim (1778–1834), married, 25 April 1799, Sir Henry Vane-Tempest, 2nd Baronet (1771–1813), M.P. for Durham, 1794–1800; for County Durham, 1807–13. She, 'the great Irish prize in the matrimonial lottery', had succeeded to the Earldom on her father's death in 1791. It was a scandalous marriage. Probably whilst the marriage settlement was being prepared he was committing adultery with a Mrs. Henderson (*née* Laurence), the young wife of a West India merchant. Because the Judge described her as an absolute strumpet, frequenting all the fashionable places of vice, the jury awarded only a shilling damages against the defendant on 20 June 1799. There was one daughter of the 1799 marriage, Frances Anne Emily, who in 1819 married, as his second wife, Charles William, Lord Stewart, later (August 1822), 3rd Marquess of Londonderry.

4. Vice-Admiral Lord Mark Robert Kerr (1776–1840), third son of the 5th Marquess of Lothian, married, 18 July 1799, Charlotte (1779–1835), Lady Antrim's sole surviving sister. In 1834 she inherited her sister's peerages under the special remainder of 1785.

43

THE PRINCE OF WALES'S REPLY

Bath, 27 Apr. 1799

Many thanks, my ever dearest mother, for your very kind letter, which gave me the greatest & truest pleasure, & your accounts of dear little Charlotte really quite delight me. The more she is with you the more she will improve, & the happier & the more content I shall be. I leave this place on Thursday for good, & shall then go to Critchill till about Monday, of which I hope also to take a final leave, as there is no longer the possibility of tolerating it, on account of the landlord Charles Sturt, who will not do anything to the place, or abide by any of the terms of the lease.[1] This place affords no gaiety to entertain you with, my dearest Madam, which must account to you in some degree for the great stupidity of my letter, as well as my being a little low *still*, owing to the medicines I have been obliged to take to expell my old enemy, *the bile*, & which, I thank God, is now accomplish'd, & I feel myself better considerably. As to Mrs. Barker you will recollect, my dearest mother, I said nothing, but merely enclosed you her letter. I was well aware that her time of life was not such as to make her either the properest or most eligible person. Either Monday or Tuesday sennight I hope to present myself to you; till then, & at all times I shall subscribe myself [etc.].

May I entreat you to give my best love to my sisters? (42280–1)

1449   THE PRINCE OF WALES TO THE DUKE OF RUTLAND

Bath, 27 Apr. 1799

I have been so unwell for some days past that it was not in my power to do what I wish'd, which was to endeavour to express my congratulations to you on your nuptials as soon as I was inform'd of their having taken place. I hope you will allow me now, though not at the first moment, to assure you that no one can participate in your happiness more than I do, or can form more sincere wishes for your wellfare & prosperity through life than myself. I will not tresspass any longer upon you at present than to beg you to beleive me [etc.] (Rutland MSS.).

1450   THE PRINCE OF WALES TO CHARLES GREENWOOD

Bath, 30 Apr. 1799

Many thanks, my dear Greenwood, for your kind letter which I received

1. The rent of Critchell House was £1,120 a year. On the 25th *The Times* announced that the Prince had given it up.

four days ago & which I should have answer'd sooner could I have obtained an answer relative to the time when Colonel Beaumont or Mrs. Beaumont might see the house in Warwick Street, but the indisposition of Lady Elizabeth Villiers, who has been at the point of death in consequence of having broken a blood vessel some few days back, will possibly make it a week before it will be possible for the Colonel to view the premises. This I beg you will mention to him with my best compliments and acquaint him that as soon as *her situation* will admit of it I will take care to acquaint you with it. Many thanks, my dear Greenwood, for your kind attention on this, as well as every other occasion. I am happy to see your letter dated from Craig's Court, as I flatter myself that is an intimation that your health is quite re-established. (Add. Georgian 38/10)

1451 THOMAS TYRWHITT TO ROBERT GRAY

Welbeck Street, Monday morning

The bearer is collector of the Charity for 'Delivering poor Women at their own Habitations'. The Prince has been long a subscriber of £20. Do arrange it so that it may not be suffered long to remain in arrear.

Used to be in Water Lane, Blackfriars, but now is No. 13 Godliman Street, Paul's Chain, St. Paul's Churchyard. £20 pr. annum. Direct to Mr. Hurst at the Office. (Has not been paid for 3 years).[1] (30053)

1452 THE QUEEN TO THE PRINCE OF WALES

Queen's House, 8 May 1799

According to yr. desire I spoke to the Kg. this morning relating to yr. conversation of yesterday.[2] He bids me assure you *that at no time in his life does he ever mean any personal offence towards you,* but as the Princesses birthday has always been kept by us ever since her arrival in England, he owes it to the world not to relinquish it at this time. Upon the cards will be put only a Dressed Ball without giving a reason for it, which I hope

1. The note is endorsed: 'Paid Mr. Waring by Mr. Brent's account, April 1799, £20, for Lying-in Charity.' Richard Waring was Secretary to the Charity.

   This Charity was instituted in 1757. The Prince of Wales was its President, and amongst the Vice-Presidents were the Earls of Dartmouth and Uxbridge. Amongst the staff were thirty midwives. The Society's meetings were held at Will's Coffee House, Cornhill.

2. The Prince had returned to London from Bath on the 6th. It was said that he was still far from well.

will in some degree satisfy you.[1] I shall be most particularly satisfyed to hear that you are better this morning, & remain ever [etc.]. (36511 and [copy] 42282)

1453 LETTERS FROM THE DUCHESS OF WURTEMBERG TO THE PRINCE OF WALES

Louisbourg, 10 May 1799

My dearest brother is I hope too well convinced of my affection to doubt that I was very much hurt yesterday at hearing from my sisters that you have not found the benefit you expected from Bath. I wish, dearest brother, that you would for all our sakes and more particularly for that of your lovely little Charlotte take care of your health; how painful would the thought be to yourself were she left without your care and protection. I always look forwards to that little girl as being as she grows up your comfort and companion. You little think how much I love to employ my thoughts in seeing your future prospects enlivened and cheered by her love and attentions.

Thank God public affairs go on well, and though it is not prudent by the post to enter much on those subjects I must ever rejoice at our being freed from our oppressors, and trust they will not again have an opportunity of returning here. The horrors they have committed in the upper part of the Dutchy are hardly to be believed.[2]

Our weather is very unpleasant as it [is] so changeable that we can never go out two days following, as the cold and rain are too apt to succeed a warm day. This place begins to be in beauty as the leaves are at last coming out. I wish you could see it as I believe you would be much struck by its extent and variety.

The Duke begs to be remembered to you and I will now, dear brother, bid you adieu.

A thousand loves to Charlotte. (51533-4)

1. The Grand Ball was given by the Queen on Thursday the 16th at Buckingham House, and the Prince of Wales was not present. Next day (the birthday of the Princess of Wales) the Queen and Princesses visited her at Carlton House and then left for Windsor. The Prince kept out of the way: he set off on an excursion into Gloucestershire.

The Duchess of York's Fete a few weeks later caused further embarrassment. The Prince insisted that the Princess should not be invited to Oatlands, and as the Duke and Duchess refused to agree to this exclusion, the Prince persuaded the Queen to express a desire that the Princess might not be invited. The Duchess then asked the Queen to name her own company (Lady Elizabeth Foster's *Journal*, 30 May 1799).

2. On 2 May *The Times* declared that the Duke of Wurtemberg had published a general amnesty for all deserters who might rejoin their regiments within three months, but that the four soldiers of his bodyguard who had deserted in consequence of a conspiracy in which they had been engaged, were excluded from the benefit of the amnesty.

Louisbourg, 27 May 1799

It gives me great pleasure to have it in my power to write you at last a letter which I am certain you will receive, and not exposed to the sad irregularity of the posts, which often makes me appear neglectful and wanting in affection to those I love dearly. Allow me, dear brother, to recommend to your notice and protection General Baron de Melius, who the Duke has named his Minister to the King, and is a man well acquainted with Continental affairs, having been employed these last thirty years by the late Dukes at the different great Courts of Europe. Last year he was both at Petersburgh and Berlin. Any attention, dear brother, you will have the goodness to bestow on him I shall feel very grateful for.

I trust you have received the two letters I have written to you on hearing from my sisters that you were unwell at Bath. I trust, dearest brother, that you are now recovered and much delighted at your return to London to find your dear little girl much improved. I should be delighted could I see that little angel. The accounts I hear of her from everybody give me great pleasure, as I look forwards to her being a great comfort through every stage of life to her dear father. I think, dear brother, this dear little Charlotte must be a great inducement to take care of yourself, who are an object so dear to all your family, but of double consequence to your child, who must ever require the attention and care of an affectionate parent. May I beg of you to allow her to wear the Cross of Ribbond-stone which accompanies a snuff box I take the liberty of offering you of Labrador. It is your known goodness to me which encourages me to offer these trifles, thinking they may be a little acceptable as they come from one who is much attached to you.

Thank God the Austrian arms continue very successful and I trust that they will prevent the monsters from again entering into the Dutchy; they treated us so ill during their stay that they have set all ranks against them. It was most providential that they did not meet with their accustomed success, as I have every reason to be convinced had that been the case in defiance of all Treaties they would have overturned the Government and made us share the fate of the Great Duke of Tuscany.[1] Our having staid quietly in the country has been very useful as on the whole it prevented dissatisfaction and very great expence. The country people are uncommonly good and behave very well, which is very much to their credit when it is known how cruelly the French have behaved, destroying the 13 best Oberämter of the Dutchy and taking away money, corn, cattle; in short, the month they were here, besides the amazing plunder under pretence of requisitions they took away for two millions seven hundred thousand florins.

1. Ferdinand III (1769–1824), a son of the Emperor Leopold II (1747–92). He succeeded his father as Grand Duke on the death of his uncle, the Emperor Joseph II, in 1790.

The Duke begs to be remembered to you and I will take up no more of your time than to assure you, dear brother, how sincerely I am [etc.].

A thousand loves to dear little Charlotte.[1] (51544–6)

1454 THE PRINCE OF WALES TO MRS. FITZHERBERT [2]

Windsor Castle, 11–12 June 1799

Save me, save me, on my knees I conjure you from myself whet., after a SOLEMN PROMISE GIVEN, PLEDGED TO MY BROTHER TO BE MINE AGAIN, *is there truth, is there honor in this world*, & YET NOT INHERENT IN YOU. Oh! my friend, my friend Payne, what will you say was it only to TRIFLE with my feelings that my HOPES WERE TO BE RAISED, THAT FUTURE PROSPECTS, THE ONLY ONES OF LIFE & HAPPINESS TO ME, *were to be held out to me* BECAUSE THE AGONIES I HAD ALREADY SUFFER'D WERE NOT SUFFICIENT. IF YOU WISH MY LIFE YOU SHALL HAVE IT. If you BREAK YOUR SACRED PROMISE, RECOLLECT I AM FREED FROM ALL TIES OF ATTACHMENT TO THIS WORLD, *as there is no reliance, no more faith existing*, I THEN HAVE NO FEARS LEFT, NOTHING BUT HONOR IN A WORLD IN WHICH I HAVE EXPERIENCED NOTHING BUT MISERY & DECEIT, *in return for* THE FINEST FEELINGS OF THE HONESTEST OF HEARTS, NOTWITHSTANDING ALL APPEARANCE MINE HAS EVER BEEN TO ME: REITER-ATE YOUR PROMISE OR RECOLLECT YOU SIGN YOURSELF MY DOOM. OH, GOD! OH, GOD! WHO HAS SEEN THE AGONY OF MY SOUL & KNOWEST THE PURITY OF MY INTENTIONS, HAVE MERCY, HAVE MERCY ON ME: TURN ONCE MORE I CONJURE THEE, THE HEART OF MY MARIA, TO ME, FOR WHOM I HAVE LIVED & FOR WHOM I WILL DIE. You know not what you will drive me to FROM DISPAIR, YOU KNOW YOU ARE MY WIFE, THE WIFE OF MY HEART & SOUL, MY WIFE IN THE PRESENCE OF MY GOD: 'TIS THE ONLY ONLY REPRIEVE LEFT. IF YOU WILL NOT ADHERE TO YOUR PROMISE I WILL *CLAIM YOU AS SUCH, PROVE MY MARRIAGE*, RELINQUISH EVERYTHING FOR YOU, RANK, SITUATION, BIRTH, & IF THAT IS NOT SUFFICIENT, MY LIFE SHALL GO ALSO, IN THE CASE YOU STILL REMAIN OBDURATE I SHALL DIE AS AN HONEST MAN IN MY OWN EYES, IF YOU WILL NOT FOLLOW YOUR HUSBAND & BE THE COM-PANION OF HIS RETIREMENT; if you will persist in not being mine again AS YOU HAVE PROMIS'D ME TO BE, IT IS THE ONLY ONLY THING LEFT ME; I SHALL AT LEAST FEEL MYSELF AN HONEST MAN AGAIN: SO HELP ME GOD, 'TIS MY FINAL DETERMINATION.

1. The Prince wrote to his friend Arthur Paget from Carlton House on the 30th: 'I am only this moment arriv'd in town, and take up my pen instantly to say how truly happy I am at the thoughts of seeing you again. Pray call on me early in the morning as there is no one living loves you more sincerely or more, than your ever affectionate' (*Paget Papers*, i.167).

2. On the cover of the letter is the following instruction: 'Private. *Mrs. Fitzherbert*, to be deliver'd into *her own hands only* by the Duke of Cumberland.'

Wednesday morn: 4 o'clock. It is now two hours since I wrote the above; I have calm'd myself & examin'd my heart, 'tis HONEST & PURE; my tears are dried up, but MY RESOLUTION IS FIX'D. This letter preceeds me, & my brother will deliver it unto YOUR OWN HANDS HIMSELF. *He knows nothing of the contents*, & UPON YOUR ANSWER THROUGH HIM TO ME IN WRITING WILL DEPEND HIS FURTHER IGNORANCE OR INFORMATION. IF YOUR ANSWER IS CONFORMABLE, WHICH GOD GRANT IT MAY, TO MY WISHES, BY ASSURANCES OF YOUR BEING AGAIN *MINE*, THERE IS NOTHING IN THIS WORLD I WILL NOT DO, & IN WHICH I WILL NOT BE GUIDED BY YOU THROUGH EVERY OCCURRENCE IN LIFE, NOW & FOR EVER. But if it is the reverse THAT INSTANT my father & the rest of my family SHALL BE ACQUAINTED WITH THE TRUTH OF MY SITUATION: AS GOD IS MY JUDGE & AS I HOPE TO RECEIVE MERCY AT HIS HANDS THIS IS *MY LAST & FINAL DETERMINATION.* ON MY KNEES HAVE I SWORN IT & ON MY KNEES DO I WRITE IT TO YOU. THUS MY FUTURE NOW DEPENDS SOLELY ON YOU, LIFE WITH YOU OR AT LEAST A QUIET CONSCIENCE, WHICH WILL MAKE ME FACE EVERYTHING: I SHALL HAVE LIBERATED MY OWN HEART, CLEAR'D THE CHARACTER OF THE ONLY BELOVED OF MY SOUL TO THE WORLD & BY VOLUNTARILY SACRIFICING MYSELF PROVED THAT I HAVE DESERVED A BETTER FATE, & TO HAVE BEEN LOVED BY YOU, AS I HAVE LOVED YOU & SHALL LOVE YOU TO THE LAST MOMENTS OF MY EXISTANCE. *The wretched experiences of the last five years have* MADE LIFE ONLY DESIRABLE IN ONE SHAPE TO ME, & THAT IS IN YOU. I AM WRAPP'D UP IN YOU ENTIRELY; AFTER SEVENTEEN YEARS ATTACHMENT [1] NOTHING CAN ALTER ME, SHAKE ME OR CHANGE ME. ALIKE YOURS IN LIFE OR IN DEATH. THE CRYSIS IS COME & I SHALL DECIDE MY FATE, THAT IS TO SAY YOU SHALL & WILL FIX MY DOOM. If your answer is SUCH TO RESTORE ME TO LIFE THERE IS NOTHING, I REPEAT, THAT I WILL NOT SUBMIT TO FOR YOUR FEELINGS, YOUR DELICACY, YOUR WISHES, & THAT I WILL NOT DEVOTE MY LIFE TO PROVE THE SINCERITY OF MY ASSERTIONS: BUT IF NOT, YOU KNOW THE CONSEQUENCE; THEREFORE DECEIVE NOT YOURSELF, I MUST REQUEST YOU. *My heart is now freer*; THE HAVING WRITTEN *my letter to my father which I bring up with me to dispatch* INSTANTLY TO HIM SHOULD YOUR ANSWER BE UNFAVORABLE *makes me feel* A CALM THAT NOTHING BUT THE SENSE OF THE INTEGRITY OF MY MOTIVES COULD HAVE INSPIRED ME WITH, & WHATEVER THE CONSEQUENCES MAY BE I AM READY TO MEET THEM, AS I FEEL, HOWEVER DREADFUL, STILL I AM ACTING RIGHT BY YOU, & PUNISH MY GUILTY SELF.

And now, GOD BLESS YOU, MY MARIA, MY ONLY LIFE, MY ONLY LOVE, THINE, UNALTERABLY THINE, George P.

Turn over.

Think not that Payne or any advice whatever will make me change my purpose, or FORSWEAR MY OATH. THANK GOD *my witnesses are*

---

1. If this statement is accurate the Prince must have made her acquaintance in 1782, not, as is generally supposed, in 1783 (see Vol. i, p. 139).

living, your uncle¹ & your brother,² besides Harris,³ who I shall call upon us having BEEN INFORMED BY ME OF EVERY, EVEN THE MINUTEST CIRCUMSTANCE OF OUR MARRIAGE. Oh!, my heart, my heart, but I am composed & calm. Whatever your answer may be & whatever the consequence STILL MY BLESSINGS WITH MY LOVE WILL EVER ATTEND THEE MY MARIA. *THY* George P.⁴ (50205–9)

1455 THE PRINCE OF WALES TO THE QUEEN, AND THE REPLY

Carlton House, 12.30 p.m., Sunday, 16 June 1799

Enclosed I take the liberty of sending you two letters upon the death of Mrs. Herbert⁵ which I could not refuse to lay before you; one of these applications I cannot help acknowledging that I feel more interested in than the other, & I will leave you yourself to find out which that is, as I do not think it will be a very difficult task. At the same time, not wishing to intrude upon the King by a letter myself, I will request of you to lay the letter which is likewise enclosed at his Majesty's feet; it comes from Alderman Le Mesurier⁶ to me, & written by the desire of the Artillery Company. You will have the goodness to express my duty to the King, & my earnest wish to be inform'd of *his pleasure* what answer *he* would have *me* return; as my only desire *can* be to do *that* that may be consider'd as most *respectful by him*, as well as appear *such* in the eyes of the world. May I not be supposed to[o] unreasonable if I request an answer *as soon as* it may be convenient, & I have therefore order'd my servant to wait your commands.

P.S. Had I felt myself sufficiently stout to have attended the Review tomorrow which I much wished, I should not have troubled [you] with so long a scrawl. (42283–4)

1. Henry Errington.

2. John Smythe. See Vol. i, p. 174.

3. Lord Malmesbury.

4. For the Duke of Kent's part in effecting a reconciliation, see No. 1462. Glenbervie wrote: 'It seems their subsequent reconciliation did not take place till the Queen sent a message herself to Mrs. Fitzherbert pressing her to it. It is believed the Queen took this step from an apprehension that the Prince would go distracted if it did not happen' (*Journals*, i.351).

5. Mrs. Georgiana Herbert, for many years a Bedchamber Woman to the Queen.

6. Paul Le Mesurier (1755–1805), M.P. for Southwark, 1784–96; Lord Mayor of London, 1793–4; Colonel of the Honourable Artillery Company.

7. The King reviewed the Prince's Regiment (the 10th Light Dragoons) on Ashford Common.

Windsor, 16 June 1799

Never did a letter arrive in better time then yours, for the Kg. was just come in from his walk, & I communicated Alderman Mesurier's letter immediately to him & he bids me say that as the Corps wishes it & it can make them happy, he can have no objection to yr. appearing with them.

I shall with pleasure remember yr. two recommendations of Miss Poyntz & Miss Mackenzie [1] when in my power, but Ldy. Carnarvon having acquainted me on the Fryday of the death of Mrs. Herbert I immediately named Mrs. Waldegrove [*sic*] [2] her successor, who as well as many others has at least been twelve years upon the list.

I am sorry to learn by yr. letter that yr. health is not so much improved as I could wish, but I hope with care & quiet it may soon be brought about again so that we may soon have a merry meeting, which can never be too often nor too soon for [etc.].

[*P.S.*] My love to the dear little angel. [3] (36512)

1456   COLONEL PAUL LE MESURIER TO THE PRINCE OF WALES

Austin Friars, 19 June 1799

I humbly beg permission to acknowledge the receipt of your Royal Highnesses most gracious letter and to express the very high sense entertained by all the members of the Honorable Artillery Company of your Royal Highnesses most gracious condescention in the very distinguished honor intended them by your Royal Highness in appearing at their head as their Captain-General on Friday next, at the inspection of the Corps by his Majesty.

Every member will receive with respectful gratitude this most honorable mark of your Royal Highnesses great goodness and gracious regard for the Corps, an honor which will ever be memorable in the annals of the Artillery Company, and which cannot fail in securing to them the

1. As Maids of Honour.

2. Described, inaccurately, in the Red Book, as Mrs. Emily Waldegrave. William Waldegrave (1753-1825), second son of John, 3rd Earl Waldegrave, married (1785) at Smyrna, Cornelia Jacoba, daughter of David van Lennep, of Smyrna. He, who became an Admiral in 1802, was created Baron Radstock [I.] in 1800. She was a Bedchamber Woman from 1799 to 1816 (*d.* 1839).

3. The Prince of Wales wrote to Arthur Paget from Carlton House on 17 June 1799: 'What can have happen'd to you, my dearest Arthur? If you cannot call early tomorrow morning which I wish you would do, pray let me know where I may write to you as you say that you are going out of town for some time' (*Paget Papers*, i.168).

protection of their Sovereign, the favour of Government and the consideration of the public.

I have now to report to your Royal Highness that I received yesterday at the Mansion House, from Major-General Ludlow,[1] the order of his Royal Highness Field Marshal the Duke of Gloucester, of which I take leave to inclose a copy.[2] Your Royal Highness will see that the Artillery Company are to meet in the Artillery ground, and to march from thence to Finsbury Square, where they are to be drawn up by nine of the clock in the morning; in consequence, orders are issued to the members to meet at seven o'clock, and the line will be formed punctually at eight, when the Corps may be ready to receive your Royal Highness, but as his Majesty may not be in Finsbury Square before ten, or half past ten of the clock, it might be too much to expect your Royal Highness to march with the Corps from their ground to Finsbury Square, there to wait for his Majesty's approach, and therefore, unless your Royal Highness should be pleased to order it otherwise, I shall march at half an hour past eight from the Artillery ground to Finsbury Square, there to take up the ground by the time ordered and wait there for your Royal Highness.

Three other Corps are ordered to join us in Finsbury Square, who will all be most happy to be considered as under your Royal Highnesses command.

It remains for me to intreat your Royal Highness will accept of my most grateful acknowledgements for the very gracious manner in which your Royal Highness has been pleased to approve of my conduct, and to beg permission to subscribe myself [etc.]. (39572)

1. See Vol. i, p. 241.

2. The order was contained in Major-General Ludlow's letter to Le Mesurier, dated the 18th:

'As the time will not, it is found, permit that his Majesty should visit each Corps at its particular Alarm Post on Friday, the 21st inst., I am commanded by his Royal Highness the Duke of Gloucester to acquaint you that it is now wished that the several Corps should assemble at two or three principal points of each division of London for that purpose.

I herewith inclose to you the description of your Alarm Post, which Post you are desired to visit and to shew to the Corps under your command previous to their being marched by you to the place where they are to receive his Majesty, which is Finsbury Sqre., where they will be drawn up for that purpose by 9 o'clock in the morning.

Description of the Alarm Post

Name of Corps	In what Division	Alarm Post	Guards detached	Patroles
Artillery Corps	Royl. Ex. Division	Artillery ground	55 at new River Head	Chiswell St[ree]t, Finsbury. The Curtain, London Wall, & Worship Street

The Corps in case of alarm to assemble on their own parades & from thence to be marched to their respective Alarm Posts.' (39573)

Donington, 19 June 1799

I have filled up the Proxy & send it by this post to the Duke of Clarence. The first time that you ride towards that part of the town after three o'clock, be so kind as to call at the House of Lords & give to Mr. Cowper,[1] on my account, a guinea for the entry of the Proxy, that his Royal Highness may not have to pay for it. I earnestly hope it is not really ill health that has brought Sir Charles Stuart[2] home. Exclusive of personal liking, I have a very high opinion of him as an Officer. The Expedition[3] will be well entrusted either to him or to Sir Ralph Abercrombie, yet Stuart has an eagerness of mind better adapted to the nature & necessities of the present war than even the sterling steadiness of the other. They are both men deserving of all the reputation that fortune can bestow upon them. I hope the effort will be made soon, for I see the possibility of the opportunity's being lost.

Ever since the termination of the frosts a continued drought has reigned here. The rich turf of this Park shows a little verdure, but elsewhere everything is almost burnt up. Still, we have the hawthorns in bloom & very beautiful. I wish you were here. Do not repose too much on the amendment which you say you feel in your health, but try to confirm its re-establishment by attention to it at a moment when you are sensible the care would be effectual.

I have not heard anything more respecting the business that came thro' the D. of Cumberland. My dispositions were probably thought indifferent, and indeed they were so, further than as it was requisite to express them, lest the supposition of any enmity on my part might have thrown a doubt on the sincerity of the Prince's gracious civilities. If the Prince be still in town, offer to him the homage of my truest & most respectful affection. (39574–5)

1. Henry Cowper (1758–1840), Clerk Assistant of the House of Lords.

2. Sir Charles Stuart (1753–1801), fourth son of John, 3rd Earl of Bute. M.P. for Bossiney, 1776–90; for the Ayr Burghs, 1790–4; for Poole, 1796–1801. Lieutenant-Colonel, 1777; Colonel, 1782; Major-General, 1793; Lieutenant-General, 1798; K.B., January 1799. Deputy Ranger of Richmond Park. He captured Minorca from the Spaniards in 1798, and was Governor there, 1798–1801.

3. On 27 August a British force, commanded by Sir Ralph Abercromby in the first instance and soon afterwards by the Duke of York, landed in Holland, at the Helder, and, assisted by Dutch Royalists, gained possession of the Dutch fleet in the Texel. A Russian force under General Hermann arrived in September, but a joint attack on Bergen failed (19 September). The outbreak of an epidemic caused the British Government to recall its troops, and the Duke of York concluded a Convention with the French at Alkmaar (18 October), by which he agreed to evacuate Holland, though he retained the Dutch fleet. This marked the end of British military intervention on the Continent until the beginning of the Peninsular War.

Donington, 21 June 1799

The bond which I gave for George Rawdon's debt to his silversmith (I believe at your intercession) is become due; I therefore enclose a draft upon Browne which I request you to get accepted & to carry for the purpose of taking up the bond to Messrs. Whigham & North, Silversmiths, Fleet Street. The bond is for £555, but the interest & the discount on the draft will bring it to the amount of the note.

This is not the only commission for you, since it is your destiny to be fagged by all the world. Donahoe's leave of absence is on the point of expiring; he is really so useful a man for any young Corps or for any Department that it is a pity he should be obliged to return to the W. Indies. Will you ask Brownrigg if the leave can be a little extended, and as soon as it shall be certain that Sir C. Stuart is to have a Command in Europe, I will labor to get Donahoe into some employment on this side of the Atlantic. Thomson, also, I am solicitous to get into better bread. They have reduced him to 14s. a day from 25s., making him an Assistant-Commissary instead of a Deputy. He is clever enough to be highly useful to anybody, especially on the Continent where his fluency in German & French would be of great advantage. Should you see Sir Ralph Abercrombie I wish you would mention Thomson to him from me, as a person for whose activity, genius & integrity I could answer. This being pretty well for one batch of commissions I will only add [etc.].

[*P.S.*] When Pizarro[1] is published have the goodness to buy it for me & send it to my mother in a frank, which you will get for the purpose from Brownrigg.

1458   PRINCESS ELIZABETH TO THE PRINCE OF WALES

Kew, 23 June [*?1799*]

I am commanded by the Queen to ask your leave to allow the child to sleep Friday night at Kew & permit her to come about twelve at noon that we may enjoy one whole day of her company. She has informed Ly. Elgin she should ask it, therefore you will have the goodness to let her know. This is totally unknown to the King & meant as an agreable surprize. (Add. Georgian 11/82)

1. Sheridan's tragedy, adapted from Kotzebue's melodrama, was produced for the first time at Drury Lane on 24 May 1799.

Carlton House, Thursday morning [June]¹ 1799

I am really, my dearest Countess, much better today, the medicine I had taken yesterday made me lower than common, & I am quite ashamed of myself for thus betraying so much weakness before the best of mothers. But my fate is so very hard a one, & the continual provocation & insult I am exposed to from the most unprincipled & unfeeling person of her sex, & whom, though I do not interfere with, still will not let me alone, drives me almost out of my senses; there is no end to her wickedness, her falsity, & her designs. These & various other circumstances for *years now*, that have been preying upon my mind, relative to my father &c, which you are acquainted with, *most* at least of them, work *dreadfully* upon me, especially as instead of the evil (particularly relative to the Princess) decreasing, I feel it is gradually encreasing & that even *those who I love the most, & who I know love me the most, are made, either by trick or by long aimed & well managed design, the instruments of planting the dagger still deeper in my heart.* I have nothing concealed from the dear Queen, therefore you may enclose her this note. I am upon my honor much better today, & have had a good night; I would see Turton, but I cannot reveal the disorders of my heart & mind to him, which neither he nor any one other physician can administer medicine to, & therefore it would be childish & useless; the disorder has *its cure* & we must hope that with the *blessing of God*, I may receive it from His *all-merciful hand.* (49234–5)

1460 THOMAS TYRWHITT'S MEMORANDUM

Carlton House, 6 July 1799

Lord Thurlow received my communication with great affability, and after expressions declaratory of his warm attachment to the Prince, as nearly as my memory will serve me, authorized me to state to his Royal Highness as follows:

That upon all occasions he had laid it down as a rule, that if he was honoured in the delivery of any message from the Princess to the Prince, he must first, in order to avoid being guilty of great impertinence towards his Royal Highness, be sure that such message would be received by him—but as in this instance, he had received sufficient authority, that difficulty at least vanished. But was I, says he, to be the bearer of any message that had respect to any other house than that lately occupied by the Master of the Horse² to the Prince, I should be negotiating for a

1. The letter is docketed June.

2. Lord Jersey.

direct seperation; which comes within the knowledge of his Royal Highness, would bring the business within the pale of his Majesty's interference, who has declared his disapprobation to the Lord Chancellor of encouraging such an idea, though, as far as it strikes my mind, I confess, without any just foundation—but was his Royal Highness to waive his objection to the particular house, I conceive a seperation might ensue nearly as efficient as if it had received the stamp of legal authority. Articles in writing as to Establishment &c. &c. &c. might be interchanged, which need not assume the title of a compact, & which would neither call for the interference or observation either of the King or the public—but should any seperate residence, save that alluded to, be touched upon, it might meet his Majesty's refusal and draw down much public observation upon the seperation of the Princess from the child— that in the house she has requested, she might have its society without interrupting its education.

He therefore prayed to have these his sentiments with his duty laid before his Royal Highness. (39578–9)

1461   THE EARL OF MOIRA TO COLONEL MCMAHON

Donington, 8 July 1799

Do not think that the Duke of Cumberland's wish has escaped my attention. I have turned & twisted the matter twenty ways in my mind; desirous of managing it, because I think it would be for the Prince's advantage. Still, I have never been able to satisfy myself how to go about it. In conversation, I could have no difficulty of submitting it to the Prince, because he would there see that it was not an attempt to get round him, which I should hold unpardonable towards him whatsoever was the subject. In a letter, one cannot go *de but en blanc*: because there is a sort of strait-forwardness that is neither more nor less than impertinent presumption; I mean the obtruding a proposition without knowing by previous questions whether it may not be exceedingly embarrassing to the person so addressed. Had the idea occurred to myself, I would have stated it to the Prince at once. As the D. of C. has suggested it (& I could not avow that particular) there would be a species of circumvention in it which, however honest the object, I never must use with the Prince. I have often thought that his Regiment really furnished the excuse for not giving him rank, since, at a time when all is to be military, he must have had some other position had he not been a Colonel. If the King made him wear a Field Marshal's uniform in the city, it proves that he must be considered in that rank whenever he appears with troops, unless tied down by a special commission of

56

inferior quality. This, I think, must lie over till I get to town, for I see I shall be obliged speedily to run up for a week.

There is an Ensign Pentland who harrasses me with letters from Newgate about his not having been gazetted in Sir T. Wallace's [?] corps; which he says was thro' mistake (*vide* enclosure) & that he thence cannot get the pay which would liberate him. When you see Brownrigg will you ask him about it; as I had conversation with him before about Pentland. (39580–1)

1462   THE DUKE OF KENT TO THE PRINCE OF WALES
3.30 p.m., Wednesday, 17 July 1799
I am just returned from Mrs. Fitzherbert's where I went agreable to your wishes, and with whom I have had a very long tête a tête. If I am any judge at all of the business, your wishes will ere long be accomplished, but it seems there are some points which she did not enter into the discussion of with me, which she says you must give up to her.[1] Not knowing what these are, it becomes not *me* to advise, but believe me, a reconciliation with a woman who possesses that attachment for a man which I am well convinced *she* does for you, is worth any sacrifice. I sincerely hope and believe everything will shortly now be completed to your entire comfort and satisfaction; when it is so I trust you will believe that none will be more happy than he who to his latest breath will be proud to profess, and to prove himself [etc.].[2] (45966)

1. Her religious scruples.

2. The Duke was back in Canada when he wrote the next letter to the Prince (15 September No. 1487). In a letter to a friend (28 September) he explained why he had again left England: 'Immediately on my recovery, I was placed as Lieutt. General on the home Staff, and that was followed by my creation to the Dukedom of Kent, and a grant of my establishment from Parliament, and every idea of my returning to America seemed to be dropped. The late King's private apartments in Kensington Palace were allotted me for my town residence, and I really thought I was settled for good at home. However, to my great surprise, when I came to make arrangements to regulate all my expences, and appropriate a part of my income for the liquidation of my debts, I found that for the sake of making a poor pitiful saving on the Civil List it had been judged expedient to cut off from me all the benefits of the table and household expences, which the Duke of Clarence had all along enjoyed at St. James' from the Board of Green Cloth, and which may fairly be computed at six thousand a year. This un-expected reduction putting it completely out of my power to live as it was expected I should, without incurring fresh debts, and much less to do that justice to my creditors which I had always promised I would the moment my establishment was granted, I determined at once to adopt some decided step that should prove to the world and to them that I had acted upon the principles I had always professed. I therefore made application, on hearing that Sir Alured Clarke wished to return to Europe, to be appointed *his* successor in the chief command of his Majesty's troops in India. I have reason to believe that had not Mr. Dundas thrown cold

Lower Lodge, Windsor, 20 July 1799

It is impossible, my ever dearest mother, for me to think of going to bed without calling here in person to enquire after you. To say how much I love you or to attempt to do so would be quite absurd, as I flatter myself that the whole of my conduct for years will express & prove what no language or words can ever pretend to do. My coming into the room tonight might excite wonder, & as it is only for *my own* private satisfaction & not for that of the world that I am anxious to know what the real state of your health is, I have stolen here & left the whole party, who are beginning to be tolerably jolly, to satisfy the first wish & object of my heart, by the knowledge of your being in perfect health. If I have been too hasty in my conclusions of your being more indisposed than really was the case you must attribute it to the warmth of that affection for you which will live & die with me.

P.S. I intend to see you tomorrow. (42285)

water upon it, my request would have been acceded to, for the Company of Directors at home would have been much gratified by one of the Royal Family undertaking the arduous duties of that situation. However, it was negatived as impossible, but at the same time the chief command in North America, that was about to become vacant by the recall of General Prescott, was offered for my acceptance. I own I was very backward at first in coming into this measure, for I am not fond of a northern climate, and I had had enough of this in a seven years residence, so that it was not until after every term I asked was granted, that at last on the 9th of May I gave my final answer that I would go out again. My promotion to the rank of General in the Army followed the next day, and my commission as Commander-in-Chief of all the forces serving in British North America accompanied it. From that moment I set about the necessary preparations for my return to Halifax, which his Majesty was pleased to approve of for my future headquarters, as Commander-in-Chief, the civil situation of Governor-General in the present instance not being held with it. However, I did not fail to stipulate in the first instance that if the Union took place, and Mr. Pitt's measure of removing the Lord Lieutenant altogether is carried, I should succeed in that case to the post of Commander-in-Chief in Ireland. Of this Mr. Pitt has given me the most positive assurances, both verbally and through Mr. Rose, besides which Dundas has repeated the same to me, and the Duke of York has added that *he would not oppose it.*

'This point being settled, I embarked on the 24th July on board of the Arethusa frigate, and having sailed the day after, arrived here on the 6th of this month, having been forty-three days at sea. Our party on board were Madame de Saint Laurent, three of my Aids-de-Camp, viz. Smyth, Hardyman, and your old acquaintance Dodd of the Artillery, Major Gordon of the 66th Regt. my military Secretary, and the Revd. Mr. Wetherall: on arriving here I was joined by his brother the Lieut.-Colonel, for whom I had procured the commission of Adjutant-General to the whole forces in North America, and by Captain Wright of the Royal Artillery, my fourth Aid-de-Camp. Vesey was prevented from being with us by having succeeded to the first Lieutenant-Colonelcy of the 52nd Regt., which Corps is one of those preparing for the expedition to Holland or Brabant. Hale is settled in Lower Canada in a post I got him for life, that of Deputy Paymaster-General to the Forces, having married Miss Amherst, niece to the late Lord and sister to the present one of that name...' (45569-77)

Oatlands, 21 July 1799

Upon the receipt of your letter of the 18th instant I lost no time in writing to the Duke of Portland upon the subject of the poor Jew, but am sorry to inform you that I received last night his answer, by which I am affraid there is no chance of saving him. As, however, I received from a Captain Cochrane an affidavit of the Jew's [illegible], I have inclosed it immediately to the Duke of Portland; what that may produce I cannot tell, though I am affraid his case has been fully considered and his fate is determined.

I mentioned yesterday evening to the Duchess the probability of my being to go abroad;[1] she was a good deal affected, though upon the whole less than I had apprehended, as she told me that she had for some days begun to suspect it from the arrangements making for Sir Ralph Abercrombie's expedition. It certainly is a hard blow upon her, and makes her regret the loss of poor Mrs. Bunbury[2] more and more, as her company would have been of the greatest comfort to her.

Colonel Brownrigg has informed me that Mr. Pitt has approved of the sum proposed for my outfit as well as of the four hundred pounds pr. month for my table, which I think exceedingly handsome.

I am sorry to hear that the Duke of Kent has had so bad an attack of the rheumatism; he ought to make one of his gentlemen write to Windsor to explain the reason of his not going there, as I told his Majesty of his intention of being at Windsor on Saturday and proceeding to Plymouth on Monday.[3] (Add. Georgian 38/11)

Berlin, 23 July 1799

Mr. Tyrwhitt being so kind as to promise me he will deliver into your own hands this letter, I can write with more sincerity than else [I] would venture to do. I have had a very long conversation with him relative to my situation and particularly about my son, whom I recommend most particularly to your protection, for as to his Majesty I never can nor will allow him to have anything to do with him. My intention is to teach him to look up entirely to you and to know that from you alone in some future day he is to expect that justice from which

1. See No. 1457.

2. The wife of H. Bunbury, one of the Duke's Grooms of the Bedchamber.

3. The Duke, who had been appointed Commander-in-Chief of the Forces in North America, took leave of the King on the 23rd, and sailed from Portsmouth on the 26th.

he is now maliciously deprived. I hope you will not refuse me this comfort, which will contribute much to my tranquillity, forced both from my situation with my father and on account of my health to live out of my country. You must see the total impossibility for my coming to England and hope you will pity me. If I could but get my Establishment and be allowed to live where I like, at least I might be less unhappy.[1] (48140–1)

1466 THE DUCHESS OF WURTEMBERG TO THE PRINCE OF WALES

Louisbourg, 29 July 1799

I can never deny myself the pleasure of offering you my congratulations on the 12th of August and begging you to believe that amongst the many wishes formed for your happiness on that day, none are more sincere than mine who am most truly attached to you and anxious for every thing that can contribute to your comfort.

Allow me, dear brother, to recommend to your notice Baron de Wimpfen, one of the Duke's Chamberlains, who will have the honour of giving you this letter. His having been with us constantly in the country may perhaps be agreeable to you as he can by that means give you very exact accounts of me.

I am happy to hear that your health is much mended and hope the military life you have lead of late will be very useful to you, as it amuses as well as gives you exercise. I believe in a few days I shall go to Hohent-weil to see the Russian troops which are to be at Augsbourg on the 4th; I hope they will meet with the same success as they do in Italy.

Everybody speaks with delight of your dear little girl. I make constant enquiries after her as I believe her to be an object of great consequence to your happiness and every day she will grow more interesting and charming to you.

The Duke begs to be remembered to you and I will take up no more of your time. (51553–4)

1. Mrs. Richard Trench, who met him in Berlin, described him as taller and larger than Prince Adolphus, and as resembling the Prince of Wales. 'His hair is too scientifically and studiously dressed to be very becoming, but on the whole his exterior is to be admired. He appears to have a fund of conversation, and great fluency. His vanity is so undisguised that it wears the form of frankness, and therefore excites no disgust' (*Remains of Mrs. Richard Trench*, ed. by the Dean of Westminster, p. 55 [1862 edn.]).

Blackheath, 4 Aug. 1799

I cannot think that you are leaving town without returning my thanks for your kind attention to come in the morning to stay a few hours with me and assuring you that it is impossible to have passed a more pleasant and comfortable day than that I have just spent in your society, which I quit with great regret. I must beg leave to trouble you with a few lines on a subject which was spoke of in our last conversation. Lord Cholmondeley mention'd to me that the Prince wish'd I should give in writing my idea to leave Carlton House, but in the same time he advised me not to write for fear it should appear to be all my own wish only; my answer was I would consider before. After that he said that the Prince would pay the stables and add twelve thousand pounds for the expenses of the house, besides the five thousand I have of my own use. Ld. C. said that as I must pay my Ladies, pages and footmen with liveries, &c., that he did not think 1200 [*sic*] would do at all. I should be very sorry to appear ungrateful for an offer of what might be so comfortable both to the Prince and me, and if you or any other person by looking over the bills of my expenses here for one or two months and calculate whether it will allow of my living in the same moderate way of which I can be no judge myself, I shall be greatly obliged to you, and I can then send a proper answer to the Prince. It is very much my wish to be as little expensive as possible while the Prince's affairs are embarrass'd; his offering Lord Berkeley's[2] house is very good to me and I hope it will be possible for me to see it before I give my answer some day when you come to town and when you can tell me whether 1200 will pay such expense as I live at now. Lord Cholmondeley tells me I had better not leave Carlton House, for that the money will not do and that it is proposed as a trap to get me into some embarrassment. About the child's going to Weymouth, Lord Chol. advised me to write to the King for permission to go there with her. I answer'd that as nothing displeased the Prince so much as my writing to the King I thought it better to submit in silence, for that I should not write to the Prince myself about it as he had brought me a message from the Prince last year that I should never write to him again. He told me that the Prince accused me of being the cause of his present embarrassment by my expensiveness here, and that he was so angry that his intention was to complain of me to the King; that the Prince is very angry with me at this time and that I should find things would not be so quiet as when he was friends with Lady Jersey, for Mrs. Fitzherbert was much more my enemy, and the real truth was

1. Rear-Admiral, 14 February 1799.

2. Frederick Augustus, 5th Earl of Berkeley (1745–1810). The story of his bogus marriage in 1785 and of his fraudulent efforts to legitimate his four elder sons is well known.

that nobody was so reasonable as I, or well satisfied without expense and that Mrs. Fitz. was extravagant in everything & would ruin the Prince, who goes now twice a day to Gray's to buy diamonds for her. This is what he told me and I think I told you before. He also said the P. got spies to watch me and that one day when I had a party he met Mr. Clark[1] on the road coming to watch who came in and out of my house. It is quite a comfort to me to think that you believe a great deal of what he has said to me is it not true [sic] as well as to think that as many bad impressions may have been given of me falsely by him and which now will be any longer believed many many things that pass'd long ago I could mention but the long time makes me afraid to trust my memory [sic]. I could speak of them to you but one must be very exact on paper. I have now reason to believe that he might be the person who prevented the Prince from performing his promise that my little girl should live in the house in the summer. I shew'd Lord Chol. this house when I took it and explain'd to him that Charlotte should have the same rooms which Lady Elgin had given her the year before; he saw the rooms in the house and in the Round Tower, which the two Governesses were to live in as they liked best, and he approved of all. Nobody else could explain it to the Prince, and Lord Chol. brought me word the Prince said there was not room fit for the child. I know he said the same to other people, that he did not think so, though he told me he did. I hope I shall see you when you come to town soon, or that you will write to me what you have calculated about the money offer'd me as I shall be very sorry to appear disrespectful to the Prince by delaying my answer.[2]

1. Probably the Rev. James Stanier Clarke (?1765–1834), the Prince's domestic Chaplain (1799) and Librarian, 1805. Canon of Windsor, 1808–34; Rector of Tillington, 1816; Historiographer to the King, 1812; Deputy Clerk of the Closet to the King, 1816.

2. *The Times* had this news item on 2 July: 'Lady Jersey has removed from the house adjoining Carlton House to that which was Lord Talbot's, in Stratford Place. The house she has quitted is destined for the residence of the Princess Charlotte and her establishment'. And on 6 August: 'The Princess Charlotte was yesterday removed from Carlton House to the house taken for her on Blackheath, late the residence of Alexander Trotter, Esq.'

Earlier, Lady Spencer had thus referred to Lady Jersey—in a letter to her daughter the Duchess of Devonshire: 'She has reigned with too much despotism to last long . . . I am unwilling to warn you or your sister [Lady Bessborough] about her, because I think most of the warnings I have given you both have generally failed completely. However, I would wish you both to remember that she has fairly dropped you, and that there is no necessity when others drop her, that you should take her up. In a good cause such a conduct is highly laudable, but surely not in a bad one' (Chatsworth MSS. [8 January 1796]).

Barracks, Guil[d]ford, 6 Aug. 1799

I am much concerned that it will not be in my power to have the pleasure of paying you a visit at Petworth today as I am unfortunately obliged to be at Windsor early tomorrow, but I trust I shall have the good fortune to make up for this disappointment very soon. I suppose that you have heard the news of a frigate being arriv'd bearing intelligence of the combined fleets of France & Spain having got out of Cadiz. The frigate I understand sail'd with them above a whole day & says that they made but little way in the course of that day. This is the only news I know worth mentioning, excepting the death of Lord Howe, which happen'd yesterday, but this I trust will be soon communicated to you, my dear friend, in a manner more agreable than merely from me, as I do assure you it is the expectation of everyone that the Blue Ribbon is intended for you, for not interfering with any private views of the Minister; there being another for Lord Camden there is no one else that it can be offer'd to, & certainly none so worthy of it as yourself. Lord Spencer, who I met by chance in my way here today, coincided in the most cordial manner possible with me in this opinion.[1]

> I am, my dear Lord,
>   ever most affectionately yours (Petworth MSS.).

Carlton House, 7 Aug. 1799

The Prince of Wales did himself the pleasure of calling upon Mr. Pitt in Downing Street this morning in the hopes of communicating to him a wish that he has so much at heart that he cannot help touching upon it in this way, being uncertain when he may have an opportunity of speaking to him upon the subject. In consequence of the death of Lord Howe it is more than probable (as the Prince understands) that some arrangements

1. On Wednesday the 14th Camden was invested with the Blue Ribband worn by the late Duke of Dorset. Lord Egremont never became a K.G. The King cannot have approved his way of life. Greville found him at Petworth 'surrounded with children and grandchildren', and he never married. It was believed that in 1802 he married a Miss Fox, who, said Glenbervie, had lived with him for years. 'She is the daughter of a low person at Brighthelmstone' (*Journals*, i.330.) Pitt, however, was not unsympathetic; he wrote to Lord Spencer on 8 August: 'I am much obliged to you for the suggestion respecting the Blue Ribband. I should be much inclined to adopt it, but I have received an application on behalf of the Duke of Somerset, whose very high rank in the peerage seems to give him strong pretensions to be early thought of, and it would perhaps be particularly difficult to pass by him in favour of a descendant of the same family, so much below in rank. In all other respects I should prefer Lord Egremont, but I rather think these considerations ought to decide' (Althorp MSS.).

are likely to take place in the Naval Department by which an opening may be made of conferring some mark of his Majesty's favor on Rear-Admiral Payne; in which event his long & meritorious services may meet that reward which the Prince trusts Mr. Pitt thinks them deserving of. The Prince of Wales cannot help adding his own extreme solicitude on this occasion, & relies on Mr. Pitt's assistance herein, of which he shall always be fully sensible [1] (Althorp MSS.).

1470 THE DUCHESS OF WURTEMBERG TO THE PRINCE OF WALES

Louisbourg, 8 Aug. 1799

It gives me great pleasure to hear from my sisters that you are perfectly recovered and able to enjoy all your military occupations and amusements. How delighted would you be, were it in your power to see the Russian troops. I regret very much that your situation prevents your having that pleasure. The Duke, who returned from Augsbourg yesterday, can talk of nothing else. Many of the Regiments have now marched nine months and never had above three days rest at a time during that period. He assures me that notwithstanding they have undergone this fatigue it would be impossible to perceive it by their looks, and that their cloathing has alone suffered. I hope General Corsakof [2] will meet with [the] same glorious successes in Switzerland as Field Marchal Surwarow in Italy. Everybody is wild with joy at the taking of Mantua, which is a most unexpected and fortunate event. General Corsakof's army is, I understand, to relieve the Archduke who to my great joy returns to the Rhine. I look on him as the protector of Germany. The end of this week I go to Hohentweil to see the army and shall then give you some further account.

The King of Naples's return has also given great satisfaction; one rejoices at the idea of seeing things on the old footing again. It is,

1. On 28 August *The Times* reported that he had been appointed Treasurer of Greenwich Hospital *vice* Lord Bridport. The salary was £200 a year.

Pitt wrote to Lord Spencer from Walmer Castle on the 9th: 'I received with some surprise this morning the enclosed letter from a Royal correspondent, with whom I have not been much in the habit of intercourse. My answer has of course been general, expressing a disposition to find any opportunity of obeying his Royal Highness's commands, and saying that I would communicate with you on the subject. You will be the best judge whether there is likely to be any opening for an officer of Admiral Payne's rank, and what are his comparative pretensions. If they are equally balanced with any others now or hereafter, you may probably think that the recommendation should be allowed to turn the scale' (Althorp MSS.).

2. Alexander Rimsky-Korsakoff, the Russian General. He was defeated at Zürich by Oudinot and Masséna on 25 September, and both he and Suvoroff were recalled to Russia a month later, the Tsar having quarrelled with his ally the Emperor.

however, very singular that throughout Italy the nobility have behaved worse than the people, though many of them were amazingly rich, and must have been reduced to beggary had this equalizing system continued. It is reported the King of Naples before he landed had the Marquis de Caraciolo[1] tried, condemned, and executed: a severe but very necessary example to be set, that this republican spirit may be quelled at once.

I hear dear little Charlotte is going into the country, which I am sure will do her good. I love her dearly for your sake and am very constant and anxious in my enquiries after her. Lady Elgin is so good as to indulge me by answering them fully, which gives me great pleasure. (39582-3)

1471 PRINCESS ELIZABETH TO THE PRINCE OF WALES

Weymouth, 18 Aug. 1799

To fulfill my promise of writing I trouble you with a few lines to say that at half after five yesterday evening we arrived here, after a very good journey. My younger sister did not arrive quite so soon, as Amelia was a good deal fatigued, but Mr. Keate assures us that she will very soon recover [from] it; one cannot be surprized at it after so long a confinement, but you may believe what I say that she is in very good spirits.[2]

I sincerely wished for you yesterday at dinner as the King spoke most kindly of your Regiment & said out & out they road the best of any.[3] You may easily imagine what a *brightener* of countenance *this was* & I flatter myself that I shall be the *first* to have told it you.

The weather is so bad & stormy that as yet we have seen nobody but I believe there are very few people we know; the place appears full, the bay very ugly & there are no ships come owing to the weather. We are in hopes of seeing Chasse, as I hear Capt. Durham is ordered from Spithead. Sir Harry Niel sail'd from Portsmouth on Wednesday but it is supposed that the severity of the gale has blown him back. The Fleet is

1. Prince Francesco Caracciolo (1732-99), the Neapolitan Admiral. Whilst the British fleet under Nelson was away in Sicily guarding the Neapolitan Royal family, a revolutionary movement, inspired by the Ideas of 1789, broke out, but it was soon suppressed by a motley force of Royalists, Russians and Turks. Caracciolo, one of the rebel leaders, was executed on 30 June by Nelson's orders, after being court martialled on board Nelson's flagship.

2. Princess Sophia and Amelia took two days over the journey, sleeping at Andover. Amelia was taken ill between Overton and Andover, and consequently arrived later than was expected. The King and Queen and the other Princesses left Windsor at 4.30 a.m. on Saturday the 17th, breakfasted at Hartford Bridge and continued their journey *via* Winchester, Romsey and Wimborne. Rather prematurely, as it turned out, the Royal family celebrated the recovery of Princess Amelia's health on 8 August, with a Fête at Frogmore.

3. The King reviewed the Prince's regiment on Winkfield Plain on the 15th, and afterwards the Prince entertained the officers at the *Bush* at Staines.

at Torbay where they are quite quiet, thank God, as this wind does not affect the sea there, but dreadful for the French which, between friends, I rejoice at.

I think mama rather fagged & tired, looking pale, but another night's rest I hope will recover her.[1] (Add. Georgian 11/83)

1472 LETTERS FROM PRINCESS AUGUSTA TO THE PRINCE OF WALES

[Weymouth], *18 Aug. 1799*

According to my promise I inform you that we all arrived here at a little after 5 o'clock. We got in before my sisters, as Amelia was so much tired the night before as to go to bed as soon as she came to Andover, & did not set out till late yesterday morning, and then stopped a good while at Blandford. She has had a very tolerable night and *Keate* is satisfied about her. She was much affected when she first arrived here, but the keeping up in her own room, indeed in bed, the whole evening and staying quiet today will be of great use to her. She is in very good spirits & will have Lady Neale[2] to spend the evening with her while we shall *broil at the Rooms*. The wind is beyond anything in point of noise, but as *we* are *up* in Torbay[3] & the French unable to get out of Brest I am perfectly satisfied, & it will give us time to prepare for the *action* which I hope to God will take place in *moderate weather*.

Mama & my sisters desire their best love to you, and tho' the mail is at the door I must add that the King mentioned at dinner yesterday how very superior your Regiment rides to all others, as they all (the men) ride in the same style, & that tho' all the horses were excellent, the *chesnut* & *black* troops were *quite* perfect.

God bless you, my dearest G.P., I shall write again very soon.

[P.S.] Amelia desires her kind love to you, & having taken something to *cause* her keeping *her bed* till its *effects are over*, cannot write herself today. (Add. Georgian 10/22)

1. The Queen sent the Prince of Wales a birthday letter on the 12th:
   'I hope to be the first whose congratulations you will receive today. They are not only truely sincere but such as an affectionnate mother's heart dictates upon the occasion & therefore comprized in very few words. May you be blessed with everything that is good; may prosperity attend you everywhere & may you be so fortunate as to enjoy the affection of the truely good & virtuous & may you never be in want of a sincere friend. This is the sum total of my heart's eloquence. To this I add an antique present which I beg you to accept of & it suits well, methinks with the unalterable attachment & sentiments of [etc.].' (36513)

2. Sir Harry Burrard Neale (see No. 1392) married (1795) Grace Elizabeth (1771–1855), daughter of Richard Neale of Melksham, Wilts.

3. Lord Keith's fleet arrived at Torbay from the Mediterranean on Saturday the 17th.

I would not trouble you again till I had very good news to give you of Emily: she has bathed three times and been as often to the Play, which she enjoys of all things, and has walked out a little on the esplanade. I really think *you* would be *perfectly* satisfied with her appearance. Her spirits are much better, and the having been at sea gave her the greatest delight. Weymouth is very full, but few people of our acquaintance. However, I think we are a *host in ourselves* & on Tuesday we shall have *our dear child*,[1] which will enliven everything.

I am very anxious to know how your *private matters stand*. Since I had the last conversation on that subject at Swinley much time has passed, and I am very desirous of knowing whether the whole *affair* is *public*, for indeed I think it would be desirable, considering how very much it stands to *your mutual credit*, that *old friends sincerely and unalterably attached* should come together again.[2] It is not like the foolish *fancy* of a day but built upon real affection & esteem. On *your* side I can answer for it & I trust for your happiness it *is the same on the other*. Write to me soon and direct it to *Lady Cathcart*. I long to hear that the first embarkation is landed; it makes me rather nervous, and when things are to be done, *public or domestic, good or bad*, I wish them *soon over*.

If you should see *Cartwright* tell him he shall have *my blessing* in the manner I am certain he will *prefer* as I send it by *you*. It is an *old saying*, that a *thing* is *doubly* done when *quickly* done, but I think *it so* according to the *manner in which it is done*. How *we* improve upon the *ancients*.

I dare say you think the sea water has *fuddled me*; well, if it will but leave me a grain of sense and feeling I shall never cease thinking of and loving my best beloved G.P. God bless him, dear angel, & may he think now and then of his most truly affectionate [etc.]. (Add. Georgian 10/23)

1. Princess Charlotte arrived at Weymouth on the 28th with the Dowager Countess of Elgin. A house in Charlotte Row, near the Esplanade, had been taken for her.

The Prince sent Lady Elgin the following instructions, dated Carlton House, the 17th: 'Lady Elgin is order'd by me to send for Dr. Turton, Dr. Underwood, Messrs. Keate & Nussey; to take such information & instructions as may be necessary to Princess Charlotte's bathing, diet & way of life'. (49236)

2. The reference is to Mrs. Fitzherbert. *The Times* commented on the 20th: 'Mrs. Fitzherbert is at Brighton, and the rumour there is that the Prince of Wales is expected. It is very probable. Admiral Payne, the former companion of the Prince, has sold his house, furniture and wines at Brompton, and is once more about to live with his Royal Highness. He has been the negotiator of a recent reconciliation!' And on the 31st: 'Mrs. Fitzherbert remains at Ramsgate expecting the honour of a Royal visit'.

Brighton, 23 Aug. 1799

I have not had time till the present moment to return my most sincere thanks to you for your letter. Garton, you may depend upon it, has done the best he can, but I hope the house *is* on the shore & close to the sea. As to Robert, if it is any comfort to *you*, you may certainly take him with you, as I wish you at all times to be as comfortably off as possible. I have only time before the post goes but to thank you for your accounts of the dear child, & to desire you will let me hear from you as soon as you have accomplished your journey. You had best write a line to Hicks, at the Grainge, Hampshire, to let him know what night you intend to be there. I already told him to apprize the housekeeper in order to have the beds air'd, & something for you to eat.

P.S. I am glad to see that Lady Charlotte Durham & her Captain are arrived at Weymouth. (49237)

1474 THE PRINCE OF WALES TO HENRY ADDINGTON

Carlton House, 27 Aug. 1799

I arriv'd late in town yesterday evening, & had not an opportunity of seeing my brother Ernest, at least of having any conversation with him till this morning, when he communicated to me what he had learnt from you of the commencement of your truly kind exertions respecting me. You may naturally conceive *my eagerness* that our plans should be crown'd with success, but at the same time that I feel (& am fully aware, as I am sure you are also) that a single moment should not be lost, as every instant at a crysis such as the present is of the greatest importance. Still the confidence & firm reliance I place in you are *such* as to get the better for the present moment of that curiosity & anxiety (which you must suppose I must naturally experience) should you feel the smallest difficulty in committing to paper the first opening of your negotiation. I have unfortunately been engaged in a manner that I cannot manage to put it off, to go down for a few days to Canterbury to see the troops at Barham Downs,[1] or I would have instantly paid you a visit at Woodley,[2] as much more is to be done & to be learnt & understood in one interview than in the longest correspondance by letter. However, as I purpose to

1. Part of the expeditionary force destined for Holland was being assembled and trained at Barham Downs, six miles from Canterbury. His own Regiment was expected on the 28th. Attended by Arthur Paget and Rear-Admiral Payne, the Prince arrived at Harbledown, near Barham Downs, the seat of George Gipps, M.P., on the 28th, and two days later he reviewed the troops there.

2. Addington's seat near Reading.

Lord Thurlow
by T. Phillips

Queen Charlotte
by William Beechey 1796

George III
by William Beechey 1799–1800

be in London again in the course of a few days, I may perhaps have the good fortune of meeting with you on my return; if not, I shall then be able to arrange where & when we may contrive to see one another, either by my coming to you or by your coming to me, in which I shall be most anxious to consult your convenience. I have, of course, as you may suppose, been revolving over much in my mind the topics we talked over, & consequently have much to say to you. I will not intrude longer upon you, except to endeavour to express the very sincere sentiments of regard & esteem with which I ever am[1] [etc.] (Sidmouth MSS.).

1475   THE PRINCE OF WALES TO THE KING, AND THE REPLY

Carlton House, 27 Aug. 1799

I am very sorry to be under the necessity of intruding upon your Majesty for a single moment, but the enclosed packet which I found on my arrival in town last night will I trust sufficiently plead my apology.[2] The contents are from my brother Augustus, & I cannot but confess I was not a little surpriz'd when I made myself acquainted with them. Though your Majesty may be equally surpriz'd at the first moment, still the Chancellor & I (to whom I immediately sent, & with whom I have talk'd the subject over) flatter ourselves that your Majesty will not see any great cause for uneasiness, if any at all. The Chancellor, who is so good as to forward this letter to your Majesty, assures me that he will accompany it with a few lines expressive of his humble sentiments. (42287)

1. The Prince's letter was sent to Addington by the Duke of Cumberland with this covering note, dated London, 28 August:

'The enclosed I received last night from the Prince which will express to you his thanks for the very truely friendly conduct of yours towards him. In the course of his conversation with me he said he had assured the Speaker he was ready to resign his Regiment to me and that he would never stand in my light. These were I believe pretty near the very words he made use of himself and which he repeated to you in his last conversation. Now I believe, dear Sir, if you was to represent to him that this moment was the very one he could bestow upon me the greatest mark of kindness in resigning now this said regiment as it was going abroad, I believe he would; and I need not say but that it would be conferring the very greatest obligation on me as in my situation the having entirely the finest Regiment in the Service would be the greatest feather in my cap. I ought to apologize to you for my troubling you so often on this same subject but, dear Sir, your goodness to me has spoilt me, and this being the wish nearest my heart, added to which the Regiment expecting to go almost immediately abroad makes me the more earnest and anxious for the completion of my wishes' (Sidmouth MSS.).

2. See No. 1465.

Weymouth, 28 Aug. 1799

You may easily believe that I am much hurt at the event that has taken place at Berlin; I had been apprized of it yesterday. I referr you to the Lord Chancellor, whose conduct during the whole of this terrible business [1] has met with my thorough approbation and therefore deserves my fullest confidence in the future steps that may be necessary. (42288)

1476   LORD LOUGHBOROUGH TO THE PRINCE OF WALES

29 Aug. 1799

I would not delay sending this letter to your Royal Highness because I am afraid it will not be possible for me to reach Canterbury from Tunbridge Wells as early as the arrival of the post, but as it was H.M. intention that I should have delivered it myself to Y.R.H., I shall have the honour of waiting upon you in the course of the morning. (39585)

1477   PRINCESS AMELIA TO THE PRINCE OF WALES

Weymouth, 29 Aug. [1799]

My dear Eau de Miel: I cannot resist sending you a few lines to tell you how happy we all are with the arrival of dear dear little Charlotte. Papa, mama & my three elder sisters are gone on board,[2] Sophy having been ill with her cramp, & though now recovered, would not venture because of the play tonight, & I likewise remained on shore as I was last time very sick on board & my stomach is not quite right. I therefore have been with dear Charlotte, & it gives me great pleasure to say I thought her looking well & in good spirits. She had just been to sleep. The dear love accompanied me home; in short, she is quite an angel & I never enjoyed anything so much as her being with us.

Dear papa [and] mama are very well; the latter I think better than she generally is by the sea. We go constantly to the play; Bannister, Mrs. Mills & Kemble, who arrived today, are all here.[3] Bathing agrees very

1. See No. 1465.

2. The frigate *St. Fiorenzo*.

3. Hughes, the Manager of the Weymouth Theatre, engaged Bannister, junior (1760–1836), for five nights. On the 29th the Royal Family were entertained with the comedy of *Ways and Means* and the farce of *The Village Lawyer*.

well with me. The dear Countess[1] appears very well, though she was a good deal fatigued with her journey.

My dear perfect Miny begs her kindest love. God Almighty bless you. (Add. Georgian 14/24)

1478 THE QUEEN TO THE PRINCE OF WALES

Weymouth, 30 Aug. 1799

I have the pleasure to inform you, my dearest son, of the safe arrival of dear little Charlotte. This I meant to have done yesterday, but a sailing day admits of nothing but idleness, & the wind proving favorable for such an excursion I was obliged to submit. The dear little angel slept well & at ½ past 8 a clock I made her my visit & she walked between the Kg. & me to the Lodge where she attended our breakfast, then saw us prepare to go on board the St. Fiorenzo & when we went away I left her with Sophia & Amelia who were to take her & Ldy. Elgin an airing on the sands, but she dropt asleep before eleven & slept till past two a clock, which was by far more refreshing for her little spirits. At my return on shore I saw her walk, & today she is preparing for her bathing & consequently not to go out. I shall pay her my visit by & by & am sure she will be very entertaining. The Kg. met Ldy. Elgin last night, & when we went to the Play he told me he had desired her to act entirely to the directions Dr. Turton had given her, & he added, 'none but those who know the child can be judges of what ought to be done.' I think this will make you easy, & I am certain will be great comfort to the Countesses mind, as she now is quite certain that Dr. Turton's name will take her out of all difficulties if any should arise.

We have gone on here very quietly & comfortably; the weather is like an intermitting fever, every other day storms & rain, but with the Royals, Grays, & Plays, the Kg. passes his time very pleasantly. The only little rub we met with is the arrival of the messenger from Augustus, of which he had an intimation on Tuesday by his dispatches. He named it not to me till the evening & said it had made him very bilious & sic, & on Thursday at two a clock he brought me all the letters. In the conversation upon the subject he told me he was satisfied with yr. conduct, but would not himself determine upon anything. I took the liberty of saying, before I had read yr. letter, that in my oppinion Augustus's return to England, & one conversation between him & the Kg. might do more than millions of letters, & in this yr. letter afterwards confirmed me, but at present H.M. is so averse to this step that I could not with any propriety press

1. Lady Elgin.

it any further. The Chancellor's letter did you ample justice & I must say to yr. comfort that the Kg. felt it much. *Tout ceci est entre nous.*

Tomorrow is Grl. Goldsworth's Revue, & we are to have after it a dejeuné dinatoire, & a Ball till six, then go home & dress for the Play, where Bannister entertains us much.[1] We have from Bath Taylor & his pritty wife, & two girl who sings tolerable & two or three tolerable actors belonging to Mr. Hughs lot [*sic*].

I am a going this morning to breakfast at Ldy. Charlotte Durrham's, where we shall have a little music I hope. Our company is increased by the Sudleys[2] & the Dutchess of Newcastle[3] & the Chancellor are expected the 1st Septbr. Lrd. Spencer arrived here on Wednesday from Torbay & staid till this morning. He sailed with us yesterday, & was very good company. This is all poor Weymouth can afford by way of amusement. Everybody here is well now. I hope to hear the same from you which is the sincere wish of [etc.]. (36514–5)

1479 THE PRINCE OF WALES TO THE KING

Harbledown, near Canterbury, 31 Aug. 1799

The enclosed note[4] from the Chancellor will account to your Majesty for my not having had it in my power to see his Lordship till this morning, when after considerable deliberation we agreed upon some certain points; but we both judg'd it most adviseable, as Mr. Pitt and Mr. Dundas are at Walmer Castle, to go over there tomorrow morning to see whether their opinions would coincide with ours, & we trust that the result when communicated to your Majesty will meet with your Majesty's gracious approbation. Your Majesty will be pleased to beleive that I shall be ever happy to obey your commands on this as on every other occasion where my humble services can be consider'd of any utility. (39586 and 42289)

1. On the 29th the Royal Family rode to Monckton Hill, five miles from Weymouth, where the 1st Dragoons, commanded by General Goldsworthy, were drawn up to be reviewed. The General subsequently entertained his guests at the new temporary barracks. After dinner there was country dancing until 5 o'clock. In the evening the Royal Family saw the comedy the *Busybody* and the farce *The Deserter.*

2. See No. 1379.

3. Thomas, 3rd Duke of Newcastle (1752–95), married, 1782, Anna Maria (1760–1834), daughter of the 2nd Earl of Harrington. In 1800 she married Lieutenant-General Sir Charles Gregan Craufurd (1761–1821). She arrived at Weymouth with her son and her brother-in-law, Lord Thomas Clinton, on the 29th.

4. See No. 1476.

Harbledown, near Canterbury, 4 Sept. 1799

Although the sincere regard & affection I have ever borne you might have tolerated my entering at any time upon a subject of material importance to your happiness, yet sentiments of scrupulous delicacy have ever restrain'd me from touching on a point of such extreme nicety before, but now relieved from all embarrassment on that score by your confidential communication, I most earnestly wish to convey to you my candid & dispassionate opinion on the very peculiar situation in which you & Lady Augusta Murray stand; & in doing so, believe me that I am far from being warp'd by any narrow or illiberal prejudice, but am solely govern'd by the purest & tenderest friendship. Reason & calm reflection, my dearest Augustus, must tell you how vain & useless it is to cherish illusions which no inward wish or desire, however reasonable or fair, can either gratify or accomplish: and be assured that nothing can be more insurmountable than the attainment of that object, namely, the establishing of your marriage with Lady Augusta Murray, & which you profess to regard as the summit of the system you have laid down for your future happiness in life, for believe me that the obstacles to its completion are insuperable & invincible. It is not only the King's determination on this point, & which I am persuaded can never be soften'd, that is to be got over, but the very law of the land must be repeal'd before you can have the *power* to confer on Lady Augusta the title you wish. This law you may consider & protest against as severe & unjust, but all opposition to it will be vain & fruitless, & all remonstrances consequently futile & unavailing, for our lot by birth & station, my dearest brother, makes us *all* amenable to it. I may for the sake of your private feelings lament those restrictions which shackle the freedom of your choice, but since fate has render'd it inevitable 'tis our duty to submit, & the more grace & cheerfulness with which we do so, the more dignified & amiable we appear. As this favourite wish of establishing your marriage with Lady Augusta Murray therefore *cannot* take place, let me conjure *you* & *her*, in the name of Heaven, whatever other terms you may choose to live upon, to summon your fortitude & good sense on this occasion, & with true greatness of mind, at once to give up the idea of marriage & to assure his Majesty, thro' me, that you *do so*. The immediate sacrifice which Lady Augusta may make will do her infinite honor, as it will not only be rescuing you, but preserving her own family from the King's displeasure, & which otherwise I fear is inevitable. As to your son, my dearest Augustus, I propose myself to take charge of him, & I do assure you that I will protect him with a father's care, therefore banish every anxiety about him, & abandon, I pray, all idea of bringing him to you, if such has been your intention, *for I am positive that will never be allowed.*

Although I am confident that neither the King nor the world would ever have interfered or questioned you about any female friend who might privately live with you, had you not weakly (pardon me for saying so) attempted to give Lady Augusta Murray a rank that was *totally* inadmissible, & she unfortunately persisting in the error you both set out with, it could not fail to attract his Majesty's notice, & naturally excite his displeasure. This, however, being the state of the case, it is my earnest advice & request that Lady Augusta Murray should immediately return to England where I shall always feel pleasure in paying her every civility in my power.

Again, I must beseech you to consider what I have so strenuously recommended, & strictly to recollect that the sentiments I have given you are dictated by undisguised friendship & affection. An acquiescence in them will, in my judgement, prove your surest road to happiness, but all opposition, my dearest Augustus, will be fruitless, or perhaps fatal to the interests of you both.

I am so solicitous & interested about you that I shall wait with all impatience for your answer. In the meantime I have only to assure you of the continuation of that love & friendship I have ever felt for you, and am [etc.]. (42290–1, and 48165–6 [copy])

1481 THE PRINCE OF WALES TO THE QUEEN

Harbledown, 4 Sept. 1799

Your letter, my beloved mother, would not have remained unanswer'd till today had I not felt so extremely indisposed yesterday with a violent billious attack that I was wholly unequal to hold my head up, much more to write at all. I cannot express my gratitude to you for your great solicitude about my little girl, & for the great care you are so good as to take of her; I hope the King is pleased & amused with her. I am sure that was a principal inducement to me to send her to Weymouth preferable to any other bathing place, especially as she would thus be placed immediately under your eye. The glorious victory with which it has pleased the Almighty to bless our arms upon the continent, quite gladdens my heart, & I must entreat of you, my dearest mother, not only to accept of my most hearty congratulations on this event yourself, but to lay me at the King's feet, & to make them also acceptable to his Majesty.[1] You gave me indeed great satisfaction at the little *entre nous* communication you was so good as to make me of the King's being content with my conduct in this business relative to Augustus, but I am *clearly still* of

1. A *London Gazette Extraordinary*, 3 September, announced the surrender of the Dutch fleet in the Texel to Vice-Admiral Mitchell.

74

your opinion, & so indeed are most everyone with whom it has been necessary for me to communicate upon this occasion, that his coming home & having one thorough, ample, yet dispassionate conversation with the King, & with his own family, would do more than correspondence for months, & probably set everything once again upon a footing of good understanding, which I am sure of all things is most to be desired. However, I have in the meantime written a long letter of affectionate & friendly advice to Augustus such as I flatter myself the King will approve of, & which I have dressed up in such a way that I think it hardly possible for him to make any further resistance.

I trust, my dearest mother, that Weymouth does not disagree with you as much this year as I think it generally does, & that you will not allow yourself to be too much fuss'd & hurried, which I well know is what is always prejudicial to your health. As to myself I cannot say how soon or how long it may be first before I shall have it in my power to make my bow to you at Weymouth, for I have just received my orders for my Regiment to march to Canterbury in the ensuing week in order to embark for the Continent, & as I have deemed it my duty as well as having promised the Regiment to see the last of them from the English coast, I mean time [*sic*] to march them to the shore & superintend their embarkation, after which & their being safely off, I shall hope to make my bow to you.[1] I must not intrude too long upon your patience, & therefore will assure you of what you already well know, que je suis toujours ma bien aimée mére, de loin comme de prez [etc.]. (42292–3)

1482 THE PRINCE OF WALES TO THE DUKE OF CUMBERLAND

Harbledown, 4 Sept. 1799

I must request that immediately on the receipt of this letter you will find out whether Lady Dunmore is in London or at Brighton, or where she is, & that you will lose no time in waiting upon her & expressly stating to her that I have authority to desire that Augustus's child may be forth-coming & produced to me as soon as I shall receive an answer to a letter I have written my brother this day on the subject by the King's im-mediate command. However painful, I cannot mince the matter in a business of this nature, & therefore I must instruct you to unequivocally

---

1. The Prince wrote to the Earl of Chatham on the 2nd from Harbledown:

    'I have this moment heard that your Brigade is under orders of march tomorrow morning; in all probability you will wish as well as Lady Chatham to be rid of me on that account. I hope in God that Lady Chatham meets this severe trial with proper fortitude, & that her good sense & nerves will support her through it.

    'My good wishes attend you always, my dear Lord' (Hoare MSS.).

assure Lady Dunmore that I have reason to know that any opposition to this demand will be attended with very unpleasant consequences to both Lord Dunmore & Lady Augusta Murray. (42294)

1483 THE DUKE OF YORK TO THE PRINCE OF WALES

Walmer Castle, 6 Sept. 1799

Understanding that you have left Canterbury for London and therefore despairing of having the pleasure of shaking you by the hand before I sail, I cannot refuse myself the satisfaction of writing to you a few lines to wish you all health and happiness till we meet again.

I had hoped to have been able to embark yesterday but the wind was quite contrary and the *Cambria* in which it was intended that I should go was not arrived, nor is she so at this moment, but as it is of consequence that I should get to Holland as soon as possible, if the wind does not increase I shall not wait for the arrival of the Cambria but embark this afternoon on board of one of the other frigates in the Downs.

God bless you my dear brother.[1] (44149)

1484 LORD THURLOW TO THE PRINCE OF WALES

Monday, 9 Sept. 1799

I am extreamly mortified that I am not able to attend your Royal Highness anywhere but in this dog-hole, where my only journey is being wheeled from bed to couch, and back again to bed. But if your Royal Highness will condescend to call here at two o'clock tomorrow I shall be happy to find it in my power to suggest anything satisfactory to your Royal Highness. (39587)

1. The Duke's letter to Charles Greenwood (6 September) throws light on his relations with the Duchess at this time:

'Ten thousand thanks for your two letters as well as for your kindness in letting me know how the Duchess was yesterday afternoon. I confess I felt more than I can express on Wednesday evening on her account; she certainly bore up most surprizingly, but one could easily see how much the struggle cost her and I dread the consequences it may have upon her health. Her situation is the only thing which could at all diminish the satisfaction which I feel at the situation into which I am placed, and which is certainly in every point of view the most honourable, the most fortunate and the most advantageous for me that could be, and if I am successful, which it certainly shall not be for want of zeal and exertions if I am not, I shall feel myself completely gratified. I am anxious to get away, but the wind is contrary, and I am affraid that I shall not be able to finish my business and be allowed to go aboard till tomorrow morning. I have not time to add more. God bless you. Let me hear from you often.' (Add. Georgian 38/12)

Austin Friars, 12 Sept. 1799

I have the honor most respectfully to transmit to your Royal Highness the copy of his Majesty's letter to the Artillery Company, appointing your Royal Highness to be their Captain-General.

I shall lose no time in getting ready for your Royal Highness's information copies of the several charters and letters from the Sovereigns of England which the Artillery Company are possessed of, and will take the liberty to add such extracts from our records as may be material to shew the ancient privileges of the Company and the rank and authority attached to the high situation of their Captain-General.

I have to promise to your Royal Highness that in the last century, during the Civil Wars, the members of the Company being divided, part remaining steady in their allegiance to the Crown and others joining the Parliament, the Charters of Henry the Eighth and his successors, together with every other record of the Company, were taken away or destroyed, except the book which contains the signatures of the Kings and Princes who were members of the Company.

At that period King Charles the First was the Captain-General, and the senior members of the Company being Royalists, it is understood that they took away those valuable Charters and Records.

During the Protectorate, Major General Shippon was the Captain-General, and your Royal Highness will find in every history of that time that he commanded all the City's forces.

At the Restoration, King Charles the Second renewed the privileges of the Company and appointed the Duke of York, afterwards King James the Second, their Captain-General, but when his said Majesty thought fit forcibly to take away the charters of the City and to annull the rights of the citizens, he revoked those of the Artillery Company which remained wholly suspended untill the accession of King William the Third, from whom we have a charter restoring the Company to its ancient rights and privileges.

Your Royal Highness will therefore be pleased to see that the privileges of the Artillery Company, like those of nearly all the corporate bodies of this country, and particularly those of the City of London, arise from prescription, and that in considering the nature of the command vested in the Captain-General of the Artillery Company, it will be necessary to take into consideration what has been the universal opinion and general understanding of the public touching that high situation.

As soon as I am able to transmit to your Royal Highness copies of the records remaining in the possession of the Company, I shall take the liberty to address your Royal Highness more at large on this important subject. (39588–9)

Carlton House, 15 Sept. 1799

I take up my pen to acknowledge the receipt of your kind letter which did not reach me till some days after your departure & for which I cannot help returning you my best thanks. I was extremely vexed that I did not see you previous to your embarking, for had I known that you was expected at Walmer the day on which you passed through Canterbury I should have with the greatest ease contrived to have seen you en passant. On my arrival in London I found so much entre nous *ingenuity* exercised on the part of my friend Cottin relative to the exchange he wished, & all the other officers of my Regiment so extremely adverse to it, & upon such *reasonable* grounds, that I was induced from principles of justice & fairness to *them*, after having talk'd the business over with them, to stop any further proceeding except what the Regulation of the Army admitted, & to oblige George Leigh, though much against his inclination, to purchase the Lt. Colcy., which has restored good humour & unanimity in the Corps. Everybody now seems perfectly content except Cottin, who is very angry at being obliged to sell for the Regulation, but this I cannot help. George Leigh is only apprehensive that he should appear in your eyes to have acted inconsistently, & it is therefore that I charge him with the delivery of this letter himself, to assure you that it was not till I took it upon myself to promise that I would write to you & explain the circumstance of its being in consequence of the application of the officers that I could induce him to assent to the purchase money being lodged by his father. At the same time I am sorry to be obliged to enclose to you a certificate [1] signed by Keate of Captn. Fuller's ill health, which will prevent his being able to join the Rt. these two months. He is laid up with a very serious venereal attack, nothing fresh but an old business which has hitherto only been patched up, but which Keate assures him now with perseverance he will make him completely rid of. As I have no news here to communicate but expect it from you from the other side of the water, & as I am sure you have letters & business enough to bore you without mine I will relieve you by concluding here. [2] (44150–1)

1. Keate's certificate is dated Arlington Street, 14 September: 'It is necessary for Captn. Fuller of the 10th L.D. to have two months leave of absence for the recovery of his health'. (44152)

2. Next day the Prince set off for Weymouth to visit the King and Queen, and, as usual, he stayed at Mr. Steward's house on the Esplanade.

Halifax, 15 Sept. 1799

From the affectionate interest you have always taken in everything that concerns me, I am sure you will be glad to learn that I arrived here in tolerable health on the 6th of this month. Our passage was very long and tedious, for instead of being about thirty days, which is the common run of a single man-of-war, we were out forty-three. However, as we experienced but little bad weather and had a most amiable worthy man for our Captain, the time passed away as well as was possible on such an uncomfortable element as the sea. My time is totally taken up with making the necessary arrangements to carry on the duties of the Command properly, which, owing to the removal of headquarters from Quebec to Halifax, will be far more numerous than I had foreseen, but I hope, with perseverance, I shall get through all, for I am determined to allow myself no recreation until everything is settled as it ought to be. The contrast between the comforts and the beauty of England, with the want of every resource and the drearyness of Nova Scotia, is certainly very glaring, but I have always made it a rule to content myself, wherever it may fall to my lot to be, and I trust this maxim will not fail me now. In the meanwhile I look forward, not without some hope, to the possibility of the union with Ireland taking place in the course of the next Session, for I believe I mentioned to you that Mr. Pitt had promised me in that event to suggest to the King the appointing me Commander-in-Chief there, on withdrawing the Lord Lieutenant. I am sure I need not urge *you* (should it be in your power) to exert your interest to forward this favorite wish of mine, for I have too often experienced your friendship not to be very certain that whenever you can serve me you will be ever ready to do it unasked. But I thought it just right to hint the circumstance in order that, when you write to me, which you promised you would do, you might think of giving me some idea whether my expectations are likely to be realised or not.[1]

I hope by this time the picture you were so good as to say, Hopner[2] should do of you for me will be completed, and that by the first frigate that comes out here you will have given Dalrymple[3] orders to send it out.

1. The Duke wrote to his friend Coutts on 28 September: 'I am in no small expectation of seeing you yet before a twelvemonth expires, at least if an Union takes place. I think myself certain of it, unless indeed Mr. Pitt has held out to me a prospect for my provision in which he was not sincere, but I cannot suppose this possible. Of course you know I allude to the Chief Command of his Majesty's troops in Ireland, if the Lord Lieutenant is withdrawn, a measure which Mr. Pitt makes no scruple of declaring to be his' (Coutts Bank MSS.).

2. John Hoppner (1758–1810), portrait painter to the Prince of Wales, 1789. On 17 January 1800 *The Times* declared that the Princess of Wales was sitting to Hoppner for her portrait, and that she was coming to town daily for that purpose.

3. William Dalrymple was the Duke's Treasurer.

I need surely not attempt even to say how much I shall value it, if the likeness is but a good one. Ernest, you know, promised me also to send out *his* picture, but *sitting* is a thing *he* does not much like giving his time to. I must therefore beg your interference if he has neglected keeping his word, for I really love him very sincerely and shall be much mortified to be deprived of this mark of his affection, which I am looking forward to with much satisfaction.

Major Jones of the 66th Regiment, to whom you desired me to shew what attention I could, is not here, being gone on leave of absence to visit a relation in the United States. This part of the world, you will easily perceive, affords nothing interesting as a subject to write upon. I shall therefore not tire you by adding anything more to this epistle except my anxious hope that every wish of yours is by this time accomplished, and in this expectation I shall beg to be remembered particularly in Hanover Square, concluding with every assurance, my dearest brother, of the most faithful and devoted attachment, with which, while I exist, it will ever by my utmost pride to prove myself [etc.].

P.S. Madame de St. Laurent requests that you will accept of *her* best wishes.[1] (45967–9)

1. In another letter (28 September) the Duke said: 'My present plan is to remain here for three years from next June if I am not called to Ireland in the intermediate time, and after that I shall look forward to other plans.' (45569)

The Duke of York's letter to the Duke of Kent (13 December 1799, not 1800 as in the copy) throws further light on his position at this time:

'I take the opportunity of the sailing of the December packet, for Halifax, to return you many thanks for your last letter, and to assure you that the Duchess and myself will not fail to have the pleasure of sending you our pictures, as soon as we can have them painted, which will be after our return to town.

I was so exceedingly occupied after you went, during the whole time I remained in England, previous to the expedition to Holland, that it was out of my power to write to you the letter which I promised; it was on the subject of the wish you expressed to Mr. Dundas of being hereafter employed either upon the Irish or Scotch Staff, and having talked the subject over fully with him, he wished me to explain to you his sentiments upon it. In the first place you do not seem to be thoroughly aware of the situation which you wish to obtain, and I should imagine, think that the Chief Command in Scotland and Ireland possesses the same powers as the one which you at present fill, which is by no means the case in either of those situations, as the Command in Scotland is merely considered, as a district completely as dependent upon the Chief Command here, as the Southern or any other district in England, and the Chief Command in Ireland is at present totally dependent upon the Lord Lieutenant, and should the Union take place you may depend upon it that it is the intention of Government to put it upon the same footing as that in Scotland, for many obvious reasons.

At the same time, my dear Edward, I trust that you will not take it ill if I state to you very fairly, that if either of these situations were such as you would wish to accept, Ministers would feel a delicacy in venturing to recommend to his Majesty to appoint you to one of them, under your particular circumstances at this moment.

It is not the business of anybody whatsoever to interfere in the private connections of any person, as long as they are not brought forward to public view, but a great deal depends upon

Berlin, 16 Sept. 1799

Having now fixed the day for Augusta's departure I take the earliest opportunity to inform you of it. She will set out from here on the 19th of the month. I flatter myself, my dear Prince of Wales, you will protect us. Our child will be here tomorrow and is to return back with Augusta. Being excessively unwell I cannot at present write a long letter. (48164)

1489 MAJOR–GENERAL GEORGE CHURCHILL [1] TO COLONEL MCMAHON

Kingston, Jamaica, 28 Sept. 1799

I have not seen your friend Capt. Wilson of the 83rd.; I was not at home when he called, and came up here (for I am not in Kingston but at a small house I have bought to be more cool and pleasant than in town) immediately afterwards. It is howr. quite sufficient that you and my friend Carter interest yourselves for him for me to take him by the hand and do all that lays in my power for him, in consequence of which I will inform you that I am without a Major of Brigade, that H.R.H. the D. of Y. promised when I left England to provide me one, but I believe forgot. I refreshed his memory some time since. Should he not yet have appointed one I shall be very glad if he will name him.

I wish you joy of the great and rapid successes of the Allies. I cannot help regretting very much to have no share in them. (39592)

appearances in this world, and every person in a public situation must avoid doing anything which may shock even the prejudices of the public.

I am the last person in the world to preach or to wish to meddle in your private happiness or connections, but at the same time I must fairly say to you you can have no idea how much the world talked of the public manner in which you went everywhere accompanied by Madame de St. Laurent. I am perfectly well aware that this may be done abroad, but you may depend upon it that it cannot be done at home, and therefore I advise you as a friend to consider this subject well over.

I must again repeat to you that I trust that you will not take ill what I have written to you, but I thought it much the fairest proceeding towards you, to state to you honestly what people's feelings are concerning you, and leave it to your own judgement to decide.

I will not trouble you with a longer letter at present, but with my hearty wishes for your health, believe me' [etc.]. (44164–5)

The Duke of York would have done well to remember his wise counsel to his brother when in 1809 his relations with Mrs. Mary Anne Clarke became matter of public scandal.

1. Formerly the Prince's Equerry. See No. 175. Major, 1781; Lieutenant-Colonel, 1790; Colonel, 1795; Major-General, 1798; Lieutenant-General, 1805 (*d.* 1808).

Berlin, 29 Sept. 1799

Any expression, any token of kindness from you, to a man who lives so neglected as I do, must be grateful in the highest degree, and indeed I must allow that upon this score your having assured me my welfare interested you makes me feel extremely happy. It has been a long time that I have not had the pleasure of seeing my eldest brother, and during the short stay that I made in England we met so very seldom that our acquaintance even then could barely be called intimacy. This misfortune was certainly mine, and on casting over in my mind past events, the remembrance of those lost moments which might have so effectually turned to my own advantage causes me the most sincere regret. However, the assurance that [I] have now received from you, my dear Prince of Wales, in this letter ensures me that the ties of consanguinity reimplace that affection which the want of greater intimacy might else have deprived me of, and consequently affords my heart comfort on a point which so materially interests it. Thus far your letter has been of infinite consolation to me; would to God the rest of its contents had been to the same purpose, and I should have been completely happy. I am sorry, very sorry, to find the wide difference of opinion that reigns through the remainder of your letter, and when I compare these sentiments to letters wrote in former times by my brother Ernest in your name, advising me that as to a left-handed marriage in Germany I ought never to think of it, as my son might inherit the Electoral States of Hannover, I am at a loss how to account for it. After having said so much perhaps my letter will afford you but little pleasure; however, duty requires me to give you that answer which the length of your letter seems to demand from me, and therefore shall venture to state my opinions on various parts of it, and as perhaps this will be an answer to his Majesty, you may freely state it as such to him, for I do not hope his favour, and have been too long accustomed to his displeasure, for to expect any change from it. Had he had the least affection for me he would not have broken his word to me when he promised me my Establishment at the same time with my brother Ernest, and which promise I have in his own handwriting; and certainly he would not have forced me to a climate which was the cause of my first indisposition thirteen years ago, and where I shall certainly die if [I] remain long, for since a whole year I have never been able to sleep one night in bed. It is impossible for me at present to enter into a discussion of what the law thinks relative to my marriage, but what [I] am certain of is, that were the law even in my favour at this moment the despotic power Government has now in its hands would doubtlessly employ it to my disadvantage, and [I] therefore think it neither prudent nor worth my while to take any step whatsoever at present. Equally useless does it appear to me to make any assurances to his Majesty on this subject for has [*sic*] the law had power sufficient to annul my marriage my consent or any assurance on my part is unnecessary, and the law only have weight, but with my approbation I ought to be the last person to be consulted on the subject and flatter myself that however different my opinions may be from those of my family they will have that respect for my character at least as to think me incapable of acting contrary to the dictates of my honor and conscience or to make use of a more general term contrary to the sentiments of a gentleman. As to the King's being able to do me harm or my wife, or any of her family on my account is a question almost too indelicate for me to touch upon, but as you have hinted it I will answer you with the same freedom. *As for me* he may certainly stint my fortune, which would be very unpleasant, but he cannot prevent my coming to England which [I] shall certainly do in that case. The consequence will be an order for my not being received at Court; agreable that would neither be, but the unpopularity of the action will fall upon him, and not upon me. *As for my wife* if he does not grant her a sufficient income and pay those debts of hers which she had contracted from having had no allowance made her the three first years of our separation, as Lord Loughborough had promised by letter, which in an unmanly and ungentlemanlike manner he got back out of her hands, but of which luckily I have an attested copy, and put her in that way of respectability as to allow for the education of our child, for her keeping her carriage, and having those comforts which she can enjoy at a distance from me, his Majesty may equally depend upon my returning to England, and if this does not avail I shall publish all the transactions, as [I] have already everything ready for the Press with attested copies of all the letters that have passed between the Archbishop of Canterbury, the Lord Chancellor, and many other persons on the subject, as also a letter from the Marquis Cenello to the Queen of Naples desiring in the name of his Majesty my not being allowed to leave Naples &c. &c. &c.

I shall not add a word more or less to the whole transaction but leave the impartial reader to judge for himself, and then we shall see upon whom the popularity or unpopularity of the business will fall. I trust therefore that as I do not enter into any explanation, but merely for to please the King, [I] have agreed to Augusta's returning to England. You will endeavour to have her comfortably and properly established as ought to be the case, if not, you know the consequence, for if a single hair of her head is touched I shall consider it as an order for my immediate return to England. With respect to the education of my son it is impossible for me to accept the generous offer you have been so kind as to make me, but it is incompatible with my feelings of honour and duty to have him either educated or treated otherwise than what I conceive is due. The loss is entirely mine but I trust a moment's reflection will make you see the impossibility of my entering into those views of yours. With a thousand apologies for the length of this letter, and with the most sincere gratitude for the affection and friendship you wish to shew me I ever remain [etc.]. (48167–9)

1491   THE DUKE OF YORK TO THE PRINCE OF WALES [copy]
Schagen Bruck, 30 Sept. 1799
I take the earliest opportunity in my power to acknowledge the receipt of your very kind letter of the 15th instant, and am very happy to hear that you have settled the Lieutenant-Colonelcy of the 10th Light Dragoons to your own and the Regiment's satisfaction.

As for George Leigh I think it would have been impossible for him to allow anybody to purchase over him, and I beg that you will assure him that I do not see any inconsistency in this conduct, and that this diffidence of himself does him credit.

With regard to Captain Fuller there cannot be the least difficulty in granting him leave of absence for two months.

News I have none to tell you from hence; since the 19th we have been obliged to remain quiet, in order to get up many things which were wanted, and the weather has been so bad and windy for some days that it has retarded us very much.

Adieu, my dear brother, I am afraid of missing the post if I add more. (44153)

1492   PRINCE AUGUSTUS TO THE PRINCE OF WALES
Berlin, 2 Oct. 1799
Having had some conversation with Mr. Tyrwhitt relative to the education of my son, & having told him in consequence of your letter I had seen myself obliged to decline your kind offer, I have assured him that as my wife and myself had the most entire confidence in Lord Thurlow and that we were convinced of the rectitude of his judgment as well as of his friendly offices, we left everything to his disposal. If consequently you will condescend to take his opinion on that matter and will agree to his proposals I shall be ready to allow of my son's being under your care jointly with him. I am the more ready to make this sacrifice as I rely on your own generous efforts in future times and that in case of any accident happening to me I have reckoned on your friendship and steadiness to accept of the guardianship of my son jointly with Lord Thurlow and his

George Tierney
by William Behnes

The Prince of Wales
June 9 . 1800

Sir,

I am this moment honour'd with Your Majesty's most gracious letter, & hope that it is not necessary for me to say, that I shall always deem an intimation from Your Majesty as a command instantly to be obey'd; of course I need not add, that I shall in consequence not attend the debate that is likely to take place in the House of Lords either today or tomorrow.

I have the honour to subscribe myself, Sir,

Carlton House.
June 9th.
1800.

Your Majesty's
most affectionate & most
dutiful Son & Subject
George P.

An exceptionally legible letter written
by the Prince of Wales to the King

mother. In full confidence of receiving a speedy, decided, and favourable answer I remain [etc.]. (48170)

1493 LETTERS FROM THE PRINCE OF WALES TO THE DOWAGER COUNTESS OF ELGIN

Carlton House, 10 Oct. 1799

I have to acknowledge the receipt of two letters from you, for which I will beg of you to accept my best thanks, but it has not been in my power from various causes to return an answer till this day. It appears to me I must say that the rent of the house at Blackheath, as well as the time it is propos'd to be let for, is very exorbitant & such an expense that I should hardly think that the Princess of Wales even could wish to put me to it, for so short a space as six weeks or two months that it would be proper for the child to remain at any rate either at Blackheath or anywhere in the country. At the same time that I think the expence of this house is very exorbitant, yet if there is anything that can be found on the other side of the Heath, even a mile or a mile & a half distant or two miles, there is no reasonable expence I am not ready to submit myself to, & no temporary inconvenience to the child & yourself, my dear Lady, that I should not wish you for a short time to put up with, sooner than that the Princess of Wales should not have the child in the neighbourhood, though I shall always expect from you during your stay that my child is not made the partaker or the puppet at her early age of any large company or society, where either she may become the object of flattery, or meet with such indulgence as is afterwards to be prejudicial either to her temper or disposition so as to injure her further education, which is one of the things I have most at heart in this world, which I ever shall attend to with the watchful eye of a parent, & which hitherto I have seen so correctly & properly carried on under your tuition. To be brief then, if any other house or any other means can be found to accomodate & meet with the wishes of the Princess of having the child in her neighbourhood without running me to such unreasonable expence, I am ready to stretch a point to indulge her, & desire that you will give such directions & make such enquiries as may be necessary. I am most truly delighted at the good accounts you give me of the state of health of my child; pray give her a kiss from her papa together with his blessing. As to my beloved mother I desire you to express what I ever must feel about her. I do not write to her, having nothing worth while saying, & as she hardly would have time to write to me again on account of her approaching departure for Windsor,[1] I have written a few lines to dear Augusta however. I will

1. The Royal Family left Weymouth on the 14th at 5 a.m., but Princess Charlotte remained there with Lady Elgin until the 23rd.

trouble you to present my best love to one & all of my dear sisters, & am, my dear Countess [etc.].

P.S. Pray remember me kindly to Chasse & to Durham.[1] I am just stepping into my chaise for Brighton. (49238–9)

Brighton, 13 Oct. 1799
As the post is this instant going out I have only time just to acknowledge the receipt of your kind letter, & to desire that you will use your own discretion about the staying at Weymouth a week longer. You have done most perfectly right respecting Christie's[2] house at Blackheath, & am in great hopes you may get it. Do not forget to write either to Hicks or to Satchwell[3] at the Grainge in time, as of course I suppose you intend the making it your half way home. You delight me with the good accounts of the dear child as well as of the rest of the family; & now adieu, as the postman is actually waiting at the door for my letter. (49240)

1494   PRINCE AUGUSTUS TO THE PRINCE OF WALES

Berlin, 15 Oct. 1799
By the time you will receive these few lines you will have already perused my long letter of the 29th of September, and the other short one written the 2d of October conveyed to you by favour of Mr. Tyrwhitt. By the first you will see the effect your letter has had upon me, by the second you will find my desire to acquiesce in your wishes as far as I conceive my duty and my honor will allow me. My determination is very firm and therefore [I] do not push the matter further, for with every wish to prove to you, my dear Prince of Wales, my sincere confidence and desire to merit your affection, I cannot forget either my own private duties or the respect I owe myself in the publick opinion. Indeed, was I to act contrary to what I conceive my own principles I never should have the assurance to shew myself in England again, which is always my view to do in time, if not necessity recalls me sooner. I hope, my dear Prince of Wales, you will be satisfied and that you will think of getting us all comfortably settled. Your promise to me before I left England makes me trust you

1. Lady Elgin's daughter and son-in-law. Captain Durham, who commanded the *Anson* frigate, was at Weymouth in September, and on the 10th of that month he and Lady Charlotte entertained the Royal Family to dinner on board.

2. James Christie, the auctioneer.

3. R. Satchwell was a Page of the Backstairs in the Prince's Household. Mrs. Satchwell was the Coffee-room Woman.

will use your endeavours for my Augusta, and overcome those insidious attempts of Lord Loughborough to prejudice her still more in the King's opinion. Her absence from me in my present bad state of health is a very severe blow indeed and a great sacrifice on my part. It merits therefore consideration, which can be done in no other way than in having her comfortably provided for, and in allowing me an independant command of my own fortune. Pray do not neglect my interests and consult about our child with Lord Thurlow. (48171–2)

1495 THE EARL OF MOIRA TO COLONEL MCMAHON

Donington, 17 Oct. 1799

You deserve a jobation, my dear Colonel, for the apologies with which your request is introduced. 'If you have any venison, I will thank you for a basket,' is the only formulary admissible, and by using any other you lay yourself open to the pains & penalties established against the crime of léze-amitié. Trusting that you will be sensible of your offence now that it is pointed out, & that you will view it with due contrition, I shall not indict you this time. Half a haver will be dispatched for Cheltenham this day.

The assurance which you gave to the Prince respecting my dispositions was perfectly right. In my professional line I am ever ready to undertake any service for which I may be ordered, howsoever hopeless the enterprize: only, if the plan be such as I think cannot succeed, I must take care that it be not fathered on my judgement. Things are now so overset in all points of our effort on the Continent that I do not conceiveMinisters can have the notion of trying any other experiment by land. There is a distant operation that might be useful if executed on a decent scale. I am, however, satisfied that it has been a deliberate determination of Ministers not to employ me; which, altho' correspondent to my private wishes & singularly fortunate for me, does not the less apprize me of a hostility that must make me tread with great caution if I be invited to serve: for such an invitation must now clearly arise from pressure of circumstances, & could be suggested only by the desire of involving me in their failures. I gave to the Prince that counsel which I thought was for his advantage, tho' it was contrary to every interest & every inclination of my own. That no suspicion of insincerity might rest upon the step which he took (as I believed they would not imagine his Royal Highness likely to withdraw his friendship from me) I deemed it necessary to disclaim any animosity: and I could do so with strict truth. Had the return to such a profession been of a nature that could bear communicating, the Speaker would naturally have been very anxious to impart it to me, since the establishment of such a sentiment might be useful to Mr. Pitt, tho' I had put it on such a footing as that it could not benefit me. The Speaker's silence, therefore, was sufficient indication to me that Mr. Pitt's temper overswayed his policy. Of course, I must be on my guard against such a disposition. Indeed, I have great reason to suspect that the Prince discovered something of that inveteracy: otherwise he would certainly have endeavored, from a foresight of possible embarrassment to himself, to have brought us together. Not having any particular object myself in the business, I never sounded the Prince as to what he had observed, so that, I own, this is all loose supposition. Whether the surmise be just or not is immaterial, for it cannot influence my conduct beyond giving me a degree of check in that sort of romantic zeal which for my own interest does require the curb.

Adieu. I will hope to see you here later in the year: for, I think service out of the question and I have no thought of stirring hence. (39593-5)

1496 GEORGE ROSE TO [?] COLONEL MCMAHON

Old Palace Yard, 25 Oct. 1799

I can assure you with the strictest adherence to truth that I left his Royal Highness the Prince of Wales, when I had the honor of attending him by his command, with an anxious wish & desire that the measure proposed by him might be found practicable. I lost no time in talking with Mr. Pitt on the subject & stating everything that his Royal Highness suggested. After considering the whole most attentively Mr. Pitt was decidedly of opinion he could not further the purchase of the late Marshal Conway's house, even for the purpose intended, in the manner proposed, and on another conversation with Mr. Pitt yesterday (having had several before) he expressed himself distinctly against the possibility of applying to Parliament at present.

It is a matter of deep & sincere concern to me that in the first instance in which his Royal Highness has honored me with his commands I should entirely fail in being at all useful. I wished to be so from the bottom of my heart, which *no consideration* should induce me to say if it was not strictly true. You will, I trust, under these circumstances, represent me properly to his Royal Highness. I feel a most unaffected anxiety not to suffer in his opinion. If I should have to undergo that misfortune it would be most unmeritedly; and I am persuaded your good-nature will protect me from danger of that. His Royal Highness's absence from town prevented an immediate access to him, & I am happy in a further delay being prevented by an opportunity of making the communication through you.

I never till yesterday understood anything about the Prince of Wales's application respecting the prolongation of the lease of the late Marshal Conway's house, but I will carry the papers down with me to Mr. Pitt & endeavor to have that point settled satisfactorily. (39596–7)

1497 THE PRINCE OF WALES TO THE DUKE OF YORK

Petworth, 25 Oct. 1799

I have only written to you once since you have quitted this country, which was upon matters of business, & knowing how much your time must naturally be taken up, engaged as you were in the most difficult & intricate service perhaps that has almost ever been chalk'd out for any man, I consider'd it but common humanity on my part not to intrude upon your leisure moments, or such as might be much more usefully employed, with letters that could not afford you much amusement, at any rate, & which perhaps you might, consistent with your usual good humour, have thought it necessary to answer, however troublesome it might have been to you. But do not suppose that though I have not broke in upon you by my letters, that therefore my silence is to be attributed either to negligence or to indifference as to what regarded your interests. You may naturally suppose that the situation of the Army under your command ever since your landing in Holland, but most especially at the present moment, creates much & indeed is the sole topic of the conversation & of the animadversion of the public. Various are the opinions & strange, very strange indeed, the opinions of people even amongst those where you would have the least reason to expect it. When a man is in difficulties (or supposed to be so by the world, which is nearly the same thing as the being really so) is the only moment when he can know his true friends, & then it is that it behoves those real friends to shew themselves such. It is therefore, my dear brother (not that I think it is necessary for me for various reasons to make any professions), that I take the earliest opportunity of writing these few lines to assure you that whatever may be the complexion or colouring it may be thought right to give or throw upon the recent events that have taken place with respect to our Army in Holland, you will find no one who will more staunchly stand by you, or prove themselves more truly your friend from having your interests most sincerely at heart, than [etc.]. (44154–7)

GEORGE ROSE TO [?] COLONEL MCMAHON

Old Palace Yard, 26 Oct. 1799

There is still a doubt in Mr. Pitt's mind as to the competency of the Treasury to grant the renewal of the lease of the house which belonged formerly to the late Marshal Conway in the manner recommended, but he is entirely disposed to do so if it shall be found the Board have the power, with a clause of resumption on paying what the premises shall be worth at the time. I hope the point may be soon ascertained. (39598)

1499 LETTERS FROM THOMAS TYRWHITT TO THE PRINCE OF WALES

27 Oct. 1799

Lindeman having missed this day's packet, I shall have ample time between this & Thursday to make up all my letters, from which I have very strong hopes of success.

In my life I never met with such boisterous gentry as those who are concerned for the Box at Drury Lane; I trust, however, they are now a little lulled, & that your Royal Highness will bear no more of their impertinencies; the arrangement shall be very shortly transmitted to you.

I heard yesterday in the City & it was believed last night that T. Grenville was going back directly to Berlin.[1] If this be true, his object can be no other than peace, as I know that neither the whole family of the Grenvilles or the whole Ministry collected will ever operate upon the present King so as to make him join any coalition where the House of Austria pulls the same way. I believe I forgot to mention to your Royal Highness at Brighton that I know for a fact that the Dutch expedition was quizzed by the King at dinner at Charlottenburg the very day the Hereditary Prince[2] set off for Lingen, & a good deal of what has since happened was foretold. I know not why, but his R.H. the Captain General[3] is not in the best of odours there. If anything occurs your Royal Highness may rest assured you shall hear of it directly from [etc.]. (39599–600)

1. Thomas Grenville left Berlin on completion of his Mission on 1 September. He arrived at Hamburg on the 5th, at the Texel on 18 October, at the Helder about the 20th and at Yarmouth on 23 October.

2. The Hereditary Prince of Orange. He reached the Helder via Cuxhaven. He was back in London on 27 October, following the failure of the Helder expedition.

3. On 7 September it was announced that the Duke of York had been appointed Captain-General of the Land Forces in Great Britain, and of the Land Forces employed on the Continent in conjunction with the Allied Armies.

5.30 p.m., 28 Oct. 1799

I am this instant returned from the City, but have not been able to do my business from the absence of the broker. Apprehensive, however, that your Royal Highness's cassette may be in want of some reinforcement, I enclose £200. I fear Lucas's draft of £630 will manger a considerable share of the balance, & which is now due. I have been the whole of the morning writing my letters to Cassel & as I think I know the two leading strings to the Landgrave's heart are avarice & ambition, I have not failed to touch them in the most forcible manner I can. I am certain the connubial connexion may be turned much to the interest of your Royal Highness.[1] Lindeman will sail without fail in Thursday's packet.

I am very happy to inform your Royal Highness that, notwithstanding strong rumours to the contrary, no money by any secret Article of the Convention[2] is to be given to the French. It is said Colonel Brownrigg carried out orders to inundate &c. &c.—but arrived too late, as the terms had been settled. The Guards have been all embarked at the Helder since Wednesday last, but have not yet arrived; the transports have orders to make the first land they can, & then immediately return for more troops. Major Coleman by the last accounts was better, but I do not find there is anything to be depended upon respecting Ld. Huntley.[3] Genl. Forbes's[4] son has never been heard of, & I am sorry to say, is not a prisoner.

Lady Elizabeth Luttrell is dead, & I believe there is no doubt respecting the fact.

If your Royal Highness has not written to Greenwood yourself, will you be graciously pleased to say whether it is your pleasure to subscribe

---

1. The reference would be unintelligible but for Lord Minto's letter of 7 December to Lady Minto: 'The Princess [of Wales] . . . told me that the Prince has just got £40,000 from the Landgrave of Hesse-Cassel, as a loan without interest. How he has brought this about, God knows, but she told me also that the Prince had proposed to the Duke of Clarence to marry the Landgrave's daughter, which the Duke of Clarence seems to have declined, being satisfied I suppose with Mrs. Jordan. He also answered that he could not say a word on such a subject without knowing the King's sentiments. The Prince wanted him to propose at once to the Landgrave, whom he has perhaps cajoled with this sort of expectation' (Minto MSS.). And on the 15th he wrote: 'I told you that the Prince has got £40,000 from Germany. This has probably enabled him to settle with Lady Jersey, who is going abroad, as the Princess says, and all this seems to have some connexion with the Prince's late advances to the Princess' (ibid.).

The Landgrave's daughter Caroline (1771–1848) was the Princess to whom Tyrwhitt was referring. She married in 1802.

2. The Convention of Alkmaar (18 October), by which the Duke of York agreed to evacuate Holland, retaining possession of the Dutch fleet.

3. Lord Huntly, who became a Major-General in 1801, was Colonel of the 92nd Foot (the Gordon Highlanders) from 1796 to 1806.

4. Gordon Forbes, of the 29th Foot. Colonel, 1790; Major-General, 1794; Lieutenant-General, 1801; General, 1812 (*d.* 1828).

100 gs. to the Fund for providing for the families of those wounded in Holland?

From what I can learn the Duke of Bedford will be obliged to submit to the Bougean system, from which, as your Royal Highness has been kind enough to enquire, I have received no small benefit. (39601-3)

1500   THE EARL OF MOIRA TO COLONEL MCMAHON

Donington, 2 Nov. 1799

The bearer, Mr. Macartney, has been working his way up to London by giving exhibitions of singing & recitation in the manner of Dibdin.[1] Some gentlemen who had heard him & believed him to be in distress, recommended him; & we have had a representation before the ladies here. Mr. Macartney's object is to get engaged at one of the London Theatres. His voice is really very good, and I think he would be found an useful performer in musical pieces. In speaking, his articulation & enunciation are such as give fair promise of him for an actor. Tho' I know no more of him than I have mentioned, I cannot refuse to give him this letter; because I believe it to be an act of charity, but the extent of my request is only that you would put him in the way of making his application to some of the Managers in such a line as may procure him an equitable hearing. With Sheridan you could probably do it easily, but then I fancy the poor man would find it requisite to eat occasionally, & it is said the Drury Lane performers are at times rather left to their wits. I know you have had negociations about Boxes &c at the Theatres; therefore I do not fear to embarrass you by this recommendation: and a man who does not know how to address himself to the Managers may at the outset take some false step that would prevent his talents from ever after having equitable consideration. (39604-5)

1501   LETTERS FROM PRINCESS AMELIA TO THE PRINCE OF WALES

[End of Oct. or early Nov. 1799]

In the first place I write to you to remind you of your kind promise of giving me a gown which I am in great want of & the pattron I sent you belongs to my dear Miny, who is very anxious that you would return it.

I am going to request a favour of you; it is not for myself, but if you grant it it will oblige me & make the family very happy. Sir Harry Neale,

1. Charles Dibdin (1745-1814), dramatist and song-writer.

before I quitted Weymouth,[1] told me how thankful he should be if I would recommend his brother, Mr. Burrard,[2] to you & beg you to make him one of your Chaplains, as belonging to you is a very creditable thing. I promised him to name it but at the same time he desired me to beg you to put yourself to no inconvenience & that you will excuse the liberty he is taking.

We left dear Charlotte very well; I was miserable to part with her. Oh! how often I look back with pleasure to the few days you were with us. I do love you dearly & every day I think if possible my affection increases. All my sisters join in love to my dear perfect *Eau de Miel*. For God's sake come & see us or at least tell me how soon I shall have that happiness. It appears an age since we met.

God bless you, my dear brother.

[*P.S.*] Sr. W. & Ly. Pitt are come today to us on a visit & they are to remain some time, to Pitty Witty's great joy. (Add. Georgian 14/25)

[*Windsor, 6 Nov. 1799*]

Many thanks for your very kind letter & all the affectionate expressions you make use of. Sr. Harry & Ly. Neale desired me to take the earliest opportunity of expressing their gratitude & thanks for your particular kindness in making Mr. Burrard your Chaplain.

Thank God we shall meet on Friday; I am looking to the hour of meeting my dear *G.P.* with great pleasure and delight. It appears indeed quite an age since I had the happiness of kissing your dear face.

The reason of my troubling you with this letter is to beg you will not name to mama having written to me, for, to tell you the truth, I forgot to shew your letter till it was too late, & she appeared anxious at not having heard of you; therefore, knowing you would see her so soon I did not say anything, but hasten to beg of my dear *Eau de Miel* not to name it to her.

I think dear Frederick looks vastly well.[3] Miny is so & begs her kind love as well as dear Sophia. We are at Windsor with Ly. C. Finch, Sr. William & Ly. Pitt.

God bless you; do come *exact* on Friday,[4] that is to say early enough, & be convinced, dear brother, of the unalterable attachment with which I remain [etc.]. (Add. Georgian 14/27)

1. Before 14 October, that is.

2. The Rev. Sir George Burrard (1769–1856), who succeeded his brother, Sir Harry, as Baronet in 1840. He was Chaplain to four successive Sovereigns; Rector of Yarmouth and Vicar of Shalfleet, in the Isle of Wight, 1801; Vicar of Middleton Tyas, Yorkshire, 1804–56, and Rector of Burton Coggles, Lincolnshire, 1822–56.

3. The Duke of York was back in London on the 4th.

4. Princess Augusta's birthday.

1502   PRINCESS AUGUSTA TO THE PRINCE OF WALES

Queen's House, 7 Nov. 1799

I am so concerned at hearing that you are still very ill that I cannot help begging you a favor not to think of coming to Windsor tomorrow for I should be miserable if you were to hurt yourself on my account, as you may believe me most sincere when I tell you that no one loves you more truly nor with more affection than [etc.].[1] (Add. Georgian 10/24)

1503   PRINCESS AMELIA TO THE PRINCE OF WALES

Queen's House, Friday morning [8 Nov. 1799]

Dear Miny has just recollected that we go this eveng. to Lady Charlotte Finches's & therefore *she* thinks *it safer* you should not dine here. Dear Miny would have written herself but being with Mr. Schrader, made me her secretary. She is very sorry we are deprived of the pleasure of seeing you, but hope you will come soon to make up for this loss. I hope my dear brother is convinced that no one is more disappointed than myself. Pray come soon again & beleive me ever your affte. sister & friend, not omiting dutiful godchild.[2] (Add. Georgian 14/28)

1504   THE PRINCE OF WALES TO LORD KENYON, AND THE REPLY

Carlton House, 15 Nov. 1799

As I am thoroughly persuaded that in the administration of justice the very last thing that could enter your Lordship's thoughts would be by any remark that might fall from your lips to unwarrantably prejudice the

1. The Prince, who had been visiting Lord Egremont at Petworth and Sir Henry Fetherstonehaugh at Uppark, near Petersfield, did go to Windsor, and was well enough to hunt the following day. He did not complain of illness on the 6th, when, in the evening, he wrote to the Dowager Countess of Elgin from Carlton House: 'I came to town so late last night that it was not in my power to write & to tell you how anxious I am to see the dear child. I therefore desire that you will bring her to town by twelve tomorrow, & after I have seen her, the King, with whom I dined this day, has express'd a wish that she should meet him at St. James's, with which command I shall be most happy to comply.' (49241)

It will be noticed that none of his letters at this time is written from Brighton. *The Times* reported on 31 October that he had lent the Pavilion for the winter to the Duchess of Cumberland, who, incidentally, had arrived at Yarmouth from Cuxhaven on 9 September.

2. On the 19th the Prince sent the following note to the Dowager Countess of Elgin from Carlton House: 'Pray bring the dear child to town tomorrow for I long to see her. If you can contrive to be in town by eleven o'clock, I could wish that you would, as I have appointed Cosway to be at Carlton House at eleven in order to finish her picture for me.' (49242)

94

publick mind against an individual of any description whatever; I am confident that your Lordship would never have used *the expression*, which in the notion of every one so decidedly alludes to me, as stated in a morning paper of yesterday which my Attorney-General has the honor to bear you. It is true that from applications from many respectable quarters I have been induced to assent to my name being placed among others as a member of a new Club to be instituted under the management, as I understand, of a Mr. Martindale, merely for the usual purposes of social intercourse, to which I can never object to be a promoter; & especially as it was represented to me that the object of this institution was to enable his trustees to render justice to various honorable & fair claimants. But if these were really your Lordship's words, which I cannot for a moment suppose, give me leave to tell you that you have totally mistaken & misstated my character & turn, for of all men universally known to have the least predilection for play I am perhaps the very man in the world who stands the strongest & most proverbially so upon that point.

I shall not trouble your Lordship further upon this strange circumstance, as Mr. Graham will convey to you my feelings & sentiments upon it, & I am well persuaded that your own knowledge of the world, as well as the urgency of the case, will suggest to you the propriety of taking such measures in consequence as are requisite & ought to be adopted.[1] (39607–8)

LORD KENYON'S REPLY

20 Nov. 1799

I have been under some difficulty in what manner I ought to act in consequence of the letter your R.H. condescended to honour me with.

I was apprehensive if I wrote immediately to you it might be deemed

1. His letter in Kenyon, *Life of Lord Kenyon*, p. 358, is substantially identical. *The Times* report of the proceedings in the King's Bench on the 13th had no reference to the Prince. The Lord Chief Justice observed that Martindale's name had frequently occurred in Courts of Justice. 'He had received letters, he dared say from very virtuous persons, stating that an event might take place which certainly ought to be guarded against. It was clear that Martindale had lost so much by gaming that no certificate could be of any service to him. It was said he was going to open another gambling house. In order to do that his Lordship supposed it would be necessary to obtain a license from the magistrates. When he considered who the magistrates for Westminster were, he took it for granted such a license would not be granted. If it were, the magistrates would certainly act contrary to their duty. There was already a sufficient number of gaming houses' (14 November).

The Times informed its readers as early as 19 February that the Prince had established a new Club on the same plan as the former *Catch Club*; that it had had its first meeting a few days earlier, and that about thirty gentlemen had dined together.

too obtrusive, and therefore I communicated what I had to say, to your Attorney-General, in writing.

Knowing that I feel all respect for every branch of my Sovereign's family, I hope that in presuming to send this letter I do not trespass on propriety.

I thought it my duty to recommend to the Magistrates not to grant a licence to Mr. Martindale, considering what had pass'd, respecting him, before me judicially. This is my settled opinion at present, and this I wished to impress.

I do not recollect the expression I used; but to assist my imperfect memory I have applied to the better recollection of the eminent practicers in the Court, and they assure me that I used no word which could be deemed offensive to your R.H. I can only add that I am confident I meant nothing offensive to you.

They know little of my sentiments who conceive me capable of using language tending to expose the higher orders of the State to censure or light observations.

May I presume to hope that your R.H. will pardon this jumble? (39661)

1505   THE PRINCE OF WALES TO THE EARL OF EGREMONT

Carlton House, 23 Nov. 1799

Many thanks, my dear friend, for your kind letter, as well as for the information it contains, which in many accounts I cannot help acknowledging to you makes me rather uneasy, & therefore with your leave I shall find myself tomorrow at dinner at Petworth & stay only one night, as I am more desirous than I can express to know all you do & to consult with you what may be best to be done under the present circumstances. You may easily imagine how truly grateful I must feel to you for the repeated fruits of friendship & regard I experience from you.

I am ever, dear Egremont, most affectionately yours [1] (Petworth MSS.).

1. On the 20th the Prince had written the following note to the Dowager Countess of Elgin, from Carlton House: 'I have the King's commands for the dear child to be at St. James's between the half past twelve & one o'clock tomorrow. Letters were received from the Duchess of Wirtemberg at four this evening. The French then had not advanced, & the Archduke had sent two strong Regiments to reinforce the Wirtemberg troops. I am, my dear Countess, in haste [etc.].' (49243)

Carlton House, Saturday night, 23 Nov. 1799

The Prince of Wales is extremely sorry that it will not be in his power to call upon Lady Augusta Murray tomorrow between three & four o'clock as he had intended; indispensible business having render'd it necessary for him to go out of town early tomorrow morning for a couple of days, & either Wednesday or Thursday, whichever is most convenient to Lady Augusta to receive his visit, he will be quite ready to have the pleasure of calling upon her Ladyship in Hertford Street either at three or four o'clock.¹ (48174)

Farm near Tunbridge Wells, 1 Nov. [? Dec.] 1799

I have great joy in enclosing to your Royal Highness a letter which I have just received from the Duke of Brunswick. It will prove to our Ministers his high ideas of your Royal Highness and of the services which you can render to this country and to Europe. It disproves the *little* tales of enemies, and announces, what I always suspected, of the disunion of the Imperial Courts: it shews his impression of the vigorous measures necessary on our part, in the para bellum.

The Baron de Jacobi has written to me a very *interesting* & friendly letter. If your Royal Highness will pay a visit to the Speaker & shew him the Duke of Brunswick's letter which I have mentioned to him, he will shew your Royal Highness the Baron Jacobi's opinion.

Mr. Pitt has the scene in his hand if he will avail himself of your Royal Highness's aid and take the continental line in his own hands. The Duke of Brunswick is on the best footing & in the same noble system with the Archduke Charles. The latter is the idol of the Emperor Paul² —*these* are the great & noble springs for a Minister possessing the confidence of King, Prince & people to give its harmony & energy to the foreign Coalition and thereby to avert the blow that is meditated against the finance & Constitution of this country.

1. Lady Augusta Murray wrote to Thomas Tyrwhitt, the letter being dated merely 'Sunday morning' (? 24 November): 'I am extremely unhappy to be obliged to do even a seeming rudeness to his Royal Highness the Prince of Wales—which the refusing to read any message coming from him may appear to be—but Prince Augustus will not permit me to receive any letter directed as the one from his Royal Highness was. May I beg you will tell this to the Prince & I trust he will have the goodness to receive this reason as a sufficient one for returning the letter unopened?' (48175)

2. The Tsar Paul (1754–1801) had succeeded his mother, the Empress Catherine II, on 17 November 1796.

United with the north of Germany (which is our natural Ally) we may defeat the combinations of the south. It has what we want & we have what it wants. Nor is there a jarring interest between us. Our fleets and finance can defend it against the world—their armies, under a Brunswick and the Ich Dien as Aid de Camp, can strike at Paris, IF OR while the enemy is aiming his invasions at our vitals.

Or if the new Frankilin [*sic*] & Washington of France[1] (like their predecessors in revolutionised America) will have peace & renounce their Counter-Revolutions *here*, on condition that we shall renounce them *there*—who so proper to *hint* this as Prussia? And who so able to heal the breaches of our former alliance with her, as the Heir Apparent of England & Hanover acting in the confidence of his father and our First Minister?—I repeat—HIS TIBI ERANT ARTES?

I shall not be easy, Sir, till I hear of a visit to the Speaker—I have just heard from him & have the highest opinion of him & of his goodwill to your Royal Highness. I shall soon have another letter from the Archduke wishing the *co-operation* of the true Prince, whom God protect. What more?[2] (39662–3)

---

1. Presumably Sieyès and Bonaparte respectively. Benjamin Franklin (1706–90), the former U.S. Minister in Paris.

2. The Duke of Brunswick's letter to Macpherson is dated 14 November:

'La lettre que vous avés bien voulu m'adresser en date du 24 Octobre ne m'a été remise que le 12 Novembre; ces retards, suites des grandes distances, et de l'incertitude des comunications, ne sont pas un des moindres empechement aux succes d'une coalition qui doit recevoir ses impulsions de Londre, de Petersbourg, et de Vienne, tandis que le foïer de toutes les secousses qui ebranlent l'Europe, je trouve concentré au Luxembourg. Si le malheur se joint à cela que les Puissances coalisés différent entre elles de principes sur l'objet qu'ils prétendent obtenir, et sur les mesures à prendre pour y parvenir, les conséquences qui doivent en deriver, ne sont pas bien difficiles à prévoir. Nous voïons dans ce moment les armées Russes, se separer des armées Autrichiennes, sur le soupçon peut-être fondé, que la cour de Vienne a entamée des negociations de paix, et nous somes à la veille du developpement d'une des plus fortes crises, dans la quelle l'Europe s'est trouvée durant cette guerre funeste. C'est avec surprise, et une douleur profonde que nous avons apris les evenemens arrivés en Hollande, nous ignorons entièrement les raisons qui ont produits les effets que nous voïons, aucune puissance n'est mediatrice dans cette affaire, et aucune Puissance n'a été invitée à l'être, le principe de la plus exacte neutralité, a dirigé come vous ne l'ignorés pas, le nord de l'Allemagne jus qu'ici. Les sentimens justes, et élévés de l'auguste Prince au quel vous avés parlé, ne me surprenent pas, il voit le mal, il voudroit y remedier, rendre des services essentiels à sa patrie ainsi qu'à l'Europe entiére, rien n'est plus digne de lui, et plus propre à inspirer la reconnoissance la plus parfaite, son intervention personelle seroit certainement de beaucoup, mais il est bien douloureux que la mobilité des affaires, et la celerité avec la quelle les evenemens se succédent détruisent souvent les plus grandes vues, et les projets les plus salutaires. Eloigné come je le suis de tout ce qui a raport à la politique, je ne puis former que des voeux pour la chose publique, et souhaiter sincérement qu'avec les vues bienfaisantes d'une pacification générale, on ne perde point de vue les preparatifs les plus serieux pour une autre campagne vigoureuse, et sur tout bien concertée. Si vis pacem, para bellum, vous en connoissés la nécessité mieux que personne, et l'Angleterre remportera outre l'extension de son comerce,

1508 THE PRINCE OF WALES TO THE DOWAGER COUNTESS OF ELGIN

Carlton House, 4 Dec. 1799

I have received your kind note, & am order'd by their Majesties to desire
that the dear child may be at St. James's at half past twelve o'clock
tomorrow. I have not been very well myself since I had last the pleasure of
seeing you or I should have sent for you up to town before this. (49244)

1509 LADY AUGUSTA MURRAY TO THE PRINCE OF WALES

6 Dec. 1799

I take the liberty of sending your Royal Highness a letter I received
yesterday from Prince Augustus, that you may not, Sir, be alarmed at the
present reports of his ill health. At the same time will your Royal Highness permit me to tell you that I have applyed several times since my
return for money due to me by the Treasury & have always had for
answer—there was none. I am therefore led to suppose, the miserable
pension of nine hundred pounds per annum is stopt by order of the
Chancellor—or should it not—such a sum *so paid*, leaves me without any
resource but writing to my Prince, which the fear of mischief has till now
prevented my doing—but now, should my future letters accelerate his
return, your Royal Highness is so just you will not impute it to me as
blame. It is impossible to live in England without a regular and permanent income—since last August (when I received two hundred &
some odd pounds) I have not had one farthing, & that sum had been due
many months before 'twas paid. I could not trouble your Royal Highness
with these details—did I not wish they should—& trust they will serve to
exculpate my conduct from any charge of unfairness.

Your Royal Highness's late extreme goodness to me makes me unwilling to do anything relative to Prince Augustus's affairs without
previously obtaining your permission—& I think, Sir, your generous
manner of being candid & just will not refuse me your consent in the
present exigencies of my pecuniary concerns, & that you will allow me to
tell my Prince his presence will not be unwelcome to your Royal Highness—that you know he is returning to England—& that your displeasure will not make his arrival painful to his feelings—on the contrary—may I tell him, Sir—that your Royal Highness will receive him
with real pleasure? (48178-9)

de son domaine, des succes brillans de ses armées navales, la gloire immortelle d'avoir sauvée
l'Europe autant par la sagesse de ses conseils, que par ses victoires. Il me seroit infiniment
flatteur d'etre aportée de rendre service à M. le Marquis Huntley, je le considérerois comme
un devoir de ma part, mais ma position m'interdit absolument de faire des demarches relatives
à des objets, qui tiennent proprement aux relations exterieures.' (39664-5)

[Carlton House, 11 Dec. 1799]

Your note, my precious life, my Maria, I have just received, & am delighted if it has been fortunately through my means that you may find an hour or two's amusement. I assure you that I had not begun the work, nor thought of it, as I am just at present in another course of reading & which will take up a good deal of my time for some days to come. As to the paper[1] I have put into your hands, it was with no view of distressing your feelings that I entrusted it to you; that I wish'd you to be acquainted with the contents I most certainly did, & next to the relief I felt when I had finish'd it, & which certainly did restore one in a manner to life after a precarious & dangerous illness, the greatest relief to my heart would be the knowing that you had perused it. As there are parts not relative to yourself which are material for you to know, & which it was so difficult next to impossibility for to explain in conversation, & which it is impossible that we must not touch upon occasionally, refer to & discuss over, the only method I knew of was, after a long hesitation & contest with myself, to lay that before you which could convince you that upon these subjects whoever talks to me speaks perfectly in the dark; that cannot be the case when you have look'd over the paper, but certainly those parts. Jack Payne,[2] who has this day look'd over one of the other copies & is perfectly master of them, may, if you please, leaving out such parts as regard you, print those that I mean & I shall tell him so before he calls upon you in the morning. Think not, my angel, that there is *one unkind expression even about you* contain'd in the whole of it; no, beleive me, nothing could be further both from the writer's heart & mind, both then & now (though it is now within a few days of four years since it was written) & indeed at all times than a thought of that nature, how I *have* lov'd & ador'd you, God only knows, & how I do *now* he also knows & you even cannot pretend to be ignorant of or to disbeleive. I have no secrets from you, nor ever will have whilst I exist; no one has ever seen it but Payne & but two others in the world know that it exists, but never have seen it. When I said no one but Payne I forgot, but as you already know it, it is almost needless for me to repeat it, that my sister[3] has seen it, but excepting her & Payne no one on my sacred honor has seen it. There is nothing in it, my Maria, to hurt your feelings; you will only know me better than ever you did, & why should you wish to remain in ignorance whilst I live of what you & the whole world must be acquainted with when I am no more? It will be an unspeakable relief, I repeat, to my heart; I

1. The Prince's Will, 10 January 1796 (No. 1067).

2. *The Times* announced on 9 November that Rear-Admiral Payne was to inhabit the house in Pall Mall next to Carlton House.

3. Princess Elizabeth.

UNIVERSITY OF VICTORIA
LIBRARY
Victoria, B.C.

am ready to receive it again when you assure me you have look'd it over, & I am sure you will not refuse me when I tell you that it is most essential to my peace of mind. As to my sister, I forgot, I suppose, to tell you that she expected no answer, & indeed rather seem'd to wish none, for she meant merely to convey her opinions, as she told me, & good wishes to you, & had but one motive, to dictate what she wrote, her sence of what was right for us both, & consequently the thorough establishment of our united & mutual happiness.

Pray, dearest life, let me see you soon again & it will be with most true & heartfelt delight that I shall meet you if I know that by having look'd that paper over you are perfectly acquainted with every feature of the heart & soul of your own, own, own George P.

P.S. My cold is something better. I was not out of my room the whole morning but have been at the Play with Treves this evening from whence I am just return'd. Pray, pray I conjure of you, let me hear of you tomorrow that you are *well* & not in *the dismals*; only think of my being oblig'd to preach to you, my beloved & adored Maria. God bless you, my only life & love, I will not positively intrude any longer upon you.[1] (50225–6)

1511 LETTERS FROM PRINCESS AMELIA TO THE PRINCE OF WALES

Tuesday morning [near Christmas, ?1799]
My dearest dear Eau de Miel: I send you with this letter the music I promised you; ten different peices you admired, & they are all adapted for your band. I have given Peck many others which he is writing out in the same manner & I hope to send them very soon.

It gives me very great pleasure to have it in my power to assure you dear mama is really much better & in good spirits. She does not look well, but better than she did when you last saw her. I was much disapointed the other day by hearing your intention was to come here after Sr. Lionel Darell's Ball.[2] I was quite delighted with the thoughts of seeing my own dear *Eau de Miel* but how cruelly disapointed when I

1. The Prince referred to his continuing indisposition in a note to the Dowager Lady Elgin, dated Carlton House, Wednesday evening, 17 December: 'I have been so much indispos'd for some days past that I have not had it in my power to send for the dear child up to town. I wish she would be in town tomorrow, & hope it will then be in my power to give you an audience, & which was not the case when I was last in town. About two o'clock I shall be ready to see you, & the child I desire may be here about me.' (49245)

2. Sir Lionel Darell (1742–1803), M.P. for Hedon, 1784–1802. A Director of the East India Company for many years between 1780 and 1803; created Baronet, 12 May 1795. On 19 September 1800 *The Times* reported that Prince Augustus and Lady Augusta Murray, on their return from Berlin, had taken Darell's house in Grosvenor Square.

found it was not you but General Hulse. I hope you will come soon and be here on Christmas Day.

All my sisters, particularly dear Miny, join in kind love to you. Miny is *much more* perfect *than ever*; every day makes her if possible more amiable. May I, my dear brother, recall to your *memory* the *gown*; I want mine exceedingly & so does Miny.

Adieu, my dear angel, beleive me ever, absent or near, your affectionate sister & grateful godchild.

[*P.S.*] My vile spasm in my throat still plagues me very much. How I long to see my dear *G.P.* (Add. Georgian 14/29)

[? *Dec. 1799*]

Many thanks, my dear Prince of Wales, for the beautiful gown you were so good as to send me which arrived this morning; it made me particularly happy as it shewed me you sometimes thought of me even when I was not with you. I do not know how to thank you for all the kindness I have experienced from you ever since I was in this world, but be assured no one is more grateful or loves you more sincerely than I do. If I could fly over to thank you myself I would, but as that is impossible this letter must do it for me. As I cannot find words to express all I feel concerning you, my dear brother, you must take the *will* for the deed; therefore God bless you & beleive I am & ever shall be your most affte. freind & sister. (Add. Georgian 14/26)

Windsor, Christmas Day, 25 Dec. 1799

My heart is so full with your constant kindness to me I cannot express what I feel, especially your kindness in writing me such a dear, dear letter. It will be my constant companion & often & often shall I read it & imprint in my mind all you say. I have, you know, always loved you most dearly both as a brother & a friend; my affection increases, & though it would be *vain* to say your present goodness makes me love you better, it gives me a particular sensation I cannot express. My beloved brother, I am well convinced of the *consequence* these last two days have been to me & that my happiness depends much upon it. The dear Archbishop's very particular goodness to me is more easily felt than described; much do I owe to him; his being the person was a very great comfort to me.[1] He has been so indulgent & kind to me. You are well acquainted with my dear papa & mama's goodness & therefore will not be surprised to hear

1. On the 24th the Princess was confirmed by the Archbishop of Canterbury in St. George's Chapel, Windsor.

of their affection to me & their goodness. I hope I may by my future conduct shew them I am not undeserving of theirs & the general kindness & affection I have experienced on this occasion. Nothing else can ever shew my gratitude.

I grieve very much at your illness but hope you will soon get better; take great care of *your dear self*. You love me & for my sake you will, for you know the joy I feel to see you in health & spirits. I own till your letter came I felt very much annoyed & disappointed at your not being here, but was vain enough to think in my own heart if you knew *about me* nothing but indisposition would prevent your attending, & *alas*! this is but too true.

I am better; you may imagine all I have lately gone through has hurried me. Now it is over I rejoice & feel much more happy & comfortable than I did before. Allow me once more to return you my thanks (though very far from what my heart dictates) for your kindness to me ever since my birth. To the last day of my life I shall love my beloved & dear *Eau de Miel & always prize* you as my friend & brother & try to preserve your good opinion & affection.

I shewed the dear Archb. your dear letter. All my sisters join in kindest & most affectionate love to you & join with me in regretting the cause of your absence.

I think my dearest mama pretty well. How great has been her affection & kindness to me & indeed how grateful ought I to be & am I in having always such a model before my eyes. The entrance into *life* is indeed a most awful thing but please God to assist me not to be undeserving of my family & the dear Archbishop's goodness.

Bless you, be convinced of the regard & unalterable affection with which I remain ever your affte. sister & godchild. (Add. Georgian 14/30)

1512 THE QUEEN TO THE PRINCE OF WALES

Windsor, 26 Dec. 1799

I was truely dissapointed in not having the pleasure of seing you yesterday as by yr. brother, the Duke of Cumberld.'s account on Saturday last he had left you so much better that you had planned a visit to the Grange, which prevented my making any enquiries after yr. health. I am sorry to learn by yr. letter that the complaint still continues, & with my very warmest wishes for yr. speedy recovery I would advise that Dr. Turton might be sent for. He is in town & may easily be found, & his skill might strike out some medicine which would sooner relieve you then what you have tryed hitherto.

Dear Amelia went through her Confirmation on Tuesday & yesterday extreamly well; she declares herself happy & uncommonly easy in her mind, which is most natural as at all times the preparation for such a sacred scene is awfull, & her very delicate state of nerves must of course have increased it considerably. She is, however, thank God, in a very good state of health & in good spirits, & the noise in the throat at times much lessened.

The Kg. orders me to say everything that is kind to you upon the occasion, & yr. sisters all join in love & good wishes for yr. speedy recovery. I return you many thanks for the very pritty almanac; it will be my constant companion for the next year & I hope it will procure me the blessing to count more hours & days of health & happiness for you in the new century than I have seen you enjoy of late, in which blessing none is more sincerely interested than [etc.]. (36519)

1513 PRINCESS AUGUSTA TO THE PRINCE OF WALES
Monday evening, 30 Dec. 1799
I have received your kind letter and hasten to send back your servant. Mama sends you a letter she wrote you this morning & which was to have gone by the post so that you will find you are not forgot. The Queen has no objection to your bringing or sending Lord Robert & Lord Charles Manners, & she will be very happy to see Arthur Paget. We shall dine at Frogmore precisely at four o'clock & you will order the *beaux* to be there a little after seven o'clock as the King wishes the Ball to be over before supper.

I am very happy to hear you are better & will bespeak *fires* as large as the *grates* can hold to warm up your appointment. I am sorry you are become of so *frigid a nature* but I hope it is only from *outside & skin deep*.

[*P.S.*] *The Ball is on Wednesday*. (Add. Georgian 10/25)

11   1800

The King enjoyed remarkably good health in 1800, but illness is a re-
curring theme in the Prince's correspondence, and on more than one
occasion people thought that his life was in danger. Mrs. Bootle Wil-
braham, who was well informed, wrote to her cousin John Loveday on
24 February, suggesting that the Prince's prolonged illness might afford
him time to 'repent of his past conduct'. 'He is low and frightened himself, and is growing very good, civil to the King's friends, and respectful
to his parents. His appearance is much altered. From the stout, athletic
figure, fat and high spirited, full of laugh and talk, he appeared at the
Ancient Music last Wednesday (which he hates and used to call dull),
but so thin, so puckered his face and so quiet that I really did not know
him. A physical man told me that I sometimes employ, that about a
week ago he took from him twenty-eight ounces of blood by cupping,
not by guess but actual weight, and about three weeks before, he was bled
at the arm twelve ounces for three days together. What constitution can
bear up under such discipline? He has great apprehensions of sudden
death, and when he feels himself oppressed, bleeds in this manner. I have
made up my mind to his going,' she concluded, 'and hope the worthy
good King may hold out till his granddaughter may be old enough to take
the Government with the aid of sensible Ministers.' Lord Bathurst said
at the end of May that the Prince was much better, 'but he is still subject to violent spasms for which he takes a great quantity of laudanum'.

His correspondence again includes a fair sprinkling of letters relating
to his indebtedness. His financial situtation called for a further reduction
in his Establishment, and the offices of Chamberlain and of Master of the

Horse were now abolished. W. H. Fremantle said in March that the Prince intended to have a Bill introduced into Parliament which would enable him to mortgage the revenues of the Duchy of Cornwall. 'I hear from pretty good authority that the Government have lent themselves to his views upon it. The object is to clear his private debts and leave him a net £100,000 per annum.' But the only measure affecting the Royal Family which received the attention of Parliament during this Session was a Bill to remove doubts about the right of the Sovereign to dispose of his and the Queen Consort's property.

The Prince had never been on friendly terms with Pitt, and it is not surprising that his attempts to secure a morsel of Government patronage for his friends failed. Lord Melbourne was refused an Irish Earldom, and Charles Pybus, though a close friend of the Duke of Cumberland—himself a warm supporter of Administration—was given neither an Irish peerage nor the office of Chief Justice in Eyre South of the Trent.

Ill health caused the Duke of Kent to return to England in August, but without any prospect of overcoming the Duke of York's opposition to his being given military employment at home. Early in May, Prince Augustus, having contrived to alienate all the members of the Royal Family, aggravated his errors by returning home without the King's leave. By that time, however, he was ready to submit to the King's will and accept the nullity of his marriage, being helped to arrive at this painful and mortifying decision by the advice of the Whig lawyer Erskine and by some disturbing and apparently unfounded accounts of Lady Augusta Murray's conduct. His departure for Lisbon in December, for the purpose of recovering his health, at a time when she was pregnant (her daughter, Augusta Emma, was born on 11 August 1801) probably made the separation easier. So it ceased to be necessary for him, a self-confessed 'miserable sinner', to offer up daily prayers for his Angel; he need no longer bemuse himself with the consoling reflection that 'what God has united, no profane hand dares, no profane hand can, separate'. He could now think about other things than 'the happiness, the satisfaction, the honour' of his wife and child. The pleasing prospect of being together again 'many a happy day and I hope also many a happy night' had for ever vanished.

1514 PRINCESS ELIZABETH TO THE PRINCE OF WALES

10 Jan. 1800

I have just received mama's commands to send a servant to town to enquire after *you*. She particularly orders me to say that she knew nothing of your being so ill till yesterday, otherwise she would have sent before, but hopes to hear from you today that you are better.[1] I trust I need not add that all the sisterhood are equally desirous to know the truth about you; we all fear'd you was very far from well the last time you was here, but Ernest assured us it was a cold. We flattered ourselves he would have been back early, but that not being the case we shall be anxiously looking out for the servant's return.

Sophia has had one of her spasms which has not lasted so long & though low she is upon the whole pretty well. Amelia's spirits are good but that strange noise continues, sometimes less, sometimes worse.

Mama commands me to say everything kind & affectionate with her love, which we all join in most cordially, but no one more sincerely than [etc.]. (Add. Georgian 11/86)

1515   PRINCE ADOLPHUS TO THE PRINCE OF WALES
From the Camp of Liebenau, 16 Jan. 1800
I seize the earliest opportunity of acknowledging the receipt of your kind letter which was sent me from Rennsburg by Sr. Home Popham,[2] and which he was prevented from delivering himself on his leaving England last Autumn. I have read it over with great attention, and though I have not the time at present of writing as long as I should wish, yet I cannot be at ease till I have answered some parts of it; and I trust you will not take ill, my dearest brother, if I write as openly as you have done. Do not think I intend to excuse myself, for if I have erred, I certainly have not done so from *intention* and still less from want of *attachment to you*, for God knows how much I love you, and I should be very ungrateful if I ever could forget the kindness you have shewn me on every occasion, and

1. On 1 January and again on Monday the 13th *The Times* reported that the Prince had been ill the previous week, and that the Princess of Wales came to town several times to inquire after him, but did not see him.

And on 1 March it declared: 'For some time past it is well known that the Prince of Wales has occasionally been very seriously indisposed. This has induced H.R.H. to make an application to the King for leave to go to Lisbon or to Madeira for the recovery of his health. As this permission could not be granted without the consent of Parliament, H.M. referred the subject to his Ministers, who, upon due consideration of all circumstances, have recommended the Prince not to make such an application, as they could not give their consent to it. H.R.H. has perceived the propriety of the recommendation, and is satisfied with remaining at home. His intention, in the event of his going abroad, was to have taken the title of Duke of Cornwall.'

2. Rear-Admiral Sir Home Riggs Popham (1760–1820). Lieutenant, 1783; Captain, 1795; Rear-Admiral, 1814. K.C.B., 1815; K.C.H., 1818. Commanded the expedition against the Cape of Good Hope, 1806, and then against Buenos Aires. M.P. for Yarmouth (Isle of Wight), 1804–6; for Shaftesbury, 1806–7; for Ipswich, 1807–12.

particularly on my last stay in England. The reason why I did not impart iṁediately that subject to you which afterwards has made me very unhappy, was what I stated to Ernest: that having heard that the King often spoke on family matters with Mr. Dundas, I thought he would be best able to judge the manner in which this subject should be mentioned to his Majesty. I did not even write to him myself, but I desired my friend General Don[1] to do it in my name, and I expected an answer on this subject which would enable me to act in a proper manner. Mr. Dundas, instead of answering G. Don's letter, immediately spoke to the King, and I then received the King's orders not to touch the subject to anybody. This is the true reason why I did not write to you, and not out of want of confidence. For had Mr. Dundas written me word that the King could do nothing for me I should have dropped the matter immediately and should not have said a word to anybody till a more favourable opportunity had offered itself. I do assure you that I have not even touched this subject to anybody except Mary till the whole was broke off, and then I received so many letters on this subject that I was forced to answer them.[2] Had Mr. Dundas sent me word that I should write to the King, you undoubtedly would have received at the same time a letter from me. I now leave the whole matter to you, and I begg you to judge if, after this candid confession of the different steps I have taken, you can impute to me with justice a want of affection. I do not at all wish to make any apology, and the manner in which you have expressed yourself in your letter is certainly a proof of your attachment, which God knows I value most highly, but nothing could make me unhappyer than the idea that you, my dearest brother, can think me wanting in affection to you. Depend upon it, that I shall never fail of informing you of anything that regards me, and I hope you will never suspect me of want of gratitude again.

Before I conclude I must add one thing, that the very long silence you have observed for these last few years, and that you have never answered

1. Sir George Don (1754–1832). Colonel, 1795; Major-General, 1797; Lieutenant-General, 1805; General, and Lieutenant-Governor of Gibraltar, 1814. G.C.H., 1816; G.C.B., 1820.

2. Lord Holland, writing from Leipzic on 26 August 1800, thus commented on the affair:
'... The Queen [of Prussia] is very pretty and he [the King] is very fond of her—so fond as to have overlooked a great indiscretion of her sister's who, while she was negotiating a marriage with our Prince Adolphus, let herself be got with child by an officer Prince Salm, & wished to conceal it till after her marriage. The King insisted on its being told to Prince Adolphus; allows her, tho' a mésalliance, to marry Prince Salm, a man worth a few hundreds a year, sconced but very little of her fortune, and provided for her husband by making him Governor of Anspach. This Princess was, as you know, widow of the King's brother Prince Louis—and this treatment in Prussia is reckoned extremely mild, for he might have seized her fortune and shut her up in a fortress, and where a pretext for seizing fortunes presents itself, it is a very unusual piece of moderation in Kings of Prussia to let it pass by. They say she is *a delightful* woman both in person and manners . . . .' (Add. MSS. 51799)

one of my letters, has hurt me a little, and I really thought you had forgot me. I do not pretend that you should answer every letter I write, but if you would only acknowledge their receipt through Ernest I should then venture to write oftener. You will be informed by him that I have asked for leave to come over to England, but as yet I have received no answer, and I own I should be very unhappy if this permission was to be refused me, as I have been six years from home, and certainly must wish to see my family again.

God bless you, be assured I shall never forget the very kind manner in which you expressed yourself on a subject Sr. Home Popham has written to me about. I am perfectly convinced of the sincerity of the good wishes you make for my happyness and did it depend me [*sic*], I am sure you would be so. I should certainly never have accepted the proposition of Sr. Home, for I am resolved never to marry before I know the object, and I will choose my wife myself, for if I am then not happy I have nobody to accuse but myself. I begg your pardon for this long letter.

All the Hannoverians belonging to the Army under the Duke of Brunswick are encamped since Tuesday last, and we shall probably remain here till the end of the month. I am writing from my tent, and my fingers are so cold that I can scarce hold my pen, and therefore I must begg you will forgive this scrawl. (48545–6)

1516 THE PRINCE OF WALES TO THE QUEEN
Carlton House, 17 Jan. 1800
Many thanks, my ever dearest mother, for your most kind letter, as well as for your most kind solicitude respecting my health. I do assure you upon my honor if I feel myself unequal to the Drawing Room, I will not be so foolish after your kind injunctions as to undertake it, but I really am so much better that I am confident I shall be able to shew myself at Court, though perhaps the whole day might be too much for me. However, your birthday is what I never have missed, nor shall it ever be said that whilst I have life, that I have ever omitted an opportunity of testifying everything that the most affectionate of hearts can feel or profess for the best of mothers. I do assure you that words fail me when I attempt to paint my gratitude for your great condescension & goodness to me, & I would myself come instantly to the Queen's House to express my thanks in person were it in my power at the present moment, & were I not afraid that I might possibly risk some fresh addition of cold which might prevent my appearance tomorrow.[1] (42295–6)

1. The Prince was not at St. James's on the 18th for the Queen's Birthday celebrations.

Fort William, 20 Jan. 1800

Since my return from Fort St. George I have had the honor to receive your Royal Highnesses gracious commands of the 28th of June 1798 & of the 18th March 1799. Your Royal Highness, I am persuaded, will do me the justice to believe that every motive of duty, gratitude & respectful attachment concur in my mind to render the execution of your orders at all times an object of the most sincere pleasure to me: but knowing your Royal Highnesses wish as well as your deep interest that the affairs of this country should be well administered, & satisfied that you will listen with indulgence to my representations on the subject of this Government, I do not hesitate to submit to your Royal Highness my conscientious opinion that Mr. Treves is not qualified to fill the office of Resident at Luknow, a station the most important and arduous in this quarter of India. It might lead to a longer discussion than it would become me to intrude upon your Royal Highnesses time, to enumerate the particular grounds of my opinion with respect to the object of your favor & protection. I trust, however, that your Royal Highness will give me credit for a full & deliberate consideration of the sentiments which I have presumed to express, and I am confident that you will pardon the freedom of a representation, proceeding from a sense of my duty towards the public & towards your Royal Highness.

I shall not fail to pay every mark of attention to the three gentlemen named in your Royal Highnesses orders of the 18th March 1799, signified to me by Mr. Tyrrwhitt.

I request your Royal Highnesses acceptance of an helmet & suit of armour belonging to the late Tippoo Sultan, & found in the Palace at Seringapatam—Major Davis, my Aide-de-Camp, will have the honor to present these articles to your Royal Highness, & I take the liberty of recommending him to your notice.[2] (39670–1)

1. The Earl of Mornington [I.] had been created Marquess Wellesley [I.] on 2 December 1799 (a 'double-gilt potato'), and was bitterly disappointed at not being given a British peerage of that rank, like his predecessor Cornwallis.

2. The following undated note about Tipu's suit of armour, written by Benjamin Sydenham, Wellesley's Aide-de-Camp, was evidently enclosed:

'This war dress was worn by Tippoo Sultaun in his campaign in Adoui in 1786 against the Nizam and Mahrattahs. He was then in the plenitude of his power. Rajah Cawn, the Sultaun's favorite slave, knew the dress immediately on its being shewn to him after the reduction of Seringapatam, and confirmed the fact above stated.

This kind of dress (made, however, of less costly materials) was much worn by the Mahomedans of Mysoor. There were few troops in the world perhaps more personally active and vigilant than Tippoo's irregular horse, and as each man generally trusted to himself alone, it became an object to improve his personal means of defence. These dresses were used as a sort of armour, and were certainly serviceable in this respect, tho' heavy and cumbersome both to the horse and rider. The latter, however, was no doubt willing to sacrifice a part of his own

Carlton House, 23 Jan. 1800

I have this moment seen Tyrwhitt who has inform'd me of your generous & kind enquiries after me, for which I assure you I am most grateful.

When Compton[1] call'd yesterday I said I would call today, totally forgetting the Drawing Room, & consequently that you would be engag'd at three o'clock. However, tomorrow I hope to be more fortunate, & if I feel myself equal to it, to dine at the Queen's House, but that must depend upon how I am. At present, thank God, I feel myself greatly better. (42297–8)

Carlton House, 3.30 p.m., 24 Jan. 1800

I find it will be impossible for me to dine at the Queen's House as I am prevented by business that at this moment is indispensible, as it regards money transactions, & I shall not be able to get rid of the people till a later hour than your dinner hour; however, tomorrow you may depend upon me.[2] Thank God I continue much better; I beg my best duty to the King, & my kind love to my sisters, & am, my dearest mother [etc.]. (42299–300)

convenience for a proportionate degree of security, and it is perfectly certain that these stuffed and quilted jackets were frequently found to resist the sabres even of our European cavalry'. (39545)

1. H. Compton was one of the Queen's Pages of the Backstairs. 'He is a favourite with the King, who frequently speaks to him. He said to him lately, in his hurried way, "Compton, have you any children?" "Yes, sir." "Sons or daughters?" "Only daughters." "Never have any sons. If you have, there must be an eldest, and he will publish your letters."' (Glenbervie, *Journals*, i.368.) The reference is to the publication of the correspondence with Addington and the King in 1803 on the subject of military rank and employment.

2. On the 21st *The Times* declared: 'On Friday last the Prince of Wales sent a message to the Earl of Jersey, purporting that H.R.H. would have no further occasion for his Lordship's services. This dismissal is no matter of surprise to us: the change of residence from Pall Mall to Stratford Place about six months ago was evidently the forerunner of what has just taken place. On the same day the Prince of Wales sent a very polite communication to Earl Cholmondeley, stating that his finances would no longer afford an allowance adequate to his Lordship's trouble and attendance; and H.R.H. therefore wished to decline his future services'.

On the 23rd this statement was corrected: 'The Earl of Cholmondeley did not receive any emolument from his situation at Carlton House, which was purely honorary'.

Finally, on the 24th: 'The Earl of Jersey is said to have received his note of dismission from the Prince of Wales as he was going to Court on the Birthday. The Noble Earl immediately alighted from his carriage, sent his servants home to take off the Royal liveries, and returned to his residence in a hackney coach'.

It was with the view of reducing still further his establishment that the Prince announced the abolition of the offices of Chamberlain and Master of the Horse.

1519   THE EARL OF MOIRA TO COLONEL MCMAHON

Donington, 24 Jan. 1800

Whether Lord Clare ever gave ground or not for the report, such use is made of the Prince's supposed declaration to him that it is essential to contradict the rumor if it be not his Royal Highness's wish to have his sentiment quoted as favorable to the Union. The violence of party is so great upon it, & bids fair to encrease to such extremity, that the most desirable position would be to be understood as not taking part on either side. I do not write to the Prince about it lest I should embarrass him & make him think it necessary to mark some decided line on the question. Do you, as if entirely from yourself, learn whether the Prince had any conversation with Ld. Clare on the subject; & let me know. Correspondent to what you shall inform me, I will do what may be necessary without in any degree committing his Royal Highness.[1] (39672)

1520   WILSON BRADDYLL[2] TO [? ROBERT GRAY OR COLONEL MCMAHON]

Earl of Derby's, Grovr. Sqr., 31 Jan. 1800

I have to hope you will forgive my mentioning to you at the request of the Treasurer of the Beef Steak Society (which his Royal Highness the Prince of Wales honour'd by becoming one of its members) that the sum of forty guineas stands opposite his Royal Highnesses name for subscription, wine &c. &c.

1. The following is the draft of an advertisement in the *London Gazette* (the printed version is slightly different):

'*Carlton House, 29 Jan. 1800*

His Royal Highness the Prince of Wales has been pleased to appoint John McMahon, Esqr. [late Lieut. Col. of the 87th Foot] to be his Vice-Treasurer & Commissioner of Accounts, and Robert Gray Esqr. to be Deputy Commissioner of Accounts.

His Royal Highness the Prince of Wales has been pleased to appoint Lieut. Col. George Leigh, of the 10th or Prince's Own Lt. Dragoons, to be his Equerry, & Mr. Gascoigne to be Clerk of the Stables.' (42301)

2. Wilson Braddyll (1756–1818) was M.P. for Lancaster, 1780–4; for Horsham, 1790–1; for Carlisle, 1791–6. Groom of the Bedchamber to the Prince Regent, March 1812–18. Farington wrote, 15 October 1796: 'Braddyll was at Knowsley in the summer. He went down with Lord Derby and returned to town with him. It is supposed young Braddyll will never inherit more than £1500 a year, so much has been wasted by his father. It is not supposed that Braddyll consumed his fortunes by gaming but by inattention to his expenses and by various profuseness of living. Though he had very expensive establishments to support, he lived much at taverns as a profuse bachelor. He proposed a *chop dinner* at the Cocoa Tree to two or three friends who were surprised to find he had ordered a turtle and haunch of venison. The dinner was about five guineas apiece. His connexion with Mrs. Billington was supposed to be attended with vast expense. Lord Derby gave him the Lieutenant-Colonelcy of the Lancashire Militia as a support'.

113

If you wd. have the goodness to mention this circumstance to Admiral Payne, I shd. be extreemly obliged to you, as I am sorry to say our funds are in that state as to make this sum an object to us.[1] (30008)

1521   THOMAS TYRWHITT TO ROBERT GRAY
Welbeck Street, 2 Feb. 1800
Colonel McMahon has sent me word he is not well enough to dine with [me], consequently I [will] not *entertain* you with a tête-a-tête, but hope to fix a day with him tomorrow when he can meet you.

I received the keys late last night from the Sieur Brent & will bring them you tomorrow. (42302–3)

1522   SIR JOHN MORSHEAD[2] TO ROBERT GRAY
Bath, 2 Feb. 1800
Mr. Michell is to be appointed Sheriff & I find that he likes it.

The new arrangement of Carlton House occasions much conversation, but people here will have it that ye Prince is extremely ill. I have had 2 letters from McMahon, with messages from ye Prince & nothing mentioned of his illness, so let me know how he is. (39673–4 & 42304)

1523   GENERAL SAMUEL HULSE TO ROBERT GRAY
Lewes, 5 Feb. 1800
I received your letter yesterday after the Prince & Admiral Payne had left

1. The receipt: 'Received the 19th May 1800 of his Royal Highness the Prince of Wales by Jno. McMahon Esqr. the sum of Forty two Pounds for subscriptions to Beef Steak Club due. John Boyd.'

2. See Nos. 249n., 539. Moira wrote to the Duke of Northumberland on 25 December 1800:
'... With regard to the Duchy, be assured that the Prince is most irksomely embarrassed by Sir John Morshead. The difficulty is, how to get rid of the Baronet. The object in nominating your Grace one of the Council was that there might be an ostensible ground for your intervention in the management of affairs there: and I know it to be the particular wish of the Prince that it should be made as gratifying to you as possible. Consult with McMahon who will know that he is fulfilling the Prince's desire by anything that can strengthen your interest: and I will answer to you for McMahon's honor in every communication you may have with him' (Alnwick MSS.).

Brighton[1] for the Grange; from what I understood from the Admiral it was not intended the arrangement should have been inserted in the Gazette so soon. Business of every description is to be done at your Office, of which the Admiral can inform you: he returns to town on Saturday. If you wish I should write to him it shall be done of course. Either Lord Cholmondeley or Mister Brent must give up the books and papers; you may recollect they had every information both from poor Robinson[2] and the Dutchy Office.

Mrs. Hulse joins me in best wishes to Mrs. Robert Gray, yourself, Esqr. Richard[3] [etc.]. (42305–6)

1524   JOHN REEVES[4] TO W. FAUKENER [? FAWKENER]

5 Feb. 1800

What I said to you about the fable of Mr. Miles[5] & Owen,[6] I now put upon paper, & you are at liberty to make what use of it you please. I never before heard of such a story as that of Owen making an affidavit of Miles consulting me about the publication of that infamous pamphlet agst. the Prince, and my advising the publication on the part of Government as a thing that would do good. I never heard such a story, nor is there a word of truth in it.[7]

However, I am a little mortified that such an imagination should be

1. *The Times* reported on 31 January that the Prince had gone to Brighton for a few days for the recovery of his health; and on 10 February that he had returned to town from the Grange on the 8th.

2. Arthur Robinson and his wife were drowned in the swollen Trent in October 1799 when the 'balloon' coach in which they were travelling from Liverpool to Birmingham overturned and fell into the river at Tittensor, Staffordshire. For many years he had been the Prince's Accountant and Sub-Treasurer and a Gentleman Usher of the Privy Chamber, and when the Prince broke up his establishment Robinson was given a pension of £500 a year. He was also Accountant and Sub-Treasurer to the Dukes of York and Clarence.

3. Richard Gray, like his brother, was a Deputy Surveyor of the Duchy of Cornwall and a Clerk of the Duchy Council.

4. The Tory journalist (?1752–1829) who, in 1792, founded the *Association for preserving Liberty and Property against Levellers and Republicans* for the suppression of seditious publications. See A. Aspinall, *Politics and the Press, 1780–1850*, pp. 63–4.

5. William Augustus Miles (?1753–1817), a subsidized Treasury journalist (in receipt of £500 a year of secret service money in 1792).

6. Possibly W. Owen, proprietor of the *Gazetteer* newspaper.

7. In 1795 Miles published a pamphlet on the subject of the Prince's debts, which went through thirteen editions. Entitled, *Letter to the Prince of Wales on a Second Application to Parliament to discharge Debts wantonly contracted since May 1787*, it appeared under the signature of 'Neptune'.

115

believed by anybody, tho' it is not unlike some of the slanders of which I have been made the object, since it has been thought worth while to say anything about me; and, considering the number, and the length of the practice, I bear them better than I used.

As to slandering the Prince, it is most contrary to my natural disposition and to the way of thinking I am used to in public matters. If any opinion of my partialities was to be formed from my supposed writings, the King, & the Prince, as his successor, are the persons in the kingdom that I might be supposed to look up to with more reverence than most men; so that my politics, & disposition are equally against such a vile design.

I think you know enough of me not readily to believe I would condescend to be a tool to the Ministers. I think I should not be much disposed to become such for a good purpose; I am sure I should not for a bad one. Indeed, I am out of the reach of such overtures, for you know I live at a distance from them, am in no confidence with them, and, I often think, they would be well content if I were at the bottom of the sea.

I hope, therefore, your friend will no longer believe me a person fit for any such employment as the one supposed.

After I am acquitted of this charge there still remains one which I think a stain upon me; namely, that I am in any confidence with the said Mr. Miles; you know what sort of knowledge I have of that gentleman. Being at Frankfort in Augst. '89 I was accosted by this gentleman, who was then resident there with his family;[1] he was very forward to oblige me and I saw him frequently but I thought him so troublesome that his civilities were lost upon me. I had never before seen or heard of such a person as Mr. Miles. When I returned to England I was made acquainted with his character, and was prepared to avoid him if ever he should happen to fall in my way. This happened, and we soon ceased to be speaking acquaintances. In this state of things between us, it was that in Nov. 1792 he accosted me in the street, and, abt. a week afterwards, he again spoke to me, saying he had been buying my pamphlet,[2] & had it in his pocket. 'If you have, then read it' said I. We parted; & now you have all the intercourse between me & Mr. M. from the year 1790, when he returned to England, & I saw him once or twice before we ceased to be speaking acquaintance. It, no doubt, was owing to this behaviour on my part that he acted as he did, with respect to my pamphlet, for you know it was he who procured the printer's men to come to the Committee, and declare I corrected the Press; it was he also, who put

1. In March 1789 Miles was sent to Frankfort on a special mission by Lord Carmarthen, the Foreign Secretary.

2. *Thoughts on the English Government*, which contained a libel on both Houses of Parliament. Sheridan, supported by Fox, demanded that it should be burnt by the common hangman, and its author prosecuted. See the debates in the Commons, 23 November and 14 December 1795.

116

it into Sturt's[1] head to take it up as he did, and begin the stir in the H. of Commons.

I never saw Miles's pamphlet till this occasion, when I was told there was more libel in his publication than could possibly be made out of mine. I thought it a poor performance—all words & rant, empty as himself. I understand it never had admirers but was generally thought highly censurable.

As to the Ministers, I never can believe they had any knowledge of Miles's intention, and I know he has made himself so troublesome to them that he is detested at Whitehall, & the last man to be trusted.

Owen happens now to be out of the kingdom, so they have chosen a good time for beginning or reviving this slander upon me.

Alas! how little these people know of the tenor of my life, what is my employment, and what are my habits and propensities! But so it is—I happen to have been once started, and am fair game, to have laid upon my head, as I escape, the sins & the curses of all who mean to disburthen themselves. Well!—*Mihi plaudo ipse domi, simulac*—not *nummos*, or anything like it, but *libros contemplor*. When I get into my arm chair in Cecil Street I forget these things, and indeed am pretty well forgotten except by those who give themselves the trouble to remember for no good, like your friend.

Excuse the length of this. (39675–7)

1525   TIMOTHY BRENT TO RICHARD GRAY

Old Burlington Street, 10 Feb. 1800

I send you herewith a book[2] you were so kind as to lend me about five years since. I am sure you will believe that I wish our friend Bob[3] joy in his nomination to assist in the management of the Prince's affairs. As his Royal Highness has thought fit to remove Lord Cholmondeley and myself it is at least a satisfaction that my emoluments devolve upon an old friend.

Remember Mrs. Brent and myself kindly to Mrs. Gray.[4] (42307)

1. Charles Sturt (1763–1812), M.P. for Bridport, 1784–1802. He had succeeded to the Critchell property on his father's death in 1786.

2. A 'book of P. Fredk.'s Accts.' (endorsement).

3. Richard's brother Robert.

4. The next letter is written on the back of this one.

Somerset Place, 11 Feb. 1800

As I generally open the letters addressed here to my brother I had the pleasure of reading yours on my return home last night, and I beg you to accept my sincere acknowledgments for its friendly contents, as also my thanks for the book. I had previously the satisfaction of hearing by several persons that you had expressed yourself in similar terms of liberality on the occasion, and I hope you are apprized that my nomination is to a part only of your late duty & emolument, and that it was unsought for & unexpected by me. (42307)

Somerset Place, 11 Feb. 1800

Since I wrote to you this morning Admiral Payne has signified to me (indeed, I had heard it before, but not so explicitly) that it is the pleasure of his Royal Highness the Prince of Wales that all accounts relating to his Royal Highness's affairs should in future be deposited in this Office;[1] and that those passed under the Earl of Cholmondeley and yourself should be given in charge to me, after they shall have been delivered up to his Royal Highness. You will much oblige me in mentioning by what time such delivery may be likely to take place, with the most perfect convenience to his Lordship & yourself. It would not be a very wise remark to say that the sooner this can be done, the sooner will those who are to be concerned in the management be enabled to obtain the necessary information for their guidance; but you well know that upon the state of the outstanding claims, of which I have seen a sketch in your hand, I believe must in great measure depend our future proceedings; and I trust you will not consider me officiously obtrusive in the request I have made. (42308)

1527   COLONEL MCMAHON TO ROBERT GRAY

Bury Street, 26 Feb. 1800

Being fully persuaded that we only & mutually wish to promote the service of our Royal master, I am sensible that no unnecessary etiquette ought to divide our confidence or weaken our exertions, and therefore once for all I entreat you will have the goodness to class me in any shape that shall prove most agreable to your feelings (whenever the plan of the Establishment is requisite to be delivered in) & which Admiral Payne may approve.

1. The Duchy of Cornwall Office.

You certainly do me but justice by what you are pleased to express in your letter, 'That it was not my intention to rank you as a person dependant on the Commissioner of Accounts or (as in the late Establishment) as Secretary or Clerk to any such officer'. Your appointment flows equally with mine from the fountain of those honors, the Prince of Wales, & our connection in office is meant to be merely a cordial co-operation in H.R.Hss.'s service. The respectability of your character was most fully acknowledg'd by the Prince himself when he named the arrangement which has taken place, nor do I believe that it ever enter'd into H.R.Hss.'s thoughts that any construction whatever should fancy you to be an officer dependant upon me. I trust therefore (knowing as I do the Prince's pleasure) that it is needless to observe that I never could have presumed to entertain for one instant so impertinent or so un-founded an idea.

While I have thus endeavour'd to ease your apprehensions on this score, I surely have a right to suppose that in fairness you will allow me the privilege to satisfy my own particular feelings, especially when they are perfectly distinct from, & do not combat with yours. (42309)

1528   LETTERS FROM GENERAL SAMUEL HULSE TO ROBERT GRAY

Lewes, 24 Mar. 1800

I had the favour of your letter and perfectly coinside with you in opinion as to the mode recomended. I will beg of you to call at Messrs. Drum-monds, and if you please in my name make the arrangement. If I am not mistaken the mode adopted which you mention by Lord Cholmondeley is the same as order'd by the Commissioners for the Prince's former debts. If you call at Mr. Coutts for five minutes in your way to Charing Cross you can gain the necessary information.

I mean to be in town on the 17th of April (the Bishop of St. David's[1] quits my house on the 16th) which I hope will be as soon as you may want *me*. Probably the payments may commence about the 25th; as you ob-serve, it will be proper to reduce the expence and the task will be difficult.

Col. Leigh came here on Thursday last to dinner with a commission to give a large sum of money for a horse which Sr. F. Pool[2] would not part with. He also told me he was to farm the hounds at either 12 or 1500£ a year; surely these sums could be dispos'd off to the credit of H.R. Highness & not for the amusement of George Leigh? Shall I beg the

1. William Stuart (1755–1822), Bishop of St. David's, 1794–1800; Archbishop of Armagh, 1800–22.

2. Sir Ferdinando Poole of Poole and Lewes (*d.* 1804) succeeded his brother as 4th Baronet, 1767.

favour of you should you perchance hear of a servant as a footman that would suit us, to ask him a question or two? Yet I am ashamed, as you must have business enough. Mrs. Hulse joins me in best wishes to Mrs. Robert Gray, yourself, Esqr. Richard, &c., &c. Mrs. H. is writing to Mary.

[*P.S.*] If a clever fellow, wages 17 gs. pr. ann. Boots & *Bris.* [*sic*] 3 ditto. Two liveries compleat pr. ann. One jacket & waistcoat also for work.[1] (42310–1)

1. The Prince of Wales wrote to Arthur Paget from Carlton House on 28 March 1800: 'Four days ago only did I receive your packet of letters, as well as the letter & pipe you was so good as to send me by Hunter, & which I shall most certainly buy & have given the necessary orders to Tyrwhitt to settle the amount as you have desir'd. With respect to the business with which you was so good as to charge yourself respecting my brother Augustus, it is impossible for anyone to have transacted it with more judgment and propriety than you have, my dearest friend, & from what we here, on this side of the water, can judge, in a manner so likely to be conducive ultimately to his advantage, as it has completely broken the ice, where we had most difficulties to apprehend.

The dear Duchess [of Rutland] arriv'd in town the day before your letters were brought to us by the foreign mails. I assure you I executed your commission & of all the creatures the most attached & the most devoted I ever saw, she certainly is the most so; in short, the more I see of her & the more I probe her heart, the *more perfect* I see her. You have really, my beloved Arthur, a jewel of the first water in her, & if you *really know her value*, your happiness will *be complete indeed*, but not more so than I wish you, or than I really think both of you deserve to be. I would have given anything in the world, as I told her, for you to have seen her last night at Lady Spencer's Assembly; she is ten times more beautiful than ever she was, grown so fat you would hardly know her, & with a forehead (to joke for a moment) that out-rivals Lady Hertford's in every respect. I complimented her much upon her looks, & she then told me she had some reason to look well and pleased as she had just receiv'd the kindest of letters from her dearest Arthur. To sum everything in a word, if you think she did love you, I assure you she perfectly adores you now, can talk of nothing else but you, & the joy she feels at the thoughts of going over to you. As to myself, my friend, with many thanks for your kind and affectionate jobation, I can only assure you that I follow most strictly your advice. I am under Farquhar's hands who I strictly obey & from whom I already have derived much benefit, but to tell you the honest truth, as things appear in a more favourable light & become *more favourable*, so my spirits & health reanimate.

We have had many dinners backwards and forwards with many of your or rather our friends, Garthshore, Legge, Bathurst, &c., but everything is flat, my dearest Arthur, without you, not a glass of wine drunk without a recollection, & I may with great safety [say] without a sigh that you are not present to partake of it with us, & to exhilarate us all. As to politicks as you are in the very spot I shall not touch upon them, as I have scarce time to write at all to you, owing to the suddenness of Mr. Haytor's departure who will convey this to you, & who I recommend to your protection. For God's sake take care of yourself in the cursed country you have gone into, & pray let me hear from you most frequently. I shall seize every safe opportunity of writing, for you well know, my dearest Arthur, how truly you are beloved by your ever affectionate friend' (*Paget Papers*, i.180–2).

Lewes, 1 Apr. 1800

Your letter of this morning mention'd the distress'd state of the stock purse at Carlton House. It is singular but true. Altho' H.R.Highness cannot find such a trifling sum as you wish for to discharge the nurses, if five or six hundred pounds were wanting to purchase a horse the sum would be found in some odd corner of a bureau or chest of drawers & paid for immediately.

As soon as the warrants are prepar'd, if you will point out what I should do to expedite payments, no time shall be lost.

Many thanks to you. Mrs. Hulse is much better. (42312–3)

1529 THE PRINCE OF WALES TO THE DUKE OF YORK

Carlton House, Monday night, 14 Apr. 1800

I feel quite unhappy at not having had the pleasure of seeing you for the last three days, but I will tell you candidly how I have been circumstanced. On Saturday I set out in my curricle but was so immediately wet through that I did not dare venture to stop in my wet cloaths. Yesterday I went to Windsor, & today I have been so unwell again that I have not been able to stir out of my house. If I am able to go out at all in the morning tomorrow I will certainly make my first visit to you, but at any rate let me entreat of you to let someone write me a line to say how you are.[1] Should I not call I hope you will beleive that it is because I am really not able so to do.[2] (44158)

1530 THE DUKE OF KENT TO THE DUKE OF YORK

Headquarters, Halifax, 19 Apr. 1800

Private. Unfortunately for me, the December mail was four months before it reached Halifax. I therefore had not the satisfaction of getting

1. On the 8th the Duke met with another accident (one day in January he had fallen from his horse and had been badly bruised). 'As H.R.H. was riding along the King's Road, a dog belonging to a drove of cattle crossed his horse, and the animal fell. The Duke's leg being entangled in the stirrup, he was dragged some distance, and two of his ribs were broken, besides his receiving a contusion in the face' (*The Times*, 9 April).

2. The Prince had not been well for some time. 'He looks dreadfully', W. H. Fremantle had remarked on 7 March. 'Indeed I think it quite impossible he can recover, but I dined in his company the other day, and he ate with a good appetite and did not drink to his former excess. He is reduced beyond idea, and still continues the dreadful remedy of bleeding' (Buckingham, *Court and Cabinets of George III*, iii.41).

121

your letter until the 15th instant; you will perceive by the date of this that I lose no time in answering it.

I must first return you my warmest thanks for the very affectionate manner in which you have promised to send me the Dutchess's picture and your own, as soon as you could get them painted after your return to town, and then request that you will offer to her my most grateful acknowledgements for this very flattering mark of her regard for me.

There was no occasion, my dear Frederic, for you to make any apology for not fulfilling your promise of writing to me sooner than you did; of your numberless occupations from the moment I left England, to that of your return from Holland, I was well aware, and being fully sensible that they were the only causes of your silence I feel not a little gratified and flattered to find that you thought of me so soon after your return.

I am very grateful for the candor with which you enter into an explanation of the nature of the two situations in Scotland and Ireland, to one or other of which I had expressed to Mr. Dundas my desire of being appointed, should either of them fall vacant during my absence. I was perfectly well aware before I left England that the command of the forces in Ireland would be ineligible for me unless the Union was concluded, and I was equally sensible from what you did me the favor to communicate when last we exchanged a few words upon the subject, that (upon that measure being carried) it would be placed precisely upon the same footing as that of Scotland, which you then told me was no more and no less than a District similar to any of those in South Britain. This knowledge, however, did by no means then and does not now lessen my desire to hold either the Irish or North British Command, for I never had a wish to be independent of *you*; on the contrary, it has always been my ambition to look up to you as my elder brother and as the person at the head of my profession, whom it was both my duty and my inclination to please, and from whom in return I expected friendship, protection and assistance to aid me in the accomplishment of those wishes which I might form for my future establishment in the line of it. At the same time I was as fully aware then, as I am now from your letter, that in holding either of those situations, I should be far more limited in point of power and authority than I am here from the commission I hold in this country. But believe me, ambition never was, is not and never will be a predominant passion with me; as such, notwithstanding this difference, it will not cost me one moment's uneasiness to move from hence to either of those stations. Indeed, could I have foreseen when it was in agitation whether I should come out or not to North America, that the General Officers then commanding the East, West and South-West Districts in South Britain were so near giving up those situations, I should never have thought of leaving England, could I have been assured that one of these would have been conferred upon me. Even now, should I be disappointed in my wish to be named to the command of the forces in Ireland or in Scotland, I shall rest perfectly satisfied for the present if you are good enough to obtain for me that of any one of these three districts (though I own, if I were permitted to declare a preference it would be for the Western, or South-Western one) and shall esteem it a great indulgence to be removed to a situation where I am near my family and more immediately under the eye of the King.

It is true that, situated as I am with an incumbrance to clear off (which you must remember my assuring you was the only motive of my return to America when I had before me the experience of the injury done to my health by my prior residence in it, and knew there was no one comfort to be met with in the country that could in the least counter-balance that certainty), the pay of ten pounds per day, which is attached to the post of Commander-in-Chief, cannot be considered a trifle to give up; but I presume this would not be insisted upon, as surely in the event of my being stationed in Scotland or Ireland, little difficulty would be made to continue me the same on *your* representation, although it might be judged expedient to give me a commission only as Commander of the Forces, and to leave out the words '*in Chief*'. Should, however, even that not be admitted as proper under the arrangements you may chuse to adopt, or if the utmost I can obtain is to be put at the head of a District on the Staff of South Britain (in which case I feel this pecuniary arrangement would be impracticable) I am perfectly willing to serve on the Staff [with the] pay of a General, being sure that with your good offices at the Treasury some mode will be found of making me amends for the loss of four pounds per day by adding to the allowance I now enjoy in lieu of table money.

I hope I have now been sufficiently explicit upon the first part of your letter, and that you will fully understand from what I have said, that any District at home, if there are objections to my going to Ireland or to Scotland, would be infinitely preferred by me to continuing any longer here. But to impress you more forcibly with my anxiety that such an arrangement should be made, I will candidly confess to you that the confinement which the faithful discharge of my duty here imposes upon me is more than my health can possibly stand much longer, as during the period of nearly eight months which have passed since my arrival, I can prove that for five days *at least* out of the seven I have been shut up eleven, and at particular times upwards of twelve hours a day.

This will not surprise you when you consider that, exclusive of those duties which I have to attend to in common with any General commanding a District at home, I have also the charge of the Commissary, the Barrack, and the Engineer Department, every estimate and account of which passes through my hands. Besides this, not a single shilling goes out of the Pay Office but by warrant under my signature. You will therefore feel the responsibility that attaches to me, and that for my own safety I cannot avoid devoting every hour of my time closely to business.

I am sensible that to a man in the habits of a sedentary life this sort of occupation might appear as nothing, but to me who require several hours of hard exercise to keep me in health, this close confinement to my Office is the greatest punishment that I could possibly undergo. It is true that from being so little exposed to cold this last winter I have been fortunate enough to escape a severe attack of rheumatism which I have had every other winter I have hitherto passed in this climate, but this benefit has been obtained by the sacrifice of what alone is conducive to the enjoyment of hearty health, and of which I have felt the painful effects in being unable for six weeks to wear anything but a pair of loose trowsers, from a very troublesome humour which, after shewing itself in several parts of my body, at length settled in my leg; indeed at this moment I am writing, one of my eyes is nearly closed from the same cause.

After what I have said I almost feel confident that your representations to the King will be such as to ensure his giving orders to recall me to a station nearer home by the first mail that may leave England after this reaches your hands, particularly as on leaving Windsor I ventured to express to him my hope that if anything fell vacant at home while I was abroad, I should not be forgot, and have since by letter presumed to re-call the same to his recollection. But if the cause you intimate as likely to prevent Ministers from recommending to his Majesty by being appointed to the command of his forces in Scotland or Ireland, is equally to operate against my being put on the Staff at home, perhaps the reply I am going to make to that part of your letter in which *this* is mentioned may not be thought sufficient to do it altogether away. Yet I must own I shall be much surprised if, after perusing the following lines, *you* should still continue to be impressed with that opinion of my conduct when last in England, which you seemed to entertain when last you wrote.

However, without further preamble I will proceed with this subject. From the moment I got home in the fall of 1798, having no one reason to shake off a connection which had then lasted eight years, and which in many of the most painful moments of my long absence from my family under the pressure occasioned by the apparent total loss of parental affec-tion, had been almost the only comfort of my existence, I studied never-theless to regulate my conduct in that particular so as to avoid giving any offence to the prejudices of the world. This motive alone induced me to establish Madame de St. Laurent in a residence altogether separate from mine, where she was attended by a distinct set of servants, and from the same principle we mutually agreed upon never appearing to-gether in the streets of London, in the Parks, or any place which could be termed public, or where there appeared to be the slightest chance of incurring either censure or even an unpleasant observation on the part of the most rigid, precise and formal. To this resolution I can solemnly declare the most faithful adherence was observed, for if I except driving her out now and then in an open carriage (in doing which we were careful to make choice of the most private rides) and going to the Prince's loge grillée at the two theatres (a part where I always understood no one was subject to the prying of impertinent curiosity) I am confident there is no person who can assert having seen us anywhere together. For my own part, so perfectly convinced was I of having fully succeeded in not exposing myself to censure by any part of my conduct with respect to her, that on leaving England it was one of the most pleasing reflections to me, and I felt the more confident in this belief, as I never once was able to find out that even in the most scurrilous public prints the shaft of satire had been levelled either at her or at me. You will easily conceive, then, what must have been my mortification at reading that sentence in your letter in which you say that 'I can have no idea how much the world talked of the public manner in which I appeared everywhere, accompanied by Madame de St. Laurent'.

That *some* people have spoken in this manner I cannot have a doubt after what you have said, being satisfied you can only have mentioned it from motives of friendship and affection for me. I therefore am sure you will not be offended if I say that I cannot help feeling that *no* one had a *right* to make this observation, as the assertion on which it is grounded is wholly unfounded. The remark made by you that 'you [were] well aware such things might be done abroad, but I might depend they could not at home' leads me naturally to say that I so fully felt this myself that I did on landing in England totally and entirely alter my mode of living with Madame de St. Laurent. Here she always did, and does now again, live in the same house with me; she therefore presides at my table, goes everywhere into company with me, and it is a rule with me never to accept of any invitation where there are ladies, unless she is asked, but I never looked forward to a similar plan of life at home, and she never had an expectation of the kind. I should have thought the little insight which you would unavoidably get into our mode of going on, by seeing how things were managed when you did us the favor to dine at Knightsbridge, would have been sufficient to convince you of the injustice of the animadversion you have heard passed upon my conduct on this point. But as it is but too clear to me that the case is otherwise, it is in vain to attempt by any comments of mine to undo the past; as it is, however, necessary that you should perfectly understand and have it from under my own hand what are my intentions with respect to my future conduct on this point, in the event of my being named to the command of the troops in Ireland, Scotland or one of the Districts in South Britain, I will communicate the plan I had intended and which I should still propose to pursue in that case.

I would in the first instance join my command *un*accompanied by Madame de St. Laurent, and establish my own residence in such place as might be pointed out for Head Quarters. This done, I would take a house for her in the country at some little distance off, where her ménage would be totally separate from mine. *She* would of course not appear at *my* house on the days I gave my public dinners, and when *I* went to *hers* I should consider myself as *her* guest, and I should avoid being seen with her at any place of public entertainment that might be in the neighbourhood, unless I could so manage matters as to be there in a private way and without exposing myself to be criticised for so doing. But in all this arrangement I desire it may be understood that not only she is the first to acquiesce, but that she has been uniformly averse to anything that brought her into public view.

Should this detail of my plan be deemed, as I am confident it ought, a sufficient assurance of the perfect propriety of my conduct, you may depend upon my strictly abiding by it, but if more is expected, and I am to understand it is the intention to make my separation from Madame de St. Laurent a term without which I am not to be employed on the other side of the Atlantic (which, however, it is too repugnant to my feelings to credit) I must at once declare that it is one which I will not admit to be dictated to me, and to which, were I to subscribe, I should consider myself as meriting every contemptible and opprobrious epithet to which those expose themselves who commit mean and despicable actions.

I will frankly confess to you, my dear Frederic, I cannot bring myself to think otherwise than that *you* will be fully satisfied with the assurances I have given you, and that no impediment can any longer exist on *your* part in the way of one or other of the arrangements I have pointed out being concluded for me. But if the case should be otherwise (as it is indispensable at this very great distance from home to guard against every possibility) I hereby declare to you, as I am sensible that my health can neither stand the labors of my present situation from the unavoidable confinement that is attached to it, nor the test of a severe winter which, according to all human judgement, the next is expected to be in the same proportion as the last was mild, my firm and immoveable resolution is not to remain in this country beyond the period when I know an answer *ought* to arrive to this letter, if it meets with that early attention from you which I trust it will be thought to merit. I must therefore request, if either I have not succeeded in removing by these lines any delicacy which his Majesty's Ministers, as you inform me, might have felt in recommending to the King for the command of his forces in Scotland or Ireland; or if by having failed in so doing, the same obstacle is intended to be considered as of sufficient force to prevent my obtaining the command of one of the Districts in South Britain, that you will lay my humble petition before his Majesty for leave of absence for a twelvemonth, a removal from this climate being essential for the recovery of my health. But should this small indulgence be refused, much as it would grieve me and wound my feelings to be drove to such an extremity, I am under the painful necessity of desiring you *in that case* to lay at his Majesty's feet my resignation of that situation to which he was pleased to appoint me in this country. For though I have hitherto considered it a most honourable mark of his confidence, I cannot but cease to feel myself happy in it the moment I am compelled to be convinced that in order to obtain the honor of serving nearer his person, which you must know I would prefer above everything, the sacrifice of my private comfort and happiness that cannot possibly injure anyone, is to be made the term sine quâ non, a condition which I am confident never sprung from *his* breast, and I trust never could spontaneously have arisen from yours.

I cannot think it foreign to the purpose here to remind you that in the whole of the last fifteen years of my life I have not been in all nine months at home, and of that time (exclusive of the eighteen months during which I commanded the Guards at Hanover, and which I do not wish to reckon anything) I have been upwards of ten years on foreign service, and undergone some of the worst and most trying climates, from which I have no scruple in saying I have contracted the seeds of disorders likely to stay by me as long as I live. I should therefore hope that this consideration would have some weight in obtaining for me that indulgence which would not be refused the meanest soldier on the certificate of the surgeon of his Regiment, and that there can be no chance of my having to apprehend a negative for leave, which would *without fail*, drive me to the painful alternative I have before intimated.

Before I conclude let me explain myself clearly with respect to my intention of returning home. The present letter according to common calculation ought to reach you before the 20th of May, which will give you a full fortnight to determine with his Majesty's Ministers and to take the King's pleasure either as to my being named to one of the situations I have pointed out, or to my receiving leave of absence for the term I have requested. I shall therefore expect your answer by the June mail, which generally reaches this sometime between the 10th and 20th of July. If by *that* I do not receive from you the intimation of my being recalled home in one of the two modes I have solicited, I shall consider myself as thereby reduced to the cruel alternative of being obliged to resign that situation which I now hold, as the proof of his Majesty's gracious approbation of my conduct during the long period I served in this country before, and you may then depend upon my embarking at latest by the 24th of July, not chusing to run the risk of delaying so long as to be at sea at the time of the autumnal Equinox, which from former experience I should not be very fond of encountering in the neighbourhood of Scilly. You will receive this within a very few hours after the arrival of the Fly [sloop] at Falmouth, for I send it by the hands of Lieutenant-Colonel Wetherall, who I trust will be permitted to deliver it to you in person, and who is also commissioned to present you with an official letter, should you think it advisable to lay that before the King, as motives of delicacy may prevent your communicating the contents of *this* to *him*.

I have now only to say that as I have by no means taken ill what you have written to me, although I must own that some part of your letter severely wounded my feelings, so I flatter myself *you* will not be offended with the candor of my reply, which, I sincerely hope, may have the effect of enabling me to owe to your friendship by recall under flattering auspices, and not under such as must give me the greatest distress, though I feel myself compelled to encounter them rather than submit to remaining abroad to the evident daily prejudice of my health, and under circumstances that I cannot but consider as pressing peculiarly hard upon me, and wholly unmerited by any conduct of mine.

After troubling you with so long and tedious a letter, I feel I ought at least to offer some apology for trespassing so long upon your time, which I am sensible must be so much taken up with business of more import-ance than attending to me, but really I cannot help flattering myself that as the subject of it is one in which I am so particularly interested, you will not judge it necessary for me to attempt an excuse. I shall therefore only add that I hope nothing that I have been under the necessity of saying will occasion any coolness on your part towards me, as on mine, what-ever may be the event with regard to myself, you may rely upon finding every disposition to prove that I sincerely am what I shall ever profess myself to be, your most affectionate brother and faithful friend. (45973–81. Another copy has slight variations.)

1531   THE DUKE OF KENT TO THE PRINCE OF WALES
Halifax, Nova Scotia , 22 Apr. 1800
Convinced as I am of your friendship and attachment for me, it becomes my first duty to acquaint you when anything occurs in which my welfare is concerned. I have therefore thought it right to enclose to you the copy of a letter I received from the Duke of York by the December mail, as also that of my answer to it which Colonel Wetherall is to deliver into his own hands. By the perusal of his you will perceive how unpleasantly situated I am with respect to those views of being provided for at home, which I had every reason to expect at the time I left England would be realised before now. However, from my reply you will observe I am neither dis-posed to put up with the terms which it appears are intended to be dic-tated to me, nor do I chuse to expose myself to the chance of another

fourteen years transportation, for you know, chat échaudé craint l'eau chaude. I have therefore judged it best at once to speak with candor, and as I conceive a man ought to do, that they may not plead ignorance as to my intentions. I own I hardly think they will drive me to the extremity of resigning my present situation to enable me to remove from a climate which I find daily more and more injurious to my health; but if they refuse either recalling me to command, in Ireland, Scotland, or one of the Home Districts, or to give me leave of absence from this station, I am perfectly determined upon not staying here an hour beyond the period when I ought to have Frederic's answer. In this case I have every reason to apprehend that the same arts which will be used to make the King negative my wishes will also be employed to paint in the blackest colours the resolution which I shall certainly put in force of giving up my post of Commander-in-Chief here, that I may have it in my power to avoid encountering a ninth winter in North America. I must therefore rely wholly on your friendship, should I be so unfortunate as to meet with the King's displeasure, to smooth the way for a better reception than without it I should probably experience. As my letter to Frederic will make you fully master of my plan, I shall only add on that subject that I think you may reckon upon my being in England by the last of August, and I shall esteem myself highly obliged if you will send me a line to Falmouth, Plymouth, and Portsmouth, which are the three ports where I am likely to land according as the wind may serve, in order that I may know which way to turn my steps when I get there. The letter to Falmouth should be directed to the care of Mr. Pender, the Agent of Packets there, with orders for him to keep it until I should either send for it myself, or he hears of my arrival in another port. Those to Plymouth and Portsmouth I conclude you will send to the care of the Commissioners at those two places. But if you should not have leisure to write yourself, which (much as it would gratify me to receive a line from your own hand) I request you will not think of doing if it is in the least inconvenient, let me entreat you to order McMahon to write the purport of your instructions to me in a letter to Major Gordon, who will certainly accompany me home. I must refer you to Wetherall, whom I trust you will permit to give you this himself for the account of my state of health: from him you will learn how severely I have paid this spring for having escaped my usual rheumatic attack last winter. You will easily conceive how anxiously I shall pray that the winds may be propitious, and that Wetherall may get back with Frederic's answer by the middle of July: but if he does not, my mind is fully made up to the necessity of taking the business for granted, and of embarking before the close of that month, not to run myself into the Equinox by a longer delay. However, I will certainly give him as much law as possible, that I may have a chance of learning my fate before I embark, for should even the event of his mission be unpleasant, which I can scarcely think possible, certainty is always better than suspense. Under the idea therefore of my seeing Wetherall before I leave this, it would be very kind of you to write by him, but at all events, if you cannot find time to do this, let me hope that you will give him a verbal message for me. Though I write a few lines to the Queen, I do not intend saying anything more than simply that I have been under the necessity of applying for leave to go home, on account of my health. I shall therefore leave it to your judgment to communicate to her or not, as you may think most fit, the correspondence that has taken place between Frederic and me. At all events I feel satisfied and perfectly at ease from knowing that the papers are in your hands, for if any misrepresentation is attempted, you will, I am sure, not suffer the truth to remain unknown.

Pray remember me most affectionately to Ernest, and tell him how happy I shall be to see him in his usual good spirits in about four months hence, which I trust nothing can now intervene to prevent. But it is time to cease tiring your patience out any longer; I shall therefore only add that nothing can make me happier than to learn that *all your wishes* are accomplished, which I hope has long since been the case, as nothing could give me more real concern than that you should doubt one moment of the sincerity and attachment with which you will find me, as long as I exist, to be [etc.]. (45982–4)

1532   THOMAS TYRWHITT TO ROBERT GRAY
Carlton House, 24 Apr. 1800
The Prince has received a present of books from the Antiquarian Society, & it is customary for the Royal Family upon such occasions to pay a fee of £3-3 –. His Royal Highness the Duke of Cumberland & Prince William of Gloucester have received the same present & paid the same gratuity.[1]
(30056)

1. The receipt: 'Received 3d May 1800 of his Royal Highness the Prince of Wales by General Hulse, Treasr, the sum of three guineas as a gratuity to the messenger of the Society of Antiquaries upon delivery to his said Royal Highness of the publications of the Society, of which his Royal Highness has lately become a member.
John Matt Cobb for
James Cobb'.

£3-3-0

[Saturday, 26 Apr. 1800]

I must once more plague you to thank you for your kindness yesy. at St. George's to Mr. Robert Keate. He came & told it me this morning & with truth I may say I never saw any person more grateful than he feels to you, my dear love. I am quite happy, for you know how dearly I love you & how much I owe to Mr. Keate & Mr. Robert Keate,[1] & therefore whatever kindness you shew them I must rejoice at. Indeed I do believe I may with great truth say he is very deserving of your good opinion.

I must now tell you that dear Ernest told me you had been talking with him about me; the interest you take in my welfare does not please me a *little*. Every day I value more your kindness, & do, my dear Eau de Miel, continue to love me. I long to see you & pray do not come to the Queen's House without calling on me. I was very sorry indeed to hear you had again been so ill; how sorry I am that you should suffer.

Dear Louisa Paget comes to town today, for *good* I hope.

God bless you, my dear, dear Eau de Miel. (Add. Georgian 14/33)

Somerset Place, 28 Apr. 1800

There will be due to the Landgrave[2] from their Royal Highnesses the Prince of Wales, the Duke of York, and the Duke of Clarence, the sum of £15,750 for six years' interest from 28th June 1794 to 28th June 1800, at 3½ p. ct. upon the principal sum of £75,000. Mr. Tyrwhitt wishes to have a bond prepared immediately to be executed by the Royal brothers for this sum of £15,750, but not to bear any interest. I presume it is not necessary to specify the preparations thereof due from each, as they are to be jointly bound, but they are as under:

The Prince's capital £30,000	6 yrs. intst. at 3½ p. ct.	6,300
Duke of York „ 33,000	do.	6,930
Duke of Clarence „ 12,000	do.	2,520

Total interest £15,750

[*P.S.*] I need not desire you to lock up this statemt. (31825)

1. Thomas Keate (1745–1821) was Robert Keate's uncle.

2. The Landgrave of Hesse-Cassel. See No. 1537.

1535 THE PRINCE OF WALES TO THE QUEEN

Carlton House, 4 p.m., 29 Apr. 1800

I had fully intended, my ever dearest mother, to have had the happiness of passing an hour comfortably with you this morning, but unfortunately I attempted yesterday to ride on horseback, which brought on last night a severe return of the spasms on the neck of the bladder, & which, being attended with some degree of fever, have made Sir Walter Farquhar desire me to remain in my room & indeed in my bed, as I am taking medicines to make me perspire. However, he gives me every reason to hope I shall be able to go out tomorrow, & if so I shall not fail to have the pleasure of dining with you. I am now thank God free from pain & consequently from spasm, & have only remaining a considerable degree of soreness, the actual attendant of the unpleasant attacks. I beg my most humble duty to the King, & my love to my dearest sisters. (42314)

1536 THE PRINCE OF WALES TO THE LORD CHANCELLOR (LORD LOUGHBOROUGH), AND THE REPLY

Carlton House, Monday night, 5 May 1800

What am I to do? The enclosed two notes which I have only this moment received on my return home from Lady Macartney's[1] will explain to you the subject, but nothing can equal my surprize. Had I not best go myself to the Queen's House tomorrow morning by the King's breakfast hour, & acquaint the King before he goes out with the circumstance & take his pleasure? Pray advise me what is best for my brother, & you will greatly oblige [etc.].

[*P.S.*] I need not say that I wish to have your Lordship's opinions as much before eight o'clock as is convenient. Perhaps it would be best for you to come to me & accompany me to the Queen's House. (48188-9)

LORD LOUGHBOROUGH'S REPLY

6 May 1800

His Majesty did not think fit to charge me with any commands respecting Prince Augustus, but I am not forbid to receive any communications the Prince may chuse to be conveyed to his Majesty by me, and I humbly submit to your Royal Highness wher. it would not be most

---

1. Jane (1742–1828), daughter of the famous 3rd Earl of Bute (1713–92), married (1768) Sir George Macartney (1737–1806), created Lord Macartney [I.], 1776; Viscount [I.], 1792; Earl Macartney [I.], 1794; and Lord Macartney [G.B.], 1796. He was Governor of Madras, 1781–5, and Governor of the Cape of Good Hope, 1796–8, resigning on account of ill health.

adviseable that Prince Augustus, after consulting with those persons in whom he has confidence, should consider well & state precisely the terms of whatever representation he would desire to be submitted to his Majesty, which I am sure your Royal Highness is convinced it would be my study to place in as favourable a point of view as my duty would permit.[1] (39683)

1537 THOMAS TYRWHITT TO THE PRINCE OF WALES

Cassel, 6 May 1800

By being so long detained at Yarmouth, I reached this place only yesterday sevennight. The course of proceeding amongst the Ministers here is so excessive slow & ceremonious that I have as yet been able to do very little. In the private audience of the Landgrave which I had to deliver your Royal Highness's letter, I took the opportunity, as the wind seemed to lay in the right quarter, to request him to purchase the jewels himself, but to this I got a positive negative, and as it seemed to sower [*sic*] his imagination somewhat, I turned the conversation.

His Serene Highness is grown so excessively avaritious that his life must be a burthen to himself, & he takes care that all those around him should not go without their share; he is also so suspicious that to this moment he has not nominated any Minister with whom I am to transact business, fearing I may have already won him over, as he terms it, to my interests.

However, I have strong hopes I shall succeed in making him take the

---

1. *The Times* announced on the 7th that Prince Augustus had arrived in the *King George* packet from Cuxhaven on the 5th, and that he was to be made a Peer of the Realm.

And on the 13th: 'On Sunday [i.e. the 11th] Prince Augustus went with the Duke of Cumberland to dine with the Royal family at Windsor, whom he had not before seen since his arrival in England. Prince Augustus, who lately arrived from Hamburg, travelled to that city from Berlin incognito under the name of Mr. Ford. By an odd coincidence a lady of quality who arrived at Yarmouth a few months since, from the same place, assumed the appellation of Mrs. Ford'.

And on the 14th: 'Some persons affect to think it very hard that Mrs. Ford is not one of the Merry Wives of Windsor'. Correcting its information given out on the 8th, *The Times* stated that the Prince had seen only his brothers, and was living in Mayfair.

On 26 June *The Times* declared: 'It is understood that Mrs. Ford is to have a pension of £3,000 a year settled on her, on agreeing to abandon all her title and claim to be one of the Merry Wives of Windsor.'

Robert Arbuthnot had written to the Prince of Wales's friend Arthur Paget from Berlin on Tuesday, 4 February 1800: '... Many of his Royal Highness's best friends have endeavoured to persuade him that the marriage being decidedly null & illegal, he is no longer bound by any ties of honour or delicacy alone to persist in maintaining its validity, but hitherto I do not think their arguments have had much effect.' (Add. MSS. 48383)

cassette for two years & make up the sum a round one. I mean to keep the advantages which will accrue to him from the debentures in the background & fairly tell him, if he does not accommodate your Royal Highness, his debt from the nation will not be paid these ten years.[1] He departs the 10th to Wesel to review the garrison as Governor, & means to be here again the 20th, but I mean if possible to make him come to something decisive before that time. His reviews went off last week much to his satisfaction, & certainly his Hussars and indeed all his other cavalry were very fine. Many of the squadron of the former could not hold in their horses in the latter part of the charge which was in line. Upon the whole I do not think it was so rapid as many of those I have seen your Royal Highness make at the head of the 10th; to please, however, H.S.H. who asked me the question, I owned it was much more rapid.

I find the Hessian Oberst in London is by no means worthy of any mark of your Royal Highness's favour; he has been constantly assuring the Landgrave that your health is daily impairing, & in short, has not only not endeavoured to second what I have in view for your Royal Highness, but also to throw cold water upon it & thwart. He avowed to me he wished the reverse, but I have good proof he has done to the contrary, & of other circumstances which I shall reserve till I have the pleasure of seeing you.

I hope in my next to be able to tell your Royal Highness something definite.

[ ]thing[2] is going so bad on the Rhine that French influence is daily gaining ground here.[3] (Add. Georgian 3/9)

1538   JAMES MANSFIELD'S OPINION

Temple, 8 May 1800

It appears to me that the books & papers above-mentioned ought to be delivered up by the late Chamberlain[4] of the Prince as being necessary for the guidance of the person who acts as his successor, in receiving the revenue & discharging the debts or expences of the Prince, & the proper remedy to compel him to do so seems to me to be a Bill in Equity against him by the Prince. The only difficulty in the case arises from a defect in

1. In July 1803 the Prince owed the Landgrave £179,470 17s. 9d. (32487)

2. Paper torn: probably 'Everything.'

3. Tyrwhitt returned home in August via Hamburg, landing at Yarmouth on the 8th. Sylvester Douglas remarked in 1801 that Tyrwhitt, 'one of the busiest of the Carlton House runners', generally made half-yearly trips to the Continent 'for the purpose of either borrowing money for the Prince, or obtaining delays of payments' (*Glenbervie Journals*, i.191).

4. Lord Cholmondeley.

the above-stated Act of Parliament, which has not provided any method by which the Treasurer or other Officer of the Prince, when removed from his office, may have his accounts pass'd & himself secured against any future demand; & the Chamberlain may think that he ought at least to retain receipts & vouchers for payments until his accounts are pass'd & himself compleatly discharg'd. If he should insist on this as a reason for retaining the books and papers, a Court of Equity might possibly order his accounts to be taken before it would decree that he should deliver them up, or at least before his vouchers for payments should be delivered up, but this does not seem to be a reason for his retaining the books.[1] (39684)

1539 LETTERS FROM THE PRINCE OF WALES TO THE KING
Carlton House, 9 May 1800
I have the honor of enclosing to your Majesty a letter which my brother Augustus has desir'd me to lay at your feet. With your Majesty's permission I shall have the honor of paying my duty to you on Monday on your return to town to receive any commands which your Majesty may be pleased to honour me with in consequence. (42315)

[Enclosure] PRINCE AUGUSTUS TO THE KING
Carleton House, 8 May 1800
The Prince of Wales having informed me your Majesty is apprized of my arrival here,[2] I venture most humbly to petition the long-wished for happiness of presenting myself before you. My view in coming at this moment to England was to enable me to make a longer stay in this country than [I] should else have done arriving at a later period, as my health is good at present, and I suffer generally in cold weather particularly travelling in the winter. My object was particularly to wait upon your Majesty

1. A second opinion is dated the 26th:
  'Since I wrote the above opinion I have been informed that Lord Cholmondeley paid no money himself nor had any placed in his hands, but that the same was lodged at Drummond's by the Treasurer and paid to the creditors upon receipts produced by them at Drummond's, authenticated by Lord Cholmondeley. Upon this representation of the case it does not appear to me how his Lordship can be exposed to any danger or inconvenience by parting with the books or papers which he retains, and though the Act is, I think, defective in not having provided some method by which his Lordship's accounts might be formally settled and himself discharged, I think this defect not a sufficient reason for his detaining these books and papers and if he shall refuse to deliver them up, a bill must, I think, be filed against him.' (39685)
2. Prince Augustus arrived from Cuxhaven in the *King George* packet on the 5th.

135

and prove to you my readiness to comply with your wishes in everything
that is in my power, which God knows has ever been my daily and most
sincere desire. If I have err'd in the manner of executing this plan I trust
your Majesty will attribute it more to an ignorance of the proper mode of
so doing than to any wish of doing anything that can savour of want of
duty. I trust your Majesty will therefore allow me to throw myself at
your feet and place myself here where duty, inclination, nature and my
own personal interest shew me I ought to be. With every sincere wish
for your Majesty's private and publick happiness I sign myself [etc.].
(48191)

Carlton House, 6.20 p.m., 12 May 1800
I have the honor of most humbly laying before your Majesty the note[1] I
have just received from my brother Augustus, which I trust will meet with
with [*sic*] your gracious approbation. I am at the same time commissioned
to express my brother's most earnest desire to be admitted, as early as it
may suit your Majesty's pleasure, to place himself at your feet.[2] (42316)

1540   LETTERS FROM NATHANIEL PARKER FORTH TO CHARLES BICKNELL
St. James's Place, 17 May 1800
I address myself to you as solicitor to his Royal Highness the Prince of
Wales, in the presence of the Earl of Moira, to tell you that in consequence of a letter written by me to his Royal Highness the Duke of York
(requesting payment of the interest due on three bonds signed by their
Royal Highnesses the Prince of Wales, the Duke of York and the Duke
of Clarence, and given to me by the Prince of Wales), the Earl of Moira
was appointed by the Prince of Wales, and Lord Kinnaird was so good as
to attend for me, as arbitrors to arrange any differences or difficulties
that might arise. Their Lordships met several times and after having
examined the bonds and a great number of vouchers, letters and other
papers, and after having carefully investigated and maturely considered
all the circumstances, their Lordships addressed me in these words on
Monday, May 5th ins.

1. Missing.

2. Prince Augustus was presented to his father by the Prince of Wales at the King's Levée on
the 14th. The date of this letter seems suspect, given the accuracy of *The Times'* information
on the 13th. See No. 1536*n*.

'Mr. Forth. We had two doubts when we came here this day, and indeed from what we had heard, they were very strong. But from the books, accounts and letters which we have just examined, they are entirely done away, and instead of invalidating your claim, they most clearly strengthen it. We have now not a shadow of doubt about your loss of the counter-security, and declare that in honour, justice, law and equity, it is to our conception fairly and clearly proved, and Lord Kinnaird said that we are ready to appear in a court of justice, or at the Bar of the House of Lords, and certify such to be my[1] impartial and sincere opinion.'

After this declaration I met by appointment on Tuesday last his Royal Highness the Duke of York, who then in presence of Lord Moira, Lord Kinnaird, Mr. Morland, Mr. Adam and yourself, after an investigation of papers and a discussion of two hours, delivered these words: 'Mr. Forth, I am not displeased with your conduct. You had a right to demand payment of the interest due on these bonds. All I pretend to say is, and I always said it, that as the Prince of Wales gave you these bonds when I was not present and without my consent, I do not think that *I* am bound to pay any part of the interest due on them. But you have answered the chief purpose of our meeting, which was for me to see the bonds, to recognise my signatures to them, and to bring back to my recollection several circumstances which I had forgotten'.

In consequence of this declaration from the Duke of York, I should only say 'That I leave his Royal Highness to reconcile it to himself as a gentleman and as a casuist, and that I shall not again apply to him on this subject'.

I have likewise to inform you, Sir, that the Earl of Moira took the trouble of calling on me yesterday, accompanied by Lord Kinnaird, and then informed me: 'That the Prince of Wales had authorized him to tell me that he did not recollect to have given the three bonds to Mr. Forth to hold them as his own property; that if they were legal instruments they must of course be paid, but he must declare his conviction that they were not returned by him to Mr. Forth'.

After this declaration relative to what I always considered as a liberal remuneration for my severe losses, expences and fatigue, I shall say with great truth: 'I should be extremely sorry to appear capable of endeavouring to exact either by law or menaces any recompence that was in the least repugnant to the wishes of the donor, and as I think it my duty to avoid hurting the delicacy or feelings of my master's son, by personally waiting on him to deliver up the bonds, I request you will be so good as to resign them into those hands, which so graciously gave them to me, with my most humble and dutifull respects'.

On this, and on every occasion, I shall be happy to acknowledge your

1. 'our' scored through.

137

politeness, candor and impartiality, at the same time that I applaud your zeal and attachment to the Prince of Wales's interest. (31627)

[*On another sheet*]

The whole affair is comprized in two questions and answers, and lies within the compass of a nutshell.

Did H.R.H. the Duke of York, by his conversation with Mr. Forth in the Closet, say or mean that he would take care that Mr. Forth should be recompensed for all his losses, expences, &c. &c. *if* he gave up the priority and got back the bonds?

If he says yes!, then let him perform his promises!

If he says no!, then Mr. Forth will never again apply to H.R.H.!

Did H.R.H. the Prince of Wales give the three bonds to Mr. Forth for his own emolument in consequence of his losses, expences, accidents & fatigues in serving H.R.H. interests, or were the bonds entrusted to him for other purposes?

If the Prince says they were given for the first cause, let him perform his promises!

If H.R.H. says they were given for the latter motive, then Mr. Forth says God forbid that I should bring before a Court of Law anything that might or might not affect H.R.H.'s peace of mind—here are the bonds!

And *now* I leave the reparation of my health and fortune to H.R.H. generous justice and candid liberality, and I leave the purity of my whole conduct to the Almighty God to whom all hearts be open, all desires known, and from whom no secrets are hid. N.P.F. (31628)

Manchester Square, 5 June 1800

As soon as Lord Moira arrived in town, I wrote to him to tell him that you had taken the trouble to call on me, and to investigate the papers and examine all the vouchers which had already been examined by his Lordship and Lord Kinnaird, and that your decision was precisely the same of their Lordships vizt., 'that it appeared to you that the counter-security for my annuities had been sold out of the India Stock and given up to accomodate their Royal Highnesses, and had not been reimplaced'. I have this moment received a letter from Lord Moira to inform me, 'that the Prince of Wales had not seen you since his Lordship had left town, but that he, Lord Moira, had written to you to know the result of your interview with me, and that you would make the report without delay'.

In this state of the affair I address myself to your candor and justice to repeat to his Lordship and the Prince of Wales what you were so good to say at my house. It appears now, Sir, that it depends on you to do me that justice I deserve, and by your impartial integrity not only be the cause of my getting some compensation for all my losses, expences & accident, but likewise prevent some measures which would cause great uneasiness and unhappiness to all parties. I request your friendship as an honest upright man, and I really have the utmost confidence in the opinion you shall give. I hope at some future period of my life to shew you [how] highly I estimate the liberality and impartiality you have already so honourably manifested. (31629)

1541 CHARLES BICKNELL'S MEMORANDUM

[? *c. June 1800*]

On Tuesday the 12th of May I met by appointment his Royal Highness the Duke of York, Lord Moira, Lord Kinnaird, Mr. Adam, Mr. Forth, and Mr. Morland at the latter's house in Pall Mall, when Mr. Forth produced the 3 bonds in question, declaring that [they] were given to him by the Prince of Wales on the 17th December 1790, when no person was present and just after the Duke of York had left the room, as a compensation for his trouble, losses and expences incurred in gettg. back 8 bonds given to the Duke of Orleans, and all which bonds had been given for the purpose of raising money on them in France where they had all been sent.

Mr. Forth said he had frequently applied by Mr. Sleigh [?] to the Prince for paymt. of the int. due on the bonds, and that his Royal Highness had in several conversations with him promised to pay him the arrears of the interest.

The Duke of York declared he did not know till he was applied to by Mr. Forth that the three bonds in question were in existence, and, upon being ask'd by the latter if he had said or done anything to offend his R.H., the Duke replied that having the bonds, he had certainly a right to apply for payment of the int. due upon them.

Lord Moira & I waited afterwards upon the Prince of Wales, who appointed to meet us the next day at Ld. Moira's, and there we related to him all that had passed, when his R.H. most solemnly assured us that he had not the smallest recollection of ever having returned the 3 bonds to Mr. Forth for the purposes abovementioned, & that he had never promised to pay the interest.

On Saturday the 17th May 1800 I met Mr. Forth at Lord Moira's, when he gave me his letter of that date and the three bonds, & appointed Thursday the 22d May to meet me at his own house, when he would shew me all his papers respecting his loss by having given up his counter-security for the payment of an anny. from the Duke of Orleans,

139

in order to enable the Duke to lend his R.H. the Prince £25,000 vested in Mr. Forth's name in India Stock.

On the same Saturday Ld. Moira & I waited on his R.H. the Prince at Carlton House, related what had pass'd & delivered the bonds into his R.H.'s hands to be cancell'd, who enquired if he shou'd do right in destroying them, & being informed they were brought to his R.H. for that very purpose, the seals & signatures were cut off & the instruments totally cancell'd & destroyed.

On the 22nd May I waited on Mr. Forth at his house in Manchester Square, when he read to me the letters he had written to the P. of Wales, D. of York & Mr. Adam, and part of a memoir which he said was intended for publication if the Princes did not recompence him for his losses, & shewed me several books, papers & accts. in which it appeared that he had consented to the sale of 15,000 India Stock, which the D. of O. advanced to the P. & which the P. returned to Forth, & it appeared that Mr. Forth had purchased some annys. of the D. of O. which he might have paid out of the int. of the India Stock as it stood in his name. (31625–6)

1542 THE QUEEN TO THE PRINCE OF WALES

Queen's House, 6 June 1800

I am beset by all sorts of people & my head is quite stupifyed, but as I see by the papers that the Duke of Wurtemberg's brother is arrived in England, I am obliged to execute yr. sister's commission, who begs in the Duke's name that nothing but common civility may be shewn to him. His Princess, as he calls her, who accompanies him, was an *actrice* whom

1. Prince Henry of Wurtemberg (1772–1833), the Duke's youngest brother, married (1798) Caroline Alexei (1779–1853).

Prince Henry arrived with his wife at Gravesend on the night of Monday, 2 June. It was said that they were obliged to lodge in a garret at the inn there, all the beds having been taken. The Royal Family probably took not the least notice of them, nor did Ministers: the Queen sent Lady Chatham a warning letter, and the contents were probably passed on to the wives of other leading Ministers:

'I see by the papers that a brother of the Duke of Wurtemberg is arrived with his Princess. I think it but fair upon you to acquaint you with her history. She was an *actrice* kept by him for some time & then married him. She is not countenanced by the Duke, & my daughter has, by the Duke's express order, desired me to shew his brother only common civility. As yr. friendship for the Duchess might perhaps incline you to take notice of a sister-in-law of hers, I think it my duty to prevent your getting into a scrape, & if you should meet with Ldy. Grenville, perhaps in her situation it would not be amiss to give her a hint of it. Excuse this scrawl' (Hoare MSS. Undated, but probably *c.* 6 June).

The Prince and his wife returned to the Continent from Yarmouth on Thursday, 9 October, in the *Prince of Orange* packet sailing to Cuxhaven (*The Times*, 11 October).

he kept for some time & ended in marrying her, & therefore not countenanced by the family, & of course cannot be received here.[1]

I have seen Riley with the drawing for the intended print you sent me.
I find the idea pritty & elegant, & if the Kg.'s likeness can be secured he
may ensure himself success. I now take my leave & am unalterably [etc.].
(36520)

1543 THE PRINCE OF WALES TO THE KING

Carlton House, 9 June 1800

I am this moment honour'd with your Majesty's most gracious letter, &
hope that it is not necessary for me to say that I shall always deem an
intimation from your Majesty as a command instantly to be obey'd;
of course I need not add that I shall in consequence not attend the debate that is likely to take place in the House of Lords either today or
tomorrow.[1] (42317)

1544 NATHANIEL PARKER FORTH TO CHARLES BICKNELL

Manchester Square, 10 a.m., 10 June 1800

I have this moment received your letter, and return you many thanks for
your kindness. Were I able I would call on you & personally thank you.
I have a sick house, and I myself am not more distressed by bodily pain

1. Nothing of interest happened in the House of Lords on the 9th. Next day the House was
virtually in secret session; all strangers, even members of the House of Commons, were
ordered to withdraw. It was understood that Lord Carlisle's Motion in connection with the
Adultery Bill was debated, but no Peer ventured to give the newspapers a *résumé* of the speeches:
the printer and proprietor would have been imprisoned for breach of privilege. See No. 1546.
The King may well have been annoyed by the prominent part which the Duke of Clarence,
inappropriately enough, had been taking in the debates on this Bill. Lord Bathurst, incidentally
thought that the Duke was 'certainly desirous of establishing a sort of princely influence in the
House which ... will in time become troublesome'.

Lord Grenville wrote to the Prince of Wales from Cleveland Row on 10 June: 'I have just
found your Royal Highness's note on my return home. No precise time is yet fixed for sending
back Mr. Paget's servant, but it will probably be in the course of next week unless I should
learn from your Royal Highness that any time either earlier or later would be more convenient
to your Royal Highness.

'From the contents of Mr. Paget's letters it seems probable that his servant when he returns
will find him still at Palermo, but I trust the King of Naples will be persuaded to return there
in the course of the summer, and in that case I should think the state of that country, and the
business which must arise in consequence will certainly detain Mr. Paget there during the
winter.' (Add. MSS. 48383)

than I am by the anguish of my mind, and grief that at my time of life, after having lived in the strictest familiarity with the first men of the age, after having been the intimate friend of my master's sons, I should be reduced to the necessity of either proving their *want of recollection* or of submitting to the imputation of endeavouring to defraud them. Oh! Mr. Bicknell, this is a sad return for all my services, care, expences and loss of health and fortune. Nor can anything compensate for the vexation they have caused.

I have had a[n] irreparable loss since I saw you by the death of my old & good friend Buller;[1] we lived thirty years in the sincerest friendship. His death is a double loss at this moment. When I told you at Lord Moira's 'that as able [a] lawyer as any in Europe, a Judge on the Bench, directed all my proceedings', and from delicacy I would not mention his name, I then meant my valuable adviser Mr. Justice Buller. He spoke to me of you in the handsomest manner and said he was glad for my sake so worthy a man was the Prince's solicitor. He gave me the necessary steps to be pursued in every stage of this business: I will shew you his advice and some of his letters one of these days. (31630)

1545 THE REV. CYRIL JACKSON[2] TO THE PRINCE OF WALES

Christ Church, 10 June 1800

I never have the honour of receiving a command from your Royal Highness without receiving at the same time a fresh proof of that uniform kindness & delicacy wth. wch. you condescend to treat me—and the permission wch. you are in all cases so gracious as to allow me of entering into an explanation wth. your Royal Highness is perhaps of all marks of your favour the one on wch. I set the highest value.

I will not therefore content myself wth. saying simply to your Royal Highness, what I might very truly say, that altho' there are certainly vacancies this year among the Studentships of Christ Church, there are none, however, the disposal of wch. falls to my lot, but I will presume to trespass on your Royal Highness a little farther. To confess the truth honestly to your Royal Highness, I feel a little indignation that Mr. Percy & his son shd. have presumed to apply to the Prince of Wales on such an occasion, without at the same time fully & fairly stating the circumstances of the case—because I am most perfectly convinc'd that if yr. Royal Highness had known those circumstances, their application wd. have been at once rejected. I am perfectly convinc'd, from the long experience wch. I have

1. Sir Francis Buller (1746–1800), one of the Judges of the King's Bench, 1778–94, and of the Common Pleas from 1794, died on 5 June. Baronetcy, January 1790.

2. The Dean of Christ Church, 1783–1809. See i.24n., 105.

had of the mind of yr. Royal Highness, that if you had been fairly inform'd that I had near three weeks ago peremptorily refus'd to admit Mr. Percy's son as a member of Christ Church in any way or on any footing whatever, no sollicitations wd. have prevail'd wth. your Royal Highness to honour him wth. your recommendation.

I cannot trouble yr. Royal Highness wth. a detail about schools & schoolboys—nor am I at all mov'd, as far as concerns myself, by the unhandsome & illiberal attempt to distress me, after my positive refusal, by the recommendation of yr. Royal Highness—but I am in truth very much mov'd & very much provoked at the total want of respect wch. Mr. Percy has shewn to your Royal Highness in the affair. But as to myself, I know that I run no risque of displeasing your Royal Highness if I humbly represent that it is of serious consequence to Westmr. School, to Christ Church & myself that my original refusal shd. be persisted in— & I venture to assure myself that your Royal Highness will suppose me to have had sufficient reason for giving that refusal.

The simple matter of fact, Sir, is this. The boy was elected to Cambridge. He very unwisely renounc'd his election, & applied to me to be admitted a Commoner of Christ Church. He was peremptorily refus'd— & his father, concealing this circumstance, presumes to sollicit the protection of your Royal Highness. The same trick of concealment was attempted by him here, during my absence, but without success. (39686–39687)

1546 THE EARL OF MOIRA TO THE PRINCE OF WALES

5 p.m., 11 June [1800]

As I had not the good fortune to find your Royal Highness at home today, I beg leave in this manner to explain a liberty which I took in the House last night of alluding to a circumstance in which your name was concerned. Lord Carlisle very properly expressed his wish that no proceeding should be adopted which might leave a painful impression on the mind of Lord Kenyon:[1] and this was so truly the sense of everybody present that the matter would have fallen to the ground without further observation, had it not been for a kind of defence rather unnecessarily advanced & assuredly not well considered. It was urged that a printer could not be

1. On 2 April Lord Auckland had introduced a Bill to prevent the offending parties in a divorce suit from marrying. Opposing it on 23 May Lord Carlisle made some uncomplimentary references to the Lord Chief Justice and to the 'monkish seclusion' of some legal luminaries. Lord Kenyon wrote in his Diary on 10 June: 'That puppy and adulterous profligate the Earl of Carlisle was to bring on his Motion ... against me for breach of privilege in alluding to his infamous speech on the Bill against adultery, but he withdrew his Motion' (Kenyon MSS.).

prosecuted by the House for a publication of the nature in question: a position which appeared to me highly dangerous in its consequences, as its effect would be to invite all kind [of] misrepresentations to lower Parliament in the eyes of the public under the screen of that subterfuge. I therefore resisted that opinion. In detailing the mischiefs which might arise from suffering the supposition of such an impunity to be entertained abroad, I stated the comments which I had myself heard from many of my neighbors in Leicestershire when an animadversion on the supposed patronage of your Royal Highness towards Martindale[1] was put into the mouth of Lord Kenyon by the newspapers. There are few people in London who are not perfectly aware of the gross incorrectness with which speeches are reported in the newspapers, and all of us further feel that, even if particular phrases be not distorted, it would be the height of injustice to decide upon the design & quality of an expression when stripped of the explanation which the context of the harangue, or the tone & manner of the speaker, gave to it when it was uttered. But in parts at a distance from the Metropolis, all that appears in a newspaper is supposed to be strictly accurate, and the impression practicable on the public mind would be dangerous in the extreme were we to establish an excuse under which any democratic editor might feel himself secure in throwing out depreciatory imputations against the Royal Family or against Parliament. Now, it seemed to me that the true distinction was this. Could it be imagined that a Judge on the Bench had slidden into any exceptionable expression, policy as well as candor should ascribe it to the incorrectness of an honest zeal in the course of business too pressing to allow time for weighing all he was about to say, and the consequence would be that such slips should never be noticed. But a record & a circulation of loose extra-judicial censures ought not to be sanctioned by any declarations in our House that such reports of speeches from the Bench cannot be a subject for our deliberation. The editors of papers ought to be instructed that they must use discretion in what they publish, & that they are not to give to the world the incidental & unweighed remarks which a Judge may make collaterally, & which have no use as to informing the public on what grounds a cause was determined. The justly respectable character of Lord Kenyon gives important weight to anything which is stated to have fallen from his lips; and it is requisite in justice to him that language should not be sent forth as his without his having had any opportunity of deciding whether it be what he would wish to say to the public. Pardon me, Sir, for this intrusion: but I thought you might hear that I had adverted to the particular which I have mentioned; and I thought it incumbent to explain in what point of view I had applied the circumstance.[2] (38927–30)

1. See No. 1504.

2. The Prince of Wales wrote to Arthur Paget from Carlton House on 16 June 1800: 'Morand

Charlton, 25 June [1800]

Apprehensive there may be some difficulty respecting the coming of my
child to Charlton, I must beg leave to trouble you with a few lines on the
subject. You may recollect having last year made me the offer of this
house for myself and my daughter, but from the lateness of the season and
other reasons unnecessary now to explain, I prefer'd remaining at Carlton
House. This summer, as I wished to be in the country for my health,
you was so good as to allow me to have this place, and I had no doubt of
being permitted to have the child with me when the weather was fine
enough. While you continued in town I did not request it because I
thought it not proper for her to come during your residence in Carlton
House. As you are now going into the country and there seems to be
some hesitation about her coming to remain at Charlton, I shall be much
obliged if you would give the order for her removal. Lady Elgin has
seen the house and she knows there is sufficient room for Charlotte,
her Sub-Governess and under-attendants. A small house might

is this instant come here & tells me he is to get off again tomorrow, though my carriage is at
the door to take me out of town, still I could not think of letting him depart without sending
you a few lines to recall myself to your recollection. How could you, my dearest friend, think
I either had forgotten you, or that my silence was owing to neglect? Indeed, Arthur, you are
ever present to my heart & to my mind, & I wrote to you by the only safe mode of conveyance
that occurred to me, which was by Mr. Hayter, & which letter I trust long before this you
must have receiv'd. Your *dear friend* [the Duchess of Rutland] I have followed your directions
& wishes about, I trust in such a manner as will prove to you my never ceasing friendship both
for you & her. Her conduct during the whole of this long winter has been most exemplary
towards you, & though wretched at your absence, still she has almost entirely confin'd herself
to her own home, where I really believe the only pleasurable moments she pass'd were those
when I could call upon her, & when the minutes rolled away without being able to count
them conversing about you, and adjusting her plans of joining you upon the Continent &
which I hope now you will not delay. I cannot speak highly enough either of her conduct or of
her affection, love, & enthusiasm about you; in short it surpasses all belief, & I trust you will
both shortly be completely happy, for I am certain you both richly deserve it. As she writes by
Morand I shall say no more about her, as she will herself tell you that I have not been unmindful, my dearest Arthur, either of you or of your concerns. My health, my friend, I am
sure you will be happy to learn is much re-established & gets more & more so as my mind
becomes more composed, & as beams of returning happiness & comfort begin once again to
shine upon me. Would you were here to share it with me, for believe me there is not a dinner
nor a party that I do not miss you & feel a drawback that always damps every pleasure from
your absence and from your not being a partaker of it with me. As to our old friends Chig,
Bathurst, etc. we dine perpetually together, and never miss drinking your health repeatedly
each time in a bumper, praying that you may soon be here again among us all who love you so
affectionately. I have no news to tell you from hence, and indeed the hurry I am in at the
present moment would prevent if I had from prolonging my epistle to greater extent, except
merely to assure you of what I am confident you are already thoroughly persuaded of, that I
am through life, my dearest Arthur, [your] most steady and most affectionate friend.

P.S. Pray write frequently be it but a line (*Paget Papers*, i.231–2).

be taken near me for Lady Elgin, who could attend as she does in town.

I hope you will aprove this arrangement and allow me the pleasure of having my child as she is my greatest comfort in this world. (42353–4)

1548   CHARLES SMALL PYBUS[1] TO THE PRINCE OF WALES

Great George Street, Tuesday morning, [*1 July 1800*]

The condescending offer which your Royal Highness was pleased to make to me at the Duke of Cumberland's, emboldens me to trouble your R. Highness with this letter, which I trust the URGENCY of the occasion will excuse.

I have just heard that Lord Sydney died last night. His place of Chief Justice in Eyre is therefore vacant. Your R. Highness is perfectly aware of my situation in *one* respect, and I hope I shall be forgiven for obtruding my own concerns upon your R. Highness's notice when I *add* that nothing but *such* a provision as your R. Highness was pleased to say that you would entreat as a personal favour from Mr. Pitt could justify me in making proposals where my *affections are engaged* and all *my comfort and happiness is at stake.*

In two words, my *happiness* or *misery* depend upon your R. Highness's success with Mr. Pitt, whom I really dare not solicit in my own person.

I have had the honour of holding a very honorable office for 9 years.[2] I mention this not as giving *me* any *claim*, but as some justification to Government for any such mark of its favour.

In addition to all the above considerations may I be permitted to add that after the literary exertions (ineffectual as they may perhaps prove) by which I have endeavoured to render some little service to the general cause, such publick notice from his Majesty, to whom my labours were addressed, would be at *this moment* the most flattering and consolatory event in my whole life.

Unless your R. Highness can see Mr. Pitt TODAY, the application would probably be too late.[3] (39691–2)

1. M.P. for Dover, 1790–1802. See No. 1403.

2. He was a Lord of the Admiralty, June 1791–July 1797; a Lord of the Treasury, August 1797–November 1803, being then dismissed.

3. Lord Grenville's brother Thomas succeeded Lord Sydney.

The following undated letter from the Prince of Wales to Pitt was probably written sometime during the next three weeks, for Thomas Grenville was presented to the King at the Levée on the 23rd following his appointment as Chief Justice in Eyre South of the Trent: 'This second letter is, I fear, a troublesome *proof* of my uncommon anxiety about P[ybus], for whom I really have the strongest personal regard, and for whose situation I do feel sincerely interested. He is, besides, the most intimate friend of my brother Ernest, whom you know to

146

Cassel, 8 July 1800

I return your Royal Highness my most heartfelt thanks for having dispatched Lindeman back again to me, who has made his passage uncommonly quick.

be amongst your warmest well wishers. P. has sacrificed his profession entirely, and I hope you will think such a provision not improperly bestowed upon him after ten years of the most active attachment to *your* interest, during *nine* of which he has held one of the *most honorable* appointments next to a seat in the Cabinet, and which, instead of encreasing a fortune which several contested elections had considerably impaired, *exacted* from him other expences in his style of living, more than proportioned to the salary he enjoyed. The vacant office, for which of course you would have his seat at the Treasury to dispose of, will be an handsome provision for him, without subjecting the country to the additional expence of one shilling; and without this provision, his circumstances will be very deplorable indeed in point of income (particularly with other contested elections hanging over his head) and he cannot, which I am sure must be a consideration with any feeling mind, have the smallest hope of ever being united to an amiable woman for whom he entertains the greatest attachment. If you think that the wishes of an Heir Apparent to the Throne ought *ever* to have the smallest weight in the scale of interest with a Minister, let me beg of you to prove it in *this* instance by bestowing Lord Sydney's office upon P. and be assured that I shall always hold your compliance with my entreaties upon this occasion in the *most grateful remembrance*.' (39693)

Pybus himself wrote the following undated letters to Pitt:

'Saturday morning. I know not whether the Prince of Wales has, or has not made any application to you in my favour. If he has not, Long will have the goodness to tell you what it *would* have been: and if he has, to mention for me, under what circumstances the application has arisen. If I may presume to make use of such a term, the Duke of Cumberland is perhaps one of my *warmest friends*, and the frequency of our intercourse has necessarily brought me more into the society of the Prince, who is perfectly aware of my situation, and professes to feel himself extremely interested for my welfare. I trust therefore that you cannot be offended that I have not been backward in availing myself of so illustrious an intercessor, whom you might perhaps feel some disposition to oblige.

'With respect to myself, I have only to add that I have never, for an instant, wavered in my attachment, and reliance upon your friendship; and that, if wretched anxiety of mind be any just criterion, I may venture to say that you have never had before you, a case of more compassion and *humanity* than mine. All my prospects of comfort as to *marriage*, fortune, and, in short, every thing that can make life desirable, depend absolutely upon your favour at the present moment. Wishing, yet *fearing* to enter upon this application, on which every thing that is most dear to me now hangs in suspense, my spirits have for some time past been such as really to unfit me for publick business in the House, and materially to affect my health. For months past I have had a serious complaint in my stomach, which no medicines have made any continued impression upon, and which I am sure never can be removed as long as my mind remains in its present state of dreadful agitation' (Chatham Papers, 169).

The second was written on 'Tuesday morning'.

'If Mr. Pitt can have the generosity to forget the feverish influence of disappointment and distress upon a mind, perhaps too sensitive in its nature, and to recollect only that the writer has sacrificed his fortune, his profession, and all the most valuable prospects of his life to his first, and he may even yet add his *predominant* political attachment, Mr. Pybus would receive with the utmost gratitude the renewal of Mr. Pitt's friendship under the present circumstances, and repay it by the most strenuous exertion of the writer's talents (such as they are) if these talents should be deemed worthy of employment' (ibid.).

147

I anticipated so much in my letter of the 4th which I sent to your Royal Highness from Minden that I have not occasion to trouble you at much length at the present moment.

I am certain had Mr. Rose sent me a promise of the whole of the Landgrave's debt being at his disposal in three days time, nothing on earth would prevail upon him to enter upon my plan which had for its tendency the vesting any more of his property in England; happy indeed am I therefore to find that for this year at least your Royal Highness stands not in need of his assistance, and it forcibly strikes my mind that you will have occasion to make no ulterior request of a similar kind.

Veltheim advised me not to trouble Monseigneur any more on the business, which advice I shall very readily follow.

H.R.H. the Duke of Clarence does not succeed in his request for the loan of £20,000.

I set out tomorrow for Berlin & shall not fail to settle with Monr. de Schack, & then immediately come to England.

I have made an arrangement with Lindemann which I think will enable Malsch & all his companions to set out without farther delay to join the 20th Dragoons.

I must do justice to Count Tauentzien's friendship for your Royal Highness, who, hearing I was here, wrote to me an extreme kind letter of enquiry into the state of your health. Most fortunately I had it in my power to acquaint him that a service of Wedgwood was arrived for him as a present from your Royal Highness.

Lindeman has made me happy in acquainting me he thinks you are looking very well but much reduced indeed.

I have sent Admiral Payne some mineral waters which are in the highest estimation all over Germany as great strengthners of the stomach. Should either of them be to your taste, any quantity may easily be procured. (39688–90)

1550 NATHANIEL PARKER FORTH TO CHARLES BICKNELL
Manchester Square, 12 July 1800
I did propose calling on you this day to return your visit, and thank you for your very candid and just conduct to all parties in the misunderstanding between H.R.H. the Prince of Wales and me. I hope now that you are enabled to convince him of what is the real state of the affair, vizt., that by the £825 Stock paid by the *Duke of York's* particular entreaties in 1790, I am now *more* than £1,250 in avance for him, even reckoning the ten years at 5 pr. co. without compound or accumulated interest (as all bankers charge) and exclusive of the different expences of postage,

presents & commission given to the Agents for their trouble in getting back the Bonds &c. This sum is due in justice and honor by the *Duke of York*. My loss of the £15,000 India Stock, as counter-security given up to oblige the Prince stands literally *thus*—after its sale in 1789:

Lost by two payments in 1790, & 1 in 1789 only		£500: 0: 0	as I received some	
do. by	do. in	91 only	487: 0: 0	other cash remittances
do. by	do. in	92 only	713: 0: 0	
do. by total loss of India Stock from 1792 to July 1800		11,250: 0: 0		
7½ years at £1,500 pr. year				
		£12,950: 0: 0		

I do not mean this *as a charge* on his Royal Highness, I leave it entirely to his liberality & generosity what part of it he may graciously please to take on himself, as well as what part of the £1,500 per annum he may judge proper to allow me untill there is a peace, and till I can recover some part of my annuities from the Duke of Orleans's great property. And as I have very great reason to believe, and the most sanguine hopes, I think it my duty in justice and in gratitude to declare that (as I expect to recover the *whole* sum due to me and the *arrears* from the Duke of Orleans's property) I will account for and reimburse any sum or sums that his Royal Highness may graciously condescend to give me now to relieve me in my distressing situation, or that he may deign to allow me as an annual pittance, untill a peace and recovery of the annuities in France. And now give me leave to say 'I cannot dig, to beg I am ashamed'!, but remember my situation and that bis dat, qui cito dat!

I shall never forget Lord Moira's & your zealous attachment to the Prince of Wales's interest, and tho' you have so examined, cross-examined & fretted me, yet I feel you have done no more than your duty.

I thank his Lordship and you for all the trouble you have taken on my account and if I ever am so happy as to meet Col. McMahon, I shall acknowledge the liberal manner in which, as Lord Kinnaird informs me, he was so good as to speak of me.

I dare not implore forgiveness from the Prince for my intemperate letters written after 6 months rhumatic headaches in a sick room; all I dare request is that his Royal Highness will forget the passionate heat of my head and recollect only the impassioned warmth of my heart when employed in his service. A broken head, and a fractured jaw often remind me of my successfull zeal for his wishes, and I hope he will not add a broken heart to them by a want of pity.

Adieu, my dear Sir, remember what Lord Mansfield say of me to the King: 'he is a gallant man, whatever is done let it be done soon & gallantly: a hair will lead him, a cable can't bind him!'[1] (31631)

1. On the 14th the Prince wrote to the Dowager Countess of Elgin from Windsor Castle: 'I have only one moment to say that I have receiv'd your kind letter, & that I desire you will bring the dear child to town at three tomorrow when I will see you; & she may afterwards return in the cool of the evening.' (49246)

Erlangen, 1 Aug. 1800

I cannot neglect recalling myself to you at the approach of the 12th, and hope when you receive the many congratulations on the day, you will think that though far distant there is a sister which loves you with the same warmth of affection as those who in person offer their wishes for your health and happiness on this joyful occasion. I hope, my dear brother, you will many many years spend this day so dear to us all with satisfaction and that every new year may bring fresh blessings and joy with it.

It gives me great pleasure to hear that your dear little Charlotte is to spend a month at Weymouth which I am sure will give great pleasure to the whole party.[1] I am always so anxious to hear something about her that I plague every English person I meet to give me some account of her. Lady Elgin in her letters frequently indulges me with little anecdotes of her which delight me.

Our situation gets worse every day. The enemy have imposed very heavy contributions on the Dutchy infinitely beyond what it is possible for the country to pay and threaten to destroy everything belonging to the Duke if their demands are not complied with in a month. In short we are most shamefully treated, abandoned by the Armistice to the enemy who till then had sent no troops into the Dutchy. (51610–1)

8 Aug. 1800

I am happy to be able to inform you that at last we have the prospect of seeing our dear Sophia restored to health very shortly. You will join with me in rejoicing at this & I feel most happy in being able to send you this good news. She is going on well. Pray, pray sweet love don't answer this, & when you come here pray take no notice to *high* or *lowe* of having heard from me.

We are all well. I often think of my dear G.P. & lamented your absence yesy.[2] For fear of the Philistines I must conclude.[3] (Add. Georgian 14/34)

1. She arrived at Weymouth on the 12th, nearly a fortnight after the King and Queen. Apartments had been taken for her on the Esplanade.

2. Princess Amelia's birthday. Princess Sophia had been rather ill for some months and had not been attending the Queen's Drawing Room at St. James's. It was not, apparently, until 31 August that she took an airing on the sands at Weymouth, though she had been there with her family for a month. The Archives throw no light on the scandalous story narrated by Lord Glenbervie in his *Journal*.

3. On the 5th Colonel McMahon wrote to George Rose from Carlton House: 'The Prince of

THE QUEEN TO THE PRINCE OF WALES

Weymouth, 9 Aug. 1800

The 12th being aproaching which gave you birth &, *par consequence*, ever dear to me, shall not pass without your receiving a few lines from me which are to convey my most sincere congratulations upon the occasion. My wishes are so uniformly the same from one year to another for your wellfare, & my affection so unalterable which I bear you, that a repetition of them would but prove tiresome to you as I am sure you cannot doubt them; therefore, to sum up all in a few words which are dictated by the heart; present or absent,[1] in prosperity or distress, you both shall & will find me prove in every situation, my dearest son, your very affectionate mother & sincere friend. (36521)

1554 THE DUKE OF KENT TO THE PRINCE OF WALES

Plymouth Sound, 10 a.m., 31 Aug. 1800

Contrary winds having obliged us to put into this port, it is my intention either in the course of this evening or very early tomorrow morning to pursue my route by land to Weymouth, in doing which, I trust, I am adopting the plan which you yourself would have directed by letter, could you have foreseen my not reaching Portsmouth as I had intended. Sea bathing having been strongly recommended to me by the medical gentleman who attended me at Halifax, I propose remaining there as long as the family stays. My health has been daily improving since I left Halifax[2] and got into clearer atmosphere. Indeed, though I have still a constant pain in my chest, and frequent violent headachs, I am generally much recovered.

I trust I need not say with what pleasure I look forward to the moment

Wales on his departure yesterday for Brighton, commanded me to repeat to you how very much he has at heart that his Majesty might be induced to raise Lord Melbourne to an Earldom in the Peerage of Ireland; and his Royal Highness entreats that you will have the goodness to represent to Mr. Pitt how greatly the Prince will feel obliged if he can with convenience and propriety, recommend this measure, at this period, to the King; by stating it as a matter, which from want of consideration, had escaped notice at an earlier moment; for his Royal Highness had not only a considerable time ago solicited from his Majesty, through the Duke of Portland, this mark of favor for Lord Melbourne; but had some little while back requested the Speaker to suggest the idea to Mr. Pitt as an entreaty from his Royal Highness' (W. Dacres Adams MSS.).

It was not until August 1815 that Viscount Melbourne was given a U.K. Barony (Baron Melbourne), which he owed to the Prince Regent. He never received an Earldom.

1. The Prince evidently had no wish to be with his family on his birthday. It was much more fun to be at the Races, at Brighton.

2. On 3 August.

of meeting you, though I scarcely dare hope for that happiness till the return of the family to Windsor; in the meanwhile, accept of the heartfelt assurance of my most warm and devoted attachment, which can only cease with my existence. (45989)

1555 THE PRINCE OF WALES TO LORD [?LOUGHBOROUGH]
Carlton House, 8 Sept. 1800

I have scarcely time to write you a few lines before the messenger sets off for Weymouth to inform you that I have seen our little friend the Admiral[1] & have also the heartfelt satisfaction to assure you that he is better in all respects than I have seen or known him for years. I have open'd myself completely to him respecting the business I had the pleasure of talking over with your Lordship previous to my departure from Weymouth; he enters into it most fully & will undertake it, but as he is so entirely right not only upon *this* alone, but upon every subject I have ever the good fortune of discussing with him, I have desired him to write his own sentiments to your Lordship, which will either accompany this letter of mine, or be forwarded to your Lordship by tomorrow's mail, when, if upon reading his letter, your Lordship's sentiments should coincide with his, we shall only wait the result of the communication you may have to make us of his Majesty's pleasure. Of course I have not open'd my lips to anyone but to Payne upon this topic. I have neither heard or seen anything as yet of my brother Augustus, & as to Arbuthnot,[2] who I sent for this morning, I find he is gone to Scotland & is not expected in town for a fortnight. Before I conclude this letter, I cannot help once more recommending to your protection & recollection my poor friend Blomberg[3] in whose prospects in life not only I, but indeed all the rest of the family are much interested. (42318)

1. Payne.

2. Robert Arbuthnot was Prince Augustus's Gentleman in Waiting.

3. The Rev. Frederick William Blomberg (1761–1847). Rector of Shepton Mallet, Somerset, 1787–1833; Prebendary of Bristol, 1790–1828; the Prince's Private Secretary from about 1785 to March 1795 when Tyrwhitt succeeded him; Chaplain to the Prince, 1793; Vicar of Bradford, Wiltshire, 1793–9 and 1808–33; Vicar of Banwell, Somerset, 1799–1808; appointed Clerk of the Closet to the Prince, January 1808; Prebendary of Westminster, April 1808–22; Prebendary of St. Paul's, 1822–47. He had a house in Weymouth, in Clarence Buildings, and the Duke of Cumberland stayed there in August 1800 whilst the King and Queen were at Gloucester Lodge. Le Marchant, the diarist, suggesting that the Prince had no taste for good society, that his connexion with Fox was purely political and that he was never at his ease whilst talking with him, added: 'He preferred the small circle of his creatures amongst whom he could drink and blaspheme and jest as the fancy seized him. His orgies were kept up long after he had reached an age at which most people have abandoned theirs. He must have been

Carlton House, 11 Sept. 1800

Your kind letter I receiv'd yesterday but not till after I had call'd in Sackville Street hoping to find you there, & it was too late when I return'd home to attempt answering you by return of post. Long ago should I have written to you had I not flatter'd myself with the good fortune of seeing you at Brighton soon after the 20th [?] of the last month, & which was the period I think you mention'd when last I had the pleasure of seeing you, at which you projected being in that part of the world, & greatly mortified I do assure you I have been at not having had that good fortune. However, my dearest friend, I have nothing to tell you from dear Arthur[1] but his expressions of the strongest & most unalterable attachment to you, & his extreme chagrin & disappointment at not being able without the greatest madness not only not to propose, but to admit of your thinking of coming to that part of the world; his judgment has proved most correct by the consequences that we are now acquainted with. He is in no sort of danger whatever, as he is on board one of our English ships & most probably with the King of Naples who is perfectly safe in board the Flagship. Of course the post must be stopp'd from that quarter; this to be sure is a very disagreable circumstance, but you will certainly not only have opportunities of writing, & secure ones too, my amiable friend, but of hearing likewise by every messenger who comes over with dispatches from that quarter. I think it infinitely probable that these late events in Sicily will expedite his return to this country, as, supposing things to remain as they are, there can be no use in the King's making any stay there, being necessarily oblig'd to remain on board of ship & in that case he probably will go & join the Queen at Vienna, & then our Minister, which our dear Arthur is, will & can be of no further service, & therefore will in all probability return, at least to acquire fresh instructions. Mr. Wyndham I have neither seen nor heard of; however, you may depend upon my making every enquiry possible respecting Arthur, & I will as immediately acquaint you with the result of all I learn. I am remaining at present & for some time in town, & shall most gladly, my dearest & most amiable friend, wait upon you whenever you lay your commands upon me to do so. As to myself, the goodness of your heart will I am sure lead you to participate with me when I say that I am *more comfortable* than I have been for time out of mind, & when I say that and *comfortable*, I know you have the most feeling & best of hearts & therefore feel the meaning & the value of that word. If I do not

sixty when old Dr. Blomberg, the Clerk of the Closet and a rich dignitary of the Church, was one day complaining at Brighton with great simplicity that he felt very unwell, for his Royal master had at two in the morning obliged him to leave his bed and make champagne punch for the party at the Pavilion' (Le Marchant's Diary).

1. Paget.

conclude here I am afraid that my letter will be too late for the post, therefore I will only add, my dearest Duchess, what I trust you have long been acquainted with, how truly I ever am [etc.].

[*P.S.*] Our dear friend[1] desires her kindest remembrances to you (Rutland MSS.).

1557   LORD LOUGHBOROUGH TO REAR-ADMIRAL J. W. PAYNE

Weymouth, 14 Sept. 1800

I received by the post this evening the letter inclosed from Mr. Arbuthnot. You will observe that Prince Augustus must now be informed that he is to find some better way of conveying to the King his request to go abroad than the mode he had adopted. Perhaps it would be adviseable to leave him for some time to his reflections, for I imagine any forward step taken towards him only gives his advisers the means of flattering him that there is more importance attached to the measures he pursues than in fact belongs to them.

His physician, who appears to be a very honest man & sincerely attached to him, is I should think the most likely person to suggest to him a proper idea of his own situation & to give him fair advice on the means by which he may be delivered from his bondage, which I am persuaded he feels sufficiently, as he must perceive that by his late conduct he has alienated all his family from him & can have no other resource but in the return of their regard.

[*P.S.*][2] Perhaps yr. R.Hs. may see the physician spoken of & give him directions for making the appeal required.

J. Payne. (39695–6)

[Enclosure] CAPTAIN ROBERT ARBUTHNOT TO LORD LOUGHBOROUGH

Edinburgh, 10 Sept. 1800

Upon my arrival here yesterday I had the honor of receiving your Lordship's letter of the 4th together with the note which you had the goodness to write to me. I have communicated the contents of your letter to H.R.H. Prince Augustus, but altho it is so obviously his interest as well as his duty to submit to his Majesty's pleasure, I am afraid that what you say will have little effect. When I took the liberty of writing to your

---

1. 'A gentleman of high rank and Mrs. Fitzherbert are once more inseparables', said *The Times*, 4 July. That, no doubt, is why the Prince was more 'comfortable'.

2. The P.S., which is an endorsement, is addressed to the Prince of Wales.

Lordship, I was perfectly sensible of the impropriety of the request, & nothing but the positive commands of his Royal Highness could have induced me to trouble you with it.

My father begs leave to present his respectful compliments to your Lordship. He is much flattered by your recollection of him, & grateful for your goodness & politeness to me. (39694)

1558   THE DUKE OF KENT TO THE PRINCE OF WALES

Weymouth, 14 Sept. 1800

I have a thousand thanks to offer for your very kind and affectionate letter of the day before yesterday, which I received just as we were all setting off for Lulworth Castle where we passed the day. I am sure, if Madame de St. Laurent knew how kindly you had spoken of her in your letter to me, she would be very much flattered. I am quite pleased to find that you think the house she now occupies is a passable pied a terre en attendant that we can do better for her. Believe me, I feel as I ought the very kind manner in which you express your regret that I do not come up to town before the 24th, but much as I should have wished to have been sooner with you, I felt satisfied you would approve of the motive which induces me to remain three weeks here, and which you will readily believe could be no other than that of marking my dutiful attachment to the King and Queen, and my affectionate love to my sisters, from all of whom I experience everything that is kind, or that I could possibly wish. Of course the very instant I arrive, after calling in Park Lane, the first place I shall turn my steps to will be Carlton House, the owner of which must ever stand foremost of all my brothers in my affection.

I shall feel infinite pleasure in meeting the request of George Hanger; first, from a desire to evince that I am never happier than when I can do anything that is agreable to you, and secondly, from the delight I always receive when I can befriend an old soldier in distress. Inclosed is a letter for him, which I must request you to direct to be forwarded to him.

The accounts from Sir James Pultney's[1] army are, as you justly observe them to be, far from pleasant, and I am sorry to see that the details of the progress of that armament, at least as far as the business has hitherto

1. Entered the Army, 1771; Adjutant-General to the troops in Flanders, 1793-4; Colonel of the 18th Foot, 1794; Major-General, 1794; Lieutenant-General, 1799; General, 1808; Secretary at War, 1807-9. M.P. for Weymouth, 1790-1811. Succeeded as 7th Baronet, 1771. (1755?-1811.) In August he had been sent to capture Ferrol. The troops captured the heights above the port, but he decided that the place was too strong to be taken without a regular siege, which would give time for Spanish forces to come to its relief. Consequently he re-embarked his troops.

gone, cannot fail of making a pitiful not to say a despicable appearance in the page of history.

The whole family here are generally in exceeding good health. The Queen now and then appears to me to suffer, though she seems to hide it, but on the whole is tolerably, I think. Sophy evidently mends daily. Amelia has a little trifling cough, but looks charmingly; all the rest, not excepting that little angel Charlotte, are as usual in great health and spirits.

I have now only to request that I may be remembered most particularly to Mrs. Fitzherbert whom I shall not fail to wait upon before many hours have elapsed after my arrival in town, and to add that I look forward with anxious expectation to the moment when I shall again shake my beloved brother by the hand. (45990–1)

1559   THE PRINCE OF WALES TO LORD [?LOUGHBOROUGH]

Carlton House, 20 Sept. 1800

Private. I have the pleasure to enclose you a letter from my brother Augustus for the King, such a one I trust as will not be dissatisfactory to his Majesty. In order that your Lordship may be a little au fait of how affairs stand at this moment respecting my brother Augustus, I will briefly state my proceedings since I received your last letter. Payne, previous to his leaving London for Brighton (which he unfortunately had done the very morning upon which I received your Lordship's letter), had called at my brother Augustus's house in consequence of a note he received from Lady Augusta Murray, stating the extreme danger my brother was in at that moment, & saying that she thought I might be ignorant of this circumstance, & that therefore she judged it right to acquaint him with it for my information. I evidently saw that this was intended to draw me into a fresh interview with her, which could answer no purpose, & I therefore requested of Payne, though my natural impulse was to go immediately to my brother & to know whether he was able or desirous of seeing me. When he was admitted Lady Augusta inform'd him that my brother was too much indispos'd to be able to see anyone, & after a long & argumentative tête a tête with her Ladyship, Payne took his leave, having receiv'd a desire from Augustus to see him the ensuing day. Accordingly Payne call'd again the next forenoon & saw my brother, when, after much conversation, he at length persuaded him to consult me upon what measures I should think were best for him to pursue, circumstanc'd as he is at the present moment. Three days after this my brother call'd upon me, & began upon the topic of his situation quite of himself, & without making it necessary for me in the least to seek for any other mode of introducing

156

the subject. Your Lordship may easily imagine I said everything that I thought could do good, without letting him into the further plans or indeed any plan that you & I have talk'd over or that you have laid before the King. He seem'd infinitely more calm than I had ever yet seen him upon this subject, & perfectly dispos'd to do whatever was respectful & his duty by the King, though he said but little, & the very next morning I sent for the doctor, with whom I likewise convers'd most fully for near two hours relative to Augustus's health & the whole of his situation, & I cannot sufficiently express my approbation of the whole of not only what he said upon the subject & of his sentiments, but of what he inform'd me had been the line of conduct he had steadily & uniformly pursued towards Augustus, & so much so that I really think him most deserving of some mark of his Majesty's gracious favour & condescension, & indeed I hope I am not too imprudent if I express my sincere wish that this may be the case, as I think him as honest & as clever a little man as I ever knew, & has truely conducted himself with great honor & integrity. The doctor call'd on me again this morning & brought me the enclosed letter for the King, & which by dint of his persuasions & by reiterating to my brother what had passed with me & him he at length procured; & tomorrow my brother is to call upon me again at Carlton House, accompanied by the doctor, that we may endeavour with some delicacy to open my brother's eyes a little more upon his *actual position at the present moment* by letting him more fully into what *has been & is actually* the lady's conduct, & which, by what I learn from the doctor, surpasses everything that your Lordship or anyone can possibly credit or beleive. However, this is a subject that I shall feel my way very delicately in, though it is a subject upon which the doctor tells me he has spoken of very frequently, & very openly with my brother, & who begins to feel it very very much indeed, though he says little upon it, & has not sufficient energy as yet to act upon it. This I trust by going gently myself, & backed by the doctor when he is alone with my brother, may be brought to bear, & I should think that the projected voyage to Lisbon will be in the end the most likely mode of effectuating what will be so much to my brother's advantage.

I ought to apologize to you, my dear Lord, for giving you the trouble of reading so long an epistle, but it would have been difficult to comprize everything for your information in a shorter letter. As to myself I shall continue to lend every aid my mind can suggest or my feeble efforts can endeavour, to forward his Majesty's wishes in this transaction, & which I trust will meet the sanction of his gracious approbation. I shall hope within a few days to hear again from your Lordship, when I hope like-wise to learn if there is anything further that his Majesty would please that I should either say or communicate to my brother, or to our good little friend the Admiral, who, I have the pleasure to inform you, writes me word that he continues to feel encreasing health & strength from the salutary air of Brighthelmstone. (42319–21)

1560 THE PRINCE OF WALES TO THE DOWAGER COUNTESS OF ELGIN

Carlton House, 25 Sept. 1800

I have to acknowledge the receipt of three letters from you since I left Weymouth, for which I am most extremely oblig'd to you, as well as for the good accounts of the dear child, who I am quite happy at learning from you continues still in such high favor with the whole family, & which I attribute much to her manners having been so constantly watch'd & directed by your good management. The Duke of Kent, who arriv'd last night,[1] inform'd me that their Majesties return is fix'd for the eighteenth, which I am sincerely glad of on account of the dear Queen, as I have long thought that the air & atmosphere of Weymouth, together with the hurrying life she is necessarily obliged to lead her [*sic*] has in no way suited her habits or constitution, & to which I am sure she cannot be too attentive. Pray present my most respectful & affectionate duty to both their Majesties, & tell the Queen in particular from me that I hope she does take good care of herself, or else that I shall certainly read her a severe lecture when we meet at Windsor. I trust that all my dear sisters are well, & that Sophia will soon be in fine shapes again. (49247–8)

1561 LETTERS FROM THE DUKE OF YORK TO THE PRINCE OF WALES, AND A REPLY

[copy]

Oatlands, 27 [?25] Sept. 1800

As it will be necessary to augment the cavalry in Portugal I take the earliest oportunity before I make any arrangement to inquire of you if you have any objection to the 10th Light Drags. composing a part of that force, as the Regt. was last year ordered for foreign service but prevented from going.

Do me the favor to give me an answer in the course of the day, as I must write to his Majesty tomorrow & propose the different Corps to be employed. (44159)

1. From Weymouth. *The Times*, 5 September, said that he had taken for his town residence the house in Park Lane which had recently belonged to Colonel Stanhope.

Carlton House, 26 Sept. 1800

I am most extremely oblig'd to you for your kind letter which I receiv'd this morning, & in answer to it I can only say that I should be most extremely sorry that my Regiment was not as ready & as desirous as any other to go upon service when call'd upon. At the same time I cannot but fairly confess to you, as you have put the question to me, that I should feel much more happy & pleas'd that any service the Regiment was call'd upon was in a part of the Continent where they might have a wider field & a greater scope for doing themselves credit & distinguishing themselves than I see any possibility of Portugal affording them; & should there be in the ensuing year an opening for troops being employ'd on that part of the Continent nearer to us, it would give me great pain that, situated as my Regiment would be in Portugal, it in all probability would be excluded from composing a part of that corps of troops which would be there employed. I have likewise to observe that we have such an amazing number of young horses that it would be absolute destruction to them. However, after having made these observations, if it would be attended with any injustice to any other Regiment, or that it would retard the service or be attended with inconvenience to you, I cannot possibly create any further objection, but I will entreat of you to acquaint me with your determination as soon as you shall have made up your mind as to the absolute necessity of my Regiment being sent upon this occasion out of the country. (44160-1)

FROM THE DUKE OF YORK [copy]

Oatlands, 27 Sept. 1800

I lose no time in acknowledging the receipt of your letter and in assuring you that there cannot be the least difficulty in sending another Regiment of Light Dragoons to Portugal in the place of the 10th. My only wish was that you should be acquainted as early as possible with the intention of sending a reinforcement of cavalry upon that service, in case you had wished your Regiment to be employed upon it. (44162)

1562   THE PRINCE OF WALES TO SIR WALTER FARQUHAR [copy]

Carlton House, 27 Sept. 1800

My dear Farquhar, Let me entreat your acceptance of the case which accompanies this note as a testimony of the true and high regard & esteem of your very sincere friend.[1]

[*P.S.*] Pray call upon me about eleven tomorrow as I feel very unwell and stand much in need of your assistance (Farquhar MSS.).

1563   THE PRINCE OF WALES TO THE DOWAGER COUNTESS OF ELGIN
Carlton House, 2 Oct. 1800

I am most extremely obliged to you for your kind letter which this morning's post brought with such very pleasing accounts of the dear child, but I am sorry to acquaint you that one part of your plan cannot be put into execution, that part I mean relative to the Grainge, as that place is now no longer mine, having entirely got rid of it & all the furniture &c. &c. &c. being taken down, & nothing that is mine will be there in the course of three days. But it has just occurr'd to me that I dare say my friend Genl. Goldsworthy, who has a house within a mile of Salisbury,[2] would allow the dear child to stop there for a day or two, by which means your journey to London or to Shuter's Hill[3] would be devided pretty nearly the same as it has been by stopping at the Grainge. I would wish you to consult the dear Queen upon this, & I am confident if she approves of this scheme & would have it hinted to the good General I am confident he would not have the smallest objection. But if this cannot be effectuated I must leave it to you to arrange the best according to your own judgment.

I beg my most affectionate & humblest duty to their Majesties, & my best love to all my dear sisters, & pray tell the dear Queen that I shall in all probability make my bow to her the day after their arrival at Windsor.[4] I am very unwell myself but only I trust momentarily so, as I have had a violent stoppage in my bowels, which has given me great pain. However, I am now, thank God, easier. Embrace the dear child for me. (49249-50)

1. Accompanying this note was a present of 'a most magnificent épergne'.

2. The King liked to travel through the night when he went on his annual holiday to Weymouth, in order to avoid the heat of the day. This he did in 1800, but Princesses Amelia and Sophia were in such a poor state of health that a non-stop journey was deemed inadvisable, and they took two days over it (29-30 July 1800), sleeping at General Goldsworthy's house.

3. Shooter's Hill.

4. The Royal Family arrived at Windsor from Weymouth on the 9th.

Carlton House, 7 Oct. 1800

My dear Sir Walter, In answer to your note, as I well know you have not much time to throw away & I hate writing long letters, I shall briefly say that your appointment in my family is physician *to my own person*, as I always am desirous of employing men of the greatest talents & abilities & most distinguish'd merit. Ever your sincere friend (Farquhar MSS.).

[*?late 1800 or 1801*]

I have received both your very obliging letters & I shall most certainly observe with all proper attention what you have there recommended, but you must allow me to observe, my good friend, that tho' I am quite ready to follow *your advice* I cannot subject myself to be eternally plagued with the attendance of others. As it was for *your* satisfaction *only* that I consented to see Dr. Blane & afterwards Dr. Hunter[1] by Mrs. Fitzherbert's desire, not knowing that he was likely to leave this place so soon, I really cannot consent to either of them coming to me here, nor indeed Keate, unless I send for them, nor even in London, for *my whole confidence is in you.* Forgive me if I scold you a little, but I really had hoped, from the various conversations I had had with you of late, & most particularly in the very last I had with you here the very day before you left this place, that you must have known that I cannot bear the being urged more than to a certain point, & that if this is done it only tends to irritate without doing anything else. This is precisely the case with respect to the letter which I received from you this morning. I know the motive that induced you to write it, & I cannot help being extremely grateful to you for it, but at the same time it has vexed me much, for as I have already told you, I place my *whole & entire confidence in you*, & wh. you ought long to have known. I feel quite satisfied in my own mind that whatever can be done for me will be done by *you*, & as to all the rest I consider it as mere stuff & nonsense & professional buckram & farce. I hoped you had too long been acquainted with me & had formed a better opinion of my mind than to think that I shall not do all that is necessary & right, but I must not be plagued, for that you might know is what my disposition when in health or otherwise does not very patiently submit to at any time.

Now, my good friend, do not run away with the idea that I am either angry or displeased, but I think it a duty as a friend thus once for all to

1. John Hunter (*d.* 1809), Physician Extraordinary to the Prince of Wales.

speak my mind to you without any reserve. You may depend on my trying the [the rest is missing] (ibid.).

1565 THE EARL OF MOIRA TO COLONEL MCMAHON

Donington, 16 Oct. 1800

I am truly sensible, my dear friend, to your kind offer of repairing to London if you could there be useful to me, but knowing perfectly the sincerity with which you make the proposal nothing could distress me more than the notion of breaking in upon that retirement which you so seldom enjoy. I shall somehow or other patch up the business. It has been singularly perplexing, & indeed has been more vexatious to me than almost any event that I have ever met. I have perfect faith in Browne's probity. I fear, however, that his embarrassments are very heavy, tho' I do not arraign him for not having been explicit with me about them, as I comprehend the repugnance of a man to disclose difficulties which he thinks he may surmount. When I saw you in town, I explained to you that I was laboring to provide for his acceptances on my account without requiring him to apply the balance which he owed to me; & I had made great lodgements accordingly. Some bills were discharged before the stoppage took place, but he now owes me between six & seven thousand pounds, & you can easily understand the distress of having thrown back upon me the demands which a large portion of that sum was to answer. He has assured me by letter that there will be funds to settle everything ultimately. At the same time I learn that the amount of bills floating between him & Corry[1] is enormous.

Monsieur, with the Duc de Bourbon[2] & four others, arrived here the day before yesterday. They go back to town on Saturday. There was no harm in a visit of this sort, but it would have been desperate had they brought their ladies & fixed themselves for a month. Do you think the Prince will come this winter? Do not speak to him about it, for I fear that he should think it an engagement, & thence do what might not be convenient to himself.[3] (39697–8)

1. Possibly Cary: the writing is not clear.

2. Louis Henry Joseph, Duc de Bourbon (1756–1830), son of the Prince de Condé (1736–1818). He commanded the cavalry in his father's Army against the Republicans, 1792–6, and in 1797 the Army passed into the service of Russia. In 1800 he accompanied his father to England and lived at Wanstead House in Essex. His son, the Duc d'Enghien (1772–1804), was shot by Napoleon's orders.

3. The following receipt is dated the 25th: 'Received the 25 October 1800 of his Royal Highness the Prince of Wales by Jno. McMahon Esq. the sum of one Hundred & five pounds, being the annual donation to the Welsch [*sic*] Charity School for the year 1799.
£105   J. J. Thomas, Secry.' (30055)

THE EARL OF JERSEY TO THE PRINCE OF WALES

Stratford Place, 28 Oct. 1800

It is with infinite reluctance, after the severest struggles, that I now presume humbly to address this letter to your Royal Highness.

The situation in which I find myself compels me to it. That situation your Royal [Highness] commanded me to submit to you by a gracious message to me some time since by Coll. McMahon signifying your pleasure to have a statement of all the circumstances attending me in the station which I had the honor to hold under your gracious favor.

The difficulties which have arisen to me from so large a deficiency have encreased into embarrassments so severe & so pressing upon myself & my family, both in the present & the future, that it is become an indispensable duty to lay the same with all submission at your Royal Highness's feet for your consideration; and I know too well the generous feelings of your mind not to be assured of the impression it will receive.

Pardon, Sir, I entreat, the anxiety of this representation.[1] (39699–700)

1567 THE PRINCE OF WALES TO THE DOWAGER COUNTESS OF ELGIN

Carlton House, Wednesday evening, 29 Oct. 1800

I have just receiv'd a message from the Queen desiring that the child may be at St. James's at half past twelve tomorrow to see their Majesties. It was my intention to have been present at the Drawing Room myself, but some disagreable appearances or rather remnants of the fever I have had make Sir Walter Farquhar desirous that I would not go there, as well on the account of others, as of myself, the fever having been rather of an epidemmical sort. I need not therefore add that I shall content myself with a message from you, my dear Lady, to acquaint me how the little woman is, & must consequently for the sake of prudence dispense with the pleasure of seeing her.[2] (49251)

1. 'Though he [Lord Jersey] has erred grievously,' Lady Spencer had written to her daughter Georgiana, 'I am confident it has been from tenderness to her and affection for his children.' She pitied him, though no one else would, she said (Chatsworth MSS.).

2. The Prince's letter to his brother the Duke of Kent, 31 October, has not, apparently, been preserved. He was still indisposed when the Duke wrote to him at 10 a.m. on Saturday 1 November, from Park Lane: 'A thousand thanks for your most affectionate note of last night. I shall certainly be with you today the moment we come in from our drive, which I think will be about three. Till then I shall now say adieu, meaning to repeat in person how faithfully and truly I ever must be [etc.].' (45992)

1568 COLONEL MCMAHON TO THE EARL OF JERSEY [copy]

3 Nov. 1800

The Prince of Wales commands me to request your Lordship will excuse my replying to your letter, which indisposition, the concern he feels for circumstances which have been so long out of his power to remedy, could only prevent H.R.Hss. from answering himself.

I am further commanded by the Prince to say that in certain arrangements which H.R.Hss. long since made, & which unexpectedly have not yet met their completion, every consideration was given to your Lordship's claims, and positive directions signified with every & all convenient dispatch to discharge them. The Prince is perfectly sensible of your Lordship's delicacy in suggesting your demand, and H.R.Hss. directs me to tell your Lordship that he has given orders it shall bear the very earliest attention as to the entire amount of it: but in the meanwhile a fund is probable to arise at no distant period that shall enable such a sum in part being remitted to your Lordship as may perhaps tend to your temporary accomodation, & of which event, by H.R.Hss.'s command, I shall have the honor to give your Lordship the speediest information. (39701)

1569 THE PRINCE OF WALES TO LORD [?LOUGHBOROUGH]

Carlton House, 4 Nov. 1800

In consequence of the gracious point of view which his Majesty has been pleased to view the line of conduct I have hitherto pursued respecting my brother Augustus, & in consequence also of the gracious message of which you was the bearer from his Majesty to me, I have exerted myself so to make every further arrangement respecting my brother, that his Majesty might not only be reliev'd from every species of anxiety or uneasiness, but likewise as far as it was possible be dissembarrass'd from any additional trouble. The conversations I have had of late with Augustus in various interviews, I have the satisfaction to assure your Lordship, have been such as greatly to facilitate the project of his intended to [*sic*] voyage to Lisbon for the restoration of his health, & to which his Majesty has already been pleas'd to signify his assent. My brother is not only perfectly willing but desirous that anyone should accompany him that the King shall think proper to nominate. He likewise without a complaint conforms to the regulations that have hitherto been laid down by the King relative to his pocket money & the further expenditure of his Household. At the same time he only hopes that if there are certain savings made upon the Household expences, *after everything* is paid, such saving may afterwards revert to him, which, if I may be allowed not only to express a wish but an opinion, I should think an adviseable circumstance, as it establishes an interest in my brother Augustus to attend to such a proper system of order & economy as is becoming, & to which from perfect inexperience he has hitherto been an entire stranger. His physicians have also been frequently with me, urging as *strenuously as possible* that his departure from this country should be delay'd as little as possible, as they conceive that should he make any longer stay in this climate, it not only may but will certainly be attended with most disagreable consequences to his future health. I therefore trouble your Lordship with this letter, hoping that you will be so good at as early a moment as possible to lay all the circumstances I have here stated to you before the King, & with my most humble duty assure his Majesty that if there is anything still that is wanting to meet his Majesty's entire approbation or satisfaction in the arrangement of this business, my feeble efforts shall ever be ready to their utmost to serve him not only in this but in every other business in which he may be graciously pleased to call for them. With the hopes of soon hearing from you my dear Lord, I am [etc.].[1] (42322-3)

1570 CHARLES SMALL PYBUS TO THE PRINCE OF WALES

Great George Street, 12 Nov. 1800

I will not attempt to describe either my obligations to your Royal Highness or the state of my mind from reiterated disappointments, which have most materially injured my health and plunged me deeper and deeper into wretchedness. But may I still be permitted to hope that your Royal Highness's benevolence will not *abandon* me in my difficulties, for I am now confident that upon that *alone* my whole and sole reliance must be placed.

There is one thing which, though not of *substantial* benefit in itself, I am from *various reasons* tempted to point out to your Royal Highness, from whose suggestion to the Minister upon the present occasion I think a refusal must absolutely be impossible.

I mean, Sir, an *Irish* Peerage, which, nominal and *barren* indeed as that honour has now become, may perhaps eventually operate as the means of ensuring some provision for me *hereafter*. Would your Royal Highness,

1. On the 11th the Prince wrote a typical note to the Dowager Countess of Elgin, from Carlton House: 'I have this day receiv'd a command from their Majesties desiring the dear child to be at the Queen's House tomorrow by twelve o'clock at the latest, as they understood that it was your wish she should go again out of town before it was dark. I therefore desire that she may be at Carlton House by half past eleven previous to her going to the Queen's House, in order that I may have the pleasure of seeing her.' (49252)

therefore, condescend to *press* it upon Mr. Pitt in your *own handwriting* and language, as a matter proceeding from your Royal Highness's *own wish* to afford some consolation to my mind under the present vexatious circumstances, and *not as any request of mine*, for I am now thoroughly convinced that *any mixture* of my *supposed desires* would of itself be sufficient to destroy all prospect of success.

May I here, Sir, without offence to your Royal Highness, and in spite of the Chancellor's most unfair and *untrue* insinuation, indulge the pride of adding that I belong *at least* to as old and respectable a gentleman's family as himself; that like himself (and *not like* Lord Carrington,[1] whose former occupations he has most inapplicably and disingenuously quoted upon your Royal Highness) I was regularly educated for, and called to the Bar as my *original and only* profession; and that *almost ever since I was of age*, I have been in one of the most honourable and distinguished offices under his Majesty's Government. When I know, therefore, with certainty, that at this very moment, a Scotchman, who is *peculiarly* patronized by the Chancellor, and of *very low* beginnings,[2] is included in the numerous list of intended Irish Peers previous to the Union, I cannot help yielding a little to the honest pride of an English *gentleman*, and I trust that your Royal Highness will not think the worse of me for giving way to it.[3] (39702–3)

1. Robert Smith (1752–1838), M.P. for Nottingham, 1779–97, created by his friend Pitt Baron Carrington [I.], 11 July 1796, and Baron Carrington [G.B.], 20 October 1797. He chose the title Carrington in an absurd attempt to conceal his plebeian origin (a Smith family had been ennobled under that title in 1643; Robert Smith's great-grandfather had been a draper of Nottingham. Later, the family abandoned any claim to a seventeenth-century Carrington descent). Robert Smith himself was a banker: one of those people whom Pitt caught in the alleys of Lombard Street and clutched from the counting houses of Cornhill (as Disraeli phrased it) in pursuing a policy of ennobling the *nouveaux riches*.

2. The reference may well be to Sylvester Douglas (1743–1823), son of John Douglas of Fechil, Aberdeenshire. He became a barrister in 1776. Chief Secretary to the Lord Lieutenant of Ireland, 1794–5; Commissioner of the India Board of Control, 1795–1806; a Lord of the Treasury, 1797–1800; Joint Paymaster-General, 1801–3; Vice-President of the Board of Trade, 1801–4; Surveyor-General of Woods and Forests, 1803–6 and 1807–10; First Commissioner of Woods and Forests, 1810–14. M.P. for St. Canice [I.], 1794–6; for Fowey, 1795–6; for Midhurst, 1796–1800; for Plympton, 1801–2; for Hastings, 1802–6. Created Baron Glenbervie [I.], 30 November 1800, but his peerage was unconnected with the Union.

3. Pybus should have known that his chances of being ennobled were slender indeed, in view of his poor financial situation, for only people who could support the dignity of the peerage were usually considered (exceptions were made in such cases as Wellington when, on grounds of highly distinguished public service, ample financial provision was made for them by a grateful Parliament). When a decayed Peer applied to the Crown for outdoor relief to save himself from the misery and disgrace of the workhouse or the Fleet Prison, his claims were apt to receive sympathetic treatment so that the dignity of the Peerage should not be unduly impaired.

Manchester Square, 14 Nov. 1800

Nothing could have imbolden'd me to presume to write to your Royal
Highness but the dread of incurring the reproach of ingratitude and of
adding this crime to those under which I have the heavy calamity of
appearing in your eyes. Altho' I had heard of your gracious liberality
towards me, yet, before yesterday, I was not assured sufficiently to
authorize me to dare to throw myself at your feet with the most respectfull gratitude.

If this condescensive goodness is meant to express your Royal Highnesses pardon for the errors of my head, and the mistaken sensibility of
my heart, it will relieve me from that melancholy dejection which has
overwhelmed me ever since I had the misfortune, owing to a six months
fever of the brain, to offend a great Prince whom it had been the pride
and glory of my life to endeavour to serve with all the zeal, fidelity and
disinterestedness that I felt to be due to so gracious and so kind a
master. But if your Royal Highnesses intentions in granting me an annuity do not comprize your Royal forgiveness, then it will be cruel to furnish the means of prolonging a life which must be miserable, as long as
it is accompanied with the reflections that even tho' my age and distresses
exacted compassion, yet my conduct had excluded me from mercy.

This, Sir, is not amplification. It is really literally the truth. I have as
yet wanted no necessary, altho' I have lost £1,500 pr. year (the interest
of £15,000 India Stock) and altho' my compensation of £600 is settled
on my wife and children, yet with £140, which is all I have left, and the
sale of my plate, trinkets &c., I have hitherto existed so as not to impor-
tune my friends.

Let it even be supposed that I dreamt the conversation between his
Royal Highness the Duke of York and me; imagining that all I believed
was the consequence of that six months brain fever for which Sr. Walter
Farquhar said he had exhausted his last hopes by such a quantity of
hemlock as he had never before ventured to give. Granting that all that
that ever accursed regicide the Duke of Orleans had told me was false,
and I do solemnly declare such to be my belief; did I not give up everything on these grounds alone, 'I must be wrong if the Prince of Wales
says so'—'I leave everything to HIS goodness of heart and generous
protection'.

That most honorable of men, that most faithfull and most affectionate
of all your Royal Highnesses friends, will tell you of my humility and
submission to your will. Need I name the Earl of Moira? Oh!, Sir, you
may say 'Mihi ipse agmen'.

If I dare trust my own feelings; if I dare presume to speak to *your
heart*, I would endeavour to describe my present situation. A faithfull

constant companion of all my distresses and sickness for ten years was last week obliged to return to her cursed country which murdered her friends and robb'd her. I could not support the prospect of her starving here.

I cannot write more. In the name of our Creator—I implore your pardon. As you expect mercy from your God, I supplicate it from your Royal Highness. Pray, Sir, be so good as to write—'Forth, I forgive you!', and it will be but prudent that Lord Moira should *see* all my papers, dreams and reveries burned. My life is very precarious, and there may come people after me who would not scruple to gratify the malignity of mankind.

In expectation of your Royal Highness's gracious forgiveness and generous pity I remain [etc.].[1] (31632–3)

1572 THE PRINCE OF WALES TO THE DOWAGER COUNTESS OF ELGIN

Carlton House, 23 Nov. 1800

It quite escaped my memory to answer your letter yesterday. I therefore take the earliest opportunity of returning you my thanks for it, & assuring you that nothing can give me more pleasure at all times than the hearing such very good accounts of the dear child's state of health. As to the other two subjects you mention'd to be both respecting Mme. de Suffrein (who I know personally) as well as the person touching who

1. Nathaniel Parker Forth wrote to Charles Bicknell on the 21st at 8 p.m.:

'The very kind manner in which you have been so good to interest yourself in the final arrangement of the misunderstanding which I have had the misfortune to have with his Royal Highness the Prince of Wales, exacts not only my acknowledgements but that I should inform you of its conclusion.

'In consequence of a very kind answer to a letter which I wrote to Lord Moira, I took the liberty of writing to the Prince of Wales and of expressing in a dutifull manner my contrition for, and sincere repentance of, my imprudent letter to his Royal Highness in April last. I have since received a letter written by Lord Moira by H.R.H.'s commands. I shall always keep it and shew it as a chef d'œuvre. Nothing can be more noble, more dignified or more gracious than the manner in which the Prince has had the generosity to forgive my intemperance. Nothing can be more able, or more eloquent than the stile and language which conveys this mark of his Royal Highnesses greatness of mind & goodness of heart.

'The last paragraph says, "You will immediately be paid by Colonel McMahon, as he was yesterday promised by Mr. Rose to send him the appointments". In a former letter Ld. Moira had expressed his surprize that I had not already received not only my disbursements, but a payment of the annuity fix'd by the Prince of Wales in May last.

'I have now only to request that you will explain to Colonel McMahon that the original sum paid by the Duke of York's orders (as per vouchers) was £825, which, with 10 years *simple* interest, amounts now to £1,237:10s, and that there is likewise a half year due of the annuity granted by H.R.H. the Prince of Wales.' (31634)

Lady Willoughby applied to you, you are quite at liberty to acquaint with their wishes [*sic*]. I hope I shall see the dear child either on Wednesday or Thursday, as their Majesties will then be in town & will most probably wish to see her. As to myself I confess I do not like much to send for her up from such a distance to town whilst the weather is so damp, so wet & so cold as we have had it here of late, especially as everybody are complaining of that nasty kind of feverish attack flying about & of which I still feel the disagreable dregs hanging about it. (49253)

1573 NATHANIEL PARKER FORTH TO COLONEL MCMAHON

Manchester Square, 28 Nov. 1800

The fear of incommoding you yesterday and of abusing the extreme politeness with which you were so kind to receive me, prevented me from communicating to you the object I had in view in taking the liberty to wait on you. As you are perfectly master of the whole misunderstanding that I have had the misfortune to lie under relative to his Royal Highness the Prince of Wales's gracious liberality towards me, I shall not say one word more than I have already said in palliation of my misconceptions. I have done those things which I ought not to have done. I have seen my intemperance, I have felt my imprudence. I appealed to the best of hearts; its possessor pitied and forgave me. His heart is not satisfied with commiseration alone; it must be gratified by affording generous protection. I shall studiously avoid naming persons or motives, because I will not, even unintentionally be the cause of anyone's being committed. I shall beg leave briefly to state my situation, the hopes I have been led to entertain and my wishes to be informed of the Prince's intentions.

After I had voluntarily given up the 3 bonds in May last I was informed of his Royal Highness the Prince of Wales's condescensive declaration, 'that Mr. Forth should be reimbursed the £825 which he had paid (by the Duke of York's order) to get up the loan bonds, together with the 10 years interest due on that sum' (amounting now to £1,237) 'and that an annuity should be granted to him adequate to the *half* of the interest of his East India Stock (which was £1,500 per annum) as a remuneration and as a compensation *untill* he should at a peace or at any other opportunity be able to recover either the whole or a considerable part of the annuities he had charged on the late Duke of Orleans's property', &c., &c.

This gracious declaration was indefinitely conveyed to me twice in the course of the summer and reasons assigned why the payment of the disbursement had been delayed.

I have lately been informed by the most respectable private authority,

169

as well as by an official gentleman, that not only such were H.R.H.'s generous sentiments relative to the reimbursement and annuity (the amount of which was *not* specified by either) 'but that it would give the Prince of Wales pain, if his intentions in that arrangement were not *exactly* fullfilled'.

As I quote the above information for no other reason than to plead in excuse for the liberty I now take, forgive me if I earnestly request you will be so very kind as to inform me (and considering you, Sir, in your official capacity I shall wait your appropriate convenience), what is the sum of the annuity thus generously granted to me, and which I feel and allow is only provisional and dependant on contingent circumstances. I am desirous likewise here to confirm what I authorized Lord Kinnaird to say, 'that any money granted to me by H.R.H. the Prince of Wales in consideration of the loss of the £25,000 or £1,500 per year (serving as a counter-security for the annuities of £2,500 received regularly from the Duke of Orleans's trustees by Messrs. Ransom & Co.)[1] shall be regularly carried to account and reimbursed when, at a peace, the arrears due by the said trustees shall be liquidated'.

I ask your forgiveness for taking up so much of your time. I shall not again thus incommode you; but I earnestly request that you will make allowance for my very distressing situation, and relieve me from the anxiety of suspence. Only mention *any time* for my receiving the reimbursement, and what is the *annual sum* graciously deigned as a provisional relief *untill* I can recover what I have lost. I only wait for this information to decide whether I shall be able to vegetate in my own house in London, or else be obliged to let it and die of a broken heart on friendless foreign soil'.

I again entreat your kindness and request you will represent me as perfectly resigned and dutifull gratefull for *whatever* the Prince of Wales shall graciously deign to allow me. (31635)

1574 THE EARL OF MOIRA TO COLONEL MCMAHON
Donington, 5 Dec. 1800
I was not a party to the final arrangement with Mr. Forth, & only heard the terms cursorily from Mr. Bicknell. From him you will get information more sure than that which my loose recollection could furnish, but I rather think the amount calculated by Mr. Forth considerably exceeds what was mentioned to me as the sum admitted.

Imagining that I might have some memorandum that would throw light upon the point, I have made a rummage among my papers. I find,

1. Messrs. Ransome, Morland & Co., the Bankers, of 56, Pall Mall.

however, that I have left every document relative to the business, as well as Mr. Forth's letters, in town. The principle submitted by me to the Prince of Wales and approved by his Royal Highness was that every expenditure made or loss bona fide incurred by Mr. Forth in his Royal Highness's service should be compensated; and as it did not appear that Mr. Forth had received remuneration for his time and trouble, it was further understood that his Royal Highness would allow him a pension. The amount was to be calculated by Mr. Bicknell with Mr. Forth, & I believe it was so done.

I hope the Prince will understand & graciously admit the difficulty which prevents my giving any active assistance to Mr. Manners at Leicester. The only direct & positive interest that I have is from such of my tenantry in Loughborough or Ashby de la Zouch as happen to be freemen of Leicester. Tho' there are a good many of that description, they are not enough to be important in a poll of 5,000 voters unless the contest be close, which here cannot be the case. By using them in this instance I should do no good to Manners & I should revolt those who on other occasions give me real weight by following my influence. Manners's advertisement was felt by all classes but the lowest as an insult & as setting at defiance the dispositions of those who have usually swayed the elections.[1] Before I come into the . . .[2] (31636–7)

1575   LETTERS FROM NATHANIEL PARKER FORTH TO COLONEL MCMAHON, AND A REPLY

Manchester Square, 8 Dec. 1800
I am very sensible of the kindness of your visit yesterday, and regret that absence prevented my having the honor to receive you. I had hoped that you would have had the goodness to *write* a few lines in answer to my letter, and indeed my principal motive in *writing* to you was that Colonel McMahon should not be committed by any private conversation, but that the Prince of Wales's Treasurer and Commissioner of Accounts,

1. Thomas Babington was elected M.P. for Leicester on 17 December, the by-election being occasioned by the death of the sitting member, Lord Rancliffe, on 17 November. Babington, one of Wilberforce's group of 'Saints', subsequently supported Pitt. It was a contested election and the poll was kept open for the full period of fifteen days, the final numbers being: Babington 1,572; John Manners, who stood as a Carlton House man, 1,418.

During the contest Manners issued an address declaring that at the next general election and at every general election, if opposed, he would keep open the poll to the very last man. According to *The Times* 'Mr. Manners had nearly thrown Mr. Babington out by calling on him for his qualification at a period when, though well qualified, he had scarcely time to produce it'.

2. The rest is missing.

after having received his Royal Highnesses commands, should officially communicate to me his Prince's gracious intentions.

On these grounds I reiterate my request of an answer to my letter of the 28th ult. on the two points of 'when I may expect to receive the £1,237 due the 1st of this inst. as disbursed by order of the Duke of York', and 'what is the annual sum graciously intended by the Prince of Wales to be advanced to me *untill* I shall be able to recover some part of the annuities due to me by the Duke of Orleans's trustees'.

In complying with this request you will oblige me exceedingly; the 'bis dat, qui cito dat' was never more applicable than in my case. (31639)

FROM COLONEL MCMAHON

9 Dec. 1800

I did myself the honor to offer you my compliments on Sunday forenoon for the purpose of explaining that no want of respect or attention on my part had caused any delay in answering your letter. It became my duty & was indispensably necessary to submit that letter to the P. of W. before I could possibly presume to venture a reply. H.R.Hss., conceiving that Lord M. could best speak to the essential points in question, commanded me to transmit it to his Lordship at Donnington, who only return'd it with his observations by yesterday's post. Ld. Moira's observations refer so much to Mr. Bicknell, who had so great a share in every conference upon the subject & who is so conversant & in H.R.Hss. sentiments respecting it, that the Prince has deem'd it most agreable to you to desire Mr. Bicknell should wait upon you for a thorough elucidation of whatever may be in doubt. I have therefore only further to add that in obedience to H.R.Hss. orders Mr. Bicknell has just informed me he proposes attending you in Manchester Square on Thursday next at 2 o'clock, when I hope & trust a final adjustment may take place.[1] (31640-1)

NATHANIEL PARKER FORTH'S REPLY

Manchester Square, 12 Dec. 1800

I received your letter of the 9th late at night; I should have expressed my obligations for your kindness immediately had I not waited to inform you of the result of Mr. Bicknell's visit.

The words 'respect and attention' which you are so good to address to me are applicable to me only on account of the consideration with which

1. The letter is endorsed: 'N.B. This is the rough copy of my letter to Mr. Forth upon which he grounds his allusion to the terms of "respect & attention". Vide his letter Decr. 12th.'

you are pleased to honor me, and, as such, they are indeed valuable in my esteem. To you, Sir, they are due, not only from the high station which you hold in the Prince of Wales's establishment, but from the *public* and *private* opinion which I have *long* known the world to entertain of *you* as an *honest* man and an *honorable* gentleman.

Mr. Bicknell, in a few words, declared the object of his visit. It was verbally to declare their Royal Highnesses the Prince of Wales's, and the Duke of York's intentions relative to their *own* declarations, vizt., to reimburse me the sum of £825 paid for *them* (according to the avowed vouchers) the 9th December 1790 and the grant of an annuity on *my* life as a recompence for my zealous services and as a compensation for my losses, fatigue, accidents and trouble.

In explanation he said, 'That as a reimbursement of the sum of £825 acknowledged to have been paid in 1790, he was authorised to offer me £1,000 to be paid in equal shares by the two Princes'. 'That as a compensation and remuneration he was also authorized to assure me of an annuity of £200 for *my* life, to be in like manner equally paid by their Royal Highnesses'.

I received this gracious message from the King's (my master) sons with all the veneration and gratitude that it merited.

I requested Mr. Bicknell to implore their forgiveness if I declined to accept of the annuity of £200. Remarking that as the Princes were convinced that I had lost £1,500 a year (the interest of my India Stock) by my zeal to serve them, I saw that they were affected by the sacrifice I had made, and compassionately gave away a part of their (already insignificant) income as an earnest of their feelings for a man who had given up the whole of his income for them. I desired that he would assure their Royal Highnesses that my gratitude was proportionate to their generosity and that at no one period of my life should I neglect to declare it.

I likewise requested, from the same motives, that their Royal Highnesses would not put themselves to any inconvenience by the addition of £175 to the £825 disbursed for them above ten years ago. I wished him only to suggest to the Princes whether they thought I was in any degree entitled to £412:10s. as *simple* interest at 5 pr. % during ten years for the money I had paid for them, especially as I myself had regularly paid *compound* interest for that very sum which I had borrowed to enable me to gratify *their* wishes.

Mr. Bicknell, with his usual candor and politeness, assured me that he would lay my humble remonstrance before the Princes, and we agreed that, to avoid mistakes, I should take the liberty of requesting you to do the same.

Upon these grounds therefore, Sir, I again trouble you officially, and request that you will take such measures as may procure me the payment of money which I have been led to expect weekly since May last; and also (in case the Prince of Wales thinks that I have no more claim to the interest due on the £825 than he appears to say I have for a compensation for the loss of my India Stock) that his Royal Highness will at least have the goodness to immediately order the reimbursement of the sum of £825.[1] (31642)

1576 LETTERS FROM THE EARL OF MOIRA TO COLONEL MCMAHON

Donington, 12 Dec. 1800

I have had a piteous letter from Surgeon Cobbe, telling me that he had been arrested, & forced (in order to get out of that scrape) to part with every sixpence he possessed at a moment when he was under orders to

1. The last of these exchanges is a letter from Forth to Moira, dated Manchester Square 17 December 1800, 3 p.m. To keep them together, it is printed as a footnote:

'In consequence of Mr. Bicknell's visit to me on Thursday last, I wrote to Col. McMahon an acct. of what had passed, and requested him to communicate it to your Lordship, especially as that visit had been in consequence of your Lordship's observations on my letter of the 28th ult. I am this moment favored with a letter from Col. McMahon informing me that his Royal Highness was gone to Donnington. I therefore take the liberty to lay before the Prince the exact state of my situation and humbly request that there may be no further delay. Mr. Bicknell made me by authority of H.R.H. two propositions: one, to give me £1,000; the other, an annuity of £200 on my life. Your Lordship has seen by my letter to Col. McMahon containing my humble remonstrance [*sic*]; as I am afraid to lose the post and write in great hurry and agitation, I hope I shall be excused if I am so concise, but here are in few words my wishes, and hope your Lordship will prevail on H.R.H. to gratify them.

1°. Reimbursement of £825 paid 9th Dec. 1790, and the ten years interest due—£412:10s.

2°. An official grant of the annuity of £100 from the Prince of Wales, and the same from the Duke of York as a mark of their satisfaction of my services & zeal, to commence in May last.

3°. An *advance* of £500 a year payable half yearly to me *untill* I shall be able to recover such part of my annuities in France as the Prince of Wales shall fix on, the different sums so advanced by H.R.H. to be refunded *then* by Mr. Forth.

I now conjure your Lordship to accomplish these my hopes. Be assured you will render the most essential service to H.R.H.; time will not permit me to expatiate. All I request is a decisive answer, and that Lord Moira may be the person to communicate it to me instead of legal men. Perhaps it is the last request I shall ever make to your Lordship and I implore you will persuade the Prince to grant it.' (31644)

On 19 December 1801 Forth signed the following receipt: 'Received 19th December 1801 of their Royal Highnesses the Prince of Wales and the Duke of York, by the payment of Mr. Chas. Bicknell, the sum of One thousand two hundred and forty pounds (for the principal sum of Nine hundred and two pounds ten shillings paid for their Royal Highnesses in the month of December 1790, by the direction of his R.H. the Duke of York) and on account of interest thereon, the vouchers for which are left in the hands of Messrs. Ransom, Morland & Cy., Bankers in Pall Mall (as evidence of such payment) as sent to by me from Paris.' (31650)

join his Regiment. As his Commission might be lost thro' his inability to pay the expense of the journey, I must help him, tho' I have no very good opinion of his prudence at least. Not having a bank note to enclose, I have written to desire that he will call upon you, & let me beg that you will give him ten guineas on my account.

Do you think the Prince likely to come hither? I ask solely because that I am preventing my Frenchmen from shooting in the coverts, from which I would not restrain them but in the view of preserving the game for the Prince. Do not ask him but just impart your own inference from what you know of his other plans. There is not a creature sends a word of news to me. This is not a hint to you to write, because I would not be so unconcionable as to lay a tax of that nature upon you whose every moment is so occupied. It is only by way of explaining to you a doubt I have about Frank Doyle.[1] He wishes to join his uncle in the Mediterranean.[2] Now I cannot judge sufficiently of the probability that war should continue, or of the course events may be deemed likely to take, to know how to decide for him.[3] When you answer me, therefore, about the Prince, just say shortly what is the appearance of affairs.

Is my mother's[4] chaise gone? (39705–6)

Donington, 14 Dec. 1800
That business at Coutts's is vexatious in the extreme, and my obligation to you for your kind exertion on the occasion is proportionate. By the account which they have sent to me I find that a note for £250 beyond what I had reckoned had been paid by them. It was one for which other provision had been made with Jefferys: but he possibly could not get it from the holder in time. I thence calculated that if Campbell could lodge

1. Sir Francis Hastings Doyle (1783–1839), Sir John Doyle's nephew, and son of Major-General Welbore Ellis Doyle; later, Military Secretary to Moira when he was Governor-General of Bengal. Created Baronet, 1828. Captain, 1794; Major, 1805; Lieutenant-Colonel, 1812; Major-General, 1838.

2. Sir John Doyle served as Brigadier General first at Gibraltar and then at Minorca before accompanying Sir Ralph Abercromby's expedition to Egypt at the end of the year.

3. 'I fear that your conjectures about a Peace are too sanguine,' he wrote to Thomas Coutts on 4 July. 'Like bad chess players we shall dash away and lose a few pieces more before we own the game to be lost . . . We seem thoroughly unfit to wage war. Professor Bonaparte has been reading lectures to Europe, but we appear incapable of understanding them. It will be rather late to attain the comprehension of them if we cannot do it until he shall illustrate them by comments upon our own territory' (Coutts MSS.).

4. Moira's father, the 1st Earl (1720–93), married, as his third wife, in 1752, Elizabeth (1731–1808), daughter of Theophilus, 9th Earl of Huntingdon. In 1789, by the death of her brother, the 10th Earl of Huntingdon, she became *suo jure* Baroness Hastings.

£500 with Coutts, I should have £250 over & above the demands. On the strength of this, I thought myself possessed of that balance when I transmitted the bundle of bills to you; and I transmitted a draft on Coutts for £100 to poor Kitty Henry, whom her worthless brother has left in difficulties at Teignmouth by neglecting to send her quarterage. I enclose to you a draft on Sir Walter Stirling & Co. for £100 which I have in their hands. It was destined for another purpose, but you must get it directly & lodge it with Coutts. Do not send the draft to Coutts's; for I had rather they should not know of my correspondence with the other house: only get the money, & lodge it specially to answer Miss Henry's bill. I have written to Coutts to thank him as I ought for his kind intervention, & I really love the man. Campbell, sure, mistakes about two bills of £500 at Hammersley's. I paid one just before I left town, which had been protected at Browne's; & I believe I omitted to tell Campbell I had done so.

I have heard from Hamburgh where all is going on right. I only fear this Emperor of Russia will thwart my poor little arrangements whilst he is striking at Mr. Pitt.[1] Thank you for the intimation about the movements. The news from France is very serious if it be true, & I credit it as a natural consequence of what I heard respecting the state of the armies.[2] The poll at Leicester will finish on Thursday.[3]

[P.S.] Sir W. Stirling's is just beyond Exeter Change.[4] (39707-8)

1577   THE PRINCE OF WALES TO THE DUKE OF NORTHUMBERLAND
Carlton House, 15 Dec. 1800
I have lived in the hope for several days past of having it in my power to pay you a visit at Sion,[5] in the first place in order to have the pleasure of seeing you, & in the next to have consulted you respecting my brother

1. The Tsar was forming the second Armed Neutrality, consisting of Russia, Sweden, Denmark and Prussia, against Great Britain.

2. On the 11th news reached London that Bonaparte had resumed hostilities against Austria following her refusal to negotiate a separate peace. On the 13th the newspapers reported that Moreau had won a great victory over the Austrians at Hohenlinden on the 1st.

3. According to the Official Return of Members of Parliament, it was on *Wednesday,* 11 December that Thomas Babington was elected for Leicester. See No. 1574 *n.*

4. Canning had dined with Sir Walter and had course to regret it. He wrote on 3 December: .. 'The fool with whom I dined yesterday gave us bad wine & a bad dinner, and so, please the fates, I will never dine with him again. He is a Sir Walter Stirling, for whom, I believe Dundas negotiated a seat in Parliament, & whom Pitt has made a Baronet just now, & who revenges himself for both by asking me to dinner. He asked Pitt & Dundas too, but they *had* dined with him—and so *have* I now' (Harewood MSS.).

5. The Duke's home at Isleworth, Middlesex.

Augustus's passage to Lisbon,[1] at which place he is immediately going to reside for some months on account of his health, & the arrangement of which business has taken up so much of my time as to prevent my leaving London of a morning for above a fortnight. Should there be anything, however, my dear Duke, that may occur to you from your perfect knowledge of & acquaintance with the Court of Lisbon, that you might deem either proper or necessary for my brother to do, I must trust to your friendship to have the goodness of suggesting it to me.

There is another subject also I wish'd much to have mention'd to you & which I must for a few moments now tresspass upon you; it is respecting a wish of our friend Lord Moira's which he express'd to me just as he was leaving London, understanding that it was my intention to pay you a visit at Sion as soon as possible. On leaving London, as nearly as I can recollect, he stated to me that from his brother Mr. Rawdon's intentions of wholly residing abroad he had made a grateful surrender to your Grace of every expectation or wish that you should further distinguish him by a fresh proof of your friendship in conferring upon him a seat at the next General Election.[2] That considering the weight of obligation he owed to you, my dear Duke, for the very handsome [manner] in which you had been so good as to bring Mr. Rawdon into Parliament (subjecting him to no political restriction or condition) he felt himself restricted by gratitude & delicacy (at the moment he signified his brother's future resignation) from suggesting anything whatever respecting your Grace's parliamentary patronage at another General Election, but he acknowledged to me that could he have overruled these scruples it would have been the eager & nearest wish of his heart to have recommended McMahon to your notice & protection, & the sincere delight it would have conveyed to his mind should this recommendation have proved propitious by meeting with your Grace's approbation & sanction. With regard to myself, my dear Duke, I can only add that (next to communicating the wishes of my friend & in that testifying my sincere esteem & regard for Lord Moira) nothing could give me more pleasure than McMahon's meeting with your protection in this instance, & the more so as, being both a friend & servant of mine, both *he & I* should feel we owed his appointment *individually* to you.[3] I am ashamed at having

1. Prince Augustus sailed for Lisbon on 28 December, arriving there on 16 January 1801.

2. John Rawdon was M.P. for Launceston, one of the Duke's pocket boroughs, from 1796 to 1802, and he then went out of Parliament.

3. The Duke brought McMahon into Parliament in 1802, for Aldeburgh, which, however, was not one of his boroughs, and he (the Duke) had to pay for the seat. Moira's letter of 25 December to the Duke of Northumberland throws further light on the situaton:

'As Colonel McMahon was to accompany the Prince hither, I thought I might have from him an explanation of circumstances which were otherwise incomprehensible to me as stated in your letter. His information, however, leaves me just where I was; and you will feel that it

tresspassed, my dear Duke, so long upon you, I shall therefore conclude after expressing the warmest wishes for the continuation of your health with signing myself [etc.] (Alnwick MSS.).

1578 THE PRINCE OF WALES TO THE DUCHESS OF DEVONSHIRE

Grantham, 25 Dec. 1800

Nothing, my dearest Sister, can ever give me more true heartfelt pleasure than any circumstance which is the occasion of happiness to you. The affection of many years which I have uniformly cherish'd in my heart for you, makes me feel no common participation in the general joy your family & the numerous circle by which you are so beloved & adored might feel at dear G.'s projected marriage.[1] That she may be as happy as she truly

was difficult for me to address the Prince himself upon the subject. Let me entreat you, my dear Duke, to believe that I have infinitely too much confidence in your friendship ever to take a round-about way of making an application to you. Had I thought myself entitled to seek from you the favor of bringing McMahon or any other friend of mine into Parliament, I should have made the solicitation to you myself. That I did not conceive myself justifiable in trespassing upon your interest in such a manner is best proved by the very circumstance on which this whole business has been founded. A considerable time ago the Prince accidentally adverted to John Rawdon's never attending in the House. I replied that I had in vain remonstrated on the subject: but that I had availed myself of his wish to go abroad, & had made it a positive condition for my furnishing him with the means of making that excursion that he should not be re-elected for Launceston; because that I could not suffer your weight in the House to be diminished by the non-efficiency of my brother as one of your members. No other communication then took place. If my memory does not deceive, I had to your Grace expressed the same sentiment & had begged that you would not think of bringing in my brother again. That would have been the moment for recommending another person, had I felt it licit so to do; but I certainly had no such notion. The night before I last quitted London McMahon came to me & said it was in consequence of a conversation with the Prince. The latter had told him that he (the Prince) intended asking your Grace to bring in McMahon for Launceston as I had declared that John Rawdon must not again represent that Borough. McMahon feared that the Prince had made some mistake, & therefore wished to learn from my own mouth that my brother was out of the question. I explained to him what had passed, & that was all our discussion of the subject. Could I have recommended anybody to you, I know not anyone whom I should have proposed to you in preference to McMahon, for I have the fullest conviction that he would have a true sense of the obligation & would exert himself honorably to requite it in every way within his power. As the case stands, therefore your Grace will not find your kindness ill-applied: but it is not the less incumbent on me to satisfy you that I am not capable of endeavoring to procure from you a favor without asking it so distinctly as to profess at the same time all the obligation attached to it. As the thing is done, I am sincerely glad that you have met the Prince's wish in this respect; for I value McMahon very highly . . .' (Alnwick MSS.).

1. On 21 March 1801 Lady Georgiana Dorothy Cavendish (1783–1858), first daughter of the 5th Duke of Devonshire by Georgiana, married Viscount Morpeth (1773–1848), who succeeded his father in 1825 as 6th Earl of Carlisle.

deserves & as I wish her to be, is the fervent prayer of my heart. I cannot say more, & I think as you know me you will be satisfied that no one can form a more eager wish than myself that her future years may prove one continued & uninterrupted series of tranquil felicity.

As to you, my ever dearest sister, though you say nothing of yourself, still I am too well acquainted not to be well aware that in the midst of all the pleasure you must naturally feel at so pleasing & so charming a union for your sweet daughter, you will [?]¹ come across a pang at the reflection that you must occasionally see less of her now & then than you have been accustomed to do, & that though you will fight & struggle against that as much as possible, yet if you do not exert yourself much indeed, my fears are (& you must pardon my apprehensions as well as the liberty I now take in preaching a little from my real affection for you) that your health will suffer, and that if you are not infinitely careful you will bring on again nervous attacks; therefore pray for God's sake, & for our sakes, for the sakes of all those who tenderly love you, do not worry & flurry yourself too much at the present moment.

Now I have done with my little sermon which I trust will meet with forgiveness when you consider its motives. I will beg of you to express to dear G. from me everything that the warmest wishes of the heart, & such a heart too *as yours*, can suggest, & let me likewise implore of you to mention to my good friend the Duke how truly I share his happiness at this event, & that were I not afraid of being troublesome I would myself have written to him to have congratulated him. I have endeavoured to say everything that heart can dictate or pen express, and now adieu ever dearest, dearest sister; may every blessing in this world attend you & yours is the constant & never ceasing prayer of your affectionate brother.

[*P.S.*] Pray let me know whether this marriage will not call you up to town sooner than you at first intended, at any rate, when you are likely to be there, as I am dying to see you. God bless you. I was just going to write to you to congratulate you when the post brought me your kind letter. I had only learnt it yesterday & that by mere chance when hunting, from Tom Cholmley (Chatsworth MSS.).

1579 THE PRINCE OF WALES TO THE DOWAGER DUCHESS OF RUTLAND
Grantham, 28 Dec. 1800
My dearest Duchess, I cannot help trespassing upon your well known goodness to entreat of you to express to the Duke how sorry I am not to be able to come over to Belvoir today, having been much indispos'd

1. Blotted out.

179

yesterday & continuing far from well today. However, as I understand the hounds hunt at Barrowby tomorrow, I trust I shall be sufficiently stout to meet them at that cover as it lays so contiguous to this place, & afterwards to proceed to Belvoir. What I feel most is the disappointment of not enjoying so much of *your society* as I should have done by passing a day more in the house with *you*. You know me too well, my dearest friend, to make it necessary for me to add anything more, except how truly I am at all times & under all circumstances, ever your most sincere & attached friend.

[*P.S.*] Mrs. Fitz. unites with me in everything, my dearest Duchess, that is most kind to you (Belvoir MSS.).

1580   THE EARL OF MOIRA TO COLONEL MCMAHON
[*Donington*], *29 Dec. 1800*

The postillion has been dismissed, & amidst the reproaches of his comrades too. I have given notice that if anyone in Loughborough employs him, that person's rent shall be doubled next year, so that I think the rascal will have to lament his insolence. I deemed the example absolutely necessary. In truth, I fear it could not but have struck you that the respect testified by the crowd at Loughborough was produced by influence which overbore deeper feelings. It is lucky that the herd have always the innate propensity to follow the sentiment inspired into them by anyone to whom they look up, rather than pursue the bent of their own dispositions. At the same time, I am from my soul persuaded that the people there regarded the Prince with greater complacency than they would have done any other individual of the Royal Family; for he is personally popular in this county: but the dista[s]te is, as I explained to you when you were here, against the form of Government, to which the multitude now ascribe all the exactions & distresses they suffer. I see this notion gaining ground with a rapidity that bids fair to overwhelm very speedily all of us whose stations & interests bind us to the Crown.

Pray give James Tackle, my porter, fifteen pounds for me. (39709–10)

III   1801

The opening weeks of 1801 witnessed two crises: one, a change of Government; the other, the threatened change of Sovereign following the King's second severe attack of mental illness.

The Catholic question overturned the British Government as it had overturned the Irish six years earlier. Pitt was in no position to give a definite pledge to the Irish Catholics to introduce and carry a Catholic Relief Bill in return for their support of the Union: the Cabinet was divided on the question, and the King was apparently implacably hostile, Lord Loughborough, the Lord Chancellor, having convinced him that recognition of the Catholic claims would mean violating his Coronation Oath, though in 1795 Lord Kenyon, the Lord Chief Justice, and Sir John Scott, then Attorney-General, had advised him that the Test Act might be repealed without any breach of the Coronation Oath or of the Act of Union with Scotland. 'I know not who he is,' Dundas had written to Pitt, 'but I am positive there is somebody about him [the King] who does much mischief by agitating his mind and inflaming his prejudices on that topic. It always renders it more difficult to bring him to think calmly and soundly on that subject, but sooner or later he must make up his mind to the plainest of all political truths, that a country where a Parliament and a free Constitution is allowed to exist, never can submit to the practice of three-fourths of the country being sacrificed to the whims, prejudices or opinions of the other fourth.'

On 31 January Pitt warned the King that he should resign if he were not allowed to introduce a Relief Bill into Parliament with the whole weight of Government. Five days later the King reluctantly accepted his resignation and asked Addington, the popular Speaker of the House of Commons, to form a Government. All the Cabinet Ministers favourable to the Catholic cause resigned, and their retirement was followed by some of the junior Ministers', in spite of Pitt's entreaties that they should stay.

The formation of the new Ministry was delayed by the King's illness, resulting from the agitation and anxiety he had had to bear. His indisposition became marked on 21 February, and for several days his life was in danger. A Regency Bill again seemed a possibility, if not a demise of the Sovereign. At first sight it seems odd that no Regency Act had been passed after the severe warning of its necessity in 1788-9, though indeed Lord Malmesbury reported that the King himself had urged the introduction of a Bill which would prevent the country from again becoming involved in disputes and difficulties (and it is noteworthy that, in spite of Princess Victoria's youth, no Regency Bill was seriously thought of until the end of 1830, long after it had become clear that no male heir to George IV or the Duke of Clarence would be forthcoming). Pitt and Thurlow agreed as to the expediency of such a measure, but differed as to its provisions, and after Thurlow's dismissal in 1792 Pitt evidently gave it no more serious thought.

On 22 and 23 February the Prince of Wales commanded both Pitt and Addington to attend him. Pitt had resigned, but because of the King's illness he still held the seals of office, whilst Addington was merely Prime Minister designate. According to George Rose, Pitt replied to the Prince: 'Sir, being *de facto* in the situation of Minister I shall have no hesitation in giving your Royal Highness the best advice and opinions in my power. But there is one thing that I must be allowed very respectfully to state. I can do so only on the express condition that your Royal Highness will forbear to advise with those who have for a long time acted in direct opposition to his Majesty's Government.' Rose reported in his Diary, 'The Prince acquiesced as to the persons immediately alluded to by Mr. Pitt, but added, he should think himself at liberty to advise occasionally with Lord Moira, which he had long been in the habit of doing.'

At this interview Pitt was said to be 'more stiff and less accommodating than he should have been'. In view of his dislike of the Prince, that may well have been the case. Pitt saw him again on the 25th, and told him that, if the necessity arose, he meant to introduce a Regency Bill practically identical with that of 1789, and in this view he was supported even by the Portland Whigs who earlier had opposed him. Pitt remarked to the Prince, 'Everyone concerned, not excepting even your Royal Highness, cannot do better than accord with what was then most evidently the clear sense of the Legislature, expressed in a manner not to be mistaken.'

On the whole the Prince seemed reluctantly to acquiesce, but said that he needed time for consideration. Some people thought that he conducted himself, as in 1789, with little good taste; and others were of the opinion that nothing he said could be depended upon. Lord Malmesbury wrote on 17 February: 'His [the King's] eldest son goes about rejoicing at what has happened and may happen. I am glad mine does not take after him.' 'He has so effeminate a mind,' declared Malmesbury in another letter, 'as to counteract all his own good qualities by having no control over his weaknesses.' Mrs. Harcourt, whose views reflected those of the Court, said that the Prince's behaviour was very bad. She believed that he always went to see the King when he was certain the King was in no condition to receive him. He saw his father for the first time since the beginning of the illness, on 11 March. A fortnight later the Prince was at the Drawing Room, behaving very rudely to the Queen (said Malmesbury), who also referred to the dancing and singing at Carlton House, and to the Prince's evident unwillingness to believe that his father was recovering. Politically, however, he seems to have acted a more prudent part than in 1789, possibly because he had the uneasy feeling that his father might after all unfortunately recover, possibly too, because his Whig friends now thought it inexpedient to go to extreme lengths in opposing a restricted Regency. 'He gives a dinner tomorrow to the new proselyte Lords, Darnley and Cowper,' wrote Malmesbury on 11 February, 'and his language in the streets is such as would better become a member of Opposition than the heir to these Kingdoms.'

The Prince had no intention of restricting political communications to Lord Moira, and Sylvester Douglas remarked on 13 February that there were 'great flockings of minor politicians into Carlton House'. As early as 24 February the Prince was busy Cabinet making, although he seems never to have finally decided who should be Prime Minister. Everyone would have been astonished if he had sent for Pitt; some (Canning amongst them) believed that Addington would be chosen. The Prince saw Addington repeatedly, and Charles Abbot reported that he always behaved to him 'with the greatest civility and propriety'. According to Charles Pybus, Addington declared, 'Nothing . . . can possibly be worse. He goes about telling everybody that his father's complaint is only a return of his former madness, which is now completely fixed.' Why should not his old friend Fox have been his choice? The answer, in part at any rate, is that he was afraid of a quarrel with Mrs. Fitzherbert, whose temper could be uncertain, and who had never forgiven Fox for his public denial of the marriage ceremony. Moreover, Fox could hardly be said to be the leader of a united Whig party. He had recently written: 'The old party is too much routed and dispersed to be rallied again,' and when, a few weeks later, a Regency again became a possibility, he was still of the opinion that he could do no good. 'I do not

183

mean to attend Parliament,' he wrote on 20 February, 'but if they think my continuing a Member, while I do not attend, is any way very hurtful . . . I will lose no time in getting out of it.' Disillusioned and dispirited, then, he seemed to have lost all ambition. Grey, too, his chief lieutenant in the Commons, said that he himself had no wish for office, and expressed the hope that a Whig Ministry would not need to be formed.

On 24 February the Prince sent a message to the Duke of Norfolk offering him the Viceroyalty of Ireland, and with full power to countenance a Catholic Relief Bill. Five days later Moira informed the Duke of Devonshire that the Prince intended to offer him any office that he chose to accept. The Prince communicated, too, with Fox, the Marquess of Buckingham, Lord Carlisle, Sheridan, the Duke of Northumberland and Lord Spencer, and it was believed that he was constantly consulting Mrs. Fitzherbert. Lord Carlisle gave him excellent advice, urging him to abandon the dangerous ground of Right, to accept whatever restrictions on his power as Prince Regent Parliament might wish to impose, and to make a strong Administration. It was with great satisfaction that Pitt and Dundas heard of this, and that the Prince had 'shut his door against the suggestions of cabal and political intrigue'. The Duchess of Devonshire believed on 24 February that the Prince was avoiding her until he had made up his mind about the new Prime Minister (he alleged that he was not stirring out from a sense of propriety), and she was confident that Jack Payne and Mrs. Fitzherbert were plotting against Fox.

The Duke of York had long since steered himself clear of the excessive influence which his brother had exercised over him, and his conduct was very different from that of 1788–9. Malmesbury remarked that the Duke 'remains firm to the King, and is as discreet in his language as proper in his conduct'. Some days later Malmesbury wrote: 'Duke of York's behaviour incomparable. He is their great and only comfort at the Queen's House, and without his manly mind and advice neither the Queen nor Princesses would be able to bear up under their present distress.' The Royal family certainly derived little comfort or consolation from the Prince. The Dukes of Clarence and Kent were believed to side with him, the Duke of Cumberland with the Duke of York. The Duke of Clarence was reported to have remarked to Lord Cholmondeley, 'Well, we shall have it all our own way now. He is not only mad, but dying, and I know my brother intends to give you a White Stick.' The Earl is said to have replied, 'Sir, I confess to you that my earnest wish is that it may yet be very long before the Prince shall have such affairs to dispose of, but when he has I can assure your Highness that having known what it is to be a servant, I am determined never to find myself in that situation again.'

Sure in any case of the support of the Old Whigs, the Prince proceeded with his plan to form a Ministry after his own heart. The Foreign

Secretaryship at first presented a problem. Believing that Shelburne (the Marquess of Lansdowne since 1784) was hostile on account of his support of Pitt's Regency Bill in 1789, the Prince asked Moira to ascertain his views. Lansdowne afterwards wrote: 'Lord Moira said that he had some time since had the Prince's directions to consider of two lines of administration; one, an eventual one in case of the King's illness being a short one, the other in case of its being permanent; that in the latter case there was no situation which the Prince would not consider to be at my choice, no competitor, of course after the Treasury. I told him I had none in view, though I wished the country saved, which could only be by settling the Government in the first instance, and by peace in the second . . . He said that the Treasury was at his option long before Mr. Addington was thought of. He said that *the six* mentioned by Mr. Grey would command in his opinion the public confidence, and Lord Thurlow was determined if he had a leg to stand upon to come forth. He talked of the Duke of Northumberland, Lord Bute and the country gentlemen; of Fox as wanting to come in for a short time to save appearances, and to go out again; that he had brought the country gentlemen at last to endure him; of Lord Fitzwilliam as *possibly* to go to Ireland; of a reform of Parliament, not disapproving it altogether, but not cordially; of peace eagerly; of economy, but not enthusiastically; that Lord Buckingham had applied to him repeatedly about stirring the question of the King's competency . . . The Queen might be gained; the Duke of York not, who had differences with Pitt about Hanover, which was the subject of two or three conversations with the King, in which Pitt proposed its being given up for British objects; that Pitt he had reason to think set out in concert with Addington. Fox was ill with Pitt, but likely to be well with the King if he recovered.'

As in the summer of 1812 when Wellesley was busy Cabinet making, various Cabinet arrangements were put on paper, but the one which seemed to meet with general approval was as follows: First Lord of the Treasury, Moira; Chancellor of the Exchequer, Sheridan; Foreign Secretary, Lansdowne; Home Secretary, Fox; President of the Council, the Duke of Grafton; Lord Privy Seal, the Duke of Bedford; First Lord of the Admiralty, Lord Wycombe (Lord Lansdowne's reprobate son and heir); Lord Chancellor, Lord Thurlow; President of the Board of Trade, Lord Hawkesbury; Secretary at War, Grey.

But these suggestions were soon nullified by the King's recovery. Towards the end of April he had a relapse, but was much better again in May, and in the summer Prince Adolphus thought he was looking as well as ever. As early as March, whilst the King was convalescing, Pitt authorized Dr. T. Willis to inform the King that he would never again agitate the Catholic question during the reign. 'Now my mind will be at ease,' the King is reported to have replied.

Many years later, the Duke of Cumberland, who fully shared his father's prejudices against the Catholics, claimed to have been instrumental in making the anti-Catholic Addington First Lord of the Treasury. He alleged that the King entrusted him with the task of conveying to Mr. Speaker his proposals for a new Ministry, but there is no mention of these activities in Pellew's *Life* of Lord Sidmouth nor in the correspondence in the Royal Archives; and in the absence so far of corroborative evidence the story must be dismissed as untrustworthy. 'I was the person whom the King employed to make the first overture,' the Duke claimed. What is certain is that he was allowed to see the King whilst he was ill, and that the Prince, who was not (until 11 March, and even then Dr. Thomas Willis remained with the King as a precautionary measure) resented this prolonged exclusion, and quarrelled with his brother. On 16 March the Duchess of Devonshire wrote: 'The Prince expressed his disgust to me at the Duke of Cumberland's conduct, who had broke thro' with him during the King's illness, and sided with the Duke of York.' She added, 'The Prince seemed also discontented with Pitt, who he thought might have acted more fairly and openly by him.'

Sir John Sinclair, M.P. for Petersfield, said, later, that the real strength of the Carlton House party, of which Moira was the head, was not yet revealed, because the Prince would not then take an active part in politics. But, in his view, the Addington Government soon needed additional support, and he suggested to Charles Bragge, Addington's brother-in-law, that Moira should be invited to take office. His military experience and his friendship with the Prince would enable him to add much to the strength and stability of the Administration. Moira seemed to favour the project, and wrote to Sinclair on 2 December: 'There could not be, *in limine*, any objection to such a junction as you indicate. Ulterior points would probably be difficult to settle. The opening which you exhibit for communication has been anticipated by a discussion of the Premier's situation, which took place long since, and, I trust, something has been matured for extricating his Royal Highness from a position intended to lower him in the estimation of the country. Thank Heaven it has had the very contrary effect, but he has suffered under it in his personal feelings too long.'

The new Government's main task was to negotiate peace with France, and the Preliminary Articles were signed in London on 1 October. The terms were far below what were needed for Britain's security, but no better could then have been obtained, and they were approved not only by the Foxite Whigs but by Pitt. On the other hand they were severely criticized by Windham and Lord Grenville and their friends who now formed the 'New' Opposition. The conclusion of peace was calculated to facilitate Addington's negotiations with some of the Whigs for an alliance, and in November Tierney had two long talks with him. Addington would have surrendered much of his power had he made overtures to the Whig party as a whole and to the Carlton House group; and his plan was merely to take in a few individuals. He was prepared to remove Lord Dartmouth from the Board of Control, and Lord Glenbervie and Steele from the Joint Paymasterships. Tierney, who had quarrelled with Fox and had ceased to have any political connection with him, refused the Mastership of the Mint on the ground that it was a sinecure, looked upon in public estimation only 'as a source of great and unmerited emolument to the person who can bargain to get it. To have held such a situation', he said, 'would be to mortify myself and by lowering my character, to render me of less value to those I wish to serve.' (This, of course, is precisely what he did in 1827 when he joined Canning's Ministry in that capacity.) Moira should succeed Dartmouth and be given the Board of Control as a Cabinet office. Thurlow was to be taken into the Cabinet as Moira's 'friend'—without portfolio so long as the Duke of Portland remained President of the Council, and to succeed to that office when the Duke could be ejected. In due course Thurlow could probably be induced to give up his seat in the Cabinet in order to make room for the Duke of Bedford, and it was thought that there would be little difficulty in finding a place at the same time for Grey. The Whig lawyer Erskine was to be appointed Chief Justice of the Common Pleas 'within a reasonable period of time'. 'A Whig Chief Justice', said Tierney, 'is a *rara avis*, and his appointment will be viewed as the surest pledge that the system of the last Administration is to be abandoned.' Tierney himself was to be sole Paymaster, with a salary of £3,000 and a house.

In December the negotiations practically broke down. As in 1797 Moira was not prepared to sit in the same Cabinet with the Duke of Portland, and, no doubt, he found quite unacceptable Tierney's absurd suggestion that though he should be appointed to an office that was to be of Cabinet rank, he should not take his seat in the Cabinet until the Duke had been removed. Moreover, Moira considered the India Board as an office much below his pretensions. Grey rejected the offer that was made to him by Lord St. Vincent, with Addington's authorization. He would have been happy only if his party as a whole had been invited to coalesce with Addington. 'What I want', he told Tierney, 'is a real security for myself, and a certain indication to the public that the Government is to be conducted on different principles from those which have prevailed of late years. This can only be had in one of two ways. Either by the adoption of some great and leading measures which would speak for themselves; or by the admission into the Administration of such a number and description of persons on our side as, combined with the removal of those whose conduct has been the most obnoxious on the other, would give us a sufficient influence over the general measures of Government, and afford an unequivocal proof of a change of system. To this I have no reason to think that Addington is disposed ... But if disposed, do I believe that he would be allowed by the Court to consent to such an arrangement? ... He is completely dependent on the Court ... All his power extends to do no more than is agreeable in that quarter.' Grey heard from Tierney that the Duke of Cumberland knew all about these negotiations and approved of what had been done. But he was not impressed. 'After all, it only comes to this, that the Court is very ready to buy us.' The Prince too must have heard of what was going on, but few of his letters written during these months have survived.

1581 THE QUEEN TO THE PRINCE OF WALES
1 Jan. 1801
I am at a loss where to find you, but whether far or near I will at least prove that you, my dear, are not out of my mind. With many good wishes upon the season I send a little remembrance; the one just imported from abroad & look'd upon by connoisseurs as well executed, the other an humble seal which marks the hour when it is used. This is the emblem of my heart where you are never forgot & ever remembered with affection by [etc.].[1] (36522)

1. On 1 January the Prince attended a meeting of the Privy Council at St. James's. Its members had to be re-sworn and to pay again the customary fees, the Privy Council of Great Britain having that day become the Privy Council of the United Kingdom. The Prince's account was later endorsed 'Not paid':

NOTE of fees on his Royal Highness the Prince of Wales taking his place at the Council Board, in his Majesty's Privy Council for the United Kingdom of Great Britain and Ireland, on the first of January, 1801.

	£	s.	d.
The Clerks of the Council	20	0	0
The Under Clerks	8	0	0
The Under Record Keeper	12	0	0
The Council Chamber Keepers	10	0	0
The Under Keeper	2	0	0
The Messenger, and his Deputy, who summon the Councils	3	3	0
The Serjeant Trumpet	4	4	0
	£59	7	0

(39713)

THE EARL OF ABERDEEN TO MRS. FITZHERBERT

Ellon Castle, 3 Jan. 1801

I have the honour of your letter of the 27th ulto. and I assure you it has given me great uneasiness that everything regarding the sale of my house in Tilney Street should have been attended with so many delays; which has no doubt been inconvenient for you, which I regret: all which would have been prevented had my health permitted me to come to town as I intended.[1]

In my answer to the first letter his Royal Highness the Prince did me the honour to write me, I mentioned that whatever the Prince and you thought the house was worth, I would agree to, as I did not intend immediately to have disposed of the house if it had not been for your accommodation: and I now readily agree to dispose of the house to you for the six thousand pounds sterg. you offer, although I am told it is worth more; and I have written so to my man of business at London.

I certainly will come to town in the spring if my health permit me to do so, and will pay my duty to his Royal Highness the Prince to return him thanks for the honour of his condescending letters.

I should have been at London more than a year ago if it had not been that I thought myself badly used by Administration in being refused being made Lord Lieutenant of this county & a British peerage, both of which I thought myself equally entitled to with many others that had had those honours conferred on them.[2] (39714)

THE PRINCE OF WALES TO THE DUKE OF YORK, AND THE REPLY

Carlton House, 6 Jan. 1801

I hope you will forgive me for troubling you with these few lines, but as I have the object much at heart that I now shall mention to you, though it

---

1. On 16 December *The Times* announced that Mrs. Fitzherbert had taken Lord Aberdeen's house at the corner of Tilney Street, in Park Lane.

2. He died on 13 August at Ellon Castle, Aberdeenshire. His claims to a G.B. or U.K. peerage were not very convincing. As a Representative Peer in the 1784–90 Parliament he had opposed Pitt's Regency Bill. As long ago as 23 October 1786 he had written to Lord Hawkesbury: 'The week after I had the honour of waiting on your Lordship at Addiscombe Place I had the honour of a[n] audience of the King, and most humbly requested his Majesty will be graciously pleased to confer the honour of a British peerage on me. His Majesty was very gracious and was pleased to say he certainly would consider of my request. As it was with Mr. Pitt's consent I asked a[n] audience of the King, I have acquainted him of my request and his Majesty's gracious answer, and begged Mr. Pitt would take me under his protection on this occasion and I should make no doubt of success. If your Lordship is pleased to interest yourself in my favour this would pay [*sic*] me under the strongest ties of gratitude to your Lordship, which myself and family will be happy in shewing on all occasions.'

does not concern myself personally, I lose not a moment in suggesting it to you. May not the occasion of our poor friend Goldsworthy's death afford you the opportunity of doing a very handsome thing by bringing in Ernest for a Regiment of Lt. Dns. which different removals may admit of. If so, for God's sake do it. (44166)

THE DUKE'S REPLY
Horse Guards, 7 Jan. 1801
It was not till late yesterday evening that I received your letter suggesting that the death of our poor friend Goldsworthy might by some arrangement or other afford an opportunity of procuring a Regiment of Lt. Dragoons for Ernest. I trust that you are thoroughly convinced how happy I should be to further any views, either of yours or of Ernest's, as far as it is in my power, & I certainly will not fail to endeavour to assist him in this instance, tho' with what success I cannot in the least pretend to say.[1] (44167)

1584   THE EARL OF MOIRA TO COLONEL MCMAHON
Donington, 9 Jan. 1801
Mr. Chancellor of the Exchequer,
There is an enormous budget to discuss: but, as the Committee of Ways & Means has been sedulously employed upon it, I hope I shall not put you to much trouble in the arrangement of the matter which I am to commit to your friendly care. A bill of £2000 drawn by Atkinson on me is payable at Ransom & Morland's on the *15th* (Thursday). Jones is employed to procure & deliver to you that sum by the *14th* (Wednesday); & Jeffereys (the silversmith in Pall Mall) is likewise occupied in raising to that amount, with instructions to pay it to you. Now, lest they should only partially succeed, I hold it requisite to send to you a bill on Atkinson & Woodward, dated on the 12th for £1000; with a correspondent draft on Nesbitt & Stewart. This I wish should not be employed without necessity; so that you must on the 13th inform yourself if my two commissioners (neither of whom should know that the other is employed) will on the morrow make out the sum between them for you. In case of deficiency, then you must carry the bill to Nesbitt & Stewart, & ask Coutts

1. General Goldsworthy died on 4 January at his seat at Wilton, Wilts. He was succeeded as Colonel of the 1st Dragoon Guards by General Thomas Garth. The Duke of Cumberland was appointed Colonel of the 15th Light Dragoons, *vice* General Lord Dorchester, on 18 March. See No. 1609.

190

to discount the accepted draft. On the 14th tell Morland you are charged to take up the bill of £2000 for me.

The £605 due to Campbell is payable at Hammersley's on the 14th according to my memorandum, but on the 15th according to yours. The sum had better be lodged with them three or four days before. I have corresponded with Campbell about the others that become due within the present month. The two of £300 each & the £900 to Moore will be renewed. Then there is no pressure on Campbell's account till the 11th February, for which period I will [make] careful & early provision lest there should be any further delay from Hamburgh.

Now for a minor commission for you. A buggy is an indispensible vehicle at this place for carrying folks down to the bridges to meet the mail coach. Six years ago I bought a second-hand one for £15. It did the State some service; for it has been in unceasing employment ever since. As nothing, however, is permanent in this world, it yielded yesterday to the weight of the Duc de Lorge & his son, & literally fell to pieces. Do make some idle fellow look out for a good strong one for me. It must be quite unfashionable, because it must have a top & an apron, & must be capable of carrying a trunk. It should be dispatched immediately by Pickford's waggon; for we shall daily be sensible of the inconvenience of not having it. The little mare arrived safe excepting a slight appearance of humor in one heel, apparently from some knock on the road, for which she has had a diuretic ball. The Loughborough Volunteers gave me a grand dinner the other day. I had heard that they were a little disappointed at the Prince's not having looked at them, so I took the opportunity of setting that matter to rights & told them his Royal Highness had commissioned me to express that he was sorry the crowd had (as they witnessed) made it impossible for him to speak to them & thank them for their attention. This compliment was received with wonderful applause.

I am sorry to tell you that his Royal Highness's pointer dog is dead. It was seized with the distemper the day after its arrival here, & had the obstinacy to die notwithstanding that Foss' body-physician pledged him for the recovery. It is a pity, for I believe it was an uncommonly good one. I have had the bitch out. She has no appearance; but I never saw anything superior in performance. As to the Club, I must beg of you to make my excuses for not accepting the honour of being one of the managers. As I never could attend to the business I should think it wrong to undertake the office. At the same time pray express that I am only too sensible to the compliment. (39715–7)

1585 THE PRINCE OF WALES TO THE QUEEN, AND THE REPLY
Carlton House, 18 Jan. 1801

I should not most certainly have omitted paying my duty to you today, but you well know how unlucky I am sometimes & that is just my case at the present moment as I was seiz'd last night with a violent inflammatory attack upon my lungs, & which has made Farquhar shut me up today, in hopes that I shall be able to make my bow tomorrow at St. James's, which I would not miss upon any account especially as I was not there the last eighteenth of January.[1] I have taken the liberty of accompanying this note with a little cadeau, which I trust you will not dislike when you see it as the subject it is meant to celebrate, is the topic of the day in the mouth of everyone. With every possible feeling of duty & affection, I subscribe myself [etc.]. (42334)

THE QUEEN'S REPLY

18 Jan. 1801

Never was poor mortal so harrassed as I have been this morning, going from one hand into another till this moment, which I looked upon as particularly unpleasant, being deprived by that means of returning you thanks for the beautifull present you sent me. I do not know which most to admire, the taste or the execution of the fan, but difficult as that is, I feel not less your kind attention to me, of which I at all times am truely sensible.

I am sorry that you are again confined & approve much of what Farquhar has done; I beg you will not think of comming tomorrow morning, nor even to Court if the day is not fine, for I will rather be deprived, tho' with regret, of your company than see you run any risk for my sake, & with these sentiments I beg you to believe me unalterably [etc.]. (36523)

1586 THE EARL OF MOIRA TO COLONEL MCMAHON
Donington, 19 Jan. 1801

Your wish for a detail of the circumstances which preceded the defeat of Gates[2] at Camden shall be gratified as far as my recollection will serve. You tell me that it is not by yourself the information is sought. I must,

1. The Queen's birthday was officially celebrated this year on 19 January.

2. Horatio Gates (1728–1806). Served under Prince Ferdinand of Brunswick and in North America during the Seven Years War. Entered the service of the Americans on the outbreak of the War of the American Revolution; defeated Burgoyne at Saratoga, 1777; was defeated at Camden in South Carolina, 1780.

therefore, express my hope that there is no intention of impeaching the just credit which has always been given to Lord Cornwallis for that battle, altho' I am not to disguise that, when I saw his public letter, I did not think myself equitably treated in his recital of the event. I was simply classed with Colonel Webster as having done my duty in the action with proper exertion at the head of the wing which I commanded: whereas I think it will appear to you that I stood upon very different ground, both as to particulars of earlier date which led to that battle & as to special services in the very decision. I have not Stedman's History,[1] but I take it for granted his dates must be correct. Tarleton's[2] narrative[3] is here. He has so strangely disjoined facts which bore important relation to each other, & has so singularly miscomprehended points with which he ought naturally to have been acquainted, that his exposition of the chain of events is as incorrect as his specific accounts of many of the actions. I could, therefore, little aid my memory by recurrence to that book.

Having been left in the command of the back country when Ld. Cornwallis went to Charlestown, I had (by my spies) kept a vigilant eye over the force which was collecting in North Carolina for the invasion of our newly acquired territory. Tho' Ld. Cornwallis had not thought it probable that the attack would be made upon South Carolina till the violent heat of the summer should be passed, I had suspected that Gates might calculate on our inability to stand the climate (especially as it was known that we were very sickly) & might then make a speedier effort. I had on that account minutely examined the country & formed my eventual plans. Camden had from the first day appeared to me an objectionable station for the army. It was a false position relative to the country, & in itself indefensible beyond any ground that I ever saw. On learning that a body of the enemy's militia had advanced to the Pedee, I considered it a sure indication that Gates would move immediately. I therefore detached Webster, a good & gallant officer, to the east branch of Lynche's Creek, & I reinforced a post which I had at Hanging Rock. As soon as I had made the necessary arrangements at Camden, I followed Webster. Of distances, I must speak loosely. I suppose the point where the road crosses the east branch of Lynche's Creek to be thirty miles from Camden; the post at Hanging Rock, thirty-five. There was a ready communication between the two by a road of about twelve miles. My object in taking this

1. Charles Stedman (1753–1812), author of the *History of the Origin, Progress and Termination of the American War* (1794). Born at Philadelphia, but served with the British under Sir William Howe.

2. General Sir Banastre Tarleton (1754–1833). Served under Clinton and Cornwallis in America. Colonel, 1790; Major-General, 1794; Lieutenant-General, 1801; General, 1812; created Baronet, 23 January 1817; G.C.B., 1820. M.P. for Liverpool, 1790–1806, 1807–12.

3. *A History of the Campaigns of 1780 and 1781, in the Southern Provinces of North America* (London, 1787).

forward position was to retard the progress of Gates' till Ld. Cornwallis should collect force from other parts of the Province, or to reduce the enemy to hazard an action where my peculiar advantages of situation would compensate for my disparity in numbers. I had 1100 men with me, all regulars or provincials; the detachment at Hanging Rock consisted of 400 provincials & 800 militia. The latter was a requisite post, because Sumpter menaced that road to Camden with a corps of militia. Gates came opposite to me. Aware of the danger of attempting to force the pass & of the difficulties that would be entailed by seeking another route, he apparently waited the issue of an enterprize that was meditated against Hanging Rock. One evening, news was brought to me that Sumpter had surprised & carried that post; & the account of the defeat of that detachment was soon confirmed by a number of fugitives from every corps composing it, except from the Legion infantry. It appeared a clear consequence that Sumpter, whose men were all mounted, would lose no time in pushing for Camden, by which, in addition to the loss of our magazines, I should have had him on my rear whilst Gates pressed my front. I addressed the Officers around me, who seemed struck with the obvious magnitude of the evil. I told them, in the hearing of the soldiers, that we were in a scrape from which nothing but courage could extricate us, & that we must march instantly to crush Sumpter before he could further co-operate with Gates. We marched in less than half an hour; and crossed the west branch of Lynche's Creek, directing our course to Granny's Quarter. In the morning, I received the information that the fate of the day had been most unexpectedly turned at Hanging Rock: Sumpter, after beating everything else out of the field, had assaulted the Legion infantry in a peculiarly steep part of that strong position, and his militia had not merely been repulsed but were so broken & dismayed by a vigorous charge with the bayonet that they had abandoned the whole ridge. That position was, therefore, still ours. I immediately hastened to occupy the bridge across the western branch of Lynche's Creek. Having sent my cavalry across it, they speedily saw the enemy's dragoons, by which I found that Gates had followed me. In the afternoon, I learned that he was encamped on the other side of the Creek. The communication from my new position to Hanging Rock was much longer than it had been from my former one; & the detachment, weakened & (except the Legion infantry) depressed, was a doubtful barrier against the future attempts of Sumpter. I therefore ordered those troops to fall back & take post behind Granny's Quarter Creek; because, altho' there was no strength of ground there as there was at Hanging Rock, I could in that situation give them ready support. You will see in this the same principle of protracting the advance of Gates untill our cavalry from Charlestown & our Light Infantry from Ninety-six should arrive. Had I repassed the western branch of Lynche's Creek to encounter Gates, I must have met him in a pine-barren even more advantageous for his superiority of numbers than a plain could have been. He had nearly four times as many men as I had with me. Had I concentrated my force at Camden, I must have stood an action before the arrival of the re-inforcements, in a position that would give every imaginable advantage to the assailant, with the certainty that the mischief of a check was irre-trievable, as there would be no space for rallying & the first success of the enemy put them in possession of our stores. Tarleton, with a childish pretension to Generalship, censures me for not having thus collected my troops at Camden, & arraigns Gates for incapacity in not comprehending that the getting round me & destroying my magazines must be fatal. Tarleton, commanding for so long a period our only corps of light troops in that country, ought to have known that which it is evident by his procedure Gates did know, namely, that there was no turning my right flank without going fifty miles down Lynche's Creek, there was no turning my left by a shorter process than heading the Creek & getting into the other road above Hanging Rock. Lynche's Creek runs thro' swamps of perhaps a mile in breadth on each side; impenetrable, except where a causeway has been made at the passing-places on the great road. The thick woods of those swamps prevented us from seeing each other's encampments across the Creek. In my second position, Gates had a post at the outlet of this causeway on his side, but he appeared never to have discovered a pass which came out about two miles from his camp, com-municating with a ford on the Creek, from which there was a path into the causeway in my front. By this track I used to send out & receive my spies. The circumstance afforded a great temptation for an attempt to surprise the enemy's camp, and when you recollect that I was then young, not backward in enterprize, & confident in my troops, you may be of opinion there was some honesty in the forbearance. I could have assigned reasons such as everyone must have been obliged to take upon trust from me to prove the expediency of the hazard; but it would, in truth, have been an unfit stake of the public interest. I might have been discovered so as that Gates might have had time to form his army, & in that case I should have to fight under signal disadvantage. On the other hand, I was well apprized that Gates's army was suffering severe dis-tress from being detained in that desart. But there was one consideration which would alone have been decisive with me: I mean that Ld. Corn-wallis was then on his way to join us; and had I atchieved a victory it must have been tarnished by the consciousness that I had availed myself of my temporary command to snatch a palm which ought to have been reserved for my General. To seduce Gates, however, into ruinous error was licit. I retired a mile from the outlet of my causeway in order to tempt him to pass the Creek; when I might have attacked him where branches of the swamp would have hindered him from profiting by his numbers: but he was too wise to make the attempt. At length, he could no longer delay a decision. If, by a march of fifty miles he crossed Lynche's Creek below me, he would still have to make his way towards Camden thro' a succession of defiles in the swamps where the Black River has its source, with almost a certainty that I should meet him there. He therefore determined to march to Hanging Rock; at which point he would be thirty-five miles from Camden, whereas in his present position he was but fifteen. My view of gaining time, of course, had succeeded. As soon as I had assured myself that this was not a feint, I broke up the bridge & causeways: and I retired to Camden, whither I summoned the troops from Granny's Quarter Creek. The motive for this was a conviction that matters must now be decided between that Creek & Camden. The banks of the Creek were not defensible; and the pine barren between it & Hanging Rock was the sort of extensive waste which we were always to shun. Ld. Cornwallis arrived, as did also the reinforcements. Having informed himself from me of the preceding movements, he asked me what had been my further purpose. I told him that, as nothing appeared to me so ineligible as receiving the enemy at Camden, I had intended to wait till my spies should apprize me of Gates's being approached within an easy march, when I meant to move forward & attack him. Ld. Cornwallis entered at once into the reasoning, adopted my plan, & reposed himself for its prosecution on the measures I had taken to secure information. In the meantime, he made all the arrangements which he judged expedient. It was I who brought to him the intelligence that Gates had arrived at Kingsley's Plantation. With a pencil I sketched for him the ground, with which I was well acquainted, indicating the position of the enemy, as I understood it by the relation of the spies, & pointing out a path from the main road by which we might possibly get undiscovered on the enemy's flank. On these data the attempt against the enemy was determined. We marched at night. At two in the morning the leading battalion, in the rear of which I was, was charged by cavalry. Their pieces being loaded, our infantry shrunk to the right & left into the bushes, thrusting at the cavalry with their bayonets. The cavalry retreated precipitately & we thought it had been only a strong patrole. When the confusion was over we resumed our march: but we soon had a heavy fire poured upon us, apparently from two battalions. A Brigade of ours immediately formed, advanced in line, & soon exchanged fire with the enemy. The latter were broken & fell back. When we came to where their dead lay, I got off my horse to feel by the uniforms if they were the Continental Infantry which I suspected them to be by the nature of their fire. I was immediately satisfied on the point. I told Ld. Cornwallis of it, saying that it certainly was the enemy's army which we had met, and I then told his Lordship that he could not have better ground to fight upon, as it was a sort of neck between two swamps which would prevent

196

the enemy from getting round his flanks. On this assurance, it being quite dark, he determined to rest till morning & then to attack the enemy. In the battle which ensued, I behaved neither better or worse than my neighbors: therefore Lord Cornwallis's mention of me in common with Webster was the fair compliment paid as a matter of course to officers of rank after a successful action; and, as far as referred to the hour of battle alone, was all that any justice could require towards me. But the preliminary events had not been unimportant, nor had the management been such, I venture to affirm, as had no claim upon Lord Cornwallis's special acknowledgement either as an officer or as a man. Lord Cornwallis had the real merit of cool decision, judicious arrangement, & steady firmness in the conduct of the action. Tho' the thickness of the fog in the morning left him to rely as much upon my representation of the nature of the ground as he had been obliged to do during the night, his claim to all the credit of the victory cannot thence be weakened: for it is a part of the skill of the General to avail himself of the lights that he may gather from any inferior officer; & the latter cannot have a pretension to share in the fame from having merely possessed an accidental piece of knowledge which might have remained unprofitable but for the judgement of the Commander. This is clearly the principle on which such a case should be determined by others. With regard to the impression left upon my mind by that chain of events, I should be disingenuous did I not avow that the final result furnished as much of that confidence which one draws from one's own successful experience as if the conclusion had been solely mine. The plan pursued without wavering, tho' with infinite anxiety, for so many days, had completely answered the end proposed & had brought the matter to an issue on more favorable terms than any lesser degree of perseverance could have fashioned; an issue which, as it had been the distinct object of my preceding movements & was prosecuted exactly according to the line which I had laid down, I have ventured to believe would not have had any different termination had the function of ordering the attack fallen to my share.

Now, my dear Colonel, in return for having given me the labor of travelling over an obsolete tale which can no longer be interesting to anyone upon ordinary grounds, let me claim from you that you shall not suffer a copy to be taken of the account. Remember that I have had the mortification of seeing one letter in print which had been intended only for a sort of confidential communication.[1] I have entered into this detail to satisfy your request: take care that I be not subjected to the disgrace of seeming to call attention to services so long gone bye & which the great scale of action in later years would make appear of miserable exiguity. (39718–27)

1. No. 1270 (15 June 1797).

1587   THE PRINCE OF WALES TO THE DUKE OF YORK

Carlton House, 20 Jan. 1801

Having heard this morning of the death of old Devaynes,[1] & knowing how ready you are to oblige me, I cannot help troubling you with this short letter to request you will appoint Mr. Nussey[2] of St. James's Street, my apothecary, to the situation which Mr. Devaynes filled. I should be very ungrateful to Mr. Nussey if I did not express to you how extremely interested I am in his obtaining this appointment, as his unremitted attention & attendance upon me for a long series of time render him worthy of anything I could do for him. (44168)

1588   THOMAS TYRWHITT TO THE COUNTESS OF JERSEY[3]

Welbeck Street, 6 p.m., 28 Jan. [*1801*]

I have just written to the Prince[4] what I trust will be thought consolatory, as Graham has given a most excellent opinion on the other side, & in which I believe he will be supported by Gruff, but he did not come to

1. John Devaynes (?1725–1801), apothecary to the King (salary, £320 a year), died on 16 January in Spring Gardens, Charing Cross. His wife predeceased him (1795) and he left no children. He bequeathed £50,000 to his brother William (*c.* 1730–1809), then M.P. for Winchelsea and a former Chairman of the East India Company; and £400 a year to the Marchioness Townshend, 'his great patroness'.

2. Nussey, the Prince's apothecary, was not appointed to succeed Devaynes, nor did he remain in the Prince's service.

3. Why this letter, which refers to the Prince's claim to the arrears of the revenues of the Duchy of Cornwall, should have been addressed to Lady Jersey is not very obvious. By this time she had practically faded out of the Prince's life, and Farington wrote on 6 July 1803: 'Lady Jersey is now quite out of favour with the Prince of Wales. She told Hoppner that she met the Prince upon the stairs at the Opera House and in such a situation as to render it necessary to make room for him to pass, which, not instantly noticing him, she did not do, as she wished, which caused her after he had passed to say a few words of apology. He went forward and the next day Col. McMahon called upon her to signify to her 'that it was the desire of the Prince that *she would not speak to him*'. She spoke bitterly of McMahon for having submitted to carry such a message' (Diary).

4. The following may be the letter referred to. It is dated merely 'Carlton House, 3 p.m.':
'Gruff [Lord Thurlow] desired me to attend him home. The instant he entered the library, "I see his Highness's handwriting; let us see". After having read not through the first page entirely, he exclaimed, "*A damned deal too much reasoning to deliberate upon at the instant; he shall keep* for my Cabinet by & by", & put the letter in his pocket. The conversation, short as it was, was interesting as he seemed to doubt on which side the popularity or unpopularity of the two Bills lay. With the letter of your Royal Highness's lay another, written in a disguised hand & anonymous, but recommending him in the strongest manner possible to have an Audience of the King. The letter begun [*sic*], "If I forget him, may God forget me!". He seemed, however, to think the King would be displeased with him, should he venture to intrude upon him. He complained of being very unwell & low.' (39751)

198

town as he promised, so I cannot say any thing decisive about him. G. maintains & proves what he says (at least I think so), that in very many old records the word *heirs* must mean *successors*, or mean nothing at all, but that if it should not, he advises setting out in the petition that Frederick Prince of Wales, &c., &c. did enjoy the Duchy &c. & no man can make Frederick a bit more the *heir* of the Black Prince than the present. In short, he seems to think there will be *no risk at all* in proceeding; if Gruff says so I think the P. will, as at all events somehow or another a certain great gentleman[1] ought & *must* refund.[2] (39728-9)

1589 THE EARL OF BUTE TO THE PRINCE OF WALES
South Audley Street, 19 Feb. 1801
In obedience to your Royal Highnesses commands I return the papers with which your Royal Highness was graciously pleased to entrust me. Happy would it have proved for Ireland, for this country, and, if I may be permitted to use such an expression, for his Majesty himself, had your Royal Highnesses suggestions been carried into execution. As matters are situated, however, I feel most happy that your Royal Highness has determined to take no opposite part in the present exigency, and this I take the liberty of saying from the affectionate attachment with which I have uniformly been impressed for your Royal Highnesses person. (39730-1)

1590 THE PRINCE OF WALES TO WILLIAM PITT[3]
Carlton House, 22 Feb. 1801
Dear Sir, I must desire you to call upon me tomorrow at twelve o'clock

1. The King.

2. Moira wrote to Addington on 24 January: 'The Prince of Wales has commanded me to seek the honour of a conversation with you respecting his claims to the arrears of the revenue from the Duchy of Cornwall during his Royal Highness's minority, a statement of which must be brought forward when the liquidation of the Civil List debt shall come to be agitated. Let me beg, therefore, the favour of an audience whenever it may suit your convenience.

As Mr. Tierney has repeated to me what passed between you in the last interview, there cannot be any necessity for our adverting to the subject of that conference when we meet, and you shall allow me to obviate any possible awkwardness on that head by offering my request that the matter may not be brought at all into discussion' (Sidmouth MSS.).

3. 'Pitt's friends', wrote Lord Malmesbury on Wednesday the 25th, 'wish and advise him to draw towards the Prince of Wales, and endeavour to form a Regency, if necessary, under his sanction. Pitt, I hear, actually saw the Prince on Monday, but they did not meet or part like persons likely to think the same. The Chancellor (Lord Loughborough) I also hear saw the

199

at Carlton House upon particular business which cannot be postponed but which I cannot enter into at present (Hoare MSS.).

1591 THE PRINCE OF WALES TO HENRY ADDINGTON

Carlton House, 22 Feb. 1801

Dear Sir, I have just seen the Duke of York & must desire to see you as soon as possible, but as I understand you are to be with the Cabinet at two o'clock, I hope you will contrive to be with me at Carlton House at three o'clock[1] (Sidmouth MSS.).

Prince this morning, but rather did harm than good' (*Diaries and Correspondence*, iv.16). According to George Rose, Pitt told the Prince that he could advise him only if he refrained from seeking advice from members of the Opposition. 'The Prince acquiesced as to the persons immediately alluded to ... but added, he should think himself at liberty to advise occasionally with Lord Moira, which he had long been in the habit of doing' (Rose, *Diaries and Correspondence*, i.311). Pitt added that he would give the Prince advice 'on the express condition that if unhappily there should be a necessity for a Regency, that H.R.H. should acquiesce in the arrangement as settled in 1789 ... The Prince then expressed uneasiness at some of the restrictions as likely to be found extremely inconvenient. Nothing, however, passed conclusive between them as to any arrangement of an Administration. The interview ended with the Prince saying that he must take time to consider all that Mr. Pitt had said ... Mr. Fox has certainly not been with his Royal Highness, and Mr. Pitt thinks he has not seen Mr. Sheridan' (ibid., i.326).

1. Addington's reply has not apparently been preserved, but the following memorandum appears in his Papers: 'Sunday, 1 March. The Prince of Wales sent Admiral Payne to Mr. Addington this morning to say that he had already intimated his wish to see Mr. A., and the Admiral added that he thought the earlier the more agreeable to H.R.H. Mr. A. explained that not having received H.R.H.'s *commands* before, he had willingly forborne to call, as it must appear either to be courting a situation which he would by preference (on personal grounds) decline, or it must seem to be seeking for that declaration of favour which he understood there was a disposition to show to him, but that being now commanded, he should go immediately. Admiral Payne added that the Prince had been told that Mr. A. obtained the King's signature on Tuesday last to the commission and had expressed great displeasure at it till Mr. Pelham had assured H.R.H. that it was impossible. In point of fact Mr. A. told me that he had positively refused to carry the commission to the King, and that when he mentioned this in the Cabinet Lord Loughborough had said he would take it upon himself, and had done so accordingly. Mr. A. told Admiral Payne this misrepresentation was one of the 10,000 falsehoods which had been circulated and which would be found to be untrue in good time, but that he should certainly not make a professed explanation on the subject. He went to the Prince, who received him very graciously, and said that if necessary *he should look to him* for this assistance, and that Lord Spencer, who had just been there, had spoken of Mr. A.'s conduct throughout as highly correct and honourable. The Prince had pressed him for his opinion on the Chancellor's (Lord L.'s) conduct about the commission, but Mr. A. uniformly contented himself with saying *he* had nothing to do with it, and he must beg to be excused giving any opinion upon the conduct of others.' Addington was evidently dissatisfied with Loughborough's conduct during this crisis, for Loughborough was not invited to remain Lord Chancellor (Cf. *Colchester Diary*, i. 248).

Carlton House, noon, Wednesday, 25 Feb. 1801

Do not accuse me, my ever dearest sister, either of unkindness or neglect at my not having as yet answer'd your most kind note; indeed the hurry of yesterday & the day before render'd it quite impossible.[1] Things still continue in the same lamentable state today, and beleive me that the very first moment I am able to stir out with propriety nothing shall prevent my coming to you, as you well know that there is no one in the world who loves you more than your ever affectionate brother (Chatsworth MSS.).

11 a.m., Sunday [? *c. Feb. 1801*]

Amidst all my troubles, I cannot resist writing a line to know how you do as I have been quite uneasy about you ever since you left town so very unwell. Can you see me today early or late, for as you may easily beleive I have much to tell you and am most anxious to see you. Early would suit me best if it is the same to you. Toujours du fond du cœur et d'âme trés dévouément à vous.

[*P.S.*] Perhaps you may prefer my coming between eight and nine this evening. If you do pray say so (Chatsworth MSS.).

1593 PRINCE AUGUSTUS TO THE PRINCE OF WALES

Lisbon, Necessitades, 25 Feb. 1801

Since some time already I have proposed writing to you, and as often have put it off from want of matter to render my letter interesting, and a natural fear, in consequence, of being consider'd intruding and troublesome. However, as I may on the other hand be accused of neglect of my duty, I have taken up my pen after mature reflection, to which a confinement of a fortnight has not a little contributed. I was sorry to have missed you the day before my departure but your occupations hurried you from town, and mine prevented me from being so exact as I ought to have been. I trust, though, that you will not attribute it to want of attention on my part, for certainly it is the last thought or inclination of mine

1. Before the 25th the Prince saw the Chancellor, Portland, Spencer and others 'who took an opposite line from Mr. Pitt in the last Regency; and it was explained that they would not now create any difficulty in passing the Bill with nearly similar provisions, if unhappily the necessity should arise' (Rose, *Diaries and Correspondence*, i.317). The Prince saw Pitt again on the 25th (*Colchester Diary*, i.246).

to be wanting in respect either to his Majesty or to your Royal Highness. I have been accused of this frequently, and I fear have suffer'd much under such an idea, but my conscience is quiet, from the conviction of my innocence, and from seeing others of the Royal Family who have labour'd equally long under a cloud. This place to me is the most horrid of any one I ever was at; climate is the only thing the inhabitants have to boast of, and as for anything else one certainly cannot find it. Strangers are never admitted into any Portuguese society, and as for any other there is none at this place; in short, everything is so disagreable here that my only comfort at the end of the day is to think that it cannot return again.

The Cabinet is at present much agitated on account of the fear there is of war, which if it does break out will be soon over, I think, for I see not the least appearance of defence in any one shape. There is not a single magazine form'd in the whole country, and I understand from very good authority that they have not provisions sufficient for themselves for the space of two months, consequently I should think the whole operation would take but very little time. The troops I have seen are wretched in the extreme, but I am told that those that are in Lisbon itself are the very worst. I have call'd twice upon Madam Silva since my arrival, and must say that seven years absence have not improved her looks. She is grown very old and ugly but still a pleasant little woman. The nobility are in general very far from being handsome. Not having been in any of their houses I can only judge by those I have seen at the Opera, which certainly is very worth hearing, but the Lent has put an end to the only amusement of this melancholy stinking place. There is no thinking of moving out on foot here, and as you ride about you are liable to have not only the chamber pots but even the digestions of the Portuguese thrown upon your head, as everything is spouted out of the windows without even their having the civility to look if any individual is passing their door. In short I believe in the annals of dirt they stand unrival'd, and as for their customs & manners, they are full three centuries behind every other European Power. I fear, my dear Prince of Wales, that this disgusting account will afford you little or no pleasure.

P.S. I hope, my dear Prince of Wales, if an opportunity offers in spite of the present situation of affairs you will endeavour to get me my Establishment, which is the only means of saving me from utter despair.[1]
(48206–7)

1. The Earl of Carlisle wrote to the Prince of Wales on 26 February 1801 (the original is not in the Royal Archives):

'The ready admission, on the part of your Royal Highness, of the motives which alone could excuse my presumption in submitting, the other day, my humble opinions to you, encourages me in the hope that you will condescend to accept those opinions in a more correct form than they could be presented to you, in that moment of agitation and first affliction.

[*Feb. 1801*]

Sunday 22nd. The King taken downstairs; the Queen saw him that day.
Monday 23rd. The Queen again, & nobody, nor her since then except on
Tuesday 24th. Mr. Addington, & nobody since then.

Wednesday 25th, Thursday 26th. Dr. Gisburne was in the room at these
different conversations but rather at a distance; they all agreed that the
King's pulse had never been above 96 but generally under 90.

Friday 27th. Dr. John Willis assured me that he not only thought that
the King could not understand what he read, were he disposed to read,
but that he could not, to the best of his judgment (Dr. J. Willis'), know
a single letter.[1]

Every hour, Sir, confirms me in the judgment, how truly advantageous to us all has already
been your Royal Highness's conduct, during the extraordinary events which have lately occurred, and that the persisting in it will lead, by the quickest and safest road, to everything that
ought to be, under any circumstances, a legitimate object to your Royal Highness's desire or
pursuit.

If the King's most dreadful malady should terminate more fatally than at present is apprehended, the humane, and dutiful attention of your Royal Highness to a parent thus afflicted,
the wise resolution of keeping at a distance all cabal and political intrigue, and the affectionate
manner of sharing with your family a distress, one of the greatest that humanity can be
visited with, must, I am confident, prove the best security against the attempts of those who
would wish to fling a cloud upon the morning of your acceptance of Power. If, on the contrary,
the disorder should so continue as to render it necessary for your Royal Highness to lend
yourself to the public and endure a temporary load of Government, I am equally confident
that this exemplary behaviour would lead to the possession of every degree of authority, in
the only manner worth your accepting, by the unanimous and willing voice of the whole
people of England, uttered through the medium of Parliament.

Consistent with these ideas, I submit to you, Sir, whether in the latter case, your language
should not be, in the first instance, most explicit, reconcileable to the conduct and pure sentiments which have gained the general approbation. The nice and dangerous ground of Right,
I would not permit again to be discussed in my hearing, but as soon as possible, entrench
myself on the safer rock of Parliamentary disposition and settlement, following the example of
that wise Prince Henry the 7th, and of Queen Elizabeth, who rested her claim solely on her
Parliamentary title. Whatever should be that Parliamentary disposition as to the conferring a
quantum of power, my poor advice would be to accept it, with the simple observation that,
if the authorities conferred were large, so would be the weight of undesirable responsibility,
and for your Royal Highness to lend yourself to the public service, without making a stipulation or demand beforehand. Should the error prevail of illiberally holding back that power
necessary for the conducting of Government, as well as for the dignity of the character you
were to assume, I am, Sir, persuaded, a momentary resignation to that painful condition would
ensure a more honourable and effectual change of that ill-timed and ill-placed severity, than
all the efforts of a party avowedly devoted to your interests.

This, Sir, you will say, is a great departure from former systems. I confess it is. So many
mistakes obtained, on both sides, in the transactions of 1789, that we ought so far at least to
profit of our errors, as not to permit them again to influence our conduct' (Historical Manuscripts Commission, Carlisle MSS., p. 731).

1. Princess Augusta wrote to the Prince of Wales on the 26th: 'The Queen commands me to

Saturday 28th. Dr. Gisburne & Dr. T. Willis (the clergyman);¹ no great alteration except the King's pulse being at 88 instead of 94 or 96; that he was much irritated from one o'clock till considerably after four. I went again in the evening; found Dr. Reynolds & Gisburne & the three Willis's. Dr. Reynolds said the King's pulse was again at 94 or 96 & certainly was more irritated than in the morning, wishing to attribute it to the food H.My. had taken in the course of the day & to the draughts with 3 or 4 grains of callemal [*sic*] the King had taken & which had not operated, but else was in general much the same.² (38479)

1595　THE PRINCE OF WALES TO [?] THE LORD CHANCELLOR [copy]

Carlton House, Sunday night, 1 Mar. 1800 [1801]

I saw Mr. Addington this morning who told me he was to call upon you by appointment at four o'clock, & I then desir'd him to acquaint you that I was desirous of seeing you at Carlton House between one & two tomorrow if that hour shd. suit your legal avocations, of wch. I am totally ignorant, but any hour sooner or later than that mention'd by me *but previous* to your attending the House of Lords will suit me eaqually [*sic*] well if you will be so good as to mention the hour at wch. you will call, or if you prefer it I will call upon you. (39678)

1596　THE PRINCE OF WALES TO THE DOWAGER DUCHESS OF RUTLAND

Carlton House, 1 Mar. 1801

Amidst the multiplicity of business I have had upon my hands for the last week, I have through hurry neglected answering a letter the Duke was so good as to write me respecting the dining with him tomorrow, as he was elected to be in the Chair at the Ancient Brittons meeting on the anniversary of St. David's Day & which is to be celebrated tomorrow. And to add to all my misfortunes I have likewise mislaid the Duke's

give her love to you and to say that the King has passed a pretty good day and the physicians are very well contented this evening. He is already gone to bed and we have all hopes of a tolerable night' (Add. Georgian 10/28). And on the 27th: 'I beg your pardon for having kept your servant but I wished to send you the latest accounts. The King is this instant gone to bed after having eat his supper with pleasure, and there is every appearance of a good night.' (Add. Georgian 10/27)

1. The Rev. Thomas Willis, Prebend of Lincoln, and a younger son of Dr. Francis Willis. Whilst in attendance on the King he lived in a house near the Rose and Crown Inn, on Kew Green.

2. The King was also attended by Sir Francis Milman and Sir Lucas Pepys.

letter, so that I know not where to address an answer to him. I therefore am under the necessity of tresspassing upon your usual good nature & indulgence to hope you will have the goodness to explain the matter properly to him, as well as to make my excuses respecting the dinner, as I am confident you will feel as I do the impropriety & impossibility of my dining at a moment like the present at so public a meeting. Once more allow me to implore your forgiveness for putting you to so much trouble, & be assured that through life & under all circumstances, no one can be more truly attached to you & to your family (Rutland MSS.).

1597 THE PRINCE OF WALES'S MEMORANDA

Sunday, 1 Mar. [1801]

I went to the Queen's House between the ½ hour & ¾ pt. four o'clock, & when I came into the Great Dining Room, where were at dinner Dr. Gisborne & the three Williss, I ask'd how the King did. Dr. John Willis then said, 'We are not as well as we were in the morning. His Majesty is a good deal more irritated,' & upon my asking him to what particular cause he attributed this irritation or if to any, he replied 'It might possibly arise from the effects of the medicine his My. had taken, that his My. expres'd a dislike to nourishment & had drank more than he wish'd to see him apply for, as it certainly indicated more fever but that possibly both the thirst as well as the apparent apathy to food might arise from the operation of the medicine.' Upon which I applied to Dr. Thomas Willis, & said, 'This reminds me of the remark you made yesterday to me, that his Majesty generally grew irritable & disturb'd from the hour of one o'clock till 4, 5 or 6 o'clock.' He then said 'That he had certainly deem'd this to be the case, & that this might possibly be the case.' (39679–80)

Sunday, 8 Mar. 1801

I went to the Queen's House about eight o'clock in the evening & had some conversation with the King's physicians respecting his My.'s health previous to their going into the King's room; & when they had left the room I remained alone with the Duke of Cumberland. The conversation then turn'd upon the general position of affairs & particularly respecting Mr. Addington who I commended much & saying I beleiv'd him to be a perfectly honest man, were I only to judge from two recent circumstances & had I not had opportunities of satisfying myself upon that head before, & upon that I mention'd the two occasions, the first his

205

having been *the only person*, & his coming of his own accord to acquaint me of the imminent danger my father's life was in about half an hour before he came to seek me, when no one else thought it proper or decent to acquaint me with the circumstance, though I had been in the House near three-quarters of an hour previous to his coming to me; & the second because he had assured me that he had positively refused the being the means of inducing the King to sign the Commission for passing the Bread Act,[1] & which he was press'd in the strongest manner to endeavour to get sign'd, which I conceive therefore he must have avoided; as an [illegible] it would be the most dishonorable action possible were he to attempt or to lend his hand to induce the King to set his name to any paper whatever when his mind was not in a competent state to do so. The Duke of Cumberland then said, & I did the same, for the Chancellor pressed me to do so, & I peremptorily refused to carry the Commission in. I then said, 'How could that be?' He then told me that positive orders had been sent to the Lodge to refuse the admittance of anyone excepting his Majesty's sons & physicians & I think Mr. Addington, & that he was greatly surpriz'd at a message he receiv'd that the Ld. Chr. was there & desir'd to be admitted; of course he was admitted & that he (the Duke of Cumd.) then carried him into what is call'd the Garden Room & there had the conversation with the Chancellor relative to the obtaining the King's signature to the Commission for passing the Bread Act, which the Duke of Cumd. then peremptorily refused; that Dr. Thomas Willis was then sent for, & upon the subject being mention'd to him, the D. of Cumd. assured me that Dr. Ths. Willis had strongly represented against it, considering the King's state of mind as quite unfit for such a circumstance, that upon this the Chanr. ask'd Dr. Willis if he knew who he was, saying that he was the Chancellor, & knew best what he was about, as all responsibility must rest with him, & that he must run every risk & that therefore Dr. Willis must obtain his My's signature. Upon this Dr. Willis carry'd in the Commission & brought it out again with the King's signature. The D. of Cumd. then added many harsh reflections on the Chr.[2] (39732–3)

1. In accordance with the Report of a Select Committee on the high price of provisions, the use of bread finer than a certain standard had been prohibited in 1800, with the view of diminishing consumption. The Act was repealed in 1801. Lord Holland suggested that had it remained on the Statute Book the unwholesome quality of the bread would have reduced the number of consumers quite appreciably. Malmesbury wrote on 25 February: 'His Majesty not better, yet signed, about 4 p.m., [i.e., on the 24th] the repeal of the Brown Bread Bill, declaring very distinctly his opinion on it, and saying it was a very good Bill' (*Diaries and Correspondence*, iv.16. See also Rose, *Diaries and Correspondence*, i.315). Returning from Buckingham House the Chancellor said that when he had carried the Repeal Bill to the King, his Majesty was in the perfect possession of his senses. But Loughborough admitted to Rose that he had not seen the King at all, and the Prince's statement corroborates this.

2. The Prince had not been allowed to see the King, and when, on Monday the 2nd, the King's

Berlin, 15 Mar. 1801

I think it my duty to give you in a few words the account of the result of my stay here. On my arrival I received the particular assurance of the King of Prussia of his abhorrence of all violent measures, and that nothing should bring him to occupy the Electorate but the utmost necessity: that both France and Russia had repeatedly proposed his taking possession of it, but that he had always refused it. That everything depended on an answer from the British Government to the Note pre-presented by Ct. Haugwitz[1] on the 12th of last month to Ld. Carysfort,[2] and that he wished nothing more than that the good understanding which had hitherto subsisted between his Court and that of London should be re-established. This was the first conversation my Aide de Camp, Capt. Deecken, had with the King. I have ever since been treated with the greatest kindness and affection, and it is by the King's desire that I have stayed so long.

Yesterday I received the authentick account of the King's being forced to occupy immediately the Electorate in consequence of Gen. Augereau[3] being ordered to march into it in case the King did not. I for this reason went this morning to the King, and mentioned to him my intention of leaving this tomorrow night. He answered me in the friendliest terms, and repeated the assurances he made the first day of my arrival: that no steps should be taken till an answer from England arrived, and he begged me to remain here still some days. I own, though I distrust too much the Prussian Ministry, not to be afraid that they will at last force the King (who has the best intentions in the world) to take a step so repugnant to his feelings. They undoubtedly wish me off, and therefore they try to spread such accounts as I have just mentioned. I probably shall be obliged to leave this in a few days, when I shall return to Hanover where I hope to receive an answer to my letter of the 24th of last month. Should however, the occupation of the Electorate take place before that answer comes I shall set off for England, as I have informed the King in my letter

life was thought to be in great danger, the Prince was not informed, though the Duke of York received the news from the Duke of Cumberland (Rose, *Diaries and Correspondence*, i.330). It was not until 11 March that the Prince saw the King (ibid., i.332).

1. The Prussian Minister (1752–1832). Prussian Ambassador at Vienna, 1792, and a member of the Cabinet at Berlin. Replaced by Hardenberg, August 1804; recalled in 1805, but retired after Jena, 1806.

2. John Joshua Proby (1751–1828), created Earl of Carysfort [I.], August 1789, and Baron Carysfort [U.K.], 21 January 1801. Joint Master of the Rolls [I.], 1789–1801; Minister at Berlin, July 1800–October 1801; Joint Postmaster-General and a Commissioner of the Board of Control, 1806–7. M.P. for East Looe, February–June 1790; for Stamford, 1790–1801.

3. One of the ablest of Napoleon's Generals; later, Marshal of France (1804) and Duke of Castiglione (1757–1816).

of today. Pray excuse this scrawl but I am writing in great haste as the messenger is waiting for my letter. God bless you.[1] (48561)

1. On the 30th Frederick William III issued a Proclamation in which he declared that he was compelled to take 'efficacious measures' against Hanover, and Prussian troops occupied the Electorate. On the 27th Addington wrote to Lord St. Vincent: 'The Prince of Wales put the enclosed letter from Prince Adolphus into my hands after dinner yesterday, and made some very judicious observations on the policy of keeping his brother at Berlin or in Westphalia as long as possible. He expressed a very anxious wish that I should communicate this to his Majesty's servants, and a hope that a messenger would be sent off today.' At 2 p.m. that day Lord St. Vincent wrote to the Prince of Wales: 'Mr. Addington, the Duke of Portland and Lord Hawkesbury concur with me in opinion that your Royal Highness's proposition to continue Prince Adolphus at Berlin or in Westphalia as long as possible, is fraught with wisdom and sound policy; and Lord Hawkesbury will send off a messenger with a dispatch to that effect the moment he is in possession of your commands to Prince Adolphus' (*Letters of Lord St. Vincent* [Navy Records Society], i.87-8). The Prussian occupation of the Electorate, however, caused Prince Adolphus to return home. He was at Cuxhaven on 12 April, and he landed at Yarmouth from the *Shark* sloop on the 16th.

The following memorandum by the Earl of Carlisle records the substance of the Prince of Wales's communications to him:

'1801, April 15.—That after an interval of nearly a month he was admitted to the sight of the King, his father, who received him with every mark of love and fondness.

He, the King, began with the happiness he felt at being able the same day to embrace his son, and dismiss Dr. Willis' keepers; that being the first day since his illness that any one of his own servants had been permitted to attend him.

The Prince was delighted to find that his mind was not poisoned on his account, but on the contrary he did him ample justice for his correct conduct during the whole period of his malady.

He continually and repeatedly talked of himself as a dying man, determined to go abroad to *Hanover*, to make over the Government to the Prince.

N.B.—Of the condition of Hanover no one had ventured to talk to him.

He insisted much on the P. accepting a white Hanoverian horse, laying the most vehement stress upon the P. of W.'s exclusive right to mount such a horse, his joy, his pride; and this went to very incorrect discourse.

He turned quick to the most violent accusation of Mr. Pitt; detailed methodically a variety of instances of his insolent conduct towards him; warned the P. against his ambition, and concluded with saying, of a bad set, Lord Grenville was the honestest.

His manner of giving the Great Seal was a mixture of neat compliment and a wandering mind. He talked of it as a trick he played. He took the Seals out of the Purse, and hid them in his bosom. When he gave Lord Eldon the Purse, he thought he was made Lord Chancellor. But the K. burst out in laughter, and said you have got the Purse, and that's all. Lord Eldon looked dismayed, not knowing how this would act [?]. But the King with a handsome recollection of his conferring that dignity upon Lord Thurlow, and a very genteel comparison of them, took the Seals from his bosom, and said, 'These, as I hid them, I give you from my heart.'

He then ran off, and talked of the device he used, by some position of his wig, to make the Council believe him in better looks and health. Here [he] was very wild.

He took the P. up to the room, the scene of the late confinement, and complained of the treatment he had experienced in terms the most moving.

He made the P. sit down to dinner with him, and expressed that once in his life he should have to say he dined *tête-a-tête* with his beloved son.

208

22 Apr. 1801

Lord Eldon came to the House between four and five o'clock, too late for me to take my seat;[1] and the business pressed too much to withdraw then. But I am to meet him at two on Monday. Unless your Royal Highness wishes to see me this evening, which I rather collect from your note is not the case, I will not fail to attend your Royal Highness tomorrow at twelve on my way to Lord Carlisle's.[2] (39734)

He eat little—a small piece of mutton, a little beetroot, a small piece of cheese, and the contents of a small apple tart. He drank 3 glasses of wine, and all to the P.'s health.

He talked of all his children in terms of the greatest affection—in terms to move tears; but particularly so when he dwelt upon his little granddaughter' (Historical Manuscripts Commission, Carlisle MSS., p. 733).

Dr. Thomas Willis wrote to Addington from the Queen's House (the letter is undated): 'Her Majesty, the Dukes of Kent and Cumberland went in to the King at half after five o'clock and remained with him for two hours. They came out perfectly satisfied—in short everything that passed has confirmed all that you heard me say today. He has desired to see the Duke of York tomorrow and all the Princesses in their turn.

I stated to him what you wished, and what I had a good opportunity of doing, and, after saying the kindest things of you, he exclaimed 'Now my mind will be at ease.' Upon the Queen's coming in, the first thing he told her was your message, and he made the same observation upon it.

I stated also the whole of what you said respecting Hanover—which he received with perfect composure.

You will not expect that I mean to shew that the King is completely *well* free from fever— but we have no reason to doubt that he very soon will be so' (W. Dacres Adams MSS.).

1. Eldon had seen the Prince on the 21st. 'The Prince told his Lordship that it was the intention of his Majesty, declared yesterday, to devolve the government on him, the Prince; that he wished therefore the Chancellor would consider the proper mode of that being carried into effect, and *that it was the King's intention to retire to Hanover or to America* ... That the Queen and his brothers wished him to take measures for confining the King; that H.R.H. very greatly disliked the Willis family being about the King, and he was therefore desirous of knowing if they were placed there by any authority, or how they might be got rid of' (Rose, *Diaries and Correspondence*, i.346).

2. The Prince of Wales wrote to Arthur Paget from Carlton House on 23 April: 'I have only this minute learnt that Morand is going to take his departure for Palermo, & indeed young Hunter is now waiting a few minutes for my scrawl. I therefore take up my pen to scribble a few lines to recall myself to your recollection, notwithstanding that it is now above four months since I received a line from you. The present situation of politicks both at home and abroad, & the various changes that have taken place since we met, my dear friend, are so curious that unless we were to meet again & converse them over *de vive voix* it is hardly possible to discuss them over, especially in so hurried a manner as that in which I am now compelled to write to you in from the sudden departure of Morand. You must have learnt the dreadful state of the K—'s health, which has thrown me into the most awkward and difficult predicament, but in which I have had the good fortune to conduct myself so as to carry with me the general approbation of the country, though one must always expect there will be in this world a certain number of grumblers, though there have been fewer upon this occasion than ever yet have been known upon any circumstance which has so much interested the public mind.

209

Monday, 27 Apr. 1801

Lord Thurlow begs leave to acquaint your Royal Highness that he has had no conversation with the Chancellor. His Lordship put off his meeting at two today on account of business in the Common Pleas: in answer to which Ld. T. proposed his dining at St. James' Square, which he also declined. Hence Ld. T. infers that he has no wish to converse on the subject. Ld. T. took his seat today and conversed with the C[hancellor] on a cause depending; but as the subject was not introduced on his part Ld. T. thought it indiscreet to force it.

Ld. T. will have the honour of attending your Royal Highness's commands tomorrow at twelve. (39735)

1600   PRINCE AUGUSTUS TO THE PRINCE OF WALES

Lisbon, 1 May 1801

I profit of the opportunity offer'd me by my friend Don Lorenzo de

Unfortunately it is not yet over, as we have had a severe relapse, and all I can say to you, my friend, upon this subject is *que je tâcherai de me conduire vis à vis de Dieu, mon père, et le pays, comme un homme d'honneur doit se conduire.* The dear Duchess is still at Belvoir, and has been there near five weeks. I have had one letter from her, in which she asks me the same question that I will ask you, my dearest Arthur, & that is, why you remain now at Palermo now that there is nothing absolutely to be done by a Minister of our Court there (at least ostensibly) & why you do not return home directly? Pray give us a little insight into what is likely to be your destiny, and when there is the smallest probability of our embracing you again; rest assured though of this, my dear friend, that whether abroad or present my affection for you can never waver or change, & shall continue, *arrivera ce qui pourra*, equally alive to your interests and ready to promote your wishes with that lively affection and friendship I ever have professed towards you, & ever must feel to the latest hour of my existence. But Chig, and the old set are still pretty *bobish*, thank God, but never cease to unite with me in lamenting your absence, who always animate us all. Mother Hump I hear a fait une fausse couche & [is] rather indisposed, but as to the rest they are all just as they were. My letter is again called for. I therefore have only time to pray God bless you, dear Arthur. Pray let me hear from you as frequently as you can, and never again send over Morand without a few lines to me, but the best thing you can do is to come yourself on any account; at all events recollect an old proverb that I am afraid has but too much to do with public life: "Out of sight, out of mind". Why I say this just now is that notwithstanding all the hints I have given in various quarters, I hear that whenever the K—— is in a situation to name a Minister to go to Petersburg, St. Helens, though a great friend of mine, is pitched upon as the man to be nominated for that Mission. Whitworth, who is now married to the Duchess of Dorset, is nominated for Paris, in case Buonaparte chooses to negotiate. In short, dear Arthur, if you do not speak for yourself and aid us a little here, I am fearful we shall not be so successful as I thought as well as Gar[th]shore we should have been a few weeks back. I must absolutely here conclude, desiring you to imagine anything that can be said that is most affectionate by you from your ever & most sincere friend.

[*P.S.*] Excuse haste and any fault there may be in this scrawl as I have not time to read it over or to correct it' (*Paget Papers*, i.342–4; Add M.S. 48383).

Lima, who is going as Minister of Portugal to England, in order to address you these lines.

It is with the most sincere interest that I write to you on the situation of the Regent[1] as the kindness and confidence he has shewn me calls for my most grateful efforts to serve him. Ignorant what turn affairs may have taken, or may take in consequence of our father's indisposition, his Royal Highness has desired me to enclose you a letter from him. This he has done in consequence of the assurances I made his Royal Highness in your name of the high esteem you had of him and the warm interest you took in his own private welfare, as well as that of his country. His position is certainly critical and not merited, for if ever a person was sincere in his sentiments and attached to our country and nation, I can answer for the Regent being so. He sees the dangers that surround him, and equally feels the advantages his country has and must reep from her intimate connection with ours. Don Lorenzo my friend is appointed the new Minister in England, and has without doubt to begin an awkward mission, but from the intimacy that has for many years existed between us, I can answer for his doing everything in his power to consolidate that harmony which the Prince has always wished should exist between the two Courts. I hope, my dear brother, that at my particular request you will shew him that kindness which he and all his family, who are sta[u]nch English, have always shewn me, and more particularly so during my stay here. Perhaps he may want friends to support him in his first outset and your protection will certainly be of great weight. The Prince is truly desirous of making peace, as far as it can be combined with his honor and principles for the advantage of his country, but if exorbitant and unjust demands are made, which may prejudice us, he is determined not to accede to them, provided he can reckon on our assistance in case of an emergency. Towards this you may certainly contribute, and by these means save a kingdom from its fall which has been the first and constant system of the whole French Revolution. The Prince has prefer'd writing to you in this way in order to prevent this letter passing through our Minister's hands, Mr. Frere.[2] He certainly is a well-meaning man but must too violent in his expressions, which of course shock here. It would be desirable therefore (was another place to be found for him) he should be removed elsewhere, for where unanimity cannot reign from private causes it is always best to make a change.

1. The only surviving son of Peter III, King of Portugal, who died in 1786. He became Regent in 1792 and King in 1816. (1767–1826).

2. John Hookham Frere (1769–1846), Under-Secretary of State in the Foreign Department, April 1799–September 1800. M.P. for West Looe, November 1796–1802. Minister to Portugal, 1800–2; Envoy to Spain, 1802–4; Minister to Spain, 1808–9. P.C., 1805. One of Canning's intimate friends.

[*P.S.*] Friza who is Marquis is brother of Lima and is a friend of mine. I recommend him to you also.[1] (48215-6)

1601 LETTERS FROM THE EARL OF CARLISLE TO THE PRINCE OF WALES, AND A MEMORANDUM

Monday night [*?end of April or beginning of May 1801*]

Unless a change I have no right to expect should take place in my gouty frame, I fear it will be very difficult for me to obey yr. R. Hss's commands. Some reasons also occur which I will explain why the conversation between Ld. T[hurlow] & yr. Rl. Hss. ought not to obtain, a third person

1. On 4 June Lady Augusta Murray wrote to the King: '*If long & unremitting suffering*—if *very sincere & acute regret* at having given your Majesty cause of displeasure, can atone for error, or plead for pardon, permit me, Sir, to approach you with this humble confession, & cast myself on your Majesty's humanity for forgiveness. I have no one to intercede for me— nobody would even venture to present this letter as coming from me; if it ever reaches your Majesty I shall owe my success to artifice; I have endeavoured as well as I could, without absolutely asserting a falsehood, to make it be believed that it came from Prince Augustus. Except on yourself, Sir, & on the goodness of your own heart, I can have no hope; abandoned & shunned by the world, for ever excluded from all my former enjoyments, believed to be the object of your Majesty's particular detestation, I am made to endure all the contempt that cruelty can inflict; it is then to the good King, that (thoughtlessly, & led away by the feelings of a fatal moment) I have displeased—it is to that good, clement King to whom I have recourse; it is in trusting to your Majesty's gracious benevolence that on my knees I implore your pro- tecting pity & patience while I also state to your Majesty's consideration my present distressed situation in point of pecuniary matters. Some time ago for the maintenance of myself & child, twelve hundred pounds per annum were granted me. After all deductions taken from it, it barely amounts to £800, & this even is paid with cruel irregularity while the price of every- thing is centupled. At the time this was granted me, I had been three years without one farthing of income, during which period I necessarily contracted debts which the then Lord Chancellor assured me should be paid. Mr. Pitt would not pay them, consequently they aug- mented, & now £600 of that £800, is annually taken from me to pay a bond. While I presume to offer such details to your Majesty, I tremble at the effects of my own presumption, but despair & misery lead me on, & oh!, Sir, behold with pity the supplications of an unhappy woman who, while she was displeasing you, was ruining herself. Educated with a strong attach- ment to religion, to principles of virtue, I suffer sufficiently by the situation to which I am reduced, by that in which I see my loved boy, to atone even for greater crimes than that I have committed. May I then implore your Majesty to mitigate my sufferings; pray place me above cruel distress—& by encreasing my income let my economy prove useful; by placing me above the contumely of debt, your Majesty will alleviate some part of the sorrows I endure; & unworthy as I am pray let me yet live to bless the clemency of the King. May I pray that if your Majesty deigns to listen to my prayer you will permit whatever money you grant me, not to be made payable on the Civil List, because of the deductions (nearly one quarter) & the long arrears. How to finish this letter I know not. I have no person to tell me, & I dread your Majesty's displeasure. Do, pray, Sir, forgive me, pity me, & do not crush the wretch you can save. I have the honor to subscribe myself your Majesty's most humble obedient servant and subject, Augusta.' (48219-21)

212

present. I trust your R. Hss. will lay the proper stress with Ld. Thurlow on Ld. Eldon's avoiding the subject with him.[1] (39737)

LORD CARLISLE'S MEMORANDUM

The first step which appears necessary to be taken, & which will be no departure from the strong ground of refusing interference (which entails responsibility) is to remonstrate with Ld. Eldon & Mr. Addington, upon their conduct & their supinely suffering the King's health to be tamper'd with by persons who can hardly can [sic] be called physicians, without applying to the best advice the country can afford.

In almost every case of a private individual, before a patient is transfer'd or returned to the care of that part of the Faculty to which Dr. Willis belongs, it is usual to require the fiat of other medical persons to sanction the placing the patient under such care. For if the Mad Doctor was to decide in the first instance upon the necessity of his having the sole management of the case, it is obvious to for[e]see to what horrible abuses this might tend. Persons perfectly sane might be buried for ever in confinement. It is to be apprehended, that Dr. Willis himself decides upon every step now taken relative to the King's malady. This, if so, is not endurable; and a protest against it might be formally made by the P. of Wales to Mr. A. & Ld. E, leaving them to take such measures as they might think fit to adopt.

If all interference on their part should be declined, will not a suspicion be fairly raised that if medical persons of eminence were consulted, the result of their enquiries into the whole progress of the King's malady might lead to a discovery of the real state of the K.'[s] mind, when the R[oya]l hand was put to instruments of the greatest consequence, & that such a discovery it would not be for their interests to encourage?

It ought to be recollected by them that it is no secret that Dr. Willis' keepers were removed on the Wedy;[2] on the Tuesday 14th preceding Ld. Eldon accepted the Seals as Chancellor from the King. On the Monday[3] following the former lamentable symptoms returned, since which time Dr. Willis' keepers were again placed about the King in the

1. On 24 March Malmesbury declared that Lord Carlisle, Lord Lansdowne, Lord Fitz-william and Fox had coalesced. 'It is said they informed the Prince of Wales, through Lord Moira, of this step, tendered him an offer of their services, and that they should hold their conferences at Carlton House. The Prince, it is said, replied that he was under too much anxiety for the King's health to think of politics; that he thanked them for their communication but not only declined their proposal but observed that, out of respect to the King, he considered it as his duty to acquaint Mr. Addington with it, and this he immediately did' (*Diaries and Correspondence*, iv.51).

2. Wednesday, 15 April.

3. Monday, 20 April.

room of his own domestics. In this lucid interval his My. makes a Chancellor. What would Ld. Eldon's answer be, as a professional man, fit as I believe him to be both from integrity & learning to be a Chancellor, were he to be asked as to the *validity of a Will made under similar circumstances; whether he, sitting in the Court of Chancery, would a moment entertain the idea* of its being *valid!*

I lay much stress upon the answer that probably would be without hesitation deliver'd.

Circumstances & particulars of the King's Will made previous to his late malady, are known to more than one of the Royal Family. Ought not the disclosure of the King's illness [to] be made to physicians alluded to, as their opinions, & statements of the case from the beginning to the present hour might be of considerable consequence, in the case of another Will being found of a subsequent date at the K's death? (39738–9)

TO THE PRINCE

The abatement of my gout permits me to endeavour to prevent yr. R. Hss. repeating yr. condescension by coming to Grosr. Place, & I have taken the liberty of inquiring at Carlton House whether yr. R. Hss. had any commands for me.

In the case of Ld. Thurlow's attempts to converse with Ld. Eldon on certain points, which are too important to be delay'd, should prove abortive, may I take the liberty of submitting to yr. R. Hss. other modes that may be resorted to, to stimulate Ministers to such exertions under a sense of responsibility as may render unnecessary the agitating any questions in Parlt., the agitation of which, they ought not to invite?

A personal conference with Ld. Eldon, urging to him such parts of the reasoning, contained in a paper delivered yesterday into yr. hands, as yr. R. Hss. thought fit either to adopt, or were found previously congenial to yr. better judgment, might be the most decisive & shortest way of going to work, particularly if he were made to recollect that many of the facts were not secrets to many persons, however their forbearance & patience might raise a hope of their ignorance of them. It is possible yr. R. Hss. might prefer treating this subject by letter.

Another mode, but in my poor opinion not the best, unless in Ld. Thurlow's hands, that of someone seeking the conversation as a deputed messenger from yr. R. Hss. Another, but perhaps more liable to objection, that of addressing him in a letter from a private, tho' informed individual. (39740)

It is a great relief to my mind to find that Ld. Thurlow gives the same approbation to all the steps taken by yr. R. Hss. as they have met with from others, whose sanction cannot be consider'd to have so much weight & importance. The steady adherence to the conduct adopted by yr. R. Hss. in his idea is the best security against everything that not only may be done, but said to render the situation in which you are placed more difficult & more uneasy.

Your R. Hss. having conversed with him this morn., makes it unnecessary for me to go over the ground of a very free & satisfactory conversation with which he honoured me, & upon one point I am not quite sure he reached the extent of yr. meaning & intentions, in regard to power whenever the time s[houl]d arrive, when you were properly called upon to accept it. He seemed to think that Mr. Addington had not collected from yr. R. Hss., that the first object to which yr. primary thoughts as well as filial inclinations would be directed, would be during the period you held a temporary rule for yr. father to hold it [in] such a manner, as to show, at the restoration of it, how affectionately & dutifully you had the wishes of the King always in your view, & consistently with this, that without committing yourself either upon the question of men or measures, those now placed in authority had nothing to fear from any *violent* design of change, the work of intrigue, in which yr. R. Hss. so happily for us, & so wisely for yourself, has not condescended to implicate yourself.

Ld. Thurlow laid so much stress upon this that I cannot resist mentioning it to yr. R. Hss., tho' at the same time I think this matter was not left in ambiguity when you saw Mr. Addington early after his acceptance of the Seals. A clear understanding upon this point I perceive he considers would smooth many difficulties; but yr. R. Hss. must be the best judge whether Mr. An. requires any more positive information on this subject.

P.S. Is it possible to conceive Ld. Eldon will have the temerity to proceed on the reliance of such a vindication as the wretched medical tribe now about the K. will on the day of account be able to afford him?[1] (39741)

1602 BASIL MONTAGU TO REAR-ADMIRAL J. W. PAYNE

Gray's Inn, 4 June 1801

It is not from any puerile impatience but from the knowledge of a fact which I ought, I think, to communicate to you that I take the liberty of

1. The Willis trio were still in attendance on the King at Kew on 12 May (Rose, i.371).

again requesting you to apply to his Royal Highness in my behalf. I have just learnt that Mr. Henry Blackstone,[1] who was a Commissioner of Bankrupts, is dead. If his Royal Highness will have the goodness to order an application to be made for me to the Lord Chancellor, it will be the means of insuring my success through life.[2]

I will call tomorrow morning about 10, and if I am not so fortunate as to find you at home tomorrow I will call on Saturday.[3] (39736)

1603 LETTERS FROM THE DUKE OF KENT TO THE PRINCE OF WALES
Saturday morning, 6 June 1801
I think it my duty to give you, (but bien entendu entre nous) a hint that the King means, if the weather is favorable, to *surprize* you on Monday at your Review,[4] and when he intimated this last night, he did it speaking in that flattering way of his inability to resist the pleasure of seeing the 10th out, which naturally was highly gratifying to your friends, amongst whom I trust your humble servant is not considered as the *least* warm. You will therefore *not* betray me but act and make your plans en conséquence. I am to attend the King with no others than Adolphus and Fitzroy[5] on horseback from Kew: and when the Review is over the King drives Adolphus in his phaeton on to Windsor. I shall return to town, trusting in your kind indulgence that you will excuse my attendance at dinner, my poor shattered head piece being very unequal to such a day. I shall pay my respects to you tomorrow between eleven and twelve at Carlton House to receive any commands you may have to give me, till which time I shall only intreat you to believe me [etc.]. (45997)

1. A Fellow of New College; son of the Rev. Mr. Blackstone of Winchester.

2. Montagu's application was evidently unsuccessful.

3. On Sunday 24 May the Prince of Wales sent the Duke of York the following note: 'I feel myself so very unwell tonight that I am afraid it will be quite impossible for me to have the pleasure of meeting you at Rumford [?Romford in Essex] tomorrow. I therefore entreat that you will not think of waiting for me'. (44169)

4. The King reviewed the 10th Light Dragoons on Ashford Common on Monday the 8th. Captain Lord Robert Manners, in one of the 'grand charges', was thrown from his horse and badly hurt.

5. Charles Fitzroy (1762–1831), second son of Charles, 1st Lord Southampton. Lieutenant-Colonel, 1794; Colonel, 1797; Major-General, 1803; Lieutenant-General, 1810; General, 1821. In 1816, six years after the death of Princess Amelia, he married Eliza (*née* Barlow), widow of Clavering Savage.

Thursday night, 18 June 1801

Conceiving that you may perhaps prefer hearing from me of the little expedition of yesterday to learning it in the first instance from other channels, I just scrawl a few lines to acquaint you that by command of H.M. Adolphus and I attended him yesterday morning to Blackheath. We arrived at half past eleven and were then dismissed by the King to go & see the Observatory and Ranger's House while he had a conversation with the Princess. We returned to the house by one, soon after which the King came with the Princess to the room where Adolphus & I were sitting with Lady Sheffield[1] and Miss Garth.[2] A half hour then passed in breakfasting and talking of indifferent matters, when the King made me send for his carriage and we returned to Kew. From what fell from the King we were led to understand that he was satisfied as to his conversation, but he did not particularise any part of it except that the Princess had declined on the Queen's account the offer of the Rangership of Greenwhich Park which he had made her,[3] and if I err not, he seemed to express a wish and a hope that it might be possible for the sake of appearance to the world that you and her some day or other should again be upon a footing of exterior civility. I feel it is great presumption in me to say even this much, and did I not recollect that the person whom I address has often and often honoured me with the appellation of his best friend I should be most fearful of incurring his displeasure. But I do not know how it is something seems to satisfy me you will receive this communication with an indulgence, knowing nothing but affection for you the most sincere and warm could induce me to make it, or to add that could I be fortunate enough to be instrumental in adding to your comfort, and at the same time to induce you to meet what I conceive to be the King's wishes in this point it would make me the happiest of men.

But I must not say more on this, but seal my lips on it for ever till you command me to speak again. I understand the Queen, Augusta and Eliza pay *their* annual visit at Blackheath *tomorrow*; yesterday they went to Oatlands.[4] Now, my dearest brother, you have my whole budget, so I shall conclude hoping to see you in the best of health and spirits Sunday

1. Lord Sheffield (1735–1821) married, 1798, as his third wife, Anne (1764–1832), daughter of Lord North, the Prime Minister. She and Lady Carnarvon were the Princess of Wales's Ladies of the Bedchamber.

2. Then, one of the Princess's Bedchamber Women. See Vol. III, *passim*.

3. Her declining the offer surprised Lord Glenbervie, 'as I know those about her . . . complain that such a house and park should remain unoccupied while she lives in a cottage on the Park wall. But there are those who think she acted prudently, as Greenwich is settled on the Queen, and it might be supposed that the grant to the Princess was the effect of temporary weakness, and that it would excite the Queen's jealousy. Besides, the Princess can live more to herself and with less restraint where she is' (*Glenbervie Journals*, i.232).

4. To visit the Duchess of York.

about one when I propose paying my respects at Carlton House: in the meanwhile I shall take leave to subscribe myself [etc.]. (45998–9)

1604 LETTERS FROM PRINCE ADOLPHUS TO THE PRINCE OF WALES

Kew, 22 June 1801

Being on the point of setting off for Windsor I have but just time to write you these lines to make you my excuses for not attending tomorrow your field day at Ashford, but I cannot yet ride and must therefore be deprived of this pleasure. I shall be tomorrow in London on business and if you have any time in the morning after 12 o'clock I will order the terrines [?] to be brought to your house. One line only to the Queen's House to let me know your hour, and I hope I shall have the pleasure of finding you quite well.

The King is, thank God, going on very well and he will be on Wednesday in town. (48567)

Weymouth, 12 July 1801

I postponed answering your very kind letter which I received at Cuffnells[1] till I had been some days here to give you a fair account how we are going on. I rejoice infinitely in being able to assure you that the King is as well as ever I saw him in my life and the sea bathing agrees with him perfectly. He is in very good spirits and enjoys very much his stay at Weymouth. The Queen and the rest of the family are well and have now quite recovered the fatigues of the sea voyage. Amelia is the only one who has hitherto bathed in the sea, but I believe they will all of them begin in the course of the ensuing weeck.

Dearest Miny, whom I have just left, has desired me to send you her kindest love and she joins with me in the hopes of seeing you here.

The King intends going to Plymouth at the end of next month and if I am not mistaken, he will be a week or a fortnight absent from this place. He will during that time reside at Saltram, Ld. Borrington's[2] estate.

You will by this time I suppose have left London and I hope you will

1. George Rose's fine seat near Lyndhurst. He entertained the Royal Family there when they were on their way to Weymouth. From the vicinity of Cuffnells they went in the Royal Yacht to Weymouth (3 July), embarking in boats from the beach.

2. John Parker, Lord Boringdon (1772–1840). Succeeded his father as 2nd Baron, 1788; created Earl of Morley, 1815, through the influence of Canning, one of his closest friends.

find yourself as well from the sea air of Brighton as we do from that of Weymouth.

I will not trouble you any longer this time, but with your permission I will write from time to time how we are going on, and be assured, dearest brother, I ever shall remain [etc.].[1] (48569)

1605   ROBERT FRASER TO COLONEL MCMAHON

Duncannon Fort, Waterford, 14 July 1801

You will possibly remember my name from having the honour thro' you to present to his Royal Highness the Prince of Wales in 1798 a paper respecting this island which he was pleased to honour with his gracious approbation, and which besides exhibiting those advantages which might be imputed from that connection since formed, proposed making a statistical survey of the internal resources of Ireland in order to lay the foundation for its future improvement, and which by his Royal Highness's commands signified to you I had the honour to lay before Lord Cornwallis. By an uncommon degree of perseverance I have at last obtained the assent of Government to proceed in those investigations I recommended, and I have been appointed to take the lead by giving an example of my design in the survey of the county of Wicklow which is now in the press and will be speedily published. As soon as it is, I will beg leave to send you a copy for his Royal Highness, and as it will be particularly remarkable for an account of the mineralogy of this interesting county I would be greatly obliged to you if you would be so good as to represent to his Royal Highness that it might be of great importance to my success in gaining attention to these objects if his Royal Highness would be graciously pleased to allow me to assume the title of mineralogist to his Royal Highness, and as I formerly held the situation of Collector of his dues or tin in the county of Devon, & in that situation had an opportunity of cultivating that knowledge which I hope is likely to be very useful to this part of the United Kingdom, his Royal Highness may perhaps think proper to condescend to grant me this mark of his favour, in return for which I shall send his Royal Highness an arranged and interesting collection of the minerals & fossills of this island. The bearer is a relation of mine who will be greatly indebted to you if you will please to obtain him a view of Carlton House.

P.S. I am now proceeding in a statistical investigation of the counties of Waterford & Wexford, and I flatter myself have greatly contributed to

3. The Royal Family did not visit Saltram at this time. They left Weymouth on 1 October, broke their journey at Andover, and reached Windsor on the afternoon of the 2nd.

excite a spirit of attention to the future improvement of this island. (39745–6)

1606   COLONEL ROBERT BROWNRIGG TO COLONEL MCMAHON
        Horse Guards, 21 July 1801
        I have to acknowledge the favour of your very kind note of yesterday and have many thanks to make for the friendly hint it contain'd. I immediately communicated with Calvert and he has written such intimation of tomorrow's intended Review to the Prince of Wales, as will I trust be acceptable to his Royal Highness and will I sincerely hope do away any idea of a want of that dutiful respect which be assured every individual of the Comdr.-in-Chief's Department entertains for his Royal Highness. It is necessary to observe that his Majesty's commands for the Review of the Volunteers was signified to the Duke of York thro' the Secrty. of State, as without that authority his Royal Highness cannot exercise any controul over them, and that what was communicated by Lord Harrington's[1] Aide-de-Camp to the several Corps of Volunteers was in consequence of that authority, and I am persuaded you will believe that nothing could have been further from the intention of any individual concern'd than to have given the slightest cause of umbrage upon the occasion.[2] (39747–8)

1607   LETTERS FROM THE DUKE OF KENT TO THE PRINCE OF WALES, AND A REPLY
        Carlton House, 4 o'clock, Friday 23 July [?24] 1801
        Agreable to your instructions I take up the pen to acquaint you that my visit to Blackheath this morning went off well beyond my expectations. The Princess received the message about the excess in her expenditure

1. Charles, 3rd Earl of Harrington (1753–1829), succeeded to the peerage, 1779. Lieutenant-Colonel, 1778; Colonel, 1782; Major-General, 1793; Lieutenant-General, 1798; General, 1803. M.P. for Thetford, 1774; for Westminster, 1776–9; Commander-in-Chief in Ireland, 1805–12; Special Mission to Prussia, 1806. Constable of Windsor Castle, 1812–29. Colonel of the 1st Life Guards and Gold Stick, 1792–1829.

2. There is a long account of this review of the London Volunteer Corps, numbering nearly 5,000 men, in the *Gentleman's Magazine*, 1801, ii.661.

1. There must be a mistake in the dating. Friday, 23 July came in 1802, but in 1802 the Duke was in Gibraltar. He must have meant Friday the 24th, and the Prince's letter of the 26th is obviously the reply.

with great good humour, expressed her acknowledgments for the communication thro' me, and fully admitted that she could not expect a larger allowance than that she had while yours continued so reduced. She desired I would say she intended to give Colonel Thomas full power to retrench wherever it could with propriety be done, and to force her servants to execute the reform that should be recommended by him in which she requested me to give that advice which my little experience enabled me to do. She then desired me to inform you she proposed reducing her three Ladies'[1] salaries from five to four hundred a year, & the vice-Chamberlain[2] to the same; her Bedchamber[3] women from three hundred to two hundred and fifty, and to dismiss Miss Coleman as handsomely as she could altogether, that orders should also be given to alter those points to which Mr. Gray's letter particularly alluded, that as a further proof of her wish to do what might be pleasing to you she would propose Lord Cholmondeley to be no longer one of her trustees, but Lord Eldon in place of him: and lastly, that although she had no fault whatever to find with Thomas for any part of his conduct, yet she did not consider him as equal to the task of regulating her household, as having had no experience of that kind; but that if you had no objection she wished to propose Lord Lewisham[4] for the situation held by Thomas, if he would accept of it; that she had long had this intention but having been lately called into the Ministry she had not thought any more of it, least it might be displeasing to you. I touched on the expences incurred by alterations and repairs to the buildings & on the great number of company invited to the house, on both which points she promised to be guarded in future. If therefore the Princess will only have command enough of herself to abide firmly by what she has said to me she would, I flatter myself, your instructions to me for this day will have been executed on my part to your satisfaction, which as you well know must be most gratifying to your [etc.]. (46095–6)

1. Lady Cholmondeley, Lady Carnarvon and Lady Sheffield. Lady Cholmondeley was no longer a Lady of the Bedchamber in 1802. Mrs. Lisle was Lord Cholmondeley's sister.

2. C. N. Thomas.

3. The Hon. Mrs. Lisle, Miss Garth, Miss Jane Coleman, and the Hon. Mrs. Vernon, so styled in the Calendars, but *Miss* in No. 1620, and, indeed, she was Lady Harcourt's sister. Miss Coleman was not dismissed.

4. The Duke evidently meant Lord Dartmouth. George, Viscount Lewisham (1755–1810), M.P. for Plymouth, 1778–80, for Staffordshire, 1780–4, Lord of the Bedchamber to the Prince of Wales, 1782–3, Lord Warden of the Stannaries, 1783–98, and President of the India Board, May 1801–2, had succeeded his father as 3rd Earl of Dartmouth only a few days earlier (on the 15th). He was Lord Steward of the Household, 1802–4; Lord Chamberlain, 1804–10. He had been summoned to Parliament by writ *v.p.* in his father's Barony of Dartmouth, on 15 June 1801, but never took his seat in that capacity on account of his father's death a few weeks later.

Brighton, 26 July 1801

Many thanks, my dearest Edward, for your kind letter: which upon the general face of affairs, as stated by you, might to anyone less acquainted with the person that you have been conversing with than I am, furnish a reasonable hope that something like a fair & honorable system might be adopted & adhered to. I cannot, though, help having my doubts from former experience; however, we will hope for the best. There are, though, some circumstances in your letter which I cannot help animadverting upon, & desire you with as little delay as may suit your own convenience to explain fully & properly to the Princess, in order to avoid any misunderstanding whatever & consequent misrepresentation.

In the first place I must desire to be completely understood that I do not interfere in any partial reduction or retrenchment whatever the Princess may think proper to make, though it is evident some are absolutely necessary to be made; a line of conduct I myself have been compell'd to adopt, & have been obliged, especially since the allowance I have settled upon her, systematically to pursue. In the next place I cannot help observing that with regard to Lord Cholmondeley, if the Princess herself chuses to dismiss Lord Cholmondeley from being one of her Trustees, she certainly is at liberty to act in that respect as best suits her own inclinations, as it is a matter of perfect indifference to me; & after what has pass'd upon that subject & which the Princess cannot fail to recollect, Lord Cholmondeley having now been so long out of my service, I cannot consider in that point of view as the smallest compliment to me, though if the Princess does intend to make a change, certainly there can be no properer person as a man than Lord Eldon. With regard to Lord Lewisham, I cannot help observing that he is, & must be quite out of the question, for though a most incomparable man, yet his rank & situation in life, besides the high office he now holds, entirely preclude the possibility of his holding such an office in the Princesses Family. As to Col. Thomas, it appears to me that there is no one who, from his well known uprightness, integrity, & honor through life, from the good character he universally bears, & from his being peculiarly well versed in pecuniary matters, & in the management of a family, as well as from the correctness of his manners as a gentleman that can be so well calculated to represent in her suite, & to enforce with due & proper respect to the Princess any commands she may charge him with, & at the same time preserve proper subordination & regularity amongst her servants & in her Family. The Princess perhaps is not aware that if she was to dismiss Coll. Thomas without any crime alledged against him, & to take another in his stead, which she must do (if Col. Thomas is dismiss'd) for she cannot do without a gentleman in his rank of life, to attend upon her, as well as to superintend her Family, there is not an instance of such a circumstance having ever taken place in the Royal Family without the emoluments of the situation being continued to the individual by way of pension.

I am afraid I have trespass'd, my dear Edward, very long upon you, but I am too well acquainted with your usual kindness not to hope you will not consider it as too great a bore my having been necessitated for the sake of clearness & complete understanding to expatiate so much at length upon those various heads, and I doubt not that your own candour & reflection, together with your extreme good understanding & fairness, will enable you to suggest to the Princess such advice as she has desired to receive from you, as will conduce, if adhered to, to the final arrangement of the matters you have so kindly undertaken, to the credit of all parties. With many thanks for all the trouble I have given, & what I fear I now give you, & hoping to hear from you soon, I remain [etc.].[1] (42335-7)

Carlton House, 4 o'clock, Thursday, 30 July 1801

I now do myself the pleasure to acknowledge with the most grateful & affectionate thanks both your letters, which I received from the hands of Col. M'Mahon, and to inform you that I have acted upon them this day in such manner, I hope, as to be able again to make that kind of report that will be satisfactory. I went to Blackheath at one and have had about an hour's serious conversation with the Princess, the result of which is as follows: that as it is a matter of indifference to you relative to Lord Cholmondeley she will let matters rest as they are, particularly as the place of trustee in fact makes him little more than a cypher in her family: of course all idea about Lord Eldon is over. With respect to Thomas, she desired me to express her perfect readiness to give him a full and fair trial in the trust now reposed in him of comptrolling her household, but she feared it would require a more minute attendance and more labour than might be compatible with the distance at which he lived from Blackheath, and the sort of indolent life she conceives him habituated to, and therefore if à la longue her apprehension on this subject should be realised, she trusts in your indulgence that *then* she may propose some

---

1. The following letter from the Duchess of Buccleuch to the Prince, dated merely Dalkeith House, 29 July, may have been written in 1801: 'Having been from home for some days I was not honor'd with your Royal Highnesses commands until this morning. I shall lose no time in giving orders to have my house at Blackheath prepar'd for the reception of the Princess Charlotte. I am afraid it is not in very good order, having been very long uninhabited. The situation, however, I flatter myself will render it agreable to the Princess of Wales.' (49254)

223

other person, it being *well* understood that he is such as shall be perfectly approved of in the *first* instance by you. As to the reduction of Coll. Thomas's salary, that being a point on which I had no commission from you to speak officially, I cannot report in a decided manner, the Princess conceiving he would be well paid if placed on a footing with her Ladies; but yet I am not sanctioned to say this point is at all concluded upon in her mind, for the last words she said to me were that as no reductions could take place till after the fifth of October, she would take time to plan them, and therefore not as yet come to any decided determination on that subject. For further particulars I beg to refer to Col. M'Mahon, with whom I have spoken in the most open manner, and who will set off in one of the early morning coaches. I hope he will be able to inform you no exertions have been spared on my part, and you may rely they shall be continued whenever you chuse to command them, from the joint motive of attachment, gratitude and duty.

I leave Castle Hill for Weymouth on Tuesday and shall certainly reach it on Thursday. I leave it again on the 17th, and shall be home on the 19th. You know I am like clockwork; you will therefore exactly know where to communicate anything you may wish me to do for you.[1]
(46004–5)

1608 THE PRINCE OF WALES TO HENRY ADDINGTON[2]

Brighton, 3 Aug. 1801

In the present anxious pressure of publick affairs, I am extremely un-

1. The Prince of Wales wrote to Arthur Paget from Brighton on 5 August: 'I am overjoyed, my dearest Arthur, at your arrival & would have flown up to town in order to have wellcomed you, had I not had my house full of people that I could not leave; however, if you are not able to come to me in your way back from Weymouth, I will meet you in town at any rate after the eighteenth of this month. My reason for mentioning this is that you may arrange your plans accordingly & I really think it would be too cruel a circumstance by a very dear & mutual friend of us both, were I to take up any part of your time, especially if your stay is to be a short one, when by my coming to town she will not be deprived of your society. Pray say everything that is most affectionate to her, & how truly I participate in her happiness, & with what pleasure I look forward to the passing a few days in your society, for I have miss'd you most cruelly, & pray tell her also that if I do come on purpose which I shall do to see you, I expect that she will give me a dinner or two with you whilst I stay in town, as I shall leave my servants & family behind me. Your letter I did not receive till late last night, as I went early yesterday morning over to the Duke of Norfolk's at Arundel & did not return till past twelve o'clock, or I should have answered it by return of post. Pray say when you go to Weymouth & when you intend to return' (*Paget Papers*, i.365, where the letter is wrongly dated the 6th [see Add. MSS. 48383]).

2. There is no fair copy of this letter in the Archives, but there is a draft (f.39749) dated merely July amended to August. The copy Addington received is in his Papers, with an inaccurate version in Pellew, i.439.

willing to obtrude the smallest additional weight of business upon you, and more especially so, to intrude any which could belong personally to myself. But the station you fill first renders it necessary that all such communications as I have to state should be made directly to you. Besides, the zeal which I am conscious animates you in the cause of all the royal family, together with the kind and obliging interest I beleive you so particularly take in whatever essentially relates to myself, induce me to communicate with you in thorough confidence, and under the impression of high personal opinion and esteem.

As I wish to make you perfectly master of the subject I am about to treat, I enclose you the copy of a letter [1] which I wrote the King in April 1798 when the alarm of invasion was then very universal, although very wide of that formidable aspect which this measure unquestionably wears at the present day. I cannot immediately put my hand on the answer his Majesty wrote me to this letter (it being among my papers in London) but it went distinctly to this, that in case of the enemy landing, my Regiment was to be foremost of the cavalry, and myself at their head. The feelings I have express'd to the King in this letter, as possessing me at that day, be assured have lived in my breast ever since, and operate at this moment with a tenfold encrease, yet, dreading even the apprehension of offering any proposition that might tend, however slightly, to flurry the King, I have determin'd not to repeat a similar mode of application to his Majesty on the present occasion, but, confiding in your friendly discretion, place these uppermost wishes of my heart entirely in your hands, requesting that you will take the earliest convenient opportunity of bringing this subject before his Majesty as a suggestion from yourself, not only founded upon the infinite anxiety you know it to excite in my mind, but from the high rank I bear in the country, as a measure of national expectation at so eventful a crysis as the present, and in its consequences materially affecting to my future character and consequence in life in the estimation of the world. I again submit, as before, to be call'd out in whatever character his Majesty shall think fit. I own that a command of cavalry would be most pleasing to me, because I think in that line I could best serve my King and country; but I have no difficulties. I am willing and ready to serve in any command and with any rank a letter of service may assign me; or even to serve under the command of any officer whatever it may be his Majesty's pleasure to place over me.

Independent of an ardent love for actual service, the consideration of my fame and character with the world engrosses, as you may readily conceive, my every thought, and will, I flatter myself & make no doubt, ensure to me your good offices and cordial co-operation in the attainment of an object I have so earnestly at heart; for I can with the utmost

1. No. 1347 (iii.427).

sincerity conclude this letter with assuring you of the truth of the declaration I made in my letter to the King, 'that death would be preferable to the being *mark'd* as the *only man* that was not suffer'd to come forth on such an occasion[1] (Sidmouth MSS.).

1609   PRINCESS AMELIA TO THE PRINCE OF WALES

King's Lodge, Weymouth, 8 Aug. 1801

It is impossible for me, my dearest dear brother, to express how deeply I feel your kind, yes, very kind remembrance of me which both Dolly & Coll. Cartwright told me. To shew you how happy I am to obey your commands I employ the first moment I have to myself in writing to you. I should long before this have written, but knowing you heard from Dolly I thought my dull letters would only be troublesome.

I must begin by telling you what I am certain will give your good heart pleasure, that our dear King's health is good; that he has improved in health, looks & strength ever since his arrival here, & that the bathing & sailing agree better this year than ever with him. I never saw mama so well at Weymouth as she is now. All my sisters are well & so have I been till these last few days, but I have now got a cold & cough which has prevented my accompanying papa & mama on board the yacht today.

This place fills amazingly; the last week has been very gay. On

1. As Addington did not reply until 11 September, and as the letter is already in print (and apparently no copy in the Archives), it is given in a footnote:

'In obedience to the commands of your Royal Highness, I laid before his Majesty, at Weymouth, the letter with which I was honoured by your Royal Highness at the beginning of last month. The satisfaction which it afforded to his Majesty was only qualified by the difficulty to which his Majesty adverted, in the most gracious terms, of giving full effect to your Royal Highness's wishes. His Majesty highly applauded the feelings by which your Royal Highness is actuated, but was of opinion that there was no military situation suited to the rank of your Royal Highness, between the chief command and that which your Royal Highness now holds. A reference was made by his Majesty to his answer to your Royal Highness's letter in the year 1798; upon which, as I had not seen it, I had nothing to offer. The conversation, from causes which it is unnecessary for me to state to your Royal Highness, was unavoidably short, but on many accounts I should not have thought myself justified in attempting to protract it. In consequence of the expedition with which I was obligd to travel, it has not been possible for me to make an earlier communication to your Royal Highness, but I have availed myself of the first minute, for that purpose, after my return. In making it I do not presume to express any feelings of my own, but those of regret arising from a consciousness that I have stated inadequately those sentiments of the King from which your Royal Highness would derive the highest gratification.

'I have the satisfaction of confirming the information of which your Royal Highness must be possessed, that their Majesties and the royal family appeared quite well. It seemed to be his Majesty's intention to return to Windsor at the end of this month' (Pellew, i.442).

Tuesday we breakfasted with Ld. Borrington[1] [*sic*]; after his Review Thursday Ld. A. Beauclerk[2] gave a breakfast & dance on board his ship, & yesy. being my birthday the dear King was so good [as] to give a dance at the Rooms. I forgot to mention a very pretty Fête mama gave last Saty. at Radipole.

Coll. & Ly. L. Erskine[3] are here; they were to have left Weymouth to-day but Coll. Erskine has got a bad knee & Mr. Keate attends him & has begged of him to remain another week, which gives us great pleasure. I never saw anything more happy then they are; Louisa's health is much better. Ld. Uxbridge is very kind to them & all parties seem quite reconciled. I passed a very pleasant eveng. at Louisa's last Thursday; we talked much of our dear Eau de Miel & she desired me to give her kind love whenever I wrote to that dear perfect *being*, for we both *agree* in thinking you a very dear *soul*. Indeed no words can express *half* how dearly I love you or how vain I am of the *place* I have in your heart. If you ever changed towards me it would break my heart, but I am sure I have no fears of that & shall ever try to merit your kindness.

The accounts of poor Ly. Holderness are very indifferent; I hear her face grows larger every day but she still keeps her health & sleeps well.[4]

Our intended journey to Ply'th. is over for this year,[5] but we do go to Bath. How long we are to remain here I have not heard but as it really does the King so much good I cannot wish to leave it. Adolphus being with us is a great comfort. Edward arrived Wedy. morning which I was very glad of. Ernest has been over for two or three days but *seems* to have so much business with his Regiment that he was in a great hurry to leave us.[6] Both Ld. Chesterfield & Ld. Walsingham[7] are here. A great

1. See No. 1604. The Royal Family, nevertheless, did not go to Saltram.

2. Lord Amelius Beauclerk (1771–1846), third son of the 5th Duke of St. Albans. Lieutenant, 1790; Captain, 1793; Rear-Admiral, 1811; Vice-Admiral, 1819; Admiral, 1839. K.C.B., 1815; G.C.H., 1831; G.C.B., 1835.

3. Sir James Erskine (1772–1825) succeeded his brother William as 3rd Baronet in 1813. Entered the Army, 1788; Captain of Dragoons and A.D.C. to General Vyse, 1793–4; Major, 1794; Lieutenant-Colonel, 1799; A.D.C. to the King, 1801; Lieutenant-Colonel 2nd Dragoon Guards, 1803; Brigadier-General, 1804; Major-General, 1808. In March 1801 he married Lady Louisa Paget (1777–1842), daughter of the 1st Earl of Uxbridge and sister of the 1st Marquess of Anglesey. His courtship of her was not sanctioned by her parents. At the beginning of the year he was made one of the King's Aides-de-Camp. In 1826 she married General Sir George Murray (1772–1846). Lady Louisa was given a pension of £600 a year, and Pitt sent the two warrants to the King for signature on 16 March. (Rose, *Diaries and Correspondence*, i.336; *The Later Correspondence of George III*, No. 2372).

4. Lady Holdernesse died of cancer on 13 October.

5. That is, their projected visit to Lord Boringdon at Saltram.

6. In March the King had offered him the Colonelcy of the 27th Light Dragoons, with the option of exchanging into the 15th when the opportunity offered. Lord Dorchester, the Colonel of the 15th, was willing to make the exchange, and it was effected immediately. See No. 1583.

7. Thomas, 2nd Baron Walsingham (1748–1818), succeeded his father, 1781. A Groom of the

friend of yours arrived yesy.; Arthur Paget. I think him looking very ill & very thin. He told me he should only remain a few days here as he was to leave England soon again.[1]

I hope, my dear brother, you will soon come here for I long to see you. I regret excessively that I shall not see my dear Eau de Miel on the *12th* but he knows his own child I hope well enough to be convinced that absent or near she loves him dearly & wishes him equally every happiness on earth & eternal happiness hereafter. To say I love you better on the *12th* than any other day is impossible except that my affection grows stronger every day & that I love the 12 of August as it gave birth to my dear brother. So be assured I hope you will live to see very many happy years & each year bringing with it fresh blessings.

Having written so lately I will not plague you with another letter on Wedy., but will soon plague you again if I find you have not really been tired with this long and dull letter. If you answer me pray enclose your letters to Adolphus. I hope you are quite well & that the Pavillions [*sic*] are going on well. It is ages since I have heard of our dear little Charlotte.[2] (Add. Georgian 14/35)

1610   THE DUKE OF KENT TO THE PRINCE OF WALES
Weymouth, Saturday morning, 8 Aug. 1801
Such has been the continued bustle of the life we have led since I arrived here on Wednesday last, that till this instant I have never yet been able to sit down for five minutes secured from interruption to write to you. I now, however, take up my pen in the first instance to acknowledge with my warmest thanks your most affectionate letter, as also to say I am more flattered than I can express at the manner in which you are so good as to speak of the way in which I executed those commissions which you have confided to my care. Believe me, you shall always find me equally zealous and interested on every occasion when my services can be useful to you,

Bedchamber, 1771–7; a Lord of Trade, 1777–81; Under-Secretary of State for the Colonies, 1778–80; Joint Vice-Treasurer of Ireland, 1784–7; a Commissioner of the India Board, 1784–1790; Joint Postmaster-General, 1787–94.

1. He was sent to Vienna as Minister Plenipotentiary and arrived there on 12 September.

2. The Queen sent birthday greetings to the Prince of Wales on the 10th. (36524) So did the Duke of Kent on the 11th (46009) and Princesses Elizabeth, Augusta, and Sophia (Add. Georgian 11/88; 10/29, 13/14). Sending the usual compliments, Princess Sophia went on: 'I am sure you will rejoice to hear the good accounts of our beloved father; he is surprisingly well since he came here, and quieter and more composed than I have seen him for years. His exercise is very gentle, & he is much more inclined to take care of himself. We go every night, two excepted, to the play, which is a great amusement & better for him than walking.' (Add. Georgian 13/14)

Princess Charlotte
by Sir Thomas Lawrence *c.* 1802

25th of Augt 1801

I hope you are well my dear Grand
Papa & that Dear Grandmamma
is so too, I hope you will accept of
the Cane String which I have made
for you, I wish it were better but
it is the first I have ever done.

I am busy at the foot stool for
my dear Grandmamma & hope
I shall see her soon & dear Aunts
pray come back soon to Kew
& send for Eggy and me.

I am Dear Grandpapa, Your
Dutiful Child
Charlotte

A letter from Princess Charlotte to the King

and if the anxious wish to complete everything to your entire satisfaction can command success, I shall never have to make you a report that is *not* satisfactory. Much as I hope for the best result of the business we have commenced, and sanguine indeed as I am that matters will eventually take a pleasanter turn than they unfortunately have for a length of time passed, I shall most assuredly profit by the hint you give me, and be upon my guard least the intention should not be (as you seem apprehensive may be the case from former circumstances) to perform rigidly according to the declaration that has been made. On my return to Castle Hill, I am to take an early day to talk over with Coll. Thomas, and Mr. Grey [*sic*] the plan that will best answer to correct in the Establishment at B[lackheat]h those principal abuses so judiciously pointed out by the latter gentleman, and to retrench the expenditure: that done, and digested into proper form I will go over to B[lackheat]h and exert myself to get it sanctioned by the P[rinces]s: it is probable by that time she may have come to some resolution as to the steps she means to take in the reduction of the Establishment of her attendants, and should this prove so, you may rely on the earliest communication from me on that subject. You know you may at all times command my attendance when and where you please. If therefore you insist upon my coming over to Brighton I most certainly shall go down, but you know also how I feel upon the subject of all absences from home, situated as I am. Indeed you were kind enough to express your approbation of my sentiments on that point, and therefore, tho' you cannot but be convinced of the happiness I ever feel in your company, I am certain if you can dispense with my attendance *there* you will do so. *Here* c'est une affaire d'obligation, for it is necessary to shew oneself frequently in *my* position to keep upon the footing with the K. & Q. which I believe you think it essential for me on *all* accounts not to lose. With *you* no such ceremony I am well satisfied is necessary, for *you* do me the justice *never* to doubt my sentiments towards you. Therefore as it is really essential to my comfort to be otherwise as little from home as is practicable, I trust if you can make it convenient to yourself to see me at Carlton House, you will dispense with my going to Brighton; you may depend on my being back on the 19th, after which day, at the shortest notice, I will attend you in town at any time you please. The three youngest girls with whom I have spoken of you, desire their kindest loves. I do not find from them that the K. has spoken either of you or the P[rince]ss at all since he has been down here; indeed I am apt to think all that business is now out of his mind. The Q. & elder girls have simply asked after you, indeed very kindly how you were when last I saw you. It is said the Plymouth journey is given up, but from something that dropped in the course of yesterday's ride, I have my doubts about it; to Bath they will *certainly* go in their return homewards. Frederic has not been here, and I think is not expected:

the K. is much improved in health and looks, and is unusually calm in his way of speaking, but I think his spirits by no means the best. All the rest except that dear girl Amelia, who has a nasty cough, are perfectly well. I believe this is all I have to say at present that can any ways interest you, and the stupidity of my letter must I am certain tire your patience. I will therefore only address my kindest remembrance to Mrs. Fitzherbert, and conclude by [etc.]. (46006–8)

1611 LETTERS FROM THE PRINCE OF WALES TO THE DUKE OF YORK, AND THE REPLIES

Brighton, 8 [?9] Aug. 1801

I meant yesterday to have thank'd you for your message by Leigh but which I was prevented doing, owing to the Races being over so very late that the post was setting off just as we came from the course. Monday the twenty-fourth will suit me perfectly if that day is equally convenient to you for the Review of the 18th Rt. in which case I will endeavour to reach Oatlands the preceeding day. On the sixteenth I am quite afraid that it will be impossible for me, though it was fully my intention to have been with you, to pay a visit to you & the Duchess. However, absent or present you are always sure of my best wishes & that we shall drink your health. (44170)

FROM THE DUKE OF YORK [copy]

Horse Guards, 11 Aug. 1801

Many thanks for the letter which I received from you yesterday & by which I am happy to learn that I have a chance of seeing you at Oatlands on the twenty-third. The 24th will suit me perfectly for the Review of the 18th Lt. Dragoons & I will take care to send the necessary orders accordingly.

It would have given me the greatest satisfaction if it had been in my power to have been at Brighton tomorrow, but you know that at this moment I am tied by the leg. I trust, however, that you are assured that nobody is more sincerely attached to you than I am & that you may see many & happy returns of the 12th of August are the hearty wishes of [etc.]. (44171)

Horse Guards, 19 Aug. 1801

I lose no time in acquainting you that by some mistake the three troops of the 18th Regt. of Lt. Dragoons which have been upon the coast duty & have been ordered at Lt.-Col. Stewart's desire to join for the Review, will not be able to arrive at Guil[d]ford till Saturday. This will therefore render it impossible to have the Review as we had agreed on next Monday, as they would have no opportunity of exercising even once with the rest of the Regiment; they ought, however, to be ready by the end of the week. I wish therefore to know whether Friday the 28th or Saturday the 29th instant would suit you, or whether you would prefer to put off the Review to the Friday or Saturday of the week following, whichever day you choose. I trust you will do the Duchess & me the favor to keep your promise of coming to Oatlands. (44172)

THE PRINCE OF WALES'S REPLY

Brighton, 20 Aug. 1801

Many thanks, my dear brother, for your kind letter which the post brought me this morning. Either Friday or Saturday will be equally convenient to me, therefore pray arrange it for that day of those two that will best suit you. If it is Saturday that you fix for the Review I will come from London to Oatlands on the Friday to dinner instead of the next Monday (which was my intention to have done after the Review, had it taken place on that day) & then take the Review on Saturday morning in my way back to Brighton. This I think will be after all the best arrangement supposing it suits you. Pray write me a few lines merely to say whether it will be the Friday or the Saturday. With my best compliments to the little Duchess I am [etc.].

P.S. Stadt[1] & I had arrang'd that we were to meet at Oatlands on Monday next to dine with you; will you have the goodness to put him off till Friday? Once more Adieu.[2] (44173)

1. The Stadholder, William V.

2. The Prince of Wales wrote to Arthur Paget from Brighton on 21 August 1801: 'I this morning receiv'd your kind letter by which I am most extremely concern'd at finding that your departure is likely to be so abrupt, and that I shall be disappointed at passing so much time in your society as I had promised myself the pleasure of doing. It was my intention to have been in town early on Tuesday morning, but as your departure is to be at so early a moment I will be in town on Monday in order to devote as much time, my dearest friend, to you as I can during the rest of your short stay here. The joy I shall experience at seeing & embracing you again, my dearest Arthur, is really quite beyond what I can express, or you can form to yourself any idea of, I am always the same, & I do assure you that nothing ever

Castle Hill Lodge, 23 Aug. 1801

Not wishing to trouble the Prince with a long letter, I am under the necessity of requesting *your* attention to the following lines, which, as they are dictated by a wish to relieve a family on the brink of encountering very serious distress, will I am confident not be considered by you as tedious & uninteresting. Not to lengthen this epistle by useless circumlocution, I will at once come to the point. Last evening I had occasion to pay a visit to Mr. & Mrs. Raynsford's at Chertsey where I found both of them evidently affected by some internal sorrow that seemed to weigh heavily upon them. Delicacy prevented *my* taking notice of what I observed, but Madame de St. Laurent, who had had some reason to suspect what was the cause of it before, learnt from Mrs. Raynsford that they were called upon for the immediate payment of a sum which, under their present circumstances, they were totally unable to raise, and that in consequence they were under very serious apprehensions of something unpleasant occurring to them unless a mode could be devised for their relief. She then intimated that there was a place, I think, called that of Receiver of the Tolls for Greenwich Hospital on the River Thames somewhere near London Bridge, at present held by a Mr. Rashleigh[1] likely to become vacant in a very short time by the death of the present incumbent, and that while Lord Spencer was at the head of the Admiralty, she had had great hopes that through the interest of some of her friends, Mr. Raynsford would have been able to obtain the reversion of it. Could their expectations on this head be realised they would have no difficulty to get over their present dilemma, but that as the same interest could no longer be of use to them, as the First Lord of the Admiralty was changed, she had no hopes left but through the Prince's kind intercession with Lord St. Vincent in their behalf. The object therefore of this letter is to obtain the Prince's authority to sanction you to write to Lord St. Vincent in his name to procure his Lordship's promise that Mr. Raynsford shall be Mr. Rashleigh's successor in the place which that gentleman now holds under the Admiralty. It is proper that I should inform you that some months back I hinted this circumstance to Lord St. Vincent, indeed, immediately after his appointment to be First Lord, when I

can or *will* alter me towards you at any time. I beg my best and kindest remembrances to the dear, dear Duchess, and am ever [etc.].'

P.S. If Charles & Bob [Manners] are with you, remember me kindly to them' (*Paget Papers*, i. 366).

1. John Rashleigh (1742–1803), First Commissioner of the Sixpenny Receiver's Office on Tower Hill, for Greenwich Hospital (so called because sixpence a month was paid by all seamen in the merchant service to the Hospital funds). His salary was £300 a year. He was the brother of Philip Rashleigh (1729–1811), M.P. for Fowey, 1765–1802. George Parker succeeded him (*Letters of Lord St. Vincent*, ii.212).

found him well disposed to do something for Mr. Raynsford out of compliment to me, though he did not appear to approve altogether of naming him to the place I had pointed out, as I had in the first instance given him to understand that he wished to do the duties of it by deputy, a circumstance which I believe the First Lord wishes to strike at as much as possible. This, however, if the *only* objection his Lordship had, is now entirely done away, for Mr. Raynsford is perfectly willing to undertake the duties himself. I would not trouble my brother in this business if I thought that my personal application to Lord St. Vincent would be sufficient, but I am well assured it will require an interference as powerful as *his*, to insure his Lordship's acquiescence with the application. I assure you you may safely paint the distress of Raynsford's family with *six* children as very pressing, and I believe the Prince, from circumstances known to him & myself, will not be sorry to be the person to relieve them from distress. I shall therefore hope I have said enough upon the subject to engage you to state it in the warmest manner you can, and to recommend Raynsford's case as standing in urgent need of the humane interference of my brother, whose heart, I know, is always open to the claims of misfortunes & more especially so where a female is the principal sufferer. It will be necessary to add that no time should be lost in making the application to Lord St. Vincent as the place may become vacant from one hour to another, owing to Mr. Rashleigh's precarious state of health, & I therefore request that you will be kind enough to take the very earliest opportunity of communicating the subject of this application to the Prince.

I request you will acquaint my brother that I returned from Weymouth on Tuesday night last & found so much writing had accumulated during my absence that I have been kept close prisoner every morning since my arrival & am likely to be so for eight or ten days longer before I can bring all up again. That done, I shall certainly attend to meet Colonel Thomas & Mr. Gray upon the affairs of the Princess, in which I shall be most happy to afford all the advice & assistance in my power. Should the Prince not have heard of it before I will thank you to acquaint him also with my having been appointed Colonel of the Royals[1] vice Lord Adam Gordon.[2] My brother, who knows how much I was attached to the Fusiliers, will feel I am sure how much it must cost my feelings to part with a corps which I have had for thirteen years, & with whom I have passed fully ten of that time; but it is flattering at any time to receive a public mark of the King's favor, & considering it in that light, I thought I could not decline the offer then made me, although it almost broke my heart at the time. Should the Prince come over to town any time this week or the next, I will thank you to let me know it that I may not omit

1. The 1st (or Royal) Regiment of Foot. Gazetted 21 August.

2. He had recently died.

calling at Carleton House. In the meanwhile you will be kind enough to assure him of my warmest & most affectionate attachment. With respect to yourself I trust you will ever be convinced of the high regard & esteem with which I am [etc.]. (46010–4)

1613 THE PRINCE OF WALES TO LADY LADE[1]

Brighton, 9 Sept. 1801

I was yesterday favour'd with your kind letter respecting Fred, & by this day's post I have written to Lord Dartmouth who is now at the head of the Board of Controul in order to have Fred's name put down upon the list immediately, so that I hope he will not loose [*sic*] a single minute when the nomination comes to his turn. You are I hope well convinced that I am happy in this as well as in every other opportunity that offers itself of obeying your commands.

P.S. I beg to be remember'd kindly to Sir John.[2] (42340)

1614 PRINCESS ELIZABETH TO THE PRINCE OF WALES

17 Sept. 1801

I was commanded by the Queen to say she would have wrote herself but was prevented; she therefore orders me to give you her kind love & to assure you how sincerely she is grieved at your accident.[3] You may believe the accounts from Mr. Keate today have eased us in some measure on your subject, yet we must continue very anxious & hope you will order somebody to write every day. You have long known the real affection the Queen has ever invariably had for you; therefore hers are not common enquiries. To know you [are] suffering must make her unhappy, therefore she hopes you will take care of yourself & implicitly follow Mr. Keate's advice. (Add. Georgian. 11/89)

1. Sir John, incidentally, was later given a pension or annual allowance from the Privy Purse (£500 in 1824). (*Letters of King George IV*, iii.499). 'Fred' was Frederick J. Darby, a nephew of the Lades. He died at Corunna on 2 January 1809 whilst a Captain in the 10th Light Dragoons (the Prince's Regiment).

2. There is a letter to the Prince from Lord St. Vincent, 8 September 1801, in *Letters of Lord St. Vincent*, ii.179, on a Portsmouth Dockyard patronage question.

3. He fell downstairs.

Castle Hill, Sunday, 20 Sept. 1801

Had I not hoped long before this to have had the happiness of seeing you at Carlton House on your passage through London either to or from Weymouth, I should have written to report that I had very nearly completed the retrenchment in the Princess of Wales's family with her own consent, which, if strictly adhered to, will, I am confident, not only keep her expences within the income allotted for her maintenance, but will also admit of a small annual saving to be applied to liquidate the past excess. The general outlines of the retrenchment are as follows; the total reduction of the place of Mistress of the Robes, and of the four Bedchamber Women, the diminution of the salaries of the two Ladies of the Bedchamber from £500 to £400, as also of the Vice-Chamberlain, who, it is further proposed, as long as he requires Mr. Grey's[1] assistance in regulating the Establishment which in my opinion will be *always*, should make that gentleman an allowance out of it of £100 a year, for in fact *he* will be the efficient man altogether: a total new arrangement of the stables, the dismissal of the chairman, a more œconomical mode of providing the liveries without deviating from the patterns established by you, and a diminution of the number of suits; and lastly the confining the servants' tables to the Princess's own people, and the exclusion of all strangers except the tradesmen who are sent for, and kept waiting, or servants of the Royal Family, who might occasionally come on business to hers. These reductions, and commencing on the 5th October to conduct the current house expences with ready money according to a plan I have given in will effect all you can wish, and if in this arrangement I have been fortunate enough to gain your approbation, I am more than compensated for the time and trouble it has taken to bring it so far. In a very few days I shall transmit the papers explaining *every* particular, and the remarks with which I have thought it right to accompany it.[2]

1. Robert Gray, the Prince's Deputy Commissioner of Accounts.

2. At a rather earlier date the Princess of Wales's Establishment had cost £5,000 a year:

	£
Vice-Chamberlain	500
Mistress of the Robes	500
Three Ladies of the Bedchamber	1,500
Privy Purse	300
Four Bedchamber Women	1,200
Two Pages of the Backstairs	300
Two Pages of the Presence	200
Cook	100
Maître d'Hotel (Bidgood)	100
Ten female Household servants	300
	——
	5,000

235

On Wednesday week I was at Blackheath with the rough draft of my arrangement to submit to the Princess, and receive her commands about the reduction of her Ladies &c., which were to the effect I have before mentioned, and I own, as far as *I* could judge she appeared very sincere in her professions of adhering to the system that was to keep her within the allowance appropriated for her use. She delivered me one communication to make to you, which she hoped you would receive kindly: this was to represent that, as she saw herself under the necessity of striking off her Establishment of Bedchamber *Women*, and it was impossible for her to have the *Ladies* resident with her, she hoped you

In 1802–3 her Establishment was as follows (32482):

Ranks	Names	Salaries	
		Qtr. ending 5 January 1803	Qtr. ending 5 April 1803
Vice Chamberlain	Chas. Nassau Thomas Esq.	125 – –	
Mistress of the Robes	Marchioness Townshend	125 – –	
Ladies of the Bedchamber	Countess of Carnarvon ..	125 – –	
	Hon. Lady Sheffield ..	125 – –	
Privy Purse	Miss Hayman	75 – –	
Bedchamber women	Hon. Miss Vernon ..	75 – –	
	Hon. Mrs. Lisle ..	75 – –	
	Miss Garth	75 – –	
	Vacant	– – –	
Pages of the Backstairs	William Cole	37 10 –	
	Robt. Bidgood	25 – –	
Page of the Presence	Thos. Stikeman	25 – –	
Maître D'Hotel	Jno. Sicard	37 10 –	
Man Cook	Thos. Vaughan	25 – –	
Gardener	Jams. Arthur	15 – –	
Coffee Room woman	Frances Lloyd		3 10 –
Housemaids	Mary Wilson		3 – –
	Ann Brown		3 – –
	Ann Bye		3 – –
	Mary Newton		3 – –
Kitchen Maids	Elizh. Ward		3 – –
	Jane Willsbourn ..		3 – –
Stewards Room Boy	Geo. Braine		5 10 –
Kitchen Boy	Henry Mathews		3 15 –
Coal Porter	Richd. Neale		8 9 –
Watch Dairyman	Edwd. Davies		13 13 –
		965 – –	52 17 –
			965 – –
	Establishment.. ..	£	1017 17 –

would approve of her having a *dame de Compagnie* to reside constantly at Blackheath; and that if Mrs. Fitzgerald (daughter of Hinuber) would accept of her offer that you would not think her choice an improper one. If you agree to this, I am to call on that lady and propose to her to come with her daughter to live in the Garden House, adjoining the Princesses, and to acquaint her that an allowance of £200 a year will be paid her for any little extra expence in her dress that might be required. The matter resting altogether with *you* to determine upon, *I* shall not presume to give any opinion upon this arrangement, particularly as I do not know Mrs. Fitzgerald, but if you had no objection to it, perhaps you would yourself like on this occasion to pay her the compliment of acceding to it.

I will now dismiss this subject to express all the regret I feel at the account I have had of your late accident, from the effects of which I hope you are now altogether recovered. You will of course have heard from Adolphus of the intention of leaving Weymouth Thursday week and reaching Windsor on Friday.[1] Indeed he wrote me word that he would give you that information or I should have done it myself. Now, my dearest brother, you must be tired of my long letter, and the sooner I let you off, the better you will be pleased, so I will only add my kindest remembrance to Mrs. Fitzherbert.[2] (46021–4)

1616 THE PRINCE OF WALES TO LORD PELHAM

Carlton House, 7 Oct. 1801

I cannot help troubling you with a few lines to request a favor of you, by which you may oblige me very much, and that is, that you will have the goodness to appoint an old & faithful servant of mine, by name John Hargrave, to a messenger's place which I understand is now vacant. I desir'd Jack Payne to write to you my wishes as I was not able to write myself, but fear as I have heard nothing from you, that there may have been some mistake about his letter.[3] (Add. MSS. 33133, f.16)

1. W. H. Fremantle wrote from Weymouth: 'Prince Adolphus has been here the whole time, and seems a remarkable gentlemanlike amiable young man, uncommonly attentive and affectionate in his behaviour to the King' (Buckingham, *Court and Cabinets of George III*, iii.173).

2. In October the Prince increased Mrs. Fitzherbert's allowance, which was paid into Coutts' Bank, from £3,000 to £4,000 a year. It was increased from £6,000 to £10,000 in April 1820.

3. The Prince's letter to Addington dated Windsor Castle, 2 October—the day after the Preliminaries of Peace were signed by Lord Hawkesbury and M. Otto, is in Pellew, i.453 but inaccurately transcribed and incomplete: 'Many thanks, my dear Sir, for your obliging communication. It is a matter no doubt of most amazing importance, and upon which I

Castle Hill, Friday night, 30 Oct. 1801

When I returned from Kew this evening, I immediately enquired of Madame de St. Laurent (previous to intimating to her your wish of meeting the rest of our brothers here on my birthday) what arrangements she had made for seeing *her* friends, in consequence of my plan of passing that day with the King and Queen and my sisters, when I found she had actually engaged sixteen or eighteen of our old American acquaintance, whom to put off now *you* would I am sure not wish, and who, from the little habit they are in of meeting company like yourself would be so much *genés* that I am confident it would be a sad bore to you to find yourself with them. Allow me therefore to propose to you to come over on Friday next instead, on which day Frederic has been for some time past engaged to dine here. Madame de St. Laurent was very pressing to put off all the persons she had asked, that you might not be disappointed in your intention of passing a few hours here; but I have ventured to insist she should *not* do so from a conviction that you would approve of my acting so. Entre nous, my dearest brother, had *you* proposed to come *alone* over on Monday I should not have thought it necessary, from the knowledge I have of your affability and readiness to accommodate yourself *to any* company, to have made any alteration in those invited here for that day, but I must frankly confess I should be very loth to expose them to the remarks of either Frederic, William or Ernest, of whose sarcastic disposition, though in each it shews itself differently, I have often had proofs; and as such I should hope you would not be offended if I request you will permit our little plans for Monday to go on as they are at present settled. This is of course, *entre nous*, altogether for obvious reasons; and I shall be much obliged to you if, when you see any of my other brothers, you will simply say to *them*, that as the debate would prevent my passing the day with the family on Tuesday (Sophia's birthday) as I had intended, it was my desire to remain with them as much of Monday as I could in place of it. I cannot of course expect or indeed *wish* that you should put yourself out of your way to meet me on my birthday at Kew, where I know the stile of life is so little suited to your taste, but I am so well satisfied of your friendship and attachment for me, that it can require no fresh assurances on your part to convince me that you will not be one of the last to wish me well upon the occasion. For God's sake therefore stand upon *no* ceremony,

most heartily congratulate you. Everything, I have no doubt, will smile upon us now. When I return through town I hope I shall have the pleasure of seeing you on every account, & which will be within a few days, as I do not intend staying here above three or four days at furthest. I am this moment summon'd to his Majesty's dinner, for my not adding anything more [*sic*] except that I am [etc.]' (Sidmouth MSS.). There was no message of congratulation, apparently, from the King to *his* Chancellor of the Exchequer.

and do not think of coming over on any account, only let me know by a line from Lee whether you will favor us with your company on Friday next. As we shall meet on Tuesday, I conclude, at the House, I do not intend being up before that, and then probably we shall have an opportunity of talking upon the business you intimated; in the meanwhile believe me [etc.]. (46025–7)

1618   PRINCESS ELIZABETH TO THE PRINCE OF WALES

1 Nov. 1801

Mama desires me to inform you that the Princess dines here tomorrow; she does not know whether there is a chance of your coming but should you think of it she would be grieved to death to have you come to meet with anything that might not be pleasant to you. Augusta desires her love; she is much better. (Add. Georgian 11/90)

1619   THE PRINCESS OF WALES TO THE KING, AND THE REPLY

18 Nov. 1801

The great kindness which I have uniformly experienced from your Majesty since my first arrival in this country, and the interest which you have done me the honor to take in everything that concerns my happiness, induces me to lay before your Majesty the uncomfortable situation in which I am now placed, wishing to be entirely guided by your Majesty's gracious advice.

When I first came to this country the expences of my household were paid by Lord Cholmondeley and amounted (as I am inform'd) to 17,000 per annum, independant of the £5,000 which I received from Parliament. In June 1800 the Prince determined to give me a seperate establishment of 12,000 per annum. I have endeavoured by every means in my power to reduce the expences of my household to this sum but I find it will be totally impossible unless I part with my Ladies, which I am very unwilling to do but which I will submit to if your Majesty commands it.

At the time the Prince determined to give this seperate income there were bills to the amount of £4,000 unsettled and which of course have since been brought to my accounts. It would be impossible for me to discharge them even if my allowance was regularly paid, but as that is now three quarters in arrear I find myself in debt and difficulty without the possible means of extricating myself. To your Majesty alone therefore I can look up for support, and whatever arrangements your Majesty may think proper to make for me I shall most readily submit to. The only favor I have to beg (and which I flatter myself your Majesty will not think unreasonable) is that whatever income is to be allowed me may be paid regularly. My present uncomfortable situation must plead my excuse for thus taking the liberty of addressing your Majesty, and I trust that my conduct will ensure me the continuance of the condescension and kindness with which I have hitherto been honored, and the idea that my future happiness comes entirely from your Majesty's kindness as a mark of your Majesty's gracious approbation of my former conduct will be the source of the truest comfort to me. (42341-2)

THE KING'S REPLY [draft]

Windsor, 23 Nov. 1801

That kindness which I could not but feel you entitled to on coming into this country is still more deserved by the propriety of your conduct in a very difficult and unpleasant situation. You have judged very properly in entrusting the letter I have received from you to the Lord Chancellor. His station in my service as well as his excellent private character particularly point him out for being employed on the present occasion. That I may not give you any advice but on good ground I have directed him to deliver this letter to you and to receive such information as you may have to communicate on the subject of your letter, or to converse with any person you may point out as best acquainted with the state of your affairs.

I cannot conclude without giving the fullest assurances of the firmest intentions that you shall never repent of the reliance you place on my affection, which is founded on the resolution of following the line of justice and rectitude. (16731)

1620 LETTERS FROM THE DUKE OF KENT TO THE PRINCE OF WALES

Castle Hill Lodge, 21 Nov. [1801]

At the same time that this reaches you, Admiral Payne will receive from me for your information a full and circumstantial report of my visit to Blackheath on Tuesday last. As such I shall not in this touch upon any of the points contained in that not to bore you with repetition; but as I have omitted giving you any information relative to what you instructed me to find out about Miss Hayman[1] and Miss Garth, I shall have to add

1. See No. 1607*n*. Glenbervie wrote on 16 October: 'Lady Glenbervie told me today the

240

that the Princess acquainted me of herself that the former of these ladies remained her Privy Purse, but that, *pour réduire la consommation de deux bouches de plus* (to use her own expression), by which was meant Miss Hayman and her maid, she had determined to lodge her only at those times when she had occasion for her attendance upon business. This being the reason held out by the Princess for not retaining this lady at all times in the house with her as before, it was impossible for me to find out whether this decision had originated in any other cause.[1] As to Miss Garth, she shewed me a letter written by her in which she complains, not altogether in the most proper manner, of the unequal share of duty that had fallen upon her, alluding to Mrs. Lisle's long absence, Miss Coleman's not being admitted to attend at all, and Miss Vernon's preciseness in doing her three months' attendance *only* without *ever offering* even to assist her on whom the labouring oar fell. I did not perceive that this had had any other effect with the Princess than to give her dissatisfaction, but whether it will influence her to take any steps upon it, I could not gather. This you will say is but a very unsatisfactory account of the circumstance, but I give it you such as I could collect. Towards the end of next week I propose leaving this for the winter; the Drawing Room is fixed for Thursday December the third; but whether the family will move to Kew or the Queen's House for the purpose appears not yet determined upon. I shall now only intreat you to remember me most kindly to Mrs. Fitzherbert, who I hope knows I called twice upon her when last she was in town, and will do me the justice to believe I was truly mortified at missing her: and conclude by assuring

reason of the coldness which the Princess of Wales has lately shown to Miss Hayman, who was so great a favourite and had really a strong attachment to the Princess. It seems on one particular occasion, perhaps about a year ago, when there was a large mixed company to dinner at Blackheath, after the gentlemen joined the ladies in the drawing room upstairs, the Princess (as she frequently does) took some young man (I believe Frere) downstairs to the Blue Room which opens into the greenhouse, and remained there some hours ... The next morning Miss Hayman took courage to execute a purpose she had long entertained of representing to the Princess that our manners and modes of society were so different from those of other countries, that what did not certainly strike her Royal Highness as at all particular would be thought so here and give rise to unpleasant and unjust remarks, which a little more attention to our prejudices would prevent. The Princess received this hint very ill, told her she neither desired nor liked nor improved by advice, that she had her ladies for attendants not counsellors ... This summer Miss Hayman has been allowed to be absent six months. Formerly she could scarcely be parted with at all' (*Journals*, i.260).

1. Glenbervie wrote on 13 November: 'Miss Hayman told Lord Sheffield that before she left Wales she had received notice that she was no longer to have her apartment in the round tower at Blackheath, but must find herself a lodging in town. The Princess therefore will have no lady established in the house with her, an extraordinary and improper situation. It seems her annual expenses since her £8,000 were raised to £12,000 and the expenses of her table, etc., have been thrown upon her, have amounted to £16,000, and she is already in great embarrassment' (ibid., i.281).

you of my devoted attachment, and of the pride I shall ever feel in proving myself to be, my dearest brother, through life [etc.]. (46028–9)

Castle Hill Lodge, Wednesday, 25 Nov. 1801
On my return from Windsor last evening I found your most kind letter, and I now do myself the pleasure to assure you that I shall punctually attend you at eleven o'clock on Friday. I am quite at a loss to conceive how it has happened that my letter to Admiral Payne did not arrive together with those for you and Mrs. Fitzherbert, for I sent all three under the same cover to Aberdeen,[1] with the injunc[tion] to forward the whole to Brighton by the first conveyance. But least that one should eventually have miscarried, I herewith enclose a duplicate of it, that before I have the pleasure of meeting you, you may be prepared upon its contents.

I left Windsor yesterday at two after having been there from Sunday. The Queen has had a slight attack of St. Antony's fire in the face. It is almost over but I believe it will be the occasion of the Drawing Room taking place tomorrow fortnight instead of tomorrow week; the Levée (which seems now to be fixed for every alternate fortnight) will be this day se'ennight. All our sisters are well except Sophy and Amelia who are slightly indisposed; our three favorites desire their kindest loves to the *dear Prince*, to use their own words. I will not take up any more of your time now than to assure you of my devoted, and warmest attachment. (46030–1)

1621   REAR-ADMIRAL J. W. PAYNE TO ROBERT GRAY
[*5 Dec. 1801*]
There is an advertisement in the papers of Mr. Jeffries the jeweller respecting the Prince. I know it to be only a grub production, but I wish if you see Gibbs[2] or Sutton[3] you would speak to them about

1. Frank Aberdeen was the Prince's porter. Earlier, he was in the service of the Duchess of Devonshire.

2. Gibbs, the Prince's Attorney-General since about July 1800. On 10 July 1800 he had kissed the Queen's hand at the Drawing Room on his promotion. See No. 1310*n*, where in line 4, 1799 should read 1800. The *D.N.B.* is in error.

3. Sir Thomas Manners-Sutton, 1st Lord Manners (1756–1842). M.P. for Newark, 1796–1805; Chief Justice of North Wales, 1797–1802; Solicitor-General to the Prince of Wales, *c.* July 1800; Solicitor-General, 1802–5, and knighted, 19 May 1802; a Baron of the Exchequer, 1805–7; peerage, 20 April 1807; Lord Chancellor of Ireland, May 1807–November 1827.

it.[1] The original I left with Mr. Addington many months ago, & he told me the Prince should not condescend to take notice of it. (32476)

[Enclosure]

1. The following statement was printed:

Statement of the Accounts of Mr. JEFFERYS, in the Affairs of His Royal Highness the PRINCE OF WALES: Shewing the Amount of the Claims of Mr. JEFFERYS, as established by the Verdict of a Jury, before LORD KENYON, and those admitted by the Commissioners for the Management of the PRINCE's Affairs; together with the Deductions and Deficiency of Payment, from the Mode adopted by the Commissioners* for the Settlement of the said Claims.

	Claims			Net Receipts		
	£	s.	d.	£	s.	d.
Amount of verdict obtained in the Court of King's Bench for jewels, on the marriage of the Prince . . .	50,997	10	0			
Received of Lord Cholmondely				25,000	0	0
A deduction was made on the balance of ten per cent. and the amount paid in debentures, which sold, on an average discount, at twenty per cent. loss, producing .				18,718	4	0
Deficiency				7,279	6	0
	50,997	10	0	50,997	10	0
Bond debts, which being admitted by the Commissioners, an appeal to a jury was unnecessary	24,700	0	0			
Ten per cent. deducted, and the balance paid in debentures, which at an average loss of twenty per cent. produced				17,784	0	0
Deficiency				6,916	0	0
	24,700	0	0	24,700	0	0
An account, including presents of jewels made by the Prince on his marriage, to the Queen and the Royal Family.	9,331	9	6			
This account, also admitted by the Commissioners, was settled by a deduction of ten per cent. and the balance in debentures, at twenty per cent. discount, produced .				6,718	14	0
Deficiency				2,612	15	6
	9,331	9	6	9,331	9	6

	£	s.	d.
Total amount of Claims . . .	85,028	19	6
Ditto of net receipts . . .	68,220	18	0
Ditto deficiency	16,808	1	6

* The Right Honourable William Pitt, Chancellor of the Exchequer; the Right Hon. Henry Addington, Speaker of the House of Commons; Henry Strachey, Esq., M.P., Master of the King's Household; William [sic] Fordyce, Esq., M.P., Surveyor of the Crown Lands; and Mr. Sergeant Walker, Accomptant General; Commissioners named in the Act for the Settlement of the Affairs of the Prince of Wales.

J. G. BARNARD, PRINTER
GEORGE'S COURT, CLERKENWELL

The amount of the account delivered to the Commissioners, in May 1795, for the jewels, for the Princess of Wales on her marriage, was 54,685*l*. and a proposal being made by the Commissioners, that I should deduct, as nearly as I can recollect, 14,000*l*. I asked if there was any appeal against the decisions of the Commissioners; to which Mr. Pitt, who was present, replied, that the act of Parliament provided redress by an appeal to a jury: to such a decision I determined to submit my claim, and, in February 1796, obtained A VERDICT for the sum mentioned in the annexed account.

Not a word was said during the trial, by the counsel for the Commissioners, of any intended deduction from the verdict; nor was any intimation made to me on the subject, till the time appointed to receive the amount (as I supposed) of the sum, to which the verdict of the jury had given me A LEGAL CLAIM. It was then, to my astonishment, proposed to me, that if I would consent to a deduction of ten per cent. the balance should be paid in debentures, bearing an interest of five per cent.; but if I refused to make such a deduction, the debentures should bear only three per cent. As I had been induced to go into a court of justice by the assurance of the Commissioners, that an appeal to a jury (if I chose to submit to it) would give me redress, and had in consequence of such appeal obtained A VERDICT, I desired time to consult my counsel, Mr. Erskine and Mr. Adam, on so extraordinary and unexpected a proposal, which the Commissioners informed me, the act of Parliament authorized. It being the opinion of Mr. Erskine, and Mr. Adam, upon consulting the act, that I had no alternative, but to submit; I was compelled by the imperious necessity of the case, and the pressing demands, accompanied with threats from my creditors, to consent (if an act under such circumstances can be called a consent) to my own ruin. The annexed account is confined solely to the deficiency arising from the mode of payment, amounting to nearly 17,000*l*.; and which, great as that amount is, forms but a part of the loss I have sustained by this unfortunate business. I have proofs sufficient to make it clearly appear, that my loss (including the deficiency of the payment) arising from a variety of circumstances that attend a state of embarrassment and distress, such as I have experienced, amounts to a sum very considerably exceeding 30,000*l*.

A variety of reports having been circulated to the disadvantage of my reputation, stating the misfortunes I have experienced to have been attributable solely to my own indiscretions; and that, having obtained a verdict, I had accordingly received (as the public imagine) the amount of my claims upon the Prince of Wales; I have thought it necessary, by the advice of my friends, to draw up the annexed statement, accompanied with a few observations (merely explanatory), for the purpose, not of conveying censure upon others, but to vindicate my own character; and an attentive perusal of the contents of this paper (which are strictly true), will, I presume, clearly point out the source of the dreadful calamities that have been experienced by my family and myself, in the transactions alluded to.

Pall Mall   NATH^L. JEFFERYS

Copy of a Letter to the PRINCE OF WALES, *enclosing the preceding Statement of Accounts, &c.*
SIR,   *Pall Mall, June 25, 1801*
FROM the difficulties I have experienced for the last four years, to provide for my family, arising from the mistaken idea of the public, that my misfortunes did not originate from the cause I state, but my own improper conduct; and the sanction this idea has unfortunately received from your ROYAL HIGHNESS totally withdrawing from me that patronage I had formerly the good fortune to enjoy, and which I am not conscious of ever having deserved to forfeit; I am most forcibly called upon, to take some method, publicly to vindicate my character in the opinion of the world, to whom I am ultimately to look for support.

I have drawn up the enclosed statement for that sole purpose; and your ROYAL HIGHNESS (I am confident), in the perusal of it, will not deny me the credit of having carefully abstained from all reflections on any individual.

The cruelty of my situation has seldom (I believe) been experienced by any man. My fortune has been ruined, my character discredited, and my health broken with excessive anxiety.

William Pitt
by John Hoppner *c.* 1805

Martha, Dowager
Countess of Elgin
by Allan Ramsay

Sir Walter Farquhar

1622 THE DOWAGER COUNTESS OF ELGIN TO THE HON. MRS. LISLE

Shrewsbury Lodge, 11 Dec. 1801

I beg the favour of you, to inform her Royal Highness the Princess of Wales with my duty, that I am disappointed of Colonel Macleod's company to meet Sr. Sidney Smith on Monday to dinner; and feeling the propriety of her Royal Highness's observation, 'that it would be unpleasant *not* to have two gentlemen of the party', which so entirely agrees with my own ideas, that unless I receive her Royal Highness's commands to the contrary, I shall decline receiving Sr. Sidney's visit till another opportunity.

If this little transaction were any way connected with the Princess of Wales's visit I should be very sorry indeed, but as her Royal Highness named Monday for dining with her dear little Princess I look forward with pleasure to that day, for which Princess Charlotte is preparing all her little store of amusement.

A servant waits for the answer, which I shall be glad to have as soon as you conveniently can, as accordingly I have to send to town, or not, this evening. (49256)

1623 THE DUCHESS OF WURTEMBERG TO THE PRINCE OF WALES

Stutgard, 23 Dec. 1801

You will I am sure believe that I was delighted to hear from Mr. Tyrwhit that you are quite recovered from your sad fall, and that dear little Charlotte improves very much. Lady Elgin has sent me her bust in wax which at this moment hangs over my writing table. I long to see the original again. She appears to be your very image, and is a great favourite with the whole family. The Queen and my sisters are very often so good as to indulge me with charming accounts of her.

All this has been produced, by placing an unlimited confidence in a quarter, where a doubt of its rectitude would have been insult.

The injury I individually complain of, Sir, is not confined to me; it extends to the public: A sacred principle of our Constitution—THE VERDICT OF A JURY—has been rendered of no effect.

Influenced by the powerful calls of necessity, and urged by no principle of resentment to any person, in the mode I adopt to vindicate my character, I hope for your ROYAL HIGHNESS's forgiveness, if any thing I have said should hurt your feelings. I assure your ROYAL HIGHNESS, nothing is farther from my intention.

I have the honour to be, Sir,
Your ROYAL HIGHNESS's obedient Servant,
NATH^L. JEFFERYS
(32477–8)

J. G. BARNARD, PRINTER,
George's Court, Clerkenwell.

I am highly delighted with the assurances Mr. Tyrwhit gives me of the continuance of your regard and friendship, my dear brother. This is a great comfort to me who have been so many years parted from my family, and I think I deserve your kindness a little from my affection for you. I hope you received long ago my thanks for the beautiful locket with my little neice's hair. It is a very favourite ornament of mine as being your gift and the little angel's hair; it gave me great pleasure and is very much admired. I regret that Mr. Tyrwhit's being in a hurry to proceed on his journey prevents my shewing him all the attentions that I should wish to shew all those who are in your family.[1]

At this moment we are all anxiety for to hear what will be concluded at Amiens, as it must in some degree have great effect on the situation of Germany. Everybody is anxious to know how far the indemnifications will be carried and to receive some compensation for the severe losses that this cruel war has brought on us all. None of the Princes have suffered more than the Duke, whose Dutchy was nearly a year in the hands of the French and was obliged to pay such heavy contributions. I am sure, my dear brother, that you would have been very much hurt could you have known all we underwent during that time, but I will not take up your time with such an unpleasant subject. May I beg, my dear brother, that you will do me the favour to accept of the trifle which accompanies this and let it put you sometimes in mind of me. (51670–2)

1. Tyrwhitt was on his way home from Vienna, and he arrived in England, *via* Paris, about the middle of January. He reported that, abroad, there was 'no confidence in the vigour or the stability of the present Ministry'.

IV   1802

The Prince's relations with Addington were much more cordial than those with Pitt. He approved the Peace (the Definitive Treaty was signed at Amiens on 27 March), and gave the Government a general support. The fact that Tyrwhitt sat on the Treasury bench, and rose '*a propos* of nothing, to express his perfect confidence in the present Administration', appeared to indicate closer relations between Carlton House and the Court of St. James's. Addington's negotiations with Moira, which had all but broken down the previous December, might have been successfully resumed in January had he been able to remove the Duke of Portland from the Cabinet. But if the Duke had been appointed Lord Lieutenant of Ireland, as was suggested, and assuming too, that something could have been done for Lord Hardwicke, this arrangement would have been an insurmountable obstacle to Grey's taking office. Addington felt that the signing of the Definitive Peace Treaty strengthened his position, and it made him less anxious to recruit new Ministers. 'Tierney', said Lord Bathurst, 'is a private trader and will sooner or later make his bargain [he accepted the Treasurership of the Navy in the summer of 1803] and I think Moira hopes to make his, although that will, on account of the Prince, be attended with more difficulties.' Some of Addington's colleagues viewed with misgivings the progress of these negotiations with Carlton House. Charles Yorke, the Secretary at War, remarked, 'I dread a connection with the Prince and his friends. No man can serve *two* masters; and then there would be jobs without end.'

On the face of it, then, it seemed likely that Ministers would view favourably the Prince's claim to the arrears of the revenue of the Duchy of Cornwall. The claim was based primarily on Edward III's grant of the Duchy to his son the 'Black Prince' when he was only eight years old, and the Prince's lawyers maintained that the consequence of the grant was to vest the Duchy in the Prince from the moment of his birth. The most astonishing thing about the claim was that it had never, apparently, been thought of in 1783 when Fox and his friends were in office and when the Prince came of age. It was not considered until 1795, when Loughborough, the Lord Chancellor, intimated that it was no part of his duty to present the claim, in the form of a Petition of Right, to the King. Since that time no other mode of presenting it having been found, nothing more had been done. Towards the end of January 1802, after a preliminary meeting between Tierney and Addington, Moira had a conversation with the Prime Minister, and on 12 February Sir John Macpherson informed Addington that what had taken place had had 'the best, the most extensive and most seasonable political effect'. He added, 'The Prince, whom I have just left, feels the happy reaction of his own good wishes to your Administration.' During the course of the debate in the Commons on 17 February on the Civil List, Thomas Manners-Sutton, the Prince's Solicitor-General, raised this question in a speech which made a great impression, but it was left over until the larger matter had been disposed of. 'The Prince', wrote Lord Bathurst on 4 March, 'considers the money as already voted, and was very active at Lady Holdernesse's auction, where everything went for double its reputed worth.' (Her furniture went to a sale room after her death.) Then, on 31 March, there was a full-scale debate which was remarkable for the absence of party recrimination and of criticism of the King. Addington and the Crown lawyers thought that the claim should be settled in the law courts, not in a popular assembly, and, largely on that ground, the Motion was defeated—by 160 votes to 103. The King was 'rather surprised, in what appears to him so objectionable a Motion, the minority should have been so large.' The voting was not altogether on party lines: among the minority were some independent country gentlemen and some of Canning's friends. Neither Grey nor his brother-in-law Whitbread voted in support of the Prince's claim. Grey, in fact, voted with the majority. He wrote (26 March) 'The Prince . . . caught me yesterday in the street and set off at once upon the subject, considering me as a sure supporter, and I was under the disagreeable necessity of taking advantage of the first pause which his want of breath afforded me, to tell him in as delicate a way as I could, that I was not quite convinced of his right. He was evidently a good deal struck by what I said, but bore it very well.' Pelham, the Home Secretary, carried the Petition to the King, who, said Lord Malmesbury, 'was very placid and good-humoured about it, and well pleased that it should not be again discussed in Parliament'.

The Prince's needs were as pressing as ever. Jefferys, the jeweller, one of his principal creditors in England, was thinking of bringing his own claims to the notice of the House of Commons. The Prince continued to spend at least £2,000 a year on his wardrobe. 'At one time,' commented Farington, 'the silver buckles were taken from him which sold as old silver for £150. They must have originally cost £900.' The Band of his Regiment, the 10th Light Dragoons, was an expensive luxury. He borrowed from Messrs. Greenwood and Cox, the Army Agents, the money for its upkeep, so that, by the end of 1804, the accumulated deficit was nearly £15,000, and by the end of 1805 exceeded £18,000. By 1804 the arrears on account of his Stables were almost £14,000.

The Carlton House group, of course, swelled the minority in the division on 31 March. Some of the Foxite Whigs were said to have placed themselves under the Prince's protection, and, remarked Lord Camden, 'I understand he is desirous of bringing a party into power to assist and prop up the present Government, and at the same time to consider themselves as under his immediate patronage.' Dundas, with some concern, noted 'that the Prince of Wales has a fixed plan to put himself at the head of as strong a party of the Scotch Peers as he can'. He added: 'It is not much to the credit of a good number of them to say that the King's age and occasional state of health creates speculations not unfavourable to his Royal Highness's views.' The Prince's friend Lord Keith seems to have been active during the General Election and at a subsequent by-election when his nephew Lord Elphinstone was elected a Representative Peer. Dundas was much concerned, and wrote to Addington: 'He [Lord Keith] has received great favours from Government, and I mistake him much if he does not look for more, and you was perfectly entitled to tell him that if he really wished to accord with the sentiments of this Majesty's Government, his nephew must not be a candidate at the present moment so as to distract the votes of the Peers. This was the language I held to all those who expressed a desire to be candidates on the present occasion, and in consequence of this representation they all deserted.'

Lord Wycombe commented on 'this very curious debate' in the Commons: 'It reminds one of the old proverb, "Child's pig—and Daddy's pork." How happened it that H.R.H. with so many able men at his disposition did not discover he had claims when he first discovered he had debts? Be his right what it may, I cannot help thinking that he has always had enough even in the worst of times to buy boots and leather breeches, or even to maintain an elderly gentlewoman, which is all the splendour I can discern about him.'

At the end of the year Addington was ready to abandon the point he had made earlier, and asked Pitt whether he thought it would be right to make a compromise with the Prince 'by setting his income clear on condition of H.R.H. waiving his claims to the arrears of the Duchy.' Pitt was against a compromise: if the Prince was entitled to the money it should be paid him; if not, the question of 'setting the Prince's income free'—free, that is, from the restrictions imposed by Parliament in 1795—should be considered separately.

The year 1802 saw the beginning of a protracted dispute between the Prince and Mrs. Fitzherbert on the one hand, and Lord Hugh Seymour's executors on the other, about the guardianship of Mary Seymour, Lady Horatia's youngest child, born in 1798. Lady Horatia, who was dying of consumption, told her friend Mrs. Fitzherbert that, whilst she was abroad, 'little Mary is to be your child'. She returned from Jamaica in 1801 but died in Bristol soon afterwards (12 July), and Lord Hugh died in Jamaica a few weeks later, leaving seven children. In his will he appointed his brothers, Lord Euston and Lord Henry Seymour, as his executors and as guardians of his children, but Mary was not named as one of them, as the will had been made before she was born. The executors naturally thought that their guardianship extended to Mary too, and they were unwilling to allow Mrs. Fitzherbert, a Roman Catholic, to bring up the child. The Prince of Wales, who loved children, had become very attached to 'Minny', and offered to settle £10,000 on her if the executors would agree to her remaining with Mrs. Fitzherbert. The offer was rejected, and legal proceedings eventually followed.

The Duke of Kent, although he had been in England since September 1801, had continued to hold his appointment as Commander-in-Chief in North America. Much to his surprise, early in 1802 he was offered the Governorship of Gibraltar, and he arrived there in May to discover that the discipline of the garrison was extraordinarily lax. The remedial measures he took triggered off a mutiny, the outcome of which is revealed in the 1803 correspondence.

The Duke of Sussex remained in Lisbon for the greater part of the year, spending, however, a few weeks in the summer with his brother at Gibraltar. He seemed to have formed the intention of settling in Portugal for an indefinite period, provided that the Prince Regent would give him a house in Lisbon for the duration of his own and of his son's life, but there was obvious reluctance to comply with this request, in view of the King's doubtful attitude. The Duke was reluctant to entertain the idea of even a brief visit to England, owing chiefly, it was believed, to a dread of being involved in disagreeable discussions with Lady Augusta and her family. Her brother, Captain Murray, who was in the Navy, was now pestering him with letters with the object of browbeating him into treating Lady Augusta as his lawful wife. Long ago, in October 1801, when Murray's ship, the 44-gun *Révolutionnaire*, was in the Tagus, they had met, and the Prince, as he then was, had promised him that as soon as he got his Establishment, following the customary parliamentary grant, he would return home to vindicate the honour of his wife and children against all opposition.

The Duke did not like being pestered in this way. He wrote Lady Augusta a letter in which he announced his intention never to see her again, and when she went to see him in Lisbon she was refused admittance to his house. By the summer she had agreed to a separation, and he expressed the hope that she would be given a title. At one moment she faced imprisonment for debt, apparently because her allowance remained unpaid.

During the year rumours that the Duke had been received into the Roman Catholic Church alarmed his family at home, but happily they proved to be unfounded. One day in March he was seen on his knees at his own window whilst the Host was being carried from a neighbouring church to a sick person, but when tackled by his Gentleman Attendant, James Trail, he treated it as a matter of no consequence, saying that he had always shown the same respect to the Sacrament in all Catholic countries. Trail was treated with no more confidence than his predecessor Livingston had been. The Duke never sought his advice, rarely took any notice of any that was offered, and told him that he would not remain in his service when he was in a position to form his own Establishment. Their relations rapidly deteriorated. Trail wrote home asking for his recall. 'Pray get me out of this terrible situation. It was Purgatory before. It is now pure Hell.' 'The Dr. [Domeier] and I often weep over our cruel destiny, but his last consolation always is, "It is such a pleasure to think that I may kill myself."' Trail commented, 'I sometimes think him half in earnest—that he will follow the path of his predecessor. I had rather follow that of one of mine—old Livingston.' His wishes were gratified and in the spring or early summer he was recalled at his own request. Nothing, he said, could be more disagreeable than to have to live with a man against his will and over whom he had not the slightest authority.

1624 THE DUKE OF CAMBRIDGE TO THE PRINCE OF WALES
Windsor, 7 Jan. 1802
I can[not] let this opportunity pass without writing you a few lines to enquire after your health. It is with the greatest concern that I have heard you have been very unwell of late and I do sincerely hope that your complaint is now removed and that I shall receive a more comfortable account today. Since my last Augusta & Minny

have both been taken ill with the cold I had, but they are a great deal better today, & Minny I believe intends dining at the Upper Lodge today. I have not yet quite got rid of my cold and for this reason I have thought it better not to come to London. I should else certainly not have missed this day and I wish you most sincerely joy of it.

The day is not fixed when the family goes to London but I will send you word as soon as I hear it.

The last two foreign mails have brought letters from Munster from Petersburgh, but as I have not seen Lenthe[1] I am totally ignorant of the contents of the dispatches.

P.S. Pray send me a line by one of your gentlemen how you are. (48570)

1625   VISCOUNT STRANGFORD[2] TO COLONEL MCMAHON

Bath, 19 Jan. 1802

I shall trust to your goodness to pardon the present boldness, to which nothing but the extremest necessity could have compelled me. I wish to be favoured with your advice whether it would be expedient to renew my application to Mr. Addington on the pension business. We are literally reduced to our lowest ebb, as the means are exhausted with which the kindness of friends had assisted us, & I know not where to look for fresh supplies. Perhaps if Mr. A. were again reminded, something might be done to deliver us from a very frightful situation. Pray forgive this intrusion. I should not thus trouble you, did not want almost stare me in the face. I hope most truly that you are perfectly recovered. (39773)

1. For some time Baron de Lenthe had been Hanoverian Minister in London.

2. Percy Clinton Sydney Smythe, 6th Viscount Strangford [I.] (1780–1855), succeeded his father, 1 October 1801. Secretary of Legation, 1803, Chargé d'Affaires, September–October 1804, May–October 1805, and May 1806–January 1807, and Minister Plenipotentiary, January–November 1807, at Lisbon; Minister to Brazil, 1808–15; Minister at Stockholm, 1817–20; Ambassador to Constantinople, 1820–5, and to Petersburg, 1825–6. K.B. 1808; G.C.B., 1815; created Baron Penshurst [U.K.], 1825. Special Mission to Brazil, 1828–9. These diplomatic appointments were almost a kind of outdoor relief. For his father's extreme poverty see No. 783 (ii. 390).

Carlton House, 22 Jan. 1802

When the letter from Mr. Otto[1] which I have now the pleasure of enclosing to you was communicated to me, I desired Admiral Payne to lay it before you. He called twice in Downing Street but missed you.

It is neither from the compliments Mr. Otto has been pleased to pay me, nor even from the justice which he renders your Administration that I am anxious to draw your attention to the contents of his letter. It is the wisdom, the temper and the pleasing harmony of the political order which it embraces that has gained my admiration.

Fortunate shall I esteem my own destiny in life if I can in any way be useful to favour a political system of such extensive good! I know what you will naturally feel upon the subject, and no one can wish you more success than I do in the arduous and noble duty you are discharging by your country.

P.S. I will beg of you to return me the letter when you have perused it (Sidmouth MSS., *Pellew*, ii.26 (incorrectly transcribed), and 39789 (draft, which varies slightly from the letter sent)).

ADDINGTON'S REPLY [copy]

Downing Street, 23 Jan. 1802

My warmest acknowledgments are due to your Royal Highness for the great satisfaction afforded me by the letters which I had the honour of receiving yesterday evening from Carlton House. I have the best reasons to believe that Mr. Otto's account of the impression made on the French Government is correct, and I am sanguine in the hope that a system may be adopted which, by keeping clear of the extreme of distrust on the one hand and of credulity and weakness on the other, will be suited to the temper, character and interests of both countries.

I may be permitted to add that I feel very strongly the value and importance of the approbation with which your Royal Highness has been pleased to distinguish my humble but sincere endeavours in the public service, and of the good wishes which you have condescended to express for their success. (38789)

1. Louis Guillaume Otto, Comte de Mosloy, French diplomatist. In 1801 the French Government had sent him to London to arrange an exchange of prisoners, and during the short interval of peace he was the French Minister in London. See Pellew, i.447*n*.

1627 THE EARL OF JERSEY TO COLONEL MCMAHON

Stratford Place, 27 Jan. 1802

In consequence of his Royal Highness the Prince of Wales's most gracious message conveyed to me in the favor of your last letter, upon the address I had humbly presumed to make to his Royal Highness, I have endeavored to avail myself of all that delay could do to ward off the repeated demands upon me, under the hopes of his Royal Highness's condescending remembrance. But these means are come to their expiration; that delay ceases to prevail, & I am daily and hourly threatened with actions & legal proceedings against me which I have not the power or ability to withstand & stop.

What then am I to do, Sir? I feel myself bound to endeavor, if possible, to rescue my family & myself from the indignities heaped upon me from all quarters, & to save them in fact from the disgrace & ruin actually hanging over their heads, & not to be averted by me.

It is to his Royal Highness I must look; this, no exaggerated statement, I will desire you to submit, with all humility on my part to his Royal Highness's recollection & sensibility. I am confident I need say no more. (39774)

1628 LETTERS FROM HENRY HOLLAND TO COLONEL MCMAHON, AND A REPLY

Sloane Place, 30 Jan. 1802

I mention'd to H.R.H. the vacant Stewardship in the Duchy; H.R.H. refer'd me to Admiral Payne, saying the Admiral would do everything that would be pleasant to me. He did so, and Mr. Gray wish me to say he had order'd to make out the deputation in favor of my friend, Mr. Colling of Okehampton, to whom I forwarded the information [*sic*]. Surely the Duke of Northumberland will not desire all this to be undone? Understanding you have some commission in the business and relying on your friendship, I have taken the liberty which I hope you will excuse. (39775)

FROM COLONEL MCMAHON

Bury Street, Saturday evening [?30 Jan. 1802]

I am extremely sorry that the commission I have had in the Cornish business should clash with any view of yours because it would afford me considerable pleasure upon any occasion to promote & not to mar whatever object might be pleasing to you. The fact is simply this. The Duke of Northumberland had solicited from the Prince, a considerable while since, one of those Stewardships (I am not sufficiently conversant in the Duchy to specify the precise one) & received in return what he consider'd tantamount to a gracious promise. On the recent vacancy by death, his Grace's Agent, Mr. Wilson,[1] requested me to repeat the Duke's solicitation to H.R.Hss. It was my duty to do so; when H.R.Hss told me that the reply he made to Adml. Payne, upon his preferring your application for the appointment in question had been 'I am always most desirous & happy to oblige Holland, but from somewhat that rests on my recollection, you must first see McMahon & know from him whether the D. of Northumberland expects it by reason of my previous promise or encouragement.'

This explanation I gave distinctly to the D. of Northumberland, who upon the faith of the hope originally given him, accepted this mark of the Prince's favor as a matter subject to neither disappointment or doubt; & accordingly I gave the name of his Grace's nominee to Mr. Gray, in order that the promised appointment should be made out accordingly.

In case the Duke has not rested on what he deem'd a promise, I am sensible of the earnestness with which the Prince wish'd to oblige you, & of the desire which Adml. Payne had to put it into execution.[2] (39778)

FROM HENRY HOLLAND

Sloane Place, 1 Feb. 1802

You will perceive by the enclosed how I was persuaded to get into the scrape I am in at Okehampton, a contested election, and the person for whom *Mr. Payne gave directions* to make out the appointment is the Returning Officer. The Duke of Northumberland may have a promise previous to August 1797, but this I am sure of, I have since that time not experienced in any instance the gracious intention of 'doing anything to strengthen my interest', while I lament this circumstance I beg leave to add my intire confidence in your good will towards me. (39776)

1. Richard Wilson (1759–1834), a solicitor, and M.P. for Ipswich, 1806–7. Principal Secretary to Lord Chancellors Eldon and Erskine, 1801–7; Bankruptcy Commissioner, 1802–31; Deputy-Recorder of Launceston, 1809–18. Unsuccessfully contested Ipswich, 1807 election. Political manager of the Duke of Northumberland's boroughs of Newport (Cornwall) and Launceston.

2. This last paragraph was scored through.

[Enclosure] THE PRINCE OF WALES TO HENRY HOLLAND

Weymouth, 27 Aug. 1797

(*Private*). Fully convinced, Mr. Holland, that the estate at Okehampton now belonging to me ought never for the interest of all parties to be seperated from that which is your brother's, I must wish you to make me an offer, and I assure you it is not my intention to part upon trifles. The estate, you know, will in a short time be a very fine property; it, however, suits me to sell it. I will order Mr. Tyrwhitt to assist and co-operate with you as the local circumstances of the town and borough may require. Things there of course will be under your arrangement. I should not press you for an answer so suddenly was I not well assured that you are so intimately acquainted with the property that it can put you to no inconvenience. I will desire you therefore to give Mr. Tyrwhitt a line to Exeter as soon as you have made up your mind to any[1] proposition. If it should strike you that the sale should not be made a matter of notoriety you have my full permission to let my name remain as the owner, and if any difficulty should arise with any of the tenants or others, my servants shall have my commands to have them removed; in short I shall be glad to do anything that can strengthen your interest.[2] (39777)

1. ? 'my' in the original (the letter is a copy).

2. The Prince of Wales wrote to Arthur Paget from Carlton House on 2 Feb. 1802: 'I have but two complaints to make of you, the first, that you have so long left me in suspense whether you have entirely forgotten me from your long & persevering silence, & secondly, from what I learn from Tom Tyrwhitt, that you could for one moment possibly doubt the full extent of that sincere affection I bear you, and which entitles you to everything that friendship can claim from one man to another. Believe me that there is not anything I am not ready, under that word, friendship, to risk or attempt for you, either to secure your happiness or peace of mind. With respect to the charge I have receiv'd respecting *Sackville Street*, I will certainly do everything I can to serve you, but I am confident your wishes are that it should be managed with all the delicacy that so painful a task will admit. I am afraid it will be some weeks if not months before I shall be able to accomplish the point owing to the absence of the parties from London. In the meantime if it is really & seriously *your wish* that *final* conclusion (as deliver'd to me by Tyrwhitt) should be drawn to *everything*, do you not think it would be more delicate, more proper, & more honourable (as well as most necessary to save you all further trouble & uneasiness) to convey to me in a parcel to be deliver'd to myself, & then again to be deliver'd solely by me to the trustees concern'd, all letters, papers & pictures that you may now have in your possession. You may depend upon it that I shall use the best of my endeavours to wound as little as possible either your feelings or those of others. It is a painful task I cannot but acknowledge, my dearest Arthur, to be under the necessity of giving pain to those one both respects & loves, but I again repeat that my friendship for you will make me waive all other considerations, at the same time I cannot help thinking the task once perform'd, I am serving others also who till then must remain in ignorance of the true state of your situation & sentiments. I have not as yet been able to see Addington, but I will not the first moment I do, cease urging him to obtain leave of absence for you from Lord Hawkesbury. Thus briefly do I write to you merely to set your mind at ease, & in order that you may never again have any foolish fancies or doubts about me, *car je suis toujours de loin comme de prés.* Many thanks for your delightful snuff box, & now God bless you.

6 Feb. 1802

The conversation yesterday at the House of Lords between Ld. Thurlow, the Chancellor & me, could only be in general terms, for the enclosed letter had prescribed that no step should be prematurely taken. All, therefore, that I could gather was a very fair disposition on the part of the Chancellor to give all advantage to the claim when the mode of urging it should be determined upon.[1]

P.S. Don't forget my commissions, & among the rest pray try whether you can pick me up a Polish, an Hungarian, or a Turkish horse or two. When you see Hardenberg, pray tell him how happy I shall be to make his acquaintance, & indeed that of everyone you approve' (*Paget Papers*, ii.36).

1. The reference is to the Prince's claim to the arrears of the Duchy of Cornwall revenues, concerning which Sir Edward Law wrote to Addington on 26 March: 'The Attorney-General presents his compliments to Mr. Addington and encloses the copy of a paper which Mr. Sutton was so obliging as to communicate to him, containing, as he understands, the principal grounds upon which the Prince of Wales's application to Parliament is founded. Mr. Addington will have the goodness to excuse his requesting that the paper should not go out of his hands, as the communication made to him by Mr. Sutton must of course be understood as of a private nature.

'The Act of the 34 H[enry] 6 is deserving of particular attention, and if the precedent were taken from a less disturbed period, would afford a good Parliamentary construction of the intended use and application of the original grant 11 Edw. 3d of the Duchy of Cornwall.

'The argument drawn from the recital in the statutes of the 8 and 16 G[eorge] 3d that the Prince stands *seised* of the Duchy of Cornwall and the possessions thereof, so as to obviate the necessity of complying with the condition of the grant, the obtaining livery from the King (or rather as recognizing the livery as in fact granted) is not well founded.

'An infant, whilst he was a ward in chivalry, was seised for many purposes and might acquire seisin by the act of his guardian, Co. Litt. 15, and yet he was not so seized as not to have occasion to sue his livery afterwards.

'The effect of Mr. Mansfield's and the other opinions taken by the Prince is that the Prince is entitled to an account of the rents and profits received during his minority—but that the expence of his state and dignity is to be defrayed out of those profits as far as they will extend—and that any advances on his account during his minority are to be set off in the account to be taken of what is due to him for the profits of the Duchy.

'The Prince is also advised by them that the proper and only way of prosecuting the claim to the profits of the Duchy was by a petition to the King in the nature of a writ of right.

'I know that Lord Rosslyn was of a different opinion, his Lordship thinking that this remedy was only competent in the case of a freehold—or rather, where a real action would be maintainable against a subject—but the authorities seem to be against him—They are most of them collected in Lord Somers's famous argument of the Bankers case, in the 11th Vol. of the State Trials 150 to 156 to which he refers.

'If Mr. Addington should wish to see the petition of right which was delivered by the Prince to Lord Rosslyn to be presented to his Majesty, the Attorney-General has a copy of it' (Sidmouth MSS.).

Lord Eldon's views are given in an undated letter to Addington (towards the end of March?]): 'I am better, but I am still harrassed by pain, feverishness, and lassitude, and the want of the use of my foot, in a degree which puts out of the question my attendance upon you today at Cabinet. I think also it is quite impossible that I should be able to attend the Lords on

The Prince requests that you will in his name get the Duke of Clarence to recommend to the Bishop of Chester[1] Doctor Gregory's application to succeed to the Living which he has so long served as Curate. Doctor Gregory desires to refer to the Bishop of London[2] for his character. (39779–80)

Monday [29 March], for, though, with good luck, I may be in a state that would admit, with management, of my voting, nursing myself during the debate, I dare not hope that I could get through the evening's *sitting upon the Woolsack*, and to be obliged to leave it would be awkward in itself, and might lead to consequences of much inconvenience subsequently. I shall, nevertheless, feel a good deal about being absent. I am at a loss what to say to you that can be useful. The Civil List part of the business I think stands on ground so arguable that I should like nothing [better] than to take part in a debate about it; but the Prince's claim is a most unmanageable matter. Put it in what way you will, I fear it never can be handsomely put, in the public mind, to our good master. And it attends as a rider, very unpleasantly, the movements of the Civil List proposition in the House of Commons. I never could find in those who act for the Prince a truly manly or sensible reason for the part which they act. Say they, all we want is to have the public know that, if the Prince had had the Cornwall revenues, he would not have been so much indebted to the public. Now that is a truism which wants no demonstration by debate in Parliament. It is equally a truism that if his *Majesty had thought* proper to accumulate the Cornwall revenues, and to have handed over the accumulations to the Prince, he *might* have done so. It wants therefore no debate to prove that, if the public have had the benefit of this fund either directly by its being applied to public uses, or indirectly by reason that the King having had the use of it he has been enabled the longer to forbear applying to Parliament for the deficiencies of the Civil List, the public have reaped this benefit from the application of that which the King *might* have given to the Prince. The real object therefore can be no other than to have it established that the King *ought and was bound* to accumulate and give it to the Prince. If this be so I can't blame the Prince (but the claim *now* is very stale) for seeking to have his *right* established. But I do not see how it is possible that it should be established in any way that does not make it almost impossible to avoid giving just offence to his Majesty. The claim so put is an imputation of misfeasance on the part of his Majesty. But if a *right* exists in law, in law there must be a *remedy* for it. Can that be a proceeding by a Committee in Parliament? Is it fit that a point of law depending upon doctrines to be understood only after research into subjects the most remote, abstruse and difficult should be decided or even discussed in assemblies not judicial? I confess I think *clearly not*. I am as anxious as any man can be that all the Royal family should, once for all, be placed in circumstances becoming their rank, but I doubt whether raising questions of this sort, as between different parts of the family, has any tendency to establish that harmony which is necessary to produce such a state of things. Upon the point itself, it is idle to be intimating what are the opinions of lawyers in the Houses of Parliament. They will differ. I am ashamed to add I fear as to some, according to their politics, and our profession will disgrace itself if this question is ever debated by lawyers in their proper persons *as Members of the Houses*. I know not what more I could say to you my dear Sir if I could have attended you today: if more is wanted from me, may I be allowed to add that in my feverish state I would rather see a deputy from the Cabinet than the Cabinet' (Sidmouth MSS.).

1. Henry William Majendie (1754–1830). Instructor to Prince William and Prince Edward, from June 1776, salary £200 a year; Preceptor to Prince William, from January 1780, salary the same. Canon of Windsor, 1785–98; Bishop of Chester, June 1800; of Bangor, 1809–30.

2. Beilby Porteus (1731–1809), Bishop of Chester, 1777–87; of London, 1787–1809.

THE DUKE OF KENT TO THE PRINCE OF WALES

Castle Hill Lodge, Sunday morning, 7 Feb. [*1802*]

The kindness you have ever shewn me, and the interest you have ever expressed in my welfare, render it my first duty to communicate to *you* a copy of a letter of mine to the King that will be presented today to his Majesty by Colonel Taylor.[1] You will perceive from the perusal of it *what* has given cause to its being written, as also that it is penned in strict conformity to the plan we talked over about three weeks since at Carlton House, and upon the adoption of which you were so kind as to express your approbation. I have also forwarded, agreable to what I *then* mentioned to be my intention, a copy of it to the Duke of York, and *all* I shall venture to ask of *you* upon this occasion, is to see *him*, and give him *your* opinion as to the part *he* OUGHT to take in the business, for his *own* sake, as, if my application should be negatived, I shall feel it my duty in defence of my character as a soldier, to make the public acquainted with the steps I have taken to reach *that* station (where I am sure *you* and the whole army will agree I *ought* to be at this juncture) and with the result of them; when, from the opinion generally entertained of the causes of my being kept from employment, you cannot but be aware that to HIM ALONE it will be ascribed.

You know my warm and devoted attachment to *you*, and therefore I will not encroach upon *your* time with the repetition of professions that never can but feebly express the extent of those sentiments, with which [etc.]. (46036–7)

1631 THE PRINCE OF WALES TO SIR JOHN MACPHERSON, AND A REPLY [copy]

Carlton House, 15 Feb. 1802

I am much obliged to you for your letter, and all I can say upon the subject is that you do but justice to those sentiments which ever must be uppermost in my heart. In *primis*, the lively interest I ever must take in whatever concerns the welfare of my own *country* and my family, and, secondly, in the restoration of order in society and the tranquillity and peace not only of Europe but of the whole globe . . .

P.S. Many thanks to Mr. Otto for his obliging communication.[2] (39790)

1. Sir Herbert Taylor (1775–1839). Clerk in the Foreign Office under Lord Grenville; Private Secretary to the Duke of York, 1799, to the King, 1805; to Queen Charlotte and William IV. M.P. for Windsor, 1820–3. Lieutenant-Colonel, 1801; Colonel, 1810; Major-General, 1813; Lieutenant-General, 1825. Adjutant-General of the Forces, 1828. K.C.H., 1819; G.C.H., 1825; G.C.B., 1834.

2. Macpherson briefly replied from Brompton on the 16th (copy): 'The letter with which your

FROM SIR JOHN MACPHERSON [copy]

23 Feb. [sic] 1802

I take the liberty to enclose a copy of my letter to Mr. Hiley Addington. [1,2] I have had access to see the original letters from the French Court on the subject of your Royal Highness's communication with Mr. Otto. Nothing can be stronger, more creditable to your Royal Highness or more useful to your country. (39792)

1632 THE DUKE OF CAMBRIDGE TO THE PRINCE OF WALES

5 Mar. 1802

Many thanks for your kind note which I received last night. I really had forgot Mrs. Andrews [?] invitation & I certainly will go there. I am going to ride to Kew & shall not be back before two. I shall certainly call then at Carlton House and should you not be at home you will oblige me very much in leaving word with one of your servants at what o'clock you will call for me for the dinner. (48571)

Royal Highness has been pleased to honour me is the best that could be written and it will produce the best effects'. (39790)

1. The Prime Minister's brother (1759–1818). M.P. for Truro, 1787–90; for Winchelsea, 1794–6; for Wendover, 1796–1802; for Bossiney, 1802–3; for Harwich, 1803–18. A Lord of the Treasury, December 1800–March 1801, and July 1802–November 1803; Joint Secretary of the Treasury, April 1801–*c.* July 1802; Joint Paymaster-General, 1803–4; Commissioner for the Affairs of India, 1806–7; Under-Secretary of State, Home Department, August 1812–18.

2. Macpherson's letter to Hiley Addington is dated 3 March [*sic*]. It is a copy only.

'In case I may not find you at home I write this note and have much pleasure in informing you that I have authority to say that a paragraph in your letter to me of the 24th of last month has had the best effect. I was most anxious to pay my respects for a few minutes to your brother on Saturday last. Most sensibly do I lament on every ground his domestic distress, and I sincerely hope it will pass soon away and that his return to health and the helm will carry everything through for the public good. *He* was the soul of the commencement of the peace; he, with the *Heir Apparent* will *conclude it*, and on the most solid, the most advantageous grounds!! I do not make this assertion *lightly*; I would pledge all that is interesting to me on the event. Do you remember my early wish that a *relation* had gone to Paris? Not till the French Government feels that the *original vital principle* of the pacification is *embraced* and *confirmed* by those who are to *conclude it*, can it be EFFECTUALLY SEALED. Even *then*, OUR PEACE at Amiens [signed 27 March] is but the definitive step to the GENERAL SYSTEMATIC PACIFICATION OF EUROPE and of the WESTERN and EASTERN WORLD!!!

Pray read the enclosed printed paper; it is the *whole*, the *necessary* system of the French Government. It must equally become that of *ours*.' (39792–3)

Manchester Square, 20 Mar. 1802

Humbly submitted to his Royal Highness the Prince of Wales.

Religious reflections and compunctive sentiments point out the necessity of humiliation, repentance and atonement. I sincerely profess them as a duty incumbent on me and as the best means of alleviating the affliction that oppresses me for my disrespect towards the Prince of Wales and the Duke of York.

In thus acknowledging my offence and my sincere contrition for it, I make all the atonement that is at present in my power, and steadfastly purpose never again to misconduct myself towards their Royal Highnesses. By these means I expiate the sin of approaching my creator at the ensuing Easter, and the only grounds on which I dare to entreat or hope for forgiveness from the Princes are 'Not as I deserve it, but (according to the precepts of our blessed Saviour) to entitle them to it in a better place'. At the same time (however much I may hope from the goodness of their hearts) I think it my duty to submit to their Royal Highnesses consideration the following real statement, to convince them that my misbehaviour is more to be imputed to the distraction of my head than to the corruption of my heart, and that, tho' very blamefull, it may in some degree be palliated.

In consequence of the many different conferences and conversations which had taken place between the Earl of Moira and Lord Kinnaird and me, and the many various remarks made and suggestions thrown out by different persons, it was agreed on with their Lordships to draw out a clear and compleat statement *of all that had passed between us* to enable us all to judge impartially, and then to consult Mr. Baldwin[1] upon it confidentially. As I was disabled in my hand by the rheumatism and unable to write; afraid to employ any person to transcribe my notes, I thought it would be more secret to have it printed under my own eye by French priests (who scarce knew ten words of English) especially as I could read my notes to their compositor without connecting the text, correct the proofs in my own room, and of course be certain that no more than four copies could be taken. The priests' well-known character for secrecy, and their being on the eve of their return to France, confirmed the prudence of the privacy.

'With these intentions four copies were taken, two of which were sent to Lord Moira and Lord Kinnaird, with an envelope cover to them on which was expressed in my own writing the following injunction *underlined* and MARKED in the most precise manner to denote my specific wishes and intentions, vizt.

"My Lord; there have been two copies of the inclosed printed for

1. The Duke of Portland's secretary.

Lds. M. & K. *private use and satisfaction*. It is not IN THE MOST DISTANT MANNER, *meant or intended to publish, circulate, disperse or give it away*. It is LENT to your Lordship *for your own private reading and consideration*, ON CONDITION that when you have well digested and made yourself master of the subject, you will *then* return it, *most carefully sealed up*. You are desired *to keep it* MOST SECRET, as it is sent *only to you*, either as a party concerned, or as an umpire by whose friendly skill the scion of equity may be grafted into the stock of justice."

'The art of man could not have contrived a more secret way to draw up the statement, nor can any language furnish words more guarded to prevent a communication of its contents. A third copy was given by me to Mr. Baldwin with a similar envelope, who returned it in a few days solemnly declaring that he had fullfilled the injunction. The fourth copy I kept myself.

'Lord Moira thought proper to carry his copy to the Prince of Wales, contrary to my positive request and intention. Perhaps he did his duty! I mean to prove only that *I* did not publish, circulate, disperse or give it away. In sending it to Lord Moira and Lord Kinnaird I sent them only a compendium of *some* of the remarks and reflections that had been made by their Lordships themselves as well as by me, and by those persons to whom their Lordships had spoken on the subject. If the printed memoir has caused any uneasiness, it is not my fault. I never meant that it should be shewed to either of the Princes. If I had I should not have inserted the frivolous animadversions and epigramatic gibes which were promiscuously made only to create a laugh in conversation. As they were totally irrelevant to the matter in the discussion, it would certainly have been the height of folly in soliciting a favor to have introduced what must be construed disrespectfull and illnatured. Malevolent intentions to *secretly* wound any man's peace of mind are contrary to the gallantry of my nature and the whole conduct of my life, and even my (perhaps too bold) language in public writing and in my letters to their Royal Highnesses will refute such a charge.

'I sincerely love them both. I faithfully served them both. I always was and am most respectfully attached to them. My zeal, my journies, my wounds and my sufferings prove all this. I was sorely grieved at the many cruel things that were reported to have been said against me. I grew intemperate and impatiens iræ, in the malady of a perturbed spirit, I lost myself. In that state I forgot who they were, and *in that state only* could I forget what was due to my beloved Sovereign and master's sons.'

In thus submitting the fact to the generous liberality of their Royal Highnesses, I throw myself in their goodness of heart for forgiveness. I mean it as an act of contrition and atonement, expressing at the same time that I breathe nothing but peace and goodwill towards all men for the remainder of my days.

In my present weak state and in the agonising pains that I suffer, I find strength only to say that I am sincerely penitent and unfeignedly lament my undutifullness. I ask no favour, I supplicate no relief, I implore no protection however exceedingly I stand in need of them. I feel that I do not deserve any and that the language that I have even privately held ought to shut the door against everything but compassion. In that light I wish them to consult only their own hearts and to gain general admiration by saying 'to err is human, to forgive, divine'. (31651–2)

1634 THE PRINCE OF WALES TO THE DUKE OF YORK, AND THE REPLY
Carlton House, 20 Mar. 1802
I call'd at your house yesterday just after you had left London, to mention to you that I had receiv'd a message from Gwynn through McDermot of my Regiment stating that Stone was quitting the Army, having receiv'd the appointment of Paymaster to the new College,[1] & that therefore he was very desirous of having McDermot as his Major of Brigade in the room of Stone. I cannot possibly have the smallest objection to what I consider is so much for McDermot's advantage especially as at the same time I know no one who is more equal to the situation; & therefore when Gwynn's request is laid before you I beg you will have the goodness to assure Gwynn that it meets with my entire approbation. Whilst I was writing the preceeding lines, the Duke of Kent has just call'd upon me, & acquainted me that O'Harra's Aid de Camp is just arriv'd with the accounts of my poor old friend's death, which I confess I am very sorry for, & Edward desires me at the same time to mention to you how anxious he is to succeed o'Harra in the Government of Gibraltar. You best know how far this is an arrangement that can take place; all I can say is that I shall ever truly participate in anything that can afford him satisfaction. Pray say how long you mean to stay at Bath. I beg my kindest remembrances to the Duchess, who I rejoice in hearing is so much benefitted by the waters. (44174–5)

THE DUKE OF YORK'S REPLY [copy]
Bath, 21 Mar. 1802
I lose no time in acknowledging the receipt of your letter & in assuring

1. The Royal Military College.

264

you that I shall have great pleasure in laying Captain McDermot's name before his Majesty to succeed Captain Stone as Major of Brigade to the Home District, for which situation he is in every respect most fit. You may also depend upon my taking the earliest oportunity of acquainting his Majesty with the Duke of Kent's wishes to succeed poor General O'Hara in the Government of Gibraltar, and trust that his Majesty will have no objection to gratify him in this appointment.

Many thanks for your kind enquiries after the Duchess, whom I have found a great deal better & who desires her best love to you. As for me, I am only come down here for a couple of days, not knowing whether I shall be able to absent myself from London again during the Duchess's stay here, & mean to be in London again without fail on Tuesday morning. God bless you.[1] (44176)

1635 THE DUKE OF YORK TO THE DUKE OF KENT, AND THE REPLY

Horse Guards, 30 Mar. 1802

I take the earliest opportunity in my power to acknowledge the receipt of your letter of Sunday, and cannot help expressing to you my surprise at its contents.

I had hoped that upon reconsideration, your own feelings would have made you sensible of the great impropriety of your wishing to delay going to Gibraltar, not only on account of the manner in which his Majesty had expressed himself concerning you, but also from the situation in which the place is left, and that no paultry private inconvenience would have been laid hold of, as an excuse to procrastinate your stay in this country.

When you asked me on Wednesday how soon I thought you ought to set out I confess that I was rather surprised at the question, but, however, told you that it was impossible for you, after what had passed, to stay here any longer than a fortnight or three weeks at the utmost; and though you may not, *as you say*, have authorised me to acquaint his Majesty with it, yet I consider myself as fully justified in having mentioned it to his Majesty when he spoke to me on the subject, as in the official capacity in which I spoke to you, a friendly hint from me ought to have been considered by you as only a more delicate way of conveying an order. Had any other General Officer in his Majesty's service been appointed to the Government of Gibraltar, I should not have hesitated in ordering him

1. According to *The Times* (22 March) the Duke had just completed the sale of his house in Piccadilly, the new proprietors being about sixty gentlemen and tradesmen who had subscribed £1,000 each for the purchase and new fitting up. The house was to be converted into a magnificent hotel and lodging house, and the purchase money was said to be £35,000.

to proceed there as soon as a frigate could have been ordered for his conveyance.

I therefore shall hope that you will not still press my speaking to his Majesty, as I shall then find myself (though reluctantly) under the necessity of mentioning all the circumstances & taking his Majesty's pleasure upon them.

With regard to the last paragraph in your letter by which you appear to imagine that your appointment to the Government of Gibraltar entitles you to draw the pay of a General Officer upon the Staff, you have perfectly misunderstood me. The pay of the Governor of Gibraltar is voted with the British Staff and therefore precludes your drawing any pay upon any other Staff. Whether you are to be placed upon the Staff at Gibraltar or not is not yet decided, but in general it is only in time of war that the Governors are allowed to receive their Staff pay. (46040–1)

THE DUKE OF KENT'S REPLY

Wednesday morning, 31 Mar. 1802

Although previous to receiving your letter last evening my mind was made up to adhere closely to the day before which I had informed you [*sic*], it would not be in my power to be ready without putting myself to the greatest inconvenience, and in fact without doing essential injury to my private concerns, the moment I read the footing upon which you urged my earlier departure, I mean, that the good of the King's service and the state of the place where I am to command rendered it indispensably necessary, I felt it a point of honor to set aside every *other* consideration and to sacrifice *everything* to *that* object, satisfied that at a future day it will *not* be forgot that I had done so at a time when everything combined to render a hurried move from home peculiarly hard and oppressive to me. As such I shall make a point *now* of leaving London by the 17th of April, and after paying my respects to their Majesties at Windsor, who I calculate will be there at *that* time, I shall proceed to Falmouth where I have settled with Lord St. Vincent to embark, in order to shorten the passage by avoiding the Channel, and consequently to render the probability of my early arrival at Gibraltar the greater.

As the feelings of men differ, I am willing to suppose some of the expressions in your letter that were very poignant to mine, were not meant to be so, and therefore I will not allow myself any observation upon them, except just to notice that you wrong me essentially if you conceive I ever sought a *subterfuge* to delay my departure. Those who know my situation in point of pecuniary embarrassment, brought on me not by extravagance but principally by the heavy losses I have sustained through shipwreck and captures while I was serving abroad, can vouch

266

that I make no small sacrifice in pressing the period of my leaving England at this particular moment.

Under the pressure of these circumstances, after the assurance I have more than once received from you of your sentiments upon the right I had to claim compensation for these losses, perhaps you would not think it unreasonable to urge Mr. Addington to make me some advance before my departure; their amount is above eighteen thousand pounds, and a small proportion of that now given would add essentially to my comfort at this moment in relieving me from some very pressing embarrassments; but this is left to your own judgement. As to my continuing to receive on the peace establishment the Staff pay which I find General O'Hara drew during the war I am fully sensible that must depend upon what shall be hereafter settled for the establishment, but I trust if the decision upon it is left to you, you will think it equitable that in a place of the importance of Gibraltar, that remuneration should not be withdrawn, when the labours of a person doing his duty there and his responsibility is considered. (46042–3)

1636   SIR FRANCIS BARING[1] TO THE MARQUESS OF LANSDOWNE
Devonshire Square, 1 Apr. 1802
I was engaged the whole of yesterday morning on business, but returning about ½ past five for a paper, I found your Lordship's note & immediately went to the House.[2] I was, however, extremely mortified that I could not stay, for I suffered so much in my head & bowels (& which I attribute to the exposing myself early in the morning to the cold wind) compelled me to retire & will oblige me to confine the whole of this day. If it is not giving your Lordship too much trouble I shall be highly gratified in conveying to Lord Moira how much I felt when I was obliged to retire, for although I was really ill when I received the note, yet my alacrity to comply with its contents made me forget what it is probable I should otherwise have attended to.

[*P.S.*] My brother is recovering fast from the gout & expects to be in town about the 14th. (39794)

1. Founder of the financial house of Baring Brothers, and a Director of the East India Company. M.P. for Grampound, 1784–90; for Wycombe, 1794–6 and 1802–6; for Calne, 1796–1802. Created Baronet, May 1793. (1740–1810)

2. For the debate on the Prince's claim to the arrears of the revenue of the Duchy of Cornwall.

Louisbourg, 4 Apr. 1802

Though you are not fond of writing I am sure that you have ever shewed me too much affection not to like to hear from me sometimes. I therefore seize with pleasure on every opportunity of recalling myself to you, and as Mr. Smith[1] has offered to execute any commissions I may wish to give him, I have begged him to deliver to you this letter and a set of Labrador buttons which the connoisseurs say are fine specimens of that stone. I wish they were more worth your acceptance but trusting to your affection am sure you will take the will for the deed.

I am delighted, my dear brother, with the accounts I hear of your charming little girl; the Queen and my sisters speak of her with great affection, and Lady Elgin is also so good as to write to me about her, knowing how anxious I am that Charlotte may turn out everything that can contribute to your happiness. Everybody speaks of her musical talents, which I am glad of as I know it will give you pleasure.

Since the 2d. we are settled here and I am very much taken up with altering my house and planting my garden, to which the severity of the winter has done much mischief. The papers mention your building again at Brighton. I hope that these alterations or additions will be finished sooner than mine which have been put a stop to by finding two beams quite spoilt. However, I am fortunate in their having been found as the whole staircase would have sunk had these beams remained.

I will not, my dear brother, take up no more of your time. (51678–9)

1638 NATHANIEL JEFFERYS TO THE PRINCE OF WALES

Pall Mall, 9 Apr. 1802

I should not have presum'd to address your Royal Highness on the subject of this letter, but upon the advice of my friend Mr. Sheridan, whom I have consulted upon the occasion. It is, Sir, relating to the future representation of the City of Coventry, where your Royal Highness has (tho' possibly you may not know it) a considerable degree of influence.

The unfavorable state of my circumstances induced me some time since publickly to decline offering myself again as a candidate, since which time & particularly within these few days the flattering opinion entertain'd by the leading people of both parties, with the principal members of the Corporation, of my conduct in Parliam't has induc'd

1. John Spencer Smith (1769–1845), Envoy Extraordinary to Wurtemberg, February–April 1804. There was no regular diplomatic representation before 1804. M.P. for Dover, 1802–6.

them to express a wish that I may again be their representative, accompanied with offers of support of the most liberal kind.

I am extremely happy, Sir, that my conduct in the House on a late occasion was such as your Royal Highness approv'd of, & it is with real concern that I reflect upon any circumstances having occurr'd to remove from your Royal Highness's mind that favorable impression of me which you have formerly with so much condescension frequently express'd. To prove to your Royal Highness the sincerity of my feelings, I beg leave to say (previous to my returning an answer to my friends in Coventry) that if there is any gentleman whom your Royal Highness would wish to bring forward as a candidate, I will withdraw my pretensions & give every possible support by my interest & exertions to promote his success—but if your Royal Highness should not have any person to propose, & should be of opinion that my future services in Parliament may in any degree be useful to your interests I certainly will in that case accept the offer of my friends, of whose success in their support of me I do not entertain a doubt. I beg leave to mention to your Royal Highness that one of my principal inducements for having declin'd to offer myself as a candidate arose from the idea I thought the world might entertain that the situation of retail trade in which I am engag'd was derogatory to a seat in Parliam't. Such a prejudice, however, if it did prevail—no longer exists, as it is my intention in consequence of the impair'd state of my health, & insufficiency of capital to carry on my business, to withdraw from my present line of business, & engage in one of a more private nature & attended with less fatigue & anxiety.[1]
(39795–6)

1639   JOHN HOOKHAM FRERE TO THE PRINCE OF WALES

[Lisbon] 14 Apr. 1802

C'est avec le plus grand regret que je me trouve forcé a faire une representation a votre Excellence sur le sujet le plus delicat possible et en

1. Jefferys was re-elected for Coventry at the general election in 1802, but he was unseated on petition on 11 March 1803. Farington wrote in his Diary on 24 July 1806: 'Mrs. Wheatley told me that Jefferies is in very good spirits respecting his *Letter to the Prince of Wales*. He said to her that in a fortnight he sold 6,050. He said he had yet more matter to bring forward. An answer to it, entitled "Diamond cut Diamond", he said, was wrote by *Gilderand*, a Jew attorney, at the instance of a man of the name of *Trieste* who formerly Jefferies had assisted. Mrs. Wheatley said Jefferies' temper is too sanguine & that his ruin has been owing to his having given up his shop upon a prospect of settling his affairs with the Prince. Mr. Jefferies' father had about £50,000. He has left her £8,000, but it is secured to herself and children. Jefferies sent his printed pamphlet, addressed to Mrs. Fitzherbert, to her house, and to insure its being received by her, got a large coronet seal to seal the cover.'

meme tems le plus urgent. La lettre que j'ai recu de Monr. Trail et que j'ai l'honneur de vous remettre c'y inclus suffira pour vous expliquer l'état des circonstances qui m'obligent a recourir a l'intervention de son Altesse Royale pour ecarter le coup terrible qui menace a la fois et le repos de sa Majeste le Roi mon Maitre, et l'honneur de son Altesse Royale, le Duc de Sussex, et la dignité de la nation Britannique qui se trouvent compromis pareillement par un concours de circonstances qui ne peut admettre aucune interpretation favorable.

L'accueil et les attentions distinguées que son Altesse Royale le Duc de Sussex a reçu de la part de son Altesse Royale, le Prince Regent,[1] ont toujours eté regarde par sa Majesté comme une preuve de consideration politique ainsi que de cette amitié individuelle que son Altesse Royale s'est plû de temoigner en diverses occasions pour la personne de sa Majesté.

Votre Excellence m'a meme assuré que s'il arriva que son Altesse Royale, le Duc de Sussex, ensuite de quelque demarche inconsiderée vint a perdre la faveur et la protection de sa Majesté, il s'ensuivrait que les attentions et les egards de son Altesse Royale, le Prince Regent, diminueraient en proportion et que la presence meme de son Altesse Royale deviendrait embarassante et penible pour cette cour. Nous craignons beaucoup Monsieur qu'une impression contraire ne soit la source des egaremens qu'on redoute de la part de son Altesse Royale et qu'il se soit persuadé que les attentions que son Altesse Royale n'a pas cessé de prodiguer a son egard derivent d'une influence qui est personelle et independente de toute autre consideration. Il importe essentiellement que son Altesse Royale soit detrompé sur ce point et vous jugerez bien, Monsieur, qu'il n'y a que votre Excellence qui pourra l'effectuer d'apres l'autorisation que vous aurez recu vous meme de la part de son Altesse Royale le Prince Regent en m'autorisant a moi ou a Monr. Trail[2] de temoigner a son Altesse Royale le Duc de Sussex combien 'une demarche quelconque qui serait deplaisante a sa Majesté Britannique changerait necessairement des attentions et des egards qui lui ont eté temoigné jusqu'a present'.

Il est penible assurement d'etre obligé de recourir a des moyens aussi extraordinaires cependant votre Excellence verra que ce n'est qu'apres avoid epuisé toutes les autres resources que nous nous sommes decidé a celle-ci. Elle verra que Monr. Trail n'a absolument rien omis de ce qui dependait de lui qu'il s'est addressé directment au Prince et encore par l'intermediaire des personnes avec lesquels son Altesse Royale vit le plus habituellement et auxquels il est naturel de supposer qu'il accorde sa confiance, quelques-uns se sont acquitté de ce devoir avec un zele qui

1. The Prince Regent of Portugal.

2. The Gentleman in attendance on the Duke of Sussex.

leur fait le plus grand honneur ils n'ont pas cependant reussi a produire sur l'esprit de son Altesse Royale aucune impression. Les instances que je me suis trouvé dans le cas d'addresser a son Altesse Royale ont eté pareillement infructueuses. J'ai trouvé qu'il persistait dans le refus de se preter a cet acte solemnel que les loix ont designé comme la preuve distinctive d'adhesion a l'Eglise Anglicane. J'ai reçu cependant de son Altesse Royale une declaration a laquelle j'attache le plus grand prix, il m'a assuré de la maniere la plus solemnelle 'qu'il n'etait pas converti a la profession Catholique Romaine et qu'il etait decidé a ne jamais se conformer a cette profession', ensuite il a declaré d'abondance 'qu'a son retour en Angleterre il serait disposé a se soumettre a tous les actes de conformité qui pourraient etre necessaires pour dissiper les inquietudes que sa Majesté aurait pu concevoir sur cet objet'. Son Altesse Royale a cru devoir aussi sanctionner cette assurance de la maniere la plus formelle.

Les assurances de la part de son Altesse Royale sont surtout consolantes en autant qu'elles renferment le dementi formel de ces bruits qui se sont repandu sur la pretendue conversion de son Altesse Royale lors de son sejour en Italie.

Il resulte cependant de cette circonstance une consideration bien serieuse et qui merite une attention particuliere, non seulement de la part des personnes qui sont chargés en quelque façon de la surveillance de la conduite de son Altesse Royale, mais aussi de la part des Ministres de son Altesse Royale qui lui meme par une suite de l'hospitalité qu'il a exercé envers son Altesse Royale est tenu en quelque sorte suivant les antiques usages de repondre pour la sureté de son hote, si par une suite des importunités auxquels son Altesse Royale est exposé il lui arrivât enfin de renoncer aux determinations et aux assurances que je viens de reciter ce serait sur nous que la faute devrait necessairement retomber. Je suis bien loin, Monsieur, de confondre les relations et les devoirs que nous avons respectivement (votre Excellence et moi) vis a vis de son Altesse Royale, le Duc de Sussex, je scais tres bien que vous etes necessairement dispensé de toute surveillance sur la conduite d'un Prince etranger et que le plus facheux evenement arrivant a votre inscu, et sans que vous en fussiez averti, ne pourrait jamais vous etre imputé. Il en est autrement, lorsque ceux qui sont chargé de cette surveillance vous avertissent du danger ou ils se trouvent et qu'ils implorent cette assistance que les Ministres de son Altesse Royale sont seuls en etat de leur accorder. Lorsqu'on cri a un asassinat moral il est du devoir de ceux qui se trouvent a portée de se lever et de venir au secours.

Enfin, Monsieur, il en est ainsi, que l'honneur de son Altesse Royale, le Duc de Sussex, et le repos de sa Majesté soient placés entre les mains de son Altesse Royale, le Prince Regent, je connois trop bien l'estime et l'attachement mutuel qui reunit nos deux souverains pour pouvoir douter de la disposition de son Altesse Royale d'accorder aux demandes que je fais au nom de sa Majesty Britannique, cette declaration condition-elle qui renferme la seule garantie specifique et efficace pour obvier au mal que nous devons redouter egalement.

Il ne tient qu'a votre Excellence de representer a son Altesse Royale d'apres les connoissances particulieres que vous possedez sur les affaires de mon pays combien celle-ci est importante et de designer d'avance les facheuses consequences qui peuvent resulter d'une reserve mal entendue.

P.S. Attendu la grande delicatesse du sujet je demanderai a votre Excellence le renvoi de cette piece aussitot que vous vous en serriez servi. (39797–81)

1640 COLONEL MCMAHON TO J. DWYER[1]

18 Apr. 1802

Although some years have elaps'd since I had the pleasure of seeing you, yet I trust you will suffer the early acquaintance I had the honor to have with you so far to operate in my favor as at least to plead my excuse for the liberty I take on the present occasion.

It has just been mention'd to the Prince of Wales that a case occurred a short time ago in which a Petition of Right endorsed by the King was transmitted by the late Earl of Clare & by him put into a course of trial in Ireland; it being stated that this business must naturally have pass'd thro' your Office, I presumed to suggest to H.R.Hss. the obliging inclination I was confident you would entertain in giving him every allowable information on the subject in question, and as it appears adviseable to ascertain a fact that would afford an important guidance in the affair which the Prince has laid before the Lord Chancellor of England respecting the mode most proper for prosecuting his claim for the arrears of the Duchy of Cornwall pending his minority, I am authorised by H.R.Hss. to request you will have the kindness to inform me what records there may be in your Office of such a transaction during the Chancellorship of Lord Clare, and also that you will be so additionally obliging as to signify whatever precedents there may be of the Petition of Right being acted upon in your Courts, together with the names of the parties & the dates of their trial.

Whatever use may be made of this information you may rest assured that your name, if you wish it, shall never appear on the occasion. (39802)

1. Secretary to the Lord Chancellor of Ireland.

1641 THE PRINCE OF WALES TO LORD PELHAM

Carlton House, 29 Apr. 1802

It has been just mentioned to me that a case occurr'd some time ago in which a *Petition of Right*, signed by the King, was transmitted to the late Earl of Clare & by him put into a course of trial in Ireland. As the intimation does not carry with it quite that authentic detail which in such a matter could not be difficult to obtain, I doubt the accuracy of the intelligence, more especially since Lord Eldon has not appeared aware of such an instance. Still, as it is stated to me that the business passed through your Office, it appears not only adviseable but necessary to ascertain without delay a fact that would afford an important guidance in the affair which I have laid before the Chancellor. Therefore I beg of you, my dear Lord, to have the kindness to inform me whether there *now exists* or *has existed* any record, or any trace of such a transaction in your Office during the time of your predecessor or predecessors.[1]
(Add. MSS. 33133, f.18)

1642 THE DUKE OF SUSSEX TO THE PRINCE OF WALES

Lisbon, 8 May 1802

On the 4th of May I forwarded through France a letter to you, as it becomes necessary from the situation in which I stand with Mr. Thrale [*sic*. ?Trail] that some speedy remedy should be found for it. In my

1. Lord Fitzharris wrote to Lord Pelham on 11 May:

'On enquiry I find that only one writ of right has passed thro' this Office in Mr. Pollock's time—that is, Mr. O'Hara's, Member for Sligo, who claimed certain lands in ye occupation of ye Custom House of Dublin. His Petition was indorsed by ye King and sent over and tried in Ireland sometime between Sepbr. 1795 and March 1796. Mr. King knows all the particulars of this case.

'Sir George will make a memorandum of Mr. White's case, inclosed in the Prince's letter.' (Add. MSS. 33133, f. 20)

Thomas Erskine wrote to Lord [? Eldon] from Carlton House on 8 May:

'I have the honor to transmit to your Lordship a Petition of Right from his Royal Highness the Prince of Wales which I beg you will have the goodness to present to the King for his Majesty's allowance in the usual form.

'When the time of the Petition's being delivered to the late Chancellor is considered (which was as long ago as the beginning of the year 1796) I am sure your Lordship will forgive my solicitude that it should now be presented at the earliest possible moment, since tho' the process by Petition of Right has been considered in the House of Commons as a legal proceeding indispensably preliminary to any other application on the part of his Royal Highness, it was not ascertained till yesterday after an interval of six years that it could be sent officially to your Lordship, & the Prince preferred any delay to a departure from regular forms, being most anxious to remove every appearance of personal controversy by only addressing his Majesty in the forms prescribed by the Constitution.' (Add. MSS. 49173, f. 14)

273

letter of the 30th of April you will already have discover'd that matters were taking a very unfavourable aspect. The day following I went to table for the first time after my indisposition, during which period I had not seen him. In the morning I had previously sent my servant to ask for some money, which he refused me, saying that if I had any orders for him I might send for him. Upon this I took a bill to which I put the order for payment, the usual manner in which I transacted business with him; this he not only refused, but would not even look at. After dinner the servants being retired, and a few of my friends at table, he began with a very *insolent tone of voice* by saying that I ought not to be surprised at the manner in which he behaved to me after the gross insult I had shewn him in refusing to see him upon business without a witness. Why would I not see him alone? That he was no assassin, and who was the d——d villain who would accuse his integrity? My answer was that when people did not agree, a third person was always of advantage to both. He continued, 'you are angry with me for having given you good advice & therefore you treat me so insultingly, which you would not dare do, unless you had the protection you have, but I have also wrote for protection and justice where I shall get it'. My only remark was, 'If you are in the right so much the better for you. You must recollect, however, that I assured you the story you mentioned of my being a R.C. was totally false, that I had never thought of it, and that therefore if you put such ideas into the head of my family you were working at a misunderstanding betwixt us, that in consequence I should look upon you as my greatest enemy and treat you as such—that by your conduct you had made me the conversation of the town, and had encouraged the King's Minister to take very improper steps relative to me'—that in consequence, if he thought my conduct insulting I was sorry for that I should still observe the same. He also remarked that when a man was insulted all ranks fell. In short, his conversation, tone of voice, and manners were so insulting as to petrify all the persons present. For my own part if it had not been for the respect I owe to his Majesty and to you, I would have thrown the bottle at his head. In order to avoid such scenes, I must again press his recall, my dear brother, for it is impossible it is the intention of his Majesty or of you that anyone should be put about me to insult me. I believe his intentions originally to have been good, but they were totally destroyed by his ruff and ungentlemanlike manners. For you must know yourself, my dear brother, that in doing anything the manner of doing it is half the business. I trust, my dear Prince of Wales, this letter will hasten some determination as to my establishment, for surely there can be no obstacle now. When in your hands I must hope for success. *P.S.* Since writing the above, a new scene has taken place which was so serious as to enforce my request again. Mr. Thrale having requested me to see him, the interview was agreed to at half after four yesterday

274

afternoon, under the excuse of his having received a letter from Lord Keith which he wished to communicate. He began by saying that he had taken this opportunity for to lay before my consideration a point which he wished I should consider myself, that he did not, and would not enter into any arguments, but he thought the subject ought to be told me. He then began again the old story of the Roman Catholick religion and said that in spite of my having taken the Communion I had treated him much worse than before; that the conclusion was that by doing this act I must have suffer'd in the opinion of the Portuguese, and that I was angry with him for this as well as with the Minister. My anger has all along been from the improper and disrespectful conduct both he and Mr. Frere have shewn me but which, if ever it comes to an explanation, will then be heard. My answer was, 'Sir, you are much mistaken in this surmise, but I can assure you after what passed, neither you nor the Minister would have either got me to take the Communion, for I saw through the whole business as an intrigue, but what engaged me to do it was a conversation with my doctor, who, without mentioning names, told me that a report had prevailed in London, that during my indisposition there I had sent for a R.C. priest. This alter'd the motives for my doing it, as then I saw a suspicion in England, & that engaged me to a step which no fear would ever have got me to have done'. He then went on to state my necessity of going to England. My answer was that if the P. of W. thought it necessary I should certainly come, but if it could be avoided it was my wish on account of my situation relative to my marriage and the derangement of my private affairs; that this even I had stated to you before and this is really my reason at present not for coming home. He continued that my conduct towards the Minister was as [the rest is missing].
(48233–4)

1643 LADY AUGUSTA MURRAY TO THE PRINCE OF WALES

9 May 1802

I have several times addressed your Royal Highness under very great embarrassment both in regard to my intrusion upon your time & in regard to the subject of my letters, but I never before felt either cause for embarrassment half so strongly as I now feel the influence of both. Your Royal Highness has formerly expressed good will for me, & an interest in my concerns, & tho' I have availed myself of your kindness, I hope & trust, it has neither been exhausted by frequency of application or forfeited by indiscretion. If you retain for me, Sir, any feelings of goodwill, I conjure you *now* to exert them in my behalf. If you incline to exercise your good nature in the cause of *justice*, I *entreat* you, Sir, to examine my claims to your support, & to act according as you shall find them. Amidst the afflictions under which this letter is written, I feel some consolation from reflecting to whom it is addressed. My present application to your Royal Highness is in favor of my *character*, which has been vilely slandered. No one knows better, Sir, than yourself the value of character, or the keenness of sorrow a generous mind feels when it is injuriously attacked. It is in your power to do *me justice*, & *only* in yours. *That justice I now ask* as the *choicest favor* you can bestow, as the kindest friendship you can exert. My gratitude can be of little or no use to your Royal Highness, but if you will serve me in this one instance my gratitude shall cease only with my life.

When I went to Lisbon a short time ago I took the liberty of writing to you, Sir, in explanation of my motives, or rather of the necessity which compelled me to the step. I then told you the *true & only, only* reason of my going. The voyage appeared to me no voyage of pleasure, & certainly the reception I met with was the utmost of insult & ill usage a woman could receive—never admitted to *his* presence—driven from his abode—the sport of his mistress & dependents—this too from the man who has sworn, & still swears ever to call me & consider me as (what he knows I am)—*his wife*. But all this is foreign to my purpose, & it is not my present business to describe the indignation & disgust I felt upon that occasion. That indignation & disgust, however, were destined upon my return to still keener exercise, & 'tis for this last *outrage* that I venture to solicit the protection of your Royal Highness. I am told, Sir, the Duke of Cumberland affirms I went to Lisbon for a different purpose than I avowed—that I went there with a view of concealing a situation which it requires the presence of an husband to support without disgrace. Some time after I returned from Berlin I heard reports of a similar nature were then circulated, & believed by some parts of the Royal Family. *Then, with my husband, & under his protection* I did not think it my business to interfere. He was satisfied; he talked to me of these reports & did not believe it worth his while to pay any attention to them. I thank him for this act of *justice*; *now*, I am told, that the Duke of Sussex's present assertions are in direct opposition to his former conviction —that he *now* disowns the girl for *his child*; that by a letter written to the Queen he lends his name to this cruel injustice.[1] I hear, too, pardon my freedom, that these reports, if they do not originate with the Royal Family, are by them *believed, repeated & spread*—that Lady Charlotte Durham is *authorized* to circulate this foul slander, which the Duke of Cumberland is become the instrument of propogating. I have endured nine

1. Lady Augusta's daughter, Augusta Emma (1801–66), who in 1845 married Sir Thomas Wilde, afterwards Lord Truro and Lord Chancellor, was born on 11 August in Grosvenor Street. Lord Glenbervie, too, said that the Duke did not acknowledge the second child, and that he demanded only the surrender of the boy (*Journals*, i.338).

years of continued affliction—I have suffered poverty & neglect all along—I have suffered persecution & I have encountered duplicity & deceit. I have borne all this patiently, but this present calamity may possibly reach my children in its consequences, & *therefore* it is that I rouse myself to the present struggle, & call upon you, Sir, by every feeling you ever had freindly to me, to exert yourself *this once* in my behalf. Do me but *justice*, Sir, & you do me a favor *boundless & inestimable*. Your Royal Highness is the only person to whom I can apply upon this occasion, & now I shall take the liberty to specify as accurately as I can *what I want*. It is, first, that you satisfy yourself that I spoke truth when I said my pecuniary embarrassment was the ONLY reason of my going to Lisbon, & that you convince the Royal Family of the same. Secondly, I beg of you to inform me whether the Duke of Cumberland's tale be true —whether the Duke of Sussex has really expressed any doubt relative to the birth of his girl—& if so I think I have a *right* to be informed of *all* particulars with respect to this cruel injury—& if he has *written it*, to see the letter, *the letter itself*, for I really *would not beleive it* upon the credit of a copy. I have also *a right* to know the object of his suspicion—the grounds of it—& every circumstance which may enable me to prove its injustice. 'Tis hard, very hard, nay cruel that my character is to be ruined without giving me an opportunity of defending it. 'Tis something more than *cruelty* to *his* child. Your brother, Sir, has accustomed me to hardship—has inured me to injury—has oppressed me with vexation— has steeped me in calamity—(let *him* remember what *was* my situation in Society when we *first* met—& what it now *is*. This sad reverse, Sir, is HIS work). This last attack, this flagrant outrage, this last injury without a name & without limit is more than I can submit to. I must struggle against this new torture—I must resist this fatal blow, which is to murder my reputation by the ruin of *my* child. It is for the sake of that child far more than for the sake of my own reputation that I now trouble your Royal Highness. The means of ascertaining these facts I will leave to your discretion, or if you please to the *malice* of mine enemies, & it shall be my endeavour to facilitate any enquiry they choose to institute. I cannot describe the indignation & disdain I feel at writing the above, but the feelings of a mother are stronger than the suggestions of pride. May I go on, Sir, & finish my request? Will it be too much to ask that the same *authority* which has circulated the calumny should contradict & repress it—that the same *organ* which was selected for the purposes of *slander* may now be employed for those of *justice*? Her zeal will *no doubt* be more ardent in the work of reparation than of injury—for sure the employment will be far more grateful. I beg pardon for trespassing so long on your Royal Highness's time, but the *cause* I trust will plead my excuse, & 'tis now *only* by seeing the length of my letter that I think of concluding it, for I would not willingly omit one word which could have the slightest influence in securing your attention to my request. Your Royal Highness cannot know what I have suffered, but for my present situation & distress you will feel, & *the time, the moment* chosen to inflict this new torture upon me, cruel, injurious & unprovoked, adds a keenness to all my present sufferings, & will perhaps very much contribute to strengthen prejudice against me. It does not escape me, Sir, that the moment *selected* for circulating this report is the most *favourable* to the Duke of Sussex, & the most *hostile* to myself. It will operate for *him* (if beleived) as an atonement in publick opinion for the cruel treatment I have just received at Lisbon & as an ample justification for the still more cruel abandonment of me, my children & our interests he is about to inflict. Towards *me* its effects (if beleived) are directly the reverse. It will both heap new sorrows & new injuries upon me & considerably augment *all* those I have long endured. I am unwilling, Sir, hastily to suspect anyone of having chosen this *malicious* moment by *design*, tho' certainly the *time chosen* is in the true spirit of the *deed*; & it does *seem* as tho' this report was *now* circulated to *excuse* the insult I lately received at Lisbon & to *justify* the injuries I receive here.

I cannot conclude, Sir, without once more asserting *upon my honor* that every one of these reports is a false & cruel calumny. May I therefore beg, intreat & conjure your Royal Highness in some way or other to do me right? I cannot presume to prescribe the manner. Your own heart, Sir, & your better wisdom will do more for me than any suggestions of mine. *Pray, pray*, represent my case & my wrongs to her Majesty & shew her my letter, if you please. I must beleive the Royal family must have been themselves imposed upon before they would *authorize* or *sanction* so injurious a report. When *they know* the wrong done me they will, I am sure, be anxious to make reparation.

Once more I intreat your Royal Highness to pardon this intrusion & to beleive that if you will interest yourself this time for me, my thanks & my gratitude shall be equal to the *favor* & benefit. Upon myself you will bestow a present kindness; upon my children a lasting advantage, & to *both* you will do an act of benignant *justice*.

P.S. Lord Moira does not know the subject of my letter, but if your Royal Highness will shew it to him I have no objection.[1] (48236-9)

1. Lady Augusta Murray wrote to her father, Lord Dunmore, (the letter is undated): 'As I trust that in your audience with his Majesty you will have an opportunity of detailing more fully my sorrows, pray remember to inform his Majesty that the calm I now enjoy is owing to Murray—his timely & generous interference prevented my being taken that day to the Fleet. He paid the bill for which I was arrested & the next morning assembled the creditors to gain from them a respite—which lasts only till the 1st of next January. No woman, however unfortunate, but has some dependence—some means of subsistence for herself & children. I only have none; tho' just liberated from the dread of immediate imprisonment—I cannot but look forward with encreasing alarm as the resources I have hitherto found in the liberalities of my friends are now exhausted. I am confident I am left thus destitute only because his Majesty

Gibraltar, 15 May 1802

As when I have not much time to myself I can get through any communication I have to make much faster by dictating my thoughts than writing myself, I have preferred in the present instance, on that account, addressing you in this manner to undertaking a letter to the Prince.[1] Having premised this, I shall acquaint you for his information that agreeably to the instructions he gave me, I wrote to my brother Augustus from Falmouth to desire him to come over to me here. My letter reached him on the 8th instant just after a violent quarrel he had with Mr. Trail, which I gathered from that gentleman's letter to me, of which the enclosed is a copy. In consequence my brother immediately determined on coming off and to my great surprise at four o'clock this morning he arrived here in his Majesty's ship Mermaid. I am sorry to say he is at this moment attacked with one of his violent spasms, but it seems already to be going off, and he is in wonderfully good spirits. From the little conversation I have hitherto had with him I gather that it is his intention to remain with me 'till he gets the official notification of his Establishment being settled for the purpose of getting clear of Mr. Trail who, he

is not informed of the helpless condition of myself & children. No person will interest himself so much in my affairs as to mention them to him but one who has the feelings of a parent. I cannot but hope I should be extricated from all my embarrassments were his Majesty informed that the pension of £1,200 a year (in fact, only £900) has been pledged by the Duke of Sussex to pay the rent & taxes of the house he himself hired. The assurances Ld. Moira was authorized to communicate to me last year of his Majesty's most gracious intention of paying my debts & granting me & my children a suitable provision for the future has not been brought into effect, for my debts still remain unpaid & myself & children unprovided for. This perhaps is owing to his Majesty having heard that the Duke of Sussex had settled £4000 a year upon me, which his Majesty imagines I am in the regular receipt of — & not one shilling of which *have* I—or *am I* to receive, H.R.H. having ordered Mr. Coutts not to pay it. Had I according to the bond given me by the Duke of Sussex been quarterly paid the amount of my annuity, I should have been precluded the necessity of contracting more debt than was already incurred before H.R.H. left England. The bill for which I was last arrested was at the suit of my boy's writing master, whom the Duke of Sussex had promised to pay. Disappointed in all these my expectations, & having exhausted all my expedients for temporary relief, I find myself compelled to recur to this last measure of entreating you, my dear father, to lay a statement of my sad situation before his Majesty, to whose parental goodness I make this appeal—this earnest request to relieve the distresses brought on myself & children by his son; & to enable me to rise from a life so degrading; an existence so painful by an establishment which I persuade myself he wants not the goodness to allow. Should you unfortunately fail in your address to his Majesty, I shall have no longer any means of supporting myself & poor children, who are abandoned by one parent, & unhappily dependent only on the poverty of the other, but by flying to my creditors & prison to a sympathizing publick [*sic*]; by publishing the particulars of my injuries, & soliciting a subscription for the maintenance of the children of the Duke of Sussex, & of myself whom he has twice in the most solemn & deliberate manner (that divine & human laws have concurred to sanction) bound himself to support & protect.' (48217–8)

1. The Duke merely signed the letter.

concludes, will then feel authorised to quit the situation he holds about him, and whom he declares no power on earth shall induce him to meet again. I am apt to think his own plan is decidedly to reside in Portugal, taking an occasional trip to England should he find the hot season peculiarly oppressive. On my urging him to explain himself fully to me on the subject of his religion, he did not scruple to declare to me upon his honor, in the most unequivocal terms, that he neither *was* a Roman Catholic nor *ever would become one*. Indeed he went farther, and said that with regard to his son it was not his intention to bring him up to that religion unless, when he got old enough to judge for himself, he should then make choice of it. He dwelt much upon his wish to have the boy at Lisbon to break him of ridiculous notions his mother put into his head, and declared that 'though he was disposed to give her a very liberal allowance he would not do anything 'till the child was first given up'. In short, in his conversation to me I found him perfectly fair and reasonable, and there shall be no exertion wanting on my part to engage him to do that which will be most to his own credit and the satisfaction of his family.

I arrived here on the 10th instant after a passage of 13 days from Falmouth, and as you will easily suppose have my hands so full of business that I hardly know which way to turn, and therefore I have not had time to attend to the Prince's commission about a barb and a Spanish horse for him, to succeed in which I am satisfied I ought not to be hurried, as it will be attended with a great deal of difficulty to procure anything that will be worthy of his possessing. (46044–7)

1645   THE DUCHESS OF WURTEMBERG TO THE PRINCE OF WALES

Louisbourg, 22 May 1802

Ever happy to converse with you I seize eagerly on Mr. Kaulla's[1] going to England to send you a few lines and to beg you will be so good as to allow him to see your horses and those belonging to your Regiment. This Kaulla is nephew to the one Mr. Wickham[2] employed as contractor for the troops in British pay, and he is at the head of the greatest banking house in the south of Germany. The whole family is now settled at

1. Jacob Raphael Kaulas, a Jewish banker (*d.* 1810). Accorded citizenship of Wurtemberg in June 1806 'in view of the various services that the Kaulas family has rendered to the country in critical periods.'

2. William Wickham (1761–1840), M.P. for Heytesbury, 1802; for Cashel, 1802–6; for Callington, 1806–7. Under-Secretary of State, Home Department, 1798–1801; Irish Secretary, 1802–4, and a Lord of the Treasury in the 'Talents' Ministry, 1806–7. Sent on a Special Mission to Switzerland, 1794–5. Chargé d'Affaires there, 1795, and Minister Plenipotentiary, 1795–7; Plenipotentiary to Bavaria, 1800, and at Vienna, 1801.

Stoutgard [*sic*] as our bankers. The present journey is undertaken by order of the Emperor of Germany who has commissioned him to purchase horses for him and Archduke Charles.

I am, my dear brother, very anxious to hear something about your dear little Charlotte; a report prevails here that she has had an ague but several posts wanting makes me hope that it is only an idle story. She must now begin to be a charming little companion. When once she can write a little I hope you will allow her to correspond with me, but forbid anybody to correct her style as I should like to judge a little of her character by her letters. Lady Elgin speaks of her with the greatest affection, and I hope that her health will allow her to continue to devote herself to this dear child who is of such infinite consequence not only to all of us but most likely to all Europe.

I hope that long before this you have received the letter I wrote to you by Mr. Smith. I will not take up no more of your time and only add my best love to Charlotte. The Duke begs me to recall him to your remembrance and assure you that he should sometimes trouble you with a letter if he did not know that writing is unpleasant to you. (51683–4)

1646   THE QUEEN TO THE PRINCE OF WALES

Queen's House, 26 May 1802

I trust not to be thought troublesome when I venture to start a remark upon a subject I am sensible I have nothing to do with. I see in the newspapers that the Ball of the Union Club is fixed for Munday the 31st; & the day following for the Thanksgiving.[1] Might not the sudden change from merrymaking to church make the ill natured, who are always disposed to find fault, encourage them to satyrise those who are at the head of it & perhaps not have considered it? I should not have ventured so far had I not understood that your garden was lent upon the occasion, & as you perhaps might be included in it I cannot withstand the feelings of a mother in representing it, as I am convinced if you see the impropriety you will endeavour to alter it for another day.

Before I conclude I beg you to be assured that neither the Kg. nor anyone else knows of this note & that nothing but my love for you could have made me write it.

[*P.S.*] I am going to make my summer visit at Bla[c]kheath. (36525)

1. The Thanksgiving for the Peace.

1647 THE DUKE OF CAMBRIDGE TO THE PRINCE OF WALES

Cuxhaven, 30 May 1802

I hasten to inform you of my safe arrival at this place. I am this moment landed after a most tedious passage of six days, chiefly owing to contrary winds and at last to a calm which prevented our landing last night. Unluckily this morning the wind blew so hard that we were obliged to put back in the barge & to get on board a Cuxhaven vessel which has brought us safe to port. Had I not taken this step I should have been detained perhaps four and twenty hours longer. I shall set off as soon as my carriage is ready and I hope to be at Hanover on Wednesday at latest.

I trust I shall soon have the pleasure of hearing from you. (48573)

1648 LETTERS FROM THE PRINCE OF WALES TO THE QUEEN, AND THE REPLIES

Carlton House, 10 June 1802

I take the liberty of sending you the first impression of a print that is going to be publish'd of me; as a fine print which it is most generally esteem'd by those who have seen it, you may perhaps not think it entirely unworthy of a place in your private boudoir at Frogmore. May I also take this opportunity of requesting to know whether you expect the Princess at Windsor on Monday, as I should feel very uncomfortable at being under the necessity of returning directly to London which I must do if she is to make one of the party at Frogmore. If she is not I hope I need not add how truly happy I shall be to pay my duty to you there, & may I also request to know at what hour we are expected to attend? (42343)

FROM THE QUEEN

Windsor, 10 June 1802

I am sorry to see that at this present moment all idea of summer is vanished, as I wish to invite you for the 14th, the day fixed for a fête a[t] Frogmore in honour of the 4th of June, where I hope to see all the Royal Family that are here at present, & was the little girl well enough & the fatigue not to[o] much, I should be happy to see her grace my fête likewise. Having said this you will of course understand that the Princess is of the party.

I trust it is unnecessary for me to say how happy your presence at all times makes [etc.]. (36526)

282

Carlton House, 10 June 1802

I trust you will forgive me for tresspassing upon you again for a few moments upon the subject of the letter that I had the honor of addressing to you yesterday. I cannot but confess I am not a little surpriz'd at the invitation of the Princess of Wales to your party at Frogmore, as it is the very first time since the year of her marriage (to the best of my recollection), especially since the *éclat* she was *so good* as to make on my account, that she has been invited to any party at Frogmore or at Windsor till the present occasion, & when there have been so many in the intermediate time to which it was never thought necessary to ask her. Whatever may have been the motives or whoever may have been the adviser of such a measure, I can only consider it as highly prejudicial to the interests of the family by disturbing its tranquillity in endeavouring to establish *a censure upon me* which I cannot pass over unnoticed, as it actually & *wantonly* revives topics of a domestic & too delicate a nature which had long, & ought ere that, to have been long committed to oblivion, & by which I have so *cruelly & unjustly* suffer'd. How contrary does this measure appear to the notions hitherto advanced by the King, or those practiced by your Majesty. Hitherto the King has always been esteem'd to set his face against any woman disobeying the *lawful* commands of the man suppos'd to be her husband; your Majesty has always been justly look'd up to as the pattern for wives, most subservient to the will & pleasure of your husband. After this what must I think, & how must I feel at this mark'd support of the Princess? I can see it but in one & in one only point of view, as an *interdiction to me*, under the *present* circumstances, to associate again with my own family as I have hitherto done; for her *triumphant and publick disclaim* of all duty to me, besides the insolence & insincerity I have in every one instance experienced from her, is alone sufficient to justify my total deriliction of a woman I never consequently can esteem. It cannot but add greatly to my regret that the feelings of my own situation compel me to be absent at the celebration of an event which your Majesty does me but justice in believing I should have heartfelt satisfaction in participating in, as well as in the general joy of my family.

Allow me to encroach one moment more before I conclude this letter. Having now submitted my humble but honest & *decided* sentiments to your Majesty, I must hope you will have the goodness to make such communication of them, either by the production of this letter or whatever other mode it may be your Majesty's pleasure, as will remove from the King's mind the possibility of supposing my absence at Frogmore could be occasion'd by the slightest want of the most respectful duty & affection. (42346–7)

Windsor, Thursday evening, 10 June 1802

I am this moment put in possession of one of the finest prints I ever saw, for which I want words to express my gratitude as well as the pleasure it has occasioned me. This was indeed a very *agreeable* surprise, & toute la bande joyeuse, by which I mean your sisters, are in hopes that you will sometime hence treat them with the same present.

I wrote this morning to you & find our letters have crossed upon the road. I must always feel sincere regret in being deprived of your company, but particularly so upon this occasion when I had flattered myself to join altogether in celebrating a birthday which this time twelve month we had so little reason to expect of doing again & in which I am sure you most heartily concur.

I will now not detain you any longer upon this subject as I am sure you will always act right. I beg once more to return you thanks for the invaluable present & beg you to believe that, present or absent, you will ever be remembered with pleasure & friendship by [etc.]. (36527)

1649   PRINCESS AUGUSTA TO THE PRINCE OF WALES

Frogmore, 11 June 1802

Mama wishes me to give you her love and to say that she hears you have a very handsome *tent* with three rooms adjoining. She would be very much obliged if you could send it her tomorrow in case that it is in London, but pray let me have an answer by this evening. Excuse the greatest haste. God bless you. (Add. Georgian 10/30)

1650   THE QUEEN TO THE PRINCE OF WALES, AND THE REPLY

Windsor, 12 June 1802

At my return from the play last night I found yr. letter & consequently was under the necessity of keeping the servant till this morning. I am truely sorry to find that the invitation of the Princess to my Fête should annoy you so much as to look upon it as a personal affront to you, which it never *could* be meant to be. You will recollect that upon yr. sister's marriage, which was also public, she was invited, & since that event I have had no other *Fêtes* but those given during the time of the camps, at which none but those of the Royal Family then at Windsor were present, the Duke of Glocester, his son & daughter being excluded at that time purposely not to shew any affront to the Princess, *as you your-*

self wished the Princess always to be treated with civility. These are the expressions you made use of in my Closet at the Queen's House, & I thought them so proper that I endeavoured to act up to them implicitely as a real proof of my affection for you, which I have proved by always informing you when she was either visited or invited by me: & as you have met with the Princess both at St. James & the Queen's House upon public days I judged that a meeting at Frogmore could not be of more consequence; add to that, that we owe something to the public, in whose power we always are, & though I am far above wishing to gain popularity by improper means, I should likewise not choose to lose the good opinion of the world by glaring incivility to anybody.

Your absence must of course, let the day be ever so bright, throw a cloud over it. You know your presence must be missed by all those who are present. All I can say is that it is to be lamented, but believe me by none more sincerely than by [etc.].

[P.S.] I shall certainly make your excuses to the King unless by an *agreable surprise* you change your opinion. (36528–9)

THE PRINCE OF WALES'S REPLY
Carlton House, 13 June 1802
I have to acknowledge with gratitude your kind letter of yesterday, together with the explanation you have been so good as to give me. You are most indisputably correct as to dates, but then you will be so good as to recollect that at that period the Princess had not thrown off as completely the mask, or gone the very great lengths she has since. I am very sorry indeed that it will be impossible for me to come to Frogmore, especially after all your very kind expressions, but I am sure you cannot be surpriz'd when I recall to your recollection that the Princess & I have never met at table nor inhabited the same appartments since that time. It would be unfair to tresspass longer upon you at present though I have a great deal more to say, but therefore I shall defer what further [remarks][1] I may have to make till I have next the pleasure of seeing you, which I hope will be very soon. (42349)

1651   FELIX MCCARTHY TO COLONEL MCMAHON
54, Piccadilly, 15 June 1802
I called on you today for the purpose of communicating circumstances in

1. The missing word is in the draft. (42348)

my humble opinion too interesting to be omitted for a moment. On Saturday & again this day I have had a conversation with Mr. Baldwin, the Duke of Portland's Secretary and *confidential friend*, the result of which is all that is necessary to trouble you with. I am satisfied if the Prince pleases he may bring the Duke and his friends over to to [*sic*] his interest. In the absence of Lord M[oira] I proposed that you, who equally possessed the confidence of both, should confer with him. He made no direct objection, but I could easily perceive that he would rather treat with Mr. Adam '*as an old and intimate friend whom he could trust*' than with anybody else. It will be for you to take such measures as your own judgment will suggest on the occasion: the urgency and importance of such a negotiation are too manifest (involving no less than the Prince's future freedom and happiness as well as that of the Empire) to need any comment; *le tems present est gros d'lavenir.* Pray God prosper your endeavours. I *pede fausto*—and save us from *Bastiles, tortures and transportations*, the necessary consequences of Pitt's returning to power which, unless measures of vigour, even a vigour beyond the law, be exerted at this moment, he assuredly will. (39803)

1652   THE DUKE OF KENT TO THE PRINCE OF WALES
Gibraltar, 16 June 1802
The multiplicity of business I have had to attend to since my arrival here has left me so few instants to myself that I trust it will plead my excuse if I have not before this written to you. Lord Keith, however, being about to leave us today I could not suffer him to sail without giving him a line just to remind you of my being alive and to assure you of my invariable and devoted attachment. Your wine (three butts of sherry) and a hogshead of a very peculiar species of the same growth, called Montillado, which I have ventured to take upon myself, is ordered today from Xeres, and you may depend upon its being forwarded by the first man-of-war after I receive it, and with special care. As yet, I have not been able to succeed in getting you any Spanish horse such as I should wish to send over to you, but I am at this moment upon the track of one which I hope will answer tolerably the description you gave me, and at the same time have the merit of being COME-AT-ABLE for the sum of between fifty and sixty pounds at the utmost. Should I proceed you may depend upon receiving him by the first man-of-war that is capable of taking him on board. Lord Keith will tell you that *he* has written to Egypt for the Arabian you wanted, so that I trust in a little while I shall be enabled to execute all your commissions. Augustus left this yesterday morning for Lisbon, and I cannot help saying notwithstanding both

286

Mr. Thrale [*sic*], and Domeier[1] think otherwise, not at all in *my* opinion tainted with the sentiments that have been ascribed to him. But I shall write fully in a few days via Lisbon by Domeier (who is to go to England) in a letter to Payne my sentiments about this business for your information. In the meanwhile God bless you.

[*P.S.*] Pray offer my kindest, and best regards to Mrs. Fitzherbert who I hope continues as I left her, in best health and looks.

Madame de St. Laurent *se recommande instantment a votre gracieux souvenir.* (46048–9)

THE DUKE OF KENT TO REAR-ADMIRAL J. W. PAYNE

1653 *Gibraltar, 19 June 1802*

Doctor Domeier, physician to my brother Augustus, being now resolved to return to England, I believe for the purpose of getting married in the first instance,[2] and next of getting into business in London, where he flatters himself, if honored with the Prince's protection, he will be enabled to make his fortune. I embrace that opportunity of writing to you, and have to request that you will obtain my brother's permission to introduce him at Carlton House, as he is particularly anxious to be honored with an audience.

The Doctor parts with my brother Augustus on the best possible terms, but as he perceives that my brother's inclinations lead him to settle at Lisbon, and his, on the contrary, to remain altogether in England, he has obtained his consent to proceed to London for the purpose of soliciting the Prince's interest to procure for him by way of retreat and pension a continuation of the allowance which his Majesty has hitherto made him for attending the Duke of Sussex. Being myself interested in the doctor's welfare, as I believe he has ever been a very faithful servant to my brother, and of essential benefit to him in point of health, I shall esteem it a very great favor if the Prince will condescend to exert himself in his behalf. I should add that Augustus has provided himself with another physician, who will join him in the course of six weeks, one who is well known to the Duke of Clarence. His name is Wright,[3] and, I believe, was many years at sea with him: he is reckoned to be a man of both merit and character.

So much for the Doctor. I have now to acquaint you for the Prince's information, relative to Augustus, that he embarked on the 15th on board

1. Physician to the Duke of Sussex.

2. According to the *Gentleman's Magazine* (July 1802, p. 684) he married Lucie Bernard, a German lady, at Lisbon, on 27 June.

3. See No. 266 (i.336).

of the Mermaid for Lisbon, having passed a month with me here, and I think from all the conversations I have had with him, I may with safety assert that there is no ground whatsoever, notwithstanding the apprehensions entertained by Mr. Trail and Doctor Domeier, to suppose that he has the least inclination to turn Roman Catholic, but at the same time that I say this, I by no means wish to insinuate that either the Doctor or Mr. Trail have wilfully misrepresented anything respecting my brother; on the contrary, I am confident that what they have stated has been in consonance with the best of their own belief. But the two principal causes which induced them to form their opinions have been perfectly explained to my satisfaction at least, by my brother. These are, first—his being so often in his own room in company with monks; secondly, his attending so frequently at the Catholic places of worship. Now, to the first of these he says that one of the monks was his music master, and the other a medical man—and to the second—that he had an affair of gallantry with a lady of fashion, whom, during the whole of the Lent season, and on festivals of the Church, according to the customs of that country, he could only meet at places of public worship, as they are not permitted at those times to receive visitors at their own houses. As to his kneeling to the Host, it is very well known that in that bigotted country everyone who meets it, and does not do so, runs the risk of being insulted by the populace. All this seems in itself so perfectly natural, and Augustus spoke of it with so much candour and openness, that as I have before said, I have not a doubt upon the subject, and am satisfied it would be as easy to explain away every other circumstance that has given rise to the idea which the gentlemen about him have taken up.

As to the other unfortunate business which has so long been like a millstone about his neck, I am satisfied that nothing is wanting to bring it to that conclusion which all his friends must wish, but some person to step forward and make a final arrangement with Lady Augusta Murray, in which nothing can be handsomer than his proposal, which is to allow her £2,000 pr. annum from his own income, if it cannot be done otherwise, in addition to the pension she receives from Government, to take upon himself every debt she made previous to her receiving the letter by which he announced his intention of never meeting her again, and lastly, to leave her the option of what equipage she chuses to retain. As such I request that you will earnestly submit to the Prince's attention to adopt some mode to assist him in bringing this essential point to issue and which appears so important for Augustus's comfort.

You will be so good as to inform the Prince that three pipes of choice old Sherry and a hogshead of Montillado have been ordered from Mr. Gordon of Xeres, and will be there forthwith embarked on board of a ship direct for London, as that is conceived to be the safest and most speedy conveyance.

I have now only to commission you to offer the assurances of my warmest attachment to the Prince. (46051–4)

1654   FELIX MCCARTHY TO COLONEL MCMAHON

25 June 1802

I did myself the honor of waiting on you for the purpose of mentioning a circumstance which shd. be *immediately attended to*, if considered of interest by you and the gentleman concerned. Hearing from the Honble. St. Andrew St. John[1] that Mr. Tyrwhitt was not provided with a seat in Parliament, I thought it my duty to acquaint you that I have been at some pains to secure one for myself in the boro' of Callington, but as the influence of H.R.Highness's name was in some measure necessary to the success of my endeavours, I shd. think myself very much wanting in respect and duty to him if I hesitated a moment in giving up to a gentleman so closely connected with him as Mr. Twtt. every pretension to the place. I have had for some weeks past an able and intelligent Agent there who is every day urging me to go down. It was my intention to do so early next week, but under these circumstances I shall chearfully relinquish all my hopes of Parliamentary honors and contentedly wait a more convenient season. Mr. St. John, as *uncle to Ld. Clinton*,[2] has it in his power to render material service and is perfectly well inclined to do so. But not a moment is to be lost. My Agent, who is a native of the country and perfectly acquainted with his duty, will I have no doubt effectually secure Mr. Tyrwhitt's election.[3] (39804)

1655   MAURICE FITZGERALD[4] TO THE PRINCE OF WALES

Merrion Square, Dublin, 26 June 1802

A report has just reached me through a respectable channel which I

1. M.P. for Bedfordshire, 1780–4, and 1784–5. Under-Secretary of State, April–December 1783; Captain of the Band of Gentlemen Pensioners, February 1806–March 1807. (1759–1817)

2. Robert Cotton St. John Trefusis, 18th Baron Clinton (1787–1832). He entered the Army, 1803, and was A.D.C. to Wellington in the Peninsular War. Colonel, 1825. A Lord of the Bedchamber, 1827–32.

3. John Inglett Fortescue and Paul Orchard were returned for Callington after a contest on 8 July. McCarthy himself was never an M.P. Tyrwhitt, who had sat for Okehampton, 1796–1802, was returned for Portarlington on 30 December 1802, *vice* Henry Parnell, who resigned his seat.

4. M.P. for Co. Kerry, 1801–31 (and in the Irish House of Commons, 1795–1800) (1774–1849). A Commissioner of Revenue [I.], 1799; a Lord of the Treasury [I.], 1801–7, and [U.K.],

trust will justify me to your Royal Highness for the liberty of thus ob-truding myself on your Royal Highness's notice. It was stated to me that your Royal Highness had mentioned in company that I had promised to vote in support of the Motion brought forward by Mr. Sutton, in the present Session, respecting your Royal Highness's claims.[1]

Never having had the honor of being admitted to any communication with your Royal Highness, I should have altogether discredited this report but for a recollection of some conversation which I held with Colonel McMahon on the subject of being presented to your Royal Highness, and which may have led to some misconstruction which my anxiety to stand fair in your Royal Highness's opinion, and regard for my own character, make it incumbent on me to clear up.

From a perfect recollection of that conversation I beg leave to assure your Royal Highness that, so far from expressing any intention as to my vote, I did explicitly mention to Colonel McMahon, that my wish to be presented to your Royal Highness arose from personal respect and a grateful sense of the partiality shewn by your Royal Highness to the Irish nation, and that it had no reference to the question before the House, nor to any political object whatever.

I certainly did express an anxiety to inform myself on the subject of the claim, a wish that it were finally settled, and an opinion, so far as I was capable of judging, that it was well founded. And with these sentiments I went into the House of Commons, where the nature of the proposition made by Mr. Sutton prevented my supporting it, because I was perfectly convinced that the legality of the claim was a question proper for the decision not of the House of Commons but of a Court of Justice. I therefore left the House rather than (even by the single vote of so humble an individual) incur the appearance of controverting your Royal High-ness's claim. Indeed Colonel McMahon had the politeness to convey to me what he was pleased to call your Royal Highness's gratification that I had not divided against the Motion.

I have taken the liberty of thus trespassing on your Royal Highness's time under a persuasion that your Royal Highness will not think it altogether thrown away if the employment of it can relieve the feelings or do justice to the honour of a gentleman.[2] (39805-7)

July 1827–January 1828. Vice-Treasurer of Ireland, 1830. A Lord of the Admiralty in the Peel Ministry, 1834–5. He inherited the ancient designation of Knight of Kerry.

1. *Parliamentary Register*, lxii, 220–63, where the day of the week is incorrectly given; *House of Commons Journals*, lvii, 282 (31 March 1802). The voting against the Prince's claim to the revenues of the Duchy of Cornwall during his minority was 160 to 103.

2. The Prince of Wales wrote to Arthur Paget from Carlton House on 27 June 1802: 'I send you the enclosed letter the contents of which I know not, but am only to desire that you will read it over patiently. I have done everything you have desired & with as much delicacy

THE EARL OF MOIRA TO COLONEL MCMAHON

Edinburgh, 29 June 1802

Your letter, my dear friend, gave me severe vexation; not so much on account of the incivility of Coutts's House to me, as from the fear that the sudden call on you may have been attended with inconvenience. Would you believe that at the moment of their refusing that bill they had a security of mine lodged in the House (with a power to them to sell it at any time) specifically worth more than £5000 beyond what they were in advance to me: and the procedure is the more discreditable for them after the cringing court which they paid to me when it was thought likely I should come into power. Do not mention this matter to anybody else. I cannot recollect whether in a former letter I desired you to write to Dawson when you wished for any venison. He has orders to send it whensoever you demand it. McCarthy's step towards Baldwin is indiscreet in a degree that would excite one's astonishment if it had no other quality, but it was so extravagantly absurd that I cannot conceive what notion he had in his head when he made the proposal. Nothing but a countryman of ours could be capable of hatching such a plan. He has, however, zeal & devotion enough to outweigh the inconvenience of his bewildered speculations. Pray get Francis,[1] or someone who remains on the spot, to apprize me from time to time of what is going forward. (39808-9)

THE DUKE OF KENT TO THE PRINCE OF WALES

Gibraltar, 29 June 1802

Sir James Saumarez being likely to sail this day for England, I embrace the opportunity just to tell you that not being satisfied with the horse I had intended for you, I have thought it best to desire Augustus to embark for England a remarkable fine one which he had intended for me,

as the subject would admit of. Everything is therefore now settled if you wish it to remain so, & you will never be troubled any more, in which case I doubt not that you will forward to me as soon as possible the packets which both Tyrwhitt & I mentioned to you in our former letters. How are you going on? I never hear from you, but I trust you nevertheless do not forget me. If you do, you are very ungrateful as no one can love you more truely or more sincerely, dear Arthur, than [etc.].

P.S. Do not forget my commissions. Chig Bathurst & myself never hold a little Club together that we do not lament each time that you do not make one with us' (*Paget Papers*, ii.56).

1. Possibly Philip Francis (1740–1818), the reputed author of the *Letters of Junius*. M.P. for Yarmouth (Isle of Wight), 1784–90; for Bletchingley, 1790–6; for Appleby, 1802–7. A Member of the Governor-General's Council at Calcutta, 1774–80. K.B. 1806; G.C.B., 1815.

but which I am sure will be much better bestowed by appropriating him in this manner. Hardyman, my Aide-de-Camp, who has asked for a few months leave to go to England, will in consequence go by way of Lisbon to take charge of the horse, in order to insure his being well taken care of, and the moment he reaches England will write to Payne to let you know where your groom must be sent to to fetch him. The agreement made relative to this horse, which Augustus got as a very great favor from a Spanish Grandee, the Duke d'Estifania, was that an English blood horse capable of carrying 15 stone (a stallion) should be returned in his room, and I have only to entreat that you will cause this condition to be fulfilled by having a horse of this description put on board of the first frigate for Lisbon, to be from thence sent on by Augustus to the Spanish Duke. If you approve of the horse when you see him, I shall be highly gratified, but if I have failed, I trust you will not ascribe it to want of zeal or anxiety to do all for the best. I shall only add that my health is as good as I had a right to expect in the midst of this trying heat, and that on the whole I think myself less bilious in some degree than I had apprehended. (46055–6)

1658 JOHN COXE HIPPISLEY TO THE PRINCE OF WALES

Council Chamber, Sudbury, 5 July 1802

From a spot on which I had the honour, 12 years since, to be distinguished by the most flattering proof of your Royal Highness's condescending protection, permit me Sir, to reiterate the sentiments of unaffected, grateful obligation.[1]

Having again the honour to be returned to Parliament, I will request permission to say that whatever may be the habits of my private friendships or attachments to public men, I shall ever prescribe to myself the gratefull duty of obeying your Royal Highness' commands, on every occasion when the personal interests of the Prince of Wales become agitated. Such a rule of conduct might indeed be adopted, without apprehension, by the coldest heart that ever professed attachment to your Royal Highness, assur'd that no question of this description was likely to be brought forward, which did not appear, in the deliberate conviction of your Royal Highness's councils, to carry with it the most unequivocal claims to the *justice* of the nation. Nor can any feeling subject of his Majesty contemplate the extraordinary privations & dignified forbearance of of [*sic*] the Heir Apparent to the British Empire without the most sensible regrets—not less arising from a jealous sense of the splendour of representation which ought to be inseparable from such an

1. Hippisley was M.P. for Sudbury, 1790–6, 1802–18.

exalted station, than from a just reverence for your Royal Highness's commanding talents and virtues. (39810)

1659 THE PRINCE OF WALES TO LORD PAGET

Carlton House, 6 July 1802

Many thanks, my dear Paget, for your kind letter which by mistake was sent after me to Sherborne the very day that I left it to return to town, & which I trust will account to you for my not having instantly return'd you an answer. I shall be most happy to appoint Mr. Lee one of my chaplains,[1] or to do anything at any time that can be agreable to you. Pray let me know his Christian name & the place of his abode, in order that I may have his warrant made out & forward it to him immediately. It is quite melancholy to see our poor wretched skeleton regiments, it really quite makes my heart ache. I expect a little sport on Saturday as the Eleventh are to be review'd, & from the little I have seen of them in their quarters, ils ne me paroissent pas grande chose, as their men are small & punchy, which I do not think meets your ideas any more than it does mine. With my best compliments to Lady Paget,[2] I remain, dear Paget [etc.].

P.S. I have bought a charming new horse for a a [*sic*] charger, & which I hope will not be unworthy of your laying your leg over when next we meet in town (Anglesey MSS.).

1660 THE PRINCE OF WALES TO THE QUEEN

Carlton House, 23 July 1802

It was always my intention to have troubled you with a few lines today in consequence of a letter which I received two days past from Lady Elgin respecting the state of Charlotte's health,[3] but as Dr. Domier is going

1. The Rev. Francis Lee (1766–1826) was appointed. Curate of Wyresdale, 1789. He committed suicide.

2. Lord Paget married, as his first wife, on 25 July 1795, Caroline Elizabeth (1774–1835), third daughter of the 4th Earl of Jersey. The marriage was dissolved, after she had given him eight children, at her own suit by the Scottish Courts in 1810. Then she married the 6th Duke of Argyll. Her former husband then married Charlotte, the divorced wife of Sir Henry Wellesley, who was awarded £24,000 damages against Paget, the co-respondent, in an action for *crim. con.*

3. The Prince wrote to the Dowager Lady Elgin on the 14th, from Carlton House: 'I write a few lines in great haste as Lord Keith is waiting for my letter to set off for Weymouth. Your letter would not have remain'd so long unanswer'd, but I have been out of town for a few days

down to Weymouth to present you with a letter which Augustus has desired him to present himself I entrust this letter also to his care. In order not to tresspass too much upon your time I will devide my epistle into three heads & treat them all as briefly as possible. In primis respecting Charlotte, Lady Elgin writes me word that the child has had a return of her aguish attack which I am afraid must prevent her bathing, but which I am in hopes may in some degree be accounted for & attributed to the uncommon wetness of the season everywhere, & consequently not to be ascribed to any particular climate, particularly not to that of Weymouth; which (I may perhaps, though, be mistaken) I rather think she hinted at as having something to do with it, as she told Lord Keith, who I immediately saw on his return, that she had had some symptoms of ague herself & that there was also one of the servants ill of the same complaint in the house. Now I entreat of you to let me know what you really think is the truth, as if the child is not sufficiently well to benefit by the bathing I would bring her back to her home when you return from Weymouth; if not, & she continues quite well, it is fully my intention to leave her at Weymouth till the end of October. Pray arrange & settle everything respecting the child as you think will be best in every respect, as I cannot fail on every account to be most thoroughly gratified, & if I may be allowed to make use of such a word, to *approve* of whatever you are so good to settle touching her, but pray have the kindness to indulge me with a line merely to say what you really think about the child.

With respect to Domier, he throws himself at his Majesty's feet, to pray for your gracious & kind support in speaking a good word for him, as he now is without a shilling of income after having served the King at his express orders in the person of Augustus for upwards of twelve years, relinquishing not only his profession & further prospects in that line, but having refused (as Mr. Livingston tells me & with whom I had a very long conversation respecting Domier yesterday) a most advantageous [?offer] from the Court of Denmark to come to Copenhagen in

& am very sorry should the delay have occasion'd you any inconvenience. There can be no doubt that I would have you accept of Mr. Tyndale's most obliging offer, for which I will beg of you to return him my best thanks, & I only lament you were not settled there at once on your arrival, as I think it would have saved you much plague & trouble. I rejoice most truly at the good accounts of the dear child, who I expect when I come to Weymouth to be much improved in strength & in looks. I beg my humble duty to their Majesties.

P.S. Pray tell dear Mary that the same reason has prevented me writing to her as to you, but that I will write soon, & in the meantime will do what she has desired me.' (49257)

The road bill for her conveyance back from Weymouth in September amounted to £58 6s. 6d., and there were ten changes of horses. Amongst the items were the following: cleaning the carriage, 10s., lodging, etc., at Winchester, £4 6s. 6d.; dinner at Hartford Bridge, £1 9s. od.; waiters, maids, etc., £3 18s. 6d.; fruit, etc., 12s. 6d.; expenses from Windsor to Shooter's Hill by stage, 12s. 6d.

order to attend upon the person of the King of Denmark,[1] which offer consisted not only in a settlement of three hundred per annum English, but his carriage, board, & lodging found him, all which he declined four years back when Livingston was with Augustus, in order that he might not have the appearance of deserting my brother from any interested motive of his own, or of disobeying the commands of his master the King, whose son he thought it was religiously his duty to attend so long as it should be his Majesty's pleasure. Livingston writes a long letter by the doctor to Lord Rosslyn[2] who he understands is at Weymouth fully explanatory of the fairness of his claims & giving the highest testimonies possible of the doctor's conduct in every point, & which Mr. Livingston as well as the doctor, both hope, my dearest mother, will be some inducement to you to say a word in his favor.

Very few words more & I will release you from the bore of reading any more of my scrawl; I cannot help mentioning to you, *entre nous*, that Ernest has again been playing the devil about me, circulating such falsehoods respecting me & the Middlesex Election (in which I have not interfered in the most trifling instance) that I was oblig'd to send him word at last, upon his having told a person that I had been supporting Sir F. Burdett,[3] that I had pressed the D. of Northumberland to do so, & that the Duke had very cavalierly refused me, in the first place that the whole of the report was FALSE & without the shaddow of a ground, & lastly, that none but a *fool* would credit it, & none but a *scoundrel* propagate it. This he was obliged to stomach, as he said he had it from a person whose name he either could not or would not name; mais cela m'est egal, whoever the cap fits, let them wear it. In short, he has blinded so many persons of high rank here in *his lies & malice*, whose names are needless here to mention, & as the whole would take up too much room for the contents of any letter from all the explanations that would be necessary to be given, that I was of necessity obliged to clear the whole business up to have the Duke of Northumberland written to, & who has

1. Christian VII, King of Denmark since 1766 (1749–1808). In 1766 he married George III's sister Caroline Matilda (1751–75).

2. Lord Loughborough had been created Earl of Rosslyn on 21 April 1801 to console him for his not being re-appointed Lord Chancellor.

3. Sir Francis Burdett (1770–1844). Radical M.P. for Boroughbridge, 1796–1802; for Middlesex 1802–4, 1805–6; for Westminster, 1807–37; for North Wiltshire, 1837–44. On 5 August 1793 he married Sophia Coutts (1771–1844) and in 1797 he succeeded to the Baronetcy on the death of his grandfather, Sir Robert (*b.* 1716). *The Times* declared on the 27th; 'Many reports have been spread that a certain person of the highest rank, and the Duke of Northumberland, espouse the interest of Sir Francis Burdett in the Middlesex election, but we have reason to believe the rumour is without the least foundation. The Duke of Devonshire's tenants at Chiswick have, however, voted for the Baronet'. The Middlesex election ended with the return of Burdett and George Byng, on 29 July. The *Official Return* (1878) wrongly says the 13th.

sent me the most honorable & ample testimony in contradiction of the scandalous & base fabrication, but couch'd in such *strong language* that I do not think it safe to trust it to a letter, but when I come to Weymouth I will bring it with me & shew it you, when you shall know everything of this most abominable proceeding.[1] I understand he is going soon to Weymouth, at least so he is supposed to have said as soon as the Middlesex election is at an end, which by some persons, by what I can find out, is likely to be today, or a day or two hence, & therefore I thought it best to put you a little upon your guard (though I know you are pretty well so in general about him) by giving you this short detail; besides, I confess I am not very anxious to meet him either at Weymouth or anywhere else, as I scarcely, I am afraid, could command myself sufficiently not to say something or other very disagreable to him. At present, my dearest mother, my intention is to pay you a visit at Weymouth, within a few days after my own birthday, therefore pray let me learn from you how long you are likely to stay & whether you think that will be as good a time as any other for me to pay my respects. I really am quite shocked when I look back at my scrawl, & must therefore repair my fault as soon as possible by throwing myself entirely upon your goodness, & subscribing myself [etc.].

P.S. Pray have the goodness to tell me how you all are, & to present my love to all the family. By the by, have you heard that Miss Frances Seymour's match, Lord Robert Seymour's daughter, with Lord Southampton is now publicly acknowledged?[2] (42355–8)

1. The Duke's letter has not, apparently, been preserved, but McMahon replied to it from Carlton House on the 24th: 'I had yesterday morning the honor to receive your Grace's letter, which I lost not a moment in laying before the Prince of Wales. His Royal Highness commands me to make his most warm & affectionate regards to your Grace, & to say that the animated & kind manner in which you have enter'd into the malicious story that was propagated respecting Sir Francis Burdett is exactly what he expected from your Grace, whose unbounded goodness & sincere attachment to H.R.H. he receives repeated & incontestible proofs of, on every possible occasion. The Prince further commands me to assure your Grace he will st[r]ictly pursue your friendly advice, & repair to Weymouth without more delay than is unavoidably necessary; and H.R.H. desires me to add every wish that the truest friendship & affection can offer for your Grace's health & happiness. The most kind & gracious notice with which your Grace has condescended to mention me, is most grateful to my heart, where it will be for ever remember'd & for ever acknowledged' (Alnwick MSS.).

2. The 2nd Lord Southampton (1761–1810) married, first, (1784) Laura (1765–98), daughter of the Hon. Frederick Keppel, Bishop of Exeter, who was a Lady of the Bedchamber to the Princess of Wales from April 1797; and secondly, 2 December 1802, Frances Isabella (*c.* 1777–1838), second daughter of Lord Robert Seymour, a younger son of the 1st Marquess of Hertford.

1661   E. LIVINGSTON TO COLONEL MCMAHON

6, Suffolk Street, Friday, 23¹ July [*1802*]

I beg you may have the goodness to inform H.R.H. the Prince of Wales that Lord Rosslyn is not at Weymouth. I waited on him this forenoon noon [*sic*] and made him acquainted with H.R.H. wish to facilitate Doctor Domeier['s] just pretentions to his Majesty's protection, and that H.R.H. the Prince of Wales, imagining his Lordship at Weymouth, had given me his commands to give Doctor Domeier a letter explaining to Lord Rosslyn the doctor's very long and meritorious service and his dissinterested conduct by refusing a very lucrative and honorable employment for life, which letter I gave Lord Rosslyn. He read it with great attention and found everything so fully explained he desired me to leave the letter with him and to assure the Prince of Wales that he would with great pleasure obey H.R.H. commands by shewing my letter to the King. If no opportunity offered soon to shew it to his Majesty he certainly would shew it to Mr. Addington, let[t]ing him know he had done it by the commands of the Prince of Wales, and that H.R.H. would be pleased if Doctor Domeier's just claims were attended to by his Majesty's Ministers.

Do me the favor to lay me at the Prince of Wales' feet and assures [*sic*] H.R.H. that it will at every period of my life give me great satisfaction to obey the Prince's commands. (39811–2)

1662   THE DUKE OF CAMBRIDGE TO THE PRINCE OF WALES

Hanover, 24 July 1802

I have not yet troubled you with a letter since my arrival here as I had nothing of any consequence to mention, and for that reason I did not like troubling you. The different letters I have received from England have given me very good accounts of your health, and I trust you know me well enough, not to doubt of the joy this news has given me. The curricle you were so good as to give me arrived about a fortnight ago with my baggage, and I return you a thousand thanks for it. I think it a very handsome one, and doubly acceptable to me as it comes from you. Indeed, my dearest brother, I feel very grateful for all the kindness and affection you have always shewn me, & particularly during my stay in England, and be assured I never never can forget it. Since my arrival here I have been very much employed, partly with the exercise of the troops, and afterwards with two Military Boards that have been sitting almost every day for this last month; my time has therefore been pretty

1. The letter is wrongly endorsed the 26th.

297

well taken up and I like very much the active life I lead. As to politics there has been a general stagnation in them for this last month. The interview between the Emperor of Russia,[1] and the King of Prussia had stopped everything, but now it seems decided that the plan of the indemnities for the different Sovereigns of Germany will be executed in a very short time. The Prussians were to march on Tuesday last, and they will get to Hildesheim in a few days; the comissariat is to be there on the 3rd or 4th of next month. The Austrians & Bavarians are also on their march so that in a very short time everything will be decided. I will not make any remarks upon the occupation of Hildesheim, but certainly if the Prussians do remain there it is a great misfortune for this country. I have ordered drawings to be made of the new cloathing of the Hanoverians & I shall send them you as soon as they are done. Now God bless you, dearest brother, I will not keep you any longer than just to beg you to remember me to Mrs. Fitzherbert. (48576)

1663   THE QUEEN TO THE PRINCE OF WALES

Weymouth, 26 July 1802

I hope you have received Mary's little note to acknowledge the receipt of your letter, & tho' my eyes are still very much relaxed, I am desirous to answer yours, as our motions depend so much upon the weather & therefore never know from one day to another what time I can command to do anything. I have the pleasure to inform you that dear little Charlotte is as well as it can possibly be expected after so severe an attack of the ague she had in town, & that by the uncommon whet & stormy season, she as well as everybody else is prevented to reap that benefit from bathing she other ways would do was the weather more favorable. Her attacks are only simptoms of the complaint, when the dampness is very great, not otherwise, & then she must not bathe, but her *sleep, appetite & spirits* are very good; moreover, I have seen Keate this morning & he assured me that she was going on very well. Ldy. Elgin has also desired *Dr. Warne* to write to Dr. Turton how she goes on, the answer to which she will not fail to communicate to you. She does so distinctly follow the priscription she received in London about the child, that you may make your mind easy that no care nor attention will be spared, nor can it be done with more zeal nor affection. As to what relates to her staying at Weymouth till October, that will be better decided by the physical people who are upon the spot, as they of course must understand the efficacy of bathing at that season, & when you come to Weymouth as you talk of

1. Alexander I (1777–1825) succeeded his father, the murdered Paul I, on 23/24 March 1801.

doing you will yourself be a better judge of what is to be done, & hear their opinion.

As to our motions I am unable to give you any account. When we left Windsor the Kg. talked of staying eight weeks, but since our arrival he has been silent upon the subject, but I think your making a visit to the child so natural that the time you have chosen to come appears to me very proper & we shall all be happy to see you, & should I hear the Kg. name the subject I shall not fail to inform you of it.

Of the Duke of Cumberland's intention to come here I am ignorant, but as he talked of taking a house here before we set out for this place, & did not do it, perhaps this proposed visit may also vanish in smoke. I am truely sorry to hear that he has again proved so unkind to you in his conduct, & feel particularly happy to know that you have given him no occasion for doing so. You may depend upon my not beleiving idle reports as I know but too well how apt the malicious world is to view things in a wrong light.

I will do everything that lays in my power for poor Domeier; when his situation is fairly represented to the Kg. I may then say more in his favour than I could do now, but believe me he shall not lose anything on my account.

I must now finish this scrawl on account of my eyes & will only add love of your sisters & assure you avec quel plaisir je me souscrit [etc.]. (36530-1)

1664 THE PRINCE OF WALES TO THE DUKE OF YORK
Carlton House, Wednesday morning, 28 July 1802
The morning proving so very wet, the not having any place to change my cloaths at till I arrive at Brighton, as well as the having been under a pretty severe calomel discipline for the last two or three days makes me afraid to encounter the Review[1] this morning; you may easily imagine how truly I lament the impossibility of coming, & beg you will express my sincere regrets to my old friend David. Depending upon seeing you at dinner on Friday,[2] I am [etc.]. (44177)

1. The review of the Scots Greys Royal Dragoons, commanded by General David Dundas. The rain fell in torrents and the review was cut short.

2. The Duke stayed until Sunday, 1 August.

Gloucester Lodge, 4 Aug. 1802

Many thanks for your kind letter I received Friday evening & which I should have acknowledged long before now had it been in my power, but all Saturday, Monday & yesterday we spent on board the yacht, & Sunday I wrote all morning to Dolly as Dr. Glass[1] left Weymouth early Monday morning.

I am truly sorry to find by your *letter* that *you* have again *met* with *unpleasant* things owing to Ernest's imprudence & must ever lament any missunderstanding between brothers: you may depend on my *being* on my guard should *he* come, but if he does I do not think Ernest likely to revive the subject to me & I should not be surprised if his intended *visit* did not take place. I hope you are quite well by this time & have enjoyed Brighton Races; the weather has *been* delightful.

Poor Sophia was taken ill yesterday with one of her cramps on her chest, attended with some inflamation; in consequence she was blooded & blistered, she is much better today, therefore, I trust shortly will be quite well again. The rest of the family are in perfect health. Lord Courtney[2] & his three sisters[3] are here & Lord & Lady Charles Somerset are expected in a few days; leaving them, the Draxes,[4] Methuens[5] and [illegible], we literaly know no soul at this place: even the plays & performers have been so very indefirent that we have only taken to go within these 10 days as Elliston & Mrs. Mills are now come & Bannister arrives when Elliston leaves us. I can continue assuring you Charlotte is quite well & bathes every other morning.[6] We shall all be delighted to

1. The Rev. Dr. G. H. Glasse, Chaplain to the Duke of Cambridge, was presented to the King at the Levée on 6 October, on his arrival from Hanover. Malmesbury described him as 'the schoolmaster at Hanwell' (iv.250).

2. William, 3rd Viscount Courtenay (1768–1835), succeeded his father, 1788. In 1831 the House of Lords accepted his claim to the Earldom of Devon.

3. The Viscount had about ten surviving sisters, including five unmarried ones.

4. Richard Grosvenor (1762–1819) assumed the additional surname of Erle Drax before that of Grosvenor, when he married Sarah Frances, daughter and heiress of Edward Drax of Charborough, Dorset. He was at this time M.P. for Chester. Both the Draxes and the Drax Grosvenors were at Weymouth at this time.

5. Of Corsham House, Wilts.

6. The Dowager Countess of Elgin wrote to the Princess of Wales from Weymouth on the 4th: 'Dear Princess Charlotte desires me to assure your Royal Highness that she is now perfectly well, good & happy; which thank God is now the case. Her Royal Highness bathes every other day, & goes out in the carriage twice a day in order to get either to the retired sands of Portland, where she delights herself with picking up shells, which she is certain are to charm her dear mama. Our other rides are among the hills that surround this place, which afford both shelter & exercise, & by the time she leaves this I dare say she will be well qualified to run races & jump over little mounds. Princess Charlotte's complexion is much improved, & I think her neck whiter than it was; in short, Madam, I hope your R.H. will find your dr. little angel

see you; when can *you* come? My sisters desire many *loves*, in particular Amelia & Sophia for your very kind message, & believe me at all times far or near your truly attached.

[*P.S.*] I was happy to hear Frederick *had been* with you at *Brighton*. (Add. Georgian 12/23)

1666 THE PRINCE OF WALES TO THE QUEEN

Brighton, 8 Aug. 1802

I have just receiv'd a packet from Augustus by the means of Lt.-Col. Fraser[1] which he has desir'd me to forward to you. I therefore take the liberty of sending it, as well as a book which I receiv'd a few days ago from Arthur Paget from Vienna & which he desires may be presented to you. Your time I know is so much occupied that I will have more mercy upon you than I had when I wrote my last, [of] the length of which I really was quite ashamed. From the nineteenth you may expect me, but you may depend upon my being with you, if nothing very extraordinary happens to prevent me, by the twenty-first at latest. Our Races[2] are just concluded last night, & I have been tolerably successful, but a good deal fagg'd by the whole week.[3] (42359)

1667 THE DUKE OF CAMBRIDGE TO THE PRINCE OF WALES

Hanover, 9 Aug. 1802

You will allow me to trouble you with a few lines to wish you joy of the 12th. I trust you know me well enough to be assured that I do most sincerely rejoice at this day, and God grant that you may see many and many happy returns of it. By this time you will be informed of the King of Prussia's having taken possession of the Bishopricks of Hildesheim, Paderborn and Munster: all this was done on the same day, the 3rd of June, the King's birthday [*sic*]. Hitherto the different countries have not

has reaped much benefit from this place, tho' the beginning of the season was so unfavourable.

I have the honor to present Princess Charlotte's affectionate duty & love to your R.H. with the most profound respect of, Madam [etc.]. (49258)

1. Probably the Edward Fraser mentioned by Lord Glenbervie as the Duke's Equerry whom he commissioned to negotiate the treaty of separation (*Journals*, i.338).

2. The Lewes Races, following the Brighton.

3. On the 9th the Queen sent birthday greetings to the Prince in a short note from Weymouth. (36532) So did Princess Augusta although she forgot to post it for three days after it was written. (Add. Georgian 10/31)

been organized, and as I understand they are to keep their present Constitutions till the Deputation of the Empire has ratified the Treaty of Indemnities that has been made at Paris. I hear that the Bishoprick of Osnaburg is destined for our family, and if the King of Prussia would consent to exchange this for the Bishoprick of Hildesheim it certainly would be a very desirable thing for this country. I understand that Mr. de Jacobi who is going back to England has orders to make some proposals on this subject, but what they are I do not know. The Emperor of Russia has, as it seems, proposed this to the King of Prussia. I do sincerely hope it may be brought about. Knowing how much you interest yourself, dearest brother, about everything that regards this country I thought it right to inform you of the little I know about this subject.[1] (48579)

1668 THE QUEEN TO THE PRINCE OF WALES

Weymouth, 11 Aug. 1802

I am to return you thanks for the letter you sent me from Augustus & the book from Vienna which arrived safely yesterday morning. I am sorry that poor Augustus has been so unwell ever since his physician left him, as I fear that he will not meet with another that can know his constitution equal to Domeyer. He had doubtless good reasons for parting with him, but I fear he will feel his loss severely.

I have the pleasure to inform you that Charlotte goes on better & better every day; even Keate assures me that her little neck & backbone grow considerably better. Lady Elgin has been seriously ill indeed; she begins to mend but it will be slow. There is no danger at present. Her attack was bilious & managed ill by herself, but timely assistance has done so well that she can now see the child, who, by the by, was wretched to a degree.

I am glad to hear you have met with some success at the races & that at last the weather proves to be fine. I trust it will continue so when you come. The time of our departure is still unknown to us & Ernest is not come, nor do I hear of his comming, tho' he has told many people in London of his intention to come.

We are to have, if the weather permits it, a sailing match tomorrow in honour of the day: that is all that can be done for there is not a soul here

1. The Prussian acquisition of the Westphalian bishoprics of Hildesheim and Paderborn, and of the city and part of the bishopric of Münster, was part of the wholesale redistribution of the territories of the Holy Roman Empire which followed the Treaty of Lunéville (February 1801). The reconstruction was carried out in Paris on principles laid down by Bonaparte, and was embodied in the so-called Act of Mediatization (February 1803).

to make up any entertainment. In the evening we go to the play where little Charlotte is to accompany us. Amelia dresses her for the day & she is to dine at our house to drink your health, which none can do with more pleasure than [etc.].

[*P.S.*] This moment Augusta comes in to tell me that Ernest means to be here by the 15th or 16th & that Brawn is to procure lodgin[g]s for him.[1] (36533–4)

1669 PRINCESS AMELIA TO THE PRINCE OF WALES

Weymouth, 11 Aug. 1802

I cannot let a day so very dear to me as tomorrow pass without sending you a few lines to tell you what I trust you are well assured of, how dearly I love you & feel all your kindness, & that among the many congratulations you will have on your birthday none will be more sincere than mine, for though I have not the talent of making *fine speeches* & expressing my good wishes in the same *elegant manner* as others may, believe me, no one can love you better or wish you more happiness than your own child. I cannot tell you how deeply I feel your invariable kindness to your *own child*, as you call me, & how delighted I was with your message which our dear Miny gave me. She is as amiable & good as ever & I hope *like* you that dear Charlotte will turn out like her, for I never saw such a dear as she *is*. I have dressed *her*, dear little love, from *top to toe* for tomorrow, & dear Miny has dressed *me* for the day.

For this last week we have had fine weather which is a great blessing for in bad weather it is sadly dull. The Freemantles came last Saty. & Ld. & Ly. C. Somerset are expected tomorrow.[2] I cannot but regret your absence tomorrow for I shuld so very much have preferred offering you my good wishes by word of mouth. I will not trespass longer on your time now than to beg you will continue to me your affection which I so much prize. (Add. Georgian 14/41)

1. Farington wrote (4 July 1803): 'The King is very much beloved by his family and attendants; they pay him great respect. The Pages are not so respectable as they were formerly in the time of Ramus. Brawn, the first Page, has a marked authority over the other Pages and seems like a Colonel among inferior officers. Compton is the most esteemed of all the Pages. The place of Brawn is estimated at £1,000 a year, the other Pages about £300. They dine after the King' (*Diary*).

2. The Fremantles had been at Weymouth in September 1801 whilst the Royal Family were there (Buckingham, *Court and Cabinets of George III*, iii.172).

Weymouth, 11 Aug. [1802]

I cannot let the anniversary of a day so dear to *all* who know you pass by without sending you, my dearest brother, one of my scrawls to *convey* the *real* sentiments of my *heart*; as it *overflows* at all times & upon *all* occasions for my dear *Eau de* Miel it is difficult for me to find *words* to express *all* the happiness & blessing I pray you may enjoy for *many many* years. I have to lament I cannot by word of *mouth* say *all* my heart *feels* on your *birthday* & I wish I had wings to fly over to Brighton to be the *first* to offer my *congratulations*. Amelia, *your old child*, has dressed little Charlotte new upon the occasion & I can assure you she will be very smart, & I flatter myself Amelia will *look* in great beauty as I have given *her* a dress *in* my own *style* to *make* her *look* less like an old *woman* than *usual*. Sophia has got quite stout & well again.

A great many arrivals this week *have* increased *our* parties very much & the Council which is on the 17[1] brings many *home* to Weymouth. As yet we have heard of no day fixed for our departure. Augusta received a letter from the Duke of Cumberland to say he intends being at Weymouth the 15 or 16.[2] (Add. Georgian 12/24)

Lisbon, 14 Aug. 1802

Now that the lot of my marriage is settled in England I am particularly anxious to get it equally determined in Germany, in order to have my arms quite free. It is a question of law and must therefore interest you all as well as myself. Could the marriage be broken, if it exists, it would afford me a great comfort as well as to her also, and therefore I am particularly anxious to have your assistance in the question. As the seperation in England is settled to which she has agreed I would humbly press his Majesty to be pleased to grant her a title and in case this should be refused, which I own, though it is but a favor, I should consider the

---

1. Its purpose was to order the Lord Chancellor to issue writs for proroguing Parliament from 31 August to 5 October.

2. He arrived on the 16th. Lord Glenbervie, who was invited to the Queen's card party one evening, said that the Duke tried Princess Sophia of Gloucester's good humour a good deal 'by a sort of quizzing jokes, which, however, seemed to be meant in great good nature, and were borne by her with equal temper and propriety. The Princess Mary', he added, 'appeared a little afraid that I might be scared at this style of raillery and said, once, "Brother, it is well we are among friends".' (Glenbervie, *Journals*, i.325).

denial of as very hard, I trust there will be no objection to my getting her a title in Germany.[1] (48246)

1672   THE PRINCE OF WALES TO THE DUKE OF YORK, AND THE REPLY

Blandford, 20 Aug. 1802

I have only just time to scribble a line before I proceed on my journey[2] to state to you that I am afraid I shall not be able upon calculation to be in town again till Tuesday, by which means I shall miss the Review of the 13th. If you can without great trouble put it off till the Wednesday you will greatly oblige me. Excuse my adding anything more.

P.S. Pray send me a line to say whether it can be done. (44178)

THE DUKE OF YORK'S REPLY [copy]

Oatlands, 22 Aug. 1802

It was not till late yesterday evening that I received your letter and have lost no time in compliance with your wishes in writing to the Adjutant-General[3] and directing that the Review of the 13th Light Dragoons which was fixed for next Tuesday should, if possible, be put off. Unfortunately I have a very particular engagement upon my private affairs next Wednesday which I cannot change, and which will therefore put it out of my power to fix the Review on that day, and therefore if the Review can be put off I have desired Colonel Wynyard[4] to warn the

1. Lady Augusta herself made inquiries about a peerage. As her undated letter was written to William Dacres Adams, Pitt's private secretary, the date is probably 1804 or 1805: 'I beg your pardon for troubling you, but will you have the goodness to ask Mr. Pitt whether he will approve of my writing a letter to his Majesty on the subject of granting a title to myself & rank to my children? If Mr. Pitt says *I may*, pray beg him to let me know whether he will be so good as to take my letter to the King, or whether I must find another conveyance for it. Will you also request him to tell you whether a foolish scribble of my own, stating my wishes, will be sufficient, or whether Mr. Pitt (I am almost ashamed of proposing it) will let me know what I ought to write? Pray, dear Mr. Adams, ask *all this* today, & do let me have an answer. What did Mr. Pitt say to my letter & the cover of the D. of Sussex?' (Wm. Dacres Adams MSS.).

2. He arrived at Weymouth that afternoon, and left for London on the 23rd, returning to Brighton on the 27th.

3. Col. Calvert.

4. William Wynyard (*d.* 1819), Major, 1794; Lieutenant-Colonel, 1795; Colonel, 1802; Brigadier-General, 1804; Major-General, 1809; Lieutenant-General, 1814. Equerry to the King. In 1802 he was Deputy Adjutant-General.

Regt. for Thursday, which I trust will be equally convenient to you.
God bless you. (44179)

1673   WILLIAM ADAM TO THE PRINCE OF WALES, AND THE REPLY
Oatlands, 20 Aug. 1802
The Duke of York some time ago sent Col. Hamilton to Hesse Cassel to
arrange his engagements with the Landgrave on a footing calculated to
relieve your Royal Highness from any obligations for him which might
remain. Col. Hamilton's success has been complete, and in his letter to
me on the subject he says that some surprise has been expressed at
Hesse Cassel that the arrangement of the concerns of your Royal Highness with the Landgrave shd. not be brt. forward, adding that if he were
authorised it was his opinion that they could be arranged most advan-
tageously by him. Having become acquainted with this circumstance—
on my arrival in town on Wednesday night—it was my duty to attempt
to have the honour to lay the matter with all humility before you. But I
found that your Royal Highness had left town. As the business presses
I hope to be pardoned for this communication & for addressing your
Royal Highness directly on the subject.

I am now on my way to Tavistock & the West of England, where I
shall be for some weeks, and Col. Hamilton's stay at Hesse Cassel will
not be long. These circumstances make me anxious that there should be
no delay—therefore in case your Royal Highness should think it proper
to employ Col. Hamilton I have taken the liberty to inclose a letter
which, if your Royal Highness thinks it proper to take any step, you
can order to be forwarded.

I hope, Sir, that my intrusion on your Royal Highness will be justified
in your eyes by the anxiety which I feel humbly but earnestly to promote
whatever may conduce to the ease & tranquility of your Royal Highness.
The matter being in its nature confidential will be an apology for this
direct address to your Royal Highness[1] (Blair Adam MSS.).

THE PRINCE OF WALES'S REPLY
Brighton, 29 Aug. 1802
I receiv'd your letter in London, & was much vex'd at not catching you
before you set off for Tavistock, as I think we could have arrang'd all
our business with very little trouble. But as it is next to impossible to

1. A much-amended draft. Adam had recently been appointed Solicitor-General to the
Prince.

306

explain any part of the circumstances in which I stand with the Landgrave without entering into the whole of the transaction, and that whole is infinitely too long a business to be compriz'd in the compass of any letter, I think it much better to refer you to Tyrrwhitt who has had the arrangement of the greatest part of the loans with the Landgrave, & is perfectly master of the whole of the circumstances, & he is luckily now in Cornwall at no very great distance at his own cottage upon Dartmoor, which he calls Torr Royal, & I write to him by this same post to proceed to you to Tavistoc without delay; you will then after seeing him & conversing the topics over with him, be the best judge whether it will be adviseable or not to employ Hamilton to negotiate with the Landgrave, & if he is to negotiate, what will be the most advantageous note to pursue. I will not tresspass longer upon you at present except to assure you, dear Adam, how truly I am ever [etc.][1] (Blair Adam MSS.).

1674 LETTERS FROM THE PRINCE OF WALES TO THE DUKE OF YORK, AND A REPLY

Lower Lodge, Windsor, 2.45 a.m., 5 Sept. 1802

It was my intention to have call'd upon you tomorrow morning in my way to London, but upon second thoughts, as it may prevent your shooting, if you will give me a bed I will be with you about nine this evening. I unluckily miss'd the Duchess this morning, & I wish much to make my bow to her, & besides I have something to say to you.[2] (44180)

1. In January the newspapers had reported that Tyrwhitt was on his way home *via* Paris. 'We some time since heard of a commission that had been sent to Vienna relative to some pecuniary concerns of a person of distinction in this country', declared *The Times* (15 January 1802).

2. On Tuesday the 7th the Prince returned to Brighton from Windsor.

There are comparatively few references to the Duchess in the Prince's correspondence but there is one of interest in the Alnwick MSS. McMahon wrote to the Duke of Northumberland on 14 December:

'I can very naturally suppose the desire which the Duchess of York has so strongly & so obviously manifested to conciliate your Grace & the Duchess into an intimacy & friendship, because I really believe her Royal Highness to be not only a most amiable woman with a most elevated mind, but the whole tenor of her conduct in this country (as I have always understood from her confidential attendants) has shewn a peculiar disposition to recommend herself to those of the highest & proudest distinctions; besides which I have no doubt that feeling as a wife, she wishes to extend the advantages of such amiable disposition to her royal husband, wherever she can.

'Nothing in my idea can be more abominable or rude than the insolent neglect & singularity of Mr. Pitt towards the Duchess of York; but it exactly keeps pace with his reprobated behaviour to the Prince at Brighton in the summer of 1801; when residing at Rotten Dean with Mr. Villiers, he rode dayly into town, & afforded the solitary instance of being the only man of any consideration in life that did not offer his duty & leave his name at the Pavilion. The Duke of York was more than an hour with the Prince before he left town on Sunday, & seems to become very pointed indeed in his attentions. He told the Prince he proposed going down to

FROM THE PRINCE

Carlton House, Monday evening, 6 Sept. 1802

Thomas has had *no interview*, but has brought back with him in writing a most extraordinary answer. I therefore shall be ready & most happy to see you & consult with you at eleven tomorrow. I have written to the Chancellor. (44181)

THE DUKE OF YORK'S REPLY

Horse Guards, 9 Sept. 1802

I take the earliest oportunity to acquaint you that in pursuance of your desire I went this day to Blackheath and delivered to the Princess of Wales your message, when she charged me to say in answer that she remains in the same determination of not receiving any message through Colonel Thomas. Not having succeeded in the first part of my commission I did not think it right to enter into the contents of the message which you had sent to her by Colonel Thomas.

I am sorry that I have not proved myself a more able negotiator upon this occasion. When I see you next week I will relate to you more fully what passed. (44182)

1675 THE PRINCE OF WALES TO THE EARL OF EUSTON

Brighton, 10 Sept. 1802

I take up my pen, my dear Lord, to acknowledge your kind letter, which I should already have done, but it only reach'd me since my return to this place, & likewise to return you my sincere thanks for the very obliging manner in which you have been so good as to communicate to me the remembrance of our much lamented friend Hugh.[1] I certainly shall ever value that testimony of his regard & shall ever endeavour to prove the sense I have of it by any mark of kindness I may have it in my power to shew at any time to any of his children, & particularly to my little favorite, Minny,[2] who I have the pleasure to tell you is in most

Bath abt. Thursday to see the Duchess for two or three days. I pray to God he may mark Mr. Pitt's insult to him, in the person of the Duchess, by a mortifying avoidance of him while there, & a rooted execration of him everywhere else.'

1. Admiral Lord Hugh Seymour died of yellow fever whilst in command of the fleet on the Jamaica station on 12 September 1801. His wife, Lady Horatia, had died in Bristol on 12 July 1801. She and Lady Euston were sisters.

2. Mary Seymour (1798–1848). In his will her father appointed his brother, Lord Henry Seymour (1746–1830), and Lady Horatia's brother Lord Euston, as his executors and

perfect health, improves daily & is the most delightful child in the world, though I am well aware that none of them can want protectors under such good guardianship as yours & that of Lord Henry. I am extremely sorry that when I was in town a few days ago I did not know of the circumstance, or I should have immediately appointed Mr. Ward[1] to have called upon me at Carlton House. The eulogium you give that gentleman I understand he most deservedly merits, & I certainly will take the earliest opportunity of seeing him when I next pass through London.

Let me entreat of you to present my best compliments to Lady Euston & to beleive me [etc.] (Ragley MSS.).

1676   LORD THURLOW TO THE PRINCESS OF WALES

Brighton, Sunday, 12 Sept. 1802

I had the honour to present your Royal Highness's letter to the Prince. His Royal Highness had received one from the Duke of York, which only referred to some conversation which was to take place on the same subject between them. Therefore I have received no commands from his Royal Highness on this occasion.

I don't presume to offer any advice to your Royal Highness upon any part of this delicate and unfortunate subject; first, because I am not sufficiently acquainted with the circumstances which have unhappily produced a fresh misunderstanding, and, indeed, if I were, your own judgement is much more competent on such an occasion. Nobody knows better than your Royal Highness how essential it is to your own dignity to observe all those forms of respect which the Prince's high rank and your own require.

I am quite sure that your displeasure taken to Col. Thomas must have serious grounds, but your Royal Highness has not mentioned them; on the contrary, your Royal Highness seems to have employed him lately in carrying a message to the Prince. But whatever his offense, your Royal Highness was certainly right in applying to the Prince on the subject, but even there I am afraid some misunderstanding took place, for neither the Duke of Kent nor Admiral Payne remember the communication which your Royal Highness quotes in your letter to the Prince. On [the] one hand the Prince would not send any person into your presence who had given you serious offense; on the other I don't know enough of etiquette to judge whether your Royal Highness would refuse to receive

guardians of his children. Lady Horatia's friend Mrs. Fitzherbert had taken charge of Mary during her mother's last illness, and wished to adopt her, but the executors would not consent to such an arrangement.

1. Lord Hugh Seymour's Naval Chaplain.

a message from the Prince by any hand, however you might decline an answer by the same person.

It is utterly improbable that the Prince would object to any arrangement which your Royal Highness might think proper to propose in your family. The rest is meer matter of ceremony, for the appointment would equally remain with your Royal Highness whether it were made in form by the Prince or by your Royal Highness with the Prince's permission, or simply communicated after being made, or not even communicated. But I humbly submit it to your Royal Highness's consideration whether the first, or at least the second, would not conduce most to your dignity, and the maintenance of that universal esteem which your Royal Highness possesses.

1677 THE PRINCE OF WALES TO THE DUKE OF YORK

Carlton House, 25 Sept. 1802

I cannot leave London with[out] writing you a line to express my regret at not having been able to come to you at Oatlands yesterday, but the agony I suffer'd from the opperation I was oblig'd to submit to in consequence of the tooth I mention'd to you in the morning, precluded me entirely from the possibility of stirring from home. However, today I am easier & just going to set off for Brighton. (44183)

1678 PRINCESS MARY TO THE PRINCE OF WALES

Amelia's room, Queen's Lodge, Windsor, 25 Sept. [?*1802*]

In consequence of having received your kind letter I *have* wrote by this evening's post to Lady Elgin and communicated *your* commands *in* regard to her not stoping at [illegible] in *which* the Queen perfectly *coinsides* with you & approves highly of the child going the forest *road* and sleeping at Windsor the 2d. night of her journey.[1]

I am very sorry you have gone through so much *pain* with your *tooth* but hope by this time you are perfectly *ease* [sic]. We are all quite well

1. Princess Charlotte, accompanied by Lady Elgin, left Weymouth on Friday, 1 October, in accordance with the Prince's instructions, sent to Lady Elgin on Saturday the 18th: 'For reasons which I will communicate to you more at length when I have the pleasure of seeing you next, I think it best that Charlotte should return from the sea coast towards the end of the next week. I have therefore sent orders that your house at Shooter's Hill should be properly air'd & ready for you from Thursday next.' (49259)

Shooter's Hill came to be in the borough of Woolwich.

& all the illustrious family desire to be most kindly remember'd, in particular Sophia & Amelia. I was very sorry not to see you yesterday, as we passed through *Staines* I saw your carriage[1] & was in hopes I had a *chance* of a visit, but I flatter myself I shall be more fortunate next week. (Add. Georgian 12/22)

1679   THE PRINCE OF WALES TO LORD PELHAM

Brighton, 11.45 p.m., 26 Sept. 1802

Private & confidential. Many thanks, my dear friend, for your kind communication. Had I been to have dictated the letter to Lord Whitworth it could not have been compris'd in words I think so judicious as those you have put it into, or so completely analogous to my feelings & intentions. I have had a long & confidential conversation with Lord Thurlow, who I am certain when you chuse to converse with him you will find most perfectly well dispos'd & most particularly so to yourself, as he has express'd himself in the strongest and handsome manner possible respecting you.

I add no more at present as I will not detain the messenger any longer in order to occasion you as little delay as possible in your intended journey. I therefore shall reserve myself till our next interview to enter into further particulars which I trust you will not find uninteresting.[2] (Add. MSS. 33133, f.26)

1. The Prince returned to Brighton on the 25th.

2. Lord Pelham wrote to Lord Whitworth on the 26th: 'Fearing that you may leave England before I return from Yorkshire, I must trouble you upon a subject which I had rather have communicated to you in conversation. I am directed by the Prince of Wales to inform you that from goodwill towards M. de Calonne he was induced to avail himself of the encouragement given him by Mr. Otto to apply thro' that Minister to the First Consul for permission for M. de Calonne to return to France; & H.R.H. conceived that this permission would of course have been followed by his name being struck out of the list of emigrants. H.R.H. feels considerable disappointment at this failure & wishes that you would take favorable opportunity of representing to the First Consul, in conversation, H.R.H.'s feelings, representing, at the same time, that it was far from H.R.H.'s intention to interfere politically or to do more than to offer a friendly assistance to an unfortunate individual whom H.R.H. had often met in private society. You, who know ye warmth of the Prince's heart, will easily comprehend how eagerly he would embrace an opportunity which he thought Mr. Otto's conversation gave him of doing an act of benevolence, & if the First Consul should be really disposed to shew a mark of personal civility to the Prince upon this subject, I know no one more capable than yourself of doing justice to the feelings which the Prince would be sure to entertain upon the occasion' (Add. MSS. 33133, ff.28–9). Calonne left London for Paris on 21 September and died there at the end of October.

311

Gibraltar, 28 Sept. 1802

Having this instant received the intimation from Captain Hillyer[1] of the Niger frigate, who sails in an hour for England, that he could accommodate a grey Spanish stallion which I purchased two months since for you, being reckoned one of the finest Andalusia produces, I hasten to scribble a few words just to call myself to your recollection and to repeat to you the assurance of my faithful and devoted attachment. I hope the horse will please, but to judge of him to advantage I beg you will not look at him till Quentin[2] mounts him on parade, for in the stable he looks dull, but in the field he is all fire and action. This completes your instructions to me about *Spanish* horses as this is the second I have sent: his price is about an hundred guineas but, as horses go here, even *that* is moderate. General Villettes[3] is looking out for an Arabian for you but has hitherto not been successful. As to Barbs from across the water out of the dominions of the Emperor of Morocco, I have lately got his Imperial Majesty's sanction to get two or three over, and I mean to take an early opportunity of sending my groom, who was poor Harvey Aston's,[4] over to Barbary to select them; should any be worth sending to *you* the *best* will of course *et de droit* be embarked a vos ordres, for I never am happier than when employed in your service.

The heat since I have been here has been literally intolerable, and I have felt it a good deal, but it *must* now soon be over, and *then* I shall hope to recover appetite and flesh, both of which have left me in great measure since I have been on the Rock. My labor, I can assure you, has been not inconsiderable to put matters to rights which I found generally in sad confusion: but all is beginning now to get systematically settled, and I trust my worst difficulties are over. Now, my dearest brother, adieu, may every blessing attend you. Pray, say a thousand kind things from me to Mrs. Fitzherbert.[5] (46057-8)

1. James Hillyar. Lieutenant, 1794; Commander, 1800; Captain, February 1804.

2. George Quintin, later, Lieutenant-Colonel of the Prince's Regiment, the 10th Light Dragoons. Major, 1805; Lieutenant-Colonel, 1808; Colonel, 1814. Knighted, 1821. A.D.C. to the Prince Regent and to him as King.

3. William Anne Villettes (1754-1808). Lieutenant-Colonel, 1791; Colonel, 1795; Major-General, 1798; Lieutenant-General, 1805. Lieutenant-Governor of Jamaica at the time of his death.

4. See No. 942n. (ii.539).

5. She was with the Prince at Brighton at this time. Lord Glenbervie wrote: 'There is no company at Brighthelmstone but him and Mrs. Fitzherbert and such divorced ladies as Lady Lucan, and women of the town' (*Journals*, i.330).

Brighton, 11 Oct. 1802

I have a thousand apologies to make to you, my dear Countess, for not having already answer'd your very obliging letter, but I have been so much indispos'd for the last four or five days, with a bad cold attended with strong billious symptoms, though not very serious ones (or otherwise I should have sent for our friend Farquhar) that it has not been really in my power to muster up resolution to put pen to paper till today. However, being now, thank God, better, I seize the earliest opportunity of answering all your questions, which I beleive may be done in answering one, which is, who is to be consulted respecting Charlotte's teeth. Old Dumergue is the person I have employ'd this five & twenty years & upwards,[1] & the only one I have complete confidence in, & the ablest most certainly in his line not only in this country but in any other, but he is unfortunately at this moment abroad; however, he will certainly be at home in a fortnight or three weeks at furthest.[2] His nephew[3] is most indisputably a very clever & genteel young man, & were the old man out of the question, one that I should prefer as a dentist to any other, & indeed who I have myself employ'd upon a late occasion since his uncle's departure. If you think it of such immediate consequence for the child's teeth that it will not admit of a delay of three weeks, of course I should wish you to send for young Dumergue, but if otherwise I should recommend the delaying sending for anyone till the return of old Dumergue. I am truly happy of hearing of your safe arrival, my dear Countess, in good health. (49260–1)

Brighton, 15 Oct. 1802

I write a few lines to acknowledge the receipt of your obliging letter, & am most extremely sorry to observe by its contents that the business of my brother Augustus, in which I have been so uncomfortably intermeddled, is not in that degree of forwardness, nor likely to be terminated so expeditiously as I was led to suppose some months ago that it would be, from the joint conversation I had at the Drawing Room on the

1. His name first appears in the *Court and City Register* as one of the Court 'Operators for the Teeth' in 1785.

2. Dumergue was supposed to have an 'allowance' of £105 a year from the Prince, but in January 1805 it was in arrear for five and a half years. (32487)

3. Charles John Joli Dumergue, born, like his uncle, in the province of Angoumois. He was the son of John Joli Dumergue and of Maria Terest, and was Dentist to the Duke and Duchess of Kent, to George IV, William IV and Queen Victoria. He married in 1802.

King's Birthday with the Minister & Lord Rosslyn. I now understand that Lady Augusta[1] has been oblig'd to abscond. I commiserate her situation most truly, but you will hear more of this from one of her sisters who will write to you by this day's post. At the same time, though I cannot but wish that his Majesty had never laid his express commands upon me to be a party concern'd in the adjustment of this business, I must consequently feel that I am in some degree bound through you to acquaint Lord Rosslyn and Mr. Addington of the disgraceful state it stands in, & of the urgent necessity there is now of bringing it to a speedy conclusion. Whenever you have a moment to spare and can run down to me for a day, I need not add how glad I shall be to see you, & I will then talk over this, as well as other business of no small import. (Excuse haste) (Blair Adam MSS.).

1683 THE PRINCE OF WALES TO THE EARL OF EUSTON, AND THE REPLY

Brighton, 15 Oct. 1802

My friend Admiral Payne in company with the Revd. Mr. Warde [*sic*] will have the honor of presenting this letter to you. I do not mean to enter into the particulars concerning which they are fully authoriz'd by me to converse most openly with you, as it would be entering upon too wide a field, and tresspassing too long upon your patience. As the Revd. Mr. Warde was so strongly recommended by you, my dear Lord, to me in your last kind letter, I thought I could not select, in consequence of what you know of him, so proper a person to accompany Admiral Payne upon the present occasion, so interesting to my feelings & so beneficial to the wellfare of the dear child of my much-loved friend Lord Hugh (Ragley MSS.).

THE PRINCE OF WALES'S PROPOSAL[2]

The Prince of Wales being fully convinced that the welfare and happiness of the child are essentially dependant on her continuance under the care of Mrs. Fitzherbert, and it appearing by the evidence before the Master that she cannot be removed without injury to her health and peril of her life, he feels it an indispensible part of the parental duty he so solemnly engaged to her dying mother to fulfil, to protect her to the utmost of his power in her present happy situation, and therefore

1. Lady Augusta Murray. Her calculated indiscretion in 1794 involved her in a sea of troubles.

2. This Memorandum was communicated to Lord Euston at this time.

314

nothing short of a stipulation that she shall remain there unmolested until she shall be of an age to chuse for herself, will satisfy his mind.

If this shall be assented to on the part of her family, the Prince, in furtherance of his designs in her favor and to obviate the exceptions that have been taken to the instrument he has already executed, intends speedily to invest the sum of £10,000 in the funds as well to answer the provision intended to be secured by that instrument as to add to it by the accumulation of the interest during her minority.

The Prince scruples not to declare his ultimate view to be to raise her up hereafter as a companion and as he hopes, a bosom friend of his own daughter. To warrant these views it is absolutely necessary that she should be bred and educated under his own eye. Her family must therefore perceive that he has a deeper interest than they have in her becoming a member of the Church of England as well as in the purity of her morals, and they cannot, he apprehends, desire a surer pledge for the security of either of those most important objects.

But his Royal Highness, far from condemning the anxiety her friends have shewn on the score of her religion, thinks himself bound to give them every satisfaction on that point they can desire. He wishes (as does Mrs. Fitzherbert most earnestly) that the freest intercourse should be kept up between the child and her family and relations, and that they also should, if they please, be eye-witnesses of the course of her education as well as the formation of her mind and manners.

This intercourse has never been prevented by Mrs. Fitzherbert, and could never have been interrupted had not the present contest taken place.

For the mutual satisfaction of the minds of her relations and his own, the Prince proposes that [he] himself, Lord Thurlow and the Bishop of Winchester[1] should be appointed, jointly with the Marquis of Hertford and Lord Robert Seymour, guardians of this infant under a previous understanding and declaration in writing that she shall remain with Mrs. Fitzherbert unless anything shall arise with reference to her religion which, in the judgment of the guardians, shall render it proper to remove her.

If this arrangement shall be approved, the contest will be put an end to, and the infant will be bred up in harmony with her family and with every protection to her spiritual and temporal welfare they can reasonably desire, but if, notwithstanding the irresistible body of evidence now disclosed to them of the dreadful consequences which would inevitably ensue, they still determine to persevere in demanding the removal of the child from under Mrs. Fitzherbert's care, he shall feel himself bound no less by the obligation of common humanity than that of the parental duty he has undertaken, to resist their efforts to the utmost of his power.

Note. It will be necessary to provide for the filling up such vacancies as may occur in the number of the guardians.

1. Dr. Brownlow North.

315

Your R.H. has done me much honor in communicating yr. intentions with regard to Ld. Hugh Seymour's youngest daughter thro' such a channel as that of Admiral Payne & Mr. Ward, & I am sure that yr. Royal Highness' candour will scarcely expect an answer from me singly upon a point of much delicacy & one on which no determination of mine can be binding without a concurrence of opinion on the part of my fellow executor & guardian, Ld. Henry Seymour.

Being placed in a situation of much responsibility &, as it has happen'd, of more than usual delicacy, it will be a source of unfeigned satisfaction to us both, I am sure, that the course which we may judge it proper to take shd. accord with your Royal Highness's wishes; that the decision we may come to will be dictated by an attachment to the memory & principles of the person for whom we are acting I trust your Royal Highness will not doubt, any more than the respect which it is our duty to bear towards your R. Highness, & to which our inclination also leads us[2] (Ragley MSS.).

1684   THE PRINCE OF WALES TO SIR WALTER FARQUHAR [copy]

Brighton, 25 Oct. 1802

I heard yesterday from your son Tom, who was so good as to dine with me, that he had learnt by a letter wh. he had recd. from one of his sisters, that it was yr. intention to come here in a day or 2 upon a visit to me; now as it is possible that I myself shall be in town either Thursday or Friday for a couple of days, I write these few lines that you may not have yr. trouble for nothing. In case I cannot come up to London I will write again & then I shall be delighted to receive you here. But even in

1. The copy is endorsed, 'Oct. 1802'.

2. Lord Euston wrote to Rear-Admiral Payne (the letter is undated): 'I lost no time in forwarding to Ld. Henry Seyr., joint executor with myself & guardian of the late Ld. H. Seyr.'s children, H.R.H. proposal of settling £10,000 upon the youngest daughter of Ld. H. Seyr. on certain conditions: the kindness of which intention both as it relates to the memory of our friend Ld. Hugh & to the worldly advantage of the child is so striking that it renders it a subject of unspeakable regret to Ld. H. & to myself to feel that we shd. not be doing our duty in the situation in which we are placed by Ld. Hugh's Will if we were not to avail ourselves of the offer made by two of the nearest relations both of the father & the mother to take the female children into their own family, which precludes the possibility of acceding to a proposal made by H.R.H. in a spirit of affectionate tenderness of which we beg also thro' you to convey our humble but most sincere admiration. As guardians to the children of our deceased friend we feel bound to act for them according to the dictates of our consciences, a principle which we are sure H.R.H. cannot disapprove, even tho' in this instance the observance of it has led us to decline H.R.H.' most liberal offer' (Ragley MSS.).

316

case of my coming to London I depend upon yr. not disappointing me afterwards in letting me have yr. company for as many days as your numberless calls will admit. Pray remember [me] most kindly to all yr. family & most particularly to Mrs. Hook whose health I hope is improving as much as everyone who has the happiness of knowing her must wish.

I am ever, dear Farquhar, very affectionately yours.

P.S. I am better than I have been for some days past. Pray say how the D. & Dss. of Devonshire are[1] (Farquhar MSS.).

1685 PRINCESS SOPHIA TO THE PRINCE OF WALES

3 Nov. 1802

If you are so good as to say that your words fall short of what you feel towards me, how *very very* unequal, my dearest, are any expressions of mine to express my gratitude & thanks for the kindest of letters you have sent me, & for the beautiful present which accompanied it. I hope you will do me the justice to beleive that I did not want anything to recall you to my mind, & though I am in extacies with my *lovely pensée*, yet dear love I will not disown that the contents of the dear letter is what I prize most, as it contains the assurance of your affection. Everything that comes from you is *valuable to Sophy*, but how far more than I had reason to expect is yr. first kindness in remembering this day. How happy should I have been to have past it with you & feel doubly sorry as you assure me that your absence is caused by illness. God grant you may soon be quit[e] well & able to join us on the 8th. At all events I shall obey yr. commands & get something for Augusta.

You will before this have received a letter from me with an account of mama. She desires me [to] say how much she feels your kind expressions concerning her & how sorry she is that you are ill. Thank God mama is really much better, & though still confined, bids me say that she is neither *ill nor well*.

All my sisters desire a thousand loves, *Miny & your child in particular.* God bless you again & again. I shall read yr. dear letter a dozen times over for I am so *happy* & gratified by it that my *words fly*, which shews you *the natural importunity* of [etc.]. (Add. Georgian 11/15)

1. The following note from the Prince to Sir Walter, dated Thursday evening, may have been written sometime in 1803: 'Pray call upon me the first place you go to when you set off upon your evening's visits. I would not give you this trouble if I did not feel myself very unwell indeed. You will find me at home here at Carlton House' (Farquhar MSS.).

1686   THE EARL OF MOIRA TO COLONEL MCMAHON

Donington, 7 Nov. 1802

On this day week (Sunday) I will be in town early enough to pay my duty to the Prince before he goes out. The arrangement which you have imparted to me has so much likelihood that I have no doubt of the accuracy of your informant. I am sure it is the best for me, and I should think it ultimately advantageous for the Prince also, were it not for the low opinion of Government which these tricks permanently impress on the multitude. No sort of confidence can attend an Administration so formed. The approaching war will require great demands on the people. They will be paid at least sullenly; and if misfortune happens much soreness of spirit will spread thro' a country which we ought to recollect has been (thro' the militia, fencibles & yeomanry) trained to arms. If we are to contest with France, we have no chance of a favorable termination but by carrying the enthusiasm of this country with Government. What hope is there of it at present? Hill says your qualification must be an English property. I can manage it; & I have sent him instructions.[1] If the Prince be in town, offer my most affectionate duty to his Royal Highness.[2] (39851–2)

1687   PRINCESS AUGUSTA TO THE PRINCE OF WALES

8 Nov. 1802

It is scarcely possible for me, my own dearest G.P., to express how dearly I love you. You know of old I am no *fine* speech maker but as Shakespeare says, 'Truth has better deeds than words to grace it',[3] and no time, no absence can change the sentiments of friendship and affection that I have ever felt for you.

I am truly sorry that indisposition prevents my having the happiness and comfort of seeing you today, but I trust when we next meet you will

1. McMahon, an Irishman, had been elected M.P. for Aldeburgh (Suffolk) on 5 July. The new Parliament met for business on 16 November. McMahon, on taking the usual oaths, would be required to deliver to the Clerk of the House an account of his qualification, in accordance with the requirements of the Act of Anne's reign which said that every English or Welsh City or Borough Member must possess an estate to the value of £300 a year, exceptions being made in the cases of the eldest sons of Peers and of men qualified to be County Members. McMahon obviously possessed no such landed property in England, but Moira was prepared to fit him up with a bogus qualification, thus demonstrating, as many other people did, how easy it was to drive a coach and four through an Act of Parliament.

2. This letter is preceded by a long account of the Despard Plot, which is not reproduced here, partly because of its length (thirty folios: 39820–50), partly because there is a full account of Despard's trial in the *State Trials*.

3. *The Three Gentlemen of Verona*, Act II, Sc. 2, line 18.

be in perfect health. *Pitty Witty* has been *cooing* over the thoughts and hopes of seeing you, & she says 'dear, sweet Prince of Wales, how very tiresome of him to be sick now', without considering that one does not send an invitation to sickness nor call out to it '*keep yourself disengaged*', *as some folks are wont to say.*

I am very happy to be able to say that the Queen is a great deal better; she is still very pale, which I believe is chiefly owing to her having staid at home for such a long time as a fortnight & therefore always living in and breathing confined air.

My sisters all desire their most affectionate love to you; your child *Amelia* is grown very *handsome* and *stout* but I wish she would *eat* a little *better* food. You must give her some advice about it when you see her again; it is now her *only fault*.

I return you many thanks for the beautifull *bracelets* little Sophy put into my hand this morning, saying, 'they come from some lady who don't *love you & who you* don't love *neither*', so I directly guessed they came from *you*.[1] (Add. Georgian 10/32)

1688   THE PRINCE OF WALES TO THE EARL OF EUSTON

Brighton, 12 Nov. 1802

Admiral Payne's hand being disabled by the gout, I hasten to acknowledge myself the receit of your Lordship's letter.

1. The following item illustrates the dilatoriness with which the Prince's bills were sometimes settled. David Robertson wrote to R. Gray on 10 November from 40, Sackville Street. 'By directions received from Mr. Tyrwhitt I beg to inclose a small bill due by his Royal Highness the Prince of Wales to Mr. Spottiswoode, incurred in June 1796 relative to an election of the Peers of Scotland, amount £16 2. 6. In Mr. Spottiswoode's absence I have his authority to receive the same. (42360–1)

'HIS ROYAL HIGHNESS the Prince of Wales in the matter of qualifying to vote at the election of the Scotch Peers in 1796

1796		to John Spottiswoode		
June	To paid Gentlemen of the Chamber to the Lord Chancellor usual fee 2 gs. extra 2 gs.	4	4	–
	To paid Clerk of the Petty Bag, usual fee £1. 11. 6, extra 2 gs. expences to Richmond 2 gs.	5	15	6
	To paid Sealers, usual fee 5 shs. extra 5/6		10	6
	To paid stamp for signed list		7	6
	To my trouble attendance &c.	5	5	–
		£16	2	6

RECEIVED the 22d January 1803 of his Royal Highness the Prince of Wales by Adml. Payne Specl. Treasr. the sum of sixteen pounds two shillings & six pence being the amount of the annexed bill. £16. 2. 6. (42362)

John Spottiswoode's receipt (42363) is dated the 25th.

Your Lordship enters perfectly into the grounds of my anxiety for the wellfare of the child.[1] Regard to the memory of my friend her father prompted my tenderness to her. A promise exacted by her dying mother made the bond more sacred. Both expressed themselves happy in the affectionate care she was then under, & her engaging manners made the task delightful. Your Lordship may judge then, if she *must* be removed, how much my anxious wishes and views for a child thus circumstanced would be disappointed if I were not fully persuaded that the affection of nearer relations will more than compensate the purposes I had formed for her education & advancement. The motives of my attachment to her, however heartfelt and sacred, give me no title to interfere with her legal guardians. I forbear therefore to ask a single question which that attachment might otherwise have prompted. It is impossible to differ from your Lordship in this, that the dictates of conscience must prescribe the duties of every relation in life, & that to provide for the wellfare & advancement of a ward is the whole duty of a guardian.

Your Lordship knows the intentions I had conceived in her favour; her fortune would have been more suitable to her birth than the present pittance, & her education would have been suitable to both. If your Lordship sees reason to deprive your ward of these advantages, that reason will doubtless afford her a satisfactory account of the matter when she comes to an age fit to judge of it[2] (Ragley MSS.).

1. Mary Seymour.

2. The Prince's second proposal to the guardians of Lord Hugh Seymour's children was written about this time:

'The Prince of Wales makes the following proposal to the guardians of the children of Lord Hugh Seymour. His Royal Highness is disposed to execute an immediate Deed of Trust empowering the youngest daughter to claim from him or his executors the sum of £10,000 on her coming of age, or at the day of her marriage, or at the moment of his own death. His R.H. proposes that the proportion of her father's fortune, to which she may be entitled, shall be placed out at interest to accumulate till she comes of age. His R.H. on the other part stipulates for only one condition, that the young lady shall continue in the hands in which she is at present placed, not intending by this arrangement to bar the access to her family, friends, and guardians, nor to exclude them from a concern in her education, but desiring in both those respects to fall in with their wishes, and that the line of instruction, religious, moral or literary shall be precisely marked out by their suggestion and recommendation.

'Nor does his R.H. wish to be understood that his disposition to promote the interests of the child is to be bounded by the arrangement specified above, but is willing to bind himself at the present moment and at all events to give effect to those propositions which are therein mentioned.

'Should the guardians be induced to accede to the proposal in question, his R.H. purposes to appoint as Trustees of the Deed in the first place themselves, and to add to their names those of the Marquis of Hertford and Admiral Payne' (Ragley MSS.).

1689   LORD PELHAM TO THE PRINCE OF WALES, AND TWO REPLIES [copy]
Wimbledon, 12 Nov. 1802
I take the liberty of humbly soliciting an audience at the time & place most convenient to your Royal Highness for the purpose of communicating to your Royal Highness a conversation which took place yesterday between the Lord Chancellor, Mr. Addington & me upon the subject of your Royal Highness's Petition, from which I am encouraged to hope that some arrangement may be made by which the public discussion of that business may be avoided.

I should certainly have taken the chance of finding your Royal Highness at Brighthelmestone if I was not afflicted with a cold, but if the return of the messenger should bring me your Royal Highness's commands to attend you at Brighthelmstone, I flatter myself that nothing can prevent me from doing so on Sunday. (Add. MSS. 33133, f.30)

THE PRINCE OF WALES'S REPLY
Brighton, 12.15 p.m., 13 Nov. 1802
I last night receiv'd your very obliging letter between 10 & eleven o'clock, & I have delay'd the return of the messenger to this late hour in the hopes of being able to have made an appointment with you in London tomorrow, but I find unfortunately that that will not be in my power. However, I shall make a point of being in town in the course of Monday, when I will immediately apprize you of my arrival & settle when we shall meet. I hope by that time you will be completely reliev'd from all the inconveniences of cold, which I am pretty well acquainted with, having had a severe attack myself of late. (Add. MSS. 33133, f.32)

FROM THE PRINCE OF WALES
Carlton House, Monday evening, 15 Nov. 1802
I am just arriv'd in town & shall be ready & very happy to receive you between twelve & one o'clock tomorrow, if that hour should be convenient. (Add. MSS. 33133, f.34)

1690   LETTERS FROM COLONEL MCMAHON TO THE DUKE OF NORTHUMBERLAND
London, 5.30 p.m., 17 Nov. 1802
The interview between the Prince & Lord Pelham has taken place. His

Lordship brought no specific proposition from the Ministers, but with vast professions of good will on their part, & personal devotion on his own, proposed that all legal proceedings should be suspended, & an amicable negociation be immediately enter'd upon. To this H.R.Hss. acceeded, & named his three Law Officers (Erskine, Gibbs, & Adam) to meet Lord Pelham at 3 o'clock tomorrow for the purpose of receiving the proposal of Ministers in writing, & discussing what may properly appertain to it, previous to the giving the Prince's determination thereon. The result of all this I shall have the honor to transmit your Grace, but fear the post of tomorrow evening may not admit of the communication, particularly as I attend H.R.Hss. to the Drawing Room tomorrow which is expected to be very late.

The Levée of this day has lasted until 4 o'clock; & the eagerness to see Andreossi[1] (who went in a new built Paris coach with a crane neck & very lumberly, & the Consular livery worn by his coachman & two footmen) almost bar'd up all the avenues to St. James's. I hope in my next to give your Grace some particulars respecting the Levée & Drawing Room.

Lord Pelham assured the Prince that everything was pacific; & that Buonaparté had not written any letter to the King as was reported.

I hope your Grace & the Duchess (to whom I beg leave to offer my best respects) have escaped colds in your journey to Bath; & I have the honor [etc.]. Whenever your Grace may have any commands to honor me with, the post at Carlton House is two hours earlier in its delivery than Bury Street (Alnwick MSS.).

London, 19 Nov. 1802

The Prince's Bar yesterday attended Lord Pelham, when again nothing specific was proposed, but Ld. Pelham express'd an entreaty that they would furnish him with an outline of the Prince's wishes, & a statement of the extent of all H.R.Hss.'s pecuniary embarrassments; declaring the sincere desire of his Majesty's Ministers to free him completely from every difficulty & incumbrance. The project that became discuss'd at this meeting & was started by the Prince's lawyers & frankly approved by Lord Pelham was—That Mr. Pitt's Bill should be abolish'd & quietly got rid of; the Prince's full income immediately restored, & all the remaining debts for which that income was originally assign'd to the Commissioners, as well as all those subsequently incurr'd, should be forthwith discharg'd. The extent of this seems to embrace a sum on a rough calculation to about £400,000. To give time for our lawyers to

1. The French General and diplomatist. Ambassador to London, 1802-3.

prepare the required statement & to allow the Ministers leisure to digest finally this outline, the next meeting between them & Lord Pelham is fix'd for Monday next at 12 o'clock, the proceedings of which I will have the honor to transmit your Grace by the post of that evening, if the report should come to Carlton House in reasonable time.

A prodigious consternation universally prevails here in consequence of the apprehension of Col. Despard[1] & about forty more who are at this instant undergoing a farther examination at the Secretary of State's Office, for a deep & horrible design of assassinating the King on Tuesday in his way either to or from Parliament, & other shocking & atrocious purposes. The great difficulty seems to be the finding out the grand movers of this treason, for Despard in the supply of money for the seduction of the soldiery can have only been an agent. It is said his corruption has extended to nearly 300 of the Guards, & those chiefly of the 3rd Regiment. King[2] (Under-Secretary of State) tells me that as yet no name of any consideration appears implicated; that they have ample means of bringing the parties to condign punishment, & that they have been nearly three months in following up & fixing the plot— but I yesterday saw Wilson[3] who told me he would learn every material particular from the Chancellor, who attended the examination, & communicate the whole to your Grace, which, presuming he has so done, there can be nothing left for me to add to your Lordship on this subject by way of information.

The Drawing Room yesterday was uncommonly crowded. The Queen look'd very far from well, & the Prince thought her so. She was extremely gracious to Andréossi, & the King had likewise been very civil at the Levée to him the day before. The Prince dined on Wednesday & Thursday at Buckingham House & nothing could be pleasanter than his reception. Lord Pelham assured H.R.Hss. at the Drawing Room that he had not a single doubt of Ministry complying with the statement I have already given to your Grace; & this the Prince commanded me, with his best love, to communicate to your Lordship.

There is nothing stirring today of any other kind worth mentioning. Wilson caught yesterday exactly as your Grace expected; I ask'd him if he heard of any of the Scotch Peers being given over, as the P. wish'd so

1. Edward Marcus Despard (1751–1803). Served in Jamaica as Lieutenant, 50th Regiment, 1772; Superintendent of H.M.'s affairs in Yucatan, 1784–90; imprisoned on account of his claim for compensation, 1798. On the 16th Despard and about thirty labourers and soldiers, most of them Irish, were arrested at the Oakley Arms, Oakley Street, Lambeth. Some were subsequently discharged. Despard was found guilty of plotting against the King's life (7 February 1803), and he and six of his associates were executed on 21 February.

2. John King (1759–1830), M.P. for Enniskillen, 1806. Under-Secretary of State, Home Department, 1792–1806; Joint Secretary of the Treasury, February–September 1806; Comptroller of Army Accounts, 1806–30.

3. Richard Wilson. See No. 1628.

much to serve Ld. Lauderdale. On this he started, & immediately, without reserve, told me both the anecdotes which Richardson had recited at your Grace's table, which will be quite sufficient for me, without adverting to where it took place, to have them set right & clear'd up (Alnwick MSS.).

Carlton House, 24 Nov. 1802

I had the honor to inform your Grace that the Prince's Bar were to meet Lord Pelham this forenoon in the hope of bringing H.R.Hss.'s business to a conclusion, but upon some difficulty occurring to his Lordship as to a particular point in the outline, which seem'd to have previously been reciprocally agreed to, the lawyers beg'd to know distinctly whether Lord Pelham on his part was authorised with full powers from Mr. Addington, in behalf of the Cabinet to treat & conclude with them, upon such arrangement as they might determine on. He reply'd that he certainly *was not*, but that he would see Mr. Addington on Friday or Saturday when he had no doubt he would completely assent to & confirm their proceedings. Here the meeting of this morning broke up & ended, & I confess to your Grace that when I think of the speciousness which Mr. Addington has practised on such various occasions, I cannot help in my superficial judgement to dislike the present complexion of our affairs, notwithstanding the pledge of fairness & sincerity which Lord Pelham's personal character may afford. The Prince now continues in town until Sunday, waiting patiently this specific answer which Ld. Pelham so confidently promises to give on Friday or Saturday next. I beg to observe to your Grace that the remainder of the debt (for which the Prince's income is assign'd to the Commissioners) is abt. £250,000; & the debt he has incurr'd subsequent to that arrangement abt. £150,000 more; both sums consequently amounting to £400,000. The sums that have been advanc'd by the nation, exclusive of his income, & which the Prince always proposed to restore from his claim, comes to nearly £160,000, so that if the outline now given in should be agreed to, H.R.Hss. will be somewhat the gainer by the bargain.

I beg leave to enclose your Grace a letter I had yesterday the honor to receive from the Duke of Kent at Gibraltar respecting the Mr. Lethbridge whom your Lordship recommended last year to the Prince, as H.R.Hss. particularly alludes to your Grace regarding that circumstance in his letter.[1]

1. There is a further reference to Mr. Lethbridge in McMahon's letter to the Duke dated 14 December: ' ... Before I was honor'd with your Grace's letter yesterday, in consequence of Mr. Wilson's report of the preceding day, I received the Prince's command to order the

The debates[1] in both Houses last night were very warm. Mr. Canning treated Mr. Addington with great severity & ridicule; & if he can be accepted as the representative of Mr. Pitt, no doubt can remain as to his hostility against Mr. Addington; besides which Ld. Grenville's speech announces the re-union of Mr. Pitt & the Grenvilles. Towards the end of the debate in the H. of Commons Mr. Windham made a violent attack on Mr. Fox respecting French politics, which it is supposed Mr. Fox will reply to this day when the report on the Address is brought up, & which excites very great expectation.

The King received the greatest acclamations on his way to & from Parliament, & everything was quite loyal & peaceable. Nothing further has been done, or has transpired respecting Despard, nor is there anything stirring worth mentioning (Alnwick MSS.).

Carlton House, 27 Nov. 1802
The letter I had the honor to receive from your Grace this morning gave me great concern in finding that your Lordship was indisposed, but I rejoice to think that the gouty attack is only a slight one, & I hope ere this has vanish'd.

Lord Pelham according to appointment has this day waited on the Prince (having previously met H.R.Hss.'s Counsel without entering on any business) & I am sorry to tell your Grace, without having the requisite & expected authority for making any specific proposition whatever. He branch'd out as before into general professions of the good intentions & disposition of H.M. Ministers towards H.R.Hss.— expatiated, in the first instance very considerably on the difficulties of repealing, or extinguishing, Mr. Pitt's Bill, from such an attempt being subject to the danger of provoking a very acrimonious discussion, & a very serious doubt as to the ability of carrying the object in the end. He afterwards combated almost the whole of the outline which had before seemingly been agreed to, & in short came to this conclusion only as the supposed sentiment of the Cabinet. To make up H.R.Hss.'s immediate income £100,000 a year (his present being £60,000) & to redeem his jewells (about £16,000).

living of Stoke to be forthwith made out for the Revd. Mr. Chas. Lethbridge. The appointment is now preparing, & when executed by H. R. Hss. I will carefully deliver it to Mr. Wilson. The living of Landulph Mr. Wilson did at the same time apply for (but not in your Grace's name) in favor of a Mr. Church whom he stated to be a useful man in Cornwall, promising to procure him speedily such a Chancery living as will cause him to vacate Landulph. The Prince directed, if nothing appear'd on the books agst. it, to have it done, but Ld. Keith stands there as a prior promise' (Alnwick MSS.).

1. On the Address of Thanks. The King had opened the Session on the 23rd.

The Prince suppress'd his astonishment, at this change of plan & diminution of intention, but (although he is highly pleased with Ld. Pelham's zeal in trying to effect a satisfactory negociation) at once rejected the entire idea & declared his resolution of proceeding forthwith in Chancery. This determination Ld. Pelham used many arguments to avert, & requested H.R.Hss. to suspend it at least until he could again see Mr. Addington, when he still hoped the business would be brought to a happy termination.

The Prince commands me to make his love to your Grace, & to say that he has given Lord Pelham until 12 o'clock on Monday to give to H.R.Hss. the final resolve & projét of the Ministers in writing, when if it should fall short of the original design, namely, to restore H.R.Hss. his whole income, & to discharge his subsequent debts, he will give the necessary orders for his Bar to make a motion in Chancery on the following day to bring on his cause.

The Grenville party, with the Canningites, threaten Mr. Addington with a system of violent opposition; & it is believed Lord Granville Leveson[1] means to come forward with a specific motion 'for the dissmission of his Majesty's Ministers'. I have been just told in confidence that the Dss. of Devonshire, & Lady Besborough on Thursday visited Mrs. Fox, who dined that day with the Bishop of Down[2] & Mrs. Dickson. Lord Moira told me the K. was remarkably gracious on *Wednesday* at the Levée to both Lord & Mr. Thos. Grenville, the day after their attack on Mr. Addington.

I shall duly acquaint your Lordship with the result of Monday, and have the honor [etc.] (Alnwick MSS.).

Carlton House, 29 Nov. 1802[3]

In compliance with the desire of Lord Pelham, the Prince's Counsel yesterday attended his Lordship & Mr. Addington at the house of the latter in Richmond Park, at 3 o'clock, for the purpose of bringing H.R.Hss.'s business to a final conclusion.

1. Lord Granville Leveson-Gower, 1st Earl Granville (1773–1846), youngest son of the 1st Marquess of Stafford. M.P. for Lichfield, 1795–9; for Staffordshire, 1799–1815. Sent on a Special Mission to Prussia, 1798; a Lord of the Treasury, July 1800–February 1801; Ambassador to Russia, 1804–6 and May–November 1807; Secretary at War with a seat in the Cabinet, June–October 1809; created Viscount Granville, 12 August 1815; Ambassador to The Hague, 1824; to France, 1824–8 and 1831–5, and 1835–41. Created Earl Granville, 10 May 1833.

2. William Dickson (1745–1804), Bishop of Down, 1784–1804. A friend of Fox.

3. This, and the remaining letters under this Number, are slightly out of order, but it has been thought useful to keep them together, as they complete the story.

After a vast deal of argument & discussion, & after a previous explanation between Mr. Addington & Lord Pelham as to some points in which Mr. A. stated Ld. Pelham to have misunderstood him, & to have consequently held out expectations that had not been intended by him, he earnestly requested to be allowed this week (which he call'd a momentous one as to Parliamentary proceedings) before he gave in writing the utmost extent to which his Majesty's Ministers could go in adjusting the matter in question: at the same time having no difficulty or hesitation on his part to say distinctly that with all possible good disposition & duty towards the Prince, & after giving the subject his most serious & indulgent consideration, his mind was finally made up to the immediate restoration of the Prince's entire income, but without undertaking to discharge any debt H.R.Hss. may have incur'd since the settlement of his affairs, when that income had been vested in the Commissioners named in the Act for the liquidation of his *then* debts. In short, my Lord, reducing this proposition to a clear point of view, it is simply this, the debt under that settlement is now as nearly as possible £250,000 remaining due, & which by restoring his income is exactly the precise sum which they give H.R.Hss. in lieu of his claim. After battleing for the payment of the subsequent debt, & the mode in which the accomplishment of the whole should be shaped, this conference broke up, & between nine & ten o'clock last night the Counsel waited on H.R.Hss. with the report of their proceedings. The Prince, tho' highly provoked at all this shufling & inconsistent proceeding, was nevertheless persuaded by the advice of his Bar (who declared their firm conviction that Mr. A. was well disposed & meant to act fairly) to agree to give Mr. Addington the week he required, but more particularly as there is no day within this week that a motion could be brought on in Chancery. Having made this determination the Prince went off to Brighton at eleven o'clock this morning intending to wait, without taking any step whatever, until Mr. Addington gives his promised ultimatum in writing, & resolved in the event of its not being such as in sound policy he ought to accept, to proceed directly in Chancery. I think it necessary to assure your Grace that this business, throughout this negociation has, on the part of the Prince, been conducted entirely by his Bar (Messrs. Erskine, Gibbes, & Adam) & without the interference of any other person whatever. I heartily hope it may terminate to H.R.Hss.'s fame & satisfaction, but I own I do not admire the prospect.

Mr. Addington in stiling this 'a momentous week' seem'd, I understand, to express a good deal of anxiety about the business in Parliament of Wednesday next, & of this day sennight, the former being the consideration of, & the Supply for, the Navy estimates; & the latter those of the Army. The Grenville party appear to encrease, & thereby to present a formidable opposition to Mr. Addington who has hitherto been entirely supported & protected by Mr. Fox against them, & the adherents to Canning. Until I may be honor'd with your Grace's pleasure & commands to the contrary, I shall keep aloof from any division, which I conceive to be the idea your Grace had the goodness to chalk out for me.

The K. & Q. do not come to town this week, & I must tell your Grace that on the last Levée day but one, the P. observed Sir Fras. Milman[1] to never leave the room where H.M. was until it was completely emptied.

Lord Say & Sele[2] just return'd from Paris, assures me that a mameluke about the person of Bonaparté attempted his life when at Dieppe, but the matter was hush'd up (Alnwick MSS.).

London, 3 Dec. 1802

Although no progress whatever has been made in the Prince's business since I had last the honor to address your Grace, nor any further communication from Mr. Addington, I think it right to apprize your Grace that Lord Thurlowe (who pass'd H.R.Hss. on the Brighton road in his way to town) has written to the Prince his decided opinion that the terms held out by the Minister, namely, the restoring to H.R.H. his entire income without any additional accomodation, should be immediately closed with, & consider'd as an equitable composition for H.R.Hss.'s claim, under all the particular circumstances which apply to the case, for instance, a difference of opinion among the Judges as to the right. A diminution of interest from 5 to 3½ p. cent on such sum as might be allow'd according to the usual practice of Chancery in such cases. A defensible charge of maintenance during minority that might be made, & a deduction of the sums paid by the nation (abt. £161,000) in 1785 & 7 —with interest on those sums from those periods. In short, his Lordship thinks the offer as fairly balancing the acct. & in that view, recommends his R.H. out of his income, which will be then £138,000 a year, a sinking fund of 38,000 a year for the liquidation of his subsequent debt, about £150,000. The moment this matter is finally arranged I shall report it to your Grace.

The extreme kindness with which your Grace has condescended so incessantly to honor me, induces me to presume the liberty of soliciting your advice on the subject of the enclosed letter which I have received from the Secy. to the Whig Club, because, humble as my situation is, I consider my conduct on such occasion might artfully be made to connect with my royal master, & that it is for this particular object I believe it

1. Physician to the Middlesex Hospital, 1777–9; created Baronet, 28 November 1800; Physician to the King (Extraordinary, 1785; in Ordinary, 1806). (1746–1821)

2. Gregory William, 8th Lord Saye and Sele (1769–1844), succeeded his father in 1788.

to be written, for I have not been at that Club these ten years past, & the last time I was there discharg'd my subscription to that period.

I trust your Lordship will have the goodness to pardon this great presumption (Alnwick MSS.).

Carlton House, 10 Dec. 1802

I have delay'd doing myself the honor of offering to your Grace my most grateful acknowledgements for the very kind advice you had the goodness to give me repecting the Whig Club, & which I have implicitly & satisfactorily pursued; because I wish'd to have acquainted your Grace of the further progress in the Prince's business, by the same opportunity.

From the period of my last writing nothing took place between Ministers, & the Prince's Counsel until this morning when Mr. Addington gave them an interview, & inform'd them that on Monday last he had submitted to the Cabinet his final proposition respecting the Prince's claim, which had met a most respectful & favorable reception there, & which had been sanction'd by his Majesty in the Closet: but that the business was not sufficiently ripe, nor the method in which it might be carried into effect so agreed upon as to leave him for the present at liberty to reveal the extent & objects to which it went; however, he would early in the ensuing week make an explicit communication on the subject, & in the meanwhile he ventured to observe that it would be of such a nature as he hoped & trusted would prove satisfactory to H.R.Hss.

The Prince came to town from Brighton last night in the expectation of finding this business entirely concluded, but H.R.Hss. commanded me this morning to make his love to your Grace & to say he cannot conceive for what purpose this unaccountable mystery prevails as to the sum of their determination, but H.R.H. does not apprehend they have anything in view beyond the restoration of his entire income of £138,000 from the present time, & from which he must consequently set apart a sufficient portion, as a sinking fund, for the discharge of the debt which now affects him, & which I think I may state to your Grace at nearly £150,000—meaning at the same time to suspend the assumption of his state until that arrear is finally liquidated & discharg'd. Whenever the promised communication is made, I shall immediately acquaint your Grace with the same.

A recess of Parliament is mention'd to take place between the 18th & the 24th, & to continue until the 10th of February.

The P. has had some fresh reason for believing that Ld. Pelham is likely to go out of office, in which case, Lord Castlereagh is supposed to be

Secy. of State in his room & Tierney Prest. of the Board of Controul.[1] Whatever may occur on those or any other heads worthy of communication I will not fail in writing to your Grace; at present there is no news stirring (Alnwick MSS.).

1691 GENERAL GERARD LAKE TO THE PRINCE OF WALES
Bareilli, 28 Nov. 1802
My dear Sir,

I have been made most extremely happy by your very kind & flattering letter dated April 20th. It gave me great satisfaction to hear from yourself that your Royal Highness had greatly recover'd your health, although you say you feel that between thirty-nine & forty one is not so young as at thirty, but I have no doubt if you take a little care of yourself & live tolerably regular that you may enjoy many years of health, happiness & comfort, & I sincerely hope much more of the latter than I fear you have for some time past experienc'd, for as well as myself I am convinc'd your Royal Highness must have suffer'd very many uneasy moments, but I trust the worst is past & sincerely hope the remainder of your days may be past in perpetual sunshine without one cloud to prevent your future prospects in life terminating in the most perfect harmony & tranquility.

I perfectly agree with your Royal Highness in thinking I may remain some years in this country before I can accomplish the first wish of my heart, the getting rid of my encumbrances & making provision for my numerous family, which, if God is pleas'd to grant me the health I now enjoy, I have very little doubt of doing. You gratify me most extremely (indeed more so than I can express) by saying that you think I shall attain this very desirable object in a highly creditable manner to myself.[2] Be assur'd, my dear Prince, you shall have no reason to alter your kind opinion of me nor have any reason to complain of my conduct in the country from whence I hope to return with that character that may entitle me to your future favour & protection. Beleive me, no one can view my former follies in a worse point of view than myself. The pangs & torment they have caus'd me are beyond all comprehension. All the hopes I now have (although I never can forgive myself) are that I

1. Lord Pelham was succeeded as Home Secretary by Charles Yorke in August 1803. Castlereagh had become President of the Board of Control in July 1802, entering the Cabinet, however, only in October. Tierney became Treasurer of the Navy in June 1803.

2. The Prince himself might have contributed to this desirable end: before going out to India as Commander-in-Chief, Lake had been the Prince's Gentleman Attendant, but his salary was four years in arrear (£2,000). (32487)

330

may be enabl'd to pay what I owe & make an honorable exit. No one can tell what I have suffer'd; at the same time I cannot avoid thinking I have been us'd unkindly by some people from whom I did not deserve such treatment. In all my cursed absurdities, not to call them by a harsher name, beleive me, my attachment to your Royal Highness remain'd pure & unalterable & will continue so to the latest hour I shall draw breath.

I rejoice it is in my power to say that I still retain the confidence & attention of Lord Wellesley in the fullest extent; his behaviour to me has been in every instance uniformly proper, kind & most flattering. I therefore feel the more griev'd that his Lordship should have neglected to pay attention to the recommendation of your Royal Highness respecting Mr. Treves & very particularly so as I feel most warmly interested in his welfare. You do him but justice in supposing his abilities & talents of the first rate, & that he is equal to any situation in India, & I can only say that I do most heartily wish that he could have gain'd any situation that would have been pleasing to your Royal Highness & himself. The present Resident at Lucnow has been appointed to that place since '99; whether your recommendation was previous to that I do not know. If it was not I fear his Lordship could not well have dispossess'd him as he is esteem'd a most excellent publick servant, a man of high honour & integrity; & as to his having a seat in Council I hardly know of late who has had the appointing to that situation as it has appear'd lately that the Court of Directors interfere very much more than they us'd to do with appointments &c. in this country. I merely mention these circumstances as they may in some degree tend to make you feel less respecting the disappointment to Mr. Treves & in some measure make you feel less hurt at the suppos'd want of attention in Lord Wellesley, who, I can assure your Royal Highness, has ever mention'd your name with the highest respect, at the same time always expressing his wish to pay every attention to any recommendation of your Royal Highness.[1]

I am at present as you will perceive at a vast distance from Calcutta, consequently can have no communication with his Lordship but by

1. The following amplifies the note in i.362 about Treves. He was the son of Pellegrin Treves, a London money-lender, formerly of Venice, and a crony of the Prince of Wales. His mother, Bathsheba, was the daughter of Moses de Paiba, broker, and the niece of Sampson Gideon, stockbroker and immensely wealthy Portuguese Jew. He was a Cadet in the Bengal Army, 1780, but returned to England in 1782. The Prince procured for him the appointment of Writer in the Bengal Civil Service (1784); he became Second Assistant to the Resident at Benares, 1787, First Assistant, 1791, and Third Judge of the Court of Appeal and Circuit at Benares, 1795. He became involved in a scandal from the full consequences of which he was saved by the friendship of Lord Wellesley, the Governor-General of Bengal, and was in retirement in England from 1802 to 1806. Returning to Bengal he was appointed Collector, 1807; Collector of Government Customs at Calcutta, 1811–18; Postmaster-General there, 1820. On 7 September 1785 he married in Calcutta, Hetty Stokes, a natural daughter of Sir Robert Sloper. He died at Lucknow, 22 August 1825.

letter. I wrote to him not long since & hinted your wishes upon the subject, at the same time in some degree express'd your feelings at being disappointed in the recommendation of all others you interested yourself the most in. All this I fear comes too late, as Mr. Treves is at Calcutta on his way home & will have the honor of delivering this letter to your Royal Highness. However, my letter may produce a conversation to Mr. Treves which I will of course communicate to your Royal Highness. I have had a conversation lately with Mr. Treves relating to your letter & wishes with which he will acquaint you. I flatter myself he is convinc'd there is nothing I would not do to serve him as it will be ever my first object to obey your commands, exclusive of which my own inclinations would lead me to exert myself on his behalf from my long acquaintance with his father with whom I have pass'd so many pleasant days & liv'd in the habits of intimacy & friendship with, added to all which I really feel most warmly interested in Mr. Treves, whose kindness & attention to me in my way up the river excited a great desire in me to afford him every assistance in my power, since which time I am happy to say, by having liv'd more with him, I am confirm'd in my disposition towards him by being most extremely pleas'd with his manners & society, & being much gratified by the open & unreserv'd way he has treated me, by which means I have gain'd much & very useful information respecting the disposition of the natives as well as the regulations & the internal managment so necessary to preserve peace & tranquility in this vast territory & with which he is so perfectly well acquainted with that it would be very presuming in me to mention anything upon the subject when he will be so near you. I can only say that I feel quite sorry that he is leaving India, not more in a private than a publick point [of] view. I have been very explicit respecting myself & sentiments upon all occasions, thinking your Royal Highness might wish to question him about me, should you be so inclin'd, he is perfectly able to give you an account of all my proceedings which may I hope prove satisfactory to you. I am confident you will like him much, be pleas'd with his society & derive much real & useful knowledge from him respecting this country.

I fear as you do that peace will not last long, in the event of which I presume our possessions in this country will be an object of no little consequence to our mortal enemy. All I have to hope [is that] our army may not be too much reduc'd to prevent us from being prepar'd for his reception, when if he does come you may depend upon every exertion on our part.

I am at present upon a tour round all the posts in the ceded districts & shall endeavour to strengthen this frontier [as] much as possible. When I have gone compleatly over them I proceed to Caronge [sic] where I have assembl'd seven Regts. of Cavalry under the command of Colonel

St. Leger[1] for the purpose of instructing & inculcating discipline among them.

My family with me are truly grateful for your recollection of them & request you will accept their humble duty; they feel truly sensible of your kindness to them upon all occasions. My son George[2] I feel proud in saying is going on most extremely well & is everything I can wish him. He is of the greatest use to me, speaks the language fluently, is diligent & attentive in business, with all the life & spirit, when that is over, attendant upon youth. He is highly gratified by the interesting manner in which your Royal Highness enquires after him & will I hope live to merit your approbation by his future conduct through life. I feel it unnecessary to ask your Royal Highness for your protection to that part of my family in Europe who will I trust be found deserving of any kindness or attention you may think fit to honor them with.

If it is not too much presumption might I entreat your Royal Highness to make my humble duty acceptable to their Majesties & to assure them that I feel the most lively gratitude for the many favors conferr'd upon me, & that they have not in all their dominions a more zealous or loyal subject or one more attach'd to their family or interests than myself.

I much fear you will think me very troublesome for this long intrusion upon [you] but will hope for your usual indulgence & beleive me [etc.]. (39853–8)

1692 THE PRINCE OF WALES TO LORD [HERTFORD]

Brighton, 2 Dec. 1802

I am more asham'd than I can possibly express at receiving a second letter from you before I had acknowledged the receipt of your first; but the real truth of the matter is this (& of which I hope you will be satisfied, as well as that it would be the very last thing I ever could be capable of, the being wanting in anything that can mark my attention & regard for you) that I trusted to having the pleasure of meeting you in London at the meeting of the Parliament when I thought by word of mouth I could better concert matters with you & second your wishes to my utmost, which ever will be my sincere inclination (whether relative to Monr. de Calonne or on any other head) than I could by letter.

With regard to Monr. de Calonne,[3] I really am afraid that till I have

1. William St. Leger. Colonel, 1797; Major-General, 1803; Lieutenant-General, 1809. (?1759–1818)

2. Mentioned in No. 49 (i.70). He became a Lieutenant-Colonel in the 20th Foot in 1803, and distinguished himself, with his father, at the battle of Laswari in the Maratha War.

3. The former French Minister of Finance died in Paris in October 1802.

had the pleasure of conversing over the business with you, we shall find great difficulty in assisting him even in the line which he, as well as Monr. de Calonne (from whom I have also receiv'd a letter) seems to point out, for you well know, my dear Lord, that it is a very easy matter to gain permission for a young man to retire from the service, but that it is the most difficult of all things, & next to an impossibility, to get him reinstated, unless he recommences from the very bottom of the subalterns. Besides, there is also another circumstance which I beleive you are not aware of at the present moment and which in *confidence* I will mention to you, my dear Lord, as I receiv'd it myself, for I know that I am safe in your hands & that you will have the goodness not to mention my name; that the Government, that is to say, the Secretary of State, has thought it necessary to seize all the papers of the late Monr. de Calonne, more I beleive to satisfy themselves that there were *no* underhand dealings & negotiations than from any information or suspicion that there really existed any such circumstance. As this is so, perhaps you will be of opinion that it may be left for a short time not to say anything respecting this young gentleman till all his father's papers have been investigated, & then, should it prove that there is nothing that can meet the disapprobation of Government, I think this circumstance will aid much in pleading & pressing his wishes & pretensions. But should you be of another opinion, I can only profess over again what I did in the commencement of my letter, that I shall ever be ready & happy to lend myself most cordially to the forwarding any object in which you interest yourself.[1]

With respect to the letter which my friend Lord Robert[2] was so good

1. Writing on 13 February 1803, Lord Malmesbury reported a conversation with Lord Pelham, the Home Secretary: 'Lord Pelham said that Calonne, previous to his going to Paris (where he died in October) had prevailed on the Prince of Wales to try to get his name struck off the list of emigrants. The Prince had actually spoken to Lord Whitworth or Merry, but as this had no effect, Calonne attempted to persuade the Prince to write to Bonaparte, stating foolishly ... as a reason, that all the Sovereigns in Europe had written to him but the King and that a letter written by the Prince would gratify his vanity and induce him to comply with any request he might make ... Lord Pelham ... represented to him the danger of such a step; that the letter would be instantly printed in the *Moniteur*, and the Prince held out to all Europe as a correspondent with the First Consul ... Fortunately Calonne died, and this foolish affair with him.

'Pelham told me that on Calonne's death he had taken possession of his papers. They filled several large coffers and were artfully concealed in closets, on the panels of which were hung the most obscene prints possible, and left in the care of a common woman ... with whom Calonne had lived for a long time. These papers contain all the secret history of Coblentz and Calonne's negotiations there and since; and from the anxiety expressed by the Prince of Condé and Duke of Bourbon to get their letters back, it should seem that the last plan was bringing *them* and *not* the King of France or Monsieur, forward' (Malmesbury, *Diaries and Correspondence*, iv.198–9).

2. Lord Robert Seymour.

as to write to you, my dear Lord, my intention was merely to enquire whether there was any chance of your coming to town in a few days, as I judged it possible that you might have had some idea of taking a journey to London to have seen Lord Yarmouth previous to his departure for France, & had that been so, I should have determined to have awaited your arrival in London, in order to have open'd another topic to you which is *most near to my heart* & to have implored your good offices & assistance with Lord Henry Seymour in my favour respecting your little neice, my old friend Lord Hugh's youngest daughter. As I have desired & empowered my friend Lord Robert (who has enter'd into the whole of the business with a zeal & kindness I never can forget) to acquaint you, my dear Lord, with all the circumstances & letters that have passed between Lord Euston & myself, when he comes to Ragley, & which I understand he intends to do in about a fortnight, and where I also understand he is likely to meet Lord Henry; I shall not therefore tresspass upon you at present with entering into this subject, but conclude, my dear Lord, with assuring you how truly I ever am your very sincere friend (Egerton MSS. 3262 ff.5–8).

1693 THOMAS TYRWHITT TO THE PRINCE OF WALES

Carlton House, 2 Dec. 1802

Colonel Crewe called upon me yesterday evening to state the circumstances attending the letter he now has the honor of being the bearer to your Royal Highness.

Mr. Brandes, the Secretary of the Regency of Hannover, has requested that if he could not deliver it to your Royal Highness himself it was immediately to be returned. It was brought over by Captain Fitzgerald of the Guards—under cover to Colonel Crewe.

Colonel C. desires me to acquaint your Royal Highness he is entirely ignorant of its contents, but that could his services be in any way useful to you, they are at your command.

The Colonel proposes returning to town soon after he has presented you the letter. (39859)

[Enclosure] BARON BRANDES[1] TO THE PRINCE OF WALES

Hanover, 4 Nov. 1802

Your Royal Highness's well known gracious and wise intentions for the

1. He signed himself 'Counsellor of the Board of Trade and Secretary to the Privy Council' [i.e. in Hanover].

wellfare of a country, the old inheritance of your Royal Family, will I hope excuse the presumption of an Address from a man totally unknown to your Royal Highness, who has no other title to approach your Royal Highness with the greatest submission than this, that if he lives he will be one day your subject and servant, a man who feels to the full the irregularity of his proceeding, but who thinks that all other considerations ought to give way to the duty he owes to his Sovereign and country on a pressing and great occasion, to the pursuing of an object in which he is *not in the least* personally interested.

Your Royal Highness is fully informed how much the security and well-being of the Electorate of Hanover has been endanger'd by the King of Prussia having the Bishoprick of Hildesheim allotted to him in the full share of the indemnities he has receiv'd. As Hildesheim is nearly incircled by the dominions of your Royal House, the acquisition of that country by a Great Power most naturally endangers to the utmost extent the security of the Electorate. Hanover is now and will be for ever in the same situation with regard to Prussia in which Bavaria stands placed with respect to Austria. On the first favourable occasion Prussia will try to acquire more or less of the Electoral dominions. Its purpose will invariably be bent on swallowing up the whole Electorate either at once or by and by.

On the breaking out of the late war I foresaw that it would most probably end by a material change in the German Constitution. The question was not what was to be wish'd for but what could be hinder'd; what, if this change was unavoidable, was to be done for the benefit of my native country for its future security, for its future independance. My unremitting endeavors went to the purpose of making people in power here sensible that in the case of an unavoidable change it ought never to be suffer'd that Hildesheim came into other hands than his Majesty's. I can name vouchers for the truth of my assertion and amongst them one whose veracity will not be question'd by your Royal Highness. I mean H.R.H. the Duke of Cambridge, to whom I open'd myself on this head most fully and proposed to him the plans to be pursued. His Royal Highness felt to the greatest extent how much the interest of his Royal House was concern'd in the matter. He took the utmost pains to be authorised to act, and after having got an authorisation he opened himself on this subject to the late King of Prussia and Count Haugwitz in the summer of 1797 at Pyrmont. Most unfortunately this opening was not pursued by a further negociation afterwards, on the accession of the present King of Prussia to the throne. My endeavors to this effect were in vain. At that time the projects of aggrandisement on the part of Prussia were not absolutely fix'd on special objects. The proposition of a change between Osnabrück and Hildesheim would perhaps have met with a favorable reception at that time at Berlin. *At that time* Prussia was the only Court w[h]were we could have opened our views on this subject.

We had no connexions at all with France. Hanover being subject to the King of Great Britain was look'd upon with the most unfavorable eye by the French rulers of the moment. When the negociations at Rastadt were on foot, I tryed again, but again in vain, to have the interest of this country with regard to Hildesheim brought forward in a decided manner. Tho' nothing was definitively arranged there, yet some connexions on this head might perhaps have been procured, and it is but doing justice to the persons employed by the Government here at Rastadt to say that they felt the consequence of this, but they had no authorisation to come forward in a decided manner.

When the league was form'd between Russia and France against Great Britain, Hanover was mark'd out as the sacrifice. Some Prussian Ministers were at least very well pleas'd to be forced to invade this country, as they certainly thought that the measure might perhaps lead to their master's retaining the possession of a part of the Electorate if not of the whole. The result was impossible to be foreseen, if the Emperor Paul had lived somewhat longer. God knows the situation we were in here at that time and how much every class of people felt and suffer'd! It is impossible for any nation to give stronger proofs of its loyalty and attachment to the Sovereign and his family than my countrymen did at that period. The state of health of our royal master at that same time was no secret for us. Amongst the general depression a letter receiv'd from your Royal Highness by the Duke of Cambridge was alone capable to dispel the gloom that hung on men's minds. As I was one of the first who heard of the admirable passage in this letter, in which your Royal Highness in the most forcible and most eloquent manner expressed your royal sollicitude and warmest attachment for the old inheritance of your family for a country you had never seen, I most humbly ask'd for an extract of this passage and the permission to make it known, a request and permission which was immediately granted, of which I did make the fullest use and of which I had the great pleasure to see the most admirable effects.

In the state we were in we had only to try if it was possible to make Bonaparte sensible how much it was against the interest of France to suffer Prussia to become master of the two great rivers of the north of Germany by retaining possession of the Electorate. This could be only done by a Mission from Hanover to Paris. Immediately on receiving the news of Paul's death I did entertain the greatest hopes that the Prussians would soon be obliged to leave this country. But I was still of the opinion that if anything could be done for the acquisition of Hildesheim it must be brought about at Paris, be negociated there by the same means employed by other Powers. Others as well as myself felt the truth of this observation. I did all I could to engage the Government in the month of April 1801 to send somebody to Paris, but this, like my former steps, was in vain, tho' at that time they were at full liberty here to act as they chose.

What every intelligent observer could foresee happened. Prussia made a definitive arrangement with France, and put itself in possession of Hildesheim. We had only the feeble support of Russia in our favor, which, according to the character of the Emperor and the system adopted in his Cabinet, must be only a feeble one.

It is not for me to decide if it was prudent that the British Ministry so absolutely neglected the interests of Hanover both at Amiens and at Paris. The two countries, tho' united under the dominion of one Sovereign, may have their separate interests, and it is certainly not my wish to have the real interests of any one of the two sacrificed to those of the other, but according to my humble opinion the interests of Great Britain can clash but very seldom with those of Hanover and certainly did the great statesmen and Whigs in the reign of George the 1st judge very wisely, when they deem'd the possession of the mouths of the two great rivers in the North of Germany in the hands of a middle and always friendly Power as Hanover, of the greatest consequence to England.

Bereft as we were of every other support we could look up only to France. It was at Paris that everything was bought and sold. The most petty Count had his agent there. Hanover alone had none. There was a decided aversion to a Mission to Paris in a quarter whose decisions everybody must respect and obey. But was it prudent to press this decision? Was it well done to wait for it, for a Government obliged so many times to act on its own strength, as every Government, very distant from the seat of its Sovereign, must do on very great and pressing occasion? Was it to be fear'd that steps undertaken only for the real benefit of a country would in the end be most ungraciously view'd by him, who could alone have the true interest of his country at heart? All these reasons were often urged but always in vain.

France resented most undoubtedly this neglect, vain as the rulers there will always be and rapacious to the extreme as they are now. They certainly expected their share of gold and frankincense from Hanover, as well as from every other German country. An overture made very late by a third hand on this head from hence, but not pursued, can have only excited their appetite, but must have ended in incensing them, because they may think that they shall be frustrated from that which was held out as a boon.

Osnabrück has been ceded to our Sovereign. Bonaparte did this certainly only with a view to gratify the Royal Family of England, to show his regard for your Royal Highness, of whose gracious disposition for Hanover he was inform'd. According to all what I know I don't doubt in the least that we could have got both Hildesheim and Osnabrück *if the proper measures had been pursued in the proper time*. Osnabrück is not by far so valuable an acquisition in itself as Hildesheim would have been, but what far outweighs everything, it does not add neither to our security nor to our independance. Hildesheim lies in the heart of the Electoral dominions, that is to say, the Prussians are got now into the centre of your Royal Highness's future possessions here.

After the occupation of Hildesheim people in power flatter'd themselves for a long while to bring about an exchange between Hildesheim and Osnabrück at Berlin, but never could I indulge in these flattering hopes. The only way capable of bringing about this exchange was to buy an order at Paris for the issuing of a Mandate to the King of Prussia to give his consent to this exchange. I know that this Mandate might very possibly have been got not two months ago for a fix'd price. Heaven knows if it is not now to[o] late!

Prussia will never on its own accord consent to such an exchange. It may open a negociation for the exchange of Hildesheim against other old and much more valuable possessions of his Majesty, propose conditions of exchanges to which no true friend of this country could give his consent. The cession of Osnabrück has been clogged by other cessions and sacrifices to be made by his Majesty, not at all immaterial in themselves. They have been acquiesced in as they ought to be. However, not content with the cessions stipulated in the first Partition Treaty, in the second still more favorable cessions to the town of Bremen have been enacted, without any equivalent at all. *Great rumors are going abroad of still more cessions to be demanded from his Majesty as Elector of Hanover.* Who can pretend to say where all this will stop? What may not be ask'd from a country known to have no interest of consequence among the Great Powers, no ally whatsoever? I know that negociations between the Hanoverian Minister at London and Mr. Otto have been going on, and useful as they may have been they are at least certainly not sufficient for our security and interest.

In this case of the greatest emergency, the salvation of this country, the hindering it to be further dismembered seems only to be possible to be brought about by the Mission of an Hanoverian Envoy or Agent to Paris, to negociate there with the usual means. I have left no stone unturn'd to effectuate this measure in the common way, but it is absolutely impossible to succeed. The only method for the adoption of this plan now left is if your Royal Highness would deign to come forward and express your fix'd determination for such a measure to the Hanoverian Minister at London. I believe the intentions of the man to be honest and if he would only strongly recommend privately the sending of somebody from hence to Paris to the Government here, the plan would immediately be taken up, as it was only by his expressing himself averse to it that it was not pursued a very short time ago. The purpose of a Mission to Paris would be according to my humble opinion:

1 The procuring from Bonaparte a decisive recommendation to Berlin for the exchange of Hildesheim against Osnabrück.
2 To hinder any other dismembrement [*sic*] of the Electorate and to try to get if possible some equivalents for the cessions that have been newly enacted.

If this Mission should not be frustrated in its purpose it would be necessary to have the proper instructions administer'd to it from England, because it then could act in a more dignified manner and with the less loss of time.

I will not venture to affirm that it will not be too late now to resort to such a measure tho' I still entertain hopes to the contrary, but the irregularity of submitting this proposition in such a manner to your Royal Highness must serve as an excuse why it has not been proposed sooner. Rational men resort only to irregular steps with the greatest reluctance. Still every consideration in them gives way to the pressure of the last moment, when they absolutely see that only by such a measure the salvation of their country may be procured and the else unavoidable degradation of their Government may be hinder'd.

I know full well that I have yet the greatest apology to make for my uncall'd for intrusion to your Royal Highness's notice and especially for having so often brought forward the man when I mention'd the measures. But in general men and measures cannot be separated, for measures will only be the result of the characters and ideas of men, and in the venturing on such a step as I have taken now on mature deliberation, it seem'd absolutely necessary to speak much of the man who undertook it, in order that the matters he submitted most humbly to your Royal Highness's consideration might appear in a less questionable shape.

Prompted by these reasons I must with the greatest submission entreat your Royal Highness's pardon for saying still somewhat more of the man.

I have no property whatever in the Bishoprick of Hildesheim, no personal friend there. To me as an individual it is *totally* indifferent to whom that country will remain. I have not the least inclination to be charged with a Mission to Paris. I know others much better qualified for this task whom I could name, nay *it would be quite impossible for me* to undertake this Mission at this moment.

I have no inclination whatsoever to inculpate individuals, tho' I know full well to whose charge the faults that have been committed may be attributed and those who are innocent of them.

Ambitious as I always shall be of serving my Sovereigns in any capacity in which they may be inclined to employ me and for which I may

340

think myself not unqualified, I shall not feel myself unhappy if I do remain exactly in the situation in which I now do stand. I do enjoy a rational independance of mind and fortune, suitable to my personal inclinations. I have no family of my own to provide for, and if I cannot act in the greatest ostensible sphere to the best of my endeavors for the benefit of my Sovereign and country I shall continue to enjoy uncontroul'd the charms of litterary pursuits and the endearments which friendship can bestow on a life fully sensible of the worth of both these blessings.

The truth of all what relates to the man could be confirm'd to your Royal Highness by H.R.H. the Duke of Cambridge, to whom I have the honor of being very well known. But H.R.H. the Duke does not know, *nor do I wish he ever should*, this my bold intrusion to your Royal Highness. According to the peculiar situation the Duke stands in I felt it to be my duty *not* to open myself to him on this subject, tho' I full well knew that the measures I have submitted to your Royal Highness's wisdom have long ago had his fullest approbation. If I am to blame for the irregularity of my proceeding, *mine* alone is the blame. I did undertake this step absolutely on my own accord, prompted by nobody whosoever.

The only personal request I must with the greatest humility beseech your Royal Highness to grant to me is *not to mention to anyone, and especially not to any one Hanoverian*, that I ventured to write to your Royal Highness. The unavoidable consequences of the contrary will be obvious, and tho' certainly I could well defend all what I have done *in due time* and in its proper place, I have the greatest reasons imaginable not to come openly forward in an unfavorable period. The measure was taken up and pursued upon general principles, according to what I thought to be for the real benefit of my Sovereign and my country. My situation will not be the better for having ventured to do what I did. The only thing I may reasonably desire is that it may not grow the worse for having deliver'd my sentiments to your Royal Highness.

I have dared to approach with the greatest openness and confidence the Heir Apparent of my native country, the man of genius and most penetrating judgment, to whose wise decisions I shall for ever most respectfully bow and submit myself and my own opinions. It is for the first and for the last time that I approach your Royal Highness without having had your special permission to do so. The only wish remaining for me is, that if I cannot be honor'd by your Royal Highness's approbation I may escape your Royal Highness's blame. (39860–4)

1694   THE PRINCE OF WALES TO THE DOWAGER COUNTESS OF ELGIN
Brighton, 19 Dec. 1802
I have, dear Lady Elgin, to acknowledge the receipt of your letter which
this day's post brought me, & to thank you for the good accounts it contains of the child, & which has given me great satisfaction. As I shall be
in London soon myself I conceive there is no immediate hurry respecting
Sir Wm. Parson's[1] attendance, & I shall then have an opportunity of
talking this over, as well as many other topics relative to Charlotte with
the Queen, & of taking her opinions & pleasure upon the subject. You
have not I think the shadow of a reason to be under the smallest apprehension relative to the safety of Lord Elgin,[2] upon which I most sincerely
congratulate you, & participate in the comfort it must afford you.[3] (49262)

1695   THE EARL OF CASSILLIS[4] TO [?]COLONEL MCMAHON
Hemells Park, Hertfordshire, 27 Dec. 1802
Under another cover I send to you the memorandum you wish'd to have
in relation to our election,[5] from which you will perceive that *my powers*

1. Sir William Parsons (?1746–1817), singing-master to the Princesses; succeeded Wiede-
mann as Master of the King's Band at St. James's, 1786. Knighted, 27 August 1795.

2. Lord Elgin, the Countess's son, was at this time Ambassador to Turkey. He was absent on
leave 29 March–4 September 1802, and left Constantinople on leave, 16 January 1803, and
was one of the many British civilians 'detained' in France by Napoleon after the rupture of
the Treaty of Amiens.

3. The letter referred to in McMahon's letter to the Duke of Northumberland on 20 December seems to be missing: 'I have had a letter this morning from Mrs. Fitzherbert informing
me that in consequence of a most *important one* which the P. received on Saturday from his
favorite & confidential sister at Windsor, H.R.H. had determined to fix in Carlton House for
the winter on Monday the 27th instant, instead of continuing at Brighton until the 16th of
January; wishing me to make some previous arrangements *secretly* for this purpose, & by
no means to have a word said on this change of plan until the P. arrived in town on the 26th
(Alnwick MSS.).
    The favourite sister was Princess Mary.

4. Archibald, 12th Earl of Cassillis (1770–1846), succeeded his father, 1794; a Scottish
Representative Peer, 1796–1806; created Baron Ailsa [U.K.], 12 November 1806; and Marquess of Ailsa [U.K.], 10 September 1831.

5. The election of the Scottish Representative Peers on 10 August 1802, following the disso-
lution of Parliament. Lauderdale was an unsuccessful candidate. Lord Keith wrote to William
Adam on 14 August: 'You see only sixty voted. We had 37. Tweeddale against us. Rollo *cut*,
also Home. Shameful. After all we had the election had it been well managed, and most of
the wealth of the peerage' (Blair Adam MSS.). Dundas wrote to Addington (the letter is
undated): 'Lord Elphinstone . . . at the instigation of Lord Keith, with whom the Prince is
much connected, was the object the Prince's friends and agents chiefly drove. I doubt if they
played fair to Lauderdale. The Prince's proxy was intended for, and I believe promised to

342

were entirely fetter'd. The list deliver'd to me by Lord Keith left no room for action upon my part; I therefore became a quiet spectator of all that was passing. What was stated to me regarding Lord *Bute's vote* is not worth mentioning; I should therefore incline that it *was put to the test.* When you speak upon this subject to his Royal Highness you will do me a kindness by saying that I shall never cease to remember with gratitude and respect the flattering marks that I have experienced of his Royal Highness's condescention and consideration. (39866–7)

1696 PRINCESS SOPHIA TO THE PRINCE OF WALES
28 Dec. 1802

I have received the Queen's commands to inform you that it is her intention to give a childs' Ball to our dear little Charlotte on Saturday next, for which mama wrote some days ago to Ly. Elgin, anxious to know if the child was well enough to come here before she asked your leave, but by some mistake the answer is never arrived; therefore the Queen is at this moment sending a servant to *Shooters Hill* desiring me at the same time to write to you, & hopes that you will have no objection if Charlotte is well that she should come to Windsor on Friday the 31st & stay till Monday. She will be lodged in the *house*, & mama wishes her to return on Monday as she should be sorry she sd. be from home *on her own birthday.*

I have faithfully delivered the Queen's commands & cannot conclude this without adding a few words from myself. I trust you are convinced how truly I wish for many many happy returns of this season & I hope the *New Year* will bring with it every blessing this world can afford. Be assured that if I could *steer your path* they would not be with thorns, for no one loves you more tenderly & affecly. than [etc.].

[*P.S.*] We had a delightful party last night at Frogmore; Mrs. Billington,[1] Barthélomon[2] & Harrison[3] were the principal performers; Sr. W. Parsons led the band & they performed all *Acis & Galatea.* The music was in the colonade and I never saw anything prettier than the effect of

Lauderdale, but that intention was departed from when Lord Keith came home [in July 1802] and the proxy was given to Lord Cassillis, but the instructions how it was to be used were intrusted to Lord Keith's discretion, who of course made the best use he could of it in bartering votes for Lord Elphinstone' (Sidmouth MSS.).

1. Charles Abbot wrote in his Diary, in June 1803: 'The *D. of Portland* keeps Mrs. Billington as his declared mistress!!!' The Speaker's astonishment was natural enough: the Duke was so dangerously ill during this summer that his physicians despaired of his recovery.

2. The violinist.

3. The singer.

the orchestra from the gay pavillion. The King was more pleased than I can express. (Add. Georgian 13/16)

1697 LETTERS FROM COLONEL MCMAHON TO THE DUKE OF NORTHUMBERLAND
Carlton House, 28 Dec. 1802

Mr. Addington according to appointment attended the Prince at 2 o'clock, saw H.R.Hss. almost immediately, & continued above an hour. A succession of visitors detain'd the Prince until almost this moment (past 5 o'clock) when I hastily got from H.R.Hss. the purport of the Minister's communication, & which he conjured H.R.Hss. might not upon any acct. transpire until he should finally assent to it, & the King ratify conclusively that assent. In the first place, he bore a message (unexpected to the P.) from his Majesty, purporting that H.M. understanding H.R.Hss. had a large demand on the publick, which the times & particular circumstances made it desireable should be quickly & amicably adjusted, had directed that what he consider'd a suitable remuneration in the most convenient mode, should be made to H.R.Hss., namely, an annuity of £75,000 to be paid out of the Consolidated Fund from the first of October last, out of which H.M. recommended that H.R.Hss. should make a sinking fund for the discharge of such debts as he had incur'd since the settlement of his affairs; & this done, H.M. had no doubt but H.R.Hss. would make such comfortable addition to the Pss.'s allowance as would seem proper; but no farther had his Majesty instructed him (Mr. A.) to either stipulate or recommend on the occasion. I write this short acct. in great haste, & do not know what day the P. has promised to return his answer to the message; but I will resume the subject to your Grace again & at large tomorrow (Alnwick MSS.).

Carlton House, 29 Dec. 1802

To resume the subject on which I had the honor to write to your Grace yesterday, I have it in command from the Prince to substantiate the message which Mr. A. bore him from the King in the manner I had already stated; & further to tell your Grace in strict confidence that H.R.Hss., being left nothing but acquiescence to anything coming in the shape of a message from his Majesty, has resolv'd to accept it graciously, but that not choosing to let the Minister immediately into the determination of his mind on the subject, H.R.Hss. has appointed 2 o'clock on

Tuesday next at Carlton House for the purpose of giving him his ultimatum, which will be deliver'd him in writing, &, before which H.R.Hss. will have seen his Majesty, as he is to pass New Year's day at Windsor, & remain there to receive the Sacrament on Sunday.

The Prince proposes to create a sinking fund of £50,000 a year in order to provide for his present debt of abt. £150,000. Another debt (which it seems Mr. Pitt never embraced in the Parliamentary settlement) of £35,000 with interest to the Landgrave of Hesse; & H.R.Hss. having always profess'd a desire to restore to his creditors the 10 p. ct. which the Commissioners had deducted from their several demands, as a point of feeling applying to his own character, has now made up his determination to institute a commission for examining & discriminating the respective accounts, & abiding their decree in such cases, to consolidate whatever may be the amount of this 10 p. ct. in the sum for which this sinking fund is to provide & discharge, & which altogether may then make somewhat about £250,000. Until after the recess it will not be possible to learn in what shape the King's Message to the H. of Commons for effecting the grant of this annuity is to be couched, & therefore no calculation as to the value of the annuity of £75,000 a year from the Consolidated Fund can be made until that is known; but H.R.Hss. has in his own possession the statement of your Grace's ideas on this subject, & intends to use it for his guidance in the matter depending.

The K. is certainly not as well as *they wish at Windsor*. The last Levée was over in half an hour. Mr. A. was courteous down to the ground with the P.—but let out no further politics than that Mr. Pitt was to be in town last night. No news. (ibid.)

V   1803

Early in the year the Prince decided, in view of what Sheridan described as the well-known glorious uncertainty of the law, to abandon his Petition of Right. This was followed up by a Message from the King to the House of Commons on 16 February, recommending to the consideration of Parliament the Prince's financial situation, with the view of resuming his dignity as heir apparent. Addington denied that the Message had anything to do with a compromise of the Prince's claim to the Duchy revenues, but Sheridan did not believe him. The object, said the Prime Minister, was to re-establish the Prince in that splendour which belonged to his rank. It appeared that in January about £563,000 of debt out of the £650,000 which had been acknowledged in 1795 had been paid off, and it was estimated that the remainder would be discharged in July 1806. Addington thought it unreasonable that the Prince should have to live in 'comparative obscurity' for another four years. The new proposal was to give the Prince an additional income of £60,000 for three years to enable him to pay off the acknowledged outstanding debts. Manners-Sutton, now the King's Solicitor-General, explained that the Prince had decided to abandon a legal contest over his revenue claims, not because he entertained any doubt as to the result, but because a contest might lead to a serious difference with the King. It was admitted that the Prince had got further into debt since the settlement of 1795, but such debts were not legal debts, only debts of honour which it was for him to judge how far they were binding. Consequently on 28 February Tyrwhitt, his private secretary, informed the House of Commons that these unrevealed debts were of so considerable a nature that a large sinking fund for their

346

liquidation would be required, and that this would in any case prevent the Prince from resuming the splendour attached to his exalted situation, with the result that the main object of the additional parliamentary grant, as Addington explained it, was not and could not be realized. On 4 March John Calcraft brought this matter to the notice of the House with the object of inquiring into the extent of these claims which, unless Parliament was given the opportunity for a further display of its liberality, would still make it impossible for the Prince to resume that state and dignity befitting the heir apparent. But the Motion was rejected by 184 votes to 139. Pitt was most indignant that Calcraft should have come forward in this way. 'Any further vote for the Prince', he told Rose, 'ought on every account to be resisted.' The proposal was 'highly indecent', founded as it was on an admission of debts contracted in the teeth of the Act of 1795 and in breach of repeated and positive promises. 'That Parliament should specifically recognise and pay such a debt', he concluded, 'is monstrous.' Ministers themselves seemed to doubt the entire wisdom and expediency of their course of action. Lord Hardwicke, the Lord Lieutenant of Ireland, thought that the King's Message threw 'a sort of ridicule upon the Motions both past and future' on the subject of the debts. The question, he added, had excited no sort of sensation in Dublin. 'Few enter into the merits of the question and few care about it in any degree.' He went on: 'I apprehend the dinners at Carlton House, and the honour of his Royal Highness's acquaintance have had the effect of flattering some of our Irish Members, particularly Newcomen and the sons of the Latouches.' Lord Redesdale, the Lord Chancellor of Ireland, was seriously concerned about the constitutional aspects of the affair, and especially the 'reversionary' influence of the Crown. He wrote on 3 March: 'I am not at all pleased with the manner in which the Prince of Wales's business has been conducted, and I think it will do Ministers no good with any party. I am persuaded the Prince will not thank them. I suspect some of the Cabinet are not pleased, and I believe a man [? Pitt] whose support of Ministers is still highly important, is much hurt.' His comments were based on 'very confidential information' —probably from his brother Charles Yorke, then Secretary at War. He added: 'It seems to me absolutely necessary that the Legislature should declare the extent of the rights of a succeeding Duke of Cornwall during his minority; for if he can claim, when of the age of twenty-one years, all arrears of the revenues, to be immediately handed over to him, such a fund may be a most formidable instrument against his father's Government.'

Once the annuity Bill had been passed, the Prince sent a Message to Parliament through Erskine, his Chancellor, expressing his satisfaction with what had been done for him. Now that the country was again at war with France, he could not think of increasing its financial burdens.

This was the final settlement of his indebtedness, so far as Parliament was concerned.

The Duke of York, whose own debts were far from negligible, felt slightly aggrieved at what had been done for his brother, and rightly believed that it would not have the effect of attaching the Prince to Addington's Government.[1] Malmesbury thought that since the Prince's additional parliamentary income was not 'appropriated to any specific purposes as the Civil List' it would be 'squandered away in the same way he has hitherto lived in, without his assuming any one single *exterior* mark of royalty or splendour—to prove that he and his hangers-on do not consider it a farce.' Addington, thought Malmesbury, had managed the business badly. 'It has given satisfaction neither to the King, the Prince nor the public, and does no credit to Ministers.'

Fox said that the Prince, 'whose strength . . . is greater in Parliament than I had supposed', was 'as hostile to Pitt as ever'. But about the beginning of December Pitt received in a very circuitous manner a characteristic letter from the Prince, saying that he had not the slightest disinclination to him, and that whenever executive power should devolve upon him he would call on him to form a Government. Pitt returned a non-committal reply, saying he hoped that a long period would elapse before he would have to decide anything on that subject, and that in the meantime the Prince, if he thought it right to interfere in politics, could not do better than support the Ministers of the King's choice. Pitt probably knew that the Prince had been anxious to promote a union of Foxite Whigs and Grenvillites (the 'Old' and the 'New' Opposition) against Addington, and he suspected that this communication was made to him in the hope that he would support the Prince's claims to military rank and employment during the coming debate on the Army estimates. 'If', said Fox, 'the Prince could be a little steady, there would be more chance of good than from anything else'—but from the Prince steadiness either in politics or in anything else was hardly to be expected.

Soon after the renewal of the war with France, when an invasion seemed imminent, the Prince made an unsuccessful offer of his personal service to the country, in letters addressed to Addington, the Duke of York and the King. Long ago the King had made up his mind—and his mind was not easily changed—that the only creditable line of action for the Prince, if he wished to gain popularity, was to serve as a Colonel in a cavalry regiment, without parade, without ostentation capable of

1. The Dukes of Kent and Clarence appealed to Addington to extricate them from an unpleasant situation. 'Delicacy forbids us from expressing the extent of our difficulties, or the consequences that must inevitably follow unless we are relieved, and that, too, without delay' (26 November 1803).

being construed into a love of pomp rather than a love of service. According to Sheridan's biographer, Thomas Moore, who apparently derived his information from Grey, the first of the published letters was written by that dashing, irresponsible soldier, Sir Robert Wilson, and the rest by Lord Hutchinson. The letters were published in several of the London newspapers on 7 December. The Prince denied responsibility for this breach of courtesy, but there is no doubt that he welcomed this appeal to public opinion (which, however, was entirely unmoved) against the advice of some of his best friends. He was, in fact, all for publicity: early in August Fox heard that the Prince wished his offer, and the rejection of it, to be mentioned in an appropriate debate in Parliament; and W. H. Fremantle wrote to Lord Grenville: 'There never was anything equal to the violence and anger of the Prince of Wales at not being employed. He is showing his correspondence right and left.'

Though Addington, in deference to the King's views, refused to support his claims, the Prince continued for a brief period to give Addington a fluctuating support, though he refused to advise Erskine as to whether he should accept an offer of the Attorney-Generalship, made to him early in the following year. Fox was sure that the Whig party would find no safe anchorage at Carlton House, yet the Prince's support could not but be useful to the cause. Whatever opinion might be generally entertained of his steadiness, his name and influence would help to smooth away difficulties and facilitate junctions. The so-called 'reversionary' interest (which took the form mainly of the Prince's post-obits, to be redeemed on his father's death or incapacity), influenced votes in both Houses: Fox referred to 'that numerous class of persons who are never easy without something that is like royal favour'. 'In the rage of royalism now prevailing', he wrote to Grey in March, 'a Prince of Wales being something like a King, will have a support which no other person or cause could have.'

The earliest of a series of manoeuvrings, as Grey described them, dated from March when the Prince gave what was described as a 'famous dinner' at which the possibility of a 'union of parties' was explored. The Prince professed a great regard for Grey, but his professions could rarely be taken at their face value, and he was not impressed. Though 'there never was such a set of fools as the present Ministers' Grey had no particular wish to see them supplanted. He would prefer to withdraw altogether from active politics. But if negotiations were opened, he would insist on far more than he had had in mind in 1801. 'I would not negotiate on any ground but that of having a majority in the Cabinet, Fox being one.' Some weeks later Grey met the Prince of Wales at two large dinner parties, one at Lord Derby's, the other at the Duke of Norfolk's: 'sad drinking dinners', he called them. He was to meet the Prince once more at Lord Moira's, where, he said, 'the same scene will be repeated'.

'These dinners with the Prince have given me the worst of my London feelings, and I am in every respect completely uncomfortable.' By mid-May Grey had convinced himself that Addington had never had any real intention of making a fair overture to the Foxite Whigs, and he ceased to have scruples about opposing the Government. He spoke of the 'excessive folly' of Addington's measures, but on the other hand he had no confidence in either Pitt or the warlike Grenville, and the Carlton House party too pursued its own way. Referring to one of the important debates towards the end of May, soon after the renewal of the war, he said, 'Sheridan would not attend, and everything connected with Carlton House either stayed away or voted against us.' In July Fox told Grey that the Prince's object at the moment was to promote a union of the Old and New Oppositions, and that he was as hostile to Pitt as ever. But Sheridan 'goes on courting the Ministers more and more every day'.

Then, on 24 October, Fox, Sheridan and the Prince went to No. 20, St. James's Place, Moira's house, to discuss the situation afresh. Both Fox and Moira doubted Addington's inclination to secure their support, but by Fox's desire it was agreed that Addington should be asked what he was prepared to do for the Prince, before they committed themselves. 'The upshot', Fox wrote to the Duke of Northumberland on 20 November, 'was that Sheridan should make use of his intercourse with Addington to bring the question *immediately* to a point, whether any coalition with him and the Prince's friends is or is not practicable.' Nothing positive emerged: Fox, indeed, suspected that Sheridan never did anything about it, and he considered the matter as closed. 'I own I am glad it should be so,' he said. He was justified in assuming that the Duke of Rutland would not have been offered a Blue Ribband had there been any serious intention of conciliating a party of which the Dukes of Bedford and Norfolk and Lord Derby were distinguished members. Tierney, then, was clearly mistaken in believing that Addington was occupied in November in planning an extensive reconstruction of his Government by bringing in leading Whigs like Moira, Fox and Grey. Grey himself was always sceptical and made no secret of his own disinclination to form part of a new arrangement. Referring to Tierney, he said, 'I don't know whether it will be possible to undeceive a man who I believe has never passed a day for the last ten years without an immediate expectation of being solicited to undertake the government of the country, but he must be credulous indeed if he still thinks that any fair offer will be made.' And Grey regretted that Sheridan had been employed to ascertain the Prime Minister's views. 'I do wish we could get rid of him and his intrigues for ever. Fox is too good-natured and forbearing, and only encourages such men as Sheridan to behave ill to him.' Fox himself wrote to Grey: 'Of Tierney and Sheridan, I think worse of the former, you of the latter, but we each of us retain perhaps a little kindness for our respective favourites'. 'Sheridan is mad with vanity and folly.' Fox justified the selection on the ground that Sheridan would no longer be able to deceive both himself and the Prince with ideas that were wholly chimerical. 'It would have been with great difficulty', he said, 'that I could have brought myself to persuade any of my friends to make part of an arrangement so formed. I would certainly have had nothing to do with it personally.' He considered that 'by supporting or even sparing Addington for fear of Pitt, we are making ourselves complete Court tools or absolute cyphers.' If only the Prince would 'take a decided part against the present system, he would soon find himself at the head of a great and respectable party ... and I think it most probable that great numbers even of Pitt's friends would (without entirely breaking with their leader) range under his standard. That the present Ministry can do nothing of what he wishes is on the other hand quite clear. I take it they can no more give him any military command or send him Lord Lieutenant to Ireland than you [the Duke of Northumberland] or I in our present situations can. I think Lord M[oira] sees this, but Sheridan either does not or *will* not see it.' Fox, then, had no confidence in Addington and his colleagues, first, because of 'the rashness with which they have produced war', and second, 'the extreme imbecility of their measures of defence'. Moreover, Addington was the head of a predominantly anti-Catholic Administration, and Fox had been sounding some of his leading friends as to the expediency of bringing forward the Catholic question in Parliament. After Fox's death the Prince's views on Catholic emancipation underwent a complete change. It is noteworthy that even in 1803 Fox felt by no means sure that the Prince would support a Motion in Parliament on that question. He wrote to Lord Fitzwilliam on 29 November: 'My opinion is as strong as yours, and if I thought I had Carlton House as much with me on this point as I once thought I had, I would not wait for other opinions; but I suspect Sh[eridan] has been successful in inspiring fears there. It is not that I shall be governed by those fears, but if the Prince is either against the thing or neuter, I must have more preparatory conversations with some friends and more authority to show them than would be otherwise necessary. His name would smooth all. It would not only be the additional force he would bring, but the effect his name would have in promoting zeal and unanimity among us. However, if we cannot have it we must do without it, if I find that others agree with you and me on the propriety of the measure.'

According to Fox, the Prince was as much concerned as the King about the impending loss of Hanover, which French troops were now threatening. 'He is in a rage about Hanover', Fox reported to Lauderdale. To Lord Pelham, the former Home Secretary, the Prince expressed a wish to go abroad and form a 'Northern Confederacy', 'He pretended', wrote Malmesbury, 'that he could manage the Duke of Brunswick, and, through him, Russia and Prussia . . . He was to be assisted by Baron Hompesch (a rank adventurer); in short, one of the ten thousand chimeras H.R.H. conceived.'

Fox thought that it was the invasion threat that caused the Prince to take an increasing interest in politics, and that if he would take a firm line on the Catholic question and condescend to take the government of Ireland into his own hands, there would be a chance of doing good. The idea apparently was that the Lord Lieutenant should be recalled and replaced by a Council with the Prince at the head, and Moira, Hutchinson and Sheridan as his assistants. 'The Prince is quite heated upon the subject,' declared Sheridan. One of the ten thousand chimeras evidently.

Men of all ranks volunteered in great numbers for national service as the invasion threat persisted, just as in 1940 their descendants flocked into the Home Guard. The Duke of Clarence enrolled as a volunteer in the Spelthorne Legion and soon became its commander. But the Prince had to be content with the prospect of fighting at the head of his Regiment. The Duke of Cumberland volunteered (without pay) and was appointed to the command of the Severn District.

Other letters during the year refer to the Duke of Kent's troubles with the Gibraltar garrison and his subsequent mortifying recall; with the successes of the British forces in India against the Marathas, in which struggle the future Duke of Wellington so distinguished himself; and with the continuing troubles of the Duke of Sussex, who withdrew the scandalous accusation against Lady Augusta Murray and tardily acknowledged her daughter as his own child. The climate of Portugal agreed with him; he felt able to lead a more active life, and he was prepared to accept the Prince Regent's offer of a military command, with the rank of General, if the King's consent was forthcoming. But in the autumn his health again deteriorated. Just before Christmas, however, on reading the King's Speech delivered at the opening of the Parliamentary Session, in which his Majesty announced his intention to take the field in person in the event of an enemy landing, the Duke begged to be allowed, if he recovered his strength, to serve as a volunteer by his father's side.

Lady Augusta, living under an assumed name in the hope of keeping out of the Fleet Prison, heard in June that, after all, nothing was to be done for her and her children who, she alleged, were threatened with starvation. 'Justice and humanity have ceased to operate in my favour,' she protested to Addington, and hinted that her collection of royal letters, bonds, certificates and other relevant papers might make it of some consequence to the Royal Family not quite to drive her to despair. How would they like to see everything she possessed appear in print for the delectation of the public? For two years and four months, she alleged, she had not received a farthing of income from the Duke, and the money which the King had granted, she said, 'his Royal Highness has taken care to make answerable for the rent of her house in Grosvenor Street'.

Carlton House, 1 Jan. 1803

Before the Prince set off yesterday for Bushy Park (from whence he proceeded this morning to Windsor) I had the honor to put your Grace's letter[1] into H.R.Hss.'s hand, because it spoke so admirably to the point in question, & was so calculated to have the happiest & pleasing effect on his mind & determination. H.R.Hss. commanded me to offer to your Grace & the Duchess 'his best love, with his sincere prayer for your enjoyment of many many happy years': & to add that after his return from seing the King, your Grace should immediately know what should be conclusively determined upon as to the line he was to pursue for the present.

The Prince's income that has been set apart for the payment of his debts under the management of the Commissrs. named by Parliament is £65,000 p. annm.—& the net residue of the Duchy of Cornwall valued at £13,000 more, making together £78,000 a year. Now your Grace will please to observe that in the proposition made, or rather the King's message borne by Mr. Addington, no mention whatever is made, nor any reference used to *that* arrangement; it is left entirely unmolested & to proceed in clearance of *that* remaining debt (abt. £230,000) belonging to H.R.Hss. & which will be extinguish'd, by those means, in 1806. It has not been even hinted at, or touch'd upon, by either party; besides which, in proof of my statement, there is a fractional difference of £3,000 a year between the sum of £75,000 out of the Consolidated Fund which Mr. A. offers in extinction of the Ps. claim, & £78,000, the income of H.R.Hss. as vested in the Commissioners originally for the payment of his former debt.

Your Grace is already apprized of the subsequent debt which at this moment affects H.R.Hss. & for the payment of which he proposes to create a sinking fund of £50,000 a year. The Princess has at present £12,000 a year for her Establishment, & £5,000 for pin money, but as H.M. has although only glanced at an encrease of her R.Hss.'s comforts, I am to tell your Grace in confidence, & as an arrangement not yet broach'd to any one, that the P. thinks it so far proper to meet this idea at once my making the Princess's 12,000 up to £20,000, so leaving her at £25,000 a year under the present circumstances. In the event of the

1. Missing.

Prince resuming his state (a measure devoutly to be wish'd if possible) I am to state to your Grace that H.R.Hss.'s Establishment as constituted in 1792 (which will not bear any diminution) cost abt. £15,600 p. annum: and that in the case of such an event taking place, I can clearly see H.R.Hss. thinks it belongs to justice & good faith to restore to their former situations in his family every man now living who is eligible, & then to fill up the vacancies occasion'd since that time by death, promotion, or dissmissal. The offices held by the Earls of Jersey & Cholmondeley will of course be to be supplied, & certainly will not be from ranks inferior to those noblemen.

With regard to the report respecting Ld. Lauderdale, I long since met Wilson who, taking the bait thrown out, told me directly the two anecdotes which Richardson had stated, & I explain'd to him clearly the falsity of both: but in addition to this, I made a point of seing H.R.Hss.'s proxy on the occasion, Lord Cassilis who not only produced to me the original proxy sign'd by the Prince (a literal copy of which in Ld. Cassilis's own writing I now enclose for your Grace's further satisfaction by special command of the Prince) wherein Ld. Lauderdale's name is the 3rd. on the list; but he likewise assured me that the said list had never been out of his possession, consequently no other person could have shewn it, & *secretly* declared solemnly to me he never had open'd his lips during his life to Mr. Richardson, nor even knew him by person. I must confidentially impart to your Grace what you will easily perceive by this list that H.R.Hss. only voted for *14* out of the *16* Peers, which certainly was owing to some manœuvre of Ld. Keith for the advantage of his nephew Lord Elphinstone who was one of the unsuccessful candidates on that occasion.

Lord Lauderdale is himself in town (on his way to Paris with his son Ld. Maitland)[1] & had not the P. bound him to secrecy, by declaring he was determined not to pretend he had heard the story he was so furious on hearing the report, that he was going open mouth'd to attack Richardson upon it, but he was entirely at a loss how such a calumny could have been fabricated.

Your Grace may confidently *rely* that Arthur O'Connor *did* dine with Mr. Fox at Paris, *for between your Grace & myself*, I can *assure* you Mr. Fox acknowledg'd it *himself* in friendship to Lord Moira, saying 'It don't signify but by God I have not a heart to meet a man in distress whom I once knew when he was worthy of esteem & not take notice of him.' Mr. Pitt did not come to sup with Mr. A. (as he expected) on Tuesday, nor send any apology. He did not even come to London, but, 'tis said, went to Ld. Grenville's at Dropmore (Alnwick MSS.).

1. James, 9th Earl of Lauderdale (1784–1860), styled Viscount Maitland from 17 August 1789 (when his grandfather died) to 15 September 1839 when he succeeded his father in the Earldom. M.P. for Camelford, 1806–7; for Richmond, 1818–20; for Appleby, 1826–32.

354

Carlton House, Thursday evening[1]

I hope & trust that this letter will find your Grace at Syon without having experienc'd any inconvenience or fatigue, in your journey from Bath.

The Prince's answer to Mr. Addington, expressive of H.R.Hss.'s grateful & ready acquiescence in his Majesty's message was yesterday laid before the King, who was pleased to agree most graciously with the reasons & motives which induced the Prince therein to submit his reluctance to an immediate resumption of his state, & to approve of the plan, suggested with all deference, of constituting forthwith a sinking fund of £50,000 for the final extinction of all his incumbrances. Mr. Addington (who was previously instructed with the Prince's wishes on this subject) was unable to make a report of what had pass'd with the King yesterday, until this forenoon; when he communicated to H.R.Hss. that his Majesty seem'd to think it would be better to name for the grand outline of this Trust, *five* Trustees of high rank & distinction, instead of *three* (as the Prince had intended) for the purpose of sanctioning H.R.Hss.'s law & other officers in carrying it into execution. The Trustees fix'd upon by the Prince were your Grace, Lord Moira, & Lord Thurlowe, but in obedience to the King's suggestion of two more, H.R.Hss. has named the Duke of Devonshire, & the Earl of Egremont in addition. Mr. Addington having entreated that the Prince would not divulge what had pass'd on this head with the King yesterday, until the names of the Trustees (which were sure of H.M.'s approbation) were laid before him, & in so doing, the finishing stroke given to the entire business; I have anticipated to your Grace, from myself, this confidential information, which will of course in a few days be formally communicated to your Grace by a regular command. I know it will give your Grace supreme delight to hear that nothing could surpass the King's kindness & attention to the Prince in his New Year's visit to Windsor, when H.R.Hss. was the only one of the male part of the Royal Family present.

I am sorry to add that H.R.Hss. is slightly indisposed with a cold which confines him to the house, & for which he was blooded (by Sir Walter Farquhar's advice) this forenoon.

I have the honor to be [etc.]. (ibid.)

1698   THE DUKE OF SUSSEX TO THE PRINCE OF WALES

Lisbon, 3 Jan. 1803

Having a safe opportunity I write you these few lines in order to hasten matters if possible. The uncertainty under which I labour is truly cruel, and instead of remedying anything is rendering my situation only more

1. Possibly 6 January 1803.

embarrassing without any one benefit whatsoever. I wish to get hold of my children at any rate and as for the rest it is perfectly the same to me. General Wemyss,[1] who is a particular acquaintance of mine, will be able to give you every possible information on my part and you would oblige me much by seeing him. He has a most excellent character and independant of this is a most intelligent cleaver [sic] officer. It was my intention to have named him as one of my Gentlemen, but being ignorant of Court etiquette I did not know whether his being a *natural son* would not be a drawback. I should wish though to appoint him one of the Grooms of the Bedchamber, if it is proper you will oblige me by mentioning it to him, relative to *affairs* in this quarter of the world I intend writing you shortly a long letter. That they are pleasing I cannot say, but that a great deal might *be done and must be done* is equally certain if the war breaks out again. We must recollect that Lisbon is the *only port* we can consider as *ours* on the Continent, and certainly if some measures were *not immediately* adopted in that instance it would go very soon, and then we should have no one place except Gibraltar. Melancholy as this consideration is, it is in my humble opinion of the *greatest importance*, and not only do I believe the *probability* and the *possibility of its being kept* but consider it likewise as being the means of making a *very important diversion*. This, though, I am not able to communicate untill all my plans are ready. I profit of this opportunity for to wish you a very happy New Year. (48248)

1699   THE DUKE OF KENT TO THE PRINCE OF WALES
Gibraltar, 4 Jan. 1802 [1803]
This letter will be presented to you by Captain Dodd of the Royal Artillery, my Aid-de-Camp and Secretary. I earnestly intreat you to grant him an early audience, as I am most anxious, from the warm friendship you have ever evinced for me, that you should learn from him all the particulars of that unfortunate business which took place here on the 24th & 26th of last month, & which Dalrymple will have intimated to you some days, probably, before this gets home, as I had just time by the mail to give him the outlines of it for your information.

You know, my dearest brother, that it has ever been my greatest pride and ambition to stand high in your opinion and esteem, as well as to prove myself deserving of that affection which you have invariably shewn

1. David Douglas Wemyss (1760–1839). Major, 1791; Lieutenant-Colonel, 1793; Colonel, 1796; Major-General, 11 May 1802; Lieutenant-General, 1808; General, 1819. He served at Gibraltar, 1797–1802, and was appointed Commander of the Forces in Ceylon, 9 May 1803. He returned home in 1806.

me. As such I feel a desire far beyond what language can express, that every doubt should be removed from *your* mind, if any arises, as to my conduct having in the most distant degree brought on those events that have almost broken my heart, as they have cast an indelible stain upon the troops that have been concerned in them. This I am satisfied will be effected at once by half an hour's conversation with Dodd, and I therefore hope I am not presuming too much in urging you thus warmly to see him the first moment it is practicable after his arrival in London. As I flatter myself the detail he has it in his power to give will be such as not to leave *any one* point upon which you may require information unsatisfied, I will not enter into any relation of the facts that took place, leaving that altogether to Dodd, but I cannot refrain from making this one observation, which to *your* open and generous mind will be a very striking one. Had the Officers been generally faithful, had the Commanding Officers of Corps been candid, had I met with support, not only the painful circumstances that will be related to *you* would not have occurred, but the garrison would have been brought to a degree of perfection beyond my most sanguine expectations.

So much upon a subject to my mind the most cruel I ever yet experienced: let me now add a few words upon my *own* situation. You will easily conceive after all the labour I had bestowed for eight months on this command, and the shocking catastrophe (for I know of no other word strong enough to convey my meaning) that has followed after all the pains I have taken, indeed I *might* add the *slavery* I have submitted to, to forward the Service, it must be painful in the extreme for me to remain where every object retraces the recollection of some one of the horrid scenes that occurred on the nights I have before alluded to, and keeps open a wound which it will be most difficult to heal. *Yet* to quit the pace at *this* moment, when the task of command is peculiarly ungracious and difficult, *honor* forbids me, and it is my firm resolution to remain till I can deliver my trust up into the hands of some abler and more *popular* man than myself, in a state in which I can say to him, 'You will receive the garrison of Gibraltar in a state of order that will not discredit the King's service. In affecting this I have gone thro' the severest trial man *could* experience; it now rests with you to keep it so, and to improve upon my system'. *Then* I trust you will agree with me it will be but fair that I should be permitted to return to England were it but to change for a time the dreary gloomy scene which this place must now ever be to me. But though such is my unfortunate situation in point of pecuniary matters, that for *some* time to come the income of my present situation will be necessary even for my existence, and on *that* account I must leave this under leave of absence, I owe it in candor to *you* to state that when I *once* quit this, it will be with the firm and decided intention of never seeing it again. My opinion is that if the Officers, seeing the injury their former

357

conduct has done me, will with cordiality and zeal *now* support me, four months of that steadiness and perseverance with which I shall devote myself to the task will bring the present garrison to as high a state of order as, under the existing circumstances, can be effected, so that I trust by the latter end of April all would be in a situation for me to turn it over with credit to myself and justice to the service into the hands of whoever may be appointed to replace me in the command. My entreaty therefore to you is that you will in my behalf take the necessary steps with the Duke of York to obtain leave of absence for me to return to England by the end of April or commencement of May. My health, which has already so severely suffered from the various climates in which I have been actively employed, was much injured by the *last* summer here, and it has not been benefited by the late events that have occurred. This therefore will afford at least a most fair and *reasonable* plea for the application, and upon that, should you approve of it, I would wish it to be made. After that is accomplished there will be time before us to reflect upon my future plans and prospects, in which of course your friendly advice will be sollicited, but I will not at this moment intrude upon you any longer, but conclude by repeating my earnest entreaties that through your good offices by the time I have named I may be enabled to leave this place where *now* I have not *one* moment more of comfort or satisfaction to expect.

God bless you; depend, while life is in me, on my faithful & unshaken attachment, and that of all your brothers none is more zealously or warmly devoted to you than [etc.].[1] (46032–5)

1700   THE DUKE OF KENT TO THE DUKE OF YORK [copy]

Gibraltar, 5 Jan. 1803

Your Royal Highness will have learnt from my letters of the 26th ultimo and of 3d & 4th instant to Major-General Brownrigg, the unpleasant circumstances that have taken place in this Garrison, in the 2nd Battalion of the Royals, and in the 25th Regiment. I therefore conceive that it will be unnecessary to trouble you with a repetition of the facts that have occurred, but at the same time I have felt it my duty to send home my

1. The Duke, who had been ordered to restore discipline in the Gibraltar garrison, set about the task with a thoroughness that exasperated both the military and the civilians. He closed about fifty drink-shops, ordered the troops to get up at 3.30 in the summer and 5.30 in the winter, prescribed the frequency with which their hair had to be cut and the manner in which they were to shave, prohibited them from entering wine-shops, and prescribed a multitude of other irritating orders and regulations filling three hundred printed pages. A mutiny broke out on 24 December 1802 and several lives were lost before it was suppressed. Three of the ringleaders were subsequently shot.

Secretary Captain Dodd, in order that you may be able to have reference to an Officer who had been an eye-witness to everything that passed, and who will therefore be enabled to give you correct information upon every point concerning which it may be your wish to receive it. By his hands therefore I transmit this letter, the principal object of which is to convey to you a candid statement of the causes that have led to the late events and to communicate my sentiments as to the only mode that will be effectual to establish for the future such a system of discipline in this Garrison as will merit his Majesty's approbation and meet your wishes.

In the first place your Royal Highness is not ignorant of the shameful state of indiscipline and licentiousness in which the troops composing this Garrison were, at the period of the decease of General O'Hara. At the time of my arrival Major-General Barnett[1] (of whose unwearied solicitude in the discharge of his duty, I never can say enough) stated to me that he had already made some changes and adopted some regulations by which a reformation in the loose system was commencing, but that the inveteracy of bad habits was such, he had not been able to make that progress which under other circumstances might have been expected. A very short time convinced me of the justness of the remark of that respectable officer, as scarcely a day passed that men were not confined from off guards for drunkenness or sleeping on their posts, for acts of insubordination, and for crimes committed upon the property and persons of the inhabitants. Punishment of course unavoidably became necessary, and the repetition of it frequent. Still the evil did not decrease, and I then felt that my whole attention ought to be devoted to form a system for conducting the several duties both public and regimental, founded upon the principle of keeping the soldier constantly employed, and thus by depriving him of the opportunities of committing crimes, prevent the frequent recurrence of them. How far I succeeded in this object your Royal Highness will best be able to judge when I inform you that since it has been inforced, the commission of crimes and the consequent punishments have been reduced by more than one half. Indeed it has been the remark of every officer who passed here that there never was a British Garrison in a higher state of discipline and good order. But while I was thus devoting every moment to the faithful discharge of my duty, many officers of the garrison, some of them I am sorry to say of the higher ranks, were commenting upon every order that was given out, complaining of every little additional duty which by the adoption of my system was imposed upon them, and that too, oftentimes in presence of the non-commissioned officers and soldiers, the natural consequence of which was that this class of men, finding the sentiments of their superiors

1. Charles Barnett (d. 1804). Lieutenant-Colonel, in the 3rd Foot Guards, 1792; Colonel, 1796; Major-General, 1801.

averse to the discipline I had introduced, began to murmur. Had the smallest intimation, however, been given either to Major-General Barnett or myself that anything of this nature existed (which has only come to our knowledge since the late unhappy business) it would have been easy for us to have prevented anything whatever occurring. But not even the most distant intimation of any discontent was ever made to me, and on my conscience I declare that till the very hour when it broke out in the Royals, I had not even the shadow of a suspicion that the slightest symptom of such a disposition was harbored.

From the foregoing statement your Royal Highness will perceive that the state of relaxation in which things were, previous to the death of General O'Hara, was the first cause of the evil, and that the second one arose from the want of that support which alone could enable me to get through the arduous task of introducing a system totally different. Had I on the contrary been cordially assisted by the officers, there is not a doubt but that no symptom of dissatisfaction ever would have been shewn on the part of the non-commissioned officers or men, and the garrison by this time would have been in a far higher state of order and discipline than that to which I have ever been able to bring it.

With respect to the 2nd Battalion of the Royals in particular, which first broke out, I believe your Royal Highness is already aware of the truly disgraceful and disordered state in which I found it; in short, no words can convey sufficiently my opinion as to their situation. I suffered, however, some weeks to elapse before I would interfere with them any farther than to deliver my sentiments to Lieutenant-Colonel Campbell as to the necessity of a reform, and the expediency of making soldiers of a set of men who were inferior in every respect to the worst militia regiment I have ever met with. However, no improvement whatever appearing, I was at length obliged to take the management of the Battalion into my own hands, and to endeavour by forming some system to bring it gradually into order. Whether my exertions were or were not attended with that success which alone can prove their efficacy may be learnt by reference on your part to any officer of rank who has lately returned from this garrison, who knew the Battalion when in its relaxed state, and has of late seen it in its improving one. But the comparison that was drawn between the strictness with which I required duty to be done, and the total relaxation which Lieutenant-Colonel Campbell suffered to introduce itself into the Corps, I fear did not please the officers, who had been long used to the old system and their unguarded conversation and remarks before the men unquestionably led to the commotion of the 24th.

With respect to the 25th Regiment, the disturbance which broke out in it arose altogether from inordinate excess in liquor, for not a man of that Corps (and I believe not above a third of the Regiment was out at all) who ran out on the night of the 26th was sober, and the riot in the Royals two days before alone occasioned their phrenzy to shew itself in that way, for it is very evident that if the former had never happened, the latter would not have been thought of, and although it was unavoidable, to punish those who were most active in the disturbance of *that* Corps for the sake of example, I must in candour say that I consider their fault as infinitely more venial than that of the Royals, many of whom I fear joined in the commotion of their own Corps, when in a perfect state of sobriety, and I only lament that our inability to bring clear proof who were the principal ringleaders in the Royals has prevented me from singling out examples from amongst them.

Having endeavoured to the best of my ability to state to your Royal Highness the causes of what has happened, I have only to request, should I not have been sufficiently explicit on the occasion, that you will refer to Captain Dodd for further particulars, who is fully qualified to give them to any extent you may require.

It now naturally follows that I should offer to your Royal Highness my undisguised opinion that the only mode to be adopted, in order to destroy the remaining leaven of the old system of relaxation and drunkenness that has so long disgraced this garrison, is a speedy and entire change of the Corps now composing it, that being a measure without which no progress whatever can be made in establishing a proper system of discipline. This will in part be effected, when the arrival of the 10th Regiment and the two foreign Corps enables me to send off the Queen's, King's, and Royal Welch Fusileers, but in them we lose the Regiments on which we can best depend, and there will remain the Second Battalion of the Royals, the detachment of the Royal Artillery, Royal Military Artificers, 25th and 54th Regiments, none of which ought to be permitted to remain any longer than the time absolutely necessary to send a relief to replace them. Of these, the companies of Royal Military Artificers and the 2nd Battalion of the Royals are those whom it is of most consequence to remove without delay. The former are composed of many of the most infamous characters in existence, have been longer than any other Corps in the practice of all the vices peculiar to this Rock, to the greatest excess, were undoubtedly active in urging the Royals on to the commission of the crime of which they were guilty on the 24 ulto. (a circumstance of which we have the most decided information) and besides are in the state of the worst discipline possible. The latter consists of an obstinate stubborn description of men, little likely to forget what has passed, and a repetition of their misconduct, on any future circumstance occurring, that is of a nature not exactly to suit their taste, while they remain in this garrison, is certainly very much to be apprehended. Next to these two Corps I should strongly recommend the removal of the 54th Regiment, for though they have certainly conducted themselves well on the present occasion, their composition (being totally Irish militia) is such that no great dependence can be placed upon them, more especially as it is well understood that their Commanding Officer, who is a young man of real merit and of the very best disposition, has found it necessary to grant them of late many indulgences in order to secure their good humour, which, but for his judicious mode of managing them, would I fear have been very dubious. As to the 25th Regiment, their penitence, regularity, and sobriety from the very moment after the ringleaders were given up, has been so marked, that were it not necessary for the general principle that every Corps composing this garrison at this moment ought to be taken from it as soon as possible, I should feel little hesitation in saying that I would retain them with pleasure, for I look on that Corps at this instant, strange as the assertion may appear, to be the one on which the most perfect reliance can be placed. As to the companies of the Royal Artillery, their conduct certainly has been without a fault throughout the whole of the trying moments we have experienced, but I feel I ought to include them in the general principle of removal, and must request you to intimate my sentiments to this effect to the Master-General. But as to the Royal Military Artificers, I must repeat my conviction that there is not a moment to be lost in relieving them, for they are unquestionably a very dangerous set of men, and in their present disposition, connected as they are with the Royals, a great deal is to be apprehended from their infamous example and the conversation which they hold whenever they have an opportunity of doing so with impunity.

I should here conclude this letter, having performed the task I imposed upon myself at the commencement of it, but I must yet trouble you with a few words upon the situation of the 2nd Battalion of the Royals.

Your Royal Highness is of course informed that Lieutenant-Colonel Campbell is the only Field Officer now present with the Battalion, that he is much advanced in years, and though possessing the best intentions, so totally and entirely worn out as to be altogether incapable of command; in short, a perfect cypher. The Second Lieutenant-Colonel, though a gallant active Officer in the field, is a man much addicted to the pleasures of the table, who very frequently drinks to excess and who carries no authority with him. Major Barnes, who has been lately promoted, though a very gentlemanlike young man, has like most of the other officers of the Royals, been brought up in the vicious habits of a relaxed discipline, and is equally unfit for either exertion or command. Thus Major Danser alone remains upon whom any dependence can be placed for firmness and discipline. Under the peculiar circumstances therefore of this unfortunate Battalion, it becomes my duty to point out the necessity of the removal of Lieutenant-Colonels Campbell & McDonald, as measures that can alone save the total ruin of the Corps or in any degree restore it to discipline. Your Royal Highness will be able from the number of officers of merit who have been reduced on half pay, to select others who are efficient to be placed at the head of it, but it will be essential that above all things in this choice the talent of supporting authority with firmness, and a complete knowledge of the command of a Battalion in all its various points should be considered, for the state of the Corps requires every aid which an able Commanding Officer can afford it. (46060–5)

1701 THE EARL OF MOIRA TO COLONEL MCMAHON[1]
Donington, 11 Jan. 1803
In the awkward uncertainty of political matters I think it most expedient to defer my journey to town, because were I on the spot a shuffler might imagine he could carry on his game of nods & smiles & half sentences & might thence suppose it unnecessary to come to any distinct position. Now, I have been taking means to bring the business with Addington to a clear understanding. Some time ago I wrote to Tierney[2] in a manner calculated to make him ask an unequivocal explanation of what was intended: because, notwithstanding all the positiveness of expression & circumstantiality of arrangement quoted in your secret letter, I did believe Mr. Addington was only continuing the silly trick which he before persuaded himself was policy; namely, that he fancied he was lulling us by expectations. From Tierney I got no answer, nor did he ever write to me on the subject at the time when he mentioned it to you. Not the most momentary suspicion of Tierney's honor ever did, or ever can float across my mind: but this I conceive as likely, that he has been unwilling to confess those doubts which he could not but feel of Addington's sincerity, & that he has been endeavoring to gain time. For my part, I am strongly inclined to put a stop to this smirking courtesy at once, & to intimate a decided hostility to the present Administration. I shall,

1. This letter is followed by a very long Memorandum, in French, on the state of Portugal, and unsigned. It is dated, Lisbon, 12 February 1803 (folios 39870–86).

2. Tierney was not yet in office: he was appointed Treasurer of the Navy at the end of May. Grey heard about it not later than 27 May: 'The reason of its being a secret is that it cannot yet be publicly declared on account of other arrangements, and if prematurely known, might endanger Tierney's re-election.' He added, 'I am sorry for it, as I cannot help feeling a real friendship for him, though I have long ceased to give him credit for much political integrity' (Howick MSS.). Charles Abbot, the Speaker, wrote on 2 June: 'The appointment of Tierney had been accelerated by the intention having transpired sooner than was meant. The D. of C[umberland] had talked of it, and the Borough [Southwark] was in a state of canvass by another candidate' (MS. Diary).

363

however, wait for an answer (which ought to come this day) to a second letter written by me to Tierney. (39868–9)

1702 PRINCESS ELIZABETH TO THE PRINCE OF WALES

14 Jan. 1803

The King & Queen have commanded me to say to you that there being no Ball they intend having an Assembly at the Queen's House *where* all the family will be together in honour of the day. Of course that takes in the Princess but they hope that will not prevent your coming, for being merely an Assembly you can always slip away.[1]

I am sorry to hear you have had so bad a cold; which I am not surprized at from the very great severity of the weather. (Add. Georgian 11/92)

1. The Queen's Birthday (19 May) was, as usual, officially celebrated in January—this year on Tuesday the 18th. The Prince and Princess of Wales were both at Court. McMahon wrote this account to the Duke of Northumberland (the letter is dated merely Wednesday, 19th 1803).

'In addition to the short note I had the honor to write your Grace yesterday, I have only to report that the several operations of the day went off in their usual manner, & the whole concluded as well as possible. The Prince enter'd the Drawing Room considerably before three o'clock, & a very few minutes after the Princess had arrived. The Duke & Duchess of York did not arrive until near four, & the Court was ended by five. All the Royal Family (save the Pss. of Wales, & the Dss. of York) dined together immediately afterward. The select card party began to assemble at the Queen's House between eight & nine, & finish'd the evening about twelve. The Pss. went home to Blackheath, which was quite an unexpected proceeding, insomuch that one of the Prince's carriages (without even a single outrider to attend it) came at ½ past 11 at night to Carlton House, when a lady got out & ran furiously into her R. Hss.'s apartments. On enquiry she proved to be one of the Pss.'s attendants who had come directly from Blackheath in order to undress H.R.Hss. by her command, for the night, as she intended to sleep at Carlton House. The woman not finding H.R.H. at home, & waiting for a length of time, grew impatient to learn what she was to do, but no one could resolve her [doubt] & therefore she remain'd for the night, as the Pss. had sent no directions whatever.

'I should have observ'd that both the Pss. of Wales & the Duchess of York were present at the Assembly at the Queen's House; & nothing could be more assiduous & pointedly attentive to the former than the D. of Cumberland was throughout the day, having handed her himself into the midst of the circle in the evening at the Queen's House.

'Mr. Pitt was at the Drawing Room, looking far from well in health, & (as seem'd generally remark'd) very indifferently dress'd. The Queen spoke, tho' with apparent graciousness, very shortly to him, & I found no one who had observ'd in what manner the King had noticed him, consequently he could not have been much distinguish'd in that quarter. He appear'd to hold more conversation with Lord Bute than any other person while he remain'd, which was not very long. He partook on that day of Mr. Addington's Ministerial dinner, where of all his bosom friends only Chas. Long I understand was present.

'Mr. Addington yesterday communicated (thro' H.R.Hss.'s Law Officers) to the Prince "that H.R.Hss.'s most dutiful reply to the King's gracious message respecting his affairs had

1703 THE PRINCE OF WALES TO SIR JOHN LADE

Carlton House, Friday, 25 Feb. 1803

I find by the returns of this day which I have just receiv'd from Brighton Fred has receiv'd orders to join the Regiment. I have already sent word down that I have extended his leave of absence & consequently that he will not join as yet. I will explain my reasons why I think this best for him the first moment I can get to myself to run up to your house. This can no ways affect him or can be possibly consider'd in any other light than the fair convenience & indulgence every young man is entitled to if his Regiment is not going upon immediate & active service, which at present is not the case as the country is at peace.

P.S. Pray excuse haste.[1] (42364)

1704 THE DUKE OF KENT TO THE PRINCE OF WALES

Gibraltar, 17 Mar. 1803

I lose no time in acquainting you with the arrival of Captain Dodd yesterday, by whom I received the King's commands to return to England. Without entering at *this* moment into a detail of my feelings upon so summary a proceeding, I shall simply inform you of my intention of

been laid before the Cabinet by his Majesty's command, when they had unanimously approved & deem'd justifiable those reasons which H.R.H. had assign'd for setting apart so large a sum as a sinking fund for the extinction of his debt; & for dispensing with his state at present; & that the motives which had actuated H.R.Hss. in this determination, appear'd to them as highly redounding to his honor & probity," Mr. Addington adding at the same time a wish that H.R.Hss. should know the Lord Chancellor was particularly loud in that opinion. This communication to your Grace, I have had the Prince's express command to make; & with H.R.Hss.'s best love to add that nothing farther in this business can be done until the King's Message is carried to Parliament by Mr. Addington after the Recess (& which he supposes may be so soon if possible as Thursday the 10th of February) when in consequence of such elucidation of the subject as the Message will afford, a formal application will be made to your Grace as the chosen friend & confidential Trustee of his Royal Highness.

'Lord Moira (for the reasons with which your Grace is already acquainted) did not come up to the Birthday.

'The Prince, although greatly recover'd from his cold, is not well enough to go out but in his close carriage, & then he seldom goes farther than Mrs. F.'s, where he nurses himself most evenings over the fire until about 12 when he returns home.

'No news worth mentioning' (Alnwick MSS.).

1. The Prince sent the following note to Lord Spencer from Carlton House on 21 February: 'I have been for some days incapacitated from indisposition, desiring you to favour me with a visit; however, being now considerably better, I do not hesitate in desiring you, if you have no other very essential engagement, to allow me a few minutes conversation with you at one o'clock tomorrow, when you will find me at home and happy to receive you' (Althorp MSS.).

availing myself of the first fair wind that may offer, after I have finally regulated matters here, which it will take me from twelve to fourteen days to accomplish. As such, I conceive that from after the 15th of April, my arrival in England may be daily expected. As you must be aware that, after the most unexpected order I have received, it is impossible for me to form the most distant idea what sort of a reception I am to expect from the King, and therefore that I must wish to see you before I pay my duty at Windsor or at the Queen's House, I hope you will approve of my proceeding directly to Carlton House upon my arrival, where you will easily conceive the joy I shall feel in again embracing my warmest and best friend. I shall not attempt to describe all the grateful affection I feel towards you for the unvaried friendship you have ever shewn me throughout life, but more especially on the present *most trying* occasion, when everything that is most dear to me, I mean my character as a soldier and as a man, is at *stake*; for my abilities are not adequate to find language sufficiently expressive to convey them. I trust, however, you will give me credit for entertaining every sentiment of devoted attachment which a feeling heart can possess.

In my present agitation of mind, you will excuse me, if I say no more, but reserve everything farther 'till our meeting. Pray remember me most particularly to Mrs. Fitzherbert, whom I shall be most happy to see again, and I hope in the best of health and spirits.[1] God bless you, my dearest brother, and rest assured that, while I live, you will ever find me, with unalterable attachment [etc.].

P.S. Never have I yet experienced a trial like the present one, but the *mens conscia recti*, and the confidence I repose in *your* friendship will, I trust, bear me through it. (46068–9)

1. If, as the Government had been hoping, the Prince were again in a position to abandon his comparatively obscure position and live in a manner more suitable to his elevated rank, Mrs. Fitzherbert's position might be altered appreciably: she might not continue to be the presiding divinity of Carlton House. From McMahon's letter of 14 December 1802 to the Duke of Northumberland it appears that there had been some discussion of this matter: ' . . . Valuing as I know he does whatever can come from your Grace, & feeling the positive conviction of the affectionate zeal & disinterested attachment which guides & governs all your Grace's advice & wishes towards H.R.Hss., I am confident it would operate on him so powerfully as to become at once a sure direction & safeguard in all his conduct & transactions. I am firmly satisfied that Mrs. F. will appreciate with the highest estimation every argument your Grace so seasonably offers, & by a fair & honorable co-operation with those sentiments will I trust chalk out exactly the line your Grace has so greatly & so wisely laid down for the Prince to pursue, not only in his general conduct, but more especially on the important event of the assumption of his full income' (Alnwick MSS.).

20 Mar. [*1803*]

I have just receiv'd your letter for which I offer you my best thanks, &
was going by this post, if your letter had not come, to give you our news
from hence, which agrees with your own, that war is inevitable & so
Bonaparte's last dispatch to your Government sufficiently indicated,
which I learnt from undoubted authority, as therein most impertinently
says he means to send 20,000 men into Holland, & 50 into Switzerland,
& that he will not allow the fleets which are fitting & which was intended
for the Colonies, but as Addington's reason, given, for *our* armament, was
on that ground, & which for the reason he furnishes, they do not mean
to employ them in that way, as it may be possible they shall have other
employment for them. I also heard Lord Melville was not to come in,
without as he says, he was quite sure of Mr. Pitt's acting with him in
office, & as far as I can gather from *that* description of persons, he will
not. I enclose you Lord St. Vincent's answer to my offers of service, to
shew the Prince. I wish you also to get a letter from me, to Thrwhitt
[*sic*], which, by what you say of his journey, I think he cannott have
receiv'd, enclosing one to be shewn to the Prince from Jack Lemon, &
do the business for me instead. I was fearful you were getting wrong
in the House of Commons upon the Prince's business, which I was
glad to see afterwards got right, by which I read in the papers. As
soon as you can speak to anything with precision I shall trust to your
friendly communication, for as you will see by the letter herewith
sent that it is necessary for me to know, and you will be surprized
at my being so bold a man when there is so much shirking. But
recover the letter for me to avoid its being improperly us'd, which
I think cannot be the case, as it speaks for peace. I enclose you
at the same time a letter from our old torment, Cockell, which you
can use as well to his advantage as I can. Yrs. truly, my dear Mac.
(39888–9)

Carlton House, 10 Apr. 1803

I am to desire you will pay to John McMahon, Esqre. 'Six hundred &
eighty seven pounds nine shillings', which sum he has disburs'd on my
private account to this period. (32481)
[Pencilled note]:

1. In McMahon's hand but signed by the Prince.

	£1,000	0	0				
The Prince	687	9	0				
A. Porrit	6	6	0				
Lord Moira for sons of Sir Patrick	105	0	0				
	£1,798	15	0	£1,798	15	0
Sir Sidney Smith	105	0	0	340	18	10
				210	0	0
	£1,903	15	0			
				£2,349	13	10[2]

2. Shortly after the 10th the Dowager Countess of Elgin wrote the following memorandum: 'On Sunday the 10th April 1803, Easter day, I had Princess Charlotte to read prayers. The dr. child told me that she was much distress'd with the Chapter on Good Friday, namely, the 19 John, which gives an account of our Saviour's sufferings. She told me the substance of the Chapter quite distinctly & seemed at a loss somehow. At last Louisa said she would tell me what the Princess meant, that she was struck with Our Saviour giving the charge of his Mother from the Cross to St. John when he was dead. 'How could He speak from the Cross?' I soon convinced her R.H. that it was previous to His death & that He drank the vinegar after the conversation. She was then satisfied, but continued to converse so much above her years that I felt it right to change the subject. The day before she had talked improperly to her French teacher [The Rev. C. de Guiffardière]; she told me of it. I told her I was sorry she was so silly, that I felt her childish but left her without any reproof. In the afternoon the maid had a pain in her breast & in the evening they were to sing hymns, being Easter eve.' (49264)

Another undated Memorandum by Lady Elgin is endorsed, 'Anecdote of my little Princess': 'A certain little person received a present of a watch about 12 o'clock just when the morning lessons of 3 hours were ended. The happiness was inconceivable, jumping & frisking like a little lamb. The letter was kissed over & over & the Governess half smothered. She then ask[ed] what she could do. 'How, my dear?' 'Why, I wish to make you happy—I will get my history by heart, I will do anything to make you happy, G.' 'Thank you, my love. You shall compose a pretty letter & thank the givers, but you have been busy all morning, & now we shall go out see the flowers.' Accordingly we went to the favourite spot & walked & jump'd till it was time to dress—then dinner, when our little wine was supp'd with uncommon spirits, & after our return to the Library. The dr. child did get two pages of this history [sic]. We then went to into [sic] the carriage & took an airing to the other side of the hill towards Eltham, where we get a shelter'd walk & met on our return in the lane our clergyman who was coming to read at 7 as usual. In this pleasing frame we arrived & she wished to shew her beautifull present to her Master but it was under the tippet, & the little person came to her Govss. to take of[f] the tippet. Unfortunately, not understanding the intention, the Govss. took it of[f] to lay it on the table—which was sadly contrary to the meaning, and the fire was kindled. The storm was violent—declaring her poor Governess very cruel & at last that she never would never do [sic] anything right again, &c. Mr. Watson, meekness itself, was perfectly astonished as well as myself. I stood still & let her go on, & when she stopt I said, quite calm, 'Sir, I am sorry you have seen this sad scene, you could not have supposed it.' 'No Madam, I could not & I grieve I have seen it.' 'So am I & thought the Princess wiser.' 'Don't you think it is my duty to punish her R.H.?' 'Most assuredly, Madam.' The little person immediately called out: 'But you cannot punish me,' & you say: 'No, my dr., I cannot whip you—that would ruin you & be so mean I should never be able to look at you.' 'I should not mind it, I assure you.' 'Come, my dr.,' said I, 'I must not talk but do. You have behaved very ill, and I am in duty

Carlton House, 14 Apr. 1803

I have receiv'd your kind letter late the day before yesterday but was prevented from answering it by yesterday's post by being under the necessity of leaving town & being detain'd in the country the whole day. My sentiments & good wishes towards my friend Lauderdale must ever continue the same, & I only wish that my abilities to serve him were equal to my feelings & inclination. I need not, I hope, add, my dear Charles, that independant of my friendship for Lauderdale, the knowing that you interested yourself for him would alone be a sufficient motive for me to exert myself on this occasion. I have already sent for Harry Erskine to consult as to the best measures to be taken for the success of our friend.[1]

With my best compliments to Mrs. Fox [etc.]. (Add. MSS. 47560, f.53)

bound to try and correct you, and I think the punishment must be the taking away the watch and I shall let the Prince know how undeserving you are of their goodness.' The countenance began its change 'and with your approbation Mr. Watsons [*sic*] I take away the watch for one week. If she is very humble & penitent for the very great fault she has committed, she may perhaps see it then.'

The dear child submitted but sobb'd & wept a little which I said could have no effect, & advised sitting down to the lesson, which she did, & all went on in quietness and made no sort of demand, went to bed with humble, silent respect.

Next morning on my giving her some little favour of a card her dr. little heart softened & she wept violently, declaring herself unworthy of my goodness & was quite penitent & never once asked [for] the watch till the time was expired.' (49265)

1. The reference is to the by-election in the Scottish Representative Peerage, occasioned by the death on 7 April 1803 of Patrick, Earl of Dumfries. Lauderdale, who was not a Representative Peer after 1796, was not a candidate on this occasion. On 29 November 1802 Fox had written to Grey, with reference to the general election on 10 August: 'À propos to the House of Lords I fancy Ministers must pretty well repent already having kept Lauderdale out, at least, they soon will, for the figure they make there is, as I learn, truly pitiable, destitute of all resource to a degree never equalled' (Howick MSS.).

Tyrwhitt wrote to William Adam on the 15th: 'I have written to Lord Glasgow and do not despair of his vote, though from what passed between me and Garthland McDowall yesterday Melville has a very powerful influence over the Peer ... T. Erskine ... is to send his brother Harry to the Prince tomorrow at one to consult what steps are ... to be taken' (Blair Adam MSS.).

The following details of the by-election on 16 June 1803 are kindly supplied by the Scottish Record Office, Edinburgh. The Earl of Kellie was defeated by Lord Elphinstone:

Voted for Lord Elphinstone:		*Voted for the Earl of Kellie:*	
Peers present:			
Earls of	Crawford	Earl of	Moray
	Kellie	Viscount	Arbuthnott
	Lauderdale	Lords	Elphinstone
	Dalhousie		Elibank
	Hyndford		

Gibraltar, 24 Apr. 1803

After our late conversation respecting your Royal Highness's intended code of orders, I sit down with great reluctance again to address you on a subject on which it is equally painful for me to write, as it probably will be for your Royal Highness to read.

Your Royal Highness is now going to England in one of the most critical and alarming situations in which a human being can well stand, as far as concerns your future character as an Officer, for if those who have recalled you are able to justify their conduct in so doing, it will be a most fatal blow to your military reputation for ever, as the universal conclusion will be that you were not fit to be entrusted with the command of this garrison.

Voted for Lord Elphinstone:	*Voted for the Earl of Kellie:*
Peers present:	
Lords Sinclair	
Sempill	
Belhaven	
Rollo	

Peers voting by Signed Lists:	
Dukes of Hamilton	Dukes of Buccleuch
Lennox	Queensberry
Gordon	Roxburghe
Atholl	Earls of Caithness
Montrose	Morton
Earls of Erroll	Strathmore
Eglinton	Haddington
Cassillis	Leven
Home	
Abercorn	Northesk
Dysart	Aboyne
Dundonald	Glasgow
Kintore	Hopetoun
Breadalbane	Deloraine
Dunmore	Viscount Falkland
Stair	Lords Napier
Rosebery	Kirkcudbright
Portmore	
Bute	
Lords Cathcart	
Torphichen	
Somerville	
Reay	
Kinnaird	

Peers voting by proxy:
Earl of Lauderdale for the Duke of Rothesay and the Earl of Galloway voted for Lord Elphinstone.
Earl of Kellie for the Earl of Balcarres voted for the Earl of Kellie.

370

At such a moment, where the most guarded prudence is necessary not to afford your enemies a pretext for the injustice they have done you, your Royal Highness is going to publish a complete code of orders for the future regulation and government of the troops in this Garrison. Such a work, which should have been the deliberate labour of months, has been composed by your Royal Highness in the course of a very few weeks, amidst the pressure of other business, and under great anxiety and distraction of mind. This, however, will not be considered by those who sit down to investigate its merits, and to criticise and publish its errors and faults to the world.

I have read your Royal Highness's intended code as far as it is now published, twice over with the greatest attention, and my opinion is that if those who have recalled you should ever in their own defence publish your orders as their justification, that the general decision would be most unfavourable to your Royal Highness, for though I readily admit that your Royal Highness's orders contain a degree of *extensive* information and *minute details* rarely to be met with on a variety of military subjects, yet recollect, Sir, that great part of such information will confer but little honor on a Prince. On the contrary, with many reflecting minds it may do you an essential injury, as they will hardly be induced to believe that you could have paid so much attention to the *minutiæ* without neglecting the *higher branches* of your profession. Independent of which, there are some parts of the orders which, if suffered to stand as at present, unexplained, will probably subject your Royal Highness to the imputation of severity or inhumanity. These, Sir, are not only my own sentiments but they are also the sentiments of another equally attached to you with myself, whose judgement or fidelity you never had reason to doubt, and surely our united opinions should have some weight with your Royal Highness, and induce you to pause before you publish a code of orders to the world at such a moment which may be attended with such serious consequences to your future military reputation.[1] (46070–2)

1. The following is a typical order issued by the Duke of Kent whilst in North America. It is dated Halifax, 4 March 1800:

'John Ballard, private soldier in his Majesty's Royal Fusilier Regiment, has my orders to proceed from Windsor to Annapolis on Friday the 7th instant, by the route specified on the back hereof, and immediately on his arrival there, to report himself to Lieut.-Colonel Urquhart, who will be pleased to furnish him with a bed in the Barracks; he is sent on purpose to cut the hair of every non-commissioned officer, drummer and private of every Corps without exception, between Windsor and Annapolis; on Friday evening he is to sleep at Winsley's, on Saturday at Colo. Bayard's, and to arrive at Annapolis on Sunday night; on Monday morning, he is to commence cutting the hair of the officers of all the Corps there; and also of every gentleman, holding a Staff situation, whether in the Commissary, Barrack, or Medical Department; precisely according to the Regulation established: after which he is to cut that of the non-commissioned officers and men and for the execution of which order at

Gibraltar, 25 Apr. 1803

The purport of this letter is the Duke of Kent's return to England, which, as it may perhaps give rise to a variety of opinions, and also to some public controversy, I have taken the liberty of writing to you on the subject; as if circumstances should unfortunately require it, I know no man so well qualified as yourself to defend his conduct and do justice to his character, and I have also the satisfaction to reflect that you possess the inclination equal to the ability.

Annapolis Lt.-Colonel Urquhart is held responsible. When this duty is perfectly compleated, he is to proceed to Digby, and cut the hair of every officer, non-commissioned officer and soldier—also of every gentleman holding a Staff situation, whether in the Commissary, Barrack or Medical Department; from whence he is immediately to return to Annapolis, there to remain during the sitting of the General Court Martial; dressing the hair of all the officers and giving all necessary instructions to the hair dressers of the 66th Regiment during that time; who are commanded to be very attentive to the instructions Ballard gives them. Immediately after the General Court Martial is closed, he is hereby ordered to return to Halifax by the same route, and in the same time as laid down for him to go. He is responsible to get a certificate from the officer or non-commissioned officer commanding at each Station, of his having cut the hair of every man on the Station; and is to obtain the signature of every officer or other gentleman in a Staff situation, whose hair he cuts. He is answerable to keep himself correctly sober on his march up, being ordered to consider himself on duty.

EDWARD, General, and Commander in Chief of His Majesty's Forces in British North America.

John Ballard is subsisted and answerable to pay his own expences on the road.' (45972)

1. Cobbett (1763–1835) had started his *Weekly Political Register* as a supporter of the 'New' Opposition, in January 1802. Windham and his friends found the necessary money, Cobbett estimating the required amount to be £600, and suggesting that twenty or thirty gentlemen might contribute. Lord Grenville's brother Thomas wrote to Lord Spencer on 5 January 1802:

'I have talked of this to my brothers and find them well disposed and even eager to promote the undertaking, but they agree with me in thinking it better to try to lessen the number of subscribers in order to have fewer hands in the pudding; pursuing therefore this more limited plan and dividing the £600 into £50 shares:

Lord Buckingham would take 3
Lord G[renville]   „   „ one
T. G[renville]   „   „ one
Lord Temple   „   „ one
Windham   „   „ one

'For the remaining 5 shares I understand Lord Fitzwilliam will readily take 2; perhaps, if you approve of it, you will be a contributor, and Dr. Lawrence and Cobbett would have a half share apiece.

'I wrote upon this project to Windham, and he appears to approve very much of the reduced number, but he was to see Cobbett and to write further to me upon it; meantime I wish to know your general opinion of this matter, but I should not forget to say that when I expressed to Windham some apprehensions as to Cobbett's violence upon the Irish question, he assured me that he found that Cobbett was grown perfectly reasonable upon that point and was entirely reconciled to the proposed measure *in Ireland* . . . ' (Althorp MSS.).

Mrs. Fitzherbert's house in Tilney Street
(now demolished)

Kew Palace

Mrs. Fitzherbert
a pastel by John Russell

In consequence of the late disturbances in this garrison, his Royal Highness received a letter from the Duke of York stating that Lord Pelham, Secretary of State for the Home Department, had obtained his Majesty's sanction for his Royal Highness to return to England, on account of his Majesty's Ministers being desirous of receiving information from his Royal Highness in person, on the subject of the mutiny which had taken place in the garrison, and intimating to him it was therefore H.M.'s pleasure H.R.Hss. should come to England for that purpose. The Amazon frigate, which brought out the despatches, was ordered to receive his Royal Highness & convey him to England in consequence.

This recall of his Royal Highness (for such it certainly is) and the fatal effects such an example may produce hereafter on the discipline of the British Army, the safety of our colonies, and even on the fate of the Royal Family itself, by the want of support so pointedly and remarkably shewn in this instance to one of its branches, certainly merits the most serious considerations.

I shall here take a short view of his Royal Highness's conduct since he was appointed Governor of Gibraltar, and explain the real causes of the mutiny, which have as yet been very imperfectly understood; and shall conclude, with offering such reflections as may occur on the subject of his recall, leaving it to your superior abilities to arrange & make use of them, in whatever manner may appear most advantageous to his Royal Highness's character, if circumstances should render any explanation upon that subject necessary.

It is well known that his Royal Highness was sent out to Gibraltar for the purpose of reforming as disorderly and licentious a garrison as perhaps ever the British Army witnessed. The late Governor,[1] from ill health and infirmity, had for some time been incapable of preserving any tolerable discipline or regularity amongst the troops under his command, and his recal had been determined upon, on this account, previous to the news of his death reaching England.

The task of reforming licentious troops must necessarily render him who attempts it unpopular, and with a victorious army it is always attended with some difficulty and danger, and we believe that no Officer ever assumed a command under more discouraging or untoward circumstances than his Royal Highness did on arriving at Gibraltar.

It is a well known fact that Gibraltar has always been reckoned, and justly disliked by the army, as one of the worst quarters for both officers and soldiers in the British dominions, and that there hardly ever was such a thing known as a contented garrison in that place under any Governor whatever.

1. General O'Hara (d. 1802).

Many causes contribute to this. The confined situation of the place itself. The wretched state of the barracks for both officers and soldiers; the men being frequently crowded, three, at times even 4, in a bed in that hot climate. The want of the common indulgencies in many respects that the British Army everywhere else enjoys, not an officer ever being allowed a single article of furniture or fuel in his barracks, and even the soldiers are not allowed the common cooking utensils, and to the disgrace of the service they are even obliged to pay for the fuel with which they cook their scanty meals. All these evils and inconveniencies his Royal Highness endeavoured to remedy by every means in *his power*, and also making the most forcible & repeated representations to Government on behalf of the troops; and previous to his departure he had the satisfaction to find that his efforts in their favor were likely to be successful.

The regiments which composed the Garrison of Gibraltar on his Royal Highness's arrival had all been in Egypt, and were extremely disatisfied both at their situation in such a garrison, and at not having been allowed to return to England after a victorious campaign, as they expected. They had been permitted by the former Governor to indulge in the greatest excesses and idleness, and the instant it was known that his Royal Highness was to be sent out to reform the state of the Garrison the utmost pains was taken by many to prejudice the troops against him and the system he meant to establish, so that from the moment of his arrival they were prepared to view all his actions and orders in an unfavourable light.

It has perhaps been an error in the conduct of his Royal Highness through life to pay too little attention to popularity or the public opinion, but we know that few officers were ever more truly the friend of the soldiers in everything that concerns his real welfare than his Royal Highness has invariably shewn himself.

His manner with soldiers ever has been to see that they are well fed, lodged, and clothed, to pay the utmost attention to their health and morals by restraining them as much as possible from drunkeness, and by keeping them constantly employed. To prevent errors, not to punish them has ever been his study.

This was the system he began to establish immediately on his arrival at Gibraltar, and the beneficial effects of it were soon seen in an astonishing decrease of the usual mortality of the troops, and a diminution of the number of court martials and punishments.

It appears from the clearest evidence (the hospital returns) that the average mortality of the troops in this garrison, for six years previous to the Duke's arrival, exceeded 140 annually, and that in the last six months he has commanded the number has only amounted to 13. And it also appears that even the punishments have not amounted to one-half of what they did, even under the former relaxed system, and the reason of this is evident. Every military man knows that there are certain crimes

374

which are hardly ever forgiven by any Commander, because the very existence of the Army depends upon their being followed by certain punishment. These, however, frequently proceed from the effects of liquor, & his Royal Highness by abolishing drunkeness prevented all those crimes and evils that usually arise from it.

There is no doubt but the restraints which were necessary to accomplish these ends did excite at first very universal discontent; as to keep the drunkard sober or employ the idle, daily experience shews to be no easy task. Habit, however, would soon have reconciled the soldier to the salutary regulations established by his Royal Highness, had he met with that support from the Officers, which he had a right to expect, instead of which, they murmured, in general at the duties required of them, and instead of supporting and promoting a ready obedience to the orders of his Royal Highness, it became the fashion to discuss and animadvert upon every order that was given in the most improper and licentious manner at the public messes, even in the presence of the servants, who being all soldiers, soon communicated the sentiments and conversation of their masters to the rest of the troops, who, encouraged by the example of their Officers, were led to entertain ideas they never otherwise would have dreamt of.

To such a length was this licentiousness of conversation carried that 'Confusion to the Governor and his orders' and 'The Royal Family of the Rock' were, we have heard, from different authorities, frequently drank as toasts at some of the messes. Can it be wondered if, after such conduct in the Officers, that some of the soldiers broke out in open mutiny?

It is rather astonishing that with such an example before them, that several of the other Regiments had not joined in the mutiny the night it broke out in the 2nd Battn. of the Royals, who certainly expected to be headed on the occasion by some of their own Officers, and also to be joined by both the 25th and 54th Regiments in their design of forcing his Royal Highness to leave the Garrison.

The world has hitherto been chiefly led to believe that the mutiny on the night of the 24th of Decr. proceeded from drunkeness, whereas on the contrary it was a cool, deliberate mutiny in that Regt., the real object of which was to force his Royal Highness on board of ship, and to bring back the garrison to that state of relaxation and licentiousness from which he had rescued it.

The riot on the night of the 26th, in the 25th Regiment, had nothing of this kind in view; it proceeded solely from drunkeness and resentment in the soldiers of that Regiment against the soldiers of the Royals, for having upbraided them as cowards in not having joined them in the mutiny on the 24th; a convincing proof of which was that their first step after breaking out of their barracks was to proceed to the barracks of the

Royals, to challenge them to come out, and fight them on account of the insults they had received.

That the imprudent conduct and conversation of the Officers was the great cause of the discontent which prevailed amongst the troops, and the mutiny which took place in one Regt., we shall only cite the example of the 54th Regt.

The Officer commanding that Corps, shortly after the arrival of his Royal Highness, had the prudence positively to forbid all conversation at the mess respecting his Royal Highness's orders, and to declare his intention to support them to the utmost, and to require the same conduct from his Officers, which they cheerfully complied with. The consequence of which was that no symptom of discontent ever appeared in that Regt.; on the contrary, they shewed the most unshaken fidelity throughout, and when the mutineers called upon the Regiment to join them on the night of the 24th they instantly fired upon them, and gave three cheers, crying 'Loyalty & discipline for ever.'

Here there is an unanswerable proof how much the conduct of the men was influenced by the sentiments of their Officers, and that had his Royal Highness met with the same support from the Officers of the other Regiments that he experienced from those of the 54th Regiment, the garrison would have been brought to that high state of discipline, regularity and sobriety in which he left it, without that difficulty & odium he had to encounter from the want of support in the Officers.

His Royal Highness has been accused of severity; we on the contrary condemn him for a mistaken lenity in not making a severe example of some of those Officers who were most forward and active in opposing his measures and censuring him & his orders. But it is a remarkable part of his Royal Highness's character that hardly any consideration will induce him to punish an offence that seems in any shape directed personally at himself, and his forbearance led many to oppose and calumniate him, knowing that they had nothing to dread from his resentment. The truth of this will hardly be doubted when it is known that no Officer was ever brought to a court martial by him during his command, though certainly several deserved it.

Having now stated the real causes of the discontent and mutiny at Gibraltar, we shall now proceed to offer some remarks on the subject of his R. Highness's recall.

His Royal Highness, as we have before stated, was sent to Gibraltar to restore discipline and regularity in a garrison where the utmost licentiousness prevailed. In his endeavours to accomplish this object a mutiny breaks out in one of the Regiments under his command, from the causes we have mentioned; this gives rise to a drunken riot in another Regt. which is also soon quelled, and the ringleaders punished. On the accounts of these disturbances reaching England, after a six weeks deliberation, it is resolved to recall his Royal Highness from his Government, at a time when the danger was over, when order and tranquility was restored and when the object of his mission was accomplished!

Here is an example for the world in these times!

An illustrious branch of the Royal Family, whose integrity and good intentions even his enemies universally admit, is removed from a high command because part of a licentious army opposed him in his endeavours to restore subordination and discipline! Had any Officer in the Service been thus deserted and sacrificed for a conscientious discharge of his duty, we should have soundly reprobated the cowardice & folly of such a measure, but when we reflect on the rank and character of his Royal Highness we confess we are lost in astonishment and indignation!!

Let the Royal Family look to themselves; this is a common cause in which they are all equally concerned. If they tamely suffer his Royal Highness to be removed in consequence of the opposition or clamours of a seditious soldiery, let them reflect *whose turn* it may be next to fall a victim to popular prejudice & discontent!

These are no times to trifle with the fate of Princes. If *they* do not support each other, by whom can they expect to be supported themselves?

The ostensible excuse for which his Royal Highness has been ordered home, is to communicate in person with his Majesty's Ministers, on the subject of the late disturbances at Gibraltar. If when this is accomplished his Royal Highness is not sent back to Gibraltar with some marked approbation of his conduct, and if exemplary punishment and disgrace is not also inflicted on that Regt. which attempted by a deliberate mutiny to expel the son of their Sovereign from the command of the most important garrison in the British dominions, it will be the most fatal and deadly blow that ever was given to all loyalty and discipline in the Army.

These are not our sentiments alone, we know that they are also the sentiments of many of the first men and best Officers in the kingdom, who justly think that even if his Royal Highness in his zeal for the good of the Service, in his endeavours to reform a licentious garrison did too suddenly enact more than was prudent, considering the temper of the troops he had to command, yet that still he ought to have been supported to the utmost against every attempt to remove him by the opposition or mutiny of those under his command; and this would have been the determination of any Ministry possessing either prudence or firmness.

That some of them did strongly condemn the measure of his recall, we know. Lord St. Vincents [*sic*] in particular declared that he regarded it as the ruining all discipline both in the Army & Navy. And even in the

377

garrison of Gibraltar, many who opposed his system now strongly reprobate the extreme impolicy of removing his Royal Highness at this moment, from the apprehension of the fatal consequences such an example may have upon the troops hereafter.

Every motive of sound policy demands that after his Royal Highness has communicated to Government such information as they may require on the subject of the mutiny, that he should be immediately ordered out again to his Government with some public mark of approbation of his conduct.

With respect to his Royal Highness's severity to the troops, about which the world has been taught to believe so much, we have already admitted that the salutary restraints he was obliged to impose, at first did cause very universal discontent, which was increased and fomented by the imprudent conduct of the Officers.

By this system, however, which they so much complained of, the average number of deaths was reduced from upwards of 140 to less than 30 annually, and the punishments diminished to less than one-half of what they were formerly.

These were the happy effects of abolishing drunkeness & restoring discipline, by which, however, his Royal Highness lessened his own income £3,500 a year.

Through life he has ever shewn the greatest zeal for the Service, and the most disinterested integrity in the discharge of his duty to his country, & he certainly expects that those under his command should in some measure follow the example he sets; but the very name of patriotism or public spirit now exerts but a smile of contempt.

With regard to his Royal Highness's conduct as Civil Governor of Gibraltar, let enquiry be made of every merchant in the city who trades to Gibraltar what their correspondents there say of his conduct to the inhabitants, and they will tell you all in one breath that so far from having suffered any tyranny or oppression under his command, that on the contrary they have found him the most mild, benevolent and upright Governor they ever beheld; that he has protected them in all their rights and property; that he has restored and encouraged the trial by jury, which had almost sunk into disuse, and that under his equitable government they have enjoyed a degree of liberty and happiness they never experienced before. This they to a man have individually & collectively declared, in every private letter, and in every public address, and that the world might see their gratitude was not confined to words, they in a few hours subscribed twelve hundred guineas to present him with a diamond star as a small parting tribute of the universal affection and admiration they felt for his character and person, and the services he had rendered them.

This will be delivered you by Capt. Dodd, with whom you are already acquainted, who is perfectly master of the subject and who can give you every further information you may require on that head.[1] (46073–81)

1710 THE DUKE OF CAMBRIDGE TO THE PRINCE OF WALES
Hanover, 8 May 1803
I hasten to return you my sincerest thanks for your very kind letter of the 16th of last month which Lindemann brought me last weeck. On his mentioning to me your wish to have one of my musicians I told him that he might settle with him & that as you had named the man I would not interfere in it, for properly in this service every musician must give two years' notice before he gets his dismission. The man, however, on account of family concerns has declined accepting for the present the offer Lindemann made him, and I think it right to inform you of this myself as I really have left it entirely to his option to do what he liked. He certainly is a very good bassoon and a very well-behaved man, and for these reasons I am glad to keep him. Should you, however, dearest brother, still wish to have him you may depend on my not preventing his going. Be assured I shall always be happy to oblige you in anything that is in my power and I shall ever feel grateful for the kindness and friendship you have always shewn me, my dearest brother.

I am very sorry to have been deprived of the pleasure of hearing from you by the horrid accident which has befallen poor FitzGerald. Not the smallest remnant of the packet has been found and even now there is no certainty where it went to the bottom.

The uncertainty of peace or war makes the situation of this country very awkward indeed. The generality of opinion seems now for war, but for our sakes I do sincerely hope the contrary. Deeken[2] has been to Berlin to see what can be done in case the French should declare war, to prevent if possible their occupying the Electorate. You may easily conceive, dearest brother, what my feels are upon this subject. God grant things may end well. (48592)

1. Captain Dodd wrote to Captain Wright from London on 25 June: 'I have not yet thought it necessary to publish your letter to Cobbet, as all seems quiet, and as to allusions you mention to have seen about cutting and dressing the hair, they appeared before we arrived, and were too near the truth to meddle with'. (46090)

2. By this time Decken, the Duke's A.D.C., was a Major. He took Francis Jackson, the diplomatist, and his brother George, to see Herrenhausen the previous November. 'There is really nothing remarkable in it. They say it was kept up in good style in George I's time; now, some people of the Court reside in it, and the gardens, which are extensive and are laid out in the formal manner of those of Versailles, are its only attraction' (*Jackson Diaries*, i.101).

1711   THE PRINCE OF WALES TO BENJAMIN WEST[1]

Carlton House, Saturday night, 8 [?7] May 1803

The Prince of Wales desires that Mr. West will be so good as to order the Exhibition[2] to be open for his private inspection with a party at three o'clock tomorrow (Huntington MSS.).

1712   THE DUKE OF CAMBRIDGE TO THE PRINCE OF WALES

Hanover, 23 May 1803

I must trouble you with a few lines by this mail as I am sure you will be anxious to hear from me. Deecken has been sent about a fortnight ago to Berlin on the first news of the probability that the negociations would be broke off at Paris in order to see what the King of Prussia would do for us. His last dispatches which arrived on Saturday give some little hope that the King will interest himself for us, and he has desired Deecken to stay till he could inform him what he can do. Our accounts from Holland which we received yesterday mention that the French are assembling near Coevorden, and that they are to have a camp of thirty thousand men between Osnaburg & Werther [?]. Our Corps is marching from all points towards the Weser, but I am afraid owing to the difficulty to get horses the regiments will not get there before the beginning of June. Our garrison will I trust be able to march off on Wednesday or Thursday. A messenger has been sent off yesterday to Berlin in order to engage the King of to try to engage the King of Prussia to do something for us. [*sic*] You know, dearest brother, my affection for you & therefore you will not doubt, I am sure, of the assurance that in every situation you will always find me [etc.]. (48598)

1713   THE DUKE OF KENT TO THE PRINCE OF WALES

Windsor, 10 a.m., Monday, 30 May [1803]

I am this instant favored with your truly kind and affectionate letter of last night and you will easily believe shall count every moment till tomorrow noon when I am to have the happiness of again meeting my best friend and benefactor. I will now only add the King's reception of me has been truly kind and his manner affectionate, but he has not touched in the least upon my unfortunate business.

1. The painter (1738–1820).

2. The Exhibition at the Royal Academy, Somerset Place.

William has been over to see me, and he as well as all the girls and the Queen me comblent d'amitiés, so that as far as my wounded feelings can suffer to feel any comfort I certainly have been highly gratified since my arrival here.[1]

God bless you, my dearest and kindest friend, rely on my faithful and unshaken attachment while I exist, being ever [etc.].

[*P.S.*] My kindest remembrance in Tilney Street[2] where I hope to be admitted for a moment tomorrow. (46084)

1714 THE DUKE OF NORTHUMBERLAND TO COLONEL MCMAHON
Northumberland House, 5.30 p.m., 8 June 1803
I herewith return you the copy of the letter from H.R.H. the D. of Kent to the Commander-in-Chief, as likewise the letters &c. belonging to Lord Hutchinson.[3] Be kind enough just to let me have one line that I may know you received them safe. I feel much obliged [to] you for having procured me a sight of these interesting papers. (39890)

[Enclosure] THE DUKE OF KENT TO THE DUKE OF YORK [copy]
Castle Hill, 6 June 1803
In the letter I did myself the honor of addressing to your Ryl. Hss. from Windsor Castle on the night of the 28th of May I expressed my expectation of receiving instructions from you upon the subject of a personal communication with his Majesty's Ministers relative to the events that took place at Gibraltar in the month of December last, agreeably to what Lord Pelham intimated in his letter to your Royal Highness of the 5th of March and assigned as the cause of his Majesty's pleasure for my return to England being conveyed to me. Nine days have since elapsed

1. The Duke of Kent had just arrived from Gibraltar. Charles Grey who thought that it would have been easy for any men of ability and desirous of peace, to have preserved it, and who described the country as 'the devoted victim of fools and scoundrels', wrote, rather uncharitably, a few days earlier, 'There is a report about the streets that the Duke of Kent is taken in his way home from Gibraltar. How true it is I know not, but it will, I think, be an instance of God's justice if the King is the first sufferer by the War' (Howick MSS.).

2. Where Mrs. Fitzherbert lived.

3. John Hely-Hutchinson, 1st Baron Hutchinson (1757–1832). M.P. for Lanesborough [I.], 1776–83; for Taghmon, 1789–90; for Cork, 1790–1801. Entered the Army, 1774; Lieutenant-Colonel, 1783; Colonel, 1794; Major-General, 1796; Lieutenant-General, 1803; General, 1813. Commander-in-Chief in Egypt, May 1801 (to him the French capitulated); created Baron Hutchinson [I.], 16 December 1801; succeeded his brother Richard (1756–1825) as 2nd Earl of Donoughmore. K.B., 1801; G.C.B., 1815.

without my receiving any directions from your Royal Highness upon this point. As such I feel it my duty to express to you in the strongest terms my extreme anxiety that an opportunity may be afforded me of meeting his Majesty's Ministers, according to his Lordship's own suggestion, in order that I may become master of their sentiments relative to the business in question, and thereby have the means of vindicating my character which as an officer I cannot but feel stands at this moment under a stigma in the eyes of my profession, from the circumstance of what *I* can *only* consider *as a recall*, whatever may be the term which those who have advised the measure may chuse to give it. Exclusive of my own feelings which, from your Royal Hss.'s own nice sense of honor you must be aware cannot but be deeply wounded, from the almost unparalleled position in which I find myself at this moment placed, and which therefore urge me to press the matter being brought forward without delay, I have an additional inducement to request your good offices, that a very early day may be named for my meeting his Majesty's confidential servants upon the business alluded to, in the approaching departure of Major-General Wemyss, of whose evidence I might otherwise be deprived, and whom I now officially report as the first & principal person upon whom I shall call to prove those facts which, in defence of my conduct & in explanation of many points connected therewith, it may be necessary for me to bring forward. Allow me therefore most warmly to press your Ryl. Hss. not to suffer any delay to arise that can possibly be avoided and in the meanwhile to give such orders as you may judge necessary to the Major-General that will ensure his being present whenever I shall have occasion to request his attendance. (39891)

1715   THE PRINCE OF WALES TO THE DUKE OF NORTHUMBERLAND, AND THE REPLY

Carlton House, 10 June 1803

I really am quite asham'd of intruding upon you so hastily, but when one has experienc'd such friendship as I ever have from you I am afraid the natural consequence is that one grows generally more impudent & more presuming. In order not to tresspass too long upon your patience I will instantly proceed to the matter which will occasion you the trouble of reading this letter. I understand that poor Richardson[1] has paid that debt

1. Joseph Richardson (1755?–1803), M.P. for Newport, Cornwall, 1796–1803. One of the proprietors of Drury Lane Theatre. He died suddenly at the Wheatsheaf Inn, Virginia Water. According to Thomas Moore (the story however, was contradicted), Sheridan, one of his intimate friends, arrived at Bagshot too late for the funeral, but succeeded in persuading the goodnatured clergyman to perform the ceremony over again (Moore's *Sheridan*, p. 603).

which we all of us must sooner or later pay; & I have greatly at heart to recommend to your protection as worthy a young man as exists, & for whom I will *be responsible under all circumstances*, as I have known him & been attached to him from the moment of his birth, & as he never has in any one instance deviated from that line of conduct which has established my partiality (& which would equally recommend him to your Grace, had he ever had the honour of being known to you), I mean my young friend Tom Sheridan,[1] & I need not add that I should not think of naming him to you, my excellent friend, if I did not know that his intentions always would be, to follow that line of politicks which you would wish those whom you countenance in Parliament to follow. Let me hope that you will pardon the liberty I am taking, & ascribe it to the sense I shall ever retain of that attachment & friendship you have testified to [etc.] (Alnwick MSS.).

THE DUKE'S REPLY [copy]
Northumberland House, 10 June 1803
I have this instant been honoured with your Royal Highness's letter, & I trust you will do me the justice to believe that nothing affords me so much pleasure as to obey your Royal Highness's commands.

The engagements into which I have already entered, & the arrangements I have made with the electors in order to secure an opening for my eldest son[2] who will now be of age in a couple of years are such that it is impossible for me now to break thro' them. I have long, Sir, foreseen & expected the melancholy event which has now taken place & therefore irrevocably fixed all these arrangements a considerable time ago.

I cannot help again repeating to your R.H. how much I am hurt at being thus circumstanced, & flatter myself that the readiness with which I obeyed your commands with respect to Colonel McMahon at the late General Election will convince your R.H. how eagerly desirous I am to do whatever is acceptable to you, Sir, whenever it is in my power to obey your commands. (ibid.)

1. Richard Brinsley Sheridan's son by his first wife, Elizabeth Linley (1775–1817). Colonial Treasurer at the Cape of Good Hope, 1813–17. He was never in Parliament. He contested Stafford at the general election of 1806. *The Times* reported on 22 October that he had been given a cornetcy in the Prince of Wales's Regiment, the 10th Light Dragoons, and that he was to accompany Moira (who had just been appointed Commander-in-Chief in Scotland) as an A.D.C. Tom Sheridan was presented at the Levée on 26 October.

2. Hugh, 3rd Duke of Northumberland (1785–1847), styled Earl Percy, 1786–1817. M.P. for Buckingham, August–October 1806; for Launceston, November 1806–7; for Northumberland, 1807–12. Summoned to Parliament, *v.p.*, 12 March 1812 in his father's Barony as Lord Percy. A Lord of the Bedchamber, 1821–47; Lord Lieutenant of Ireland, 1829–30.

Castle Hill Lodge, Friday morning, 10 June 1803

Having yesterday, as I left Dumergue's about eleven o'clock with the intention of turning my steps towards Carlton House, seen your post chariot and four turn up Half Moon Street, I concluded there could not be a chance of my meeting with you at home, and being very much wet I therefore went directly to the Queen's House where I dressed for the Drawing Room. From *that* time the rain was so incessant that having no equipage *monté* it was impracticable to attempt getting at you, so that when the King's dinner was over I made the best of my way home *here*.

I had nothing new relative to myself to communicate, my letter of Monday last remaining yet unanswered from Headquarters, but I was anxious you should know what had prevented my fulfilling the intention I mentioned in my note to MacMahon of calling on you yesterday. It is most probable I may be detained two or three days here without going into town, having many letters by me to answer, and some business in my own private concerns to transmit; in the meanwhile, should you have any commands for me, on receiving the slightest intimation of your requiring to see me I shall at all times quit everything to attend you.

Pray accept the renewed assurance of my unalterable and most warm attachment.

[*P.S.*] Pray say everything that is most kind from me to Mrs. Fitzherbert.[1] (46086)

1. Next day the Duke of Kent wrote to his brother, the Duke of York:

'A report having just reached my ears that it was in agitation to send British troops over to his Majesty's Hannoverian dominions in order to aid his Electoral ones in the defence of the country, although, as you will easily conceive, I cannot form the most distant judgement whether the same is [well] founded or not, I feel I should be greatly deficient in the duty I owe and the attachment I feel to the King were I at such a moment as the present one and *on such an occasion*, notwithstanding the peculiarly distressing situation in which as an Officer I now stand, to be backward in making the humble offer of my services to his Majesty, should they be acceptable to him or he be pleased to conceive that they can in any shape be useful. Knowing therefore of no channel so proper to convey this tender of them to him as yourself, I earnestly request that you will not lose a moment in communicating these my sentiments to the King in such manner as you may judge to be most proper. In the event of the measure of sending British troops to the Electorate being adopted, and my humble offer of serving with them being graciously accepted by the King, I beg to add that although Adolphus's military rank is inferior to mine, it is my particular wish his Majesty should dispose of me in any manner he may think proper, *without reference thereto*, and fully understand that as my view is *to aid* in a cause which cannot but be considered as *that of the whole family, not a difficulty of any kind* will be made by me to take *any* station where it is thought I can be useful.

P.S. You will of course understand that the subject of these lines is in no ways to affect the discussion of my Gibraltar business, which every sentiment of honor as an Officer and every feeling I possess as a man forcibly compel me to insist upon as the only means now left me of vindicating a character which, during the many years I have been employed in the King's Service in situations of trust, it has ever been my study to preserve without reproach, and which

Carlton House, 17 June 1803

My dear Frederick,

I take the opportunity of the Honble. & Revd. Mr. Twisleton's[2] going out to Ceylon (with the appointment of Chaplain to the Garrison) to write you a few lines in order to thank you for the kind letter I some time back received from you, & to assure you how sincerely I rejoice at the pleasing accounts you give me of your health, as well as of the satisfaction you feel in your situation. This gentleman I understand is not unknown to you, which may possibly in some degree facilitate the kindness with which you are ever ready to meet any request of mine, & which *is* in the present instance to admit him into your society & when in your power to be useful to him. Allow me to seize this opportunity of thanking you for your attention & kindness to my protégé Johnson, who I am certain will ever be sensible of your goodness, & endeavour to prove himself worthy of it. I am ever, my dear Frederick, your very sincere friend (Kent Record Office).

at *this* moment *must from the measure of my recall* stand stigmatized in the eyes, not only of the garrison late under my command, but in those of my profession at large. (46087)

1. Frederick North, 5th Earl of Guilford (1766–1827), third and youngest son of Lord North, the Prime Minister. M.P. for Banbury, 1792–4; Secretary of State in Corsica, 1795–7; Governor and Vice-Admiral of Ceylon, 1798–1805. He succeeded his brother Francis in the Earldom, 11 January 1817. He replied to the Prince's letter on 3 May 1804 from Colombo: 'Your Royal Highness's gracious commands have been delivered to me by Mr. Twisleton who arrived here during my absence at the Pearl Fishery after a long passage of eight months, with his wife and charming children. I am very happy that so old a friend of mine as Mr. Twisleton has obtained your Royal Highness's notice, and if our spiritual concerns receive the same benefit from his exertions which our temporal ones have from those of Mr. Johnston, we shall have great reason to be grateful for the distinguishing manner in which your Royal Highness has exercised your protection. My desire to return to England has been much quicken'd by a year of public and private misfortune. I am happy to add, however, that with the want of every thing but vigour, unanimity and a good cause, we have been able to repel our enemy in every direction and to establish a system of successful aggression against his territories, which will I hope by the blessing of Providence continue till we obtain a sufficient addiction to our disposable force to take final and satisfactory vengeance at him. May I request your Royal Highness to accept the assurances of the sincere veneration and gratitude with which I am [etc.]' (Kent Record Office).

2. Thomas James Twisleton (1770–1824), son of Thomas, Baron Saye and Sele. Rector of Broadwell cum Addlestrop, Worcestershire, Vicar of Woodford, Northants, 1796–1803, and of Blakesley, 1797–1824; Secretary and Chaplain to the Government of Ceylon, 1803; Archdeacon of Colombo, 1815–24.

1718   THE DUKE OF CAMBRIDGE TO THE PRINCE OF WALES

Windsor, 3 July 1803

I was very sorry to have been prevented calling upon you the two last days I was in London, but I really had so much to do that I could not get to Carlton House. I delivered your message to Frederick about the Review, and he desired me to say it was a fault of the Adjutant-General who has order[s] to give you notice of every Review that takes place, and he has spoke to him on the subject. Yesterday four Lt.-Generals were put on the Staff, Ernest, P. William,[1] Harrington, & Cathcart. The first is to have his headquarters at Gloucester, the second at Liverpool, and the two last in London. This is all the news I have to write. I must now beg you will send me word if you go on Wednesday to Woolwich, and at what o'clock I am to be with you as I shall be very happy to attend you. And now God bless you, dearest brother, all my sisters desire their kind love, & Sophy a thousand thanks for the feather. Little Charlotte desires her duty too. (48602)

1719   PRINCESS SOPHIA TO THE PRINCE OF WALES

Queen's Lodge, Windsor, 4 July 1803

Although Dolly has already thanked you *de ma part* for the feather, yet I cannot feel satisfied until I have endeavoured *myself* to say how much I feel your kindness in indulging me with *one* you have *worn*; believe me it will be highly valued by your *own Sophy* as everything is that comes from her beloved *G.P.*, though I fairly own that the feather will be *doubly endeared* as you have made use of it first. I am very happy to hear from Dolly that you are well; he as usual speaks with the greatest affection of you & gratitude for the invariable kindness you shew him. I think it is a very long time since we have met, but I assure [you] the old proverb of '*Out of sight, out of mind*' does not stand good with me as absent or present my heart is ever with you & no one loves you more affectionately than [etc.]. (Add. Georgian 13/17)

1720   THE PRINCE OF WALES TO HENRY ADDINGTON, AND THE REPLY[2]

Carlton House, 18 July 1803

The subject on which I address you presses so heavily on my mind, and

1. Prince William of Gloucester.

2. In this 'Royal Correspondence', as it was called, there are one or two trifling differences between the MS. version and the printed.

daily acquires such additional importance, that, notwithstanding my wish to avoid any interference with the disposition made by his Majesty's Ministers, I find it impossible to withhold or delay an explicit statement of my feelings, to which I would direct your most serious consideration.

When it was officially communicated to Parliament that the avowed object of the enemy was a descent on our Kingdoms, the question became so obvious that the circumstances of the times required the voluntary tender of personal services. When Parliament, in consequence of this representation, agreed to extraordinary measures for the defence of these Realms alone, it was evident that the danger was not believed dubious or remote.

Animated by the same spirit which pervaded the nation at large, conscious of the duties which I owed to his Majesty and the country, I seized the earliest opportunity to express my desire of undertaking the responsibility of a military command.

I neither did, nor do presume on supposed talents as entitling me to such an appointment. I am aware I do not possess the experience of actual warfare; at the same time I cannot regard myself as totally unqualified or deficient in military science, since I have long made the Service my particular study. My chief pretensions were founded on a sense of those advantages which my example might produce to the State by exciting the loyal energies of the nation, and a knowledge of those expectations which the public had a right to form as to the personal exertions of their Princes at a moment like the present.

The more elevated my situation, in so much the efforts of zeal become necessarily greater, and I confess that if duty had not been so paramount, a reflection on the splendid achievements of my predecessors would have excited in me the spirit of emulation. When, however, in addition to such recollections the nature of the contest in which we are about to engage was impressed on my consideration, I should, indeed, have been devoid of every virtuous sentiment if I felt no reluctance in remaining a passive spectator of armaments which have for their object the existence of the British Empire.

Thus was I influenced to make my offer of service, and I did imagine that his Majesty's Ministers would have attached to it more value. But when I find that, from some unknown cause, my appointment seems to remain so long undetermined; when I feel myself exposed to the obloquy of being regarded by the country as passing my time indifferent to the events which menace, and insensible to the call of patriotism, much more of glory, it then behoves me to examine my rights and to remind his Majesty's Ministers that the claim which I have advanced is strictly constitutional and justified by precedent, and that in the present situation of Europe, to deny my exercising it is fatal to my own immediate honour and the future interest of the Crown.

I can never forget that I have solemn obligations imposed on me by my birth and that I should ever shew myself as foremost in contributing to the preservation of the country. The time is arrived when I may prove myself sensible of the duties of my situation and of evincing my devotion to that Sovereign who, by nature as well as public worth, commands my most affectionate attachment.

I repeat that I should be sorry to embarrass the Government at any time, most particularly at such a crisis, but since no event in my future life can compensate me for the misfortune of not participating in the honours and dangers which await the brave men destined to oppose an invading enemy, I cannot forego the earnest renewal of my application.

All I solicit is a more ostensible situation than that in which I am at present placed, for, situated as I am, as a mere Colonel of a Regiment, the Major-General commanding the Brigade of which such a Regiment must form a part, would justly expect and receive the full credit of pre-arrangement and successful enterprize.[1] (39900–1)

ADDINGTON'S REPLY

Downing Street, 20 July 1803

I have been honor'd with your Royal Highness's letter and will not fail to lay it immediately before the King. It is my earnest hope that I shall not incur the imputation of presumption if I venture to assure your Royal Highness of the strong impression made upon my mind by the sentiments which your Royal Highness has so forcibly express'd and which must command respect and admiration wherever they are known. (39908)

1. Lord Thurlow drafted the following paper, 'for the Prince of Wales to submit to Government': It has been suggested that the promotion now about to take place in the army offers a suitable occasion to tender my services in a manner more formal and official than I have hitherto pursued.

In the pre[se]nt posture of this country I am sensible that no opportunity of urging my claim to an active and efficient post in its military service can be omitted without derogating from that character which I wish to preserve in it, but views more enlarged and publick zeal prompt [the ambition to crown my life with glory or close it with honour in defense of the nation*].

These considerations lead me not to forego the present occasion of pressing my claims upon the Commander-in-Chief, by whose counsels, the Constitution presumes, the military department of the Empire is administered.

If his Majesty's advisers should deem my pretensions to be the only ones of all the Royal Family fit to be rejected, they will at least think it just and honourable to explain that I am laid by in virtue of that judgement and not in consequence of my own slackness. (39929–30)

* The passage in square brackets was scored through and the following substituted: 'me to require a forward station in the service upon the present emergency.'

Shooter's Hill, 19 July 1803

Be assured 'tis with the utmost regret I trouble your Royal Highness to beg your instructions at a time I well know you are so engaged. But I dare not take things on myself, and you alone are the person I wish to speak to respecting your dear little Princess. I must therefore beg to have your authority for some things that ought to be done if your Royal Highness cannot as I fear have leisure to direct me yourself.

I have first to request your permission to send for Mr. Angier, the person that undertakes to remove defects in speech. Princess Charlotte had got much the better of the hesitation to which she was so much inclined when very young. Her reading master, Mr. Trew (whom the Queen saw & approved of at Weymouth) declared from the first and does so still that there is no defect in her organs of speech, which is evident from her repeating long pieces of poetry & changing her voice as the subject requires. Mr. Trew says it is occasioned by a redundancy of ideas and words which she cannot utter so quick as she wishes & occasions a nervous agitation. I have allways observed that when anything affects her nerves; damp weather, any little disappointment brings it on a little, but to my sincere grief I find it has increased very much since the hot weather began, and I was quite in agony at her being greatly affected while we were at Windsor. She has used the cold bath since her return & I have kept [her] as cool as possible yet her Royal Highness does not get the better as she used to do. Mr. Trewe [*sic*] is gone to the country for 3 or four weeks, and it occurr'd to me that if I had your R.H.'s permission I would send to Angier & hear what he says on the subject. This your Royal Highness will allow I ought not [to] do of myself, & if you you [*sic*] will send me one word on a slip of paper to say I may send for Mr. Angier it will be sufficient. I have likeways a great wish to have some masters for Princess Charlotte, but what I have to say on that subject I shall defer, having received this evening a letter from poor Miss Hunt[1] telling me tho' her time of absence is nigh compleated she is unable to return to her duty & that she did not think she ever should, & means to write your Royal Highness herself. I have long wished to have talked on that subject with your Royal Highness on Miss Hunt's situation but felt the point too delicate to write on. Many things one can say to those they esteem & can confide in, which in writing (at least mine) appears unkind or exaggerated. One thing I am sure of, that your R.H. will not be in any great hurry. I expect Charlotte from Portsmouth in a few days & she will stay with me till a proper person is found—one qualified for the situation and not one who the situation may suit. It now becomes of the greatest consequence, I shall be in town on Wednesday and be truly happy to have a summons to attend your R.H.

1. The Sub-governess.

I am informed by a letter from Mrs. Hamilton Nisbet that a gentleman who saw Elgin very lately says he was in full hopes of getting Lady Elgin[1] sent home, they wait a few days to see, before they set out for Scotland & till they give up hopes of seeing Ly. E. I am very unwilling to meddle with my son's packages, finding the presents are so mixed, and allso I should be sorry to deprive her of the great pleasure of presenting them herself. I know there is a very fine sword for your Royal Highness & he wrote me of some Collections, I understood (from himself), but he did not give me particulars & I am afraid to say anything. If Lady Elgin don't get a passport I shall apply directly to your Royal Highness & get the packages from the Custom House. I wrote Elgin a letter under feigned names begging his directions & begin to be afraid he has not got it. Your R.H. may be assured I would not delay the delivery one moment did it depend on me who am in truth [etc.]. (49266–49267)

1722   COLONEL MCMAHON TO THE HON. J. C. VILLIERS[2]
26 July 1803
I am commanded by his Royal Highness the Prince of Wales to express the strong sense of approbation which every part of your conduct toward him respecting the Corps[3] proposed to be raised under your command has impress'd upon his mind. His Royal Highness feels very sensibly the propriety, delicacy & respect of your sentiments and offers upon that subject—but his Royal Highness commands me to say that he will on no account hear of accepting your offer of surrendering the Corps to his

1. Thomas, 7th Earl of Elgin (1766–1841), was Ambassador to Turkey, 1799–January 1803. He married, as his first wife, 11 March 1799, Mary (*d.* 1855), daughter of William Hamilton Nisbet of Dirleton and Belhaven, Haddingtonshire. He and Lady Elgin, being in France when war was renewed in 1803, were imprisoned at the Château Trompette in the Pyrenees, but they were released in 1806.

2. John Charles Villiers, 3rd Earl of Clarendon (1757–1838). M.P. for Old Sarum, 1784–90; for Dartmouth, 1790–1802; for the Tain boroughs, 1802–5; for Queenborough, 1807–12 and 1820–4; Comptroller of the Royal Household, 1787–90; Chief Justice in Eyre North of the Trent, 1790–1838; Special Mission to Portugal, 1808–10. Succeeded his brother Thomas as 3rd Earl of Clarendon, 7 March 1824.

3. A Royal Corps of Volunteer Cavalry. An advertisement in *The Times*, 3 September, invited eligible people to enroll, but the project came to nothing. Colonel Villiers sent out the following circular on 12 September: 'It appearing to the Committee for directing the affairs of the Royal Corps of Cavalry to be raised under the command of the Right Hon. J. C. Villiers, that the views of Government would at present be better answered by discontinuing the raising of the above-mentioned Corps, the Commanding Officer has the honour to inform you that the proceedings in this undertaking are stopped . . . ' (*The Times*, 16 September).

390

command. His Royal Highness declares his conviction that the actual duties of raising, forming, training & commanding such a Regiment cannot be in better hands than those in which his Majesty has placed them by his gracious acceptance of your offer.

His Royal Highness at such a crisis could not with consistency, or as he hopes may soon be manifest, with propriety apply himself to those duties. His Royal Highness therefore directs me to inform you that whatever was his disposition to comply with the desires of those who requested him to place himself at the head of a Corps proposed to have been assembled on a similar but more extended principle of service, he now entirely forgoes it, and so far from countenancing any plan that can in the slightest degree interfere with yours, now form'd & officer'd, accompted and sanction'd by his Majesty, he will by every means in his power promote its completion & success.

At the same time I have it in command from the Prince to say that if it be the general idea of the gentlemen connected with your plan (as you have declar'd it to be yours that there wou'd be a peculiar and distinguishing propriety in his name being at the head of the list of such an association of the young nobility & gentry not otherwise employ'd in the defence of their country, he is perfectingly [sic] willing and indeed with feelings highly gratified under such a call to accept of the honor of being named as their Colonel, but upon the same terms as attach to those officers whose rank does not allow of their interference with the detail, discipline or general command of their Regiments. These his Royal Highness again repeats cannot be more fitly entrusted than to you.[3] (39909–10)

1723   THE PRINCE OF WALES TO HENRY ADDINGTON, AND THE REPLY

26 July 1803

A week has now elapsed since the Prince of Wales transmitted to Mr. Addington a letter on a subject of the highest importance; though he cannot anticipate a refusal to so reasonable a demand, he must still express some surprise that a communication of such a nature should have remained so long unanswered.

When the Prince of Wales desired to be placed in a situation which might enable him to shew to the people of England the example of zeal, fidelity and devotion to his Sovereign, he naturally thought that he was only fulfilling his appropriate duty. As the first subject of the realm in which as it has pleased Providence to cause him to have been born, so he is determined to maintain himself by all those honourable exertions which the exigencies of these critical times peculiarly demand. The

3. This is a draft in Sheridan's hand.

motives of his conduct cannot be misconceived or misrepresented. He has, at a moment when everything is at stake that is dear and sacred to him and to the nation, asked to be advanced in military rank, because he may have his birth-right to fight for, the throne of his father to defend, the glory of the people of England to uphold, which is dearer to him than life, which has yet remained unsullied under the Princes of the House of Brunswick, and which he trusts will be transmitted pure and uncontaminated to the latest generations. Animated by such sentiments, he has naturally desired to be placed in a situation where he can act according to the feelings of his heart and the dictates of his conscience.

In making the offer, in again repeating it, the Prince of Wales considers that he has only performed his duty to himself, to the State, to the King, to Europe, whose fate may be involved in the issue of this contest. If this tender of his services is rejected, he shall ever lament that all his efforts have been fruitless, and that he has been deprived of making those exertions which the circumstances of the Empire, his own inclinations, and his early and long attention to military affairs, would have rendered so particularly grateful to himself, and he trusts, not entirely useless to the public. (39911–2)

ADDINGTON'S REPLY

Downing Street, 27 July 1803

Upon receiving the letter with which Mr. Addington was last week honor'd by the Prince of Wales, he assured his Royal Highness that it should be immediately laid before the King. This was accordingly done, and the letter is still in his Majesty's possession. A communication was afterwards made to his Royal Highness the Prince of Wales, in a mode and thro' a channel which Mr. Addington humbly hoped his Royal Highness would approve. Mr. Addington, however, now finds it to be incumbent upon him, in consequence of the expectation which has been express'd by his Royal Highness, to state that his Majesty, on being inform'd of the sentiments and wishes of the Prince of Wales, applauded in the strongest manner the feelings by which his Royal Highness is actuated, but referr'd nevertheless to the answers which his Majesty had judg'd it necessary to return to similar representations, and which, in obedience to the commands of his Royal Highness, had been laid before his Majesty upon former occasions. (39913–4)

Donington, 28 July 1803

The letter to Mr. Addington is very well written, & puts the question upon true & fair ground. Some indulgence is due to Mr. Addington on the score of the parade which he makes of entering into the Prince's feelings on the subject, because he could not but make that profession in consistency with his former declarations, & in truth (I am persuaded) with his real sentiment. At the same time it would have been more manly in the first instance to have said that the point could not be carried. There is this disadvantage in the Prince's having renewed the application in such strong terms before any actual attempt of the enemy furnished new ground, that his Royal Highness might be thought engaged to some step on the refusal, and what that step should be is very difficult to decide. The remonstrance of the Prince is against the unimportant functions of a Colonel in such a contest as is apprehended: and indeed there does seem nothing fitted to his rank between an essential command & a station which may mark devotion to the country by a temporary rejection of the distinctions due to his birth. If not suffered to hold that pre-eminence in the field which naturally appertains to the Prince of Wales, I should rejoice to see him in the ranks as a volunteer with that corps of gentry which might be first opposed to the invader. Perhaps an intimation quietly & temperately given that his Royal Highness has such a procedure in contemplation may make others reflect better on their conduct toward him, for they will be little inclined to risk the construction which would follow his being forced to take the step; still less would they relish the popularity likely to attach to him upon it. As for me, I should be at his side; & so many others would be actuated by the same ardor of accompanying him that the onset of that squadron would not be the least formidable which the enemy would have to encounter. There would, in this hazarded stake of his person to set example to the valor of his countrymen, be a proud contrast with the cold policy which has so ruinously prevailed in other instances: and the general clamor of the country would avenge him of the slight attempted to be put upon him. The notion is worth considering: therefore submit it to the Prince with the assurance of my most affectionate & unceasing devotion. (39917–20)

1725 THE PRINCE OF WALES TO HENRY ADDINGTON, AND THE REPLY

Carlton House, 28 July 1803

The Prince of Wales has receiv'd Mr. Addington's written communication of the last night. The Prince of Wales has only to observe that he requires Mr. Addington to submit to his Majesty his last note dated the 26th of this month. (39915)

ADDINGTON'S REPLY

Downing Street, 11.30 p.m., 28 July 1803

Mr. Addington is just honour'd with the commands of the Prince of Wales, and will not fail to lay his Royal Highness letter, dated the 26th of this month, before the King. (39916)

1726   HENRY ADDINGTON TO THE KING, AND THE REPLY[1]

[Downing Street, 11.30 p.m., 29 July 1803]

Mr. Addington humbly transmits to your Majesty two letters with which he has been honor'd by his Royal Highness the Prince of Wales. (10967)

THE KING'S REPLY

Windsor, 30 July 1803

The King has just received Mr. Addington's note enclosing the two letters from the Prince of Wales. His Majesty could but chooses not to comment on the hint of the former, but authoriz[e]s Mr. Addington to communicate to the Prince of Wales he having laid before the King [*sic*] who had referred Mr. Addington to the orders he had before given him, with the addition that the King's opinion being fixed, he desired no further mention should be made to him on this subject (Sidmouth MSS.).

1727   HENRY ADDINGTON TO THE PRINCE OF WALES

Downing Street, 1 Aug. 1803

In obedience to the commands of your Royal Highness, I laid before his Majesty the letter dated the 26th of July with which your Royal Highness had honor'd me; and I have it in command from his Majesty to acquaint your Royal Highness that 'The King had referr'd Mr. Addington to the orders he had before given him, with the addition

1. This letter, and the King's reply, were not, of course, included in the published correspondence.

that the King's opinion being fixed, he desired that no further mention should be made to him upon the subject'. (39921)

1728   THE PRINCE OF WALES TO THE KING, AND THE REPLY

Brighthelmstone, 6 Aug. 1803

A correspondence has taken place between Mr. Addington & myself on a subject which deeply involves my honor & character; the answers which I have receiv'd from that gentleman, the communication which he has made to the House of Commons, leave me no hope but in an appeal to the justice of your Majesty. I make that appeal with confidence because I feel that you are my natural advocate & with the sanguine hope that the ears of an affectionate father may still be open'd to the supplications of a dutiful son.

I ask to be allowed to display the best energies of my character, to shed the last drop of my blood in support of your Majesty's person, crown & dignity. For this is not a war for empire, glory or dominion, but for existence. In this contest the humblest & lowest of your Majesty's subjects have been call'd on. It would therefore little become me who am the first & who stand at the very footstool of the Throne to remain a tame, an idle, a lifeless spectator of the mischiefs which threaten us, unconscious of the dangers which surround, & indifferent to the consequences which may follow. Hanover is lost, England is menaced with invasion, Ireland is in rebellion, Europe is at the foot of France: at such a moment the Prince of Wales, yielding to none of your servants in zeal or devotion, to none of your subjects in duty, to none of your children in tenderness & affection, presumes to approach you and again to repeat those offers which he has already made through your Majesty's Ministers. A feeling of honest ambition, a sense of what I owe to myself & to my family, & above all, the fear of sinking in the estimation of that gallant Army which may be the support of your Majesty's crown & my best hope hereafter, command me to persevere & to assure your Majesty with all humility and respect, that, conscious of the justice of my claim, no human power can ever induce me to relinquish it.

Allow me to say, Sir, that I am bound to adopt this line of conduct by every motive dear to me as a man & sacred to me as a Prince. Ought I not to come forward in a moment of unexampled difficulty & danger? Ought I not to share in the glory of victory when I have everything to lose by defeat? The highest places in your Majesty's service are filled by the younger branches of the Royal Family: to me alone no place is assigned. I am not thought worthy to be even the junior Major-General of your Army. If I could submit in silent submission to such indignities I should indeed deserve such treatment & prove to the satisfaction of *your enemies & my own* that I am entirely incapable of those exertions which my birth & the circumstances of the times peculiarly call for. Standing so near the Throne where I am debased, the cause of royalty is wounded. I cannot sink in the public opinion without the participation of your Majesty in my degradation: therefore every motive of private feeling and of public duty induce me to *implore* your Majesty to review your decision, & to place me in that situation which my birth, the duties of my station, the example of my predecessors & the expectations of the people of England entitle me to claim.

Should I be disappointed in the hope which I have form'd; should this last appeal to the justice of my Sovereign and the affection of my father fail of success, I shall lament in silent submission his determination, but Europe, the world & posterity must judge between us.

I have done my duty. My conscience acquits me. My reason tells me that I was perfectly justified in the request which I have made, because no reasonable arguments have ever been adduced in answer to my pretensions. The precedents in our history are in my favour, but if they were not, the times in which we live, & especially the exigencies of the present moment, require us to become an example to our posterity.

No other cause of refusal has or can be assigned, except that *it was the will* of your Majesty. To that will & pleasure I bow with every degree of humility & resignation, but I can never cease to complain of the severity which has been exercised against me & of the injustice which I have suffered, till I cease to exist. (42365–8)

THE KING'S REPLY

Windsor, 7 Aug. 1803

Though I applaud your zeal and spirit, of which I trust no one can suppose any of my family wanting, yet considering the repeated declarations I have made of my determination on your former applications to the same purpose, I had flattered myself to have heard no further on the subject. Should the implacable enemy so far succeed as to land, you will have an opportunity of shewing your zeal at the head of your Regiment. It will be the duty of every man to stand forward on such an occasion, and I shall certainly think it mine to set the example in defence of everything that is dear to me and to my people. (39922)

Welbeck Street, Sunday, 7 Aug. 1803

I have receiv'd your letter of the fifth of August, in which you express the regret his Royal Highness feels at not finding me at my station, when he visited my Brigade on the second instant; on my part, I am to express much concern that you never communicated to me the intention of his Royal Highness the Commander-in-Chief. Had he, through you, intimated any wish that I shou'd be present, I shou'd (postponing every other business and sacrificing every other duty) have seiz'd with the utmost satisfaction such an opportunity of paying my personal respects to his Royal Highness, to whom, I trust, I never have been deficient in that obedience which I owe to him as an officer, and in that deference & respect which are due to him as the son of my Sovereign. But, Sir, I have also other duties to perform, and those of a most important kind. As a Peer of the realm I claim it as my undoubted privilege to attend the proceedings of Parliament, and that privilege I never will relinquish, as long as I continue on the Home Staff, except in cases of the utmost emergency. When his Royal Highness, without any solicitation on my part, impos'd the command of a Brigade upon me I accepted it as a duty and not as a favor; I then address'd a long letter to his Royal Highness in which I enforc'd my claims to a more extensive command, specifically stating that nothing wou'd have induc'd me to accept a situation so inferior to that which I had once fill'd, but gratitude to the King and a sense of the dangers which threaten the people of England; but I do not recollect that I ever pledg'd myself to be present at any particular hour or in any particular week. That I meant to take upon me the command is evident, because a house has been hir'd for me at Hastings, and my servants are there. The urgency of public affairs can well account for my absence hitherto. It was but the last week that Bills of the utmost importance to that country in which I was born, & in which my family have a deep interest, pass'd through Parliament. During the whole of this week the House of Commons has been occupied in discussing military points of the greatest importance. I wish'd much to be present at their debates, because it is my duty to form an opinion on such subjects. There is even, at this moment, a notice given in the House of Lords by a noble Peer, that he means to bring forward the same questions that were agitated in the House of Commons on the second instant.[1] I certainly thought, and do still think, that I have been engag'd in pursuits much more material to the public, than the command of a Brigade mostly dispos'd of in two barracks, under the orders of two experienc'd Colonels, with another

1. On 2 August Lieutenant-Colonel Robert Craufurd, M.P. for East Retford, 1802-6, initiated a debate on the defence of the country (*Parliamentary History*, xxxvi. 1680-92). The debate is poorly reported because a Member moved the Standing Order for the exclusion of strangers and the Gallery was shut.

General Officer at the distance of a few miles. Without any responsibility, and, from peculiar circumstances, almost without a command, I did not suppose that I was plac'd there for the purpose of drilling a Brigade, for which pursuit the habits of my life and the dispositions of my mind but little qualify me. I am perfectly willing, however, to bring any knowledge and experience I may possess, to the public service, and I lament that it shou'd have been deem'd expedient to remind me of 'the necessity of every Officer in his Majesty's service, giving the strictest attention to his military duty'. I can without vanity say that I have never yet been deficient in my duty or show'd an example unworthy of imitation. I was a volunteer for two campaigns on the Continent; I was wounded at the head of my Brigade in Holland; I commanded the Army in Egypt; I think, at least, such conduct might have exempted me from animadversion. I shall immediately repair to take the command at Hastings, where I shall remain 'till the proceedings of Parliament may again require my attendance, unless the danger of invasion shall be eminent, and in that case, no man will be more unwilling to quit his post than he who has the honor [etc.]. (39923–4)

1730   THE DUKE OF NORTHUMBERLAND TO COLONEL MCMAHON

Alnwick Castle, 10 Aug. 1803

Many thanks for your letter with its contents. I sincerely wish our Royal master had taken the step at first: I have always advised him to do. It woud have saved him a deal of trouble, & you see he is forced to it at last, & now it does not come with the same grace as at first.

We got down here on Friday to dinner, & our reception was of the most flattering nature. I wish Ministers had been present. It woud have been a lesson to convince them how very unavailing all their efforts have been to ruin my interest & influence in this county, notwithstanding I have been absent for seven years & they have moved heaven & earth to overset that influence.[1]

Lord Percy has been very successfull with his Corps of tenantry, nearly 1500 of the tenants having instantly enrolled themselves to serve under him. This is a proud situation for a young man just entering into life, & with the enthusiastic attachment & joy they showed on my return

1. Lord Holland wrote: 'The Duke of Northumberland, who was now utterly disabled by the gout, and who at the commencement of the war had served in a very fatiguing campaign as a volunteer in the Pyrenees, was, on the pretence of the invasion called upon to join his militia or resign the command of it, as if the rank and name of a colonel of militia was not of greater importance than his presence and activity' (*Memoirs of the Whig Party*, i.130). He felt obliged to resign his office of Lord Lieutenant of Northumberland in 1798.

amongst them will tend to make him feel his future weight & consequence in this kingdom.

We are here in a terrible state for defence, Sr. H. Dalrymple[1] having only one weak & incomplete battalion of Militia & 3 troops of Dragoons within this county for its defence. It is a shame. They trust I fancy to the Volunteer Corps, & yet by their conduct to them, & the frequent changes they make in the terms they offer them, & the difficulties they fling in their way, they do everything to disgust them.

Adieu my dear Col. When do you set off for Cheltenham? (39925)

1731 THE DUKE OF KENT TO THE PRINCE OF WALES

Castle Hill Lodge, Wednesday evening, 10 Aug. [*1803*][2]

It is with infinite regret I find myself deprived of the pleasure I had looked forward to with so much joy, *that* of passing tomorrow and your birthday at Brighton: but the determination of his Majesty to go to the House on Friday, on which occasion I understand it is considered an indispensable duty on our part to attend him, renders the thing altogether impracticable. I have heard that the Duke of York and Adolphus intend rattling down after the attendance on the King is over, but as their object is to see the troops out the ensuing morning, and in my present situation, je n'ambitionne pas de briller en militaire a pareille fête sous les auspices du chef actuel. I know you will approve of my *not* doing the same, *but* notwithstanding that I shall not have the happiness of giving you joy *in person* on the 12th of that happy day, I trust you will do me the justice to believe that of the whole family *none* will *wish* you every blessing and comfort this world can afford, and very many returns of the day *each* happier than the preceding, with more warmth and sincerity *than myself*, whose firm profession through life will ever be that of the most faithful and devoted attachment to you. I was commissioned jointly by Mary and Amelia to give you a small snuff box as a token of their love and affection, and to say they knew you would take the *will* for the deed, but

1. Sir Hew Whitefoord Dalrymple (1750–1830). Lieutenant, 1766; Major, 1777; Colonel, 1790; Major-General, 1794; Lieutenant-General, 1801; General, 1812; created Baronet, December 1814. Signed the Convention of Cintra, 1808.

2. The letter is endorsed 1804, but this is impossible. 10 August 1803, not 1804, was a Wednesday. The King delivered the Speech from the Throne at the close of the Session on Friday, 12 August 1803 (in 1804 Parliament was not sitting at that time). There was a Grand Review of troops in the presence of the Duke of York on Saturday, 13 August 1803 on Newmarket Hill, four miles N.E. of Brighton.

Princess Amelia sent birthday greetings to the Prince on the 8th. (Add. Georgian 14/42)

I shall now transfer the commission to Adolphus. Allow me to offer my kindest remembrances to Mrs. Fitzherbert and believe me [etc.].

Madame de St. Laurent desires me to express *her* best wishes also, and to offer her kindest compliments upon the 12th. (46230–1)

1732 THE DUKE OF YORK TO THE PRINCE OF WALES

Horse Guards, 10 Aug. 1803

I had fully intended to have arrived time enough at Brighthelmstone tomorrow to have had the pleasure of dining with you, but it having been determined today that the Parliament is to be prorogued tomorrow, I cannot avoid attending his Majesty at the House. I shall, however, lose no time as soon as that ceremony is over in setting out for Brighton and hope to be with you before you are up from dinner.

Inclos'd I send you a letter from the Duchess. (44184)

1733 COLONEL GEORGE THOMAS TO THE EARL OF EGREMONT

Dale Park,[1] 11 Aug. 1803

Presuming your Lordship to be at Brighton and in the daily habit of communicating with his Royal Highness the Prince of Wales, I beg leave to address you the enclosed plans for *a Corps of Honor*, requesting you (should it meet with your approbation) to submit it to the consideration of his Royal Highness. I should wish our county to take the lead in such a business and to have at least a squadron composed of Sussex men, if possible. Should his Royal Highness decline the proposal I trust he will forgive the liberty I take in suggesting the measure. I beg he will be assured I am actuated by no other motives than a sincere attachment to his Royal Highness's person and family and a zealous wish to defend to *my last shilling and last drop of blood* our country and our Constitution. In the *situation* in which the *Commander-in-Chief has thought proper to place me*, whatever may be my inclination to exert myself for the public service, the common feelings of honor and a gentleman forbid me to aspire at *any commission*, but if you will do me the honor to recommend me to his Royal Highness my personal services *as a private* are at his disposal. (39926)

1. Near Arundel, Sussex.

Proposals most respectfully submitted to the consideration of his Royal
Highness the Prince of Wales, &c., &c., &c., thro' the medium of the
Earl of Egremont *for establishing a volunteer Guard of Honor* for the
safety and defence of his Royal Highness's person during the war, by his
Royal Highness's most devoted, most faithful and obedient humble
servant, George Thomas.

A Corps of noblemen and gentlemen to be form'd immediately for the
above purpose, on the following plan:

1 Colonel	⎫	To be named by his Royal Highness; to be
2 Lt.-Colonels		composed of noblemen and gentlemen not
2 Majors		being professionally military.
6 Captains	⎬	
12 Lieutenants		N.B. Without any pay, emolument or allow-
12 Cornets	⎭	ance whatever.

35 Total officers volunteers

2 Adjutants	⎫	Officers of merit selected by his R. Highness
6 Quarter Masters	⎬	from the half pay and to receive full pay and
8 Total	⎭	all emoluments and allowances.

Six troops, comprehending:

    12 Sergeants

    12 Corporals

  180 Privates at 30 pr. troop—Total *204.*

These, as above stated, to be composed of noblemen and gentlemen
recommended by the Field Officers and Captain and to be approved by
his Royal Highness.

N.B. A band will of course be establish'd from which six trumpeters
may be taken.

Conditions

To volunteer their services *as a Guard of Honor* to his Royal Highness
during the war without pay or any emolument whatever.

His Royal Highness to appoint all the Commissioned officers and to
approve all the non-commissioned officers and privates, they being
recommended by the Field Officers and Captains.

His Royal Highness to order the uniform and to fix the colour of the
horses for *each* troop, fixing also their height, that the whole may be
uniform and exact.

The uniforms, horses, accoutrements and arms to be found by each
individual according to his Royal Highness's wish and command.

In case of invasion the whole to assemble round his Royal Highness's
person at any spot fixed upon by his Royal Highness.

Their services to be unlimited *within* the Kingdom.

During the war one troop to be always on duty on his Royal Highness's person *month and month about*, wheresoever his Royal Highness shall think proper to reside and command their attendance.

The whole to assemble during the month of May in order to be train'd and exercised.

No forrage to be allow'd by Government except to Adjts. & Q. Masters. Each officer and private to keep his own horse and to have his groom well mounted, to attend, wearing whatever livery his Royal Highness shall command and a broad sword. The grooms to be form'd into a Corps. (39927–8)

1734 PRINCESS AUGUSTA TO THE PRINCE OF WALES

12 Aug. 1803

I fear, my ever dearest brother, that I shall not have the happiness of seeing you today to offer you my warmest and most heartfelt congratulations upon it. Be assured, my dearest G.P., that present or not present no one is more tenderly attached to you than I am.

I am delighted in acquainting you that our dear Amelia is better. She goes out morning and evening in the open carriage, which is of great use to her and her spirits are a great deal better.

I am going to send this to town to beg Adolphus to carry it to you. God bless you.[1] (Add. Georgian 10/33)

1735 CHARLES JAMES FOX TO THE PRINCE OF WALES

St. Anne's Hill, 18 Aug. 1803

I have the honour to return to your Royal Highness with many thanks the papers which you were so good as to leave with me. It appears to me that though Dumouriez's plans are rather upon too extensive a scale for our present means, a partial application of them might be very adviseable. Your Royal Highness has not I am sure failed to observe that with respect to offensive operations, he considers continental alliance as the first necessary preliminary. With regard to the possibility there may be of forming such alliance your Royal Highness is far better informed than I can pretend to be, but I confess I have little hopes upon that point unless some previous attempt were made towards peace, and in any case I suspect the character of the present Ministers is so low that every foreign Power would be very loth to engage with *them*. Your Royal Highness's

1. There are birthday letters from the Queen (36535), Princess Sophia (Add. Georgian 13/18), Princess Mary (Add. Georgian 12/26) and Princess Elizabeth (Add. Georgian 11/93).

account of their conduct in respect to Hanover strengthens me very much in this opinion.

I cannot express sufficiently my gratitude for your Royal Highness's condescending visit, and for the kind manner in which you opened yourself to me upon the important subjects which were brought into conversation. With regard to the business most personally relating to yourself, I mean your offer and the rejection of it, whether or not it ought to be brought forward in Parliament appears to me to be a question upon which your Royal Highness can take no counsel so good as your own, and whatever therefore your determination may be, I shall implicitly obey your commands without presuming to interpose my advice. But if your Royal Highness should determine that it *shall* be brought forward, I think there can be no doubt but it should be done with all the strength both of numbers and authority that can be had, and that no terms should be kept, in the manner of doing it, with the Ministers. The refusal should be considered distinctly as *their* act. With a view to strength, I would recommend (not *now* but a week or two before the meeting of Parliament) that the affair should be stated to Ld. Grenville, the M[arqu]is of Buckingham, Windham, aye and even to Pitt, to know their sentiments upon the matter. This might be done in as cold and formal manner as may be thought fit, more or less so probably according to what one may learn of the respective dispositions of the persons to be applied to. There need be no party appearance, still less anything like solicitation in the communication. The persons applied to should be considered merely as weighty Members of Parliament whom your Royal Highness wishes to apprize of the intended proceedings of your friends upon a point in which you are so much concerned. I have not mentioned Thurlow, Fitzwilliam, Spencer, Carnarvon, Carlisle & others, because I conclude there will be opportunities before the time I mention of consulting with them either personally or through common friends. I will, if necessary, speak to Grey, Whitbread,[1] the Dukes of Bedford,[2] Northumberland and others. Though I do not think very highly of Canning as a speaker, yet from his talents, and still more from the influence he seems to have upon his acquaintance, he is of some consequence in such a business, but I do not think (though I may be mistaken) that he or even Morpeth[3] or Lord Granville would give a decisive answer before they

1. Samuel Whitbread (1764?–1815), M.P. for Bedford, 1790–1815, Grey's brother-in-law and a Foxite Whig. His father founded the brewery business.

2. John, 6th Duke of Bedford (1766–1839), succeeded his brother, 2 March 1802. M.P. for Tavistock, 1788–90 and 1790–1802. Lord Lieutenant of Ireland, 1806–7.

3. George, 6th Earl of Carlisle (1773–1848), succeeded his father, 4 September 1825. Styled Viscount Morpeth until 1825. M.P. for Morpeth, 1795–1806; for Cumberland, 1806–20. First Commissioner of Woods and Forests, May–July 1827; Lord Privy Seal, July 1827–January 1828, and June–July 1834; Cabinet Minister without portfolio, November 1830–June 1834.

know that Pitt has been applied to. When he *has* been applied to, I think that even if he should refuse they will think themselves at liberty to come forward in your support. Your Royal Highness will of course expect to receive great support from your friends in Ireland especially if the notice to them is early enough to enable them to come without great inconvenience. I have reason to think that not only the Ponsonbys, the D. of Leinster & their friends, but even Mr. Foster[1] would come upon any question in which your Royal Highness conceives yourself to be materially interested. I am afraid your Royal Highness will think me very tedious upon this subject, but if the thing is to be undertaken I am extremely anxious it should be done with every advantage. Whether it should be undertaken at all, I repeat, is a question for your Royal Highness's sole determination.

The concern which your Royal Highness seems to feel upon the affairs of Hanover and of Ireland does you great honour. With respect to the former it appears to be very doubtful whether anything can be usefully done in Parliament. With regard to Ireland, it is a different question, and I think both for your reputation and your interest it behoves your Royal Highness to turn your most serious thoughts to the state of that country with a view to forming some system to be recommended in Parliament and countenanced by your Royal Highness's approbation. I have no doubt but, if you will apply your mind to the subject, your good sense as well as your humanity will incline you to the system of conciliation & equal participation between Catholicks & Protestants of all the advantages of our Constitution and even of the honours & emoluments belonging to the Administration of it in its different parts. I feel myself certain that this is the system which Ld. Thurlow, Ld. Moira & Ld. Hutchinson would recommend, and I name them because I conceive them to be persons in whom your Royal Highness has a just and well grounded confidence. I would not conceal from your Royal Highness that there are some very good & very respectable friends of your Royal Highness whose opinions may lean another way, particularly for instance Mr. Foster and Lord Roden[2] whom you mentioned on Tuesday. What I would recommend therefore is that when you shall have formed your opinion you should declare it unequivocally (in private I mean of course) and the question of Catholick Emancipation may make as good a test as any other to discriminate those who are willing or otherwise to adhere to

1. John Foster, 1st Baron Oriel (1740–1828), M.P. for Dunleer [I.] 1761–8; for Co. Louth [I.], 1768–1800, and [U.K.], 1801–21; Irish Chancellor of the Exchequer, 1784–5; Speaker of Irish House of Commons, 1785–1800; Irish Chancellor of the Exchequer, 1804–6 and 1807–1811; a Lord of the Treasury [U.K.], 1807–11. Peerage, 17 July 1821 [U.K.].

2. Robert, 2nd Earl of Roden [I.] (1756–1820). Styled Viscount Jocelyn, 1771–97. M.P. for Maryborough [I.], 1776–8; for Dundalk [I.], 1783–97; succeeded his father, 21 June 1797; Irish Representative Peer, 1801–20.

your Royal Highness's Irish politicks. Affairs are so much altered since Mr. Foster and his friends considered that question, that I should not be without hope that he would acquiesce in your Royal Highness's opinion if it should be favourable to the measure, but if not, it is right at all events that your opinion should be known. There is another important question relative to Ireland upon which I can give your Royal Highness no opinion because I confess I have not yet heard enough to make up my own. The question I mean is *whether or not the Union should be dissolved*. I lean to the negative but would advise your Royal Highness to consult Ld. Moira, Ld. Hutchinson, Mr. Foster and George Ponsonby. To the latter as well as to Grattan I will myself apply upon the whole of the subject. I consider this as a new era in your Royal Highness's life in which the importance of the crisis has led you to pay more attention than you did formerly to political affairs, and that Ireland, as it is the most endangered part of the Empire, is that on which you most employ your thoughts. I understand that if it were necessary you would yourself condescend to take the Government of it, and I am convinced that your doing so would afford far the best chance of any good being done there. Now tho' a motion for that purpose in Parliament might be objectionable, yet by proposing measures which might be known to make a part of your Royal Highness's system, one might direct the publick consideration to that object (I mean that of your personal Government of Ireland) and, though unsuccessful for the present, open hopes to the dissatisfied people in that country from a new reign which might in some degree divert them from their connections with France.

I owe you, Sir, a thousand apologies for this very tedious and perhaps in some parts unintelligible prose, but the importance of the subjects and my attachment to your Royal Highness must plead my excuse. I will only trouble you with one word more of general advice. If you do come forward at all, let it be with all the dignity & authority which belongs to your character & to your situation. Let it be thoroughly understood that you are in earnest, and that with respect both to men and measures you are taking a part, not for the present only but with a view to the future.

P.S. As I have taken the liberty of writing so very unreservedly I trust your Royal Highness will consider this letter as confidential, but on the other hand I have no objection if your Royal Highness thinks it convenient to its being shewn to any person in whom your Royal Highness has a real confidence, such as Thurlow, Moira &c.[1] (39931–6)

1. Cp. Fox's letter of the same date to Grey (Russell, *Memorials and Correspondence of Fox*, ii.423). Fox wrote to Grey on 21 August: 'I hear that on the very day I was writing my long letter to the Prince, he and Sheridan were getting drunk *tête à tête*, and, that the latter boasts that he had convinced his Royal Highness that all he had done was right. It is not the *boast*, which may be all false, but the dining *tête à tête*, in the present circumstances, which makes an impression upon me' (ibid., iii.427).

1736   FELIX MCCARTHY TO COLONEL MCMAHON[1] [copy]

Cleveland Court, Saturday [*endorsed 20 Aug. 1803*]

In taking the liberty of requesting that you would be so kind as to ascertain either thro' Mr. Tierney or others in the secret whether the Russian Fleet is to act with us, and in making this request in Lord Moira's name I know I but anticipate his own intention. You are, I am sure, Sir, persuaded that I would not presume to do so without being *fully warranted*.

The fact is that some of his *best friends* in the City, such as Rowcroft and Hornyold, have been *cut to the quick* by the DOCTOR'S[2] fallacious statement last winter and that their wounds are not yet healed, which operates *very injuriously* in certain arrangements. This is a crisis which may enable them to recover those losses, for if Russia should be with us it will necessarily excite great confidence. I am well aware of the delicacy belonging to this subject which [I] will thank you to apprize his Lordship of. (39937)

1737   THE MARQUESS OF LANSDOWN[3] TO [?] CAPTAIN CHARLES PALMER[4]

Bowood Park, 23 Aug. 1803

Dear Palmer, I should be proud and happy to execute any commands of the Prince however convey'd, but I must submit that I have very great doubts of the propriety of committing my own name in the present moment, much more that of his Royal Highness, without which there would not be the smallest possible hope of success. Besides all this I find that neither release nor exchange remains with the Minister of the Foreign Department, but with the Minister of War, of whom I have not the slightest knowledge nor of any of his connections. But the matter shall not be off my mind, and if any means shall unexpectedly offer of carrying the Prince's wishes into execution, I will not fail to avail myself of them, or at any rate to submit what may occurr to me upon the subject. (39938)

1. The letter is unsigned; the writer's name is learnt from the endorsement.

2. Addington's.

3. Unlike his successors, he spelt his name without a final *e*.

4. Charles Palmer (1777–1851), son of John Palmer, the theatre proprietor who reorganized the mail-coach service. M.P. for Bath, 1808–26 and 1830–7. Major, 10th Light Dragoons, 1805; Lieutenant-Colonel 1810; Colonel, 1814. Later, A.D.C. to the Prince Regent.

London, 26 Aug. 1803

I have made a fresh copy from the opinion given to the case that was formerly submitted to Messrs. Mansfield & Co., which I have now the honor to enclose your Royal Highness, because it is not within my recollection that it was ever laid before the King or even regularly submitted to the Minister at that time.[1] An observation which fell from Tierney when I shew'd him this opinion, 'Has the King seen it?' has suggested to my mind, after bestowing all my thoughts on the subject, that in the event of Y.R.Hss. making your determination to write another letter to his Majesty, this opinion would either prove a powerful ingredient in such a letter or constitute new & good ground for a fresh one to Mr. Addington. I hint this merely with a view to keeping the business alive during the recess, & this at all events must be done by every possible means. At the same time this correspondence stands on such perfect & unshakeable ground towards Y.R.Hss. at the present moment that it certainly requires mature consideration whether another step may tend to strengthen or weaken it, and I own the more my doubt arises on this question when I recollect that Y.R.Hss. in your letter to the King uses these words, 'Should this *last* appeal to the justice of my Sovereign & the affection of my father', but presuming that Lord Hutchinson is with Y.R.Hss., I barely throw out the idea for his judgement.

Still not one word of news.

[*P.S.*] The letter yesterday in the *M*[*orning*] *C*[*hronicle*] was extraordinary well done, & has had an extreme good effect. So has Lord Moira's speech at Leicester. (39939–40)

1739 THE PRINCE OF WALES TO THE KING [draft]

Brighton, 27²Aug. 1803

I have delay'd thus long an answer to the letter which your Majesty did me the honor to write from a wish to refer to a former correspondence which took place between us in the year 1798.[3] Those letters were mislaid & some days elaps'd before I could discover them. They have since been found. Allow me then, Sir, to recall to your recollection the expressions you were graciously pleased to use, & which I once before took

1. The letter is endorsed, 'Opinion of Counsel as to whether H.R.H. is competent to hold certain rank in the Army'.

2. Dated the 23rd in one of the copies in the Archives (39906), and one printed copy is dated the 22nd.

3. Nos. 1347, 1353, 1357–8, 1361 (iii.427, 431, 435, 438).

the liberty of reminding you of, when I sollicited foreign service upon my first coming into the Army. They were, Sir, that your Majesty, upon my solliciting foreign service did not then see the opportunity for it at that moment but that if anything was to arrise at home I might be first & foremost. There cannot be a stronger expression in the English language or one more consonant to the feelings which animate my heart. In this I agree perfectly with your Majesty; I ought to be *first* & *foremost*. It is the place which my birth assigns me, which Europe, which the English nation, expect me to fill, and which the former assurances of your Majesty might naturally have led me to hope I should occupy. After such a declaration I could hardly expect to be told that my place was at the head of a Regiment of Dragoons.

I understand from your Majesty that it is your intention, Sir, in pursuance of that noble example which you have ever shewn during the course of your reign to place yourself at the head of the people of England. My next brother, the D. of York, commands the Army; the younger branches of my family are either Generals or Lieut.-Generals, and I, who am Prince of Wales, am to remain Colonel of Dragoons. There is something so humiliating in the contrast that those who are at a distance would either doubt the reality or suppose that to be my fault which is only my misfortune. Who could imagine that I, who am the oldest Colonel in the Service, had ask'd for the rank of a General Officer in the Army of the King, my father, & that it had been refused me? I am sorry, much more than sorry, to be obliged to break in upon your leisure & to trespass thus a second time on the attention of your Majesty, but I have, Sir, an interest in my character more valuable to me than the throne, and dearer, far dearer, to me than life. I am call'd upon by that interest to persevere, and I pledge myself never to desist till I receive that satisfaction which the justice of my claim leads me to expect. In these unhappy times the world, Sir, examines the conduct of Princes with a jealous, a scrutinizing, a malignant eye. No man is more aware than I am of the existence of such a disposition, and no man is therefore more determined to place himself above all suspicion. In desiring to be placed in a forward situation I have perform'd one duty to the people of England; I just now perform another & humbly supplicate your Majesty to assign those reasons which have induced you to refuse a request which appears to me, & to the world, so reasonable & so rational.

I must again repeat my concern that I am obliged to continue a correspondence which I fear is not so grateful to your Majesty as I could wish. I have examined my own heart, I am convinced of the justice of my cause, of the purity of my motives. Reason & honor forbid me to yield. Where no reason is alleged I am justified in the conclusion that none can be given.

In this candid exposition of the feelings which have agitated &

depress'd my wounded mind I hope no expression has escaped me which can be construed to mean the slightest disrespect to your Majesty. I most solemnly disavow any such intention, but the circumstances of the times, the danger of invasion, the appeal which has been made to all your subjects oblige me to recollect what I owe to my own honor & my own character, and to state to your Majesty with plainness, truth & candour but with all the submission of a subject & the duty of an affectionate son, the injuries under which I labour, which it is in the power of your Majesty alone at one moment to redress. It is with the sentiments of the profoundest veneration & respect that I have the honour [etc.]. (39944–6 and 42371–2)

1740 THE DUKE OF NORTHUMBERLAND TO [?] COLONEL MCMAHON

Alnwick Castle, 31 Aug. 1803

Altho' it is long since I received your letter of the 17th I am certain you will excuse my not acknowledging the receipt of it sooner, when I relate to you the melancholy cause of my silence. My youngest daughter, Frances, a charming girl of twelve years old, was taken ill three days after our arrival here, & having suffered for fourteen days under a most violent illness, expired on Saturday last.

I am much obliged to you for the papers (marked 8 & 9) & lament extremely things having taken this turn. How much better woud it have been to have applied in the first instance, where I have always advised the first application to be made. The answer woud have been given, & tho' an unpleasant one, a tedious correspondence which only serves to irritate both parties woud have been avoided. I confess I am much surprized at the K.'s answer. For the P. to have an opportunity afforded him of distinguishing himself at the head of his Regiment (perhaps under the command of his younger brothers) was not what I shoud have expected to have come from that quarter. I own I expected a refusal; but more in caracter. As it is, H.R.H. can do nothing but submit in silence to the orders he has received; any further steps in the present temper of things woud not only be unbecoming his dignity, but I fear unavailing. The answer must have been given in a moment of irritation & displeasure, which if kept up, can only tend to the worst of consequences, but if left alone must die away of itself, & I have no doubt but things will come right of themselves, if time is left for proper reflection. At all events, perfect silence & moderation is the only adviseable line to be pursued at this moment. At least this is my opinion, which I fear, however, will not be followed. The word *command* which H.R.H. asks for, is what it is very easy for him to obtain without mentioning it; & I fear it is this word that

409

causes an alarm, which is the foundation of the refusal that is given H.R.H. It is now too late to repeat what I remember saying to you, that my advice was to have seen the K., & to have said that as H.M. woud possibly himself put himself at the head of his regular troops, with the De. of York under him as Commander-in-Chief, the P. intreated permission under H.M. to place himself at the head of the Yeomanry, Volunteers, & other armed force of the country, & to endeavour to rally them round the Royal Standard in support of his Majesty, without interfering with those to whom H.M. thought proper to confide his regular forces.

As I am ignorant where you are at present, I shall direct this to Carlton House. When you see, or write to the P. pray do not forget to present my duty, & assure him of my attachment.

Depend upon it, the less *the particulars* of the correspondence is made publick, the better. If anything is said of it, it shoud be in *general* terms; that the P. offered his services & to take a command, but that it was thought to confine those services solely to the command of his Regiment of Light Dragoons as a simple Colonel.

We are left here in a curious state of defence. In this county, only the Anglesey & Westmoreland Regts. of Militia, with two troops of the 5th Dragoon Guards. The first of these Corps are not above 200 men, & are attached to the artillery, & the Westmoreland are not more than 300. Four thousand volunteers, of which 3800 are without arms, & not a single armed vessel on our coast. In the county of Durham to support these, the Northd. Regt. of Militia, about 900 effective men, with the 2d. Battalion of the Oxs. now raising from the men enrolled for the army of reserve. To this force is trusted the defence of Newcastle—the collieries &c. I forgot indeed to mention that the fortified town of Berwick, which woud serve as a depot in which the enemy might secure his stores &c. & keep up a communication with his own country, is left with a garrison of not more than 30 invalids!!! This is nearly as bad as in 1778 when I commanded [*the rest is missing*]. (39948-9)

1741   COLONEL MCMAHON TO THE PRINCE OF WALES

Private. London, 2 Sept. 1803

Wilson having gone down to Petworth, he will of course acquaint your Royal Highness with regard to everything that relates to the Duke of York & Greenwood; & also that no mention whatever of Y.R.Hss. on the point in question took place in the interview Lord Hutchinson had this morning with the Duke. Notwithstanding what Wilson says Greenwood told him, & notwithstanding the desire I believe Greenwood has to bring the interposition of the Duke into play, I am of opinion he will never touch upon that subject with Hutchinson; neither do I believe, from all I can collect, that the King will, in his present temper, be induced to revoke his cruel & unwise decree. I am given to understand, certainly not. I have myself considerable doubt as to the Duke of York's interference, although I can conceive him to wish the measure success more now than at any other stage of it, for Brownrigg I know fears that he will not venture to attempt it. I think it so much the better that no answer has been made, for while it magnifys your wrongs, it serves distinctly to prove that Y.R.Hss. could not possibly make another effort in that quarter. Thus circumstanced, there seems little to remain to be done until the meeting of Parliament but to keep the subject alive in all directions.

Dumourier dines tomorrow with Lord Moira to meet Lord Hutchinson. No news from France or anywhere else. Poor Astley's[1] Theatre was burn'd down & entirely consumed at 4 o'clock this morning. The mother of young Astley's wife was burn'd to death. (39950)

1742   THE DUKE OF KENT TO THE PRINCE OF WALES

Castle Hill Lodge, Friday, 2 Sept. 1803

I trouble you with these lines to sollicit your acceptance of a Spanish and an Egyptian stallion, which have arrived with the residue of my cavalry from Gibraltar, having been embarked there purposely for you. The Spaniard is of what is termed *la race bleue*, reckoned the best in Andalusia; he has one fault in common with every Spanish horse I have met with, that is, a heavy head, but a beautiful barrel and good limbs, & he is fully equal to your weight, tho' like all the rest of the breed, of low stature. The Egyptian is *but* four year old off [*sic*] and promises to be uncommonly fleet. Lieut.-Colonel Moore[2] of the 23d. Light Dragoons who procured him for me has assured me he is a very valuable and choice breed. I have sent both the horses to Carlton House, and shall feel highly gratified if they can prove at all acceptable to you; I only wish they were more worthy of *him* to whom they are offered, but they are the best it was in my power to procure.

1. Philip Astley (1742–1814), the equestrian performer and theatrical manager. In 1798 he opened Astley's Royal Amphitheatre, London, which had been burnt down in 1794 and which was rebuilt a second time in 1804. It was situated within the triangle formed by Westminster Bridge Road, Felix Street and Stangate Street. Mrs. Astley's mother, Mrs. Woodman (Woodham according to the *Gentleman's Magazine*), was an elderly, infirm lady living in the Astleys' house in front of the Theatre. It was thought she could have been rescued by ladder had she not lingered in the house in the hope of retrieving some valuables.

2. James Moore, Colonel, 1811; Major-General, 1814; Lieutenant-General, 1830 (*d.* 1848)

411

I now, beg to inform you that yesterday morning having received notice from Mr. Yorke[1] that the result of the determination of the Cabinet on my business was that they could not, consistent with their duty, interfere in it at all, I determined upon meeting the Duke of York on it *without* delay, and we had in consequence a very long conversation together at the Horse Guards, which, as you may suppose, was a very painful one to me. However, the result of it, as far as my comprehension goes, was decidedly that he should recommend to the King to sanction the conduct of Sir Thomas Trigge[2] in the suspension and alteration of my code of orders, and consequently be averse to my returning to Gibraltar at all, affirming that my regulations accounted to *his* mind satisfactorily for the causes of the mutiny. He added that he thought the whole business was a very awkward one, expressed his wish to save my feelings in it as much as was practicable without deviating from the opinion he had formed, and concluded by appointing me to meet him again this day week, by *which* time he would see what could be done in it; at the same time he asked me to come over to Oatlands tomorrow, when their Majesties and my sisters had espressed their intention of paying their annual visit to the Dutchess. By this you will perceive my prospects do not improve, and that I am most probably destined to continue under the sufferance of severe mortification. The times, however, I am sensible, command me to submit to the evil with patience for the present, and I only live in hope of better ones to come. Should you *not* have heard it before, I beg leave to inform you that Fox[3] is *certainly* coming back from Ireland, and Lord Cathcart the man on whom the Cabinet have pitched to succeed him. I conclude that every attempt will in consequence be made for me to vacate Gibraltar *for Fox*, who is the person for whom that Government was originally meant in the event of my not having got it when O Harra died.

I have now only to add my kindest regards to Mrs. Fitzherbert, and to assure you of that unalterable friendship and attachment with which [etc.]. (46105-7)

1. Charles Philip Yorke (1764–1834), second son of Charles Yorke (1722–70). M.P. for Cambridgeshire, 1790–1810; for St. Germans, 1810–12; for Liskeard, 1812–18. Secretary at War, February 1801–August 1803; Home Secretary, August 1803–May 1804; Teller of the Exchequer, 1810; First Lord of the Admiralty, May 1810–March 1812.

2. Lieutenant-Colonel, 1778; Colonel, 1782; Major-General, 1793; Lieutenant-General 1798; General, 1803; Lieutenant-General of the Ordnance, November 1804–February 1806, and 1807–10. K.B., 1801; Lieutenant-Governor of Gibraltar, 1796 (later Governor, to 1802) (*d.* 1814).

3. Lieutenant-General Fox had been Commander-in-Chief in Ireland for only a few months (gazetted, 28 May). Lord Cathcart succeeded him, and he was appointed Lieutenant-Governor of Gibraltar in 1804.

1743　THE DUKE OF YORK TO THE PRINCE OF WALES [copy]

Portman Square, 8 Sept. 1803

I have been desired by young Astley, not knowing whether you was in town, to transmit to you the enclosed Memorial, begging your assistance and protection to enable him to rebuild his Theatre which was burnt down last week, by which his poor father and himself are compleatly ruined.[1]

The protection which you have always given to them makes it I am sure perfectly unnecessary for me to press you in their behalf, particularly when any favor you may shew them will really be an act of charity towards two very loyal and industrious persons. I will therefore not take up more of your time, but only beg you to be assured how sincerely I am [etc.]. (44185)

1744　THE DUKE OF KENT TO COLONEL MCMAHON[2]

Carleton House, 4.30 p.m., 9 Sept. 1803

Not having had the good fortune to meet either the Prince or you at home on my return from Mr. Greenwood's, where I was obliged to go upon my own unfortunate business, I adopt this mode of acquainting you for the Prince's information with my having been unable to learn anything whatsoever relative to the effects produced by the Prince's last letter to H.M. Indeed, so completely were my sisters in the dark about it, that when I made my enquiries of them they told me they had themselves intended questioning me whether the letter had been sent at all, as nothing relative even to the receipt of it had in any shape transpired. As to my own affairs they are literally worse then ever, for the Duke of York has intimated his intention of speaking to the K. relative to them tomorrow, and I am apt to believe it will be to obtain his authority to confirm officially the total subversion of my system, as reported by Sir Thomas Trigge. I conceive the determination of my not returning to Gibraltar to be irrevocably fixed, but that there is no intention of employing me otherwise, altho' it is clear from the hints that are dropt that it is the wish I should give up Gibraltar; but you may assure the Prince that nothing short of a positive command from the King will wrest it from me. I am appointed to meet the Duke of York at his office on [*sic*] half-past one on Tuesday and do not propose being in town again 'till that day. It is thought the King, Queen & my older sisters will be at Kew from Wednesday till Friday next, and that a Review will take place

1. 'Young Astley' died seven years after his father.

2. Only signed by the Duke.

413

of the Brigade of Horse Guards under Lord Cathcart on Thursday. Pray assure the Prince of my warmest and most faithful attachment. (46108–10)

1745 THE EARL OF MOIRA TO COLONEL MCMAHON

Margate, 10 Sept. 1803

I received your letter this morning; and I despatch this as a parcel (since there is no post today) that you may not remain in any uneasiness about Vere & Lucadon. Their letter must have been written in the morning. Before two o'clock your check would be taken out of their hands. You have only to write a line to them to say that you had arranged to have the check taken up, which was of course effected before that time.

Can you get anybody to hint to Colonel Sherborne Stewart (of the Life Guards) that the charger which he has sold to me is lame: but not accidentally so, but from defect of long standing which may be palliated for a moment but never cured. My groom told Colonel Stewart's, when he delivered this horse, that it was lame. It continued so; & a very few miles of the journey hither showed the complaint in its full extent. It is the most restive brute imaginable. Neither that, however, or my objection on the score of its figure, make, & insufficiency of strength, would have been urged against what I considered as a bargain concluded. The contract, of course, implied that it was to be a sound horse. It certainly was not so, tho' I have not the remotest conception that Colonel Stewart had a suspicion of the horse's malady. Indeed, I only want the hint to be given to him from the knowledge that he would be anxious to repair the mistake. If you spoke to Ld. Harrington, as if entirely from yourself, ascribing the error to Stewart's groom in his not apprizing his master of the horse's condition, it will probably set matters to right: otherwise I shall never have a ride, even in Rotten Row for my two hundred pounds.

Were the Prince to offer to the Princess to purchase the house at Ramsgate for her, she would probably (by what I hear) decline it. She has never wished it, they say, as a permanency.[1] The attention would tell well. (39951–2)

1. The Princess had been living in a villa at Ramsgate which had belonged to John Hopkins, probably the Hopkins (*c.* 1745–94) who was M.P. for Ilchester, 1784–90, and for Malmesbury, 1790–4.

1746 THE DUKE OF KENT TO THE PRINCE OF WALES[1]

Carlton House, 3 p.m., Tuesday, 13 Sept. 1803

Pursuant to *your* desire I herewith enclose a hasty sketch of my interview this day with the Duke of York, upon which I shall make no comment as the facts speak for themselves. I shall feel highly flattered if my conduct meets with your approbation; at *this* juncture it appeared to me there was a necessity for its being different from what under *other* circumstances it would undoubtedly have been. My heart is quite broke with *all* that has passed, and I am quite *care worn*, in the literal sense of the word, so I trust you will forgive me, if I only add the repetition of those sentiments of unalterable friendship and devoted attachment with which I shall ever *through life* remain [etc.]. (46111)

1747 THE DUKE OF CAMBRIDGE TO THE PRINCE OF WALES

St. James's, 15 Sept. 1803

I am desired by Augustus from whom I heard about a fortnight ago to inform you that he has sent by the Diana frigate, Captain Myling,[2] a pipe of Malaga sherry for you. Not having read in the newspapers the arrival of this ship, I should advise you to have an enquiry made about it at Portsmouth or Plymouth and to give your orders where the wine should be sent to. Since I have had the pleasure of seeing you I have been for five days in Essex where I have seen some very fine brigades. Some of the militia have wonderful fine men and very well drilled for the time. The last fortnight I have spent at Windsor where everybody is well excepting poor Amelia, whose recovery goes on but very slowly indeed. I hope very soon to be able to write you word when I can come to Brighton. Till then God bless you. (48603)

1748 THE PRINCE OF WALES TO THE DUCHESS OF DEVONSHIRE

Brighton, 17 Sept. 1803

Gracious God, ever d[eare]st Dss., what an account I have heard by mere chance, of you today! I am alarm'd & terrified beyond all discription. What has been the matter with you? They tell me that you were suppos'd to be in great danger, & still I knew nothing of it. Let me implore of you to let me have one line from anyone about you; if you are not

1. Only signed by the Duke.

2. Thomas James Maling. Lieutenant, 1797; Commander, 1798; Captain, 1800.

able as yet to write yourself, to say what has been the matter & how you are now, in order to quiet the alarms & apprehensions of my mind. I am confin'd myself by illness to my room, & the hurry of the last week must account to you for my long silence. God bless you, ever dearest Dss. Ever most devotedly yours.

P.S. God grant my next account may be a good one. I shall not rest till I receive it (Chatsworth MSS.).

1749   THE DUKE OF KENT TO CAPTAIN WRIGHT
Castle Hill Lodge, 27 Sept. 1803
Dodd, whom I commissioned to acknowledge every communication, with which I have been favored by you, previous to your letters of the month of August, all of which from the 4th to the 17th I have now before me, will have fully acquainted you, I conclude, with all my proceedings, and have informed you that, if I did not write myself, it was solely because I had nothing pleasant or satisfactory to relate. From his letters you will have learnt that no effort was left by me untried, no exertion unused, to bring my conduct at Gibraltar to an investigation, the result of which could not have failed of being honorable to myself and completely satisfactory to all my friends and wellwishers; but so determined an opposition was made to this by the Commander-in-Chief, *I presume*, that after every pretext was spent that could lead to delay, I was at length informed, on the 9th of *this* month officially, that the Cabinet did not conceive that, consistent with its duty, it could interfere with the business at all, and that the words used by the late Secretary of State for the Home Department, communicating his Majesty's pleasure for my return, were the same always used to Governors or Commanders-in-Chief when it was judged expedient to call them home from their commands from motives of policy, without attaching any censure to their conduct, and consequently without intending to require or allow of an investigation. This compelled me at length to demand an audience of the Duke of York, a measure I never should otherwise have taken, since, when I had previously seen him on the 3rd of June at his Office he had himself shewn the greatest disinclination to enter into a discussion upon the subject in question, by never suffering a word to escape his lips that had any connexion with it. The meeting took place the same day as that communication was made to me which I have just related to you. It lasted two hours, and was, as you may suppose, of a most painful and unpleasant nature, for it gave occasion to a great deal of warmth, which between brothers ought never to be the case. The result of it was briefly this. He condemned my conduct from first to last as marked by cruelty

416

and oppression. To those causes, he said, he ascribed the origin of the mutiny, and intimated his intention of submitting to the King Sir Thomas Trigge's report upon my Code of Orders, and recommending it to his Majesty to authorize him to confirm the alterations which the Lieutenant-Governor had made in many articles, and to cancel those which he had provisionally suspended. A hint followed this, that probably under such circumstances it might not be pleasant for me to return, and that it was supposed I should not like to retain the Government.

To the two first observations I replied naturally as my feelings dictated, and complained of the manifest injustice there was in condemning me *unheard*, but this seemed to have no effect whatever. With respect to the intention he had expressed relative to my orders, I endeavoured to obtain that they should first be submitted to the examination of a Board of General Officers, but he replied that he considered himself perfectly adequate to pass a determination upon them without consulting anyone else. Upon the latter subject of the conversation, vizt., the hints relative to my vacating the Government on account of the unpleasantness that must attend my return to it after the Lieutenant-Governor had obtained tantamount to the annihilation of my Code, I never made any reply whatsoever, for obvious reasons. The conversation concluded by my being informed that I should be again sent for shortly, and that till then I must wait in patience. The next day I saw Mr. Greenwood, with whom I had a long interview, and who appeared perfectly disposed to urge the Duke of York to abandon his intentions with regard to my orders, upon the score of the dangerous example it would be to the service, exclusive of the wound it would inflict on my feelings, and I was led to imagine that, if it was judged expedient, that I should not immediately return to the Garrison. I should either be named to the command of the forces in North Britain, or be sent to Malta as Commander-in-Chief in the Mediterranean, in order to prevent illiberal remarks being made on my non-residence at my Government. But having seen him on a subsequent day, I found that he had in vain pressed these different points, and though the Commander-in-Chief appeared deeply agitated at all he had said to him by my directions, he had gained no ground whatever. A fresh attempt was made by Mr. Greenwood on the 12th, but equally without success, and on the 13th I was summoned to the Horse Guards, when with evident confusion and the greatest awkwardness I ever beheld in any man, the Commander-in-Chief communicated his letter to Sir Thomas Trigge, which exactly corresponded with what he had at our prior meeting intimated to be his intention of conveying to that Officer. *My name*, however, was totally left out in it, and he took much merit to himself for his forbearance. His Majesty's name being made use of in the dispatch, I felt it my duty, having fortunately a perfect command of myself, to state that I should ever bow to *his* commands with humble submission

417

and without remonstrance, but that I must deeply lament that misrepresentation, dictated by malice and *conveyed in the dark*, should have had weight enough upon the Duke of York's mind to induce him to recommend to his Majesty to sanction an act *the most cruel*, the *most unjust* and the *most arbitrary* any Officer had ever experienced. I then with great composure observed to him that however I might feel after what had passed, it was still my wish that he should report to the King my readiness to go out to Gibraltar *whenever he thought proper*, that I was ready for it *at the shortest notice*, and therefore only waited for his commands to that effect. The surprise evinced when I made use of these words is not to be described (for it was fully expected that I should throw up the Government at once). However, as I began to feel rather roused beyond what it might have been prudent to shew, I then withdrew, leaving the Commander-in-Chief, as I have since found by his own confession to one of my sisters, perfectly confounded at the coolness and determination with which I had received his communication to me; and *thus matters stand at this moment between him and me*. I have since seen both Mr. Addington and Mr. Greenwood, and to both I have stated, least my forbearance hitherto should be misconstrued, that were I simply an individual, and to consider only my feelings as an Officer, no earthly tie should induce me to remain any longer in the Service after the infamous injustice I have experienced at the hands of the Officer at the head of it, but as *the King's son*, at a moment of awful crisis like the present, and when it is of the utmost consequence that his Majesty's family should at least *appear* united, that I felt it incumbent upon me to stifle my own feelings and to refrain from an act that might wound him deeply; that the same motive had led me to form the resolution, from which nothing should divert me, of *never resigning the Government of Gibraltar*, but that if the same power that had hitherto been used to oppress me were equally exerted to induce his Majesty to *take* it from me, my feelings could not withstand such an indignity, and this act should be followed by *the instant resignation of every commission I held*, and a publication to the world how I had been used, and of my motives in relinquishing that Service to which I had devoted the best years of my life so fruitlessly to my interest. Whether this will or not make the party that has hitherto so prevailed against me alter from their determination of wresting Gibraltar from me, I cannot at present say, for all has been quiet since then, but the Government of Gibraltar was certainly already promised to General Fox as his reward for having nearly lost Ireland by his supineness. It is possible they may be satisfied after giving Sir Thomas Trigge, the first 20-shilling Government that falls vacant, with appointing Fox Lieutenant-Governor, and sending him out to command and enjoy there, with that commission, the Staff pay of Lieutenant-General, the bât and forage as Commander-in-Chief, and the £3000 a year for his table

418

expences; but after what I have already experienced, I should not be surprised at anything they may do. Were I to write to you volumes I could not make you more completely master of my situation up to this day. If a Spanish war takes place, which, from what unaccountable policy I know not, his Majesty's Ministers seem most anxiously to avoid, I shall again renew my offer of returning to Gibraltar, but I cannot pretend to form any idea how it may be received.

The kindness I receive from the Queen, the Prince, and every member of my family, and all my old military friends, is not to be described, and the personal goodness of the King was never more marked than it has been from the moment of my return, and continues to be, which is as much as a tacit avowal that he laments in his heart the part they make him take. The very Officers of all the Regiments that have returned from Gibraltar are so grateful for the superiority they now feel above every Corps they meet, from the perfect knowledge they have of their duty, that they express themselves everywhere with enthusiasm as to the obligation they conceive themselves to be under to me, and *none more so* than those of the *Welch Fusileers*. In short, if you except the circles about the Horse Guards and those immediately dependent on the smiles of the Commander-in-Chief, there is not an Officer of any respectability in the Service that has not expressed himself most warmly in my behalf, and who does not reprobate the conduct that has been adopted towards me. To shew you the opinion which the most experienced Officer in our Service, Sir William Fawcett (who was upwards of 30 years Deputy Adjutant and Adjutant-General), entertains of my Code, I herewith send you a copy of his note to me, upon returning the book which I had sent him, at his own express desire. I think you will admit after that, that I have no reason to be ashamed of my labors on that occasion.

Of General Barnett's conduct, I can assure you there is but one opinion, and I believe there is scarcely a character in the Army at present more despised by every well thinking man than his. I do not think his triumph will be long; indeed, had Gibraltar remained under the Home Department, I am confident Mr. Yorke would have made a point of his removal.[1]

Captain Ramsay will, I have reason to believe, be ordered back to Gibraltar, for the Duke of York does not chuse that any Officer belonging to a Regiment in that Garrison should be on the Staff elsewhere, unless he has the King's Commission, and even Captain Maule, who was Major of Brigade, has been obliged to vacate his situation and is now going out. At all events Captain Ramsay will not be in Lord Charles Somerset's family, for that Officer happening to be on the most intimate

1. In July 1801 colonial business was taken away from the Home Secretary and handed over to the War Department, the Secretary then becoming Secretary of State for War and the Colonies.

terms with me, I have thought it my duty to convey to him my opinion relative to him, in consequence of which, even if the Duke of York should consent to his staying at home, his Lordship has declared he will have nothing to do with him.

Dodd has been absent for this fortnight past, bathing at the Isle of Wight, to endeavour to get the better of the ulcers on his arm, which are again broken out and are very troublesome to him. On his return from thence, the Treasury Board will probably be reassembling, or at latest in a fortnight or three weeks time, when I shall make a fresh attempt to carry the business through with respect to the Secretaryship, and upon the result of that will depend my determination relative to his immediate return or otherwise to the Rock.

I lament from my heart that Sir Thomas Trigge, whom I am very ready to consider as an honorable man, should have been so weak as to become the dupe of General Barnett. If he had only had common firmness and resolution, and as much activity as was necessary to have made him see things with his own eyes, all would have been well, but unfortunately his indolence has been the cause of much evil, and I hope it may not eventually bring ruin and disgrace upon himself. Is it not singular that he has not ever had the civility to write me once or send me a single report since I left the Rock?

You will oblige me by writing a full account to my worthy friend General Villettes at Malta of all my proceedings, as you have learnt them from Dodd, together with an extract from this present letter. I shall not myself have time to write him any more by this opportunity than a very few lines to this effect, but as he is the oldest friend, almost, I have in the world, and I know he will be very uneasy about me and most anxious to hear what is going on, I therfore rely upon you not omitting to do this *by the very first opportunity*.

I need not say the pleasure I shall feel in meeting that worthy fellow Colonel Ross;[1] you will of course have, long before this, heard that he is Lieutenant-Colonel of the 44th Regiment, and an irreparable loss he will be both to Gibraltar and the 54th.

The lioness is arrived at Plymouth and I am now taking the necessary measures for getting her removed to the Tower, for you will easily conceive she would not be a very pleasant pet at my house.

The inclosed petition I have some time since received from poor Wyatt. You will of course make him understand that, from the footing on which I stand with Sir Thomas Trigge, I cannot interfere in his behalf, but I think it will be right for you to remind Colonel Fyers of what passed between us at Landport Gate on the morning of the first of May, and of the promise he made to see justice done to the old man,

1. Andrew Ross (1773–1812). Lieutenant, 1791; Major, 1794; Lieutenant-Colonel, 1800; Colonel, 1809; Major-General, 1812. A.D.C. to the King, October 1809.

and that I hope he will feel it incumbent upon him not to leave the Lieutenant-Governor in peace till the engagement with regard to Mr. Wyatt [is] fulfilled.

This letter will be delivered to you by Lieutenant-Colonel Keane,[1] a most worthy young man, and one who sees things in their proper light or I am much mistaken indeed.

Having nothing further at present to add, I have only to assure you of the continuance of my best wishes [etc.].[2] (46121-6)

1750   THE EARL OF MOIRA TO THE PRINCE OF WALES

London, 30 Sept. 1803

Colonel McMahon will detail to your Royal Highness a curious circumstance which has occurred. Respect & propriety would without any consideration of policy have led me to receive the expressions with all due acknowledgement, but it struck me that it might chance to promote your Royal Highness's service were I to encourage the disposition professed, & at all events no inconvenience could flow from it. I think some sense of growing difficulties has produced this communication, and I shall not be surprised if the same cause gives rise to similar advances from the Ministers. It is, I trust, unnecessary for me to say that the mode in which I should correspond to any overtures of this nature would be guided exactly by your wishes. You will signify them to me, Sir, without shackling them by advertence to any supposed interest of mine, because I speak literally when I say that there is no object whatever which could stand in the slightest degree of comparison with the gratification of proving my devotion to you. If ever I have been able to persuade myself that I have been set aside on account of my attachment to your Royal Highness, the sentiment has really made the loss of any possible advantage seem nothing to me. And this is not the cold observance of a fidelity which I might have prescribed to myself in return for your kindness. It is a heart-felt sensation that pays itself. There are many points in which I know you understand me as well as I read you without explanation on either side, and there is nothing that proves confidence so much as that very omission of explanation. You do not, I am sure, Sir, think I either hoped or wished to evade your perspicacity when I did not

1. John Keane, of the 13th Foot (1781–1844). Entered the Army, 1793; Major, 1802; returned to England from the Mediterranean, March 1803; Lieutenant-Colonel, 1803; Colonel, 1812; Major-General, 1814; Commander-in-Chief at Jamaica, 1823–30, and in Bombay, 1833–9; Lieutenant-General, 1830. K.C.B., 1815; G.C.H., 1831; G.C.B., 1839; created Baron Keane, 1839.

2. Only signed by the Duke.

propose to return with you to Brighton, nor did I for an instant fear you would misconstrue me, or thence doubt the happiness I should have had in paying my duty there. As far as regarded you, I could have confessed my excuses with perfect openness of heart, & it was only the inveterate habit of silence on such topics that made me shun discussion. This is in itself an avowal in which I could not feel justified but from the secrecy & delicacy of your friendship, tho' in allowing it to myself I enjoy the proving to you that my heart labors when it has the appearance of concealment towards you. You will laugh at this, but your honor will approve the shyness & will guard the acknowledgement. In the confession, I feel myself as safe with you as if it rested in my own breast. As to public matters, Colonel McMahon can furnish better information than I can. My only object in this letter is to do that which is an indulgence to myself tho' superfluous to you, to repeat the ardent affection & unalterable devotion with which I remain [etc.]. (39962–5)

1751   LETTERS FROM THE DUKE OF CLARENCE TO THE PRINCE OF WALES
Bushy House, Friday night [*?September or October*] *1803*
My time has been so constantly taken up by the Volunteers that when night comes I am too tired to hold a pen, but the situation of the country now requires every exertion and I write to inform you I expect every hour orders to march, and then it will not be in my power to inform you of it. The Artillery Company march tomorrow and some Corps are ordered to have packs and greatcoats. I expect our arms and accoutrements in the course of the day, but our cloathing will not be ready these six weeks. However, I hope before three weeks are out to have the caps and stocks for the men. I wish we had our uniform[s], tho' we can fight without them.

You may perhaps remember Serjeant McCrowe who you discharged into the Norfolk Cavalry: he now drills at Feltham and has requested me to recommend to you his son Nathaniel McCrowe, a remarkably fine boy who knows something of musick and is desirous of belonging to your Band.

McMahon has of course told you and written all I know. My love to Mrs. Fitz. We may perhaps meet in the field. I really believe at last the French will come.

We are in want of a bugle and perhaps you can give us one for the cavalry. (44913–4)

Bushy House, Saturday night [*? Autumn 1803*]
My motive for troubling you is relative to Cottin who is Second Major

422

to the Royal Spelthorne Legion. He cannot buy a horse and I cannot well afford to purchase one for him, but if you would make him a present of a horse I shall be able to maintain it for poor Cottin at my stables here.

The uniform of the troop will be beautiful: it will be in red blue and gold what your fine regiment is in blue, yellow and silver. The pantaloons are to be red, the officers to have felt caps with red and gold tassels, the privates leather caps like yours and no helmets. The accoutrements of the whole corps are to be black. The officers of the infantry will have a neat plain jacket with blue lappels with a gold epaulette blue pantaloons and Hussar boots with a black tassel in front and a plate to their black sword belt with a plain G.R. with the Crown over it and the King's regulation sword: the Field Officers to have two epaulettes and to wear a sabre round the waist: the serjeants and privates to have jackets according to the regulation without any lace, and blue pantaloons and half black gaiters: the drummers laced down the seams and over the arms with white lace: the serjeants and privates of the troop the same in red and blue and white and silver as your regiment in blue, yellow and white and silver. I hope all the volunteers except the officers, the serjeant and drum majors will wear their hair round in their necks. I shall be happy to shew you the different patterns of everything when you come this way and will inform you how we get on and what may arise.

I send this to Carlton House as Macmahon told me when I saw him last Wednesday in town he thought you might arrive there as tonight or tomorrow. I will endeavour to see you, tho' my time all next week must of necessity be taken up in enrolling the men in the different parishes, to which I must attend, as there will be great difficulties: indeed, what I have undertaken is no easy task and will require great good humour, coolness and at first constant application. The presence of the Field Officers will be necessary: without them nothing can be done and I feel great pleasure in having such men as Braddyll[1] and Cottin. Serjeant Marshall has been and will be very useful in keeping ill-disposed people quiet and is very zealous and desirous to learn his duty: Chambers has the troop. My best wishes and compliments attend Mrs. Fitz. (44916–7)

1752   LETTERS FROM LORD THURLOW TO THE PRINCE OF WALES

[? 28 Sept. 1803]

Lord Thurlow has the honour to submit to your Royal Highness's

1. Probably Lieutenant-Colonel Thomas Richmond Gale Braddyll (1776–1862), M.P. for Bodmin, 1818–20; son of Wilson Gale Braddyll (1756–1818), M.P. for Lancaster, 1780–4; for Horsham, 1790–1; for Carlisle, 1791–6.

consideration the scroll of a letter, wherein the D. of R.'s ideas are turned and accommodated to the new plan.

He still finds himself somewhat at a loss to discern the utility of the measure; at least, of any part of it but the last paragraph, which, *perhaps*, may facilitate the publicity of your Royal Highness's conduct. But he cannot presume to offer advice upon a subject with which he is so little familiar. The advice of your military friends would be more authoritative, and that of your Parliamentary supporters more apt for the occasion, but your Royal Highness's judgement will, as it ought, not only controul the measure, but but [*sic*] frame the representation to suit your own ideas.

Ld. Thurlow's main object has been a care not to prejudice the place your Royal Highness has taken in the publick opinion.[1] (39966–7)

Thursday [*? 29 Sept. 1803*]
In the scroll submitted to your Royal Highness yesterday, Ld. T. forgot, he fears, to make an alteration which occurred to him on reading it over; viz., instead of the words, *in which I may better correspond*, to insert the words, *more correspondent*. They seem to mean the same thing, expressed with more ease. But this, and all the rest is submitted to your Royal Highness.[2] (39970)

1. Endorsed. 'Relating to the question of his Royal Highness's desire to hold higher rank in the Army'.

2. Moira's letter to McMahon, dated Thursday night, may well have been written about this time:

'I have studied & weighed with all attention the papers you left for me. Ld. Thurlow's letter is perfect, if the ground be deemed adviseable to proceed upon; but I am doubtful whether a specious plea may not be furnished to Ministers by pushing the matter on this footing, & I wish you to submit the suggestion to Ld. Thurlow. The excuse to which the King originally resorted was that the station of Prince of Wales superseded all Army rank; consequently, that the latter was incompatible with the former. Now this would be plausible enough as a position in any question on the subject in Parliament. What the Prince wants is command, not specific rank. The consideration of public advantage arising from his example applies to the former, not to the latter. Might not the brevet be made the occasion of marking this distinction & of introducing the discrimination so ably advanced by Ld. Thurlow (the rejection of all views of patronage or influence) without incurring the answer which I have stated would be given to the application for a defined rank? There is time enough to have this point considered & to signify the opinion to me. I enclose Cavendish Bradshaw's letter; so do not put it up with the other papers.

I waited for you as long as I could, but I suppose you had an engagement of which I could compute the force.' (39976–7)

Moira's note to the Prince of Wales, dated Friday, could have been written the following day:

'Lord Thurlow has sent to say that he will call upon me at two o'clock, not being able to come sooner, so that it will not be till after that hour when we can have the honor of waiting upon your Royal Highness.' (39978)

[*Brighton, 2 Oct. 1803*]

An extensive promotion has taken place in the Army,[2] wherein my pretensions are not noticed; a circumstance, which it is impossible for me to pass by [at this momentous chrysis] without observation.

My standing in the Army, according to the most ordinary routine of [promotion, had it been followed up, would have placed me either at the bottom of the list of Genls. or at the head of the list of Lt.-Genls.] When the younger branches of my family are promoted to the highest military offices, my birth, according to the distinctions usually conferred on it, should have placed me first on that list.

I hope you know me too well to imagine that idle, inactive rank is in my view. Much less is the direction and patronage of the Military Department an object which suits either my place in the State or my inclinations. But in a moment when the danger of the country is thought by Government, so urgent as to call forth the energy of every arm in its defense, I must needs feel myself degraded, both as a Prince and a soldier, if I am not allowed to take a forward [& distinguish'd] post in defense of that Empire and Crown, of the glory, prosperity, and even existence of that people in all which mine is the greatest stake.

To be told I may display this zeal at the head of my Regiment, is a degrading mockery. If that be the only situation allotted me I shall certainly do my duty, as others will. But the considerations to which I have alluded intitle me to expect and bind me withal to require a situation more correspondent to the dignity of my own character and to the publick expectations.

It is for the sake of tendering my services in a way more formal and official than I have before pursued, that I address this to the Commander-in-Chief, by whose counsels the Constitution presumes that the Military Department is administered.

If those who have the honour to advise his Majesty on this occasion shall deem my pretensions among all the Royal Family to be the only ones fit to be rejected and disdained, I may at least hope, as a debt of justice and honour, to have it explained that I am laid by in virtue of that judgement, and not in consequence of any omission or want of energy on my part. (39968–9)

1. This is Thurlow's draft of the Prince's letter to the Duke. The words enclosed within square brackets are in the Prince's hand. The published version varies but little from this draft. See 39971, 40006, 44186–7.

2. *London Gazette*, 1 October.

Alnwick Castle, 2 Oct. 1803

I shoud not have delayed writing to you so long, but I was uncertain where to direct my letter, & I beg therefore that the same thing may not again happen. You will be kind enough to let me know in your next whether it is proper always to direct to you at Carlton House, & whether your letters will be regularly conveyed to you from that place.

I am very sorry to hear that you have been confin'd with so troublesome a disorder as the rheumatism, especially as in this part of the Kingdom we had the finest weather that ever was known.

If the information you mention in your letter can be depended upon by Ministers, they are under a most dangerous responsibility, for [they] have left this maritime county, with all its collieries, in the absolutely defenceless state in which it is; not a single man in it that ever saw an enemy & but few who ever handled or fired a musquet; Berwick a regular fortress with a garrison of only sixteen invalids, & of 4,700 & odd volunteers considerably upwards of 3,000 without arms. We have indeed been promised arms, but none are arrived. If therefore the enemy was now to land in this part of the Kingdom poor Sir Hew Dalrymple has little to oppose them with. Nothing coud be easier than for the French to seize upon Berwick with a crew of a frigate, & then they will have a most charming fortified depot where they may land in perfect quiet & security what troops, provisions, forage &c. they chuse, hold it with four or five Battalions & from thence make predatory excursions into this county & Scotland, nor coud they be dispossessed of it but by a regular siege in force. The only regular Regt. Sr. Hew is even promised is the 53d., consisting of Officers & Serjts. & the men ballotted for the Army of Reserve in the West Riding of Yorkshire who are to join the offrs. & serjts. at Sunderland as soon as they are compleated, and this they call a regt. of his Majesty's regular troops! I had indeed forgot two troops of the 5th Dragoon Guards which Sr. Hew has under his command!!!

I have last night received the eleventh edition of regulations, allowances, &c., &c., &c., for the volunteer corps, with various alterations (I wish I coud add also emendations) in consequence of which I have 60 more letters & copies to have written for the 12 volunteer corps of this county. I had much rather have received the arms & accoutrements for them.

I shoud have been alarmed at H.R.H. the Prince's indisposition had I not been sure that if it was anything serious I shoud have heard from you on the occasion.

I beg you will assure him of my duty & attachment, and accept yourself of the compliments & best wishes of myself and family. Adieu. (39972–3)

Horse Guards, 6 Oct. 1803

Nothing but an extraordinary press of business should have prevented me from acknowledging sooner your letter of the 2d. instant, which I received while at Oatlands on Monday evening.

I trust that you are too well acquainted with my affection for you, which has existed since our most tender years, not to be assured of the satisfaction I ever have felt and ever must feel, in forwarding, when in my power, every desire or object of yours, and therefore will believe how much I must regret the impossibility there is upon the present occasion of my executing your wishes of laying the representation contained in your letter before his Majesty.

Suffer me, my dearest brother, as the only answer that I can properly give you, to recall to your memory what passed upon the same subject soon after his Majesty was graciously pleased to place me at the head of the Army; and I have no doubt that with your usual candour, you will yourself see the absolute necessity of my declining it.

In the year 1795, upon a general promotion taking place, at your instance, I delivered a letter[1] from you to his Majesty, urging your pretensions to promotion in the Army, to which his Majesty was pleased to answer[2] that before ever he had appointed you to the command of the 10th Light Dragoons, he had caused it to be fully explained to you what his sentiments were with respect to a Prince of Wales entering into the Army, and the publick grounds upon which he never could admit of your considering it as a profession, or of your being promoted in the service, and his Majesty at the same time added his positive *commands and injunctions* to me, never to mention the subject again to him; and to decline being the bearer of any application of the same nature, should it be proposed to me; which message I was of course under the necessity of delivering to you, and have constantly made it the rule of my conduct ever since, and indeed I have ever considered it as one of the greatest proofs of affection and consideration, towards me, on the part of his Majesty, that he never allowed me to become a party in this business.

Having thus stated to you fairly and candidly what has passed, I trust that you will see that there can be no grounds for the apprehension expressed in the latter part of your letter that any slur can attach to your character as an officer, particularly as I recollect your mentioning to me yourself, on the day on which you received the notification of your appointment to the 10th Light Dragoons,[3] the explanation and condition attached to it by his Majesty. And therefore surely you must be satisfied

1. No. 973 (9 March 1795. iii.43).
2. No. 980n. (iii.50).
3. Nos. 723, 725 (ii.335–6).

that your not being advanced in military rank proceeds entirely from his Majesty's sentiments respecting the high rank you hold in the State, and not from any impression unfavourable to you. (40007 and 44188–9)

THE PRINCE OF WALES'S REPLY
Brighton, 9 Oct. 1803

I have taken two days to consider the contents of your letter of the 6th inst. in order to be as accurate as possible in my answer, which must account to you for its being longer perhaps than I intended or could have wish'd.

I confide entirely in the personal kindness & affection express'd in your letter & am for that reason the more unwilling to trouble you again on a painful subject in which you are not free to act as your inclination, I am sure, would lead you, but as it is not at all improbable that every part of this transaction may be publicly canvass'd hereafter it is of the utmost importance to my honour, without which I can have no happiness, that my conduct in it shall be fairly represented and correctly understood.

When I made a tender of my services to his Majesty's Ministers, it was with a just & natural expectation that my offer would have been accepted in the way in which alone it could have been most beneficial to my country, or creditable to myself, or if that fail'd, that at least (in justice to me) the reasons for a refusal would have been distinctly stated, so that the nation might be satisfied that nothing had been omitted *on my* part & enabled to judge of the validity of the reasons assign'd for such a refusal. In the first instance it was referr'd to his Majesty's will & pleasure, & now I am inform'd by your letter that before 'he had appointed me to the command of the 10th Lt. Drs. he had caused it to be fully explain'd to me what his sentiments were with respect to a Prince of Wales entering into the Army'. It is impossible, my dear brother, that I should know all that pass'd between the King & you, but I perfectly recollect the statement you made of the conversation you had had with his Majesty & which strictly corresponds with that in your letter now before me, but I must at the same time recall to your memory my positive denial at that time of any condition or stipulation having been made upon my first coming into the Army, & I am in possession of full & complete documents which prove that no terms whatever were then propos'd, at least to me, whatever might have been the intention, & the communications I have found it necessary subsequently to make have ever disclaimed the existence of such a compromise at any period, as nothing could be more adverse to my nature or more remote from my mind. As to the conversation you quote in 1796 (when the King was

428

pleas'd to appoint me to succeed Sir Wm. Pitt) I have not the most slight recollection of its having taken place between us; if your date is right, my dear brother, you must be mistaken in the exactness, or at least in the conclusion you draw from it, for in the intimacy & familiarity of private conversation it is not at all unlikely that I should have remember'd the communication you made me the year before, but that I should have acquiesc'd in, or referr'd to a compromise which I never made, is utterly impossible. Neither in his Majesty's letter to me nor in the correspondence with Mr. Addington (of which you may not be fully inform'd) is there one word or the most distant allusion to the condition stated in your letter, & even if I had accepted the command of a Regiment on such terms, my acquiescence could only have relation to the ordinary situation of the country & not to a case so completely out of all contemplation at that time as the probable or projected invasion of this Kingdom by a foreign force sufficient to bring its safety into question. 'When the King is pleas'd to tell me that should the enemy land he shall think it his duty to set an example in defence of the country, that is to expose the only life which for the publick wellfare ought not to be hazarded,' I respect & admire the principle which dictates that resolution, & as my heart glows with the same sentiments I wish to partake in the same danger, that is with *dignity & effect.* Wherever his Majesty appears *as King* he acts & *commands.* You are Commander-in-Chief; others of my family are high in military station & even by the last Brevet a considerable number of junior officers are put over me. In all these arrangements *the Prince of Wales* alone, whose interest in the event yields to none but that of the King, is disregarded, omitted, & his services rejected, so that he has in fact no post or station whatsoever in a contest on which the fate of the Crown & the Kingdom may depend. I do not, my dear brother, wonder that in in the hurry of your present occupations these considerations should have been overlook'd. They are now in your view & I think cannot fail to make a due impression.

As to the rest, with every degree possible of esteem for your judgment of what is due to a soldier's honor, I must be the guardian of mine to the utmost of my power.[1] (44190-2)

1. Thurlow's much-amended draft of the Prince's letter is so different from that which the Duke received, that it is given here (the passages within square brackets were scored through):

'My letter was an official tender of my services, founded intirely on the peculiar crisis of these times, and my object was to draw from *Government* either an acceptance of those services, tendered on that principle, or, at least, an open acknowledgement that they had been so tendered and rejected: the last I claimed as due to justice and honour.

'H.M. has been pleased to communicate to me his intention of taking the field in case of an invasion; a purpose well suited to his great situation and spirited character. The Prince of Wales would in that case have remained the only idle spectator; if accident had not placed him at the head of a Regiment, would Government have thought that circumstance an advantage to the general cause in such a crisis as the present? Or does it now think that simply the

Horse Guards, 11 Oct. 1803

I have this moment upon my arrival in town found your letter, and lose no time in answering that part of it which it appears to me highly necessary should be clearly understood.

Indeed, my dear brother, you must give me leave to repeat to you, that upon the fullest consideration I perfectly recollect your having yourself command of a Regiment in which he may be & indeed must be commanded either by the younger branches of his family or by other officers that have been put over his head & particularly by the last Brevet a situation for the Prince of Wales in such an emergency?

'Those considerations (in the hurry of your pres[en]t occupations it is no wonder) you have overlooked, & which I am sure now that they are brought before you, you cannot but feel.

'As to the present question, it is really a matter of no consequence whether I received my first commission under a declaration that I was to expect no further rank or even obtained it by acquiescing in such a condition. The present crisis supersedes those trifling points and if either had been the case I should have been equally bound to urge my present claim upon the attention of *Government*, but the fact was otherwise and I have documents to confirm this assertion.

['My first commission was in 1792 and it was proposed to be that of Major-General, but the post of Colonel was recommended to me as affording readier means to become acquainted with regimental details; the objection was that being junior I should be commanded by all the existing Colonels: to obviate this my commn. was antedated 1782.]

'H.M. was pleased to inform you in 1795 that before I had my commission, that is 1792, *he had caused it to be fully explained to me what his sentiments were with respect to a Prince of Wales entering into the Army, and the publick grounds upon which he never could admit of my considering it as a profession or of my being advanced in the Army.* Whatever H.M.'s intentions were, that explanation was never made, nor do I at this moment know what the publick grounds are which should exclude the P. of W. from the military service of his country. In the correspondence which has already passed on this occasion (with which perhaps you are not fully acquainted) no hint of such grounds appears, but very emphatick expressions are used of a contrary tendency; nor till your letter was any hint dropt of the supposed conditions. This either proves that no such fact exists or at leas[t] that it was thought nothing to the purpose. It certainly affords no sort of answer to my present application.

'I rem[em]ber in the year 1795 your communication of the language H.M. was pleased to hold with you, but I must at the same time recall to your recollection that I then assured you that whatever explanations H.M. might have thought of *causing to be made to me*, nothing of that sort had been said.

'3. As to the conversation you quote in 1796 when the King was pleas'd to appoint me to succeed Sir Wm. Pitt. I have not the slightest recollection of such a conversation taking place between us. If your date is right you must be mistaken in the exact terms or at least in the conclusion you draw from it, for in the intimacy and familiar[it]y of private conversation it is not at all unlikely that I should have remembered the communication you made me the year before, but that I should have acquiesced in or referred to a compromise which I never made, is absolutely impossible.

'4. [If I had, you must have imputed that circumstance to H.M., but when I went to return my humble thanks to H.M. for my appointment not a word passed upon any such subject.]

'5. For the rest, with every degree of esteem for your judgement of what is due to a soldier's honour I must be the guardian of mine to the utmost of my power. [My sentiments upon that head are also confirmed by the publick voice that it cannot stand right but by an open avowal that my services have been tendered in the manner I have already mentioned.'] (39941–3)

told me at Carlton House in the year 1793, on the day on which you was informed of his Majesty having acquiesced in your request of being appointed to the command of the 10th Regiment of Light Dragoons, of which Sir William Pitt was then Colonel, the message and condition, which was delivered to you from his Majesty, and which his Majesty repeated to me in the year 1795, as mentioned in my letter of Thursday last, and I have the fullest reason to know that there are others to whom at that time you mentioned the same circumstance. Nor have I the least recollection of your having denied it to me when I delivered to you the King's answer, as I should certainly have felt it incumbent upon me to recall to your memory what you had told me yourself in the year 1793.

No conversation whatever passed between us, as you justly remark, in the year 1796 when Sir William Pitt was promoted to the King's Dragoon Guards, which was done in consequence of what was arranged in 1793, upon your first appointment to the 10th Light Dragoons, and I conceive that your mentioning in your letter my having stated a conversation to have passed between us in 1796 must have arisen from some mis-apprehension, as I do not find *that* year ever adverted to in my letter.

I have thought it due to us both, my dear brother, thus fully to reply to those parts of your letter in which you appear to have mistaken mine, but as I am totally unacquainted with the correspondence which has taken place upon this subject I must decline entering any further into it. (40010 and 44193–4)

FROM THE PRINCE OF WALES
Brighton, 12 Oct. 1803
By my replying to your letter of the sixth instant which contain'd no sort of answer to mine of the second, we have fallen into a very frivolous altercation upon a topic which is quite foreign to the present purpose. Indeed, the whole importance of it lies in a seeming contradiction in the statement of a fact, which is unpleasant even upon the idlest occasion. I meant to assert that no previous condition to forego all pretensions to ulterior rank under any circumstances had been imposed upon me, or even submitted to me in any shape whatsoever upon my first coming into the service, and, with as much confidence as can be used in maintaining a negative, I repeat that assertion.

When I first became acquainted with his Majesty's purpose to with-hold from me further advancement it is impossible to recollect, but that it was so early as the year 1793 I do not remember, & if your expressions were less positive I should add or beleive, but I certainly knew it, my dear brother, as you well knew, in 1795, & possibly before. We were

431

then engaged in war, therefore I could not think of resigning my Regiment, if under other circumstances I had been disposed to do so, but in truth my rank in the nation made military rank in ordinary times a matter of little consequence except to my own private feelings. This sentiment I convey'd to you in my letter of the second, saying expressly that mere idle inactive rank was in no sort my object, but upon the prospect of an emergency where the King was to take the field & the spirit of every Briton was roused to exertion, the place which I occupy in the nation made it indispensable to demand a post correspondent to that place, & to the publick expectation. This sentiment I have the happiness to be assured, in a letter on the occasion, made '*A strong impression upon the mind & commanded the respect & the admiration*' of one very high in Government.

The only purpose of this letter, my dear brother, is to explain, since that is necessary, that my former ones meant not to give you the trouble of interceding as my advocate for mere rank in the Army. Urging further my other more important claims upon Government would be vainly addressed to any person who can *really* think that a former refusal of mere rank under circumstances so widely different or the most express waving of such pretensions, if that had been the case, furnishes the slightest colour for the answers I have receiv'd to the tenders now made of my services. Your department, my dear brother, was meant, if I must repeat it, simply as a channel to convey that tender to the Government & to obtain either their attention to it or an open avowal of their refusal. (44195-6)

THE DUKE OF YORK'S REPLY

Horse Guards, 13 Oct. 1803

I have received your letter this morning and am sorry to find that you think that I have misconceived the meaning of your first letter, the whole tenor of which, and the military promotion which gave rise to it, led me naturally to suppose your desire was that I should apply to his Majesty in my official capacity to give you military rank, to which might be attached the idea of subsequent command. That I found myself under the necessity of declining, in obedience to his Majesty's positive orders, as I explained to you in my letter of the 6th inst., but from your letter of today I am to understand that your object is not military rank, but that a post should be allotted to you, upon the present emergency, suitable to your situation in the State.

This I conceive to be a purely political consideration and as such totally out of my department, and as I have most carefully avoided at all times and under all circumstances ever interfering in any political points, I

432

must hope that you will not call upon me to deviate from the principle by which I have been invariably governed. (40012 and 44197)

Carlton House, 14 Oct. 1803

It cannot but be painful to me to be reduced to the necessity of further explanation on a subject which it was my earnest wish to have closed & which was of so clear & distinct a nature as in my judgment to have precluded the possibility of either doubt or misunderstanding. Surely there must [be] some unlucky fatality obscure my language in statement or leave me deficient in the powers of explanation when it can lead your mind, my dear brother, to such a palpable misconstruction of my meaning (for far be it from me to fancy it willfull) as to suppose for a moment I had *unconnected my object with efficient military rank* & transferr'd it entirely to the view of a political station, when you ventur'd to tell me 'My object is *not* military rank but that a post should be allotted to me upon the present emergency suitable to my situation in the State'. Upon what ground you can hazard such an assertion, or upon what principle you can draw such an inference, I am wholly at a loss to determine, for I defy the most skillful logician in torturing the English language to apply with *fairness* such a construction to any word or phrase of mine contain'd in any one of the letters I have written on this (to me most interesting) subject. I call upon you to *reperuse* the correspondence. In my letter of the 2d. instant I told you unequivocally that, 'I hoped you knew me too well to imagine that idle inactive rank was in my view' & that sentiment I beg you to observe I have in no instance whatever for one moment relinquish'd or departed from. Giving as I did all the considerations of my heart to the delicacy & difficulty of your situation, nothing could have been more repugnant to my thoughts or disposition than to have imposed upon you, my dear brother, either in your capacity of Commander-in-Chief or in the near relationship which subsists between us, the task, much less the expectation, of causing you to suffer any displeasure from his Majesty by disobeying in any degree his commands, though they even militate *against myself*: but with the impulse of my feelings towards you & quickly conceiving what friendship & affection *may* be capable of, I did not, I own, think it entirely impossible that considering the magnitude & importance which the object carries with it, you might officially have advanced my wishes (as matter of propriety) *to military rank & subsequent command*, to his Majesty's Ministers for that direct purpose, especially when the honour of my character & my future fame in life are so deeply involv'd in the consideration. I must here therefore *emphatically* repeat, '*That idle inactive rank was never in my view*', but that military rank with its consequent command was never *out of it*.

Feeling how useless as well as ungracious controversy is on every occasion, & knowing how fatally it operates on human friendships, I must entreat that our correspondence on *this subject* shall cease here, for nothing could be more distressing to me than to prolong a topic on which it is *now clear* to me, my dear brother, that you & I can never agree. (44198–9)

1756   THE EARL OF MOIRA TO COLONEL MCMAHON
Donington, 19 Oct. [*1803*]
Yesterday brought me the offer of the command in Scotland, which, of course, I accepted with due acknowledgement, tho' beshrew me if anything could be much less convenient. There is one point which I must get you to explain to Greenwood. When it was before rumored that I was to be put upon the Staff, application was made to me that Ridge might be my Agent for that Commission. As he had been attentive to us, I said it should be so: for, as the appointment was then expected to be put upon a footing merely to answer the public clamor at my not being employ'd without any regard to me, I did not feel it necessary to shew any complimentary attention by appointing Greenwood. Now, tho' the matter has taken a different cast, I did not leave any eventual reservation; so that Ridge must have it in consequence of my former promise. Any person recommended by the Prince must be most cordially accepted by me: but the young gentleman at whom you have hinted ought to have a devilish deal of lecturing before he comes to me, as a buckish *Aide-de-Camp* would have a bad time of it in my military family. Say to the dear Prince everything that respectful affection & earnest devotion of soul must unremittingly suggest to me. (40004–5)

1757   GENERAL G. LAKE TO THE PRINCE OF WALES
Agra, 23 Oct. 1803
Private. Before this arrives your Royal Highness will have heard of the total extirpation of the French faction on this side India & the capture of Alighur,[1] Delhi[2] & Agra & the deliverance of the Nizam Shah Allum,

1. Marching from Cawnpore, Lake captured Aligarh at the end of August, causing Perron to retire from Sindhia's service.

2. Lake defeated Perron's successor, Louis Bourquin, at Delhi in September, and in November vanquished Sindhia's remaining forces at Laswari.

434

King of Delhi & the representative of the House of Timur from the power & controul of the French faction which has long govern'd this part of the country, & where it was intended to plant the standard of Buonaparte the first moment they could. This part of the country had been long in the hands of a Monsr. Deboign who has been for very many months a constant resident with the First Consul, for what purpose may be easily imagin'd as a constant communication has been kept up between him & Monsr. Perron who succeeded him in command, & although nominally a subject & officer belonging to Doulet Roo Scindia[1] was in part the ruler of a prodigious tract of territory affording an immense revenue which he collected in a most arbitrary & in my opinion a most atrocious manner; in short, I would not enter into all the horrors attendant upon collecting these revenues. The conduct of Doulet Roo Scindia which has been most perfidious which brought on hostilities [sic] in consequence of which I have been with my army most actively employ'd. I commenc'd my march from Cawnpore on the seventh of August & flatter myself you will approve the proceedings & conduct of the troops under my command. They have behav'd uncommonly well as you may perceive by my official dispatches. I could dwell long upon their merits but as all I could say would not do them justice & might appear vanity on my part, I must leave your Royal Highness to draw your own inferences of their conduct from the plain & simple tale I have told in my publick letter. I can only say that Col. Monson behav'd like an angel & will I trust meet with the approbation of his Majesty & your Royal Highness. Major Macleod of the 76th, after Monson was wounded, did everything that man could do. Nothing can exceed the gallantry of that Regiment & I believe it seldom has been equall'd—but what will not British troops do?

I cannot express to your Royal Highness the satisfaction I felt in releasing the poor old blind King of Delhi[2] from his captivity. He embrac'd me in the most affectionate manner, & testified every mark of joy at coming under the protection of the British Government, & I trust since I have had him under my care he has experienced every mark of deference, respect & attention due to the exalted situation of Royalty, & to the descendant of one of the greatest Emperors upon the earth at one time. His Majesty made me accept the second title in the Empire, & would have given me the first had it not been already possess'd by Dowlet Roo Scindia. He also gave a title to my son, of whom he had heard a most flattering account.

These titles are in such high sounding language according to the oriental custom & language that I feel asham'd of sending a translation from the fear of being laugh'd at.

1. Daulat Rao Sindhia.

2. The titular Mogul Emperor, Shah Alam.

435

I have sent Major Nicolson, my late Adjutant-General, with a dispatch to the Duke of York for the information of his Majesty respecting the conduct of the troops brought under my command. He will have the honor of delivering this letter to your Royal Highness & is very equal to give you every information respecting our movements &c. I have now to return you [thanks], my dear Sir, for the very handsome sword I received by the handsome sword [*sic*] convey'd to me by Col. Monson. The sensations I felt cannot be express'd, as it evinc'd to me in so flattering a manner that I was still in your recollection & that I had retain'd the affection & friendship you had ever shewn me & which I trust will never be forfeited by any improper conduct on my part.

Now, my dear Sir, allow me to say that it is not possible for me to describe in terms in the smallest degree adequate to my feelings the treatment I have met with from Lord Wellesley; the unlimited powers he invested me with, the full confidence he has ever repos'd in me & the affectionate friendship he has ever favor'd me with, has made such an impression upon my mind that while I have life my heart will ever overflow with gratitude, esteem & admiration.

The encrease of territory & revenue to Government will be immense, & the boundary will afford most secure & ample protection to all our possessions which certainly would have been in a most precarious state had Buonaparte sent assistance, as he intended, to the French already establish'd & which certainly were intended to be sent here from the large Staff landed at Pondicherry, which fortunately from the alarm at the appearance of our Fleet off that port reimbark'd & have not since been heard of. It is with pride & pleasure I can assure your Royal Highness that the inhabitants of Hindostan are astonish'd at our mildness & humanity, & say that 'till now every victorious army had commited every excess such as devastation, rapine & murder throughout the country, burning, destroying everything they could not carry away with all the horrors of war, instead of which they are living in their houses, their families & property protected & every indulgence granted them, by which means the whole of the country with the exception of a few disorderly people are ready to join us. I am happy to add that most of the Chieftans on this side India are most desirous of alliances with the British Government, many of which I have enter'd into Treaties with & others are coming in hourly. I really beleive that no army ever behav'd better than the one I have the honor to command in point of spirit or good order & discipline.

It is with extreme satisfaction that I can assure your Royal Highness that my son Major Lake has in every situation he has been engag'd merited my most sincere praise, & I do really think that in all my service I never saw a young man of his age display so much zeal, energy & ability, from whence I am led to believe that he will make a great figure in his profession. This you may perhaps say proceeds from the fond partiality of a father, but let me entreat you to be assur'd it is from justice due to a young man I have long forborne to mention from his near connection with me but now think it my duty as a parent & an officer to bring to the notice of your Royal Highness & solicit for him your patronage & protection.

I flatter myself this war will terminate very shortly & that your Royal Highness will believe me with the most affectionate regard [etc.].

I write in great haste, therefore trust you will excuse all inaccuracies. (39953–61)

1758 HENRY ADDINGTON TO THE PRINCE OF WALES, AND THE REPLY
Richmond Park, 23 Oct. 1803
In consequence of some intelligence which has reach'd me, I am impelled by a sense of duty to your Royal Highness, and to the public to express an earnest and anxious hope that you may be induced to postpone your return to Brighton until I shall have had an opportunity of making further enquiries, and of stating the result of them to your Royal Highness. (40013)

THE PRINCE OF WALES'S REPLY
Carlton House, 25 Oct. 1803
By your grounding your letter to me upon intelligence which has just reach'd you, I apprehend that you allude to information which leads you to expect some immediate attempt from the enemy. My wish to accommodate myself to anything which you represent as material to the public service would of course make me desirous to comply with your request. But if there be reason to imagine that invasion will take place directly, I am bound by the King's precise order, and by that honest zeal which is not allow'd any fitter sphere for its action, to hasten instantly to my Regiment. If I learn that my construction of the word 'intelligence' is right, I must deem it necessary to repair to Brighton immediately. (40014)

1759 PRINCESS AMELIA TO THE PRINCE OF WALES
[*? End of Oct. 1803*]
As dear Edward is writing in my room I cannot resist adding a few words

437   29—C.G. IV

in the cover to tell you how truly I do lament your absence, particularly the cause. Do, dear love, take care of your dear self & if possible be here Augusta's or Edward's birthday.[1] It is ages since *eleven* of us have been together. God bless you; think of her who is & ever will be [etc.].[2] (Add. Georgian 14/44)

1760   PRINCESS SOPHIA TO THE PRINCE OF WALES

4 Nov. 1803

How can I find words adequate to express my gratitude for your beautiful present, but *perfect* as it is, what gratified & pleased me more than all was your thinking of me. Your affection, my beloved G.P., is of more, far more, value to me than all the *jewels* you could give me, & if I may hope that I have a little corner in the *original* heart of which this dear one is a representative it will make me happy, for I do love you *de cœur & d'ame*, & though silent I do feel the loss upon this present occasion & must live in the hopes that the day is not far off when, please God, *this sad affair* may be cleared & then we shall enjoy you in comfort.

The loss of yr. society is no small mortification, but believe me *absent* or *present* I am ever the same, lamenting in silence that any coolness should subsist *between two*[3] I do *dearly love*. Your beautiful present is the admiration of everyone who sees it; indeed my words fail me, but if you cd. look into my heart you wd. see that you have not a more grateful, affect., attached & faithful friend or sister than your own. (Add. Georgian 13/19)

1761   THE DUKE OF NORTHUMBERLAND TO COLONEL MCMAHON

Alnwick Castle, 6 Nov. 1803

I have to thank you for your letter of the 21st of last month with the copy of the correspondence between the Prince & the Commander-in-Chief. I confess I coud wish that the Prince woud leave this business where it is, as far as any further correspondence on the subject. It cannot possibly do any good. H.R.H., if he stops now, will indisputably have the nation with him, & the less he talks of advancement in the army, & the more he

1. The Prince apparently joined his family neither on 2 nor on 8 November, the birthdays of the Duke of Kent and Princess Augusta respectively.

2. Watermark, 1798.

3. The Prince and the Duke of York.

438

regrets in publick that a station is not assigned him suitable to his birth & the rank he holds in the country in a crisis like the present when everything dear to man is at stake, the more in my humble opinion he will act properly and becoming his dignity.

I had the pleasure of seeing Lord Moira & Sr. Wm. Keir here, as they passed in their way to Scotland. Having travelled all the preceding night Lord Moira was too sleepy to talk much, & forgot to tell me many things which he mentioned the next morning to Mr. Grey, who afterwards communicated them to me, not without some surprise that Lord Moira has forgot to tell me of them. I cannot say I envy Lord Moira his Command. He has a whole Kingdom & an extended coast to defend, & if my experience of forty-five years service & three wars in which I have been pretty actively engaged, can entitle me to form a military opinion, his Lordship's force, considering of what stuff it is composed, is not adequate to the undertaking. This I fear is the case everywhere at a distance from the capital; here for example I am told Sr. Hew Dalrymple has fifteen thousand men for the security & defence of the Northern District, but when it is considered that 9,000 of these consist of sea fencibles (fishermen) dispersed along a coast of an hundred miles, in little knots of 17 or 20 in each, armed only with pikes, & of volunteers who have not been armed more than three weeks, & some not completely armed & accoutred even now, & that all the remainder is composed of corps formed from the men ballotted for the Army of Reserve or Supplementary Militia, half armed, half cloathed, half accoutred, & who hardly know how to load their firelocks, except 1,000 old militia, about 150 artillery, & two troops of the 5th Regt. of Dragoon Guards (the only efficient cavalry that Sr. Hew has in his District) & that not one corps except these two last ever yet saw the face of an enemy, I think you will agree with me that such a force of fifteen thousand men cannot be very formidable against such troops as the French will bring over. But we are 300 & odd miles from the capital.

I shoud not be in the least surprised if the plan for carrying off the Prince had really been formed. The execution of it coud certainly be very easy for an enterprising partisan. I trust, however, effectual steps have now been taken to prevent the possibility of it.

It has been asserted in a letter I received from town, and further confirmed to me by Mr. Grey, that Mr. Addington has vanity enough to look up to one of the two Garters which are now vacant. It was bad enough when H.M. chose to decorate the son of a country attorney with that Order,[1] but to give it to the son of a mad doctor, whose grandfather too

1. Lord Camden (1759–1840), who was invested K.G., 14 August 1799, was the son of a barrister, Charles Pratt (1714–94), afterwards Earl Camden (1786) and Lord Chancellor, 1766–1770.

was, as I have been assured, a common day labourer,[1] & would be no great compliment to those noble personages whose ancestors & themselves have thought it an honor to belong to the Order; not to mention the Sovereigns & Princes both of the Royal blood, & foreigners, who were proud of being Knights of the Garter. But it has been too much the fashion for some years to debase everything in this country, & then cry out against levelling principles. Pray let me know whether there is the smallest foundation for this report, for I confess I cannot believe it. Surely, at all events, the King will never consent to it.

Adieu my dear Colonel. The Duchess[2] unites with me in compliments to you & Mrs. MacMahon. Where are you now? If at Brighton present my dutifull respects to H.R.H. (40024-5)

1762   THE MARQUESS WELLESLEY TO THE PRINCE OF WALES

Fort William [Calcutta], 9 Nov. 1803

Having understood from Lieutenant-Colonel Monson that it was your Royal Highness's pleasure that I should occasionally submit to you such intelligence respecting the affairs of India as might appear to merit your Royal Highness's notice, I have the honor to transmit to Mr. Tyrrwhitt by this dispatch a series of Gazettes[3] comprehending the official reports of our late rapid & splendid success in India against the confederate forces of Scindiah & the Rajah of Berar with their French artillery & French officers.

By Major Nicolson, who proceeds to England in the course of a few days, I propose to have the honor of soliciting your Royal Highness's attention to a more particular & detailed statement of this glorious triumph of the British arms.

In this first communication, however, I am anxious to offer my congratulations to your Royal Highness upon the brilliant & highly useful services of General Lake: his masterly operations, his unexampled alacrity & honorable zeal, the judgment, skill & promptitude of decision which he has manifested in every crisis of difficulty or danger, combined with his irresistible spirit of enterprise and courage entitle him to the gratitude & admiration of every loyal British subject & of every heart & mind which can feel for the honor or can understand the interests of the British Empire.

Your Royal Highness's gracious disposition towards my family will

1. The statement is inaccurate. See Pellew's *Sidmouth*, i.2.

2. The Duke married, 25 May 1779, as his second wife, Frances Julia (1752–1820), sister of the 1st Baron Gwydir, and daughter of Peter Burrell of Langley Park, Kent.

3. *Calcutta Gazettes Extraordinary*, 29 August–2 November 1803.

induce you to receive with pleasure the official report of the memorable & decisive victory gained by the forces under the command of Major-General Wellesley[1] on the 23d of September, & I am persuaded that, in addition to public sentiments, your particular favor will incline your Royal Highness to read with satisfaction the accounts of the noble & gallant spirit & distinguished ability with which my brother has seconded the victories of his illustrious Commander-in-Chief.

Intending to have the honor of addressing your Royal Highness by Major Nicolson, I shall now request you to accept the sincere assurance of the sentiments of gratitude & attachment with which [etc.]. (40026–7)

1763   THE DUKE OF KENT TO THE PRINCE OF WALES

Windsor Castle, Wednesday morning, 9 Nov. 1803

The enclosed letter from Sophy, my dearest brother, was given me the day subsequent to her birthday to forward *to you*, but by some unaccountable mistake of my servant's was found to have been neglected. I must entreat your forgiveness for this, which has made the dear little girl quite miserable lest you should think she had not felt as she ought your most kind and affectionate remembrance of her on *that* day.

I had yesterday a long conversation with the Queen upon the subject you directed me to negotiate, but I am much concerned to say was not as successful as I ever must wish to be when my object is to forward any wish of yours. This evening or tomorrow morning I shall commit to paper a correct summary of what passed between us and on Friday I will attend you in town with it.

Pray remember me very particularly to Mrs. Fitzherbert, and do me the justice to believe, *que tant que souffle de vie existera* I shall ever remain [etc.].

[*P.S.*] I am just going to leave Windsor for Kew, and shall send this by the King's chaise to town. (46127)

1. Arthur Wellesley, Duke of Wellington (1769–1852). Entered the Army 1787; A.D.C. to the Lord Lieutenant of Ireland, 1787–93; Lieutenant, 1787; M.P. for Trim [I.], 1790–7; Captain 1791; Lieutenant-Colonel, 1793; Colonel, 1796; took a leading part in the war against Tipu of Mysore, 1799; Governor of Seringapatam and Mysore, 1799–1805; Major-General, April 1802. Defeated the Marathas at Assaye and Argaon, September and November 1803. K.B., 1804; G.C.B., 1815. M.P. for Rye, 1806; for St. Michael, 1807; for Newport (Isle of Wight) 1807–9; Irish Secretary, 1807–9; a Lord of the Treasury [I.], 1807–9; Lieutenant-General, April 1808; Commander-in-Chief in Portugal, 1809; created Viscount Wellington, 4 September 1809; Earl of Wellington, 28 February 1812; Marquess of Wellington, 3 October 1812; and Duke, 11 May 1814. K.G., 1813. Master-General of the Ordnance, 1818–27; Prime Minister, 1828–30 and November-December 1834; Foreign Secretary, 1834–5; Commander-in-Chief of the Army, January-April 1827 and 1842–52.

Edinburgh, 9 Nov. 1803

Lord Lauderdale has requested me to ask if the Prince will condescend to allow his dedicating to his Royal Highness a work which he has now in the press. It is a Treatise on the Sources of National Wealth, containing no allusion to Party or Party principles, but is chiefly a controversion of Adam Smith's positions.[1] Nothing could be wiser than the offer of the Wardenship to the Duke of Northumberland.[2] I see by the Gazette that he must have declined it; on the consequences of which I sincerely congratulate you, but the kindness of the attention will not be forgotten by him.

I shall be much obliged if you will take the trouble of seeing McCarthy as speedily as [possible] respecting a bill concerning which Newton has written to me. I have written to McCarthy about it; therefore he will understand it completely. It was in the hands of one Abbot; & there are circumstances that give it a very awkward appearance. I have every reason to imagine no money was ever procured for it. Should it prove otherwise, the ingenuity of Campbell must be summoned into play.

I slave like a dray-horse: but I have the consolation of seeing things go on with that quiet activity which is the soul of arrangement: and the people are quite surprised at being shown by me that they possessed resources which they did not know how to compute, nay which they did not suspect existed. Believe me, all your political speculations are false. Addington thinks he over-reaches me in making me an insignificant instrument. Looking no further than the day, he imagines this to be wisdom. (40030–1)

1765 THE EARL OF MOIRA TO THE PRINCE OF WALES

Edinburgh, 13 Nov. 1803

Your Royal Highness knows so well the eagerness of my heart to fulfill any wish you signify, that I never can have a fear in stating obstacles where they stand in the way of your commands. With regard to Lt.-Colonel Grey, I had, before I was honored with your Royal Highness's message, relieved him from the principal discomfort which hung over

1. In his *Wealth of Nations* (1776).

2. The reference is to the office of Lord Warden of the Stannaries and Steward of the Duchy in Devon and Cornwall, which Rear-Admiral Payne must have resigned shortly before his death (17 November). Tyrwhitt succeeded him in that office, which, one would have thought, was not one that so grand a person as the Duke would have accepted—but he was offered it. He already had the office of Constable of Launceston Castle, one of the Duchy offices. See No. 1767.

him, for I had given him leave to remain at Edinburgh instead of going into exile at Fort George. To take him into my family as a supernumerary *Aide-de-Camp* would require application to the Duke of York, & it would be an application which I could not but be conscious I ought not to make, as on the face of it the solicitation was to withdraw an officer from the head of a Regiment. I therefore humbly trust your Royal Highness will be satisfied with my having assured him that should the enemy actually land here I will use the exigency of the moment as a pretext to attach him to my family for the occasion. He is sensible that more was not in my power.

I have apprized Sir Granby Calcraft[1] that you have done him the honor to recommend him to my attentions; & I have professed to him that I shall rejoice in any opportunity of showing how I respect the instruction.

My reception here has been very gratifying. I am on the best terms with the Magistracy of every description: and I find from all classes of people the most cheerful activity in facilitating anything I deem necessary for the public service. My arrangements have now got a little into form; but I had laborious work before I could satisfy myself that I had a just notion of the best mode of defence for this country. (40032–3)

1766   THE EARL OF MOIRA TO COLONEL MCMAHON

Edinburgh, 14 Nov. 1803

By today's post I send to the Prince a letter about Col. Grey, which will be a voucher for his Royal Highness's recommendation of him. Sheridan is not yet arrived. I go on upon excellent terms with all classes & descriptions here: but I have toil beyond measure as it is imagined I can remedy all omissions & neglects & I am of course assailed with applications from every quarter. What you tell me of the expected union of the civil & military power of Ireland in the person of Ld. Cathcart is very probable. It would afford a most intelligible comment upon my appointment, the intention of which has from the outset been very equivocal. In the military light alone, a decided preference was given to Ld. Cathcart, for he was sent to command a much more ample force; in a quarter more the object of attack, & thence more honorable; with allowances greatly superior to mine notwithstanding the difference of our army rank. Without depreciating the services of Ld. Cathcart, past years did not give him the opportunity of exerting himself so much as they

1. Sir Granby Thomas Calcraft (1770–1820), younger son of John Calcraft (1726–72), and brother of John Calcraft (1765–1831). Cornet, 1788; knighted for protecting the Emperor Francis II at Villiers-en-Couche, 1794 (the Order of Maria Theresa); in command of the 3rd Dragoon Guards, 1800–13; Major-General, 1813. M.P. for Wareham, 1807–8.

enabled me to do, therfore I cannot be flattered when I am placed in a professional station secondary to his. Were the Lieutenancy¹ to be also granted to him, it would be a distinction which would render my present situation degrading. In truth, there is nobody that would not put upon the matter this construction, that I was sent hither merely to become by having an ostensible employment less a marked object of Ministerial neglect. I wish Tierney to know that I was not the dupe of the courtesy which his new friends affected towards me before my departure. I met their smiles with smiles & their bows with bows, but it was always with a reservation of confidence & a determination to guard myself against implied connection till I should have better proof of their real dispositions. I own I doubt those dispositions grievously. (40034–5)

1767   THE DUKE OF NORTHUMBERLAND TO COLONEL MCMAHON, AND THE REPLY
Alnwick Castle, 16 Nov. 1803
I always feel myself much obliged to you for your letters, but particularly for the last of the 11th as it explained to me a circumstance about which I was totally left in the dark. I have not from any other quarter received the least intelligence of the plan adopted for the ensuing campaign in St. Stephen's, or of the measures which it was intended shoud be pursued. I confess I do not quite like the idea which has laterly been taken up by some of our friends, that I am, with those I can influence, to follow as a matter of course, & in the crowd, those measures which others chuse to adopt, without any previous communication with me on the subject, & shall in future consider myself in such case at liberty to pursue those measures which shall appear to me most beneficial to the country in general, without any other consideration. And when it is resolved to carry on negotiations for arrangements, in order to please the D. of Bedford, Lord Moira & Mr. Grey without any previous consultation with me, or consideration of what may be agreable to me for myself or my friends, I shall think myself equally justified & at liberty to negotiate for myself & my friends without consideration of those gentlemen. I am tired of being deemed only one in the crowd, except where money or a seat in Parliament is wanted of me. I beg you will assure his Royal Highness that I feel myself singularly obliged to him for the communications thro' you, which otherwise the other gentlemen woud never have thought of making,² & that the honour he has done me by shewing me this

1. Lord Hardwicke remained Lord Lieutenant of Ireland until 1806.

2. Fox, however, wrote to him on the 20th, inviting his comments on the political situation, with particular reference to the state of Ireland and the expediency of bringing forward the crucial Catholic and tithe questions. The Duke replied from Alnwick on the 26th: 'Your

letter has relieved me from considerable embarrassment. Many of those who are kind enough to listen to my opinion had written to me to inform them of the line of conduct I shou'd wish them to adopt during this Session of Parliament. To this question, altho' the House was to meet in a day or two, I was unwilling to give any answer, till I cou'd learn your sentiments on the subject; & not learning a syllable either from you or any other person, I confess I was much distressed; & the more so as I was led to conceive, from an accidental conversation with Mr. Grey, that you had thoughts of coalescing with Mr. Pitt, shou'd he be inclined to wish it. For my own part, holding in utter detestation the principles of Mr. Pitt, & doubting his abilities as a statesman altho' I acknowledge his eloquence, I am free to own that nothing cou'd ever induce me to unite with him. In addition to this, the personal insults he has offered me, are such as I shall never forget. I am besides further convinced that by you & your friends openly supporting Mr. Pitt's measures you will indeed probably remove the present Administration, but it will only be to place Mr. Pitt & his party at the head of affairs without any of your friends partaking of the advantage. Let me ask you, my dear Sir, in what a situation wou'd you then be? How will it be possible for you & your friends to act in unison with, & support the measures of that man whose conduct when in power you have reprobated in the severest terms? What will the publick think? What will they say of you? I know full well the weakness & imbecillity of the present Administration; & it is on this very circumstance that I found my wish that they wou'd make the proper overtures to you. Amongst such weak men it is impossible but you must take the lead, & might thus have an opportunity of rendering essential service to your country. How they can be so blind to their own weakness & their own interest as not to court an union with you, is beyond my conception. They cannot possibly go on as they are without some accession of abilities in the present critical situation of the country. Their plans of arrangement, as far as relates to military matters, of which forty-five years experience has made me perhaps a better judge than of their political measures, are totally misconceived & ridiculous; and it is clear to me that those who direct in these matters are wholly ignorant of the very first rudiments of defensive war. I confess it appears to me that were you to lay by awhile, without absolutely taking up the gauntlet against them & rendering all reconciliation impossible, at least till some time after the holydays, they will be under the absolute necessity either of coming to you or calling in the aid of Mr. Pitt & his friends, or totally relinquishing the government of the country. In thus giving you my opinion you may rest assured it does not proceed from any interested motive; as in any event I shall never consent to take any employment myself. My wish to dissuade you from an union with Mr. Pitt proceeds entirely from my regard for your honour & consistency. With regard to the particular point with respect to Ireland, altho' I am very liberal in my ideas, with regard to the regulation of tithes, & indulgence to be offered the Catholics of that country, I cannot say that I can approve of the entire emancipation of them; as I can readily form to my mind many insurmountable difficulties which wou'd occur, shou'd every restriction be removed. As one instance for example, how cou'd you allow an Irish Catholic to sit in Parliament as the representative of an Irish county or borough, when you refuse the same advantage to an English or a Scotch person of the same religious persuasion? I can have no objection, my dear Sir, to authorize you to state my opinion in *private* consultations with H.R.H., or with others. Bread a soldier, I am perhaps more bold in speaking my opinion than is consistent with that cautious prudence usually assumed by person[s] connected with party & politicks. With respect to the Prince's feelings on this business, if I am to judge of them by my own, I confess I shou'd be more inclined to favour those who, altho' they had not the power to bring about the accomplishment of my wishes, had never outraged my feelings by indignities & insults, than to run the risk by oversetting them of bringing back to power the man who, during the whole time of his former Administration, had treated me with impertinence & hostility. I am ashamed to have troubled you with so long a letter, but as you were pleased to ask my opinion, I was determined to give it fully to you. This therefore must be my excuse. When any plan is formed or anything finally

mark of his confidence is more than an equivalent for the slight put upon me by his counsellors. I have been very sorry to have observed for some time past that a great jealousy of me has arisen amongst those who are H.R.H.'s advisers. In abilities, many of them may surpass me, but in attachment, zeal or fidelity towards his Royal Highness I will assert that no man can surpass me. God knows I have no other view on earth in my conduct towards him but the advancement of his happiness & dignity, and whatever advice I may at any time have presumed to give his Royal Highness has been founded on a thorough conviction that it was for his interest. You yourself must be sensible of this, from the conversations we have had together on various subjects; & I believe I may add without vanity that it would sometimes have been better for his interest had he listened to it & followed it. On the present occasion, I coincide perfectly in opinion with Mr. Sheridan; the insults which H.R.H. has received from Mr. Pitt are such as I hope he never will pardon or forget, & the disinterested support of Mr. Addington is more becoming H.R.H.'s dignity than any coalition with Mr. Pitt. When Lord Moira signified to me his Royal Highness's flattering mark of confidence in appointing me of his Council,[1] his Lordship added that he had it in command from H.R.H. to signify to me that the whole direction of everything in Cornwall shoud pass thro' my hands. My never having assumed the least pre-eminence or consequence in Cornish business, notwithstanding this gracious message, ought to be a convincing proof that I am not eager either for power or patronage. They have gone on settling & directing everything there just as they have have [*sic*] pleased, without any interference of mine, & sometimes even, as you may well know, contrary to his Royal Highness's wishes. What cause therefore they have to be jealous of my zealous & disinterested attachment to his Royal Highness I cannot conceive, but so it is, & I have only to trust to your & Mrs. F[itzherber]t's good offices to preserve me his Royal Highness's esteem & regard. Her interest is compleatly blended with his, & her good sense & understanding can easily distinguish between those whose motives for the advice they give proceed from ambition & self interest, & those whose advice proceeds purely from their regard for & attachment to H.R.H.'s person & interest.

determined upon by you, & those whom you consult on these subjects, I trust you will do me the favour to make me acquainted with it' (Alnwick MSS.).

Fox had no great respect for the Duke, and, communicating his views on the political situation to Grey on 29 January 1804, gave him this caution: 'Take care that your foolish Duke knows nothing of all this till I communicate to him myself, unless you would undertake to do it on my behalf, which, if you see occasion, you have my authority to do' (Howick MSS.).

1. The Duke of Northumberland and Moira appear in the Red Book as members of the Prince's Council of the Duchy of Cornwall for the first time in 1802—replacing Lords Cholmondeley and Jersey—appointments which are not noticed in the *Complete Peerage*.

I am sorry to receive such an acct. of the state of health of a great personage.[1] If you hear anything particular on that subject, or any other which is interesting, do give me a line.

The Duchess desires I will offer her compliments with mine to you & Mrs. MacMahon.

[*P.S.*] Whoever advises a coalition with Mr. Pitt consults their own interest more than H.R.H.'s honour or dignity. (40036–7)

COLONEL MCMAHON'S REPLY[2]

Carlton House, 22 Nov. 1803

The flattering mark of confidence which your Grace has confer'd upon me by your last letter I shall ever value as one of the proudest distinctions of my life, & I trust that the faithful use I shall make of it will best declare the happiness it has afforded, & the gratitude I feel for it, & I hope I may prove myself not unworthy of the continuation of it.

I never was more forcibly struck with the conviction of the truth & justice with which your Grace has placed the many essential points alluding to the present times & state of things, than by the arguments contain'd in the letter I have had the honor to last receive from your Grace: but I am at the same time grieved to the soul to learn that your Lordship should imagine that anything like jealousy or neglect should prevail towards your Grace in the minds or conduct of those in the higher class who are in the habit of surrounding the Prince: for I *am certain* that his Royal Highness's heart beats with every sentiment of love, affection & respect to the Duke of Northumberland; & if jealousy does inhabit their breasts, it can only arise from their envy at, & knowledge of, this fact. In proof of my belief as to the bearings of the Prince's mind, I yesterday had the honor to receive a letter from H.R.Hss. at Brighton dated on Sunday, in answer to an express I had forwarded him with the news of Admiral Payne's death. This letter relates to so much other business, & mixes with so many different things, that it is not in a state to transmit your Grace for your occular demonstration, but I will here upon *my solemn word of honor* give your Lordship a true & literal copy of an extract in that letter which relates to your Grace. 'With respect to the Lord Wardenship of the Stannaries, & to which I have never been able to give my mind since I heard of poor Payne's death, until today, I own frankly to you, that a sounding as to his feelings upon it, or a tender of it, if found agreable, should be made to our good friend the Duke of

1. The King.

2. The reply is very slightly out of chronological order.

447

Northumberland, but to be extremely cautious against the possibility of wounding those feelings (& which might perhaps arise in his idea of becoming the successor to a private gentleman, whose chief eligibility to that office, whatever the partiality of his friends as to his private worth might be, must have proceeded principally from his gallant services in the Navy, & to the rank he held in that service as a Vice-Admiral; added, however, to the personal affection I bore him) by any deficiency of high respect in the suggestion, & if a proffer may be made, it must be made in the most delicate & respectful manner, & in terms of the warmest friendship & regard from me to the Duke. Now in my opinion the best & most proper mode to have this done would be for you, whom he knows to have my entire confidence, to write a private letter to the Duke, stating to his Grace that *you* knew it was *my* earnest wish & intention to do so, if I thought it could in any way be agreable to him, & that he might be induced to consider it as a small but sheer proof of my personal esteem & attachment to him.'

Whatever may be your Grace's pleasure on this head, I have only to rejoice that the idea flows from the fountain head, & cannot possibly have had the intervention of any councillor of his Royal Highness whatever. The selection being a grand one, the motives are pure & properly dignified, they proceed alone from attachment & affection, & they come alone & spontaneously from the Prince of Wales to the Duke of Northumberland. For God sake, my dearest Lord Duke (pardon a freedom warm from the heart), give this ostensible & great support to the Prince, & by placing your Grace's name at the head of *us all*, so elevate *us all*. I know the Prince will be delighted with your Grace's declarations towards him in your last letter, which he was quite ignorant of when he wrote the foregoing, & which I am sure H.R.Hss. has ever been highly sensible of (Alnwick MSS.).

1768   THE DUKE OF CLARENCE TO THE PRINCE OF WALES

Bushy House, Friday night [18 Nov. 1803]

We are next Sunday inspected on Ashford Common and shall be cloathed tho' not properly fitted. I have received an order from General Fox to prepare to be reviewed after the first of December and should therefore be anxious you would present the Colours before the end of the month. I make this request because the Bishop of Salisbury[1] has just informed me that a Chapter of the Garter is to meet at St. James's next Friday the twenty-fifth instant, at which if you attend it may be convenient to you

1. John Douglas (?1721–1807). Canon of Windsor, 1762; Bishop of Carlisle, 1787–91; of Salisbury, 1791–1807. He was the Chancellor of the Order of the Garter.

448

to give us the Colours on Sunday the twenty-seventh on Ashford Common and dine with the Corps &c &c at the Toy afterwards: let me know as soon as you can that I may make every arrangement as we are so widely dispersed.[1]

Mrs. Jordan was yesterday brought to bed of a girl.[2] (44918)

1769 LETTERS FROM THE DUKE OF KENT TO COLONEL MCMAHON

Castle Hill Lodge, 18 Nov. 1803

The enclosed paper ought to have been delivered by me to the Prince on the 9th instant, as the conversation of which it is a report took place on the preceding day with the Queen; but the Prince saw her Majesty himself before I had an opportunity of putting it into his hands, and thereby became master of her sentiments upon the point on which he had directed me to receive them, so that it was perhaps unnecessary to trouble him any farther on the subject. However, conceiving he might like to keep it as a memorandum amongst other papers, I do myself the pleasure of sending it to you with a request that you will deliver it to him when he comes to town, or at any other convenient moment.

Not having had the pleasure of hearing from you on the subject of the exchange between myself and the Duke of Northumberland of boxes at Covent Garden Theatre, concerning which you were so good as to say you would make some enquiry for me, I conclude you have not as yet had it in your power to give me any satisfactory information on that point. I only beg to remind you that I am still very anxious it should be accomplished, and shall feel very grateful to you for any exertions you are so good as to make to that effect. I now will trouble you with a message for the Prince relative to his box at Covent Garden Theatre on those nights when their Majesties honor it with their presence; but at the same time

1. 'On Sunday next the Royal Spelthorn Legion [Volunteers] commanded by H.R.H. the Duke of Clarence, will have their first field day on Ashford Common, previous to their receiving their Colours from H.R.H. the Prince of Wales. The Duke of Clarence is indefatigable in his exertions to perfect the discipline of the corps, the dress of which we highly approve as it is both plain and soldier-like' (*The Times*, 17 November).

'On Sunday last the Spelthorne Legion, commanded by H.R.H. the Duke of Clarence, were inspected on Ashford Common by Lieutenant-General Dalrymple . . . They mustered about 840 strong. After the inspection H.R.H., accompanied by the officers, adjourned to the Toy at Hampton, where they were entertained with an elegant dinner. H.R.H. the Prince of Wales is to present their colours in about a fortnight' (*The Times*, 22 November).

2. Augusta FitzClarence (1803–65), born 17 November. She married (1) on 5 July 1827, the Hon. John Kennedy Erskine (*d.* 1831), second son of the 1st Marquess of Ailsa; and (2) on 24 August 1836, Lord Frederick Gordon, who assumed the name of Hallyburton.

449

I beg to premise that if you think it is one that will not be agreeable to him or is in itself improper, you will then use your own judgement and drop it altogether. You are of course aware that in consequence of a change which took place about two years since, their Majesties, when they go to Covent Garden Theatre, now occupy the Prince of Wales's box, which occasioned Mr. Harris[1] to stipulate, when he acceded to construct one opposite to it for the Duke of Cumberland, that on those nights when their Majesties deprived the Prince of his, it must be given up for his accommodation. This I have directly both from Harris and Brandon. The message therefore I wish you to deliver to the Prince from me is to convey to him the request that on such nights when the King goes to Covent Garden, and the Prince does not chuse himself to go there, he will indulge me with an order to have the Duke of Cumberland's box in *his* right. Should he approve of this, I should wish to commence on Monday next, when I presume the Prince has not a thought of making his appearance, as the Dukes of Orleans[2] and Montpensier[3] have expressed a wish of going there with me. As there is no post on Sunday, if you are enabled to favor me with an answer in the course of that day, I will thank you to send it to my porter at Kensington Palace with directions to forward it immediately here.[4] (46131–3)

Castle Hill Lodge, 1 Nov. 1803
Having, from a very severe cold, been prevented going up to town today as I had intended I have only this moment received both your obliging notes of yesterday and today. I feel infinitely obliged to you for your friendly and immediate attention to my wish relative to the box at Covent Garden Theatre, but if Mr. Brandon's statement is correct, that it was only to be given up to the Prince *in person*, and *not* to be subject *to his order* when his own box was occupied by their Majesties, I most readily withdraw my request, as the use of that box can only be considered a favor by me when it comes from the Prince, and I by no means wish to be under any obligation to anyone else for it but him. You and I both know the Duke of Cumberland well, that he will not give up an iota of what he considers his right, to any man breathing, and I should be miserable to have the slightest discussion arise between the Prince and him on my account, which would ill accord with my devoted attachment to the

1. Thomas Harris (*d.* 1820), proprietor of Covent Garden Theatre.

2. Louis Philippe (1773–1850), son of the Duke of Orleans (*Égalité*) who was guillotined in 1793. King of the French, 1830–48.

3. Louis Philippe's brother (1775–1807).

4. These letters are only signed by the Duke.

former. I am infinitely obliged to you for all the trouble you are so good as to take about the exchange I am anxious to effect with the Duke of Northumberland, and feel confident that nothing will be wanting, on your part, to have it arranged in the manner most consonant to my wishes. (46134)

1770 LETTERS FROM THE DUKE OF CLARENCE TO THE PRINCE OF WALES
Bushy House, Monday morning [? *21 Nov. 1803*]
We yesterday made a better inspection than I could have expected after all the noise that has been made about the cloathing and the infamous conduct of the taylor who never till yesterday morning sent the uniforms to Sunbury where the focus of sedition had been. We had six hundred and sixty in the field besides the cavalry, the officers, serjeants and drums. I should hope to have the whole fitted in a few days and am therefore to request you will not think of presenting our Colours till Sunday sennight which is December the fourth and on which day I shall hope to show you eight hundred cloathed and fitted in the field. (44919)

Bushy House, Thursday night [?*24 Nov. 1803*]
I am to acknowledge yours of the 21st instant and feel happy we have both agreed on the same day for the presentation of the Colours. Sunday is the only day we can assemble and by Sunday sennight I hope we shall all be cloathed.[1]

You need not be afraid of your room as I shall sleep in your bed and consequently have constant fires in the room till you come up. As Mc-Mahon is to be with you next Saturday you will settle if he is to meet you. I suppose you will come here Saturday sennight and stay till the following Monday. I will ask whoever you please for the Saturday and on the

1. There is a long account of the ceremony in *The Times*, Monday, 5 December. 'The business of the day being over, the Prince with his party returned to the Bush Inn at Staines, to dine, where they were met by the Duke of Clarence and the Officers of the Spelthorn Legion. The volunteer who attracted most notice . . . was the second son of the Duke of Clarence.'

The Times added, on the 8th: 'The Royal Spelthorn Legion, who received their colours from . . . the Prince of Wales on Sunday last, is a corps formed by the different volunteer companies in the neighbourhood of Bushey Park, of which the Teddington Volunteers make a part, in which Company the Duke of Clarence was, on its first formation, a private, but, on the Companies being joined together to form a Legion, his Highness was requested to take the command. The Duke also commands the Royal Spelthorn Cavalry, and H.R.H. has paid great attention to bring them to a very high state of discipline'.

451

Sunday if you have no objection Braddyll,[1] Cottin, Lord Lucan,[2] George Grey[3] and Chambers shall with Dalrymple make the dinner party.

The papers will tell you what passed in both Houses yesterday:[4] the King was not particularly agitated but was anxious to get away. I heard nothing new today. McMahon will tell you my remarks and I will say nothing more as he will see you so soon.

I will invite if you like it the Dukes of Kent and Cambridge. (44920)

1771 CHARLES JAMES FOX TO THE PRINCE OF WALES

London, 24 Nov. [1803]

Your Royal Highness will have heard from others of the opening of Parliament and how little of importance has passed. I just said enough about Ireland to leave it open for me to bring forward that business or not as shall be thought most proper,[5] but my reason for troubling your Royal Highness with these few lines is an extreme anxiety that where your Royal Highness's name is concerned I should not say anything which you may disapprove. I should therefore very much wish to know whether on the day when the Army is considered it would be contrary to your Royal Highness's wish that the complaint of your not being properly employed should be repeated.[6] I should naturally make such a complaint a part of my speech but if I understood that (as I have heard hinted) your Royal Highness would not like that the subject should be renewed, I shall most certainly conform my conduct to your wishes. I am with every sentiment of duty and attachment [etc.].

P.S. I am going home today, and if your R.H. should condescend either to write or order a line to be written to me, you will have the goodness to have it directed for me St. Anne's Hill, Chertsey. (40040-1)

1. See No. 1751.

2. Richard, 2nd Earl of Lucan [I.] (1764-1839), styled Lord Bingham from 1795 when his father was made an Earl, to 1799, when his father died. M.P. for St. Albans, 1790-1800; Irish Representative Peer, 1801-39. For his wife see No. 1392, where, in note 2, '3rd Earl of Lucan' should read '2nd Earl of Lucan'.

3. Possibly one of Charles Grey's brothers (1767-1828), created a Baronet, July 1814. George Grey married Whitbread's sister Mary (Whitbread married his sister Elizabeth).

4. The King then delivered the Speech at the opening of the Session.

5. *Parliamentary Debates*, i.1541 (the debate on the Address, 22 November).

6. Fox made a long speech on 9 December when the Army Estimates were debated in Committee (ibid., i.1729). He did raise the question of the Prince of Wales's rank in the Army (col. 1744). See No. 1774.

[c. 25 Nov. 1803]

I have much reason to believe that my prediction will be verified. You are about to be appointed to a very honorable station where your services are most likely to be required—namely, 'the Eastern District'.

Yr. *friend Sheridan* may indeed prevent this arrangement, for the King is certainly not a little indisposed towards you in consequence of information given to him of the author of the Prince's letters, and that information could alone proceed thro' the named channel.

Be assured that the Duke has had a very difficult task to perform in consequence of the King's insane prejudices and obstinacy. It was only one week before Ld. Moira's appointment that the King declared he never should again be brought forwards. And I am of opinion that *he* was always the obstacle, but the Duke preferred to bear the odium in preference to committing his father. At the present moment Addington and the Duke by our friend Sheridan's *tattle* are at daggers drawn, therefore of course every attempt will be made to thwart the Duke and expose him to general animadversion for measures he has not the power to control. However, as far as relates to yourself I should imagine that neither King or Ministers dare to oppose the recommendation of the Duke to *add you* as an [   ] Genl. to the Eastern Staff . . .[2]

I have given you this information in consequence of some conversation which pased between me and a man of some consideration. Greenwood I assure you is not my author and therefore do not blame him if my hopes are not realized. However, I trust that you will have cause to praise the superior intelligence and authentic report of yr. sincere friend —R.W.

Taylor is come to London just in good time. There is no news beyond the statements in the newspapers but there is a rumour that tomorrow a very extraordinary Message will be sent to the House . . . (40038–9)

LORD HUTCHINSON'S REPLY [copy]

Brighton, 25 Nov. 1803

I shall fight, I shall die, if necessary for the King, but never will I flatter his unjust prejudice against his son; never, never will I consent to adulate any created being at the expence of truth & honor. I fear nothing but

1. General Sir Robert Thomas Wilson (1777–1849), one of the officers responsible for saving the Emperor Francis II from capture by the French at Villiers-en-Couche, 1794, being rewarded with the Cross of the Order of Maria Theresa, and knighted, 1801; served at the Helder, in Egypt, at the Cape, in the Peninsula and in Germany in the War of Liberation. Whig M.P. for Southwark, 1818–31, and, until 1827, friend of Lord Grey.

2. The paper is badly burnt.

God, and on the great & solemn occasions of life it requires no effort from me to place myself above the pitiful wrath of man. I certainly am amongst the most attach'd of his Majesty's subjects: my allegiance is passion & sentiment, and not the cold effort of interested judgment. My proud heart detests the wild, the sanguinary, the dirty ravings of democracy; I wou'd rather even submit to the tyranny of a King. I do not know who is the author of those letters. If his Majesty does me the honor or the injustice to attribute them to me, before he proscribes me, I wou'd recommend it to him to peruse them a second time, and then ask his conscience, with the candour of an honest mind, and the devotion of a religious man, whether there is a word or a sentence which his son and his successor ought not to have address'd to his father & his Sovereign.

As for the Duke of York, if he supposes that I shall endeavour to widen the breach between him & his brother, he does me great injustice. I am entirely and irrevocably attach'd to the Prince. I will share his fate & fortunes whatever they may be; no human power shall ever seperate us, but I shou'd little consult his honor, his interest or his dignity if I endeavour'd to set him at variance with any branch of his family, particularly the Duke of York. As for myself, whenever he shall treat me with that attention which I think I deserve, he shall ever meet with a just return on my part. Though intimacy is impossible, we shall preserve those external appearances which decorum and the circumstances of the country require. If he will be but fair and open, and shew no farther proofs of idle jealousy against me, that is all I desire. As for the favor, the affection or the friendship of the Duke of York I neither wish nor hope for them. I have so little vanity and so much pride that I am not desirous perpetually to put him in mind that I commanded the Army in Egypt, unless, when he appears to be dispos'd to forget it; 'though I know this to be the true firm [sic], & front of my offending. (40042–3)

1773 THE EARL OF MOIRA TO COLONEL MCMAHON
Edinburgh, 27 Nov. 1803
Of the £2000 which will be paid to you by Mr. Clarke, I will beg you to lodge £500 directly with Cap. Ridge, 43 Charing Cross.[1] There will be £270 to pay to Campbell. Then I shall be obliged to send to Dawson by this post a draft upon you for £1000 at ten days date, tho' I hope it may not be wanted as it was only to guard against the non-payment of a bill which I thought doubtful when I endorsed it to a Leicestershire banker; I mean doubtful only as to exact punctuality of discharge. The money

1. The banking house of Biddulph, Cocks and Ridge.

454

was otherwise intended to answer some of your notes soon becoming due the dates of which you promised to send to me.

You would be pleased if you could know into what a state of good humor & confidence I have brought this country, when it was in the extreme of the opposite temper at the time of my arrival. I hazard deeply, however, for I am appearing satisfied to meet a very probable attack from a force much superior in number with a body of troops absolutely raw. Should accident happen, it will be said, why did he not make representation? I would by no means have you hint at the bareness of our defence, because it would appear as if I were making indirectly those applications which I would not urge openly. Assietti, whom you recommended to me, is a very gentlemanlike & serviceable man; very pleasant also to do business with.[1] (40044-5)

1774 THE PRINCE OF WALES TO CHARLES JAMES FOX, AND THE REPLY
Brighton, 27 Nov. 1803
Yesterday's post brought me your kind & friendly letter, for which I beg you will accept of my best acknowledgements. So far from not meeting the question with respect to the indecent treatment I have experienc'd on the subject of the military situation in which I am placed, & so far from my not wishing it fairly to be understood by the country, nothing can be more comformable to my inclinations than that the topic should be revived, as I consider it a point of absolute duty on my part to the country, that my character should stand quite clear in its eyes, especially as the correspondence has been subject to much gross misrepresentation, as for instance, instead of the King's having told me, as you know in his letter that he did, that my place was at the head of my Regt., the courtiers, not the Ministry, have artfully & industriously circulated that my being here at my post was entirely contrary to his Majesty's will & pleasure, & arose solely from a willfull *opposition* on my part, the King having desired *me to be on his right hand* whenever he took the field. I feel quite

1. The following letter from Moira to McMahon, dated merely Edinburgh, 22 November, was almost certainly written in 1803, though it was believed to be an 1804 letter and preserved with the 1804 correspondence. Moira was in London, not Edinburgh, on 22 November 1804.

'Mr. Clarke is desired to pay into your hands the £2000 arising from the bond, which you will retain for the present. As I could not get him to come to any account for his journey hither, I must get you to press upon him the necessary remuneration. I was thinking that £50 would answer for time, trouble & compliment. Get the Prince to allow you to recommend Mr. Greaves (Assistant Inspector of Hospitals here) to the good offices of Keate, but do not mention to Keate my intervention.

'The 26th Foot, two thousand men, is ordered away from me to Ireland. I have now only one battalion of regulars for field service. Do not make any complaint about it.' (40326-7)

secure in your hands, & therefore wish you to follow exactly what your own excellent judgment will suggest, & from what has dropp'd from the King in his last Speech of his determination to set a *personal example*,[1] I think it affords you the fairest & most inviting opportunity whenever the Army estimates are brought forward.[2] It is not my intention, unless something very particular should arise, to be in town for some time. Pray remember me most kindly to Mrs. Fox, & tell her I have not forgot her wine, but that as soon as I install my family in London & my butler consequently returns, I will instantly dispatch it to St. Ann's Hill.

P.S. I am afraid you will hardly be able to read this horrid scrawl, but I have not time to copy it over.[3] (Add. MSS. 47560, ff.65-6), and (draft) 42269, where the last sentence and the P.S. are wanting)

FOX'S REPLY

St. Anne's Hill, 29 Nov. [1803]

I received this morning your Royal Highness's most condescending letter, for which I return you my heartfelt thanks, and will certainly obey your Royal Highness's orders to the best of my ability.

After having troubled you upon a subject of such importance, may I be permitted to apply to your Royal Highness upon one of a very different kind? I applied some years ago to the Duke of Gloucester to know if I could have leave to shoot once or twice in the year in Bagshot Park, and received an answer that it was kept entirely for your Royal Highness. If this is the case perhaps your Royal Highness might be so good as to give or to obtain for me leave to shoot there this winter. I should not wish it for more than two or three times at most, and would of course

1. ' ... Embarked with my brave and loyal people in one common cause, it is my fixed determination, if the occasion should arise, to share their exertions and their dangers in the defence of our Constitution, our laws and independence' (*Parliamentary Debates*, i.1523 [Speech from the throne at the opening of the Session, 22 November]).

2. Bragge, the Secretary at War, initiated a debate on the Army Estimates on 9 December. In the course of it Fox referred to the Prince's situation, and suggested that Ministers, by their advice to the King to decline the offer of military service, might 'take away from him an opportunity of rendering himself popular, and becoming one of the most beloved Princes in our history' (ibid., col. 1745).

3. The letter is printed in Russell, *Memorials and Correspondence of Fox*, iii.446, but in-accurately: the 'horrid scrawl' was evidently too much for the editor.

Fox referred to the Prince's letter when writing to General Fitzpatrick on 2 December: 'I have a letter from the P. which makes it all safe upon the subject of mentioning his business, and I am sure the more persons speak of it the more he will be pleased. I will speak to Francis of this before the debate, but do not mention my having had a letter *yet*. What Sheridan said, tho' I knew it was a lie at the time, gave me an opportunity of asking orders which I did, however, without naming Shn., but of this when we meet.' (Add. MSS. 47581, f.138)

take care not to go at any time that might interfere with your Royal Highness's sport. I intreat your Royal Highness not to give yourself the trouble of writing upon so trifling a subject, but to direct any of your servants to write me a line signifying your pleasure. As woodcocks are the chief object your Royal Highness knows that the next three or four weeks are the best. I would not have given your Royal Highness this trouble if I had known who was with you at Brighton to whom I might address myself. Mrs. Fox desires to present her duty and many thanks for your kind remembrance. (42332–3)

1775 THE DUKE OF KENT TO CAPTAIN R. WRIGHT

Castle Hill Lodge, 28 Nov. 1803

I have now before me your letters of the 15th and 19th of September and of the 2nd and 13th of October, all of which were severally received on the 15th of the latter, and 12th of this present month.

I trust, long ere this, mine of the 27th of September will have reached you, for, as I sent a duplicate by Lisbon immediately after the sailing of the Amazon (which opportunity I unfortunately missed owing to Colonel Keane's losing his passage) I think it impossible but that either the original or duplicate must have found its way to you in all October. In *that*, I gave you a most circumstantial account of all my proceedings up to the 13th of September, the day of my final interview with the Commander-in-Chief, and I then expressed my extreme impatience for the declaration of war with Spain, as affording the only opportunity, which could give me a suitable opening to renew my offer of returning to Gibraltar. At *that* time, there was a daily prospect of this taking place, but the same system of pusillanimity, which we pursued with France and Holland, has been exactly followed in our proceedings with the Cabinets of Madrid and Lisbon, and *now* a rupture with either Spain or Portugal is considered as a very distant event. How far Ministers will be inclined to put up with the admission of French men-of-war and privateers into the Spanish ports, and the condemnation and sale of British vessels captured by them, while ours are refused admittance, I cannot foresee; for such is the apprehension and tardiness of his Majesty's present servants, that one can form no estimate upon any former established principle of the manner in which they will act. God grant they may at length be roused for *my* sake against Spain, for I really see no other pretence but that of being actually at war with your neighbours, that can, after the manner in which I have been treated, and especially after the readiness that I have *since that* expressed to return to my command, justify me in spontaneously coming forward with a repetition of the same.

457

Sir William Fawcett is still alive, consequently no vacancy has occurred, and General Fox, on his return from Ireland, was put into the command of Lord Cathcart's District, comprehending all the country in the vicinity of London, which I have strong reasons to believe was kept so long open (I think not short of two months) from a hope that I should have applied for it. But I am fully¹ determined that, till I am reinstated in what is my right, I shall ask *for nothing*. I am sure you must coincide in opinion with me upon this point, and admit that my judgment upon it is correct. Nothing can be *personally* kinder to me than the King is; indeed, I am more with him than ever I was, but it is evident he studiously avoids the possibility of my talking to him about my business, which must arise from his feeling that, after having once given up the point to the Duke of York, contrary to his own opinion (*which is a well understood and an admitted point*), it is too late for him to recede. It is, however, a great satisfaction to me to know that he has expressed himself, in confidence to one of his family, both as to the hardship of the treatment which I have experienced, and as to his high approbation of the line of conduct I had taken up. You will therefore see that, knowing this, I can undertake nothing at this moment, but must necessarily remain quiet and upon the watch to take advantage of whatever may offer, which, you may rest assured, I shall not fail to do, being most thoroughly disposed, however great the sacrifice may be, to grasp at anything that can reland me on the Rock, were it ever so short a period, provided I could do it with honor and without submitting to a sacrifice that must be repugnant to my feelings. The Prince, I know, thinks that, in the event of a Spanish war, my application to go out cannot be resisted. I heartily wish his opinion may prove correct. Should that event take place you may rely upon my bringing out with me such a Second as I can depend upon, as also upon my making those arrangements for the defence of the Gut, which we have so often talked of, and for which I have already prepared my old friend Lord St. Vincent.

Colonel Ross, who, you know, was promoted to the Lieutenant-Colonelcy of the 44th Regiment, was, soon after his arrival here, moved to the 70th, in consequence, I believe, of what I said of the merit and talent he evinced in forming the 54th Regiment; for the 70th was in the most wretched order possible, and he was selected to reform it. Unfortunately however, in marching from one part of England to another, the Division under the command of the senior Lieutenant-Colonel (a son of the unfortunate Lord Kilwarden)¹ got into a quarrel with some of your

1. Arthur Wolfe, 1st Viscount Kilwarden (1739–1803). M.P. for Coleraine, 1783–90; for Jamestown, 1790–7; for Dublin, 1797–8. Irish Solicitor-General, May 1787, and Attorney-General, August 1789; Chief Justice of the King's Bench (I.), July 1798. Created Baron Kilwarden [I.], 3 July 1798, and Viscount [I.], 29 December 1800. He was murdered in Dublin on 23 July 1803.

Corps, in which some of the latter fell. In consequence, the Regiment was immediately ordered to the West Indies, and poor Ross has been shipt off with them. He behaved, whilst here, just as nobly as he ever did at Gibraltar, and spoke his mind with a degree of freedom which did him the greatest honor, to many, and some of those too, pretty closely connected with the Horse Guards, both on the subject of General Barnett's conduct and of the injury done to the Service by the measure of removing me.

Tomorrow I am to have a meeting with the Secretary at War[1] relative to the Secretaryship, having previously arranged with Mr. Addington that this is to be the channel through which it is to be concluded. Mr. Yorke has behaved in the handsomest manner about it, and declared to his successor, Mr. Bragge, that he [?considered] the business as a settled point even before he left the War Office, so that I really am extremely sanguine that *this* matter at least will shortly end to our satisfaction. Dodd will certainly not leave this till he has his commission in his pocket, for I cannot myself look forward to any other termination of this long protracted matter, notwithstanding the swaggering of Raleigh's sons, and his own menace of going out.

With respect to the Government of Gibraltar, my firmness has, I believe, totally stopt the views of wresting it from me, and Sir Thomas[2] will certainly be baulked in his expectations of succeeding to it if such he had formed. I shall be curious to see *his* Code of Orders, whenever it comes out in print, and I will thank you to send me half a dozen copies of it. At the same time, of *my own* I shall wish to have two or three dozen, for, ever since the Prince of Wales at his late visit at Portsmouth expressed his admiration of the Regiments that had lately come from Gibraltar, my system is become the fashion with all those who are attached to him, *even* among the Militia Corps, and I am literally now stript, in consequence of repeated applications, of every copy almost that I had. Indeed, such has been the rage of militia regiments after it, that the King's, and Welch Fusileers, are daily called upon to furnish every drill they have, to instruct them, and poor Robertson is in such request that the Commanding Officers of Corps in the vicinity of Portsmouth were literally squabbling who should get him.

I trust by this time the fever at Malaga has abated, and that every

---

1. Charles Bragge [afterwards Bragge-Bathurst] (*c.* 1754–1831). M.P. for Monmouth, 1790–1796; for Bristol, 1796–1812; for Bodmin, 1812–18; for Harwich, 1818–23. In 1788 he married Addington's sister Charlotte. Chairman of the Committee of Ways and Means in the House of Commons, 1799–1801; Treasurer of the Navy, November 1801–May 1803; Secretary at War, August 1803–May 1804; Chancellor of the Duchy of Lancaster, June 1812–23, with a seat in the Cabinet; President of the Board of Control, *ad interim*, January 1821–February 1822.

2. Sir Thomas Trigge.

precaution has been taken to prevent its getting into the garrison; but I fear you will upon that occasion have particularly experienced the want of that nervous police [*sic*] which I took so much pains to establish; although, from what you tell me of my measures relative to the establishment of a police officer being confirmed from home, it would not have been difficult to have maintained it, *at least such as I left it*.

With respect to my plateau, I received the inclosed letter from General Barnett, but, as it is the *only* one with which he has thought proper to *honor* me since I left the Rock, I certainly shall not answer it, *for obvious reasons*—I therefore request you will inform him of your having my instructions to take the trouble of forwarding it off *his* hands, and you will embrace the first opportunity of a man-of-war or a storeship *coming directly to Deptford*, to send it home addressed to me, observing to enter it as a part of my equipage which had been left behind at the time of my coming away, and to write me such a letter respecting it as I can shew to the officers of the Customs; you will of course not forget to thank Captain Campbell of the United States frigate Adams, for his politeness in bringing the plateau from Leghorn.

The inclosed letter from General Jacome I received a very few days since from the Continent; pray desire our friend Viale to answer it for me, saying everything that is kind and affectionate from me to him, and, at the same time, let him assure Castaños of my regard, and of my regret that those arrangements I adopted with him for the Cartel, which were so beneficial to both nations, should have been broken through.

Your brother of the Engineers was so good as to ship some boxes of preserved sweetmeats for me from St. Vincent, as will appear from the inclosed note that I received on the 12th of last month; for this attention, although the boxes have never as yet found their way to me, I request you will thank him most kindly. I am not yet without hopes of getting them, as I know the ship by which they were sent, and of which your father informed me, has arrived safe.

I cannot at present think of anything farther to communicate to you, and shall therefore only assure you of the continuance of my friendship and regard.

P.S. 30 Nov. Not having made up my letter, I am enabled to acquaint you with my having received yours of the 24th ultimo last evening, by which I saw, with much concern, that the fever at Malaga still continued to rage so violently: you will of course have heard from Dodd very fully by Captain Parker, as, being at the time of the Amazon's sailing under Buffa's care at the Isle of Wight for the cure of his arm, he was enabled to get *his* on board *in time*, although I was disappointed in that opportunity of sending mine.

I have now the pleasure to add, that I had yesterday a very long circumstantial conversation with Mr. Bragge upon the subject of the Secretaryship of Gibraltar, and I really conceive it is now in a fair train of being brought to a speedy and favorable issue, as the Secretary at War has promised to follow up Mr. Yorke's recommendation of a pension being granted to Raleigh, from the Civil Revenues of Gibraltar, which will be submitted to Mr. Addington immediately. I believe he means to propose the amount to be £250 per annum for the old man's life, and the half of that, after his death, to be continued to his wife. This being once arranged, the rest will follow as a matter of course, and therefore, as it was in my power yesterday to answer every other objection to the arrangement that was started, I believe, most fully to Mr. Bragge's satisfaction, I cannot see any reason to prevent everything terminating now, according to our wishes without much delay.'¹ (46137–40)

1776   THE DUKE OF CLARENCE TO THE PRINCE OF WALES
Bushy House, Tuesday afternoon [?*29 Nov. 1803*]
I am to request in the name of the Deputy-Lieutenants, Magistrates and Officers of the Hundred of Spelthorne that you will do them the favour of dining with them next Sunday at the Bush Inn at Staines after you have presented the Legion with their Colours. I did all I could to prevent this invitation but I found it was necessary to comply and hope therefore you will sacrifice one day to bad port wine and a mixture of company: there are coming the Deputy-Lieutenants and Magistrates, many gentlemen and some who are known to you. As for the Officers of the Legion you will I am sure make an allowance and recollect what difficulty we must have in getting subalterns. However, it is well meant and perhaps the party may afford you some amusement.

I shall expect you on Saturday to dinner: adieu till then. (44921)

1777   THE DUCHESS OF DEVONSHIRE'S MEMORANDUM FOR THE PRINCE OF WALES
[*Nov. 1803*]
Lest I should make any mistake in the statement you have done me the honour to desire me to submit to my mother,² I write down what I understood and shall [be] extremely obliged to you to write at the end of this one line, either of approbation or alteration.³

1. Only signed by the Duke.

2. John, 1st Earl Spencer (1734–83), married, 20 December 1755, Margaret Georgiana (1737–1814), daughter of Stephen Poyntz, of Midgham, Berks.

3. 'Nothing, dear Duchess, can be more correct. Addio. G.P.'

I understand that the Queen approves of Miss T[rimmer][1] in every point except the etiquette of rank, and that she thinks the sub-Governess should be a person of rank to attend the Princess[2] to Court. I understand from your goodness, dear Sir, to obviate this difficulty which had not occurred to you, that you propose to attach Miss T. to the Princess under the denomination of Companion and teacher enjoying the appointment of sub-Governess in every respect except the attendance to Court, being to be always to be always [*sic*] with the Princess, to dine with her, and have every appointment belonging to the sub-Governess's place, and that to obviate all difficulties you have thought of appointing Louisa Pointz[3] as sub-Governess, as she would attend the Princess to the Queen, but in every other respect would give Miss T. the full power of education by going hand in hand with her.

I will not trouble you now with observations which you feel I know as much as I do. It is a pity the situation could not be at once fix'd as you intended for the success of the object in view, but I feel most gratefully your kindness in thus trying to obviate the difficulty and in thinking of my cousin, as I am aware that the Queen's resolution is taken.

I understand that I am to desire my mother not to mention the subject of Louisa at present, but to give it due consideration, as well as to the whole of the arrangement, till the return of your Royal Highness for the meeting of Parliament[4]—till which time I understand you will have no intercourse with the Queen, and Miss T. is at liberty to remain with her friends.[5]

Will you kindly just add if you are perfectly satisfied with my stating this to my mother, or, if I have in any one instance misunderstood my commission? (Chatsworth MSS.).

1. Selina Trimmer (1765–1829), who had been governess to the Duchess's children. She was the daughter of Mrs. Sarah Trimmer (1741–1810), well known in her day as the author of *The Œconomy of Charity*, etc.

2. Princess Charlotte.

3. The Duchess's cousin. The Duchess said that she was 'really the best kind of woman that ever was, and her only fault *is not her fault*, I mean her being an old maid, but this gives her a fidgetty spirit of tidiness and order that works me to death' (*Georgiana*, ed. by Lord Bessborough, p. 71).

4. The memorandum, then, was probably written some days before the meeting of Parliament on the 22nd.

5. Mrs. Campbell and Mrs. Udney were subsequently appointed sub-Governesses to the young Princess.

Brighton, 2 Dec. 1803

I am sure you will beleive me when I say that nothing in the world would give me more real pleasure than the contributing by any exertion of mine either to your amusement or satisfaction, were it in my power, but unfortunately in the present instance I can be of no use at all to you. In the first place I gave up Bagshot to the Duke of Gloucester above ten years ago, since which I have never set my foot within the gates, as it has by some arrangement between the King and the Duke of Gloucester been settled upon Prince William, nor has the smallest reservation been made as to my shooting in any shape either in Bagshot Park or in the Manors belonging to it. Neither the Duke of Gloucester nor Prince William have been upon the very best terms with me for some years, therefore I should feel no small degree of difficulty in making any application to them either upon this or any other subject. However, notwithstanding these apparent difficulties, I will endeavour to find out if possible some way of getting at them. It gives me the truest & most heartfelt pleasure to find that your ideas & mine so completely meet, as they do, upon the subject of our late letters. (Add. MSS. 47560, ff.67–8)

33 Fleet Street, Thursday, 8 Dec. 1803

I am sorry, ashamed, and mortified beyond description that my paper[1] has sustained a very serious injury by your omitting to favour me with the correspondence of his Royal Highness the Prince of Wales, &c. &c. which appeared in yesterday's Morning Chronicle and Morning Herald.[2] A marked preference for more than a twelvemonth by articles of less importance in these prints, I have noticed with some temporary vexation. I contemplated, however, these transitory misfortunes in sullen silence, not wishing for a single moment to interrupt your better avocations, and attributing such deviations from the first channel of his Royal Highness's confidence to some unaccountable accident or mistake. But a continuation of the same system, in the very same papers, together with the very formidable shape which it now assumes, renders it incumbent upon me to make a firm but a respectful remonstrance.

To a gentleman of your experience and discernment it would be an insult to your good sense to insinuate the most remote belief on my part

1. The *Oracle*, the copyright of which newspaper he had bought in 1794 for, it was said £80, amalgamated with the *Daily Advertiser* in 1798.

2. Also in the *Sun*.

that the correspondence, which reflects so much honour on his Royal Highness, was not issued from and sanctioned by the chief officers of his confidence; and why I should be excluded from a share of the first honours of such a publication remains for those who have taken upon themselves the direction of this affair to determine. Of this fact, however, they may rest assured, that a pride of character—not a little cherished by the gracious condescensions of the Prince, through your kind medium—precludes me from remaining any longer with indifference in the background. I beg, therefore, leave firmly to urge and respectfully to maintain those claims to which my long and faithful services entitle me.

It requires no wonderful effort of memory, my dear Sir, to charge your recollection with the time when my paper *alone* had the *singular* peculiarity of daily and uniformly vindicating his Royal Highness against the wanton and bitter aspersions of his enemies. Pardon me for saying that they had so far succeeded as to have produced a very great and wonderful abatement of the Prince's popularity. Another paper also soon took an active part with me in the same cause, and the tide of public opinion was suddenly changed by the judicious and indefatigable use of the two engines alluded to.

Then why should I professionally be deprived of the distinction resulting from the publication of such a correspondence? Have I ever been reluctant or dilatory in my duty to his Royal Highness? Have I ever in any instance violated the confidence with which I was honoured? I say *no*, and defy the bitterest effort of malignity to overturn my assertion. But perhaps this liberty may be taken with my property because the Prince, in the plenitude of his favour, has been pleased to approve of my conduct by a certain grant of which you have had the proper and honourable management.[1] Be it so. Then take back, I pray, that bare recollection of past services, and I shall sit down in the quiet enjoyment of my independence. Let all my former exertions and all the past sacrifices of my paper be at once sunk into oblivion. Let it never be remembered that I stood forward in his Royal Highness's cause when the whole tribe of Jacobins were prepared to hunt him down, and if possible to wound and destroy his fair fame. But above all let it never be remembered that the very persons who then openly reviled him, appear now—to the astonishment of every loyal and patriotic man—entrusted with his Royal Highness's confidence — at least so far as regards the subject-matter now in question. When you gave me, my dear Sir, the account of the Spelthorne Volunteers, to serve his Royal Highness and his Royal brother, I had no idea that my property was next day to sustain a severe shock from a quarter that ought by no means to be suspected. It would

1. The *Oracle* had received a subsidy from the Treasury so long as it supported Pitt's Government (A. Aspinall, *Politics and the Press*, p. 68). Evidently, for a time, it was subsidized by Carlton House.

certainly be irksome and disagreeable if the cause of his Royal Highness were to suffer by the obloquy exercised against those who have ever been zealously & warmly bent on the vindication of his character and conduct. But I am so confounded at the marked and unmerited insult that I beg you will excuse me for thus expressing the operation of my feelings. (40046–7)

1780   THE PRINCE OF WALES TO THE EARL OF MOIRA

Brighton, 11 Dec. 1803

(*Private*). I should long since have thank'd you for your last most affectionate & kind letter, had I not in addition to heartfelt grief, been occupied by much disagreable & painful business arising from the death of poor Payne.¹ The goodness of your own most excellent & valuable heart will not fail to suggest to you what I have suffer'd on this occasion. An old & steady friendship of upwards of twenty years standing is not easy to be obliterated. I will not, however, tresspass further upon you upon this topic. You must, my dearest friend, before you receive this, have seen that the correspondance has found its way into the public papers, & the only way I can account for this is, that about a fortnight since, McMahon receiv'd a letter from a friend at Bath, stating that he understood there was a spurious publication of the correspondance coming out, & actually then at that moment in the press in that city. McMahon (I beleive through the means of Palmer) immediately had every sort of enquiry made, & finding the circumstance to be as it was stated, stopped it, & preserved [?] the whole of the impressions that were ready for distribution excepting 30 copies which had already been clandestinely dispos'd of, and succeeded also in having the press destroy'd. Who gave the first copy for this publication we can nohow trace, not even guess at. But it is evident that some of these thirty printed copies must have been sent & probably sold at a large price to the various presses & newspaper proprietors in London, & which were all so greedy after it that they were all running at one another which should publish it first, & to such length was this spirit carried, that, notwithstanding McMahon had various interviews with several of the editors, & I beleive some letters also passed between them, it was wholly impossible to stop the publication of the correspondance, & all he could obtain & which I approve most extremely in his exerting himself in doing, was the preventing Mr. Addington's *first private* note to me from being brought forward with the rest, & which he only succeeded in doing by saying that it would give me great personal offence & hurt my private feelings, as an ungentlemanlike &

1. Rear-Admiral Payne died on 17 November, following a paralytic stroke.

465

illiberal act. Thus the circumstance is, that I confess to you after all I have indured, & the very offensive, oppressive & degrading treatment I have experienc'd, though no one has a right to ask a question of me upon the subject, my wounded mind & my pride will not allow me to say the publication was not authoriz'd by me though I knew no more of how it came to the public press than you who are in Scotland. It has run like wild fire all through London, & already through all the Southern Counties, & the call for it, I understand, is immense from all quarters. The general impression, I am happy in learning, is the approbation of my conduct & sentiments by all who have look'd it over, & a thorough conviction of the base and scandalous illtreatment I have experienc'd. The courtiers are very sore upon it, as they had propagated many most gross & villainous falsehoods respecting it, in which they are detected, & the one good effect at least of the correspondance, is that they have had the lie given them most completely by it. The only footing, I understand, upon which they now indulge their malevolence is the saying how injudicious the publication is at such a moment, as it shews the enemies of the country that not only the country is not so united as it should be, but that there are private dissentions in the Royal Family; but they dare not open their lips in any other tone. To you, my dearest friend (to whom I ever have through a long series of years unveil'd the most secret thoughts of my heart & soul, & to whom I shall continue to do so whilst I have life), I have stated the whole of this proceeding, but honest pride forbids me to justify myself even though blame might be attach'd to it, to anyone but such a friend as you are, the friend of my heart. Pray tell me what people say of it in your part of the world. You will see how ably & handsomely Fox handled [it] in the House on Friday, as well as how greatly he spoke upon the whole state of the country, but which I understand is badly stated in all the papers, as a personal friend of Pitt's assured me that he never since he was in Parliament ever heard such a great speech as Fox's was, particularly his reply to York[e] & Addington; in short, that it was the greatest effusion of genius, of argument, truth [and] oratory; that he never witness'd anything like it, such was the rapturous strain in which he talk'd of Fox's speech, in so much, he added, that it not only completely silenc'd the ministerial phalanx, but left neither friend nor foe a single word to say either respecting me or any other head. You will likewise see the honorable mention Fox made of you, & also that he & Pitt are totally at variance, & never further from coalescing than at the present moment; that Wyndham & the Grenvilles also appear to differ widely with Pitt, & inclin'd to draw another way, that Pitt himself seems to be trimming back to Addington, or at least from his affected moderation, to ingratiate himself in high quarters with the powerful aid he has underhand from the Horse Guards, to avail himself of the momentary displeasure there may be against the present Premier for having perhaps espous'd my cause, as may be industriously represented, in the representations he judged right to make upon it, & whilst this displeasure exists, to totally get rid of him if possible; but if that is not to be done, at any rate his guarded line bespeaks his desire of return, & of conciliation with the Minister, & which if ever Ad—— is fool enough to give way to, I think cannot fail of terminating in his being speedily chasséed [?] by his re-created [?] friend.

I find if I do not here close this long scrawl, I shall be too late for the post. I will therefore add nothing more at present except the assurances of the invariable and unbounded affection, of [etc.][1] (Huntington Library).

1781   JOHN WALTER[2] TO COLONEL MCMAHON

Teddington Grove, 12 Dec. 1803

I am favour'd with your reply to my letter[3] & had I adverted to the debate which took place on Friday, should not have sent mine circuitously to Brighton which would have induc'd me to suppose you were in town.

I am at present confin'd with a sore throat but it seems mending, & having been engag'd sometime to dine with Mr. Scott on Wednesday in the Adelphi Terrace, if I am well enough, I will come to town & have the honour to pay you my personal respects.

As nothing could have tended more to the celebrity of the TIMES than the publication of the early part of the correspondence you did me the honour to let me peruse, you may be assured I would readily have publish'd it, had I not been withheld by the delicacy of the subject—the personages attach'd to it & the blame which might have follow'd in adding to the coolness which must naturally be augmented between his Majesty & the Heir Apparent to the throne.

I am told that the correspondence has been in the hands of individuals for some time & that the foreign Ambassadors had a copy of it, from some of whom it might have reach'd the press, as you assure me it was without the privity of his Royal Highness or any of his confidential servants.

1. The Prince wrote to Lord Moira the following note, dated merely Monday, 5.30 p.m.: 'Fox is arriv'd, I have seen him, & he wishes to see you, either now before dinner or at any time in the afternoon at your own house that you may please to appoint, as he wishes to return back into the country early tomorrow morning. Pray send me an answer directly.' (ibid.)

2. One of the proprietors of *The Times*, and sole manager and editor, from January 1803 (1776–1847). Second son of John Walter (1739–1812), the founder and chief proprietor of the newspaper.

3. Missing.

As the Prince's letters are very popular & highly spoken of, contrasted to those that have appear'd from his brother which are shifting & evasive, & as the two letters written to Mr. Pitt in 1796 & 1797 are illustrative of his Royal Highness's desire of a more active situation in the State, & were hinted at in the debate on Friday, I shall be happy in having his consent to lay them before the public, if you will take the Prince's sentiments on the subject; as I have heard opinions given that had his wishes been attain'd, Ireland would have been tranquil & rebellion extinct in that arm of the British Empire.

We will commune together on this matter when we meet, & if your engagements do not permit you to remain at home, if you will have the goodness to leave word where I can see you, I will follow your footsteps if I am able to come to town. (40048)

1782   THE EARL OF MOIRA TO COLONEL MCMAHON

Edinburgh, 12 Dec. 1803

I think that in my last letter I omitted apprizing you that the Trinidad papers which I gave to you the night when I left London belong to General Picton.[1] They should be sent to him. I have explained to him that I never had time to look at them.

I have expressly declared to everybody here that the publication of the correspondence was without the privity of the Prince or anyone belonging to him. I never disguised my regret that the matter had been pushed after the first refusal by the King, for I saw the risk of a publicity which I am sure is painful to the Prince, notwithstanding all the advantage he has in the ground. Vexed as he has been on the subject, his affection to the King is such that I know he will grieve at anything that frets his Majesty, which I fear this will do bitterly. That the King cannot by this be more estranged to the Prince & all attached to him than he was before I can fully believe. This unfortunate coldness, however, was never met with any similar sentiment by the Prince, so that I have observed the most kind anxiety in the Prince whensoever the King was ill or even mortified, & I thence judge his feelings on this occasion. Thank his Royal Highness for me, with all the earnest devotion which his unvarying friendship demands, for what he commissioned you to say to me. Never did I think for one moment that there was a tittle of sacrifice in any preclusion or proscription which I had entailed upon myself thro'

1. Lieutenant-General Sir Thomas Picton (1758–1815). Captain, 1778; Lieutenant-Colonel, 1796; Military Governor of Trinidad, 1797–1801, and Civil Governor, 1801–2; Brigadier-General, 1801; Major-General, 1808; commanded the Third Division in the Peninsular War; K.B., 1813; Lieutenant-General, 1813; G.C.B., 1815; killed at Waterloo.

Hugh, Duke of Northumberland
by R. E. Pine

Mary Isabella, Duchess of Rutland
after Sir Joshua Reynolds

profession or attachment to him: and had I been more appetent [*sic*] in disposition than I think I am, my sensations on the subject would have been just the same. Nor will the supposition of anything of this sort ever in any future day give color to a claim upon him. I have expressed myself heretofore to you upon that point sufficiently. Where I can be useful to him he shall command me to death, but it will be for my own gratification, and his kindness has not left him the power of incurring a shadow of debt to my adherence. His behaviour to you is nobly like himself, & my heart echoes all you say upon it.

McCarthy writes me word that Ogle has paid to Wilkes & Dickenson the sum which I paid to the Leicestershire Bank for him. If so you must get it, for there are £200 to be paid to Newton on the 20th & £1000 on the 26th, which you will furnish out of that £2500. (40049–51)

1783 THE PRINCE OF WALES TO RICHARD BRINSLEY SHERIDAN

Brighton, 16 Dec. 1803

I should some days ago have answer'd your letter had I not been oblig'd to write other letters that were of more immediate import. I ever must lament anything that causes you uneasiness, as I hope that you are well assured that there is no one in the world who entertains a higher regard for you than I do, nay, I may even say entertains a sincerer affection for you than I do. With regard to the publication of the correspondence you may know the real truth of the circumstances from McMahon, but my mind is too proud to stoop to make further explanations or apologies when there is not the smallest shadow or reason for censure, as I had nothing to do with the business. And such an accusation you must clearly see can only proceed from such as feel their plans developped, & the lies they had circulated contradicted by the appearance of the correspondance, the authenticity of which they cannot now dispute. No one that knows anything of the world can doubt the quarters, & their motives for doing so; but as I have already said, I have too long put up with the most ignominious, cruel, & oppressive treatment arising from yours as well as the arguments of other friends, but the just feelings I have for my own reputation & character will not admit of my submitting to be thus kick'd about any longer. You may ask McMahon any questions you please. As to Government I do not lay anything to their charge, but if they have tried to aid any cry against me they are very ungrateful. After the Recess if you have nothing better to do you may run down here perhaps for a day or two, & bring with you what intelligence you can as to the prospect we have to look for for future politicks; I trust you have good accounts from Tom, & that he continues pleas'd with his

situation.¹ With my best regards to Mrs. Sheridan,² I remain, dear
Sheridan [etc.]. (40052–3)

1784   THE EARL OF MOIRA TO THE PRINCE OF WALES
Edinburgh, 16 Dec. 1803
It has been with the truest emotions of gratitude that I have received
your Royal Highness's letter. If the knowing how to appreciate your
condescending kindness can afford any pretension towards that partiality which you deign to profess, I will venture to say that I am not
unworthy of the gracious friendship with which you distinguish me.
Your anxiety that I should be persuaded of your having no previous
knowledge of the publication of the correspondence was very superfluous, but is at the same time most justly estimated by me. In the long
course of time thro' which your Royal Highness has indulged me with
the freedom of expressing my sentiments undisguisedly to you, there
has been no instance in which I have felt so much confidence requisite
in the manliness of your character as when I urged objections to the
prosecution of that correspondence. I was sensible that the object in

1. 'Provision is to be made for Mr. Sheridan's son as a reward for the father's services; but to
avoid wounding the delicate feelings *of both*, there is an intention of giving Sir John Morshead
an employment, that the Prince of Wales may appoint Thomas Sheridan to the situation Sir
John now has under him' (Rose, *Diaries and Correspondence*, ii.59 [2 October 1803]).
    The office to which George Rose referred was that of Surveyor-General of the Duchy of
Cornwall, which, however, Sir John continued to hold. On 11 September 1803 Lady Bess-
borough reported that Sheridan had rejected the offer of 'a great place for Tom' at Malta.
She added, 'A few days ago Mr. Greenwood sent to him to say Tom was appointed *Aide de
Camp* to the D. of York, with some place in the Household', but Sheridan had refused all offers
(*Correspondence of Lord Granville Leveson-Gower*, i.430).
    Dr. Laurence wrote to his friend Lord Fitzwilliam on 11 August: 'Sheridan will not join
them [Ministers]. He would not even suffer his son to accept a good place in the particular
patronage of Lord St. Vincent, who offered, it is said, to give the father a license at the same
time to abuse Ministers as much as he would. He did indeed abuse them very fairly to me as
we walked away together after one of his late panegyrics upon them. I regard neither the one
nor the other. He has too much pride and ambition to accept anything which Mr. Addington
can or will give him. He will not, if I know him at all, submit to be subordinate to the present
Cabinet and placed on a level with Tierney, following too in his wake. On the other hand, he is
daily losing, or rather has already lost, the regard of all his former connections; has merely
confirmed himself in the favour of the newspapers, gained possibly some popularity among the
Volunteer Corps who do not see through his policy; and not yet succeeded in his attempt of
drawing after him the following of an Irish party' (Fitzwilliam MSS.).

2. Sheridan married, 27 April 1795, as his second wife, Esther Jane, daughter of the Rev.
Newton Ogle, Dean of Winchester (1776–1817): a woman of whom he was as unworthy as was
the Prince of Mrs. Fitzherbert. The Duchess of Devonshire described her as 'a good-hearted,
odd little thing' (Chatsworth MSS. To her mother, Lady Spencer, 2 September 1795).

question did interest you, & rightly, in the tenderest point. In reason & equity nothing could be advanced against it; it roused all your magnanimity, and the rejection of your claim to a prominent station in that contest which was to decide the fate of Britain was injustice if not insult. Your plea could not be thought stronger than what I held it. I had only the apprehension that in pressing it after the first refusal, as it could not be done without energetic expostulation, that publicity might follow which has occurred: not from any notion that your demand would not be sanctioned by the opinion of almost every individual in the country, but from the dread of a consequence which I knew would be more painful to you than to any other man breathing. I was aware how irritable the King's mind was upon the subject, & I trembled lest the agitation should affect his health. Once you were embarked in the controversy, the notoriety of such an application's having been made & resisted made it unavoidable that the arguments on both sides should have a circulation supposed to be confidential: and the ultimate appearance of the correspondence in print seemed to me equally inevitable thro' the indiscretion of individuals, whatsoever care your Royal Highness might take to prevent it. If the King shall not feel it in the manner I feared, the publication cannot but benefit you in universal estimation. Indeed, the sentiment, both here & in every quarter from which I have heard, is uniform. Warm applause is given to the generous zeal which you have manifested, & I can assure you, Sir, no less tribute is paid to the forbearance which you have shown in the discussion of a refusal that wounded you so deeply. I am truly happy that your Royal Highness has enabled me to destroy the only insinuation that could have been attempted by malicious artifice against you, namely, that this was an appeal to the public on a matter of disunion in the Royal Family. It would have been a false description of the procedure had your Royal Highness sanctioned the publication, for this is a national concern, & not a question of family arrangement. I am not deceiving you from a view of gratifying you momentarily when I say you have cause to be highly satisfied with the impression made here. Need I paint it stronger than by saying it is such as meets all the wishes of him who is with devoted affection [etc.]. (40054–7)

1785 THE EARL OF MOIRA TO COLONEL MCMAHON
Edinburgh, 19 Dec. 1803
Ogle's shuffling about the £500 bill makes me fear still more that he will not repay the former sum advanced by me out of which you were to make provision for Newton. Have the kindness therefore to send for James (No. 1, Albany Place, Piccadilly) whom I have desired to confer with

you on the business of the Exchequer. I do grievously suspect (but do not hint at it) that there has been connivance between McCarthy & Ogle for temporary convenience about these bills, and that they have been cashed for their accommodation whilst we were told they could not be discounted. I cannot comprehend to what the enclosed alludes if it be not to a bill which McCarthy professes never was discounted, as Newton will explain to you from a letter which I enclosed to him. Do make Newton enquire into this.

They have at last found out at the Horse Guards that it would look awkward to refuse to me the allowance for a Secretary when they had given it even to Vyse, so they have offered it if I will apply for it. As I cannot accept it on the footing of compliment it will not do now to make a sinecure of it. Of course it makes no opening for Ld. Delvin;[1] indeed an efficient Secretary to copy & keep papers in order would be a material aid. Sutton did think of taking a house here for a winter for the education of his daughters. If it would suit him he would suit me, therefore I have written to sound whether in that case he would relish such an evocation.

Adieu. I lead the dullest & most slavish of lives, but I do my business & please the people, which is always a comfortable consciousness. (40059–60)

1786   THE DUKE OF KENT TO THE PRINCE OF WALES

Castle Hill Lodge, 26 Dec. 1803

General Burton[2] of the 3d Regiment of Guards has just left me and

1. George, 8th Earl of Westmeath [I.] (1785–1871), styled Lord Delvin from 1792, when his father succeeded as 7th Earl, to 30 December 1814, when his father died. Entered the Army, 1800, served in Egypt under Sir Ralph Abercromby (1801); Lieutenant, September 1803; Commissioner of Barracks [I.], 1813–15. Created Marquess of Westmeath [I.], 12 January 1822; Irish Representative Peer, 1831–71.

2. Napier Christie Burton (1758–1835), of the 3rd Foot Guards. Entered the Army, 1775; Lieutenant, 1779; Lieutenant-Colonel, 1789; Colonel, 1795; Major-General, 1797; Lieutenant Governor of Upper Canada, 1799–1802; on the Staff of the North-west District, 1803–5; Lieutenant-General, 1805; General, 1814. M.P. for Beverley, 1796–1806. On 6 December the House of Commons was informed that he, one of its Members, having been charged with a breach of military discipline, had been arrested, with the view of his being court-martialled (*House of Commons Journals*, lix. 33). The General Court Martial at Chelsea ended on Tuesday, 10 January 1804, and the proceedings were communicated to the King. *The Times* announced on 23 January: 'The decision of the court martial . . . sentenced that officer to be broke, on the ground of indiscretion. The King confirmed the sentence, but the next day restored him to his rank in the Army'.

If Lord Glenbervie is to be believed, the affair gave rise to violent dissensions in the Royal Family. The evidence which produced Burton's conviction 'was a letter to the Duke of York and exhibited by him in support of the prosecution. This letter, Burton's friends say, was of a

having anxiously entreated me to solicit your humane and benevolent interference with the Duke of York to prevent, if possible, his being brought to a court martial in consequence of his unfortunate duel with the Honble. Captain King,[2] I cannot possibly refuse submitting his request to you who I know are ever ready to lay aside your own personal feelings when the motive that actuates you is that of serving a meritorious officer. Twenty-nine years devoted to the military profession in various quarters of the globe, with an unblemished character, are the claims of General Burton, and I am sure stronger ones will not be wanting with you to induce you to lend him an assisting hand, if there are not insuperable obstacles to your interference. You are, of course, fully sensible that however favorable the result of the court martial might be to the General, the consequences of a trial of *that* nature are ever unpleasant in the extreme. If therefore through *your* good offices these can be averted by preventing the trial from taking place, the act will be truly worthy of yourself.

If I had had anything interesting to communicate to you I should have written long ere this, but *that* not being the case, I have been unwilling uselessly to intrude, well knowing you would never consider my silence as proceeding from any other cause. I shall now only add a request to be most kindly and particularly remembered to Mrs. Fitzherbert and repeating the assurance of my most warm and devoted attachment [etc.]. (46141–2)

private, confidential nature, and his cause has been very warmly espoused by the Dukes of Clarence and Kent, and one day lately, before the King was taken ill, those two brothers and the Duke of York being with the King, the Duke of Kent is reported to have said to his Majesty, "Pray, Sir, what would your Majesty think of a man who should injure another by a breach of private confidence?" The King replied, "I know not why you put that question to me, but, as a general position, such a breach of confidence must be considered as very culpable and dishonourable".

"Then", said the Duke of Kent, "my brother there", pointing to the Duke of York, "is the man who has been guilty of that culpable and dishonourable act". Here, it is said, a very furious altercation between the brothers ensued till the King, in great agitation, ordered them all out of the room' (*Journals*, i.365).

2. Henry King (*d.* 1839), a younger brother of George, 3rd Earl of Kingston (1771–1839). Ensign, 1794; wounded in the Helder expedition; Captain, 1796; Major, 1804; Lieutenant-Colonel, 1809; Colonel, 1814; Major-General, 1825; Lieutenant-General, 1838. K.C.B., 1835.

VI   1804

The year opened with further displays of the Prince's irritability, provoked not only by his having been refused a military command but also by the removal of his Regiment from the coastal area around Brighton, where the French might be expected to land, to the inland town of Guildford, where he would have no opportunity of showing his courage. Though he said that he would never forgive his brother, the Commander-in-Chief, for allegedly insulting him in this way, they were soon on speaking terms again, Sheridan being given the credit for the reconciliation. Some people believed that the recent publication of what had become known as the 'Royal Correspondence' was partially responsible for the frightening collapse of the King's health once more in February.

In the meantime the popularity of the Addington Ministry both in the country and in the House of Commons was declining, as the belief gained ground that he was incapable of conducting the war. He still commanded a substantial majority in Parliament when the King's health again broke down. Early in February the Duke of Kent was reporting unfavourably on his father's condition, and his worst fears were realized on the 15th when the 'mad' doctors were sent for to the Queen's House by order of the Cabinet. The Prince was reported to be in great agitation. He 'talks all day without ceasing to Mrs. Fitzherbert'. 'Sheridan', said Grey, 'has seen him occasionally and is the only person engaged in politics who has done so except Lord Thurlow.' Some days later he was still 'in a fever of uneasiness, and anxious that questions should be pressed in Parliament without delay'.

474

The possibility of a Regency in any case made Addington's position insecure, and Lord Glenbervie reported that Fox was to be Prime Minister if the Prince became Regent. But there was Pitt to be reckoned with, even though his personal following was not large, and he himself wrote to Lord Melville on 29 March, 'I should be very sorry that either Lord Moira or through him the Prince should suppose that there is any chance of my changing my opinion'—the opinion that he himself must be Prime Minister. Moira shared Thurlow's view that if need be the Prince should accept the restrictions embodied in the Regency Bill of 1789. But Melville was confident that Pitt would be unable to establish a Regency such as he had proposed in 1789, and the mere attempt would ensure his unpopularity. The situation had changed. On the earlier occasion he had been at the head of a powerful and popular Government, and the country peaceful and prosperous, whilst the Prince had failed to conduct himself with discretion and had led the public to believe that he was in the hands of an unpopular faction. But now Addington's Administration was neither powerful nor popular, nor was there in existence a compact, consolidated faction of which the country was in dread. It seemed likely that if the situation arose, the Prince, though Pitt feared that 'no very certain dependence is to be placed on any language which he holds,' would be discreet enough to call into his service able men belonging to different party connections and possessing the confidence of the nation. According to the Duke of Portland he had become perfectly reconciled to the Queen, had avoided caballing with every description of people, and had dined daily with Mrs. Fitzherbert with only such intimates as Tyrwhitt and Colonel McMahon to keep him company.

The process of Cabinet making never got under way: the King happily recovered before the end of March, though the probability of a change of Government increased during the next few weeks as the various Opposition groups came closer together in a joint effort to defeat Addington, whose position was fatally compromised by the defection of many of his influential friends in the House of Commons, the independent country gentlemen. (Governments in those days were defeated, not by their enemies but by their friends.) Fox was told early in April that Erskine would very reluctantly refuse an offer of the Attorney-Generalship. 'He has behaved very meanly to a degree that makes me quite sorry for him.' Sheridan too was 'desirous of getting right again' and was certainly 'out of humour with the Doctor'. The Grenvilles coalesced with the Foxites, and the Government's majority fell from 71 on 15 March to 52 on 23 April (after which, Charles Yorke, the Home Secretary, admitted that the game was up) and to 37 on the 25th. On this last occasion the minority did not include either Sheridan or Grey, and other Foxites too were absent. On the 29th Addington decided to resign to avoid outright defeat and consequent embarrassment to the King, whose mind, it was believed, had been conditioned for a change by the Duke of York. Addington believed that the Prince could have averted a change of Government if, during the last few days of April, he had decided to stand by the King—but he had 'thrown himself entirely into the Opposition'. At one of the Princess of Wales's dinner parties she impishly displayed for the amusement of her guests (one of them Lord Hawkesbury, a Cabinet Minister) a new caricature of the State Waggon in distress, drawn by *donkeys*, whilst John Bull's *horses*, with political faces, were standing by, rubbing one another at the prospect of being harnessed together.

1787 THE DUKE OF KENT TO THE PRINCE OF WALES

Castle Hill Lodge, 2 Jan. 1804

I have a thousand thanks, my dearest brother, to offer you for your most kind answer to my letter, which was everything I could wish, and precisely what I expected it would be, as I told General Burton at the time I was writing to you, that I did not conceive you could possibly comply with his request, however you might wish to serve him, of interfering in his behalf with *the Commander-in-Chief*. I am sure the perusal of what you have written, and which you have so kindly permitted me to indulge him with, must be extremely consolatory to this unfortunate officer in his present truly melancholy situation; I dare beforehand answer for his utmost gratitude. I understand his court martial comes on on Friday, and I am apprehensive, if his sentence should be *that* which, by the articles of war, attaches to the sending of a challenge, there is no intention on the part of the Duke of York, to recommend his case to the King's clemency. I wish I may be mistaken in my judgment.

I must now reply to your most affectionate message by the Duke of Orleans, which he delivered to me last evening by saying that I feel very sincerely and highly flattered by the most kind wish you express of seeing me at Brighton, in consequence of which, should it suit your convenience, I propose running down on the 20th, passing the 21st and 22nd with you, and returning home on the 23d: but should any of your own arrangements move you from Brighton before that, then I shall make a point, should you wish it, of coming over to you at an earlier day.

I have not yet seen William, as I only returned last evening from Windsor, where I went over to see poor Adolphus, who, as you know, has broke his collar bone. I left him without pain or fever, but much

476

mortified at the prospect of continuing so many weeks in a helpless state. He charged me to present you his kindest love, and to say how happy he had been made by your affectionate remembrance of him. I intend going over again to see him in the course of next week, and shall be happy *then* to deliver him any message you may chuse to give me for him, which I well know will make my visit doubly welcome.

Madame de St. Laurent desires me to say qu'elle est infiniment flattée de vos bontés en vous rappellant d'elle, and to offer her best wishes for your welfare and happiness. May I request of you to say from me everything that is most kind to Mrs. Fitzherbert, for whose friendly attention to me I feel truly grateful. And now receive the assurance of my most warm and devoted attachment.

P.S. Will you permit me, when I come over to Brighton, to bring Colonel Smyth with me, who is a very excellent musician and would be highly gratified in the opportunity of hearing your Band. (46148–50)

1788   RICHARD WILSON[1] TO THE PRINCE OF WALES

Bildeston, Suffolk, 2 Jan. 1804

I humbly beg your Royal Highness's pardon for presuming to trouble you about a private in the 10th Dragoons, but as I know your Royal Highness interests yourself so readily & feelingly about the lowest individual in the Regiment, I have the less hesitation in addressing you upon this occasion.

Last summer, the son of a tenant of mine at this place wished to enlist into your Royal Highness's Regiment, having sometime before been in the yeomanry cavalry. I then took the liberty of writing to Colonel McMahon, mentioning the circumstance & begging of him to solicit your Royal Highness to make him a non-commission'd officer when he should be fit for it. His name is John Read & is in Lord James Murray's[2] troop. If your Royal Highness will have the condescension to order some enquiry to be made about the poor fellow & if found deserving of the promotion I have mentioned, I humbly beg of your Royal Highness to think of him, & it will give great comfort to his parents who are extremely respectable farmers.

I cannot omit this opportunity of stating for your Royal Highness's

1. See No. 1628.

2. Second son of John, 4th Duke of Atholl [S.]. (1782–1837). Entered the Army, 1798; Lieutenant-Colonel, 1806; Colonel, 1813; Major-General, 1819; Lieutenant-General, 1837. M.P. for Perthshire, 1807–12; a Lord of the Bedchamber, 1812–32; A.D.C. to the Prince Regent and to the King, 1813–19. Created Baron Glenlyon, 17 July 1821, a 'Coronation' peerage.

satisfaction & information that wherever I go in the country I hear the most general & unqualified approbation of your Royal Highness's conduct upon the subject of the cruel rejection of your fair & just claim to military rank. Your Royal Highness, however, has this consolation, that you are placed upon the highest pinnacle of fame, from which they will feel it very difficult to pull you down.

Forgive me, Sir, for thus presuming to say so much on this occasion, but it comes from the heart of one who feels the most dutiful attachment for your Royal Highness & with all deference subscribes himself [etc.]. (40061–2)

1789   PRINCESS MARY TO THE PRINCE OF WALES

Windsor, 4 Jan. 1804[1]

I am desired by Dolly to return you many thanks for your kind inquiries & I have the happiness of assuring you he is going on very well. The collar bone is certainly broke but he suffers very little pain; the most unpleasant part of the business is Keate having told him he will not have the use of his arm for some weeks.[2]

The Queen & my sisters have desired me to say everything kind in return for your recollection of them.

Dolly hopes you will have a pleasant party at Sir H. Featherston's & is very sorry *he* must now give up all thoughts of belonging to it.[3] He also joins with me in wishing you every happiness this world can afford.

Amelia certainly is better though her recovery is but slow.

I am always happy in having an opportunity of assuring you, dearest brother, you will ever find me your truly affte. friend and sister. (Add. Georgian 12/27)

1790   LETTERS FROM COLONEL MCMAHON TO THE PRINCE OF WALES

London, 5 Jan. 1804

I write for the purpose of merely informing your Royal Highness that still no order is gone for your Regt. to march. They must mean either to

1. The letter is wrongly endorsed the 1st.

2. The Duke of Cambridge met with this accident whilst hunting.

3. On 30 December the Prince and the Duke of Clarence had set off from the Pavilion to Uppark for a shooting party.

make the movement on the 14th instant as they profess, or intend to abandon the design altogether.

I saw Mr. Hague this morning at 12 o'clock; he is a dark, good looking young man of, I should suppose, nearly forty: is a solicitor I find & has been in business for some years in Greek Street. He appears to me to be a sensible, clever fellow with rather too much of the democratic taint 'declares himself actuated by no other motive than a desire to indulge the manly spirit of an Englishman by giving praise where praise is so justly due & to rescue the character & honor of a brave & gallant man from all doubt & aspersion; in short, to take *one* good man out of the hands of *two* bad ones'. He is outrageous at the removal of your Regiment & very willing to follow it up in any way, but I think him too violent & intemperate to be hurried; therefore (as he goes into the country on Saturday) I have made another appointment with him for Monday next at 12 o'clock, which will not only afford me time to make further enquiries about him, but likewise to consider what use should be made of his letter to the —— as well as of himself generally.

No distinct news of any kind, but the rumour as loud today as ever that the Brest fleet have been seen at sea standing to the westward & that the Boulougne flotilla is also out.

P.S. I wrote last night to the D. of Norfolk. The Living is not in Y.R.Hss.'s gift, which I took care to observe how much you lament. (40063)

London, 6 Jan. 1804

Notwithstanding the Enniskillen Dragoons are to go to Brighton I think it is yet likely to happen that they will remove the 4th Dragoons & not your Royal Highness's Regiment, for the removal of it has already made so much noise & excited such general disapprobation that it is probable they will stop where they are.

The Duke of Kent intends being at Brighton on Tuesday to meet yr. R.Hss. The D. of Clarence I understand told Princess Amelia in conversation on Wednesday last that the order for Y.R.Hss.'s Regt. to march from Brighton to Guildford, at the moment of alarm, was an indignity you could never pass by, & that it would produce an irreperable breach for ever between Y.R.Hss. & the D. of York. This conversation it seems Princess Amelia repeated in confidence to the D. of York, who, I have reason to believe is considerably alarm'd at it, for the old shelter for everything is again resorted to: 'It is all the King's own doing', and 'Nobody has had a hand in it but the King.' The alarm of invasion has subsided today, for the frost has now set in with such severity that there can be no co-operation from Holland; but the Brest fleet is not yet accounted for. In all other particulars town is barren of every kind of news.

Sir Chas. Green[1] goes immediately to the W. Indies, where he is either to continue in command, or hold it, until a Commdr.-in-Chief goes out. (40064)

1791   THE DUKE OF KENT TO THE PRINCE OF WALES

Brompton Park House, Friday, 6 Jan. 1804

Having been absent from Castle Hill *since Wednesday* it was not till last evening that I got your most kind and affectionate note of the 3d, I now hasten to inform you that on the 10th (Tuesday) I shall not fail to avail myself of your most welcome invitation and make my appearance at the Pavillion. With your permission, unless your own arrangements should take you from thence earlier, I shall make mine to remain with you Wednesday and Thursday and return to Castle Hill on Friday, on which day I have the Duke of Orleans and his Twickenham friends, Stahremberg,[2] &c. to dine with me. Yesterday's account of Adolphus continues to be good and I trust nothing is wanting for his perfect recovery from his accident but a little time and patience.

I take the liberty of enclosing to you poor General Burton's letter to me as the best mode I know of to convey the expression of his gratitude to you. You will perceive by it that his court martial comes on today and that I am to attend as an evidence to his character. I heartily wish the result may be more favorable to him than from present appearances and the hints that are dropt I am led to apprehend.

I shall now only add my most kind and particular remembrance to Mrs. Fitzherbert and repeat the unfeigned assurance of those sentiments of the warmest and most devoted attachment with which I shall to the last day of my existence remain [etc.]. (46152–3)

1. General Sir Charles Green (1749–1831). Lieutenant, 1769; Lieutenant-Colonel, 1793; Civil Governor of Grenada, 1796–1801; Colonel, 1797; Brigadier-General, 1798; on the Irish Staff, 1803; knighted, May 1803; appointed to succeed Grinfield *ad interim*. General, 1819. Created Baronet, December 1805.

2. The Imperial Minister.

480

1792 PRINCESS CHARLOTTE OF WALES TO THE KING

6 Jan. 1804

I am very glad to hear my dear grandpapa is well. Lady Elgin has allowed me as I shall be eight years old tomorrow to write to ask his blessing and assure him I shall do all in my power to be his most dutiful and affectionate grandchild.[1] (49274)

1793 THE DUKE OF NORTHUMBERLAND TO COLONEL MCMAHON

Alnwick Castle, 6 Jan. 1804

I had the pleasure of receiving your letter last night, & have not a moment's hesitation in recommending it strongly to the Prince to keep his Regiment. His language on this, as on every occasion, shoud be dignified. 'Whatever appearance the removal of the 10th Regt. of Dragoons from Brighton to Guilford may have, he has too much reliance of his Majesty's promise that shoud an invasion take place he woud give him an opportunity of distinguishing himself at the head of his Regiment, not to be convinced that this removal is intended rather to carry it thro' Guildford to the probable scene of action than to remove the Regt. from it.' By holding this language, & appearing easy on this subject, shoud the removal have been ordered to mortify the Prince it will appear as if it had failed in its effect, & his avowed reliance on H.M.'s promise will force them to employ H.R.H. shoud any invasion take place. At any rate they will completely fail in their principal object, which is to get the Regt. from him by his own resignation. It is for the same reason that I much advise his going to the Birthday. Every act of his which tends to make the world believe that he is not mortified will vex them, as all this is done solely with the view to mortify him; & the less he appears so, the more will they be provoked. He must on this occasion, as on all others where he cannot help himself, endeavour to disguise his feelings. For it is the true & proper line of conduct in a person of H.R.H.'s

1. Her mother wrote to Lord Melville on the 3rd: 'The Princess of Wales takes the liberty of inviting Lord Melville to dinner at half after five o'clock at Kensington Palace next Friday the 6th of January, to meet Princess Charlotte to celebrate her birthday. The Princess also desires that all the gentlemen appear in dress coats on the occasion.' Melville endorsed the letter, 'Excused myself on the score of indisposition.'

The Princess wrote to him again on the 6th: 'The Princess of Wales is more than sorry at Lord Melville's indisposition—and trusts that his Lordship will soon recover to enable him to dine at Kensington on the 18th of this month, after the Drawing Room at seven o'clock. Princess Charlotte will regret very much when informed of Lord Melville's not being able to attend her on her birthday. The Princess wishes to his Lordship many returns of the season, and that Lord Melville may enjoy many many years more of earthly happiness to which he is so much entitled' (S.R.O., Melville MSS.).

consequence to appear to suppose it impossible that an indignity or insult can be intended to be offered him till it is so very gross as to admit of no palliation. In such a case as the present, fifty plausible excuses may be offered for the removal of a Regt. of Dragoons. All this mischief & vexation, however, proceeds from the ill-advised step of publishing the correspondence, & I cannot help again repeating that whoever advised that step was certainly no sincere friend to the Prince, or at best so very ill judging a person that his advice ought not to be taken. I sincerely wish the idea I once suggested had been adopted by H.R.H. instead of seeking a Commission of General, to have asked leave to place himself at the head of the armed peasantry & yeomanry of the country, & I think I coud have put the request into such words that it coud hardly have been refused. Three or four hundred thousand British freemen voluntarily following the Standard of the Prince of Wales woud have placed him in a proud situation.

I [am] much obliged to you for what you mention relative to the Living of Stratton. I shall feel myself much obliged to H.R.H. if he will do me the honour of presenting a particular friend of mine, the Revd. Mr. John Rowe, A.B. to this Living. Mr. Rowe is a Launceston man, & son to one of the Aldermen, & is the person for whom Mr. Wilson has applied, as I understand from him.

I have entered very fully into the P.'s business respecting the resignation, from the desire which you informed me Mrs. F. had to know my sentiments on the occasion. I have therefore given them very freely. I wish my opinion may have weight in this instance, as I am convinced shoud H.R.H. resign he will repent it himself whilst he makes them happy. Let them, if the enemy lands, keep him at Guildford unemployed if they dare; but I know they dare not do it. They must employ him, & they know it; & the only way by which they can escape the consequences of not doing so, is to endeavour to make him resign in ill humour. Adieu my dear Colonel, accept all our best wishes. (40065–6)

1794   THE EARL OF MOIRA TO COLONEL MCMAHON

Edinburgh, 10 Jan. 1804

Yours on Parish business which I received this morning would have distressed me still more than it has actually done were it not that I got at the same time one from James. By the latter, he would be able to apply nine hundred & odd pounds which I had sent to him to the liquidation of the bills you mention; for I had requested him so to dispose of it if he could suspend (which I now find he has done) another application of it. This consoles me in a delay that had taken place about getting money for drafts on you, which I still expect this afternoon but not before three o'clock when the post goes out. McCarthy's behaviour about the West India bill of Ogle's is inexplicable to me.

I earnestly hope the Prince will not give up his Regiment. Alas! how I always lamented those letters. My situation here is laborious & heavy beyond measure; not cheered by a single gratification or by the most indistinct prospect. By Heaven if it were not for the Prince I would give up every public walk of life tomorrow. Adieu. (40067–8)

1795 THE PRINCE OF WALES TO THE QUEEN, AND THE REPLY

Brighton, 17 Jan. 1804

The eighteenth of January cannot pass without my endeavouring to express & to lay at your feet those good wishes which a truly attach'd & much devoted son must ever, in the most lively sense, feel for a rever'd & beloved parent. All your children who are bless'd with seeing you on that day cannot help feeling the same, but none can with more truth or fervency than myself pray that you may enjoy many happy returns of it through a long series of years; though I shall unfortunately be absent, you will do me the justice to beleive that none of them can look up to you with a greater degree of veneration & tenderness than I do.

Repeated attempts have been most unjustly & cruelly made not only to wound my feelings & honor as a man, but to degrade & ruin me both as a Prince & an Officer in the eyes of my own country as well as of Europe. At this awful crysis to our nation, a military Command suitable to my birth has been refus'd me; the 10th Dragoons is also at this moment remov'd from the advanc'd post of the Army only because *the Prince of Wales* is its Colonel; so circumstanc'd I must recollect that I am the Heir of these Kingdoms, & that it is therefore impossible for me to appear in a place where my presence cannot but be disagreable to those who, notwithstanding their conduct to me, it is still my duty to respect. I cannot help expressing to you, as a mother, an anxious wish that those with whom I stand so nearly connected had treated me with the same degree of fraternal affection which I will defy even the malice of my greatest & bitterest enemies not to acknowledge I have ever wish'd to testify to all the younger branches of my family. I in return have experienc'd a treatment which my proud soul can neither now brook nor hereafter forgive.

I am sorry to mix any complaint with my congratulations to you on this day, but my heart is so full & so sincere that neither feeling nor candour permit me to be entirely silent on a subject which has given me more pain than any event of my life. To require an opinion upon this question of,

483

to you, so delicate a nature, would excite too keen a sensation in your breast. I therefore hope, my dearest mother, you will not trouble yourself farther than to acknowledge through the Duke of Kent the safe receipt of this letter.[1] (42377–8)

THE QUEEN'S REPLY

Queen's House, 19 Jan. 1804
I did not receive your letter till this morning after breakfast, as the Duke of Kent could not find an opportunity of giving it me yesterday. I seize the first moment I can call myself at liberty to return you thanks for the kind & affectionate expressions towards me, & I trust that you are fully persuaded that none can be more sensible of your continued & unalterable kindness than myself. I lament having been deprived of your presence on my birthday. Your absence must always be a loss, but to none more so than to myself, & I trust *at least I may hope* that our separation will not be long, & that ere long we shall all be again united as in former times, which none can more anxiously wish & pray for than [etc.]. (36536 and (copy) 42379)

1796 LETTERS FROM THE DUKE OF KENT TO THE PRINCE OF WALES

Brompton Park, Thursday afternoon, 19 Jan. 1804
I hope when you have read the inclosed, you will admit that I am not a bad commissioner. I received it from the Queen's own hands about an hour since in Eliza's room, and if I may be allowed to judge from the manner in which it was given to me, I should not hesitate in saying, although she has never opened her lips to me, on the *contents* of your letter to her, that it excited no *one* sensation in *her* breast, but what, if it could have been witnessed by you, would have been most consolatory and gratifying to your afflicted mind. I sincerely hope the perusal of her answer will *not* prove that I have misjudged the expression of her countenance. I have conversed much with Minny and Sophy about you, and to *them* I have shewn the copy of yours: *both* felt your kindness to *them most sensibly*, and the former, who is bolder than poor *little Barnacles*, spoke with infinite fairness of the D. of Y—— as far as related to his conduct about the Regiment, the particulars of which conversation I will reserve, if you will permit me, as you are informed of the essentials (qui sont *le cœur pour vous*) till we *meet*; the latter was all tenderness, but her shaken nerves are not equal to speak out as roundly as the placid,

1. The two drafts of this letter (40069–72) are dated the 16th.

484

The 1st Marquess of Hastings
by John Hoppner 1794

Sir Thomas Tyrwhitt
attributed to R. Miller

Georgiana, Duchess of Devonshire
by John Downman

firm Minny. As to Emily, she is so perfect an enthusiast about you, that weak as *she* is, and agitated with every wind that blows, I did *not* chuse to shew the letter to *her*, but confined myself to the expression of your affection for *her* which was received with every unfeigned demonstration of the greatest joy. As to Augusta and Eliza, the obligations they are under of eternally hearing whatever *may* pass relative to you between the K. & Q. deterred me from putting *them* in a predicament that might have been delicate, and therefore I did *not* shew the letter to *them*; but they are both most attached to you, et gémissent intérieurement de tout ce qui se passe. *William* has of course seen it, and approves of it most fully. Mrs. Fitzherbert will explain to you how I was prevented from delivering it in *propria personâ* but I trust the result will prove that the commission has not the less had its effect.

So much on this subject; I shall just add that, with respect to the ball, if *agreable* to *you*, Thursday the 26th will be the day *I* should wish, and it will be perfectly agreable to William also, who is disengaged for *that* day. I shall not fail to bring the Duke of Orleans, and il Pittore. We propose leaving this at *ten* in the morning with your horses, and, as you are so good as to say that we are to have them also from Cuckfield, we trust we shall be with you by *four*, and depend on your indulgence to permit us on *my* account to return the *next* day, as it is *that* fixed for my taking possession of Kensington, et vous êtes trop gallant pour ne pas sentir quelle seroit la dureté de laisser Madame de St. Laurent veuve pour la première nuit.

Now having answered your kind invitation, permit me as your truest and most faithful friend to entreat your serious attention to a message I took the liberty of sending thro' Mrs. Fitzherbert on the subject of the expediency of your taking up your residence *soon, at least nominally*, at *Guilford*. It is the opinion of *all* your *real* friends, it should be so, and your enemies only wait for your fixing at Brighton or in London to publish, that you staid with the Regiment *only* to gratify your *own* convenience, and *not*, as you ever have professed, from a determination to adhere to what the K. had pointed out as your post. I know *you* will not be offended at my saying this, for you cannot mistake *my motive*. God bless you my dearest brother, remember me most kindly to Lord Hutchinson, Blumfield,[1] and all *with you* whom *I* have the pleasure of

1. Benjamin Bloomfield, 1st Baron Bloomfield (1762–1846), Lieutenant, 1781; Captain, 1794; Major, 1805; Lieutenant-Colonel, 1806; Colonel, 1812; Major-General, 1814; Lieutenant-General, 1830. Knighted, 1815; G.C.H., 1819; G.C.B., 1822. Appointed a Gentleman Attendant to the Prince of Wales, 21 October 1808, *vice* Lord Lake; Clerk Marshal and Chief Equerry to the Prince Regent, 1812–17; A.D.C. to the King, 1811–14; Auditor and Secretary of the Duchy of Cornwall, 1816–17; Receiver-General of the Duchy of Cornwall, Keeper of the Privy Purse, and Private Secretary to the Prince Regent in succession to McMahon, 1817; Envoy to Sweden, 1823–33. Irish peerage, 14 May 1825.

knowing, and accept with your usual indulgence the renewed assurance of the unalterable, and devoted attachment [etc.].

Mad. de St. Laurent is most grateful for your remembrance, and begs to offer her best wishes. (46154–6)

Brompton Park House, Saturday evening, 28 Jan. [1804]
Having by my unexpected detention at Kensington Palace to a later hour than I intended been unavoidably prevented from writing by the post, I shall send these lines by the Brighton coach which will reach you tomorrow afternoon.

The K. I saw both last night and this morning. His legs being wound round with bandages it is next to impossible to judge of their real size, but as far as I could form an opinion from the look of the ankle and foot the swelling is much reduced. His looks are good except I think rather a bilious eye, the speech if *anything* a little quick and agitated, but this in so trifling a degree that were it not from a retrospect to past events it would scarcely be perceivable; in short, tho' not *quite* dans son assiette ordinaire, he is but in a trifling degree removed from it and as yet I see *no grounds* to form an opinion that one has to apprehend a relapse into his former state. As I know you will not leave Brighton till Tuesday after post hour, I will give you a few lines again by Monday's mail, but should anything unexpected occur, you shall *then* hear earlier from me.

The Queen and my sisters received me *all* most kindly and seemed much pleased at what I told them of the fête as well as of your particular injunction to me to say everything most affectionate from you to *all*. Now I must bid you farewell pour le present . . .

[*P.S.*] Pray say a thousand kind things from me to Mrs. Fitzherbert. (46157–8)

1797   THE PRINCE OF WALES TO SIR HENRY FETHERSTONHAUGH
Brighton, 29 Jan. 1804
I hope that you never will conceive that I can ever think that you can entertain two opinions about me, or that I can entertain two opinions about you. The sincere wish of my heart is, that upon the footing of friendship upon which we ever have liv'd, & I trust *ever* shall live through life, you are at perfect liberty to follow whatever is most convenient or suitable to yourself; but I should feel most unhappy if my home is at any moment of my life open for the reception of my friends, that an

invitation should be not be sent to you, who I consider as one of the first & firmest.

P.S. Send me the Old Major without fail, & spare Welch if you can (Uppark MSS.).

1798 THE DUKE OF KENT TO THE PRINCE OF WALES

Brompton Park House, Sunday evening, 29 Jan [1804]

Since the note I wrote you last night I have seen the K. whom indeed I only quitted at *two*. The lameness is now very trivial indeed,[1] but he complained a good deal of bile and the colour of his eyes and face shewed a strong tinge of that disorder. The hurry is certainly *not* increased nor *yet* can I say it is diminished, and I believe the truest report I can make is that things are in statu quo. His general state of health seems upon a balance; that is, *if* his bile *works off* he will again be just what we have known him since his last illness, but if it prevails *then* it will be difficult to say to what extent it may affect him. As yet there is nothing of moment enough to notice and it is certainly possible nothing may occur, yet I cannot help thinking que nous sommes dans une position chatouilleuse et *vacillante*.

Having now fulfilled my promise to you and nothing else occurring worth troubling you with, I shall only add the assurance of my unalterable and devoted attachment [etc.].

[*P.S.*] I of course confide all this in you, trusting that it will never go further than to our friend Mrs. F[itzherbert]. Vous en sentés toute la consequence et pour vous et pour moi. Pray say a thousand kind things then from me. (46159–60)

1799 THE DUKE OF KENT TO CAPTAIN B. BLOOMFIELD

Kensington Palace, 7 a.m., Thursday, 2 Feb. 1804

Dear Blumfield,

Having, by the merest chance, heard yesterday evening that Sir W. Farqhar and Walker had been suddenly sent for to the Prince at Petworth[2] in the morning, I cannot help feeling excessively uneasy and

1. 'The King had a slight attack of the gout in his foot', wrote Charles Abbot on the 17th (Colchester, i.476).

2. According to *The Times*, 2 February, the Prince was taken ill whilst at Brighton. Lord Glenbervie alleged that the illness was occasioned 'by an excessive debauch of eating and drinking' (*Journals*, i.364). The Duke of Clarence, too (so Farington reported), said that 'it

therefore hasten to entreat you to let me have *without delay* some tidings of my brother in whom you know I feel so *very lively an interest*. At the same time pray give him my kindest love and tell him that on Tuesday and yesterday I did not write as I should only have had to repeat my report of Sunday and Monday. However, when I left the Q.'s House last night towards *eight* there was a great change from the hurry and agitation (which for the last five days had been predominant) to calm and indeed to drowsiness. I find the physician was much pleased with this symptom and expressed a confident hope things would now take a favorable turn; if *any* change takes place I shall write directly but if I am silent the Prince may be satisfied that things are as they stood. (46161)

1800   THE PRINCESS OF WALES TO THE KING

5 Feb. [*1804*]

The Duke of Cambridge just informed me that his Majesty has been so very kind to send me the picture of my father to Carlton House. I never could have words sufficiently to express to his Majesty how very deeply I am indebted and penetrated with this new proof of his Majesty's particular attention and great goodness to me: it will make certainly the finest ornament in my room except it is not too presumptuous of me to aske for the honor to be allowed to hope one of this days to possess the picture of his Majesty, which would be the greatest happiness and satisfaction for me. (42380)

1801   THE EARL OF MOIRA TO COLONEL MCMAHON

5 Feb. [*1804*]

Infinite thanks to you for your having somewhat eased my mind respecting our beloved Prince. With what a calamity this country was menaced by his illness! I do assure you that the anxiety occasioned here by the

was the effect of drinking hard three days successively with the Duke of Norfolk, *his guest*, and other company' (*Diary*, 3 February 1804). Farington added, on the 15th: 'Dr. Burney ... said he had lately seen the Duke of Norfolk and Lord Guilford who were of the Prince of Wales's party at Brighton while for a week they drank to such excess that the Duke said he was not yet perfectly sober.' Speaker Abbot wrote on 19 February: 'Colonel McMahon told me that the Prince had lost eighty-four ounces of blood in his last illness, but was *now quite well*' (Colchester, i.480).

report that his malady was serious proved most gratefully the exalted estimation in which he personally stands.[1]

[*P.S.*] Eyes much better. (40075)

1802   THE DUKE OF NORTHUMBERLAND TO COLONEL MCMAHON, AND THE REPLY

Alnwick Castle, 5 Feb. 1804

An attack of my old complaint in my hands has prevented me from acknowledging sooner the receipt of your letter of the 21st of last month, & indeed it is with so much pain & difficulty that I write even now, that nothing but my having last night seen an article in the newspaper, mentioning that the Prince was ill, woud have induced me to trouble you now. Interested, however, as I am by gratitude as well as duty in whatever concerns his Royal Highness, I cannot delay taking the very first opportunity of enquiring thro' you after his health. Sincerely hoping the article is ill founded, or at least that his Royal Highness is perfectly recovered, I must beg that, with the assurance of my most dutifull attachment, you will return my thanks to the Prince for permitting me to see the letter he wrote on the Queen's birthday, & his Royal Highness may rest assured that neither this nor any other confidential paper with which I may be trusted by him shall ever go out of my hands or be communicated to any other person but by the order of his Royal Highness.

I undoubtedly think the Prince perfectly right in attending to the duty of his Regiment at Guildford. The same reason which induced him to continue with it at Brighton is equally valid for his removal with it to its new quarters, for by so doing, the Prince will act with that consistency which I hope will ever be the guide of all his actions.

From this last motive, I trust in God H.R.H. will never consent to any coalition with Mr. Pitt. The indignities & insults offered to the Prince by that arrogant & insolent man have been such as can neither be overlooked nor forgiven. It woud be inconsistent with H.R.H.'s dignity was he to do so.

As Parliament has now met again, I take it for granted some kind of arrangement must soon take place. Do pray let me know what you hear on this subject. It appears to me that if Ministers do not take great care, they are in danger of burning their fingers with the Volunteer Corps.

I see by the papers Lord Cornwallis has contrived to worm himself again into command.[2] I wonder whether it was his conduct at Yorktown

1. *The Times*, 8 February, reported that he was out of danger.

2. *The Times* announced on 21 January that Cornwallis had been appointed to the command of the Eastern District.

489

or Amiens which has recommended him for a situation of such material consequence to this kingdom on the present occasion.

As I have no other information relative to his Majesty's state of health except what I see in the papers, I shall feel myself very much obliged to you for any information on this subject which may come to your knowledge.

I am very glad that my opinion of the propriety of H.R.H. keeping his Regt. coincided with that of Mrs. F. She may depend upon it that any advice I presume to offer the Prince will be founded on the sincere regard I have for his dignity, honour & welfare, & that as I can have no other object in view but H.R.H.'s welfare, having myself no views of ambition to gratify, that my advice will ever be the pure dictates of my heart. I understand a certain great Lady[1] is soon to return from Bath. Mrs. F. should keep a strict eye on the proceedings & intrigues of that cabinet. (40073–4)

COLONEL MCMAHON'S REPLY[2]
Carlton House, 11 Feb. 1804
Most Confidential
I had the honor to receive your Grace's most kind favor of the 5th at Brighton, from whence I return'd last night. In the first instance, as a subject in which I well know your Lordship's mind to be most interested, I will speak of the Prince's immediate health, & I have the happiness to assure your Grace, *most confidently*, that H.R.Hss. is as perfectly well as your wishes can possibly desire, which I think to be prononcing enough. His fever has entirely abated, & not one symptom of complaint, thank Providence, now remains. H.R.H. was most sensibly affected with the assurances I gave him (for Mrs. F.'s name being mention'd in your Grace's letter, together with the just precaution agst. the cabals of a certain house, it became impossible to give him occular demonstration of the fact) of your Lordship's most affectionate & constant anxious enquiries about him. H.R.Hss. observation was in his bed, *so help me God*, exactly as follows 'I have, my dear Mac, but few such friends on earth as the dear Duke, God bless him, do not tell him how ill I have been, but tell him that in whatever rumours he may hear of the causes of my indisposition, that my mind, at my past cruel treatment, which he will understand, although the foolish commentators on my actions either do not or chooose not to comprehend, has been the main spring of my illness; pray speak of me & remember me with that real love & affection

1. ? Lady Hertford.
2. The reply is slightly out of chronological order.

490

you must know I always bear him.' I will here close the subject of my beloved master. The K. is unquestionably in a very alarming state, the bandages on his legs remain; his agitation & hurries are great, but seemingly operate on alternate days; the discipline of riding in his Riding House is entirely given up, and (although reported to be in perfect health) the airing even in a close carriage is not substituted. The parties at the Queen's House are totally omitted for two evenings in a week, & on the others are composed but of three or four who invariably & exclusively form them. He raves for a Play, but that is not allow'd; & the Ancient Music (his hobby horse) has been defer'd from Wednesday to Thursday sennight. In short, his malady at this moment is dropsy. There is, however, a strong alarm for his mind, & the Willis's have refused their attendance, unless sanction'd by an Order of Council, which will not be ventured to be attempted on this occasion. The D. of Cumberland, who ostensibly came up from his Command on *private* business for a fortnight, has renew'd his leave of absence for another? [*sic*] Your Grace will readily guess all this manœuvre. I do not think the generous nature of the Prince will so soon forgive the D. of Y. as that nature & the Duke's expectations might afford reason to suppose. Sir Frs. Milman & Dundas of Richmond, are the only medical men who see the K.

The Government *certainly* received bad accounts from Ireland yesterday. The intelligence is kept a great secret. The general report is that Mr. Fox & the Grenvilles have joined. The Coalition is far from being pleasing to the friendly or public eye. Mr. Pitt will not have anything to do with it, but undoubtedly he looks to profit by it. I have so far the presumption to think your Grace will not approve it. God bless all belonging to Anwick Castle, prays your Grace's grateful [etc.] (Alnwick MSS.).

1803   THE EARL OF MOIRA TO THE PRINCE OF WALES
Edinburgh, 7 Feb. 1804
Most fortunately I did not learn your Royal Highness's illness till I was at the same time assured that all uneasiness repecting it had subsided. Even then I could not but feel a severely painful shock at the thought that the attack was of a nature which might have become formidable. For mercy's sake, Sir, take care of a life so precious not merely to those who are devoted to you but to your country. Believe me, the alarm excited here by the supposed extent of your indisposition proved in the most gratifying manner with what anxiety the public mind fixes itself upon your energy & talents as a resource in the growing difficulties that surround us. Had it not been for the occasion, which was too high a price for

the gratification, I should have delighted in the unfeigned exhibition of people's feelings which the circumstance called forth. Thank God, the crisis is over. Suffer, however, your interest for the sensibility of those who are bound to you by grateful affection to make you take that care of yourself which you would not do on your own account. I have been undergoing a tedious & painful inflammation in my eyes; now much better, but not quite subdued. Poor Sheridan is confined with a teazing erysipelas. Your Royal Highness will be glad to know that he behaves with great attention & perfect propriety. He has an excellent heart. (40076–7)

1804 THE DUKE OF KENT TO THE PRINCE OF WALES

Kensington Palace, Thursday night, 9 Feb. [*1804*]

The unbounded attachment I have ever felt for you, and the lively interest which I take in your welfare, will I trust induce you not to be offended with me if I venture to advise you against moving to town so early as the day after tomorrow, which I understand to be your intention.[1] My reason for presuming so far upon your indulgence is in the first place the apprehension I feel lest, after the severe fit of illness from which you are but just recovering, so *early* a move should prove prejudicial to your health, which is of so *much* moment to us all: but exclusive of that I fear much that your settling in London might be the means of affording to those who are ever prone to construe your conduct, however correct in itself, in the most unfavorable manner, the opportunity of fabricating fresh tales to your prejudice. I believe I may go so far as to assert that your *best* friends, *those* who are now immediately about you, coincide with me in *this* opinion. Pray, therefore, my dearest brother, weigh the matter well *before* you take the step and condescend to bestow a moment's reflection upon the counsel I have presumed to offer. I feel, when I say this, that I am taking a very great, perhaps indeed an unwarrantable liberty, but I place such confidence in your knowledge of the sincerity of my attachment that I am satisfied, even if my advice be not followed, it will not be considered as offensive.

The state of things here is still very much the same; yesterday evening there was *more* hurry, and this morning again less; indeed we are quite at a still stand. I certainly think there is *no* amendment, but yet no fall off either. The symptoms of bile yet shew themselves strongly, and the case, to the best of my poor judgment, appears very precarious.

1. Charles Yorke wrote to Lord Hardwicke on the 13th: 'The Prince came to town last night, and Addington has written to him and seen him since. He behaved very properly and with feeling.' (Add. MSS. 35705, f.99)

I will not venture to add more than that *all* here rejoice most cordially in the late comfortable accounts we have had from you, and none more sincerely than [etc.]. (46162–3)

1805 THE PRINCE OF WALES TO THE DUKE OF YORK, AND THE REPLY

[*13 Feb. 1804*]

The Prince of Wales is extremely concern'd that the Duke of York has given himself the trouble of calling so frequently of late at Carlton House. But one moment's recollection & reflection must convince the Duke of York that it is impossible for the Prince of Wales, whatever may be his regret, to receive the Duke, after *all* that has so *recently* passed.[1] (44200 and 44201)

THE DUKE OF YORK'S REPLY

Horse Guards, 13 Feb. 1804

The Duke of York takes the first oportunity upon his return to the Horse Guards to acknowledge the receipt of the Prince of Wales note delivered to him while at Carleton House by the Page Lucas, and has only though with the deepest regret to attend to its contents.[2] (44202)

1806 THE DUKE OF KENT TO HENRY ADDINGTON [copy]

Kensington Palace, Monday night, 15 [13] Feb. 1804

In consequence of the wish expressed by you that I would state in writing the purport of the communication I made to you in our interview of this morning, I herewith enclose a faithful narrative of what I then expressed,

1. Endorsed, 'Received by the Prince's Page Lucas at Carleton House, February 13, 1804'.

2. Glenbervie wrote on 1 March: 'It seems a reconciliation has taken place between the Prince and the Duke of York. The newspapers ascribe this to the good offices of Sheridan' (*Journals*, i.369). George Rose wrote, in his Diary, on the 25th: 'Mr. Sheridan stated confidently this morning that a perfect reconciliation had taken place between the Prince of Wales and the Duke of York, and that it was effected by him exclusively.' But Lady Uxbridge wrote to her son Arthur on 28 February: 'You will be happy to hear Paget [her eldest son] has brought about a complete reconciliation between the P. and the D. of Y., and they both thanked him most cordially for having effected it' (Lord Hylton, *The Paget Brothers*, p. 17). Lord Minto heard of the reconciliation not later than the 24th, and he said that the Duke of York had been left a good while waiting in the hall at Carlton House (*Life and Letters of Lord Minto*, iii.306).

made out according to the best of my recollection, and in order that you may be satisfied that the sentiments of the Duke of Cumberland perfectly coincide with mine upon this highly interesting subject, I have requested him to affix at the foot of the paper his signature and declaration to that effect; to which I beg to refer you.

Sir,

On my arrival at the Queen's House this morning, I was informed by the Duke of Cumberland that the Doctors John & Robert Willis[1] were in the house, whither they had been brought in consequence of an order from the Cabinet Council, with the intention of their being introduced into the King's apartment to attend him as his physicians. This measure impressed us both with the conviction that it was our bounden duty not to lose a moment in acquainting you with his Majesty having *subsequent to his last illness*, when his mind was perfectly restored, and at different periods *since that*, required a solemn promise & engagement from the Duke of Cumberland & myself that, in in [*sic*] the event of its being the will of Providence that he should again be afflicted, as he had been before, *we* should use every means in our power to prevent anyone of the Willis family from being placed about him. In consequence I repaired directly to Downing Street, & commenced my communication with you by relating this circumstance, and acquainting you that at each of those times when such promise was exacted from us, we did both jointly and seperately give it to him in so full and unqualified a manner that, were we at this moment *not* to represent against their admission, we felt we should be guilty of a flagrant breach of our words so solemnly pledged to him.[2]

1. Charles Yorke wrote on the 14th at 3 p.m.: 'The physicians (Milman and young Heberden) have been consulted on the necessity of calling in either the Willises or some other person of that description, and I am told that they are of opinion that in the present state of the King's health, such a measure would in all probability produce *convulsions* which might be *fatal*. The Cabinet have just separated and are to meet again tonight at half past eight for the purpose of examining Milman and Dr. John Willis. Mr. Addington saw the Prince yesterday ... It is said that the Prince went afterwards to Mrs. *Fitzherbert's* where he had a *Council*, but I have not yet learnt who was there.' (Add. MSS. 35705, f.105)

Pitt thought that the difficulties facing Ministers (whoever they might be after a temporary Regency had been settled) would probably be 'not a little heightened by the uncertainty of the Prince's disposition, the avowed breach which had unfortunately taken place between him and the King (extending in its effects to the Duke of York), and finally the new state of parties' (Melville MSS. To Melville, 16 February 1804).

George Rose wrote in his Diary on the 16th: 'The physicians in attendance on his Majesty are Sir Francis Millman and Dr. Heberden. Neither Dr. Willis nor any of his family have been sent for. In their stead a person of the name of Simmons is in attendance on his Majesty, which I think is deeply to be regretted, as well on the account of the superior skill of the Willis's as of the strong attachment one of them at least I know has personally to the King.'

2. Rose wrote on the 20th: 'I this day received from the Bishop of Lincoln a letter written to him from a physician of great eminence in London (a friend of Dr. Willis's) dated the 17th,

Having said this, I proceeded to represent to you that, from the repeated opportunities we had had of hearing the King deliver his sentiments relative to *every* member of the Willis family, we were decidedly of opinion that their introduction at this moment would be productive of an irritation of mind for which the worst consequences might be apprehended; but that, exclusive of the effect likely to be produced upon his Majesty's mind by this measure, we were fully convinced that, if it were persisted in, another evil of the greatest magnitude would in all probability ensue—no less a one than that of his Majesty taking up a rooted prejudice against the Queen; for that no argument however strong, no proof however direct, would be sufficient, after his recovery, to persuade him that her Majesty had not been privy to the doctors Willis being placed about his person—that we formed this opinion from a knowledge of the manner in which he had expressed himself over and over again to the Queen on the subject in our presence, and that the consequences to be apprehended from such a calamity—in which the destruction of the peace of the whole family would be involved, more especially that of the female part of it, whose every comfort depended on the uninterrupted continuance of that harmony which they had ever before witnessed— were such that we could not allow ourselves from motives of delicacy for a moment to advert to them.

I then stated that we conceived the Duke of Cambridge to stand equally pledged with ourselves on this subject, who therefore would not hesitate in joining us in this representation, and farther added that we were impressed with a very strong belief that the Queen might be similarly situated also; but having, from an anxious wish not to commit her Majesty by anything we conceived *ourselves* bound to state, judged it most respectfull and dutifull to her not to make her acquainted with the step we were about to take until it had been carried into effect, we could not presume to assert this as a fact, although we were persuaded, if such a pledge *did* exist on *her* part, she would inform you of it, previous to the admission of the Doctors Willis into the King's apartment.

I concluded by saying that having fulfilled our promise to the King we thought it right to request that this representation might be treasured up in your recollection, with a view that, if at some future period it might be

in these words: "The history of the King is purposely involved in mystery. What I know is that Dr. Simmons's men have been about the King for three days. Most people think the Doctor himself is at the Palace also. The Willis's have not seen the King, but have been very often before the Cabinet Council. They were to have met Reynolds and Pepys this morning at Buckingham House, but they did not. In fact I fancy they are all in confusion, and I fear the King will lose his life if they do not change their mode. My opinion is that the Willis's will be sent for at last, I hope before it is too late. There certainly appears to have been some foolish engagement in some quarters that the Willis's should not attend the King. It is quite ridiculous to consider such an engagement, under the circumstances, as binding, as the very request on the King's part must be attributed to false impressions, and probably an unsound mind."

found necessary to make the same known to the King, in order to convince him of our having faithfully discharged our duty to him during his illness, you, Sir, might then come forward with the relation of what had passed and do us justice.

THE DUKES OF KENT AND CUMBERLAND TO HENRY ADDINGTON
Kensington Palace, Wednesday night, 15 Feb. 1804
Sir,

The foregoing communication having been committed to paper at your express desire, we now jointly request that it may be laid before the Cabinet Council, and entered on the Minutes as the substance of our sentiments; at the same time we trust it will be fully understood that if, notwithstanding this representation, the two phy[si]cians, Doctors Willis, are called upon to attend his Majesty, the measure is to be considered to be totally and entirely that of the *Cabinet*, and that *we* in no shape whatever have participated in it. (46164–6)

1807 PRINCESS MARY TO THE PRINCE OF WALES
Tuesday, 9 p.m., 13 [?14] Feb. [1804][1]
I should have answered your kind letter sooner but I am sure you will excuse it when I inform you the King never left us till half passed 7 o'clock & such a *day* I never went through in my life. The poor Queen keeps up wonderfully but the *trial* is a most severe one. She desires me to thank you for your kind attention & for the affte. expressions contained in your letter concerning her as well as all my sisters. I am happy to add mama's health has not suffered yet from all *she* has gone through in mind & body since *we are* come to town.

I hope, my dearest brother, you will take care of *yourself*; most truly sorry was I to hear you have been so ill & still suffer from sickness.

Excuse this hurried scrawl. I must return to the Queen, & believe me, far or near & in *every* situation in life [etc.]. (Add. Georgian 12/28)

1. The year is endorsed. Tuesday fell on the 14th. The newspapers of the 15th contained alarming accounts of the King. Lord Glenbervie wrote: 'Some people about the Court are of opinion that the King's present attack has been chiefly owing to two causes, the publication of what is called the Royal Correspondence (which is known to have been the direct act of the Prince, contrary to the sound advice of the few sensible people he consults with, although he makes McMahon and others of that description assert everywhere that it was done without his knowledge), and the loss of Hanover' (*Journals*, i.367).

Alnwick Castle, 14 Feb. 1804

It is impossible for me to express the pleasure which your letter of the 11th afforded me by the account it gave me of re-establishment of the Prince's health. I trust, however, H.R.H. will not allow the subject he mentioned to prey upon his mind. He stands clear in the eyes of all the country from any want of zeal or spirit upon this occasion. He has done everything in his power, & if he shoud not be employed in case of invasion in such a manner as his birth & high situation in the country entitle him to expect, the blame will not lay upon him. But I cannot bring myself to believe that seriously anything else can be intended. The answer I trust proceeded from the hasty anger of a moment which, upon cool reflection, must have passed off, & although persons in very high situations are unwilling to retract, let us hope that when the time comes H.R.H. will have such a command as his rank & abilities deserve.

What you mention of another person corresponds much with what I have heard. I think the Williss have acted perfectly right for their own honour & for the good of the country. These are not times to trifle upon such serious subjects. In such a crisis as this, the kingdom at large have a right to know whether they are governed by a King or his Ministers. As the information I get from you on this subject is I know authentic & therefore to be depended upon, let me beg you if you hear anything particular to let me know it. I shall leave this place on the 22d or 23d; if therefore you write any day before Sunday, be kind enough to direct it to me here; after that day, till Sunday following I must desire you to direct to me at the Post Office at Newcastle-upon-Tyne, & I hope to be in town by the 2d. or 3d. of March.

A letter I had from London mentions the K. being bilious. We know what that means. I hope in God he will get well, for these are not times for any person to wish to occupy the uncertain & constrained situation of a temporary Regent, & I trust that if the necessity of appointing a Regent shoud occur, that the P. will insist upon proper & full powers, without which nothing can be done for the service of the country. Pray have you ever heard that the K. has made no Will as yet? I always understood that Lord Thurlow had made his Will for him some years ago. I am now told he has positively not made any. This is a matter of the utmost consequence for the Prince to know, & I should think, considering his intimacy with Lord Thurlow, H.R.H. might easily have it from his Lordship. If no Will is as yet made, it may be a matter of doubt how far, in his present state of mind, a Will made now may not come to be disputed hereafter. This of course is for the Prince's own ear only. I can hardly yet write legibly, but I know you will excuse the trouble you will have in deciphering it.

You will be kind enough to assure the Prince that I feel as I ought to do those flattering expressions in which his message to me has been conveyed, & that I trust my conduct will prove that I am not wholly unworthy of them. No person I will venture to say can surpass me in attachment to his person, zeal for his service, or anxiety for his honour, dignity, & welfare. (40080–1)

1809   THE DUKE OF SUSSEX TO THE DUKE OF KENT [copy, and extract]
Lisbon, 15 Feb. 1804
It was only by the preceding packet that I had the least information, of a suit laid against me in Chancery by Lady Augusta Murray, which I confess with some reason, has astonished me, as I was in no way prepared for it, but by a letter she wrote to Colonel Muller, dated the 29th of November, & which he communicated to me, as soon as received. By that very packet I got a letter from Mr. Coutts, dated the 3d of December, in which he mentions the circumstances, promising to give me further intelligence, and at the same time informing me that he would not take up my quarterly allowance, which would be shortly due, for the present, as it might be of detriment to my interests. Thus was I situated 'till the day before yesterday, when two packets arrived at the same time, bringing the mails, from the 31st of December to the 2d of February included. By one of those I received a letter from you, dated the 29th of December in which you hint at the subject, & promise to gain information. However, the only real intelligence I have of the state of the business is by the newspapers. Recovering as I am at this moment from an indisposition which has confined me almost constantly to my house ever since the month of September, it is impossible I can be prepared for such a transaction, neither can I get any legal assistance, therefore all I can do for the moment is to relate to you fairly the whole circumstance because I can rely upon your activity, steadiness, and friendship; and secondly, to take precautions.

When Captain Murray[1] arrived here, you may recollect that at first I did not receive him. Upon some explanation taking place, and a *solemn promise* of no pecuniary subjects being started, I saw him. His reasons for coming over were, 1° To ask me to get a title for Lady Augusta Murray, if not in England, at least abroad, which I promised, if in my power should be done. 2° To obtain a divorce in Germany, to which I consented upon the same conditions. 3° To write a letter to the Queen, on the subject of my daughter, which I did. 4° a letter to the Prince, which was also sent, & 5thly to obtain copies of these letters which had

1. Lady Augusta's brother (1764–1842).

498

been found in Germany and sent to the Regency at Hannover, which I refused, saying I had them not here. After these subjects were settled Captain Murray told me that either the very day or the day before he left London, he had met Mr. Tierney in the street, who had told him that my Establishment was to be augmented to sixteen thousand pounds a year; that his sister was to have her debts paid by his Majesty, & that a maintenance was to be given her which would be no less than four thousand pounds a year, & that as no pensions were regularly paid but those of the Royal Family, she would be obliged to me if I would advance her the money, and get myself reimbursed by the Treasury. This seemed to me no unreasonable demand, and though I was firmly resolved to have no further communication, & which I have strictly observed, I conceived this to be an attention towards her which any man of delicate feelings would submit to, the more so as Captain Murray said to me himself, 'You have my word of honor that on Government's paying her—you shall be repayed.' After some more conversation on this point I consented, upon condition that my son should be given up to me, which he over-ruled by saying that either the Prince of Wales or the Duke of York was to have him under his protection, but that he did not know exactly which. Upon my agreeing to this he took a paper out of his pocket saying that it was for this purpose. All I recollect of it was that it was a parchment. Having not the least suspicion, I signed it immediately, and upon calling Colonel Muller to witness the paper, who wished to look at it—I said, 'This is a private transaction between Lady Augusta and me,' upon which he signed, conceiving it, as he told me since, articles of seperation be-twixt her and me. As soon as this was done the paper was put into Captain Murray's pocket, and I heard nothing more on the subject 'till I received a letter from him, when arrived in England, in which he talked of a *deed*, & that he forgot to ask me *certain letters* (though he remained three or four days afterwards here) copies and forms of which he sent me, & without which he said no money could be obtained. The moment this letter reached me, I saw something was not right, but was perfectly quiet as he had wrote me nothing could be done without the letters, which I had determined not to send, finding no new pension granted to her by his Majesty, no augmentation of my Establishment, neither were her debts paid. To tell you the truth, I am not sorry that these circumstances will appear, because the conduct of the whole family will thus be known, but I should wish that if the lawyers can make it illegal, that it should be rather made by them than by me, for I would rather lose my whole Establishment than that I should be suspected by anyone for a moment of a dirty action. Therefore having heard & taken council, I am ready to submit to any arrangement the Lord Chancellor may think proper to make for me, & by that I will abide. Untill then it is impossible for me to enter into any business with my other creditors, but I am determined immediately to reform the greatest part of my establishment in order to avoid useless expence. The method of precaution I have taken is to send a Power of Attorney to Powell, to annul the one I gave Mr. Coutts, and I have wrote to the Lords of the Treasury to inform them I have drawn upon them for the money, and in future to deliver up none of my money but upon bills signed by me, which I shall draw, as the quarters become due. I have ordered Powell to hear Council, & to do nothing without speaking to you, as by this means you will be able to communicate with the Prince on the subject, and of course with Mr. Adams [*sic*]. Indeed I enclose my letters to Powell open to you, in order that you may peruse them. It is absolutely necessary that Mr. Coutt's Power of Attorney should be annulled as soon as possible. The whole transaction is shocking. However, it has made the whole family known to me, with whom I am determined never to have the least communication whatsoever. My conduct has always been delicate towards Lady Augusta, though she certainly did not deserve it, but from a [blank] principle I conceived her my wife, though I knew perfectly well the law could not acknowledge her as such. You may easily imagine, my dear brother, the confusion in which the whole transaction has thrown me, but as I am certain of clearing my honor, as to the rest si j'ai fait des imprudences il faut que je les paye—As to the house in Grosvenor Street, I desired Lady Augusta through Mr. Coutts in the month of February or March 1802, to leave it, and I would pay her back her pension. Mr. Coutts in his letter of the 27th of April 1802 says—

'The inclosed answer which I received from Grosvenor Street (and which at this moment I cannot find) suspends for the present my power of executing your Royal Highness's commands, relative to that house, as the Lady Augusta does not chuse to give it up'. He afterwards goes on —'Meanwhile I shall endeavour to see Sir Lionel Darrel & to learn if he will be willing to take back his house, as I understand by the agreement your Royal Highness is not authorised to let it again, and that you are obliged to keep it for seven years, at the rent of £600 per annum.'

To this latter part, I have also to make a remark, which is that when this paper was shewn me, I observed to Lady Augusta the great imprudence of the step, as my health might perhaps not allow me to return, & that perhaps you on your return to England, not having a house, might be glad to take it, & I should then be deprived of an advantage. Her Ladyship told me she had been with Sir Lionel Darrel, who would have no objection to any one of my brothers taking the house. I believe you will not find in this letter any violent expressions, for that is beneath me, mais on m'a joué cruellement.[1] (48253-7)

1. The Duke of Sussex's letter to the Duke of Kent of 23 April, from Lisbon, throws further light on his unpleasant situation there: 'Words can scarcely convey the unpleasant situation in which I find myself with a large household on my hands and already seven months elapsed,

DECLARATION OF THE QUEEN, AND NINE OF HIS
MAJESTY'S CHILDREN, WITH MEMORANDUM FROM
THE DUKE OF KENT[1]

Queen's House, Wednesday night, 15 Feb. 1804

In the present dreadful and alarming illness with
which it has pleased Almighty Providence to
afflict the King, we, the Queen and nine of his
Majesty's children at present assembled at the
Queen's house, think it a duty we owe to his
Majesty, to our country and to ourselves, to state
in writing the reasons which have induced us, after
having duly weighed the melancholy circumstances
under which we stand* to accept with thanks the
offer which has been made to us by his Majesty's
confidential servants to relieve us from the care
and superintendence of his Majesty on this trying
occasion.

We are fully sensible that we are bound both by
duty & affection towards the King, in our respective
situations of wife and children, to fulfil, as far as is
in our power, every personal wish and intention of
his—but considering his Majesty's public situation
in this country as King, the interest which the nation
has in the preservation of his life, & the restoration
of his health†; ⌜how much its dearest interests and
even the very existence of his Majesty's Throne and
Government may depend upon the measures which
are now to be decided upon⌝,‡ and lastly, being
fully aware that the law does not authorize us to
take upon ourselves the arduous duty of determin-
ing upon the means to be adopted for his Majesty's
recovery, we conceive this important charge cannot

* The following words were proposed by the Duke of Kent, but objected to by the Duke of York and the sentence as it now stands, from 'to accept' to 'trying occasion' inserted—
'to express our grateful satisfaction upon the communication made to us by Mr. Addington, of its being the disposition and intention of his Majesty's confidential servants to take altogether upon themselves the responsibility attending the care and superintendence of his Majesty's person during the continuance of his present calamitous, and alarming disorder'.

† The Duke of Kent from the moment he first read this paper felt a strong wish, that the words between ⌜and⌝ should be altogether omitted, as he was apprehensive they might admit of a construction that would be justly offensive to some of the family, but he felt, judging from himself, a conviction that no such meaning could be intended to be implied, & therefore, for obvious

not only without receiving a shilling, but with the additional aggravation of protested bills.
For a man who has a character to support in the world these are severe trials but I have courage
to undergo everything, although my health certainly suffers more severely by it than I can
describe. Should it become necessary for me to leave Lisbon you must be sensible I cannot
move without liquidating all claims that may be made upon me here, and unless I am enabled
to receive my Parliamentary allowance to its whole extent up to the day of my departure, that
cannot be effected. This makes me the more unhappy as I am aware of the urgent necessity
there must be for my going over to England for a short period to settle my affairs and recover
my unfortunate boy before he is totally ruined by the wretched education his mother gives
him. But nothing would make me yield even to the expediency of this move were I otherwise
enabled to make it, but the dependence I place on the Prince and yourself to prevent her
having any communication with me and to establish an impossible barrier between us until
the accomplishment of which I never shall be at ease' (Chatham Papers).

1. 'Put into the Prince's hands Sunday, February 19th, 1804'.

reasons, did not start
any objections ; reserving
however, to himself to
make a private note of
the manner in which
they had struck him,
in case, at a future day,
it should be the subject
of discussion.

‡This sentence, from
'and lastly' to 'call to
his Councils'—was
proposed by the Duke of
Kent, was unanimously
agreed to, and
accordingly inserted

rest in any hands with so much propriety as in those
of the persons whom the King has himself been
pleased to call to his Councils.

Having thus stated the reasons which have
actuated us under the present dreadful circumstances, we can only add our fervent wish that,
should the Almighty restore his Majesty to us & to
the country, our conduct may meet, after full consideration, with is approbation, as it does with that
of our own consciences.

(Signed)   Charlotte
           Augustus   Frederick
           Eliza   Edward
           Mary   Ernest
           Sophia   Adolphus Fredk.
           Amelia   (36537–8, and 36539)

1810A   THE DUKE OF KENT TO THE PRINCE OF WALES

Kensington Place, Thursday, 16 Feb. 1804

I conceive it my duty to lose no time in transmitting to you, copies of
two papers, *the one*, a letter which I had occasion to write last night to
Mr. Addington, *the other*, a declaration drawn up by the Duke of York,
and signed by the Queen, as well as every one of the family, who were
present at the Queen's House at the time, when the Minister communicated the disposition of the Cabinet to take wholly upon themselves, the
care, and superintendance of the King's person, during the continuance
of his present melancholy complaint.

The *former* of these, you will perceive, was written in consequence of
Mr. Addington's having requested me to commit to paper the verbal
communication I had with him, in Downing Street, in the morning. I
do not conceive, from my knowledge of the little intercourse you have
had with the King since his last illness, that you can possibly stand similarly pledged to him, with myself; but lest, contrary to my opinion,
you should be acquainted with any circumstances that might induce
you to affix any remark or declaration of yours to that paper, I have
thought you would approve of my submitting it to you for your
consideration.

With respect to the *latter*, I am perfectly sensible that, as you were not
present at the Queen's House when the Minister made his communication to the Queen, and those of his Majesty's children who happened to
be there at the time alluded to, and when we declared our sentiments

thereupon, I cannot with propriety suggest, *even* to your *consideration*, whether *you* would affix *your* name to it also. But, I feel I should be wanting in what I owe to you from duty, as the eldest of the family, and from the truest personal attachment, especially after having heard from the Minister the very handsome and feeling manner in which you have expressed yourself, not only upon the present melancholy situation of the King, but upon also upon everything connected with it, if I did not submit the paper in question to you, in order that you may have it in your power to make such use of the communication as to you may seem expedient.

It is my intention to transmit a similar copy of each of these papers to the Duke of Clarence, as I conceive it possible that, although his situation with regard to the King is different from that of the rest of us, he may perhaps wish to have an opportunity of expressing *his* sentiments also: but I shall delay doing this, till you have favored me with your acknowledgments of this letter. (46167–8)

1811   THE DUKE OF NORTHUMBERLAND TO COLONEL MCMAHON

Alnwick Castle, 17 Feb. 1804

Your two letters of the 14th & 15th have reached me safely, I cannot say that the news contained in them was totally unexpected by me, from what I had observed previously in the papers.

My letter of the 14th will have informed you that I purpose leaving this place on the 22d & after spending two or three days in the neighbourhood of Newcastle in visits, I shall proceed directly to London.

I cannot suppose H.R.H. can have the least wish to have my opinion or advice on the present occasion, as H.R.H. has many persons whom he honours with his confidence in these very critical situations, whose abilities & advice are far superior to mine. But if my presence in town, sooner than I at present intend, is desired, or that I can be in any way usefull, I shall with pleasure obey any commands of H.R.H. communicated thro' you. Any letter wrote between Saturday the 18th & Saturday the 25th will come to my hand if directed to me at the Post Office, Newcastle-upon-Tyne. For God's sake let the P. be cautious whom he consults, or into what promises he is drawn by artful persons. Let him not give himself up too much into the hands of any one individual till he has a little time to look about him. Windham & the Grenvilles will most assuredly hamper him with Pitt. Hint this to a certain quarter. Beware of the Great House & Cabinet formed there. At this moment it is more dangerous than ever. May H.R.H. be prevailed upon to act with great caution, & to wait patiently to take a proper advantage of events as they arise; & I trust that above all things he will rather appear to hang back than come forward too readily just at this critical moment. If the news I told you about the Will is true, it is of the greatest moment on this present occasion. Before this I hope the Prince is satisfied on the subject, one way or other, by Ld. Thurlow.[1]

Yours in great haste to save the post. (40087)

1812 MEMORANDUM

17 Feb. 1804

That the communication between Mr. Fox and Lord Grenville began about the time, or a little before his Royal Highness's illness,[2] which prevented him from sending a person on purpose to Brighton to make H.R.H. acquainted with all that had past. That he was again prevented from waiting on the Prince for the same purpose in town by Mrs. Fox's sudden illness;[3] and that, when he came to town on Tuesday, he found a prevalent report of the King's indisposition, which for the present produced a situation that made Mr. Fox particularly unwilling to intrude himself on his Royal Highness.[4]

That the offers to him on the part of Lord Grenville and his friends were fair and liberal, viz. that they should unite in endeavouring to remove the present Administration, and to form a new one on a broad comprehensive principle, which he thought the state of the country required. In these general views he had concurred, but that he was bound to nothing beyond the natural result of that general concurrence—that he had declined entering into any formal declaration or positive demonstration of union, and had given it as his opinion to Lord Grenville that it would be more advisable to let that conclusion come gradually of itself, as the regular consequence of a previous agreement in Parliament on some of the great points depending—in which opinion Lord

1. George Rose wrote on the 16th: 'I am confirmed in the last observation ['It is not probable the Prince of Wales will require him [Pitt] to form an Administration'] by a *certain account* that Ld. Thurlow was with the Prince of Wales more than two hours this morning!! What advice a man can give who has entirely secluded himself from *all parties* and any description of gentlemen almost (except in occasional visits to Brighthelmston), living only with low Jacobins, it is difficult to guess' (Diary).

2. At the beginning of the month (No. 1799).

3. Fox said he was prevented from hearing Whitbread's excellent speech on 8 February by his wife's severe illness, 'not dangerously, indeed, after the first day, but [she was] in dreadful pain from a bilious attack' (*Fox Correspondence*, iii.454).

4. George Rose wrote on the 15th: 'I heard through Ld. Granville-Leveson and Mr. Bourne that Mr. Fox had been sent for by the Prince of Wales' (National Library of Scotland, MS. 3795 [Rose's Diary]).

Grenville had concurred. So that Mr. Fox is under no engagement whatever. (40088)

1813 LETTERS FROM PRINCESS ELIZABETH TO THE PRINCE OF WALES

20 Feb. 1804

As you have expressed a wish to hear how our dear mother bears up under her present severe affliction I am happy to say she is composed, but her nerves considerably shook, & Sir Francis Milman[2] has prescribed for her today. She is equally anxious as we all are about you, & we beg you to let us know how you really *are*, for our enquiries are very sincere & full of anxiety about you. (Add. Georgian 11/94)

Queen's House, 21 Feb. 1804

I am commanded by the Queen & my sisters, to which I most cordially join, our sincere thanks for your very affectionate expressions about us, which we feel as we ought. Your being well is a great comfort to us & we anxiously hope you may long continue so. With respect to your kind offer, my brother Edward will explain everything, therefore I will take up no more of your time but to add that the dear King has had six hours good sleep, which has considerably raised our spirits. (Add. Georgian 11/95)

1814 THE PRINCE OF WALES TO THE DUKE OF KENT

Carlton House, 21 Feb. 1804

I return you my best thanks for the copies of the papers which I have just receiv'd from you. I applaud the very honorable motives that you have acted upon, but as you justly observe, it is impossible for me as an honest man to set my name to any paper containing any matter which to me is

1. Glenbervie wrote on the 22nd: 'The Grenvilles now acknowledge their junction (they will not call it coalition) with Fox. Windham avowed it to Lord Bayning, who told it to me. They have settled no preliminaries nor had any explanation further than having agreed to a joint co-operation for removing the present Ministry on the ground of incapacity . . . Pitt has positively declared against either joining Fox or engaging in a systematic opposition. He says he will act according to his own opinions as circumstances arise. It is understood that Fox is to be First Lord of the Treasury under the Prince, if he is appointed Regent' (*Journals*, i.368).

2. He was one of the five physicians who signed the daily bulletins relating to the King's illness, the others being Sir Lucas Pepys, H. R. Reynolds, S. F. Simmons and W. Heberden.

not *personally* known. With respect to the other paper which likewise appears to me to have some reference to the specifick declaration which you & the Duke of Cumberland have signed, besides my absence from the Queen's House, as you also remark, it is for the reasons I have above stated that it is equally impossible for me to affix my name to that paper; & the only observation I can make upon the contents of the 1st paper signed by you & the Duke of Cumberland is that at present as to myself I cannot nor would it be proper for me to form any opinion as to the necessity, propriety or impropriety of introducing the Doctors Willis, or Dr. Symmonds[1] or any person in that professional line to my father. My earnest wish must ever be that whatever is done may be *that* that is best & most conducive to the King's safety & the perfect re-establishment of his health, which as a dutiful & affectionate son & as a subject I must so ardently wish & pray for.

You have done most properly & discreetly in communicating the circumstance for the considerations of his Majesty's Cabinet & of his physicians. (42382–3)

1815   RICHARD BRINSLEY SHERIDAN TO THE PRINCE OF WALES[2]

21 Feb. 1804

I will not attempt to describe the strong impression of gratitude under which I address these few lines to your Royal Highness. No one but

1. Samuel Foart Simmons (1750–1813). M. D., 1776; physician to St. Luke's Hospital. Physician extraordinary to the King (gazetted, 15 May 1804).

2. This is the reply to the Prince's letter dated Monday night, 20 February 1804 (W. Fraser Rae's *Sheridan*, ii.243). 'You will know that I never forget my old friends. The death of Lord Elliott affords me the opportunity of offering you a trifling proof of that sincere friendship I have always profess'd & felt for you through a long series of years. I wish to God it was better worth your acceptance.'

Sheridan wrote to Addington on the 21st: 'Convinced as I am of the sincerity of your good will towards me, I do not regard it as an impertinent intrusion to inform you that the Prince has, in the most gracious manner, and wholly unsolicited, been pleased to appoint me to the late Lord Elliot's [*sic*] situation in the Duchy of Cornwall. I feel a desire to communicate this to you myself, because I feel a confidence that you will be glad of it. It has been my pride and pleasure to have exerted my humble efforts to serve the Prince without ever accepting the slightest obligation from him; but, in the present case, and under the present circumstances, I think it would have been really false pride and apparently mischievous affectation to have declined this mark of his Royal Highness's confidence and favour. I will not disguise that, at this peculiar crisis, I am greatly gratified at this event. Had it been the result of a mean and subservient devotion to the Prince's every wish and object, I could neither have respected the gift, the giver, or myself; but when I consider how recently it was my misfortune to find myself compelled by a sense of duty, stronger than my attachment to him, wholly to risk the situation I held in his confidence and favour, and that upon a subject on which his feelings were so eager and irritable, I cannot but regard the increased attention, with which he has since honoured me, as a most gratifying demonstration that he has clearness of judgment and firmness of spirit to distinguish the real friends to his true glory and interests from the mean and mercenary sycophants, who fear and abhor that such friends should be near him. It is satisfactory to me, also, that this appointment gives me the title and opportunity of seeing the Prince, on trying occasions, openly and in the face of day, and puts aside the mask of mystery and concealment. I trust I need not add, that whatever small portion of fair influence I may at any time possess with the Prince, it shall be uniformly exerted to promote those feelings of duty and affection towards their Majesties, which, though seemingly interrupted by adverse circumstances, I am sure are in his heart warm and unalterable—and, as far as I may presume, that general concord throughout his illustrious family, which must be looked to by every honest subject, as an essential part of the public strength at this momentous period' (Moore's *Life of Sheridan*, ii.321 (4th edn.]).

George Rose wrote on the 21st, in his Diary: 'The Prince of Wales has given to Mr. Sheridan the office of Receiver-General of the Duchy of Cornwall vacant by the death of Lord Eliot, worth £1,200 a year; this, with H.R.H. seeing Lord Thurlow every day, strongly confirms the probability of my former conjectures respecting what may be expected from a Regency Government. And I have been assured this day that notwithstanding the promising appearances of convalescence in the King, a Regency Bill is thought of. The Duke of York in that event to be completely given up and a Council of War to be established.'

He added, on the 25th: 'Some doubts are entertained whether the Prince of Wales's intention of giving the Receivership of the Duchy of Cornwall to Mr. Sheridan can be fulfilled as his Royal Highness had made a reversionary grant of the office some years ago to General Lake before he went to India, but it seems probable as the General is now in a situation of great profit that the Prince will prevail with him or with his brother Warwick Lake in his absence, to waive the grant and let Mr. Sheridan into possession'.

Lord Glenbervie commented: 'On the report of the present intended appointment of Sheridan, Warwick Lake, the General's brother, went to the Prince and reminded him of the grant to his brother. The Prince seemed confused—said it was so long ago he had forgot it, but he hoped he would not object to the grant being now made to Sheridan. Lake answered, it did not become him to object; he had only thought it his duty to remind H.R.H. of his former grant to his brother. How such a grant in favour of a person not here to resign or surrender it can be or has been got over, is a mystery' (Glenbervie MSS.).

Sheridan wrote to Colonel McMahon (the letter being dated merely 'Thursday evening'): 'I have thoroughly considered and reconsidered the subject we talked upon today. Nothing on earth shall make me risk the possibility of the Prince's goodness to me furnishing an opportunity for a single scurrilous fool's presuming to hint even that he had, in the slightest manner, departed from the slightest engagement. The Prince's right, in point of law and justice, on the present occasion to recall the appointment given, I hold to be incontestable; but, believe me, I am right in the proposition I took the liberty of submitting to his Royal Highness, and which (so far is he from wishing to hurt General Lake) he graciously approved. But understand me—my meaning is to give up the emoluments of the situation to General Lake, holding the situation at the Prince's pleasure, and abiding by an arbitrated estimate of General Lake's claim, supposing his Royal Highness had appointed him; in other words, to value his interest in the appointment as *if he had it*, and to pay him for it or resign to him.

'With the Prince's permission I should be glad to meet Mr. Warwick Lake, and I am confident that no two men of common sense and good intentions can fail, in ten minutes, to arrange it so as to meet the Prince's wishes, and not to leave the shadow of a pretence for envious malignity to whisper a word against his decision' (Moore's *Sheridan*, ii.358).

Moore commented: 'On the death of Lord Lake all difficulties were removed, and the appointment was confirmed to Sheridan for his life'.

yourself, Sir, could have so greatly enhanced the value of a favour & honor by the manner of conferring it. I trust that I feel and prize every word of your most gracious letter as I ought. It was not possible to encrease the devotion and attachment to your Royal Highness's character & person which have so long been among the warmest feelings of my heart, but diligence & exertion on my part may be encreased—and they shall be. To the end of my life I will strenuously employ every faculty of my mind in your service—and never can there arise any reward so grateful to my feelings as will be the consciousness of contributing in the slightest degree to the advancement of your Royal Highness's happiness and the maintenance of your renown and power. (40090–1)

1816 THE DUKE OF NORTHUMBERLAND TO COLONEL MCMAHON

Alnwick Castle, 21 Feb. 1804

I feel sensibly your kindness in writing to me at this time. I cannot understand the sudden changes which appear to take place in the K.'s disorder, nor indeed clearly what the nature of the disorder itself is. From what one hears I shoud conclude that this is no more than a third attack of his old complaint.

I hear from the Inn at this place that Mr. Grey has been sent for in a great hurry & is gone to town.[1] Probably to be consulted on the present occasion & on the arrangements to be made in consequence. I only hope, loving & reverencing the Prince as I do, that those in whom H.R.H. places his confidence & thinks proper to consult in this critical situation of affairs, may give H.R.H. such advice as will contribute to his comfort, honour & dignity, without any selfish views of their own. I have no doubt but H.R.H. will recollect on *this occasion* that Ld. Thurlow's advice cannot be quite impartial. He was at a former period the Ld. Chancellor & one of those who were the strongest for laying the intended Regent under the severest & most disgracefull restrictions. It cannot therefore be expected that he will, by contrary advice on this occasion, & owning that under these restrictions the Government of the country cannot possibly be carried on, openly declare to the nation that he was actuated on the former occasion by the most unjustifiable & criminal motives.

1. 'Some *pressing* consideration has, it seems, induced Mr. Grey once more to attend his *duty* in Parliament' (*The Times*, 27 February). The information was accurate enough. On the 20th Grey was at Darlington. 'I . . . intended to sleep there, but I found the house so full and was shown into so uncomfortable a room that I determined to come on, and have travelled all night [to Ferrybridge] . . . I slept more in the chaise than I should have done in a bad bed,' he informed his wife. On the 21st he reached Grantham, and London on the 22nd or 23rd (Howick MSS.).

I clearly foresee the game that will be played with the Prince by three different sets of men, & shoud H.R.H. *implicitly* comply with the wishes of any one of them, I must fear he will find cause hereafter to repent his having so done. God grant H.R.H. may take into his confidence & consult wise, experienced, & above all *disinterested* & *honest* men on this occasion, the most critical perhaps that ever will be offered to him in the whole course of his life, & upon which his future happiness or misery may perhaps greatly depend.

I have now lived long in the world, & have had great experience in it, & I therefore feel all the danger attending the situation in which the Prince is placed. I love H.R.H. most sincerely, & therefore tremble for the line of conduct he may be advised to follow. But neither the subject nor what I coud say upon it ought to be conveyed thro' the medium of the Post Office. (40092–3)

1817 THE EARL OF MOIRA TO COLONEL MCMAHON

Edinburgh, 21 Feb. 1804

Lord Thurlow is certainly right in the opinion he has given as to the policy of the Prince's not combating any of the Articles of the Regency Bill, if it be indeed what the last was. Leave it to the general clamor of the country to reprobate the attempt of palsying the executive power at a moment when the circumstances of the country require it to possess unusual vigor & energy. Should the enemy be really about to move, I should be sorry to leave this place on the eve of an attack because, right or wrong, there would be a want of confidence in the person who would then command, which might make a great difference in the behaviour of our young troops. I do not advert to this from any appetence of distinguishing myself, but from a disinterested view to the Prince's service: therefore let his Royal Highness decide as to time exactly in the way that at the moment strikes him as most for his own convenience. I much doubt whether Ld. Melville has any intention of going to town. I have peculiar reasons for thinking that he had not, two or three days ago, any notion of such a procedure on the part of Pitt as what you have mentioned. Persons of his intimate society argued strongly, speculating on probable necessities, against such restrictions as were proposed for a Regent heretofore. The Ministers cannot play double with the Prince; therefore I give them no credit for their frankness. (40094–5)

Kensington Palace, Wednesday night, 21 Feb. 1804

In consequence of the wish you intimated to me this morning that I would commit to paper the message I was commanded by the Queen to deliver to you on the subject of your offer to call at the Queen's House, I herewith inclose the purport of the same, which, I trust, will be found to convey as correctly to you the meaning of the Queen, as, according to my recollection, it does the words which I made use of to you. (46169)

ENCLOSED MESSAGE FROM THE QUEEN

The Queen has directed me to express in the most affectionate manner the satisfaction, which your note to Eliza has afforded her, and particularly the kind attention which you have shewn in offering to come to the Queen's House to see her; and that nothing would afford her more pleasure than to accept of it, as she really would be most happy to see you. But, as circumstances, to which she will not advert, have prevented you from coming on her birthday and from seeing the King previous to his indisposition, she trusts you will enter into the delicacy of her situation, and, from the same motive on your part, feel that on both your accounts it would be better for the present to give up the idea of meeting, however reciprocally you may feel grieved that such a necessity should exist. At the same time, she added that, the moment his Majesty was so far recovered as to admit of her communicating with him, she would not fail to represent in the fullest manner to him not only the constant and anxious enquiries made by you relative to his health, and your repeated expressions of affection and tenderness for her conveyed through the medium of your sisters, but particularly your offer of coming to the Queen's House to see her, for which purpose your letter to Eliza containing it would be carefully preserved. (46170)

THE PRINCE OF WALES'S REPLY

22 Feb. 1804

I lose as little time as possible in acknowledging your kind note, enclosing the Queen's message. What I wrote in my answer to Eliza I wrote from my heart in the wish I express'd to see the Queen & my sisters, as it was & is fully as much my anxious desire to see them, as they can possibly wish to see me; & it is therefore the cause of no inconsiderable degree of pain to me that I see myself necessarily compelled to relinquish that gratifying hope; but I consider it as my duty to submit to whatever the Queen's sentiments & wishes are upon that head. (42381)

1819   SIR ROBERT WILSON TO COLONEL MCMAHON

23 Feb. 1804

If your time be not totally occupied, or if you are not unmindful of my anxiety, pray give a confidential statement of the nature of the King's disorder, its progress, and probable termination. Every thought is directed to that particular event, and the publick feeling throughout this part of England is most strongly excited. I have no news to communicate. We are taught to expect the French and we are directed to *beat* them, but I doubt much whether we can presume to *fight* them. The Volunteers are resigning, disputing, and daily becoming a more fearful force for this country. If want should menace to pinch them, it is my firm opinion that this immortal deed of the Doctor's will establish a maximum by beat of drum and cram the bellies of the land proprietors with cold iron.

My duty is most unpleasant, harrassing, expensive and unsatisfactory. I have no military authority, a district of 400 miles in circumference to ride thro', no travelling expences allowed, only allowance for 3 horses, and 13s. 10d. per day pay. I dare not resign but I would be very glad to receive my dismissal. Perhaps pride operates to disgust me, for I presume that I should have a better employment than what the situation of Adjutant to yeomanry offers.

Lord Hutchinson has I suppose withdrawn from me his acquaintance. He threaten'd in a letter to do this if he found that the District of Genl. Myers[1] was offered him. The newspapers have informed me that the Duke did make the proposal. I confess that I never was so surprized. It was a thunderbolt which has smote me heavily, for Ld. H.'s friendship I valued much, but explanations and protestations avail nothing with him. However, I think you will do me the justice to believe that I knew nothing of the matter—on the contrary that I was most egregiously duped by a certain friend of ours assuring me that Ld. H. was to succeed some English General who was to be removed to Ireland for the sole purpose of making a vacancy on this Staff. However, the *mens conscia recti* is a very satisfactory sensation and must eventually operate to my advantage and the restoration of the opinion of those whose esteem I covet.

Simcoe is still here, but entre nous, he is not so good a General as I

1. Lieutenant-General Sir William Myers (*d.* 1805). Lieutenant-Colonel, 1786; Colonel, 1794; Major-General, 1796; Lieutenant-General, 1803; created Baronet, July 1804. He died at Barbados whilst Commander-in-Chief of the Windward and Leeward Islands. 'He makes fourteen out of eighteen of his family who have died after their arrival in the West Indies' (*Gentleman's Magazine*, 1805, ii.881).

thought him to be. His head is full of plans but he cannot arrange any system. However, I respect his talents and admire his zeal. From him I have received every possible attention and for my own sake should regret his absence from this Disct. but on publick grounds I wish that no General served where his own property and views were centred.

I will not trouble you with a longer letter. If the Prince ever honours me by a remembrance I wish you would express my sincere joy at his recovery and my unceasing devotion to his interest.

I have just returned from a tour thro' Somerset. The ev[en]ing papers should contain some paragraphs similar to Cobbett's remarks of last Sunday. (40096–7)

1820 AUGUSTUS CAVENDISH BRADSHAW TO COLONEL MCMAHON

Dublin, Friday, 24 Feb. 1804

I received your letter of the 20th this morning & instantaneously commenced *that office* which gratifies me more than the most lucrative place any Government could give me. *Confidentially* & *secretly* I have communicated with each individual, & to those that *I know* would vote against us I have said *nothing*.

Mr. Ponsonby[1] & Mr. George Ponsonby (the latter in the midst of his law business) have determined to sail tonight; they are warm & powerful friends. B. Dayly,[2] Falkener[3] & Hamilton,[4] Ld. Mathew,[5] two La

1. William Brabazon Ponsonby (1744–1806), M.P. for Co. Kilkenny, 1783–1800, and [U.K.], 1801–6. See No. 410.

2. Denis Bowes Daly (*c.* 1745–1821), M.P. for Galway borough, 1776–90; for King's County, 1790–1802; for Galway borough, 1802–5; for Galway County, 1805–18. Joint Muster Master General of the Forces in Ireland, 1806. See No. 410.

3. Sir Frederick John Falkiner (1768–1824), M.P. for Dublin County, 1801–7; for Carlow borough, 1812–18. Created Baronet, 21 December 1812.

4. Hans Hamilton (*d.* 1822) M.P. for Dublin County, 1801–22. Lord Hardwicke, the Lord Lieutenant, wrote from Dublin Castle on 30 April: 'Falkiner and Hans Hamilton ... are attached to the Prince of Wales, and the former told Sir Evan Nepean [the Chief Secretary] that on that account he thought it would be better he should remain here, more especially as he has undertaken to raise a regiment. Whether he is right in supposing that it is more agreeable to the Prince of Wales that he should remain in Ireland I cannot pretend to say. I own I should think not, for if his Royal Highness wishes to turn the balance, the more of those who attach themselves to his standard who are on the spot, the more his object is answered.' (Add. MSS. 35705, f.302)

5. Francis James, 2nd Earl of Landaff (1768–1833), styled Viscount Mathew from December 1797, when his father was made Earl of Landaff [I.], to 30 July 1806, when his father died. M.P. for Callan, 1796; for Co. Tipperary, 1790–2, 1796–1800, and [U.K.], 1801–6. Entered the Army, *c.* 1785; Lieutenant-Colonel, 1794; Colonel, 1805. K.P., 1831. On 10 July 1797 he married Gertrude Cecilia, daughter of John La Touche of Harristown, Co. Kildare.

Touche's,[1] Sir M. Somerville[2] & Mr. Hume[3] have promised me they will sail tomorrow night. I have writen to Ld. Ormonde[4] to send his brothers.[5] I shall most assiduously persevere in my canvass with due discretion.

As to myself, my dear friend, I do not consider my interest one moment when put in competition with any service I can be of to the *best of human beings*. If my coming into Parliament will be of use, purchase the seat at any price—but let there be a clause in case I vacate, to bring in a friend in my place during the Parliament or purchase at a larger price for a term of years. Say everything dutiful & attached from me to a certain person. I shall attend to all your orders with heart and soul.

I send you by this post a statement of my own grievances which peruse at your leisure. (40098–9)

1821   THE PRINCE OF WALES TO MRS. HOOK[6] [copy]

Carlton House, 24 Feb. 1804

It was quite out of my power either to see Hook this morning or to acknowledge the letter dictated by dear Sr. Walter in Hook's handwriting. It is impossible for me to express to you the anxiety I feel about his present state & the necessity which I understand his physicians have thought it incumbent upon them to represent to him of change of air. Gratitude alone for his invariable attention to me, but particularly in

1. The La Touche family had four representatives in Parliament at this time: David La Touche (1769–1816), M.P. for Carlow County, 1802–16. John La Touche (1775–1820), M.P. for Dublin, 1802–6; for Leitrim, 1807–20. Peter La Touche (*c.* 1775–1830), M.P. for Leitrim, 1802–6. Robert La Touche (*c.* 1773–1844), M.P. for Kildare, 1802–30. From No. 1822 it would appear that David and Peter are here referred to.

2. Sir Marcus Somerville (*c.* 1772–1831), M.P. [U.K.] for Meath, 1801–31. Succeeded his father as 4th Baronet, 1800.

3. William Hoare Hume (1772–1815), M.P. for Wicklow, 1801–15.

4. Walter, 18th Earl and 1st Marquess of Ormonde (1770–1820), succeeded his father, 30 December 1795; created Baron Butler [U.K.], 20 January 1801, and Marquess of Ormonde [I.], January 1816. K.P., 1798. A Lord of the Bedchamber, 1812–13. His Marquessate expired with him.

5. Two surviving brothers: James, 19th Earl and 1st Marquess of Ormonde [I.] (1774–1838). M.P. [I.], for Kilkenny City, 1796, and for Co. Kilkenny, 1796–1800; [U.K.], for Co. Kilkenny, 1801–20. Succeeded his brother in the Earldom, 10 August 1820; created Baron Ormonde [U.K.], 17 July 1821, and Marquess [I.], 5 October 1825. Also, Charles Butler (1780–1860), M.P. for Kilkenny City, 1802–9, 1814–20; for Co. Kilkenny, 1820–30.

6. Sir Walter Farquhar's daughter Anne (*c.* 1774–1844) in 1797 married the Rev. James Hook, D.D. (*c.* 1772–1828), Dean of Worcester, 1825–8. See No. 6 (i.8) where his dates are not given. He was at this time one of the Prince of Wales's Chaplains.

the late instance, and which never can be obliterated from my mind, would at all events & under all circumstances have created an uncommon interest in my breast relative to every circumstance respecting him, but particularly as to whatever relates to his health. Pray tell me the truth & let me daily learn from you, my dear madam, whatever accounts you may receive of my much respected friend. Should you at any time yourself wish to join him during his residence in the country, which I most devoutly pray may be beneficial in its effects to him, as you & I most cordially wish, I have a coach most easy in its motions & with a most easy & well contrived bed which might at any time, if you wish it, facilitate your journey with as little difficulty & with as little inconvenience or risk of bad consequences as can possibly be expected; in short, with none that I know of or else I should certainly not think of mentioning the circumstance to you. Excuse the trouble I am now giving you, but you must ascribe it to the true motive, which I am certain your usual liberality & well-known goodness of heart will induce to do, the anxious & lively interest I take in everything that concerns our dear Sr. Walter, & indeed any of his family, but most particularly yourself.

P.S. I need hardly add that the coach will be at your orders whenever you wish to send for it (Farquhar MSS.).

1822 AUGUSTUS CAVENDISH BRADSHAW TO COLONEL MCMAHON

Saturday, 25 [Feb. 1804]

I am not for half measures, therefore do not hesitate in geting me a seat in Parliament. I may be of use, & if I have a power to vacate it will be of no inconvenience to me. But do not even let that clause prevent your getting me in if necessary.

Peter La Touch [*sic*] & young David La Touche [*sic*] & Mr. Fitzgerald,[1] late primus Sergeant, will be off in two or three days at furthest, & I think Col. Leslie[2] will go on Monday—I hope by Thursday I shall have sent you thirteen County Members & two City. The moment I receive your summons I shall attend to it the same day. In haste. (40100)

1. James Fitzgerald (*c.* 1742–1835), M.P. for several Irish constituencies before 1801; for Ennis, 1802–8 and 1812. He was appointed Prime Serjeant [I.] in 1787 but was removed from that office in January 1799 on account of his refusal to support the Union.

2. Charles Powell Leslie (*c.* 1767–1831), M.P. for Monaghan, 1801–26; for New Ross, 1830–1831.

1823 PRINCESS SOPHIA TO THE PRINCE OF WALES

Saturday, 25 Feb. 1804

It is with the greatest pleasure that I take up my pen to recall myself to your mind, for I have ever experienced such kindness from you that I have longed for an opportunity of assuring you that though absent, *little Sophy* thinks of you perpetually. I am also anxious to tell you how very very anxious I have been about your health & how happy I am to learn you are now so much recovered. I pray God you may long continue well & trust every earthly happiness may attend you.

Mama's cough I think rather more troublesome today but our *present* mauvais situation is such that one is only surprised we get on as we do. Dear Amelia is certainly better but not yet as *free from pain* as I could wish. She joins with all my sisters in kindest love towards you & though *last* believe not the *least* attached to you is [etc.]. (Add. Georgian 13/20)

1824 LETTERS FROM PRINCESS ELIZABETH TO THE PRINCE OF WALES

Queen's House, 26 Feb. 1804

I have received the Queen's commands to return you thanks for your many kind enquiries concerning her. I am happy to say she is better today & she hopes you will give a good account of yourself if you answer this note, as we are all equally desirous to hear you are quite well again.

I wish it were in my power to give you a better bulletin of our dear Amelia's health; for some days she has been sadly troubled with her old complaint, besides that she has caught a bad cold which makes her cough very much, but both Dr. Turton & Sir Francis Milman hope that in a few days she will be better.

The Queen & my sisters desire their affectionate love. (Add. Georgian 11/96)

Queen's House, 27 Feb. 1804

As I think you will be anxious to know how Amelia continues today I trouble you again with a note to assure you she is considerably better, & tho' her cold is still very heavy upon her, that is so trifling compared with what she went through yesterday that both Dr. Turton & Sir Francis Milman give us the greatest comfort about her. She desires her kind love to you. The Queen is better & always desires me to recall her affectionately to your mind; my other sisters join me in everything most kind [etc.]. (Add. Georgian 11/97)

1825 THE EARL OF LAUDERDALE TO COLONEL MCMAHON

Dunbar, 27 Feb. 1804

I have just received your letter from Cheltenham. I cannot express to you how much I feel his Royal Highnesses kindness towards and his activity in executing [*sic*]; he has in short left nothing untryed that I would have suggested even had I been on the spot. When you come to town there is only Grey,[1] Falkland[2] and Kirkcudbright[3] about whom nothing is done.[4] I am afraid nothing can be done about Glasgow.[5] (40101)

1826 PRINCESS ELIZABETH TO THE PRINCE OF WALES

Queen's House, 28 Feb. 1804

I flatter myself that I can give you a much better account of Amelia. Fortunately a violent *rash* has come out in the night about her legs which has considerably encreased today which the *wise heads* assure us is a great thing in her favour. Dr. Turton has always wished this to happen. Her other complaint is better. At *present* she is very easy & exceedingly obliged to you for the interest you take about her; she desires her kindest & best love. The Queen is very much obliged to you for your very kind expressions in regard to herself & *us*. (Add. Georgian 11/98)

1827 AUGUSTUS CAVENDISH BRADSHAW TO COLONEL MCMAHON

Dublin, 28 Feb. 1804

I find it very difficult to stir the Irish Members. All that I have *secretly* communicated with are *steady friends* but they say it cannot come on so soon, that their own accounts differ from mine—but they are all determined to go in a few days, & I will keep working at them.

1. William John, 13th Lord Gray [S.] (1754–1807), succeeded his brother, 18 December 1786. He committed suicide. He was given a pension of £200 a year in May 1788.

2. Charles John, 9th Viscount Falkland [S.] (1768–1809), succeeded his brother in May 1796. He was mortally wounded in a duel. In July 1802 he had been given a pension of £200 a year.

3. Sholto Henry, 9th Lord Kirkcudbright [S.] (1771–1827), succeeded his father, 24 December 1801. In November 1805 he was given a pension of £100 a year, and in March 1807, on Lord Grenville's recommendation, one of £200 a year on the Scottish establishment, having already been in receipt of one of the same amount since July 1802.

4. In any case these three were not Scottish Representative Peers.

5. George, 4th Earl of Glasgow [s.] (c. 1766–1843), succeeded his father, 7 March 1775. A Representative Peer, 1790–1815. Created Baron Ross [U.K.], 11 August 1815.

516

Mr. O Hara[1] & Mr. Caulfield[2] (who sail tonight) beg to be added to the list I sent you before.

Ld. Mathew is gone—the La Touche's tomorrow or next day. If I was in Parliament I should not be so lukewarm and I hope by procuring me a seat you will give me an opportunity of proving my words. (40102)

1828   LETTERS FROM PRINCESS ELIZABETH TO THE PRINCE OF WALES

29 Feb. 1804

I have very great pleasure in assuring you that our dear Amelia is going on very well; the physicians are perfectly satisfied with her today & tho' she has still fever, think that of much less consequence than the other complaint. (Add. Georgian 11/99)

Queen's House, 1 Mar. 1804

You will be glad to hear we are much more comfortable about our dear Amelia; she has been very sick, which has done her a great deal of good. The physicians which [*sic*] her to keep quiet, which she thinks very necessary herself as she has had very little sleep in the night. The worst of her complaint is very much removed so we are much easier about her.

The Queen desires her kind love to you; she is better but suffers from her eyes. All my other sisters are pretty well & join me in everything kind. (Add. Georgian 11/100)

2 Mar. 1804

Many thanks for your note which I received last night. It is with great satisfaction, to myself I can assure you of both the Queen & Amelia being better. I am desired by them both to say everything most kind to you with thanks for your enquiries. My other sisters always wish to be remembered with affection. (Add. Georgian 11/101)

1. Charles O'Hara (1746–1822), M.P. for Sligo County, 1801–22.

2. Henry Caulfeild (1779–1862), M.P. for Co. Armagh, 1802–7, 1815–18, and 1820–30.

3 Mar. 1804

The Queen commands me to express to you with every sentiment of affection her thanks for your kind message & the interest you take about her eyes; she is now using some eye water which has been of great service to her, but if they get worse she will follow your good advice & see Mr. Dundas.

Amelia is going on slowly but better & having received great benefit from what she has taken she is in great hopes that in a few days she will be about again. (Add. Georgian 11/102)

4 Mar. 1804

Amelia is going on well but is not to come into company yet, quiet being necessary. The Queen pretty well & desires with my sisters & myself every kind thing that can be said by [etc.]. (Add. Georgian 11/103)

Q[ueen's] H[ouse], 5 Mar. 1804

I beg, tho' I am ever happy to receive your notes, that you will never think it necessary to answer me when it is in the least troublesome. I am much delighted in having it in my power to assure you that the Queen is pretty well & Amelia much better.

[*P.S.*] My mother & sisters all desire their kind love. (Add. Georgian 11/104)

Queen's House, 6 Mar. 1804

Amelia being better she might have come out of her room yesterday eveng. but the Queen thought [it] too damp for her to venture across the cold staircase; therefore she is still in her room but going on well.

The Queen desires me to recall her as well as my sisters affectionately to your mind. (Add. Georgian 11/105)

1829   JOHN HOOKHAM FRERE TO THOMAS TYRWHITT

Madrid, 6 Mar. 1804

At the dispersion of the property of the House of Alba, I was fortunate

518

enough to get possession of a sword which had belonged to the celebrated Duke[1] who commanded in the Low Countries. If it should be thought worthy of a place in his Royal Highnesses armoury, I would beg of you to make an offer of it as a token of my humble duty and respect. (40103)

1830 THE PRINCE OF WALES TO RICHARD BRINSLEY SHERIDAN[2]

Tilney Street,[3] *8 p.m., 6 Mar. 1804*

I have just learnt that Tom[4] is arriv'd with Lord Moira, but *I must absolutely* see you for two minutes *here* tonight, having heard some fresh news that it is absolutely necessary you should be acquainted with as soon as possible.[5] (42384)

1. Ferdinand Alvarez de Toledo, Duke of Alva (or Alba) [1508–82], whom Philip II sent to the Netherlands in 1567 to subdue the revolt.

2. On the 5th, at 11.30 a.m. the Prince had written to Sheridan from Carlton House: 'Pray come here as soon as you can, for I have got hold of almost all the circumstances that have happened respecting the interview of yesterday, and which is most essential should be communicated previous to the debate of today. The sooner you come the better' (Rae's *Sheridan*, ii.245. Rae did not accurately transcribe letters, and the accuracy of this one cannot be vouched for).

3. Where Mrs. Fitzherbert lived.

4. Sheridan's son.

5. Sheridan wrote to his wife on 27 February: 'There never was known before anything equal to the agitation of people's minds at this moment, and the Prince, just recovered from an illness in which his life was despaired of for two days, is so nervous and anxious that it is not easy to thwart him, though he runs a great risk of making himself ill again. I now see him openly, but till lately I never saw him till twelve at night, and he has often kept me till 4 in the morning, not supping or with a drop of wine, but in his bedroom' (Rae's *Sheridan*, ii.249).

Charles Grey's letters at this time illustrate the suspicion with which Sheridan was regarded by the leading Whigs on account of his Carlton House connection. 'The Prince', wrote Grey on 24 February, 'is in great agitation, and talks all day without ceasing to Mrs. Fitzherbert and McMahon. Sheridan has seen him occasionally and is the only person engaged in politics who has done so, except Lord Thurlow. Through Sheridan everything comes to Fox, a terrible channel, I think, tho' Fox seems at present satisfied with his conduct. Sheridan has also had communications with Addington which I distrust very much, tho' Fox on this head also seems perfectly secure. But I am not at all relieved from the forebodings I have felt from the beginning of disgusting intrigues and some arrangement at last in which I shall refuse to have any share' (Howick MSS.).

On the 27th he wrote, again to Mrs. Grey: 'I saw Sheridan at Fox's for the first time, looking more fiery and horrible than ever. I only saw him for a minute as I went with Fox into the inner room with the Grenvilles, with whom he is not yet quite cordial.'

And on 9 March: 'I feel more and more every day the mischief of Sheridan's favouritism with the Prince.'

Creevey fully shared Grey's suspicions, writing on 2 April 1804: 'His insuperable vanity has suggested to him the brilliancy of being first with the Prince and of governing his councils.

519

Queen's House, 7 Mar. 1804

Amelia continues to mend tho' not as speedily as we wish. Poor little Sophy this morning has been seized with one of her spasms; she is going on well but at present in great pain. The Queen not as well as *you* or *I* would wish her, very nervous, all the rest pretty well & desiring every kind love possible to you. (Add. Georgian 11/106)

Q[ueen's] H[ouse], 8 Mar. 1804

Many thanks for your very kind note. I can with truth say all *are better* here today but we have been much alarmed about our dear little Sophy who was seized with a most dreadfull cramp yesterday morning which appeared to abate towards night but at ten o'clock she had so severe a return of it that at twelve it was necessary to send for Sir F. Milman, who remained with her till two this morning when she was asleep & remained so till five & has slept a great deal since & has kept everything on her stomach since last night. All danger is *now* over & only quiet necessary to restore her strength, which is greatly wanted now. Amelia is better but still very delicate & the Queen is certainly more comfortable today, but her nerves not at all the better for the various anxieties she has to go through. She has been dreadfully alarmed about Sophia. She desires me to thank you very kindly for your kind messages to her & all my sisters join in everything most affectionate to you. (Add. Georgian 11/107)

1832   THOMAS TYRWHITT TO COLONEL MCMAHON

8 Mar. 1804

I apprehend Mr. Lorentz will be satisfied as he states with some *satisfactory assurances* that H.R.H. has ever expressed his anxious inclination to liquidate the debt of the Elector,[1] as well capital as interest, & that most undoubtedly when his own private Commissioners have had time to make any arrangements, his Electoral Highness will be always kept

He will, if he sees it practicable, try, and is now trying, to alienate the Prince from Fox, and to reconcile him to the wretched Addington. The effect of such a diabolical project is doubtless to be dreaded with a person so unsteady as the Prince' (*Creevey Papers*, p. 25 [1906 edn.]).

1. 'Landgrave' scored through. The reference is to the Elector (formerly Landgrave) of Hesse-Cassel.

in view. A letter to this purport will stop all further importunities, though the stronger it is worded the better.

Respecting Mr. Lorentz himself, I can see no earthly reason why he is to bore the Prince by demanding an audience; his situation in life is not of that calibre to expect it; he is by no means in the confidence of his master, but being a great schemer, and as the Elector thinks, by being a good calculator, likely to squeeze a farthing more for him, he sends him here.

I know nothing at all to the discredit of Mr. L. excepting that his zeal to feed the avarice of his master leads him to be very persevering & troublesome.

Adam is, I believe, master of all the accounts.[1] (40105)

1833 LETTERS FROM PRINCESS ELIZABETH TO THE PRINCE OF WALES

[9 Mar. 1804]

It is with great satisfaction to myself that I can assure you both Sophia & Amelia are better. The former is still very *tender* from the violent pain she has been in but is going on well. Amelia is more comfortable some hours than others, but also will get quite well as she gains strength. The Queen commands me to say to you she has followed your advice & asked Dundas about her eyes. He approves of what she is doing & she is obliged to you for your good advice. (Add. Georgian 11/108)

10 Mar. 1804

You may depend, my dear brother, that as long as my sisters remain unwell I shall not fail to write to you constantly. My sisters are both better thank God today, Sophia going on a[s] well as possible; Amelia very quiet & patient & certainly much better than yesterday. My other sisters well. I have been very unwell but not stopt from doing everything I

1. Lorentz is next mentioned in McMahon's letter to William Adam, 16 January 1806: 'I send you a prospectus of finance from the Hessian Minister M. Lorentz which he has submitted to the Prince for the purpose of inducing H.R.Hss. to become either a real or an ostensible subscriber.

'Now, *in confidence*, the truth is, the Prince does not wish to either give his money or lend his name, for he knows but little of Mr. Lorentz. Still, however, as he is Chargé des Affaires for the Landgrave, & that it is incumbent to hold a candle to the —— [*sic*], he has refer'd Mr. Lorentz to you, & begs you will use the best means of declining his proposition, without dissatisfying him' (Blair Adam MSS.).

ought & am much better today & have been out with the Queen who desires her kind love to you. (Add. Georgian 11/109)

11 Mar. 1804

The Queen is a great deal better for her airing, which I am sure you will be glad to hear. My sisters are both going on very well, Sophia getting very charmingly; Amelia, who has so long been an invalid, will take more time to recruit her strength. You must be sick with the sight of my handwriting, therefore will only add the Queen's & my sisters love. (Add. Georgian 11/110)

12 Mar. 1804

I am happy to say my sisters are going on just as you could wish, my dear brother. The Queen pretty well & with kind love from her & my sisters. (Add. Georgian 11/111)

Queen's House, 13 Mar. 1804

Both my sisters desire me to thank you for all your kindness to them. I am very happy to be able to say that they have both had a remarkable good night & they appear to be going on as well as possible.

The Queen is much better for her airings. (Add. Georgian 11/112)

1834 THE EARL OF DARNLEY TO THE PRINCE OF WALES

Berkeley Square, Tuesday, 13 Mar. 1804

After the conversation with which your Royal Highness has lately honor'd me, I think it my duty to inform you that I can state from undoubted authority that Mr. Pitt neither has, nor (as I firmly believe) ever will, enter into any compromise or co-operation with his Majesty's present Ministers, of which the hostile Motion which he is about to bring forward in Parliament on the subject of the Navy, and which I know he intends to support with all his strength, affords additional proof.[1]

1. Pitt's motion for an inquiry into the state of the country's naval defence (15 March) was defeated by 201 votes to 130 (*Parliamentary Debates*, i.874–927).

Having enter'd upon this subject, I trust to your Royal Highness's usual condescension when I venture to pursue it a little farther, and to state the opinions in writing which induc'd me on a late occasion humbly to offer to your Royal Highness a suggestion which your better judgment has induc'd you to reject.

The first position, on which I wish to ground all subsequent argument and which my zeal for your Royal Highness, with whom the welfare of the country is inseparably connected, has induc'd me so frequently and so urgently to press upon your notice is this—*that of all men existing Mr. Pitt is beyond comparison the person most capable of rendering effectual service to both.* On this point I beg leave to stake all the credit I may possess with your Royal Highness in opposition to anything you may hear to the contrary from other quarters. Independent of all other considerations which may induce the publick to look up to him at the present moment, the circumstance of the convicted imbecility of Government on the one hand, and the national honor which the manifest sacrifice of every principle to ambition excites in the minds of men, and which the late Coalition appears to present in such glaring colours on the other, place him in a situation of eminence which neither his splendid talents nor his former services, without such a concurrence of circumstances, would ever have enabled him to reach.

But your Royal Highness appears to think that he is your enemy, and that he having heretofore fail'd in that respect and deference which is due to your Royal Highness and to your exalted station, it would not become your dignity to take any step which might by possibility be construed into seeking or courting the assistance of such a person from the unworthy motive of mere self-interest, or the still more unworthy impulse of fear.

In the first place permit me to state to your Royal Highness that he is not your enemy to my certain knowledge, and that I have every reason to believe that he might easily be converted into a firm, & certainly a most useful friend. But this in the first instance depends on your Royal Highness, from whom any overture must necessarily come. On a late occasion it struck me very forcibly that an opportunity occurred in which, without committing the dignity of high station, without deviating from those exemplary rules of conduct which have with so much wisdom been adopted without appearing either to court or to fear, your Royal Highness might, if you had thought fit, have oblig'd the man who (if I am right) is most capable of doing it, to do you justice. For what was the situation in which your Royal Highness then stood, & may perhaps now stand? The subject is a delicate one, and nothing but my zeal & anxiety for your Royal Highness should induce me to enter into it. The Chancellor had in the most solemn manner pledg'd himself & his colleagues to the assertion that the Royal functions were not suspended. They had even gone so far as to act upon this assertion, and to induce his Majesty to give the Royal Assent to Acts of Parliament. On the very day after this transaction had taken place one of the physicians solemnly assures your Royal Highness that his Majesty was actually at that moment in a state which notoriously incapacitates all men from doing any act of discretion whatever. The inference drawn by your Royal Highness and express'd on this occasion was irresistible. Either the physicians deceiv'd your Royal Highness, or the Ministers the Parliament and the nation. In either case your Royal Highness was materially interested, but in the latter, the rights of the Crown, of which your Royal Highness was then the natural and the only guardian, were usurp'd. Under such circumstances it appear'd to me that something ought to be done, & thinking as I do of Mr. Pitt, I earnestly wish'd that your Royal Highness should render it impossible for him to plead ignorance of the real state of the case hereafter, and even supposing (which I could not believe) that he was acting with the Ministers, or likely to act with them in such an usurpation, that he should at least know that your Royal Highness was in possession of proofs against him and them. Besides, setting aside for a moment all the circumstances of his situation which appear'd to render him the person best able to afford your Royal Highness advice & assistance, a natural and plausible reason presented itself for sending for him in preference to any other man, and thereby deviating from the rule which had so very properly been laid down. *He had been the King's Minister during a large proportion of his Majesty's reign, and during the periods of the two former suspensions of the Royal authority.* I firmly believe he would have given the best, the most upright and even the most friendly advice. But supposing the contrary—how could he, if he would, have denied the *evidence of facts* which your Royal Highness had ready for him, or how could he have avoided pledging himself to your Royal Highness to maintain your just rights & those of the Crown? He must have known that if he had dar'd after such an interview to act a false or double part, your Royal Highness had in your hand the means of convicting him. But supposing what I believe, your Royal Highness would have rivetted to your interest the best & most effective friend you can possess. Besides, as it strikes me, no point of etiquette would have been compromis'd, no pledge of future favor would have been given. But the man who was able most efficaciously to serve your Royal Highness would have been held fast to your interest by the united operation of the two most powerful springs of human action, hope and fear. In his hands your Royal Highness would have deposited a dignified protest against any invasion of the rights of the Crown, or of your own interests as connected with them, and you would have left him without excuse if he had not strenuously and anxiously supported them.

I forbear to adduce many other arguments which present themselves on this subject, having already trespass'd too much on your Royal Highness's time, for which I must trust to your accustomed goodness to pardon. (40106–9)

1835   THE PRINCE OF WALES TO CHARLES JAMES FOX

Carlton House, 10.45 a.m., Tuesday, 13 Mar. 1804
I have just receiv'd a note from Sheridan, which was brought to my house at five this morning, by which he says that you will be at Lord Thurlow's in George Street, Westminster, at three today. Lord Thurlow wish'd much, if you did call upon him, that it might be before three, as at that hour he leaves town to return into the country to his dinner. I have therefore mention'd that you will be with Lord Thurlowe [*sic*] about two o'clock. I hope I have not done wrong.[1] (Add. MSS. 47560, f.69)

1836   LETTERS FROM PRINCESS ELIZABETH TO THE PRINCE OF WALES

14 Mar. 1804
My sisters are all going in as well as possible & I now begin to hope that in a few days the house will no longer wear the appearance of an hospital,

1. Next day the Prince sent Addington a brief note:
'The Prince of Wales requests to have the pleasure of seeing Mr. Addington at Carlton House tomorrow between one & two o'clock' (Sidmouth MSS.).
On the 15th (or, more accurately, perhaps, at 1 a.m. on the 16th) the Government had the unexpectedly large majority of 71 (201 v. 130) on Pitt's Motion for papers relative to the conduct of the country's maritime defence. 'Sheridan, Erskine and Colonel McMahon (a sort of manager for the Prince of Wales) divided with Government. This circumstance gave occasion to a great deal of observation. Addington had been met in the morning coming out of Carlton House, and the Duke of Norfolk, who has been wavering for several months, is said to have declared himself in favour of the Ministry. Sheridan's entire separation is now expected more than ever. He has always been a doubtful and hollow friend' (Glenbervie, *Journals*, i. 372). 'Sheridan', wrote Creevey on 2 April, 'displays evident distrust of his own projects, and is basely playing an under game as Fox's friend, in the event of defeat to him and his Dr. I never saw conduct more distinctly base than this' (*Creevey Papers*, p. 26). Fox commented, in a letter to Grey (6 April): 'Sheridan has been here, and as I judge is very desirous of getting right again, but you will easily believe my dependence on him is not very firm.'
The Government's majority was deceptively satisfactory: the reality was that Ministers were fast losing the confidence of the House. Of the seventy-one, forty or fifty were men who in general voted with Fox on all political subjects, but who would not on this occasion join him against Lord St. Vincent, the First Lord of the Admiralty. And it was said that as many Government supporters went away without voting. Charles Yorke for one was now convinced that the Administration, of which he was a prominent member, could not go on much longer.

which it has of late done. The Queen desires her affectionate love to you. (Add. Georgian 11/113)

15 Mar. 1804

I am delighted to be able to assure you that all the sick are going on as well as possible. Poor Augusta is confined with a wholesome but most suffering complaint, which is a large boil, but we hope in a day or two she will be quite well. (Add. Georgian 11/114)

Queen's House, 18 Mar. 1804

I have the pleasure of assuring you Sophy is quite well & only wants strength, & desires me to thank you very particularly for your goodness to her. Amelia is going on well & in two or three days will be out. Augusta is still confined & suffering cruelly from a boil; Mary very well. The dear Queen pretty well, but her nerves to say the truth sadly shook.[1] I hope I shall be soon able to say she is well, but as you like the truth I write it. They all desire their kind love to you. (Add. Georgian 11/115)

1837   CHARLES JAMES FOX TO THE PRINCE OF WALES

Albermarle Street, Tuesday [? *20 Mar. 1804*]

I cannot leave town without thanking your Royal Highness as well for your general condescension to me, as particularly for Mr. McMahon's vote last night which, circumstanced as I was, was of most material consequence to me.

May I be permitted to repeat to your Royal Highness the advice I humbly offered to you on Saturday, not in the present suspended state of affairs to say or do anything that may make any of the parties in opposition to the Doctor totally desperate with regard to the possibility of your Royal Highness's future countenance?

I suspect the King's state to be such as may make it necessary for Ministers to come forward with some project for carrying on the Govern-

---

1. The Queen must have had some terrifying experiences. Glenbervie wrote (27 June): 'Mrs. Trail, who is much acquainted with Miss Planta, says the Queen's temper is become intolerable, and that the Princesses are rendered quite miserable by it. Alas, there is much ground for accounting for this and pardoning her' (*Journals*, i.383).

526

ment in the King's name in a few weeks. Never believe me again, Sir, if what *they* will bring forward will not be offensive & hostile to your Royal Highness in the highest degree, but if I should be mistaken in this, it will be always open for your Royal Highness to act as you please. But if I am right the great object will be to procure a junction of *all* the parts of Opposition which will be strong enough, I am satisfied, upon such a subject to controll the Ministry. Of us, of course, your Royal Highness is sure. I have little doubt but you may be nearly equally so of the Grenvilles &c., but Pitt in such a case I am sorry to say would be a most material card and his decision will, I suspect, entirely depend upon how far he may consider himself as proscribed by your Royal Highness. If there were good hopes of his Majesty's real & perfect recovery I am convinced there would be no chance of him, but as things are I think he might be gained for the purpose of resisting any improper measures of the Administration in regard to a Regency. At the same time let me observe that any overture from your Royal Highness to him would I think be very much below your dignity and at present prejudicial rather than useful to your interest. I repeat it, till he shall have given up all hopes of the K. there is no chance of his assistance, but when these hopes shall be gone, if he does not think his case absolutely desperate with your Royal Highness, I think he would not be averse to taking his share in destroying the present men.

Pardon me for this trouble, which I trust your Royal Highness will impute to its true cause, the perfect attachment with which I shall always be desirous of shewing myself, Sir, [etc.]. (40356-7)

1838 THE EARL OF MOIRA TO COLONEL MCMAHON

Edinburgh, 27 Mar. 1804

You are to accept two bills drawn in favor of Joseph Atkinson; one for £1200 at 70 days from yesterday, the other for £1400 at 65 days. By this arrangement I shall in a day or two transmit £2000 to you, & within the fortnight £1200 more to make good the impending payment up to the 20th April inclusive.

Somebody was congratulating Harry Erskine the other day on the favorable bulletin in the newspaper. 'I am rejoiced', answered he, 'to see it stated that his Majesty is in so fair a way; but I shall never think him really recovered till he has sent away his *Doctor*.'

Offer my most affectionate devotion to the Prince; and tell his Royal Highness that General Dalrymple was the person at the Duke of York's dinner whom I labored so fruitlessly to recollect. (40110-11)

Louisbourg, 29 Mar. 1804

Though I know that you are not fond of writing I flatter myself you will allow me to express to you how much I have been distressed at hearing that you had been dangerously ill. My sisters, who are so good as to keep up a constant correspondence with me, mentioned with great vexation your having an inflammation on your chest. I hope that with care you have been long recovered, and that dear little Charlotte, as soon as you was able to [be] settled in town, was your companion at breakfast. The whole family speak of her [with] raptures, and whenever you allow her to spend a week at Windsor all my letters are filled with accounts of the dear child who, I am assured, is your picture. I hear frequently of her by Lady Elgin who is very much attached to her.

I have, my dear brother, been very unhappy of late with hearing of the King's illness, which, owing to contrary winds, I was first acquainted with by the French newspapers. You, who have never been at such a distance from your family, cannot imagine all I went through till dear Elizabeth's letters arrived. I can never forget her kindness to me in writing at a moment that she was so much afflicted herself and was also taken up with attending in so exemplary a manner on the Queen who I fear will suffer essentially from this fresh trial.

We have had a very dreadful event take place in our neighbourhood. On the 15th the French crost the Rhine with a small body of troops, marched into the Electorate of Baden and have carried off several émigrés who are accused of having taken an active part in the conspiracy against the First Consul. It makes on[e] quite shudder to think what the consequences of this step may be.[1]

The Elector desires me to present his compliments to you. May I beg of you to give my love to Charlotte, who I have taken the liberty to send a little ivory and gold fan for to the Queen [*sic*]. (51703-4)

Kensington Palace, 30 Mar. 1804

The inclosed letter I received yesterday from old Montague, Equerry of the Crown Stable to his Majesty and formerly Clerk of the Stables to the Prince. Having reason to believe that the Prince has a regard for the old man I conceive I may without presumption request of you to take a favorable opportunity of laying it before my brother and receiving his commands upon it. I understand Mr. Montague is at present involved in

1. See No. 1841.

difficulties from which a compliance with his request would tend essentially to relieve him, and I am well aware from the goodness of the Prince's heart and his well known justice and liberality, that a if promise [*sic*] of the nature mentioned by the old man was ever made, it will be scrupulously observed on his part. (40112)

[Enclosure] JAMES MONTAGU TO THE DUKE OF KENT

The King's Mews, 27 Mar. 1804

May it please your Royal Highness. The kindness I have continueally experienced from you emboldens me to lay before your Royal Highness a few particulars relative to the situation in which I stand in respect to his Royal Highness, the Prince of Wales, in the hope that you will condesend to become my advocate on the occasion.

When, at his Royal Highness's request, I resigned my place of Clerk of the Stables, he kindly bestow'd uppon me a compensation of £120 p. annum which was to continue not only for my life but during Mrs. Montagu's also if she survived me, but after enjoying it some few years one halfe was suddenly taken from me, and about five years since the other halfe also, unknown to, I am persuaded, and contrary to the intention of his Royal Highness, who, with the greatest kindness and condesention, confirm'd the original grant by a letter to each, which I have now in my possession.

Prompt'd by the consideration of the advance in price of every article of life and by the inconvenience occasion'd by the Civil List being so much in arrear that I have been under the necessity of selling out part of my little stock, by the persuasion that through your Royal Highness's intercession I may be again placed on the compensation list, I have taken the resolution to trouble your Royal Highness with the above, hopeing that if I have innocently done wrong I shall at least obtain your pardon. (40113-4)

1841   THE DUKE OF KENT TO THE PRINCE OF WALES

Kensington Palace, 3 p.m., Tuesday, 3 Apr. 1804

Since I took my leave of you on Sunday the state of matters has been as follows. Sunday afternoon, and evening, much agitation; the subsequent night very restless, and great hurry the Monday, until about twelve, when he was thought so much calmer as to be able to see the D. of Y[ork]. The interview lasted about half an hour, but I have reason to believe it was not satisfactory, and that the C.-i.-C. came away impressed that *the* K. was not so well as at their former interview. This was followed by his being *very high* afterwards till night: nevertheless he did sleep five hours and awoke much calmer this morning. *Yesterday* he walked in the garden at 11 & just before sunset. *Today* he has been in the riding house, and it was expected would see the Chancellor. I do not conceive anything is yet settled about Kew, nor do *all agree* in sentiments as to *that* point.

The military changes settled at yesterday's interview are as follows: Sir D. Dundas to be Govr. of Chelsea,[1] Dalrymple to be Govr. of Fort Augustus & Fort George,[2] Trigge to be Lt.-Govr. of Chelsea,[3] Fox to be Lt.-Govr. of Gibr.,[4] Vyse to have the 3d Dragoon Guards;[5] Wilford,[6] Vyse's present Regiment,[7] & it is surmised that Gwynne has the promise of Craig's[8] on *his* death, as also that Churchill will succeed to Gwynne's.[9] *Voila tout* that I have been able to learn, except the massacre of the poor Duc d'Enghien[10] which I have just learnt by a hasty note from the Duke of Orleans.

I shall write again the day after tomorrow. I was told at the Queen's House that Dundas retires from his District, but no successors are yet talked of for either him or Fox. (46185–6)

1842 LETTERS FROM THE EARL OF MOIRA TO COLONEL MCMAHON

Edinburgh, 4 Apr. 1804

Since my return hither I have not had any political information whatsoever from London. Frequently, however, distance affords the means of

1. The Royal Hospital there, *vice* Sir William Fawcett, *deceased*.

2. *Vice* General Sir David Dundas.

3. *Vice* General Dalrymple.

4. *Vice* General Sir Thomas Trigge.

5. *Vice* General Sir William Fawcett.

6. Richard Rich Wilford (*d.* 1822). Colonel, 1795; Major-General, 1797; Lieutenant-General, 1805; General, 1814.

7. The 29th Dragoons.

8. General Francis Craig (*c.* 1726–1811) commanded the 13th Dragoons. Lieutenant-General 1777; General, 1793.

9. The 22nd Dragoons.

10. Louis Antoine Henri de Bourbon, Duc d'Enghien (1772–1804), the son of the Duc de Bourbon (1756–1830) by Marie Louise (1750–1822), sister of *Égalité*, Duke of Orleans. Napoleon, violating the neutral territory of Baden, seized and carried him off to Vincennes. He was sentenced to death by a military tribunal as an *émigré* in arms against his country, and shot, 21 March.

obtaining intelligence which is not to be had directly: therefore I apprize you that an arrangement is far advanced for bringing in Pitt again to the head of affairs.[1] Possibly the Prince has been informed of this. If that be not the case, the collusion of Mr. Addington is very censurable. (40126)

1. Moira had definite news of this from Lord Melville, whom he saw that day. Melville reported to Pitt, 'He did not seem to receive the communication with either surprise or dissatisfaction, but gave no symptoms of acquiescence from which I could draw any conclusion.' Melville wanted to know 'the extent of Mr. Fox's connection with the Prince, and his influence over him in a comparative view with that of Lord Moira himself.' Upon this subject, Melville informed Pitt, Moira was 'certainly very explicit. He reminded me that in the first conversation he had with me when I came first from the North, and when a Regency was every day expected, he expressed his conviction in pointed terms, that the Prince would act most unwisely if he did not set out immediately with an avowal of forming the strongest Government he could, founded on an extinction and oblivion of party prejudices and animosities, and as the best groundwork for doing so, to begin with banishing his own. I certainly acquiesced in the fairness of that statement, and admitted that the advice he, both through the Advocate, and personally, represented himself to have given to the Prince, was in unison with what he held out previous to his going to London. He further distinctly stated that previous to his arrival in London, the Prince had stated to Mr. Fox and Mr. Grey, that he could not see either of them till he had seen Lord Moira from Scotland, that he accordingly adhered to that intimation, & did not see either of them till after his arrival, and had received a full communication from Lord Moira of all his opinions, and particularly of the propriety of his embracing with cordiality the support and connection of Mr. Pitt and Lord Melville, and he makes no doubt the Prince stated all this to Mr. Fox when he did see him. He distinctly states that he himself made a full communication of all these opinions to Mr. Fox, as those which he had given to the Prince, and that Mr. Fox seemed without hesitation to acquiesce in the propriety of them, nor does he entertain any doubt that Mr. Fox still remains in those sentiments. At this period of the conversation he threw out a surmise, but whether he meant to convey only a suspicion or to express an idea for which he had some ground, I could not distinctly collect. It was as if Sheridan, whom by *some means* Mr. Addington seemed to have got hold of, was playing or would play a game for the purpose of impressing the Prince that the easiest mode by which he could gain any object, even that of an extensive plan of Government on the footing recommended by Lord Moira, was by admitting into his friendship and confidence Mr. Addington, whose interest and inclination it certainly was to cultivate the friendship of the Prince. I should have liked to have probed this part of the conversation a little further, but I did not see an opening for it. He mentioned that either in his communications with the Prince or Mr. Fox (I am not certain which) he stated doubts how far too strict a league and union with the Grenville interest was an eligible or wise measure. He admitted it to be very proper if it went only to considering that interest as a part of the weight and talents that was on his principles desirable to unite in one mass of general strength and exertion for the safety of the Empire, but he hinted that difficulties would arise if it went further, for that they were unpopular and full of pretensions. He said that except accidentally one day at the Duke of York's when Mr. Addington came into the room, he had never seen him till a few hours before he left London, when in consequence of a note from Mr. Addington, he called on him. There was nothing very pointed in the conversation. There were great regrets that Lord Moira's duty rendered it necessary for him to leave Town, as he would have been the happy instrument of reconciling the King and the Prince, which was of all others the most desirable thing at that moment to be attained. There was likewise some general hints to what an eminence it would raise Lord Moira if he should beat the French &c &c., but as there was no point to be gained by any discussions of that nature the conversation ended between Mr. Addington and Lord

Edinburgh, 7 Apr. 1804

Since I last wrote, I have made out a good deal more of politics. Pitt & his friends are aware of Addington's insincerity, & pay him in his own coin. He will be flung by them, but you may depend upon it that they are truly sensible to that generous oblivion of the past which the Prince has so magnanimously professed, & their success would not be injurious to his Royal Highness's interests, or be attended with any preclusion of Fox.

You had singularly forgotten my having apprized you that the £900 was lodged for Thomas before I quitted town. All the others will be settled thro' James.

If this finds you at Brighton with the Prince, offer to him from me all that most respectful affection which my heart owes to him & does most truly pay. (40127–8)

Edinburgh, 13 Apr. 1804

I can give you some further political intelligence on which you may depend. Addington has been plain [*sic.* ?playing] loose with Pitt: the latter knows it, & is quietly collecting all his forces to strike at him. We ought to assist this as much as possible, for what can be more false or more hostile to us than the present Administration? Even if one had not that private interest, it is urgently important to get rid of men whose incapacity will ruin us all if they have much longer the conduct of our affairs.

I do not wonder at the forged excuse which you tell me is circulated about the 3d Dragoon Guards, because it was necessary to say something to prevent the inference which was sure to suggest itself to everybody. Let me assure you that not the most distant hint of an offer was ever made to me. As I neither expected or cared about the Regiment, I cannot have felt disappointment. Indeed, the sensation I have had on the subject has been simply surprise that people should be so silly as not to be aware of the construction the world would put upon the procedure. Undoubtedly, the pitching upon my second in command (possessing a Regiment already) for such a mark of attention, will appear the most ingenious mode of giving unnecessary & impolitic affront that ever occured to wise heads. It will not slacken my energy in the trust I have undertaken.

Moira, and for the same reason he soon dropped it, and our conversation ended by Lord Moira asking me to name the first day I could to dine with him. I named this day and I understand he has asked a good number of friends to dine with him today to *meet* Lord Melville.' (Add. MSS. 40102, f.133. To Pitt, 6 April)

James will tell you all about financial matters. Cannot you get somebody to hint to Baron Graham how earnestly I am interested about Davison? Graham's report must decide much: old Graham is partial to me. (40129–30)

Edinburgh, 17 Apr. 1804
Confidential. All the Scotch Members are going up to join Pitt in a thundering blow against Addington.[1] It is our interest, in my judgment, to add every weight to this attack, for I can say to you I am *satisfied* that Pitt's line would be quite different from any which he has hitherto pursued. At all events, nothing can be more injurious to the Prince's interests than Addington's conduct. If this sentiment be adopted do you speak in my name to Chapman,[2] Ram,[3] & others whom they will indicate; & make Sir John Sinclair write to Loveden[4] as well as speak to the friends who are in town. (40131)

1843   PRINCESS ELIZABETH TO THE PRINCE OF WALES
       18 Apr. 1804
I have not troubled you of late as my brothers always promised me to mention how all went on here, but I cannot now resist to recall myself to your mind & to assure you that all here are well excepting poor Augusta, who is still confined to her couch, tho' nearly well. The Queen has been indifferent but is now better. She desires her affectionate love to you. We all had great delight in seeing you the other day & trust you saw us kiss our hands to you, tho' at a distance it made us truly happy,

1. Pitt himself wrote summonses to some of them (Stanhope's *Pitt*, iv.145); and he wrote to George Rose on 12 April: 'My answers from Scotland are favourable, and from all I hear I have little doubt that there will be collected in town, of different descriptions, not less than from 200 to 220 persons ready to vote on a good question against Government. Some deduction must be allowed in estimating the number that will actually divide, but I think the force must be nearly sufficient to answer the purpose' ('to bring the contest of parties to an issue for the present Session'). (Add. MSS. 42772, f.195)

2. Charles Chapman (*c.* 1754–1809), M.P. for Newtown, 1802–5. He was reckoned one of the Fox-Grenville party in May.

3. Abel Ram (*c.* 1756–1830), M.P. for Co. Wexford, 1801–6, and 1807–12. He was considered a supporter of Pitt in 1804 (and in 1805), and he supported the Perceval Ministry later.

4. Loveden's politics were considered 'doubtful' in 1804—one of Addington's friends 'on whom some impression might be made'.

& we trust that ere long the unfortunate barrier will be removed which has seperated us so long.[1] (Add. Georgian 11/116)

Edinburgh, 24 Apr. 1804

Pray tell Mr. Fox that I have sent my proxy to the Prince of Wales, to be made over to whomsoever his R. Highness shall think proper. I have one for Ld. Eglinton's[2] signature, which will be similarly forwarded to the Prince.

Ld. Melville carries up the proxy of every other Scotch Peer who does not attend in person. His Lordship set out this morning with the Ld. Advocate.[3] The line is thoroughly understood by them; &, from their assurances, I consider Mr. Pitt is equally pledged: but the Prince is not bound by any implication connected with these conversations, which have on my part only extended to declarations, professedly unauthorised, that no personal animosity was cherished by H.R.Highness. I could have made efficacious head against the Scotch portion of the storm against Addington; for I declare to you very few from this country would have taken the steps they are now pursuing had I expressed a contrary senti-ment. Mr. Addington's slights have, therefore, not been altogether politic. (40132–3)

Edinburgh, 29 Apr. 1804

I enclose to you a draft for £600 to meet your acceptance of £500 due the 3d of May. Tell James that I will write to him tomorrow, but this being

1. Lord St. Vincent wrote to the Prince of Wales on 21 April: 'I have the honour to acquaint your Royal Highness that I have received the King's commands to dispatch a frigate to Lisbon to convey his Royal Highness the Duke of Sussex from thence to Malta. The Revolutionaire, Captain Henry Hotham, is fixed upon; and the orders will be dispatched from this Office on Monday night. In the meanwhile, I shall be proud to receive the commands of your Royal Highness' (*Letters of Lord St. Vincent*, ii.120).

2. Hugh Montgomerie, 12th Earl of Eglintoun (1739–1819). Entered the Army, 1756; Lieutenant-Colonel, 1782; Colonel of the Glasgow Regiment, 1793–5; Whig M.P. for Ayr-shire, 1780–1, 1784–9, and June–October 1796. Succeeded his distant cousin in the peerage, 30 October 1796; Scottish Representative Peer, 1798–1806; created Baron Ardrossan [U.K.], 15 February 1806. K.T., 22 May 1812.

3. Charles Hope, Lord Granton (1763–1851), M.P. for the Dumfries burghs, 1802; for Edin-burgh, 1803–4. Lord Advocate of Scotland, 1801–4; Lord Justice Clerk, 1804–11; President of the Court of Session, 1811–41.

Sunday when the post goes out at two o'clock & my time is occupied by a long attendance at Church, I cannot this day answer a financial letter which I have just received from him.

With regard to politics, I can have no other pledge of Pitt's disposition to attend properly to the Prince than Ld. Melville's assurance. That I might not bind the Prince by any implication, I only professed my conviction (founded on my knowledge of his magnanimity as well as on the conversations which had passed between us) that he would spurn any notion of petty vengeance for past transactions, or any system of proscription. This was communicated, & was met becomingly. The best security, however, is that no change could be for the worse. We have experienced Addington to be hostile to us as an interest, notwithstanding all the cajolery of his language, and I am sure we may say that every man of us has found him false in the conduct which he has held to us as individuals. (40134–5)

1845   LORD NELSON'S MEMORANDUM

Apr. 1804[1]

In my plans respecting naval matters, although I have not been so fortunate (in the opinions of those who have had the power of acting upon my ideas) as to be successful in seeing them carried into execution, yet I am by no means convinced that they would not have done some good especially as no other modes have been substituted in their places.

Yet at a time like the present it behoves every man in the station of life in which I have the honor of being placed to submit his ideas upon maritime subjects, and surely never a more important one presented itself that [*sic*] the defence of our native land.

I am not one of those who hold the French in contempt as an enemy. I know them to be indefatigable in their pursuits and by no means deficient in courage to carry their schemes into execution. I am one of the last men to believe that the French cannot be beat by an equal number of English. I have seen the contrary both at shore and at sea, but I am satisfied you cannot make a Frenchman surrender without fighting him and that sometimes very hard.

Therefore it is not for want of a thorough conviction that if the whole French army was landed in England but that it would be beat.

My ideas extend farther, that we should be able to say to France and not as a Gasconade, but be able to carry what we assert into effect,

1. Endorsed by him, 'Thoughts upon small vessels for the defence of our coasts—April 1804'.

535

'you cannot land in our country if there is a breeze; our ships of war shall annihilate your embarkation; if it is a calm our flottilla.'

It is a known fact and if not known I venture to assert it, that nothing but a first-rate is fit to go alongside a first-rate, and that nothing but a gun boat is fit to fight a gun boat; the chances of fortunate events does not take away from the principle I have laid down.

It therefore in my humble opinion without in any manner aping the exertions in our naval yards for the equipment of our fleets, becomes a very material object to have a flottilla to a certain extent: I will say one hundred gun brigs or schooners and 50 gun & mortar boats. It may be said, what a time these vessels will take to build, where is the wood, where are the shipwrights? &c. &c. My answer would be this. Shall it be admitted that at a time when our inveterate foe is using every exertion to destroy us, that Britons are incapable of as great exertion or even greater than Frenchmen? I am sure the exertion of my countrymen in every department only requires to be called forth and they will exceed those of France, for I should consider it as disgraceful to be outdone in exertion in defence of our country as I should to be defeated in battle.

With much deference I merely submit my idea of the mode of getting in six weeks or two months the 150 vessels which I have thought absolutely necessary.

The gun brigs for the present service are not wanted to be built of such stout materials as those formerly, for the service being temporary, if they last a little longer that [sic] the French flottilla it is all that is required: of course the vessels can be run up in a much shorter time than heretofore and being slighter will both tow and sail better. I do not speak of the less cost because I consider the dirty consideration of a few pounds w[h]ere *all* is at stake as unworthy the thought of a Englishman. A plan should be given in to the Admy. from not only our surveyors but should be requested from other builders or gentlemen who have turn'd their thoughts to this subject.

The builders of London, Bristol, Liverpool, Glasgow, Leith, Newcastle, Whitby, Lynn, Yarmouth and every port on the north coast & in the channel should be desired to say how many they can procure wood for building.

The time necessary must depend upon the number of workmen employ'd; therefore the greatest possible number should be employ'd upon each vessel and throughout the Kingdom (if necessary) every man who can be made useful in building these vessels should be called forth. True patriotism will shew itself and as many as are wanted will come forth; they should be carried free of expence to the place they are wanted at and their families not to be deprived of any comforts in their absence.

The shipbuilders of Great Britain are such a truly respectable set of men that every reliance may be fairly placed upon their exertions in rendering such an important service to their country, masts, sails and rigging may be procured & fitted in a week at farthest.

It may now be said w[h]ere are the men to man them? We want men for the fleet and cannot get them. To such people I should reply, when the enemy are at our door can it be supposed that no man or sett of men will step forth when we see so many volunteers on shore to volunteer their services in these vessels? Forbid it heaven that it should be said that the seafaring people of Great Britain are the only class who will not volunteer their services. Many, many plans could be hit upon to man these vessels. There are parts of the sea fencibles which might go in them; they would never be sent out of the Kingdom; a good Lieutenant ought to command and 20 men ought to regularly belong to them who would know everything relative to their management & fighting; these 30 sea volunteers would naturally fall into their places and the vessels would be fit for any service. In winter they could be secured in the ports opposite Bolounge, such as Dover, Rye, Hastings, Shoreham, &c. I would have every 20-gun vessels under the command of a Master & Commander, and over each fifty I would place a Post Captain with a broad pendant, and farther if necessary an Admiral to command and keep in order the whole of them, which command should to a *certain* degree be independant of any other Admiral, for the management of these vessels must be attended to in a uniform manner and as an inducement amongst many others which could be thought I would call them by the names of the places w[h]ere they were built, vizt., Whitby No. 1, 2, 3, 4, the Lieuts. I would appoint, if equally fit, of that country and the sea volunteers from that place & environs should go on board those vessels. The corporate bodies might be induced to grant certain little priviledges to such men as volunteer'd their services, such as porters unloading ships, watermen, &c., in short, as every man in the Kingdoms must have an interest in not allowing the enemy to set foot upon British soil, many inducements would naturally be held forth to sea volunteers.

I would send a Master of the Navy and a boatswain to see their rigging & sails fitted at the different building places, the rope for rigging and canvas for their sails can be there purchased and the old seamen of the place and sailmakers would fit them very easily.

With respect to arming them, that must depend upon how the enemy are armed. (40121—5)

VII   Some Undated Letters

THE EARL OF MOIRA TO COLONEL MCMAHON

26 Apr. [? *1797*]

A thousand thanks to you, my dear Sir, for your kind exertions. Sanguine as you still appear, I doubt the solidity of your expectations, for I think there is a spell upon my affairs that is always to raise an obstacle to whatsoever arrangement I may attempt. I have to fear considerable interruption in the receipt of rents from Ireland, and sale in that country is at present totally out of the question.[1]

You cannot see the state of this country in a more formidable light than I do. I am persuaded that Pitt sees it in the same point of view; but that, thinking a public convulsion not more formidable for himself personally than the immediate loss of his place would be, he has made up his mind to let matters run to confusion. The interests of either the King or the nation have never been objects of his attention, so that he is indifferent to the fatal consequences of the scene that is approaching, unless as to the degree in which they may effect him individually. To such of us as have property to lose, this plan of the Ministers is not very agreeable. Nothing but the union & efforts of those independent gentlemen in the House of Commons can afford a chance of our escaping the mischief, but the members of that Party have not yet brought each other's minds to concurrence in a specific measure. Sir William,[2] thro' prejudices against some individuals & partialities which make him desirous of

1. Ireland at this time was seething with rebellion, and a French invasion was daily expected.

2. Probably Sir William Pulteney.

538

saving others from the Ministerial wreck, throws without knowing it infinite embarrassments in the way of his object. Such a purpose does not admit of management or intrigue. It cannot succeed but by such an open procedure as may be distinctly intelligible to the whole country, & may thence carry general opinion in support of the measures to be pursued.

Pray show the enclosed to Brownrigg, who will understand it. Pelham, because I censured the measures of Irish Government, presses upon Clavering, to whom he knows I am attached.[1] (39681-2)

1847   THE PRINCE OF WALES TO CAPTAIN J. W. PAYNE

[*Before Feb. 1799*]

I have just heard & from pretty good authority that there is five hundred stand of arms now conceal'd at one Gough's at the Minories, wh. were intended to have been sent to the French, but wh. he dares not venture to send fearing yt. they may be seiz'd, but I suspect they are intended for another purpose. Pray send Nepean word of it, for if no good, no harm can come of caution. I am glad, dear Jack, to learn yt. you are so much better. (39865)

1848   THE PRINCE OF WALES TO LORD GRENVILLE

The Prince of Wales presents his compliments to Lord Grenville, and knowing that there were dispatches received from Arthur Paget a day or two ago, wishes much to know from Lord Grenville whether his courier is likely to be order'd back soon and when. The Prince of Wales would likewise be much oblig'd to Lord Grenville if he could without any impropriety give him a hint whether Paget is likely to stay the ensuing winter on his Mission, as the Prince of Wales has in commission to send him over several things, which in the case of his not being likely to stay some time, he would not forward[2] (Fortescue MSS.).

1. The letter is endorsed 1800, but this seems incorrect.

2. As the letter was obviously written before 1801, the date must be either the summer of 1794 (which is unlikely, since Paget was merely Secretary of Legation and *Chargé d'Affaires* at Berlin during Malmesbury's absence (July 1794-January 1795)), or the summer of 1800 when Paget was at Palermo (this is also unlikely as the Prince would probably not require anything to be sent to him from Sicily), or the autumn of 1798 when Paget was Envoy at Munich (from 27 September 1798 to May 1799). 23 November 1798 seems a reasonable suggestion: on that day Tyrwhitt wrote to Paget, 'His Royal Highness has commanded me to see the

For the performance of the Deserter (Louisa) ten nights at the Little Theatre in the Haymarket; Subscription tickets 1 guinea. Mr. Weltjie requested to have five dozen for his Royal Highness . . . . £ 63 – –

His Royal Highness honored me every night with his presence, with company. According to the rules of the Theatre it is customary for the Royal Family not to pay at the door—but at the end of the season the Treasurer makes out his account. But by the order of Mr. Weltjie this was not to be delivered, as he said he would settle it. Therefore, ten nights for his Royal Highness's Box, at £3 pr. night . 30 – –

The Masquerade of the Fair of Venice, at the Pantheon, which I made on purpose for his Royal Highness after seven weeks labor and study, I was three hundred guineas out of pocket. Mr. Weltjie took the receipts of all the money, and promised to see everything made good to me by his Royal Highness.

Ten tickets given to Mr. Weltjie for his Royal Highness for the above Masquerade, at two guineas each . . . . 21 – –

My two last Benefits, at Covent Garden Theatre, his Royal Highness had twelve tickets the first year, and six, the next 4 10 0

———————

118 10 –

(30007)

Tuesday evening

Tomorrow the Income Bill is in a Committee in the H. of C. & it is *very* material that I should attend. On the other hand, after what you communicated to me yesterday, I am particularly desirous of an opportunity to make my acknowledgments to his Royal Highness. Tell me whether there will be any impropriety in my sending an *apology* from

enclosed safe to the Foreign Post Office. Thank God he was never better or in better spirits. You were luckily out of the way when he had the shocking fall at Canterbury, but pray give him a hint (which will be attended to) to be somewhat more cautious as to the strength of the horses he rides' (*Paget Papers*, i.137).

1. Weltje died in October 1800.

2. A possible date is 18 December 1798. On the 19th the House went into Committee on Pitt's Bill to impose an income tax. The Prince was at Carlton House at that time.

the H. of C. that I am detained there, or whether it would be a sufficient excuse for my coming *too late* for dinner that I could not get away from the debate, and lastly whether I may, without disrespect to the Prince, go back to the House before he rises from table.

To know these things is very material to my arrangements tomorrow, and I will thank you much for an answer. I am sure you will excuse the trouble I give you, and attribute it to my my [*sic*] being so awkward a novice in proceedings of this kind. (40355)

Wednesday morning

The Herald of this morning makes me, in speaking of the Prince yesterday, to have said that I had *some authority* for what I did. Now the fact is that I took very particular care to have it understood that I spoke merely from public report. The substance of what I stated was 'that it was not from the fear of disaffected persons obtaining arms that Government acted, but from a wish to reject the services of every man not friendly to Ministers. I instanced Tarleton, hinted at others & added that even a high personage who could not possibly be suspected of *disaffection* had, as it was reported, experienced nothing but coldness and discouragement in return for offers of the most patriotic nature, & which, coming from one whose ardour must necessarily be so gratifying & animating to the affections & zeal of the people it was the more inexcusable to slight.' I observed further 'that if this report was correct, & I knew no more than what came from report, it attached the more blame personally to particular persons amongst his Majesty's Ministers as from the affection which was known to subsist between the Commander-in-Chief & the high personage to whom I alluded it was obvious that the application must have received every degree of countenance & recommendation from the highest military authority.' (40365)

1851 CHARLES STUART[1] TO [?] COLONEL MCMAHON

Tuesday afternoon, Lambeth Terrace

I have done some business for the Captain, which I had prepared last week, and which I wait to deliver to you. Although ill I came to town yesterday evening and waited for you all this day. Believe me, that no

---

1. Daniel Stuart's brother, and, like him, a journalist. *See* A. Aspinall, *Politics and the Press.*

exertions of mine will be wanting to promote *that* cause which I have always had nearest my heart for the last *twelve* years.[1] (39704)

1852   COLONEL MCMAHON TO ROBERT GRAY
Bury Street, Wednesday evening [? *11 Feb. 1801*]
I return the warrant signed as you described. I likewise enclose you a letter from Miss Robinson[2] (Mrs. Robinson's daughter) expressing her desire that the arrear of annuity should be paid to her order *only*. You will best judge how far this request ought to be complied with (supposing the Exchequer capable), but I own it strikes me that so far as her mother's claim goes it requires some previous administration. In the case of her *own* annuity of £200 a year I judge it to be admissible.[3] (29860)

[Enclosure] MISS MARY ELIZABETH ROBINSON TO COLONEL MCMAHON
Englefield Cottage, near Egham, Surrey. Thursday morning [*wrongly endorsed 4 Feb. 1801*]
Permit me to apologise to you for the liberty I am guilty of in addressing you, though a total stranger to you, but from the respect which my dear mother ever expressed for your character. The cause of your time being intruded upon by the perusal of this letter is to request as *the most particular favour* that you will *once more* exert your interest for the payment of the *last quarter* my adorable parent ever lived to trouble his R.H. for. I mean that due on the 25th of Decr. last (1800). I need not explain the *many, many* demands (which *now* fall on *me*) occasioned by the *long* and lingering illness and death of my mother. Your own good judgement will point them out. If then, Sir, you would entreat his Royal Highness to confer this *first* favour to me, and *last* he can pay to the memory of my blessed mother, you will very materially oblige, Sir [etc.].

You will oblige me very much by ordering Mr. Gray to pay it to *my receipt only*.[4] (29859)

1. The letter is endorsed 26 Nov. 1800, which may be the day (a Wednesday) when it was received or answered. These endorsements are very untrustworthy.

2. Mary Elizabeth Robinson (*d.* 15 January 1818). She was always financially embarrassed, and generally received one quarter's pension in advance. (30416)

3. 'Perdita' had died on 26 December 1800 at her cottage on Englefield Green. 'She had been several months in a declining state of health, which worldly troubles greatly aggravated. In her last moments, however, she was consoled by the tender attentions of her daughter and many friends' (*Gentleman's Magazine*, 1800, ii.1300).

4. The letter was endorsed: 'Answ'd it can't be paid at present, & when the time arrives it cannot be paid to her unless she administers'. 5 February 1801 was a Thursday.

542

Friday, 17 Dec.[1]

I write with the Queen's leave to inform you that a young woman of the name of *Saxton* gave her a Petition yesterday stating her *situation* as most distressing and as she is Mrs. Scot's daughter and your foster sister, we promised her to inform you of her situation. She having married against her mother's consent has no claim upon her, though reconciled to her will do nothing *for her.* Her husband is in *trade* & upon the point of breaking & this poor woman ready to lie-in & in immediate *want,* as the husband must give up business. Their wish *is* to get any place that will afford them a *subsistence but stating* no one situation whatsoever. You must know, my dearest brother, however anxious the Queen may be to help them it is *quite* out of her power to assist them in *that way* as far as momentary relief goes, I am sure she will do what she can as *well* as all of us.

As I am writing I cannot help just mentioning that the King sprained his leg getting on horseback the other day; as he put his foot in the stirrup the horse started, in consequence he has not rode out for these last two or three days, but he is so much better today that I hope he will soon be able to do as usual. The rest of the family are in perfect health & desire to be most kindly remembered to you. (Add. Georgian 12/25)

1854 THE PRINCE OF WALES'S MEMORANDUM FOR HENRY ADDINGTON 'IN DECEMBER LAST'

The Prince of Wales was not relieved from all his debts by the arrangement made under the Act of Parliament of 1795, the circumstances of which are known to Mr. Addington. There still remains a large part of the debt of the Landgrave, and other sums which will not be discharged by the Commissioners—these now must rest upon his Royal Highness—there are besides some additional incumbrances, not

1. Possibly an 1802 letter. McMahon wrote to the Duke of Northumberland on 20 December 1802: 'A very material piece of information has just been *confidentially* imparted to the Prince which I lose not a moment in communicating to your Grace, & to whisper it as coming from Lord Sandwich who was present on the occasion. The K. riding on Friday last, turn'd round suddenly to Col. Fitzroy the Equery who was near him & said "I hope Col. Fitzroy you did not hurt yourself in the blow you gave me." "Good God (cried F.) your Majesty, I was not close to you & hope you received no blow, Sir." "Why then", observ'd the K., "Tis odd, but something must have snap'd then." H.M. immediately gave up riding, & has not stir'd out since.

'A Levée is, however, announc'd in the Gazette of Saturday for next Wednesday, & it will be somewhat puzling & curious if, under those circumstances, it should take place, as 'tis supposed at least, it was the tendon Achilles' (Alnwick MSS.).

considerable, created by necessary expences, which could not be avoided, and which need not be enumerated.

In addition to these his Royal Highness feels it to be due to his own character to consider the situation of those creditors, from whom 10 pr. ct. was deducted by the Commissioners, though his Royal Highness is aware that this was a bargain which it was lawfull to make, and which in many instances might be a fair and full payment of their demand, still in other cases it may have been less than the just debt. His Royal Highness therefore proposes to have the particular cases investigated, and to reimburse such as may have suffered by the deduction.

These various demands upon the justice of the Prince, and the arrears already mentioned, make it impossible for his Royal Highness to resume his state, or any part of it, unless they are liquidated by the public, as he knows by dear bought experience that a premature resumption of his state must inevitably involve him in fresh difficulties, therefore to be henceforth free from all debt, induces him to wish it may be distinctly understood that unless a sum could be provided by Government to discharge those demands, he must himself place an effective fund in trust for that purpose, and it is his Royal Highness's object explicitly to declare that his state cannot be resumed until, by the operation of the trust or an adequate aid from the public, he is enabled to discharge all his existing obligations.

Under this explanation his Royal Highness could not fail to receive with gratitude such a proof of his Majesty's goodness as had been communicated by Mr. Addington.

The Prince is fully sensible of the propriety of resuming his state, and of the very gracious manner in which his Majesty has been pleased to desire such an idea to be conveyed to him.

He therefore trusts that Mr. Addington will take an opportunity of humbly explaining to his Majesty that the Prince will not postpone such resumption one moment beyond the time required to discharge the demands alluded to, and he confides in the gracious disposition which induced his Majesty to direct the information, justifying this explanation and resolution on the part of his Royal Highness.[1] (42327–8)

1. The Prince sent Addington the following note, dated merely Carlton House, Sunday, 11 o'clock:

'Can you call upon me for a few minutes this morning, or will it be more convenient to your present arrangements to come to me tomorrow, as I have a very great desire to have a few minutes conversation with you, having miss'd you at the Levée on Friday I am sorry to be obliged to intrude upon you by this note' (Sidmouth MSS.).

My present advantages exclusive of my allowance from Parliament are as follows.

Half pay as Commander-in-Chief in North America
viz. £10 per day (with the usual deductions) making 3300 nearly
Table allowance from the civil expenditure of Lower
Canada, made to me *personally*, but *not* connected
with the military command . . . . 2700 nearly

N.B. the above was arranged by Mr. Pitt & Mr. Rose to make my American income £6000 per annum.

Exclusive of this, the advantages of the house, garden, fuel, candles, and rations make upon an average when resident there about £2000 more.

On giving *this* up my wish is this. That I should be
appointed a General on the British Staff and have the
Command of the Plymouth District, and which with
the Staff pay, attached to the rank, viz., £6 per day,
with the usual deductions will give me about. . . 2000

That my civil allowance which might be termed *table*
should be augmented from £2700 (in order not to
diminish the sum total of the receipt per annum), to. 4000

Lastly that at Kensington Palace I may be allowed my fuel & candles as the Duke of Clarence has them at St. *James's* Palace.

As by the above arrangement I shall lose all the *local* advantages which I had when resident in America and which at a moderate computation as above mentioned amounted to about £2000 per annum, I request in return to make me amends for that, the promise of Plymouth government whenever that becomes vacant either by the death of the present possessor, or his removal to another, in case, if Portsmouth should fall soonest, he could be prevailed upon to take that in lieu thereof.[1]

I found my request on these several points:

First, on my having received my Parliamentary allowance only when I was 32 years of age,[2] whereas the Duke of York had his at 21, and the Duke of Clarence his at 24.[3]

Secondly, that from the moment of the Duke of Clarence getting his establishment to the present hour, a period of 11 years,[4] he has enjoyed an unlimited table at St. James's for himself and his servants, and that

1. Lord George Henry Lennox (1737–1805), a son of the 2nd Duke of Richmond, and a General (October 1793) was Governor of Plymouth and Sir William Augustus Pitt Governor of Portsmouth, and there was no vacancy during these years.

2. £12,000 a year (March 1799).

3. In 1789.

4. Assuming the accuracy of this statement, the Memorandum was written before the spring of 1801, but the reference to Addington implies that Addington had become Prime Minister.

except the £2700 per annum which I have had for two years and an half,[1] I never received a *stiver* for *my* table.

Thirdly, that I have been nearly twelve years on foreign service,[2] that in that time I have never till within this last twelvemonth been in all nine months absent from my duty and then only from ill health.[3]

On these grounds I sollicit the Prince's good offices with Mr. Addington (who I believe is already well disposed towards me) to get the arrangement I have submitted *adopted*, in order that I may not be obliged to cross the Atlantic Ocean an *eigth* time and return to a climate where my health has so severely suffered, to which measure pecuniary difficulties would otherwise compel me.

If the Prince would also touch upon the subject of my heavy losses at sea from shipwrecks and captures by the enemy amounting fully in the course of the war to £18000, and which the *late* Lord Chancellor, (the Prince will recollect), *promised* should be provided for, it would add most essentially to my comfort. (45994–5)

1856 LETTERS FROM PRINCESS AMELIA TO THE PRINCE OF WALES

Queen's Lodge, Tuesday night[4]

Thinking over what you mentioned to be about the *Palenquin* I cannot recollect where it is & it was just big enough to hold a little doll, but if you wish to have one I will speak to Mr. Williams & he shall get one made & I will make him promise he will not mention it. Only send me one line before we set out tomorrow that I may know what you wish me to do. God bless you, my dear love. (Add. Georgian 14/31)

I take up my pen this time with great pleasure as I have just heard from Mrs. Williams that the man has promised that the *Palenquin* shall be ready in time. I gave your message to Elizabeth & likewise told her of your plan which she approves highly of, & her *dear head* is now at work

1. He was Commander-in-Chief of the Forces in North America from July 1799, so this statement would seem to indicate that the Memorandum was written about the end of 1801.

2. He was sent to Gibraltar in January 1790 (ii.66), so 'nearly twelve years' would put the date of the Memorandum slightly earlier than January 1802.

3. The Duke returned home from Canada in November 1798 on sick leave (iii.483), went back in July 1799, and was home again owing to ill health caused by his accident, in August 1800.

4. This, and the two succeeding letters, may have been written in 1800. Little Princess Charlotte was evidently to be given a present.

thinking of what can be done should this not succeed, but by what I have already mentioned in the first part of my note I hope all will succeed according to your wishes. I shall see Mrs. Williams tomorrow morning.

[*P.S.*] I enclose Mrs. Williams's note. (Add. Georgian 14/32)

1857   PRINCESS ELIZABETH TO THE PRINCE OF WALES

I have through Amelia received your kind message & have really racked my brain to think of something to fill up time. Amelia desires me to tell you the palanquin is bespoke & will be finished *in time*, but Mrs. Williams is desirous to know about Charlotte's dress; it ought to be a gold muslin, the turban the same. Mrs. Williams, if you had no objection, would come to be with Lady Elgin at Carlton House or Downing Street that she might see you & talk the matter over as several things will be wanting. Will you appoint an hour & let us know *very early* (as we are to quit London by eleven o'clock) & we then will send to her. If this scheme does not do, what should you say to Astley's monkeys which the King has heard much of & has never seen? That is what is come into my head, & if you think of anything else & want any assistance as far as my poor ability's can be of any use, you may depend upon me. God bless you. The heat has nearly overcome the whole family. (Add. Georgian 11/84)

1858   THE PRINCE OF WALES TO THOMAS COUTTS[1]

My Dr. Sir,

The Prince[2] desires me to say that he wishes for no other company than yours and Mrs. Coutts.[3] Adl. Payne will be out of town otherwise would have been happy to wait upon you. I pray, dear Coutts, after what Mrs. Fitz. has written, *my old friend* Mrs. Coutts as well as yourself and my friend the Marquis will be all I can wish to meet. Ever sincerely yours (Coutts' Bank MSS.).

1. Between 1800 and November 1803.

2. ? One of the French Princes.

3. Coutts married, 18 May 1763, as his first wife, Susannah Starkie, one of his brother James's maids. She died on 4 January 1814, and a fortnight later he married (when he was almost eighty) the actress Harriot Mellon, afterwards (1827) Duchess of St. Albans (1777–1837).

Saturday morning [*?1802*]

How can I, my dear perfect Eau de Miel, thank you for the most beautiful bracelets[1] I ever saw which you were so good to send me yesy.; nothing but my dear angelic brother could have given me anything half so pretty. You are already convinced of my affection for you, therefore it is needless to tell you how dearly I love you & how much obliged & grateful I am for your invariable kindness to *me*, but indeed was I to try, volumes would not contain all my heart dictates to you concerning my affection for my dear Eau de Miel & my constant wish & prayer for your happiness.

When will you come to Windsor? I hope very soon. Your *own child* (for I will always call myself so) is very anxious to see you. I am very sorry dear Charlotte has been so tormented with her chilblains; mine are not broke but very tormenting, I assure you. I really am much better, but feel very sensible of your kindness & well assured of my beloved brother's good wishes for my health & happiness; the thoughts of possessing your friendship is *great* joy to me. God bless you, my dear angel. (Add. Georgian 14/37)

Kew House, Saturday [*1802 or later*]

I cannot delay thanking you for the very beautiful horse you have given me & which appears to be everything I could wish. Papa likes it very much & cannot possibly express to you how dear it will be to me as coming from you. I trust you are convinced how dearly I love you. The pleasure this mark of your kindness has given me I cannot tell you: indeed most dearly do I love you & feel your constant kindness to me, which believe me is deeply engraven on my heart & never will be forgot by me. You know I have always been *so vain* as to consider myself as your *child* & be assured at all times & in *all situations* my feelings for you are the same & my good wishes & prayers for your welfare & happiness ever attend you. I trust you will never forget *me*.

I cannot conclude this letter without saying what perhaps I ought not, but you will, I trust, take it as I mean it. It really is that I *feel* that I cannot help hoping ere long I may have the blessing of seeing you, my own dear love, again, & telling you myself how dearly I love you. God knows that day will be a joyful one to me, for I can be silent, but that does not prevent my *feeling*. This last year has been a most unkind one to me in every sense; pray God we may see better days. I am *sure* you *guess*,

1. Obviously not a birthday present, possibly a New Year one.

know & *feel* all I wish to say; your own good heart will *explain* better than I can all I feel. God bless you; how happy I feel to converse with you even in this way. (Add. Georgian 14/38)

Windsor Castle, Tuesday night [*?1802 or later*]

Reports are so easily spread & exagerated that I take up my pen to inform you of what your kindness at all times to me makes me feel certain will interest you & alarm you unless you hear the truth, but your beautiful horse fell down with me today & cut his knees very much. I fortunately, kept my seat & escaped quite well; I believe, & so does all the gentlemen, that the fault was owing [more] to carelessness of servants than to the poor dear annimal, as the grooms do not pay that attention they ought to ladies' horses. It has vexed me more than I can tell you, for as being my dear G.P.'s gift it was a very precious horse to me. Edward was with me at the time so he will be able to explain it to you, but I could not bear not to tell you the truth myself & some *illnatured person* wld. have represented it quite different to what it is.

I hope you are quite well & that we shall meet soon, & be assured at all times your own *child* will love you above all things & that absent or near her heart will ever remain the same to you. You will ever find, could you see it, that you are in possession of *not the smallest part* of my heart & that could my prayers or good wishes be of any avail you wld. be as happy as any human being can be. God bless you. (Add. Georgian 14/39)

Saturday, 3 p.m. [*1804 or later*]

I am very sorry you are unable to come to us. Mama says some of the *sisters* shall come to you this eveng. at six o'clock & I write from Miny & myself to say if it can be any amusement to you we will bring Sr. William Parsons, our musick & my pianoforte, only have the goodness to let me know whether you will like it or not. (Add. Georgian 13/46)

1860 RICHARD BRINSLEY SHERIDAN TO REAR-ADMIRAL J. W. PAYNE

Saturday evening

I send a man who will call on you very quietly, and without causing any reports, which the motion of a finger does at present. I had reason to beleive that I should have heard the result of a meeting which was to have been in *Downing Street* this eveng. but it is put off. Ld. Brudenell's[1] intelligence and its consequences are in *full circulation*—and great pains seem to be taken to make people believe it. It appears to me that the interdiction on the papers should *in part* be taken off, and a general line of intelligence, omitting every hint which respect requires should be omitted, be permitted. I think in justice to the Prince it ought to be so.[2]

After you went I informed Mrs. Fitzherbert that I should have a person at Windsor tonight to learn whether there was anything essential to the Prince's service to be communicated, and she express'd great anxiety to have a line to be informed how his R.H. was, &c.

There is a mail from the Continent in which there is rumour'd to be news of importance, but I have heard no particulars. (42267)

1861 LETTERS FROM THE DUCHESS OF DEVONSHIRE TO THE PRINCE OF WALES

Saturday [? *5 Mar. 1803*]

I was very unwell yesterday which prevented my writing. I am much better today but a good deal teazed. For Parker I find will deliver nothing unless 1000 is paid in money. This is very tiresome but I will try all I can to get it, that your kindness to me in trying so generously to relieve me from care may not be disappointed.[3]

War I think is inevitable,[4] but Mr. Pitt seems trying everything to get in again;[5] I am afraid he will succeed. Our friends will be very moderate I am sure, and if the Address[6] is properly worded, support it, but if

1. James Brudenell (1725–1811), who in 1790 succeeded his brother as 5th Earl of Cardigan, was created Baron Brudenell in 1780, and in default of male issue the Barony became extinct on his death. He was Constable of Windsor Castle, 1791–1811.

2. If the reference is to the King's illness the letter was probably written early in 1801.

3. She divided her debts into two classes. The First Class were debts of honour, which need not be paid until the Second Class were liquidated—money owing to tradesmen, etc. Amongst the First Class creditors were the Duke of Bedford, Lord Egremont, Charles Ellis and her cousin Charles Beauclerk.

4. War with France was renewed in May 1803.

5. In March Addington had offered to give way to Chatham as First Lord of the Treasury, with himself and Pitt as Secretaries of State, Melville conveying this proposal to Pitt at Walmer Castle. Further, in April Pitt rejected Addington's offer to resign the premiership to him on condition that the Grenvilles and Windham were excluded from the new Ministry.

6. On 9 March the House ordered an Address to be presented to the King in reply to his Message of the 8th which announced that in view of the military preparations in French and Dutch ports, the Government had adopted precautionary measures for the security of his Majesty's dominions. Fox was somewhat critical of the conduct of Ministers, but the Address was carried *nem. con.*

Pitt's friends make any motion to remove Ministers for the purpose of bringing him in for war it is impossible they can support that, having disapproved of the conduct of the last war.

God bless you, dear Sir. I hope I shall be better when you return but hitherto I have returns of pain and faintness. (Add. Georgian 21/71)

Sunday [1803]

I had a headache, dearest Sir, yesterday which vexed me as I wanted to write to you again. In my two long letters I purposely overwhelmed you with business of every kind because I would not allow myself to write on a subject that made me very nervous and which was fresh in mind from letters from Hart as well as yours: I mean the death of poor Payne.[1] I know all you must feel and indeed there is nothing like the pain of the loss of a friend. His state of health, tho' perhaps it may be so far a consolation that he was released from suffering, is none in fact to those who have lost him. I would not allow myself to mention him when I wrote the other day and eloignéd the idea, for from what you and others said, and knowing all you felt, brought the poor D. of B[edford] so strongly to my mind that it overcame me, the more so as I had met here a person who knew the D. of B. and who has made the sad moment of his loss appear quite recent.[2] You have the only real consolation, your constant acts of kindness to your poor friend, for even in the short difference and coolness that existed between you (and what friendships have been ever quite uninterrupted) I know from a letter my brother shewed me how generously you acted in trying to serve him in his profession at the very moment you was a little hurt with him; few friends and still fewer Princes would have acted in this manner.

I ought not now to write so much on this subject, but as I would not allow myself at first I could not help saying one little word.

Every hour makes me rejoice in the wisdom of the line of conduct you have adopted. All *our business* too will do very well. I hope you will not think of distressing yourself to send me anything. I entered into my situation more to give you some occupation to turn your thoughts than for anything else; owing to you I am really very comfortable.

As to Miss T.[3] there is not the least difficulty, for Miss Hunt[4] was not sub-governess I believe and she really has no idea or thought but to

1. Rear-Admiral Payne died on 17 November 1803. The letter may well have been written on the 20th.

2. The Duke of Bedford died on 2 March 1802. See Buckingham, *Court and Cabinets of George III*, iii.196.

3. Miss Trimmer, the governess at Devonshire House. See No. 1777.

4. See No. 1721.

make herself of use. Her letter is exactly her sentiments as she often expresses them to me.

Was not Mrs. F. very much distressed at poor Admiral Payne's death? Pray say everything most kind to her.

God bless you, my dearest Sir. We are gone into lodgings[1] and have escaped the neighbourhood of Ly. Pomfret.[2] I hope I shall hear from you soon, and that you will forgive me when I do not write, for the writing sometimes affects my head so much that I am obliged to abstain from anything that can affect or agitate me. God bless you.

Sunday. I must add one word to tell you that I have just seen in the newspapers that the D. of N[orthumberland] has the Warden's place.[3] What a very good thing it is, as he seems to be particularly attached to you.

God bless you, dearest Sir. (Add. Georgian 21/71)

Bath, 24[4]

A thousand thanks for your kindest of letters: I think the waters will agree with me but hitherto they rather heat me and particularly confuse my head if I attempt to write, read, or even think with application. As I have millions of things to say to you I am happy that today is a day of *discipline*, which enables me to write without feeling intoxicated.

We have Duncannon with us and expect Hare, the Fosters and perhaps Lima, otherways I never saw so few people whom I knew. We are not yet in our house. I have been at one play and once to Bristol, and that has been all our gaieties, but as we walk a great deal and have a good pianoforte we are as comfortable as we can be in an hotel. We get into our house tomorrow which is a very good one, near Sidney gardens. I wonder what the history of a Lady Pomfret is who lives next room to ours and I believe, by the figure she is when I meet her on the stairs, must be a little mad. She sat at the play in the next box and le[a]nt her whole weight against me so that I was obliged to use some dexterity to get rid of her neighbourhood.

I am very glad you are not in town. The whole of your line of conduct seems to me to have been as prudent, as dignified and, I think, is likely to bring about some discussion highly to your honour. I am the more glad as I think the present state of politics very unsatisfactory. The

1. At Bath.

2. George, 3rd Earl of Pomfret (1768–1830), married, 29 August 1793, Mary, (1769?–1839). daughter of Thomas Trollope Browne. They soon separated.

3. See No. 1764.

4. Probably November 1803.

552

Ministers can inspire no confidence, and it must be a great regret to see at such a moment all the talent which England possesses (equally to what it could boast at any period) absolutely banished from notice and the great means of exertion left to the hands of mere idiots. I do own, when I reflect on this, I think Sheridan's reasoning that every encouragement is to be given to these foolish people merely to keep out one man,[1] as selfish as it is weak and unpatriotic. But the truth is that Pitt has no idea of coming forward and is skulking under pretence of military duty to avoid taking a part, and in the meantime Sheridan, to avoid this phantom of his own creating, is giving all the support he can to Ministers.

I shall always think that the only place that could do good was the one you had, dearest Sir, last year, for you to have made yourself the centre of a coalition of all the talent and character of the country, for you to have assembled around you the Old Opposition, Lord Moira, the Grenvilles, Lord Fitzwilliam and Windham and have desired them to waive all old feelings and animosities. Nay, if under the principles laid down by you, Pitt and his friends had chose to join in this view, so much the better. But the moment I fear is gone by and the plan which was entirely your own and comprehensive as it would be efficient, must wait, tho' I hope not be for ever lost. For as to helping out the Doctor[2] it never can be more than a temporary measure, very inadequate to the crisis we are now in.

This being my opinion I doubly rejoice in your absence as I fear Sheridan tormenting you with his jealousies and idle dreams, tho' I give him, as I always have done, the credit of believing he will not be entirely seduced away, but he will give constant cause thro' his vanity to be often suspected.

I think by staying away now and letting things take their course and *pledging* yourself to nothing, you will after Christmass have opportunities of exerting *that influence* your rank, abilities and growing popularity gives to you alone, and the events that may have occurred will be your guide how to employ that interest for the advantage of your country, which is so dear to you.

I know you will forgive this long boar, tho' I write you another letter not to make this too heavy, containing a very satisfactory one I think from Miss Trimmer.

How extremely good you are to and about poor La Canea. I have been very negligent, but the case is that I was so harrass'd and so poor when I came to settle everything after so long a residence in London that I could not muster what I meant to send him. I sent him all I received;

1. Pitt.

2. Addington.

the last was the D. of Portland's 25, which I gave Burchell[?], by I intend to give him 25 for myself and 25 for the Duke. I have promises from Miles Andrew[1] and many which I cannot get till London but which will be about 100 more, but if he wants the 50 and you are so extremely good as to advance it, I shall ask the Duke for it in London and give it you and I think La Canea may depend on the 100 more, for tho' I do not always depend on the promises made me, these are some who requested to be put down and who ought to have paid me long ago.

When I talk to you of poverty, dearest Sir, it is only comparative, for owing to your extreme goodness in Parker's business, I have enjoyed a degree of care and comfort which I could not have looked to. But notwithstanding when I was about to leave London I feared so many things owing to my illness, &c. that I am in great actual poverty. I do not mean to ask the Duke for trifles because I am in some hopes of bringing him to a regular arrangement at my return. Instead, dearest Sir, if you should happen to be at all rich, a very small *cadeau* would make me very comfortable, and if you do, send it by a half note in two letters, but if you are not rich, I entreat you not, for owing to *you* I have been less tormented than I could have supposed when you found me in that anxiety last spring.

You perhaps do not know *all* you have done, but I do, and keep a very grateful account of it in my heart. God bless you, my dearest Sir. I do assure you that if you are a *poverino* as well as me I can do very well, only I am doing all I can to avoid all little plagues that I may return to London *better than I ever was in my life*.

You tell me nothing of your health but I hope you are quite well now, and Mrs. Fitzherbert, and Minny, once more. Addio. (Add. Georgian 21/71)

1862   THE EARL OF MOIRA TO COLONEL MCMAHON

Wetherby, Monday morning [1804]
Be so good as to accept the enclosed which you are to deliver to Price or any one sent by him for it, and then you are to scratch out from your book, as paid, the £900 due on the 29th inst.

Send to Sir John Sinclair as by my desire when any question is coming forward in the House, for he will transmit the instruction to others in my name.[2] (40362)

1. Miles Peter Andrews, the dramatist (*c.* 1742–1814). M.P. for Bewdley, 1796–1814.

2. Cp. No. 1842 (17 April 1804).

554

1863 THE DUKE OF CAMBRIDGE TO THE PRINCE OF WALES

St. James's, 6 p.m., Monday

I lose no time in sending you the enclosed which has been sent me from Blackheath. It was been brought over by a Major Gleisher who has been sent here by the Duke of Brunswick with letters to the King. Had it not been so late I should certainly have called at Carlton House, but being obliged to go out to dinner I was already [*sic*] & therefore I trouble you [with] this note. (48613)

1864 THE EARL OF MOIRA TO THE PRINCE OF WALES

11.45 p.m., Wednesday night

Secret. For the want of documents which could not be copied in time, it has been necessary to adjourn the further consideration till Friday night, but all wears as good an appearance as possible and I think your Royal Highness may calculate on dining at the Queen's Palace on Monday without chance of disappointment. (39752)

1865 THE PRINCE OF WALES TO THE DUCHESS OF DEVONSHIRE

Brighton,[1] [   ] *1802*

I should not, D[eare]st Dss., have troubled you so soon again with my scrawl, but an article which I saw in two of the papers today has alarmed me to the greatest degree, purporting that you had been run way with in your curricle and nearly destroy'd, though the horses were fortunately stopped by some labourers who were at work near the spot where the

---

1. This letter is printed in *Georgiana*, edited by the Earl of Bessborough, p. 251, under date 21 October 1803. The postmark, which is not clear, may be 21 October. The Prince's dating is obscured by a smudge. On the 24th Lady Spencer wrote to her daughter: 'I am really terrified, my dear Georgiana, at the accounts which all the newspapers here are full of—that your horses run [*sic*] away with you in a curricle & of the narrow escape you had of being dashed down the cliff. If there is any truth in it you must have been dreadfully frightened—too much so, I dare say, to write yourself, but I am quite angry with Harriet, who on such an occasion might have written a few lines to say how you were. If I get no letter today I shall be very uneasy as I cannot then have any till Tuesday' (Chatsworth MSS., No. 1655). Then, Lord Bessborough printed (p. 252) a letter dated London, 24 8bre, in which she says that the accident happened three weeks ago: 'It was most stupid in me, dst. mother, not to suppose and prevent your alarm. It was founded on nothing but that three weeks ago I was going with Hart in the coach ... '. It seems odd that the newspapers were three weeks late in getting hold of the story, and also that the Duchess's letter bears the same date as her mother's, for the Duchess's seems to be the reply to her mother's letter dated the 24th.

horses were running to. I hope in God this is not true, as I am confident that if it is, the alarm you must have receiv'd from so dangerous a circumstance must have made you extremely ill & nervous ever since. Pray forgive me for requesting, be it but a line, to say how you are, & if you are really well to explain to me what can have occasion'd so extraordinary an accident & still more providential escape, in which no one can rejoice so truly from the very bottom of their heart & soul than I do [*sic*]. It is impossible for you to conceive how anxious & uncomfortable I shall feel till I hear something of you. God bless you ever, [dst.] Dss., de loin comme de près, ever most devotedly yours (Chatsworth MSS.).

Appendix

Select List of Officeholders,

1799–1804

THE CABINET, 1799–APRIL 1804

	PITT		ADDINGTON			
	From June 1798	Feb.–April 1801	June–July 1801	Oct. 1802	17 Aug. 1803	Nov. 1803
First Lord of the Treasury and Chancellor of the Exchequer }	*Pitt*	*Addington* (20 March)	*Addington*	*Addington*	*Addington*	*Addington*
Lord Privy Seal	Earl of Westmorland	Westmorland	Westmorland	Westmorland	Westmorland	Westmorland
Lord President of the Council	Earl of Chatham	Chatham	Portland (30 July)	Portland	Portland	Portland
Lord Chancellor	Lord Loughborough	Lord Eldon (14 April)	Eldon	Eldon	Eldon	Eldon
Home Secretary	Duke of Portland	Portland	Lord Pelham (30 July)	Pelham	*Charles Philip Yorke*	*Yorke*
Foreign Secretary	Lord Grenville	*Lord Hawkesbury* (20 Feb.)	*Hawkesbury*	*Hawkesbury*	*Hawkesbury*	Hawkesbury[3]
Secretary for War (and the Colonies, from July 1801)	*Henry Dundas*[1]	Lord Hobart (17 March)	Hobart	Hobart	Hobart	Hobart
First Lord of the Admiralty	Earl Spencer	Earl of St. Vincent (19 Feb.)	St. Vincent	St. Vincent	St. Vincent	St. Vincent
President of the Board of Control				*Viscount Castlereagh*[2]	*Castlereagh*	*Castlereagh*
Master-General of the Ordnance			Earl of Chatham (27 June)	Chatham	Chatham	Chatham
Chancellor of the Duchy of Lancaster } President of the Board of Trade	Earl of Liverpool	Liverpool	Liverpool	Liverpool	Liverpool	Liverpool[4]
Secretary at War	*Wm. Windham*					
Minister without portfolio	Lord Camden					

Members whose names are italicized sat in the Commons.
1. Dundas was also Treasurer of the Navy (until May 1800) and President of the Board of Control.
2. President of the Board of Control from 12 July, but not in the Cabinet until October.
3. Peerage, 15 Nov. 1803.
4. Crippled with rheumatism, Liverpool probably never attended a Cabinet meeting whilst Addington was Prime Minister, but no evidence has come to light to suggest that he resigned his seat in the Cabinet, and there *is* evidence of his being sent Cabinet papers. He remained Chancellor of the Duchy of Lancaster until November 1803, and President of the Board of Trade until the Government resigned in 1804.

Junior Lords of the Treasury	Hon. John Thomas Townshend, John Smyth, Sylvester Douglas, Charles Small Pybus
From July 1800	John Smyth, Sylvester Douglas, Pybus, Lord Granville Leveson-Gower
From Dec. 1800	John Smyth, Pybus, Lord Granville, Leveson-Gower, John Hiley Addington
Joint Secretaries of the Treasury	George Rose, Charles Long
Junior Lords of the Admiralty	Lord Arden, Sir Philip Stephens, James Gambier, Wm. Young, Thomas Wallace, Robert Man
From July 1800	Lord Arden, Sir Philip Stephens, Gambier, Young, Man, Hon. William Eliot
Secretary of the Admiralty	Evan Nepean
Under-Secretaries of State	
Home Department	John King and William Wickham
Foreign Department	George Hammond and George Canning
	Hammond and John Hookham Frere (from 1 April 1799)
	Hammond and Edward Fisher (from 25 Sept. 1800)
War Department	William Huskisson
Commissioners of the Board of Control	Henry Dundas, Duke of Montrose, Viscount Belgrave, Earl Bathurst, Lord Hawkesbury, Sylvester Douglas, William Dundas
From 28 March 1799	Henry Dundas, Duke of Montrose, Viscount Belgrave, Earl Bathurst, Sylvester Douglas, Wm. Dundas, George Canning
From 28 May 1800	Henry Dundas, Duke of Montrose, Viscount Belgrave, Earl Bathurst, Sylvester Douglas,[1] Canning, Thomas Wallace, Earl Temple
Secretary to the Board of Control	Hon. William Brodrick
Master-General of the Ordnance	Marquess Cornwallis
Lieutenant-General of the Ordnance	Viscount Howe
Surveyor-General of the Ordnance	Major-General Alexander Ross
Clerk of the Ordnance	John Sargent
Surveyor-General of Crown Lands	John Fordyce
Surveyor-General of Woods and Forests	John Robinson

1. Created Lord Glenbervie, 30 November 1800.

Paymasters-General	Thomas Steele and Dudley Ryder
	Thomas Steele and George Canning (from 28 May 1800)
Treasurer of the Navy	Dudley Ryder (from 28 May 1800)
Postmasters-General	Earl of Leicester and Lord Auckland
	Lord Auckland and Lord Gower (from 22 Feb. 1799)
Master of the Mint	Sir George Yonge
	Lord Hawkesbury (from 6 March 1799)
Vice-President of the Board of Trade	Dudley Ryder
Judge Advocate-General	Sir Charles Morgan
Master of the Rolls	Sir Richard Pepper Arden
Attorney-General	Sir John Scott
	Sir John Mitford (from 17 July 1799)
Solicitor-General	Sir John Mitford
	Sir William Grant (from 17 July 1799)
Lord Advocate of Scotland	Robert Dundas of Arniston
Solicitor-General of Scotland	Robert Blair

THE IRISH GOVERNMENT

Lord Lieutenant	Marquess Cornwallis
Chief Secretary	Viscount Castlereagh
Lord Chancellor	Earl of Clare
Chancellor of the Exchequer	Isaac Corry
Attorney-General	John Toler
	John Stewart (from 23 Dec. 1800)

ADDINGTON'S MINISTRY, 1801–1804

Junior Lords of the Treasury	John Smyth, Charles Small Pybus, Lord George Thynne, Nathaniel Bond
From July 1802	Pybus, Ld. George Thynne, Bond, John Hiley Addington
From Aug. 1803	Pybus, Ld. George Thynne, Bond, William Brodrick
From Nov. 1803	Ld. George Thynne, Bond, Brodrick, Edward Golding
Joint Secretaries of the Treasury	John Hiley Addington (from 24 March), and Nicholas Vansittart (from 9 April)
From 8 July 1802	Vansittart and John Sargent
Junior Lords of the Admiralty	Sir Philip Stephens, Hon. William Eliot, Sir Thomas Troubridge, James Adams, John Markham, William Garthshore

(from 10 Jan. 1804)	Stephens, Troubridge, Adams, Markham, John Lemon, Sir Harry Burrard Neale
Secretary of the Admiralty	Evan Nepean (Baronetcy, July 1802)
	William Marsden (from 21 Jan. 1804)
Under-Secretaries of State	
Home Department	John King and Edward Finch Hatton
	John King and Sir George Shee (from *c*. Aug. 1801)
	John King and Reginald Pole Carew (from 17 Aug. 1803)
Foreign Department	George Hammond and Lord Hervey
	George Hammond and Charles Arbuthnot (from *c*. Nov. 1803)
War [and the Colonies]	William Huskisson
	John Sullivan (from May 1801)
President of the Board of Control	Viscount Lewisham (Earl of Dartmouth, 15 July 1801)
	Viscount Castlereagh (from 12 July 1802) [in the Cabinet from Oct.]
Commissioners of the Board of Control	Viscount Lewisham (Earl of Dartmouth, 15 July 1801), Duke of Montrose, Earl Bathurst, Lord Glenbervie, Wm. Dundas, Thomas Wallace, Lord Arden, Thos. Pelham, Edward Golding
From 6 July 1802	Viscount Castlereagh, Duke of Montrose, Ld. Glenbervie, Wm. Dundas, Wallace, Ld. Arden, Edward Golding
From Oct. 1803	Visct. Castlereagh, Ld. Glenbervie, Wallace, Golding, Thomas Maitland
Secretary to the Board of Control	Hon. William Brodrick
	Benjamin Hobhouse (from Nov. 1803)
Secretary at War	Charles Yorke
	Charles Bragge (from Aug. 1803)
Master-General of the Ordnance	Marquess Cornwallis (to June 1801)
Lieutenant-General of the Ordnance	Viscount Howe
Surveyor-General of the Ordnance	Major-General Alexander Ross
Clerk of the Ordnance	John Sargent
	William Wellesley-Pole (from July 1802)
Surveyor-General of Woods and Forests	John Robinson; Ld. Glenbervie (from 5 Jan. 1803)
Surveyor-General of Crown Lands	John Fordyce
Paymasters-General	Thomas Steele and Ld. Glenbervie
	Thomas Steele and John Hiley Addington (from 1 Jan. 1803)

Treasurer of the Navy	Dudley Ryder; Charles Bragge (from 17 Nov. 1801)
	George Tierney (from 1 June 1803)
Postmasters General	Lord Auckland and Lord Charles Spencer
Master of the Mint	Lord Arden
	John Smyth (from 2 July 1802)
Vice-President of the Board of Trade	Dudley Ryder
	Ld. Glenbervie (from 17 Nov. 1801)
	Nathaniel Bond (from 8 Feb. 1804)
Chancellor of the Duchy of Lancaster	Lord Pelham (from 11 Nov. 1803)
Judge Advocate-General	Sir Charles Morgan
Master of the Rolls	Sir Richard Pepper Arden
	Sir William Grant (from 21 May 1801)
Attorney-General	Sir Edward Law
	Spencer Perceval (from 15 April 1802)
Solicitor-General	Spencer Perceval
	Sir Thomas Manners-Sutton (from 11 May 1802)
Lord Advocate of Scotland	Charles Hope (from 12 May 1801)
Solicitor-General of Scotland	Robert Blair

THE IRISH GOVERNMENT

Lord Lieutenant	Earl of Hardwicke (appointed 27 April; sworn in, 25 May 1801)
Chief Secretary	Charles Abbot (from 25 May 1801)
	William Wickham (from 13 Feb. 1802)
	Sir Evan Nepean (from 6 Feb. 1804)
Lord Chancellor	Earl of Clare
	Lord Redesdale (from 13 Feb. 1802)
Chancellor of the Exchequer	Isaac Corry
Attorney-General	Sir John Stewart
	Standish O'Grady (from 28 May 1803)

Corrigenda and Addenda

VOLUME I

pp. 229–30   No. 164, line 2, and Index. *For* Hogmagog *read* Gogmagog. This was Lord Francis Osborne's seat in 1802 (*Auckland Correspondence*, iv. 168).

p. 235   *n.*, line 2, *for* Lord *read* Gentleman (as on p. 37, *n.* 1).

p. 414   *n.* 2, line 1 (and Vol. II, Index), *for* 1807 *read* 1802.

p. 519   Marquess of Cholmondeley. First reference should be 152, not 151.

p. 520   *for* Featherstonhaugh *read* Fetherstonhaugh (as on p. 143, *n.* 2).

p. 522   *for* Hardenburg *read* Hardenberg.

p. 524   *under* Martin, Mrs., line 3, *for* 149 *read* 150.

p. 527   *delete* Townshend, and add the reference, 70, to the following line.

p. 528   *under* Willis, Dr. Francis, *for* 1717 *read* 1718.

There are a few misprints in the Duke of Orleans's letters, but the remarkably bad handwriting and punctuation largely account for some errors which are here corrected:

p. 147   No. 112, line 8, *for* he *read* je.

line 20, *for* gagni *read* gay ni.

line 21, *for* longtemps. Je *read* longtemps je (though there is a very definite dot and space after longtemps).

p. 170   line 2, *for* écrit *read* écrite.

line 5, *read* reconnoissance.

line 12, *for* qui *read* que (the Duke's 'e' is almost indistinguishable from his 'i').

line 14, *for* fusse *read* fasse.

line 19, *for* it *read* il.

line 22, *for* où *read* ou.

p. 170   line 25, *read* changeoient.

p. 171   line 3, *read* jusques.

p. 249   No. 192, line 8, *read* entends.

p. 250   line 5, *read* douterez (the very peculiar 'z' looks like a 'c' or an 'r').

p. 263   No. 204, line 1, *read* avez.
          line 10, *read* garde.
          line 14, *read* croyez.
          line 15, *read* amis.

Very curiously, the Duke did write 'Quand a votre voyage,' 'ni l'ayez pas effectué' and 'touts les temps' on page 170; 'quand au' and 'je n' ourois me servir' on page 263.

See also Corrigenda and addenda (Vol. I) in Vol. II, p. xi.

VOLUME II

p. 5   *n.* 2, and Index. *For* 1732? *read* 1733. The more usual spelling seems to be Nolcken.

p. 145   *n.* 1, and Index. Delete *c*.

p. 160   *n.* 2, line 1, and Index. Delete the query.

p. 267   Add to *n.* 1: 'It was because she was a Princess of Savoy that her murder might, as the Queen said (No. 686) "draw the resentment of other Powers".'

p. 271   line 5. The child there mentioned was Léontine de Noailles (1792–1881) who in 1809 married her cousin, Vicomte Alfred de Noailles.

p. 271   *n.* 1, line 1, and Index. *For* 1753 *read* 1747. Also add to this note: 'The Duchesse de Biron (1751–94), *née* Amélie de Boufflers, was also guillotined.'

p. 507   Add the following to *n.* 2: 'The Marquise was Marie Petronille de Roquefort de Marquin; she married Vaudreuil as his second wife, in 1767.'

Index

p. 546   *under* Charlotte, Queen, line 3, add 858; line 13, *for* 870 *read* 871.

The following references are slightly expanded, and dates added:

Belzunce, Antoine Louis, Marquis de (1741–96).

Bezborodko [Besborodko], Count [1784], Prince [1797], (1747–99).

Bouillé (1739–1800).

Carignan, Marie Josèphe Thérèse of Lorraine (1753–97), sister-in-law of the Princesse de Lamballe, and wife of Prince Victor Amadeus of Savoy-Carignan (1743–80).

Choiseul, Claude Antoine de Choiseul, Duc de (1760–1838).

De Coigny, the Marchioness (1759–1832).

De Ligne, Charles Joseph, Austrian Field Marshal.

d'Hervilly, Comte (*d.* 1795).

Épernon (1554–1642).

Jarnac, Comte de (1740–1813).

For L'Oménie *read* Loménie de Brienne (1727–94), Archbishop of Toulouse, and Minister of Finance, (1787–8).

Monaco, Prince Joseph of (1763–1816). Delete his entry under Joseph, and his wife's under Josephe.

Monaco, Princess Josephe of (*née* Françoise Thérèse de Choiseul (1767–94), 471.

Noailles, Comte Charles de, later, 3rd Duc de Mouchy (1771–1834), son of Philippe, Prince de Poix (1752–1819).

Poix, Philippe, Prince de (1752–1819), 2nd Duc de Mouchy.

Worontzov [Woronzow], Count (1744–1832).

VOLUME III

p. 75   *n.* 1, and Index. *For* Radzivil *read* Radziwill.

p. 95   *n.* 3, *for* Stewart (the Royal family's usual spelling) *read* Steward. Francis Steward married Martha Seymer on 11 May 1768. He was a member of the Weymouth Corporation in 1773, the Corporation Treasurer in 1784, and Mayor in 1770, 1782 and 1793. Gabriel Tucker Steward, the Weymouth M.P. from 1794 to 1810, whose dates are still uncertain, must have belonged to some branch of this influential family. (Information *ex* Mr. J. A. C. West, Chief Librarian of the Weymouth and Melcombe Regis Public Library.)

p. 381   *n.*, line 4, *for* 1799 *read* 1800.

p. 386   last para., line 8, *read* unpopularity.

p. 461   *n.* 1, line 1, and Index. *For* 1765 *read* 1756.

p. 465   line 11. The reference is to Garth's disfiguring portwine birthmark.

p. 479   *n.* 2, line 6, *for* 3rd *read* 2nd.

p. 512   line 3, *for* in liquidating *read* for liquidating.

Index

p. 506   *after* Beaulieu, M. de, *add* (1725–1819).

p. 507   *for* Caylus, Duke of *read* Caylus, Duc de (1764–1823).

p. 513   *delete* ? *from entry under* Hoche, General.

p. 515   *for* Oenhauser *read* Oenhausen.

p. 516   *after* Peck, *insert* Charles, the Prince's maître d'hôtel.

p. 518   *delete entry under* Ukscull, Count. *Insert entry* Uxkull-Gyllenband, Count (1716–1801), 1309, 1316, 1341.

Index to Letters

Index to Letters

Chatham, Mary Elizabeth, Countess of (1762–1821), 1481n.
letter to, 1542n.

Chester, 1420n. 1421, 1546n., 1599n., 1655n.

Chesterfield, 5th Earl of (1755–1815), 1609

'Chig', *see* Chester

Cholmley, Tom, 1578

Cholmondeley, Charlotte, Marchioness of (1764–1838), 1432, 1434–5, 1440, 1607
her children, 1432, 1435
her sister, *see* Willoughby de Eresby

Cholmondeley, 1st Marquess of (1749–1827), 1467, 1526, 1528, 1538n., 1607, 1619, 1621n., 1697A
letters from, 1435, 1440, 1442
inquiries about his children, 1432, 1434
dismissal of (1800), 1518n., 1523, 1525, 1538

Christ Church, Oxford, 1545

Christian VII, King of Denmark (1749–1808), 1660

Christie, James, the auctioneer, 1493

Church, Mrs., 1690n.

Churchill, Lieutenant-General George (d. 1808)
letter from, 1489

Churchill, William, (d. 1835?), 1435

Clare, John Fitzgibbon, Earl of (1748–1802), 1519, 1640–1

Clarence, Duke of, *see* William Henry, Duke of Clarence

Clarke, 1773, 1773n.

Clarke, Sir Alured (?1745–1832), 1462n.

Clarke, Rev. James Stanier (?1765–1834), 1467

Clavering, 1846

Clinton, Robert, 18th Baron (1787–1832), 1654

Closet, the (the Queen's Closet, now King Edward IV's Chantry in St. George's Chapel), 1432

Cobb, James, 1532n.

Cobb, John Matt, of the Society of Antiquaries, 1532n.

Cobbe, Surgeon, 1576

Cobbett, William (1763–1835), 1709n., 1819
letter to, 1709
views on Catholic emancipation, 1709n.

Cochrane, Captain, 1464

Cockell [*sic*], 1705

Coke, Lady Mary (c. 1727–1811), 1432

Coleman, Miss Jane, Bedchamber Woman to Princess of Wales, 1607n., 1620

Coleman, Major, 1499

Colling, of Okehampton, 1628

Commander-in-Chief, the, *see* Frederick, Duke of York

Compton, H., one of Queen's pages, 1518, 1668n

Commissioners for the Prince's debts, the, 1528

Conway, Lady Anne Horatia Seymour (1762–1801), 1683, 1688–9

Conway, Henry Seymour (1721–95), Field Marshal, his house, 1496, 1498

Conway, Lord Henry Seymour (1746–1830), 1675, 1683, 1683n., 1692

Conway, Lord Hugh Seymour (1759–1801), 1675, 1683, 1683n., 1688, 1688n., 1692

Conway, Lord Robert Seymour (1748–1831), 1660, 1683, 1692

Copper exportation prohibition Bill, (1799), 1443

Corfu, capture of (1799), 1440

Cornwallis, Charles, 1st Marquess (1738–1805), 1462n., 1487, 1586, 1605, 1802

Corsakof, *see* Korsakoff

Cosway, Richard, portrait painter (1740–1821), his picture of Princess Charlotte, 1503n.

Cotes, 1446

Cottin, 1486, 1751, 1770

Court of Directors of East India Company, and patronage, 1691

Courtenay, 3rd Viscount (1768–1835), 1665

Coutts, Mrs. Susannah (d. 1814), 1858

Coutts, Thomas, (1735–1822), 1528, 1576, 1584, 1643n., 1809
letters to, 1487n., 1576n., 1858
his banking house, 1656

Covent Garden Theatre, 1769, 1849

Coventry elections, 1638

Cowper, Henry (1758–1840), Clerk Assistant of the House of Lords, 1457

Craig, General Francis (c. 1726–1811), 1841

Crewe, John, Lord (1742–1829), 1693

Critchell House, Dorset,
Prince means finally to give up, 1448

Cumberland, Duke of, *see* Ernest Augustus

Dalrymple, Sir Hew Whitefoord (1750–1830), 1730, 1754, 1761

Dalrymple, William, Duke of Kent's Treasurer, 1487, 1699

Dalrymple, General William (c. 1736–1807), 1770, 1838, 1841

Daly, Denis Bowes (c. 1745–1821), 1820

Danser, Major, 1700

Darell, Sir Lionel (1742–1803), 1511, 1809

Darnley, 4th Earl of (1767–1831)
letter from, 1834

Fremantles, the (William Henry Fremantle and his wife), 1669

Frere, John Hookham (1769–1846), 1600, 1642
letters from, 1639, 1829

Frogmore, 1648, 1650

Fuller, Captain, 1486, 1491

Fyers [*sic*], Colonel, 1749

Gainsborough, Margaret, the painter's daughter, 1424

Gainsborough, Thomas (1727–88), 1424

Gardiner, Major-General William (1748–1806) *letter from*, 1428

Garter, the Order of the, 1761

Garth, Miss (*b.* ?1772), 1603, 1607*n.*, 1620

Garthshore, William (1764–1806), M.P. for Weymouth and Melcombe Regis, 1528*n.*, 1599*n.*

Garton, 1473

Gaskoin, [Gascoigne], John, Clerk of the Prince's Stables, 1419, 1519*n.*

Gates, Horatio (1728–1806), 1586

Gazette, the, *see London Gazette*

George I (1660–1727), 1693

George II (1683–1760), 1462*n.*

George III (1738–1820), *passim*
letters from, 1475, 1619, 1726, 1728
letters to, 1475, 1479, 1539, 1543, 1600*n.*, 1619, 1726, 1728, 1739, 1792, 1800
his pages, 1668*n.*
difficult to deceive him, 1434
illness in 1801, 1594, 1597–8, 1598*n.*, 1599*n.*, 1601
talk of retiring to Hanover (1801), 1598*n.*, 1599*n.*
illness in 1804, 1796, 1798, 1802, 1804, 1806–1807, 1810, 1813, 1841
the *Ancient Music* his hobby horse, 1802
sprains his leg (1802), 1853

George, Prince of Wales (1762–1830), *passim*
his Attorney-General, *see* Gibbs, Sir Vicary and Graham, Sir Robert
his Solicitor-General, *see* Graham, Sir Robert
visit to Belvoir, 1420*n.*, 1422
visit to Woburn, 1421, 1427
anxiety about Mrs. Fitzherbert's illness, 1422, 1425, 1427, 1436
his attorney, 1425
ill at Bath, 1439*n.*, 1441–2, 1444, 1447
his claims to arrears of Duchy of Cornwall revenues, 1446, 1588, 1588*n.*, 1629, 1640–1, 1655, 1689, 1689*n.*, 1690
threatens to commit suicide, 1454
threatens to reveal his 'marriage' to Mrs. Fitzherbert, 1454
his disordered mind, 1459

George, Prince of Wales—*cont.*
his rank and employment in the Army, 1461, 1720, 1735, 1753, 1755, 1771, 1774
appointed Captain-General of the Artillery Company, 1485
portrait by Hoppner, 1487
is no gambler, 1504
his Will, 1510
and the Beef Steak Club, 1520
his debts, 1534, 1537, 1540–1, 1621*n.*, 1673, 1697, 1697A, 1702*n.*, 1832, 1854
wants an Irish Earldom for Lord Melbourne, 1552*n.*
his Privy Council fees (1801), 1581*n.*
his memo. regarding King's illness (1801), 1594, 1597
application for military employment (1801), 1608, 1608*n.*
injured by a fall (1801), 1614–15, 1623
a fine print of him, 1648
proposals respecting Mary Seymour, 1688
quarrel with the Duke of York, 1753, 1755
insulted by Pitt, 1767
illness of (Feb. 1804), 1801–2
reconciliation of the Prince and the Duke of York, 1805*n.*
memo. for Addington, 1854

Gibbs, Sir Vicary (1751–1820), 1446, 1621, 1690

Gibraltar, the mutiny at, 1699–1700

Gisborne, Thomas (*d.* 1806), physician to the King, 1594, 1597

Glasgow, 4th Earl of (*c.* 1766–1843), 1707*n.*, 1825

Glasse, Dr. G. H., Chaplain to D. of Cambridge, 1665

Gleischer, Major, 1863

Gloucester, Princess Sophia of (1773–1844), 1650

Gloucester, William Frederick, Duke of (1776–1834), 1532, 1650, 1718, 1778

Gloucester, William Henry, Duke of (1743–1805), 1456, 1456*n.*, 1650, 1774, 1778

Goldsworthy, General Philip (*c.* 1738–1801), 1478, 1583
his house near Salisbury, 1563

Gordon, Mr., of Xeres, 1653

Gordon, Lord Adam (1726–1801), 1612

Gordon, Duchess of (1748–1812), 1440

Gordon, Major James Willoughby, Duke of Kent's Groom (1773–1851), 1462*n.*, 1531

Gough, 1847

Graham, Sir Robert (1744–1836), 1446, 1842
the Prince's Law Officer, 1446, 1504, 1588

Grange, the Prince at the (1800), 1523, 1563

Moira, Elizabeth, Countess of (1731–1808), Lord Moira's mother, 1457

Moira, Lord, *see* Hastings

'Monsieur', *see* Artois, Comte d'

Monson, Lieutenant-Colonel William (1760–1807), son of 2nd Lord Monson and M.P. for Lincoln, 1806–7, 1757, 1762

Montagu, Basil
letter from, 1602

Montagu, James, 1840
letter from, 1840

Montague, Mrs. James, 1840

Montgomery, Bob, 1420*n*.

Montpensier, Antoine Philippe, Duc de (1775–1807),
brother of Duke of Orleans, 1769

Moore, 1584

Moore, Lieutenant-Colonel James (*d.* 1848), 1742

Moore, John, Archbishop of Canterbury (1730–1805), 1490, 1511

Morand, 1546*n*., 1599*n*.

Morland, William, banker, 1540–1, 1584

Morning Chronicle, the, 1738, 1779, 1850

Morning Herald, the, 1779

Mornington, Lord, *see* Wellesley, Marquess

Morocco, Emperor of, 1680

Morpeth, Viscount, *see* Carlisle, 6th Earl of

Morshead, Sir John (1747–1813), 1522*n*., 1783*n*.
letter from, 1522

'Mother Hump', 1599*n*.

Muller, Colonel, 1809

Münster, Prussian occupation of (1802), 1667

Münster, Count (1766–1839), the Hanoverian Minister, 1624

Murray, Lady Augusta (*c.* 1762–1830), 1480, 1482, 1488, 1490, 1492, 1494, 1559, 1644, 1653, 1671
letters from, 1506*n*., 1509, 1600*n*., 1643, 1643*n*., 1671*n*.
letter to, 1506
joins Prince Augustus in Berlin, 1480
returns to England, 1494
in Lisbon, 1643
obliged to abscond, 1643*n*., 1682
her pension unpaid, 1643*n*.
asks for peerage, 1671*n*., 1809
her daughter, *see* Truro, Lady
her suit against the Duke of Sussex, 1809

Murray, Captain Alexander, (1764–1842), 1643*n*., 1809

Murray, Lord James, Baron Glenlyon (1782–1837), 1788

Myers, Lieutenant-General Sir William (*d.* 1805), 1819

Naples, King of, *see* Ferdinand IV

Naples, Queen of, *see* Caroline

Napoleon, Emperor (1769–1821), 1507, 1576*n*., 1599*n*., 1679*n*., 1690, 1693, 1705, 1757, 1839

Neale, Sir Harry Burrard (1765–1840), 1471, 1501

Neale, Lady (1771–1855), 1472, 1501

Nelson, Horatio, Viscount (1758–1805)
memo by, 1845

Nepean, Sir Evan (1751–1822), 1820*n*., 1847

Nesbitt and Stewart, Messrs., 1584

Newcastle, Anna Maria, Duchess of (1760–1834), 1478

Newport (Cornwall), elections, 1715

Newspaper reporting, inaccurate, 1546

Newton, 1764, 1782, 1785

Nicholson, Major, 1757, 1762

Niel, *see* Neale

Nisbet, Mrs. Hamilton, 1721

Nizam, the, 1517*n*.

Norfolk, 9th Duke of (1746–1815), 1607*n*., 1790

Norman, Lady Elizabeth (1776–1853), Duke of Rutland's sister, 1444, 1448

Norman, Richard, 1444, 1448

North, Dr. Brownlow, Bishop of Winchester, half-brother of Lord North, the Prime Minister (1741–1820), 1683

North, Frederick, 5th Earl of Guilford (1766–1827),
letter from, 1717*n*.
letter to, 1717

Northumberland, Frances Julia, Duchess of (1752–1820), 1674*n*., 1690, 1697A, 1761, 1767

Northumberland, Hugh, 2nd Duke of (1742–1817), 1628, 1660, 1735, 1764, 1769, 1861
letters from, 1714–15, 1730, 1740, 1754, 1761, 1767, 1767*n*., 1793, 1802, 1808, 1811, 1816
letters to, 1522*n*., 1577, 1577*n*., 1660*n*., 1674*n*., 1690*n*., 1694*n*., 1697, 1697A., 1702*n*., 1704*n*., 1715, 1802, 1853*n*.
views on Catholic emancipation, 1767*n*.
complains of lack of consultation, 1767
insulted by Pitt, 1767*n*.
his daughter Frances (1791–1803), 1740

Nugent, Admiral Sir Charles Edmund (? 1758–1844), 1417

Nugent, Mrs. Charlotte
letter to, 1417

Nussey, the Prince's apothecary, 1472*n*., 1587

Observatory, the, at Blackheath, 1602

O'Connor, Arthur (1763–1852), 1697A

586

St. John, St. Andrew, 14th Baron St. John (1759–1817), 1654

St. Laurent, Mlle. [or Mme.] de, 1462*n.*, 1487, 1487*n.*, 1530, 1558, 1612, 1617, 1652, 1731, 1787, 1796

St. Leger, Colonel William (? 1759–1818), 1691

St. Vincent, *see* Jervis

Salisbury, Bishop of, *see* Douglas, John

Sandwich, 5th Earl of (1744–1814), 1853*n.*

Salm, Prince, *see* Solms-Braunfels

Satchwell, R., a page of the backstairs in the Prince's Household, 1493

Saumarez, Sir James, Baron de Saumarez (1757–1836), 1657

Saxton, a tradesman, 1853

Saxton, Mrs., 1853

Saye and Sele, 8th Lord (1769–1844), 1690

Schack, M. de, 1549

Schrader, Mr., 1503

Scott, 1781

Scott, Mrs., 1853

Scott, Sir John, 1st Earl of Eldon (1751–1838), 1598*n.*, 1599, 1601–2, 1607, 1619, 1629, 1640–1, 1674, 1689–90, 1702*n.*, 1809, 1834, 1841
letters from, 1629*n.*, 1689*n.*
letter to, 1641*n.*

Scottish Peers, election of, 1687*n.*, 1695, 1695*n.*, 1697A, 1707

Seringapatam, Palace at, 1517

Sévigné, Mme. de (1626–96), 1420

Seymour, Miss Frances, *see* Southampton, Frances Isabella, Lady

Seymour, Miss Georgiana, Lord Cholmondeley's ward, 1432
not to be presented at Court, 1434–5

Seymour, Mary (1798–1848), 1675, 1683, 1688, 1688*n.*, 1692, 1861

Seymour, Lord Robert, *see* Conway

Shah Alam, the titular Mogul Emperor, 1757

Shakespeare, William (1564–1616), 1687

Shee, Sir George (1754–1825), Under-Secretary of State, H.O., 1641*n.*

Sheffield, Anne, Lady (1764–1832), 1603, 1607

Shelburne, Earl of, later, Marquess of Lansdowne (1737–1805),
letter from, 1737
letter to, 1636

Shelley, 1422*n.*

Sheridan, Mrs. Esther Jane (1776–1817), 1783

Sheridan, Richard Brinsley (1751–1816), 1500, 1638, 1766–7, 1772, 1774*n.*, 1803, 1830*n.*, 1835, 1835*n.*, 1842*n.*, 1861

Sheridan, Richard Brinsley—*cont.*
letters from, 1815, 1815*n.*, 1860
letters to, 1783, 1815*n.*, 1830
offered office of Receiver-General of Duchy of Cornwall, 1815, 1815*n.*
Whig suspicions of, 1830*n.*

Sheridan, Tom (1775–1817), 1715, 1783, 1783*n.*, 1830

Shippon, Major-General, 1485

Shooter's Hill, 1563, 1678*n.*

Shuckburgh, Sir George Augustus William (? 1751–1804), 1429

Sieyès, Emmanuel Joseph, Comte (1748–1836), 1507

Silva, Mme., 1593

Simcoe, Lieutenant-General John Graves (1752–1806), 1819

Simmons, Dr. Samuel Foart (1750–1813), 1806*n.*, 1814

Sinclair, Sir John (1754–1835), 1842, 1862

Sindhia, Daulat Rao, 1757, 1762

Sleigh (?), Mr., 1541

Smith, Adam (1723–90), 1764

Smith, John Spencer, (1769–1845), Envoy to Wurtemberg, 1637, 1645

Smith, Admiral Sir William Sidney (1764–1840), 1622, 1706

Smyth, Lieutenant-Colonel George Stracey, Duke of Kent's Groom, 1462*n.*, 1787

Smythe, John, Mrs. Fitzherbert's brother, 1454

Smythe, Mrs. (*d.* 1808), Maria Fitzherbert's mother, daughter of John Errington and widow of Walter Smythe), 1422, 1425

Solms-Braunfels, Prince Frederick of (1770–1814), 1515*n.*

Somerset, Lord Charles Henry (1767–1831), 1665, 1669, 1749

Somerset, Edward Adolphus, Duke of (1775–1855), 1468*n.*

Somerset, Lady Elizabeth (1766–1815), 1665, 1669

Somerville, Sir Marcus (*c.* 1772–1831), 1820

Sophia, Princess (1777–1848), 1477–8, 1501, 1617, 1620, 1665, 1670, 1678, 1687, 1718, 1763, 1796, 1831, 1833, 1836
letters from, 1609*n.*, 1685, 1696, 1719, 1760, 1823
illness of (1800), 1514, 1552, 1558, 1560

Southampton, Anne, Lady (*d.* 1807), 1444

Southampton, Frances Isabella, Lady (*c.* 1777–1838), 1660

Southampton, 2nd Lord (1761–1810), 1660

Southwark elections, 1701*n.*

Wilson, Richard—*cont.*
land's Agent, 1628, 1690, 1690*n.*, 1697A, 1793
letter from, 1788

Wilson, General Sir Robert Thomas (1777–1849),
letters from, 1772, 1819

Wimpfen, Baron de, Duke of Wurtemberg's Chamberlain, 1466

Windham, William (1750–1810), 1556, 1690, 1709*n.*, 1735, 1780, 1811, 1861

Wombwell, Lady Anne (1768–1808), 1439, 1441

Wombwell, Sir George (1769–1846), 1439, 1441

Wood, Miss (*d.* 1799), 1424

Wright, Captain R., Duke of Kent's A.D.C.
letters from, 1708–9
letters to, 1709*n.*, 1749, 1775
his brother, 1775

Wright, Dr. Robert, the Duke of Sussex's physician, 1653

Wurtemberg, Duchy of, invaded by the French, 1437, 1453, 1551, 1623

Wurtemberg, Caroline Alexei, Princess of, later *cr.* (1807) Baroness von Rottenburg, and (1825), Countess von Urach (1779–1853), 1542

Wurtemberg, Frederick, Duke of (1732–97), 1453

Wurtemberg, Frederick, Duke of (1754–1816), 1441, 1453, 1466, 1470, 1542, 1542*n.*, 1551, 1623, 1645, 1839

Wurtemberg, Prince Henry of (1772–1833) visits England with his *actrice* wife, 1542, 1542*n.*

Wyatt, 1749

Wyndham, *see* Windham

Wynyard, Lieutenant-General William (*d.* 1819), 1672

Wynyard, Lady Matilda, 1434*n.*

Yarmouth, Francis, Earl of, and (1822) 3rd Marquess of Hertford (1777–1842), 1692

York House, 1448

Yorke, Charles Philip (1764–1834), 1742, 1749, 1775, 1780, 1804*n.*, 1806*n.*, 1835*n.*

THE HOUSE OF WURTEMBERG

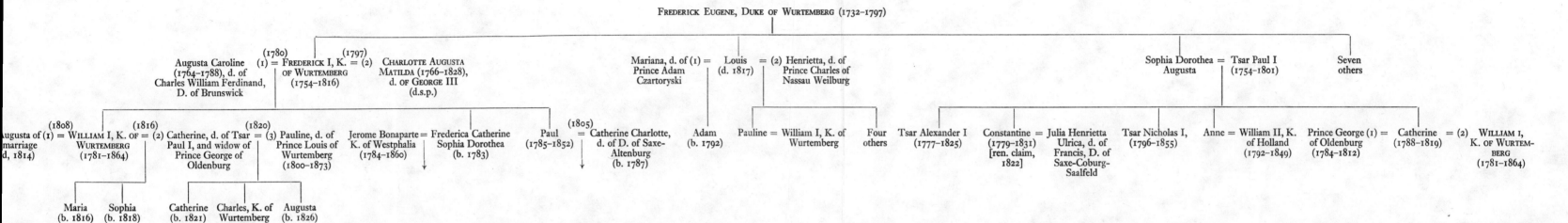

Frederick Eugene, Duke of Wurtemberg (1732–1797)

Augusta Caroline (1764–1788), d. of Charles William Ferdinand, D. of Brunswick — (1780) (1) = Frederick I, K. of Wurtemberg (1754–1816) = (2) (1797) Charlotte Augusta Matilda (1766–1828), d. of George III (d.s.p.)

Mariana, d. of Prince Adam Czartoryski (1) = Louis (d. 1817) = (2) Henrietta, d. of Prince Charles of Nassau Weilburg

Sophia Dorothea Augusta = Tsar Paul I (1754–1801)

Seven others

Augusta of (1) marriage [d. 1814] = William I, K. of Wurtemberg (1781–1864) = (2) (1816) Catherine, d. of Tsar Paul I, and widow of Prince George of Oldenburg = (3) (1820) Pauline, d. of Prince Louis of Wurtemberg (1800–1873)

Jerome Bonaparte, K. of Westphalia (1784–1860) = Frederica Catherine Sophia Dorothea (b. 1783)

Paul (1785–1852) = (1805) Catherine Charlotte, d. of D. of Saxe-Altenburg (b. 1787)

Adam (b. 1792)

Pauline = William I, K. of Wurtemberg

Four others

Tsar Alexander I (1777–1825)

Constantine (1779–1831) [ren. claim, 1822] = Julia Henrietta Ulrica, d. of Francis, D. of Saxe-Coburg-Saalfeld

Tsar Nicholas I, (1796–1855)

Anne (1788–1819) = William II, K. of Holland (1792–1849)

Prince George of Oldenburg (1784–1812) (1) = Catherine (1788–1819) = (2) William I, K. of Wurtemberg (1781–1864)

Maria (b. 1816) Sophia (b. 1818)

Catherine (b. 1821) Charles, K. of Wurtemberg (1823–1891) Augusta (b. 1826)

THE HOUSE OF MECKLENBURG-STRELITZ

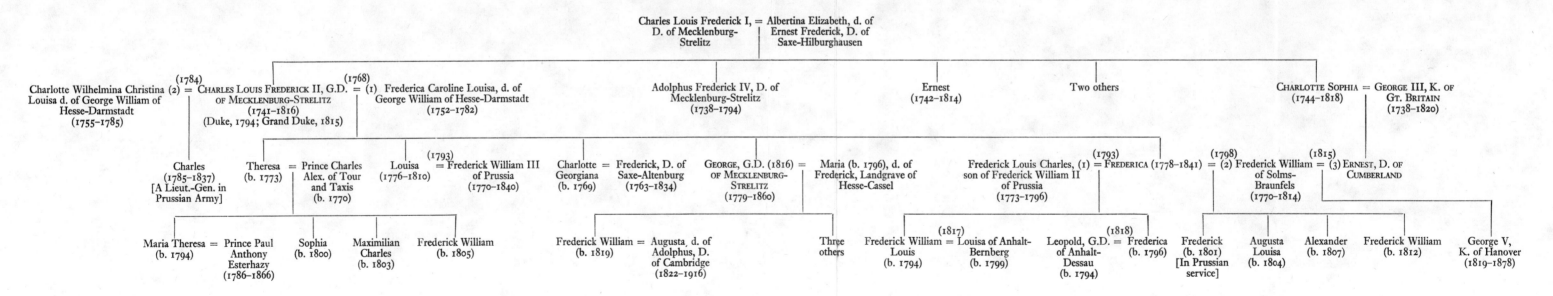

Charles Louis Frederick I, D. of Mecklenburg-Strelitz = Albertina Elizabeth, d. of Ernest Frederick, D. of Saxe-Hilburghausen

Charlotte Wilhelmina Christina Louisa d. of George William of Hesse-Darmstadt (1755–1785) (2) = (1784) Charles Louis Frederick II, G.D. of Mecklenburg-Strelitz (1741–1816) (Duke, 1794; Grand Duke, 1815) = (1) (1768) Frederica Caroline Louisa, d. of George William of Hesse-Darmstadt (1752–1782)

Adolphus Frederick IV, D. of Mecklenburg-Strelitz (1738–1794)

Ernest (1742–1814)

Two others

Charlotte Sophia (1744–1818) = George III, K. of Gt. Britain (1738–1820)

Charles (1785–1837) [A Lieut.-Gen. in Prussian Army]

Theresa (b. 1773) = Prince Charles Alex. of Tour and Taxis (b. 1770)

Louisa (1776–1810) = (1793) Frederick William III of Prussia (1770–1840)

Charlotte Georgiana (b. 1769) = Frederick, D. of Saxe-Altenburg (1763–1834)

George, G.D. (1816) of Mecklenburg-Strelitz (1779–1860) = Maria (b. 1796), d. of Frederick, Landgrave of Hesse-Cassel

Frederick Louis Charles, son of Frederick William II of Prussia (1773–1796) (1) = Frederica (1778–1841) = (2) (1793) Frederick William of Solms-Braunfels (1770–1814) = (3) (1815) Ernest, D. of Cumberland

Maria Theresa (b. 1794) = Prince Paul Anthony Esterhazy (1786–1866)

Sophia (b. 1800)

Maximilian Charles (b. 1803)

Frederick William (b. 1805)

Frederick William (b. 1819) = Augusta, d. of Adolphus, D. of Cambridge (1822–1916)

Three others

Frederick William Louis (b. 1794) = (1817) Louisa of Anhalt-Bernberg (b. 1799)

Leopold, G.D. of Anhalt-Dessau (b. 1794) = (1818) Frederica (b. 1796)

Frederick (b. 1801) [In Prussian service]

Augusta Louisa (b. 1804)

Alexander (b. 1807)

Frederick William (b. 1812)

George V, K. of Hanover (1819–1878)